TEENAGERS
with ADD
A Parents' Guide

Chris A. Zeigler Dendy, M.S.

WOODBINE HOUSE  1995

All rights reserved under International and Pan-American copyright conventions. Published in the United States of America by Woodbine House, Inc., 6510 Bells Mill Rd., Bethesda, MD 20817. 800–843–7323.

Cover illustration & design: Marcie Wolf-Hubbard
Cover Photograph: Alex Zeigler & Chris Dendy
Illustrations p. 12 and p. 13: Derek Engram
The photograph on p. 14 is reprinted by permission of *The New England Journal of Medicine*, Alan J. Zametkin, M.D., Volume 323, p. 1365, Figure 4, 1990. Copyright 1990. *Massachusetts Medical Society*. All rights reserved.

Library of Congress Cataloging-in-Publication Data

Zeigler Dendy, Chris A.
    Teenagers with ADD : a parents' guide / Chris A. Zeigler Dendy.
        p.   cm.
    Includes bibliographical references and index.
    ISBN 0–933149–69–7 (paper)
    1. Attention-deficit disorder in adolescence—Popular works.
I. Title.
RJ506.H9Z45 1995
616.85'89'00835—dc20
                                        95–524
                                        CIP

Manufactured in the United States of America

10 9 8

This book is dedicated to my extraordinary teachers—
my sons, their friends, and my husband.

About the Author:

Chris Abney Zeigler Dendy, M.S., is a mental health consultant with twenty-five years experience. Her varied professional roles have included counselor, teacher, school psychologist, administrator, advocate, and parent support provider. She is the co-founder of the Gwinnett County CH.A.D.D. chapter in Georgia. Her book draws upon her extensive professional experience, as well as her own family's experience with ADD, including raising two teens with ADD.

TABLE OF CONTENTS

Part V: Parent Advocacy

Part VI: Teenagers Speak

ACKNOWLEDGMENTS

Many friends and colleagues from across the country who have lived or worked extensively with ADD have given considerable time being interviewed or commenting on drafts of the book. This book could not have been written without their invaluable assistance and encouragement. I am *deeply grateful* to all the contributors listed below whose unique insights have so greatly enriched this book!

Several people provided essential information regarding *medical* aspects of ADD: Edward M. Gotlieb, MD, (Adolescent Medicine Specialist), and his staff, Kathleen Allen, MA, (Licensed Counselor) and Gail Doggett, (RN), Pediatric Center, Stone Mountain, GA; Bill Buzogony, MD, (Psychiatrist, former WI Commissioner of MH), Madison, WI; Calvin Sumner, MD, (Psychiatrist, Dir. Public Sector Psychiatry, WVU), Buckhannon, WV; DeLane Long, Pharm.D., and Joyce Rimmer, BS, (pharmacists), Lawrenceville, GA; Clyde Rountree, MD, (Psychiatrist, Medical Dir., GRN CMHC), Lawrenceville, GA.

One group of people was especially helpful because they provided priceless expertise from a broad range of perspectives: *treatment and educational issues, parent advocacy, and/or personal experiences with ADD.* Their wonderful common sense advice strengthens the book: Beth Dague, MS, (Dir. Stark Co. Family Council), Canton, OH; Christina Kloker Young, (Chair, FMHI Children's Board), Stow, OH; Paula Finley, MS, (Dir., Continuum of Care, Governor's Office), Columbia, SC; Elaine Mizell, MS, (Dir., Northampton Associates), Charleston, SC; Doris Cobb, MS, (Dir. Regional IPPC Committee), Hinton, WV; Judy Sturtevant, (VT FFCMH), Montpelier, VT; Helen Snyder, MS, (WV Dir. Children's Mental Health Services), Charleston, WV; Bob Friedman, PhD, (Prof. & Dir., Research and Training Center for Children's MH), FMHI/USF, Tampa, FL; Cathy Roberts Friedman, MS., (Coord., Children's Clinical Case Management), Tampa, FL; Dixie Jordan, (Family Advocate, PACER Center), Minneapolis MN.; Barbara Friesen, PhD, (Dir. Family Support/RTC/Portland State U.), Portland, OR; Beth Stroul, MS (CASSP Consultant), McLean, VA; Bobby Robbins, (Dir., GRN CMHC), Lawrenceville, GA; Barbara Huff, (Dir., Nat'l Federation of Families for Children's Mental Health), Alexandria, VA; Sue Smith, (Dir., Parent Support Network), Atlanta, GA; Priscilla Casciolini, (Chairman GRN Regional CMHC Board, Past Pres. GA AMI), Stone Mountain, GA; Jerry and Creasa Reed, (Parent Advocates, Past Pres., nat'l FFCMH), Wichita, KS.

Critical *educational* issues were addressed by several educators: Claudia Dickerson, PhD, (School Psychologist), Dick Downey, PhD, (Dir. Special Education), Candy Steventon, (Spec. Ed. Supervisor), and Dale Carter, PhD, (Dir. Psychological Services), (Gwinnett County Schools), Lawrenceville, GA; Steven Forness, EdD, (Prof. and Inpatient School Principal, UCLA), Los Angeles, CA; John Clark, MS, (Administrator, Nebraska Dept. of Ed.), Lincoln, NE; Alice Smith, MS, and Jerry Randolph, (GA Dept. of Ed.), Atlanta, GA; Mary Kay Clyburn, (SLD Teacher), Snellville, GA; Virginia Brickman, MS, (Ed. Consultant, GLRS), Atlanta, GA; Joan Maril, MS, (Ed. Consultant), Macon, GA; Al Duchnowski, PhD, (Dept. Dir., FMHI/USF), Tampa, FL; Rev. James and Carolyn Wofford, (minister and teacher), Menlo, GA; Joan Teach, PhD, (Prin., Lullwater School), Decatur, GA; Sue Seldenridge, (Vice Prin., SLD teacher, Duluth Middle School), Duluth, GA; Naomi Karp, (Special Assistant, OERI, U.S. DOE), Washington, DC; Sandra Dendy, (teacher), Buford, GA; Linda Lawton and Rosemarie Gill, (Special Education), Hartford, CT.

Input on *treatment and research* was provided by: Steven Evans, PhD, (Assistant Prof., Western Psychiatric Institute and Clinic), Pittsburgh, PA; Ann Abramawitz, PhD, (Clinical Dir., ADD Program, Emory University), Decatur, GA; Beth Morrison, (Dir. IPPC Committees), Charleston, WV; Debra Rugg, PhD, (Researcher, FMHI/USF), Tampa, FL.; Mark Prange, PhD, (FMHI/USF), Tampa, FL; Maria dePerczel, PhD, (FMHI/USF), Tampa, FL; Jonathan Greenstein, PhD, (St. Joseph's Hospital), Tampa, FL; John White, LCSW, (Dir. Children's Services, Suncoast Center), St. Petersburg, FL; Jan Smith, MA, (Assistant Dir., Family Connections), Glen Dale, WV.

Substance abuse and family advocacy issues were addressed by: Ari Russell, (Dir. GUIDE Program), Lawrenceville, GA; Bruce Hoopes, MS, (Dir., Regional CMHC Board & former SA Dir.), Gainesville, GA; Bob and Robbie Revel, Woodland Hills, CA.

Judicial and delinquency issues were discussed in interviews with Scott Henggeler, PhD, (Prof., Medical University of South Carolina), Charleston, SC.; Judge Billy Shaw Abney, LaFayette, GA and Judge Virgil Costly, Covington, GA (Juvenile Court Judges).

Excellent information regarding *post high school* issues such as the GED, technical schools, community colleges, and universities was provided by: Ann Phillips, PhD, (Dir. Student Services), & Ann Ball, MS (Developmental Studies), and Gerald Hall, PhD, (Dir. Student Development, West Georgia College), Carrollton, GA; Rhonda Holmes, MS, (Dean of Students, DeKalb College), Sandra Causey, (Admissions, Gwinnett Tech), and Joe Purvis, (Dir., GED Program, Gwinnett Tech.), Lawrenceville, GA.

Several *members of CHADD* and other *parents* have shared family experiences that have greatly enriched this book: Amber Bertolini, Buford, GA; Carol Lewellan, Duluth, GA; Helen Frick, (CHADD Coord.), Lilburn, GA; Don and Penny Dieckman, Snellville, GA; Steve and Marsha Clippinger, Larry and Becky Doster, Judy McCarty, Lawrenceville, GA; Sandy Tyson, Perry Hall, MD; Jamie Hartman, (CHADD Co-Coord.), Macon, GA; Jack and Debbie McMurray, Gate City, VA; Milton and Marian More, Milledgeville GA; Sheila Anderson, (Sec., Nat'l CHADD Board), Renton, WA; Belinda Cunningham, (CHADD Coord.), Charleston, WV; Sandy Johnson, (CHADD Co-Coord.), Norcross, GA; Randy Medley, Chattanooga, TN; Audrey Grabowski, Mendota, IL; Kay and Jimmy Dendy, Lillian Abney, and Dr. Billie Abney, LaFayette, GA; Gaye Smith, Ringgold, GA; Vicki Ragsdale, Highland Heights, KY; Ed and Emma Zeigler, Orange Park, FL.

Finally, I would like to express my deepest appreciation to my extraordinary editor, Susan Stokes for her guidance and support! Her literary gifts were invaluable in publishing a book that provides much needed practical advice and hope for parents.

A special thanks to our teenagers who live daily with the challenges of having ADD. They have taught us so much!

Alex	*Cassie*	*Lee*	*Mandy*	*Andrew*
Steven	*Elizabeth*	*Scott*	*Kevin*	*Tonya*
Lewis	*Chad*	*Matt*	*Brian*	*Bart*
Shawn	*Robert*	*Damian*	*Michael*	*Katie*
Travis	*Cooper*	*Jeremy*	*Kansas*	*Kristin*
Jason	*Evan*			

INTRODUCTION

Much has been written about children with Attention Deficit Disorders (ADD).* However, little material about *teenagers* with ADD has been available to parents when their children reach the challenging years from 13 to 20. When faced with the day-to-day reality of raising a teenager with ADD, many parents experience overwhelming feelings of frustration, inadequacy, guilt, and fear. The lack of information about the unique problems of adolescence has made the job of parenting these teenagers more difficult. Parents have had to trust their instincts about raising their teenagers and hope they were making the right decisions.

Teenagers with ADD was written to fill the information void about the special issues and challenges confronting adolescents with ADD. This book may be helpful to several groups of people: 1) parents of adolescents who were diagnosed with ADD as children; 2) parents who have recently discovered that their teenager has ADD; 3) parents who suspect that ADD may be the culprit behind their teenager's underachievement in school; 4) teenagers who want to understand themselves and ADD; and 5) educators and mental health professionals who want specific suggestions for interventions with teenagers with ADD.

Most books describe ADD and its impact on the family in academically sterile terms. Yet coping with ADD can be an intensely emotional experience for teenagers and their families. If parents are aware of the troubling behaviors some teenagers with ADD exhibit (skipping school, sneaking out at night, receiving speeding tickets, not telling the truth, acting out sexually, or experimenting with alcohol or drugs), they may be less likely to be shocked by misbehavior, overreact emotionally, or jump to the erroneous conclusion that their teenager will become a juvenile delinquent. Personal vignettes are shared throughout this book to more accurately portray the highs and lows, troubling and positive behaviors, and hope and anxiety that accompany ADD in many teenagers. Through these vignettes, success stories achieved in spite of challenging struggles are shared.

This book discusses typical issues, including inattention, impulsivity, academic difficulties, and disobeying parents. It also covers seldom-addressed topics, such as sports participation, driving privileges, speeding tickets, sleep disturbances, drug and alcohol experimentation, and college attendance. It includes the most up-to-date diagnostic criteria and research findings about the causes of ADD.

Because success in school is so critical to building strong self-esteem, there are several chapters on common academic and behavioral problems in the classroom. Included are discussions of learning problems common to teenagers with ADD and specific classroom adaptations that can be made under federal regulations. Much space is also devoted to explaining the most common interventions for teenagers with ADD: medication, academic and behavioral interventions, activities to build self-esteem, and counseling.

Parents will find many suggestions for protecting and strengthening their teenager's self-esteem. By following these suggestions, parents can help their teenager understand the impact of ADD on his school and home life; encourage him to pursue activities in which he will achieve success; teach him skills to cope more effectively with ADD; and ultimately, encourage him to pursue a career in which ADD will not present a handicap.

---

* Note on terminology: The term "ADD" will be used throughout the book to describe all attention deficit disorders, including the old diagnostic categories of both ADHD (Attention Deficit Hyperactivity Disorder) and Undifferentiated ADD (without hyperactivity) and the categories of Attention-deficit/Hyperactivity Disorder established in 1994 in the *Diagnostic and Statistical Manual of Mental Disorders, Fourth Edition* (DSM IV).

My unique perspective on ADD comes from experiences as a former teacher, school psychologist, mental health counselor, mental health administrator, lobbyist, and state and national mental health consultant. However, my most valuable education regarding ADD comes from the humbling experience of being the mother of Alex and step-mother of Steven, both of whom have ADD. I have great admiration for my sons, who have struggled to cope with this disorder. They are delightful young adults and have done well: Alex is a college junior and Steven graduated from college two years ago. I have also gained valuable insights from several relatives with ADD who are very successful as adults.

My approach to writing this book was to provide the information on raising teenagers that I *desperately* needed, but could not find, when our family began its journey through adolescence nine years ago. Because I know from experience that this difficult journey can be completed successfully, I have shared personal insights that have given me a very positive outlook regarding the future of teenagers with ADD.

Several deeply ingrained philosophical beliefs provided the foundation for this book. First, as a mental health professional with over 25 years experience, I believe in a *"wellness treatment model"* which builds on the strengths of the teenager and family. I see the family as *an essential part of the solution rather than the problem.* Unfortunately, mental health treatment is frequently built on finding the "illness" or pathology. Second, I believe that *parents know their teenagers best* and have strengths that are not used and in fact, are often overlooked in the treatment of ADD. Consequently, I do not talk down to parents but share this information as one professional with another. Third, I believe that if parents have the needed information, they are the most effective and tenacious advocates for their teenager's successful adjustment. *Parents are in the best position to coordinate* the wide range of educational, mental health, and medical services, plus community activities needed by the vast majority of teenagers with ADD. Last, *I always assume good intentions* of other people and seldom do they disappoint me. Most teachers, educators, and medical and mental health professionals *want* to help teenagers with ADD but may not know how. ADD can be a complex disorder and the best methods for treating it effectively are not always clear. Since information in this book may also be helpful to professionals, you may want to share it with them.

Teenagers with ADD has been written in collaboration with three sets of "experts": parents, teenagers, and educators/treatment professionals. I have interviewed over a hundred people, including parents, teenagers, parent advocates, CHADD members, teachers, learning disabilities teachers, guidance counselors, principals, county directors of special education, psychologists, mental health counselors, a pharmacist, nurse, physicians, psychiatrists, state education and children's mental health administrators, and national leaders in the field of children's mental health.

These experts provide a richness of theory tempered with real-life experiences, since many have dealt with ADD from both a professional perspective and personally, in their own family. The powerful stories they shared are incorporated throughout the book. I am deeply grateful to my friends and colleagues who have been so generous with their time. Their personal interviews and comments on the book over the past five years have greatly enhanced its practical value. Personal insights provided by these contributors will help families cope in a healthy and loving way with this stressful disorder.

Several of my colleagues are physicians, researchers or psychiatrists who specialize in treatment of ADD or conduct disorders: Edward M. Gotlieb, M.D., adolescent medicine specialist, The Pediatric Center (GA); Bill Buzogany, M.D., psychiatrist, Medical Director, Lad Lake Treatment Services and former Commissioner of Mental Health in Wisconsin; and Cal Sumner, M.D., psychiatrist, Director Public Sector Psychiatry, WVU and staff physician, young adult unit, Westin State Hospital; Steven Evans, Ph.D., Assistant Professor of Psychiatry, ADD Program, Western Psychiatric Institute and Clinic, University of Pittsburgh; Herb Quay, Ph.D., formerly Chairman, Department of Psychology, University of Miami; and Steve Forness, Ed.D., Professor and Inpatient School Principal, UCLA. They have been extremely generous with their time for interviews, sending relevant research articles, or reviewing and commenting on my book. I am deeply grateful for their guidance and insights.

In Chapter 14, the teenagers themselves share powerful insights into their confusion and pain as they have learned to cope with ADD. They also share their success stories. By the late teenage years, a teenager's ability to articulate feelings about having ADD and how it affects his life has usually improved significantly.

> **"Up until my ADD was diagnosed, I had never done very well in school. During class I tended to be real tired and sleep a lot. I guess I thought I was lazy and stupid. Since I started taking Ritalin, I'm making mostly A's and B's."**
>
> —*Shawn at age 16*

> **"Academically, school wasn't challenging. I didn't get any gratification out of the academics. I always felt I could do the work. The work was always easy but I couldn't concentrate. I'd get attention from [doing] academics but everyone got the same attention. But I could get limitless attention if I misbehaved. I always had good intentions. I always wanted attention but I hated bad attention. But it was the only attention I could get.**
>
> **"You forget things when you have ADD. So you forget to take your medication which is supposed to help you remember things. Dang, if I can just remember to take my medicine I would be fine. When I was younger, people would always say, "Why? Why? Why?" And now I know why I had problems in school. But I can't remember to take my medication."**
>
> —*Robert, age 18*

Information from national and international experts in the field also enhances the book. I have relied heavily on the work of two researchers who have studied this disorder for the past 20 years and have made profound contributions to understanding and treating ADD: Russell Barkley, Ph.D., and Sydney Zentall, Ph.D. Dr. Barkley, a clinician, educator, and researcher at University of Massachusetts Medical Center, is considered the national authority on ADD. His book, *Attention Deficit Hyperactivity Disorder*, an encyclopedia on ADD, is the most comprehensive one written regarding this disorder. I am also extremely impressed with the respect and caring attitude that Dr. Barkley has for parents and children with ADD. I have quoted liberally from his book since many parents may never read this 700–page volume. Sydney Zentall, Ph.D., Professor of Special Education at Purdue University, is one of the few educators who has researched the educational strengths and learning problems of youngsters with ADD. Dr. Zentall's upbeat approach to ADD provides an inspirational boost for parents.

Research on ADD without hyperactivity has been very limited. According to Dr. Barkley, between 6,000 and 10,000 studies have been done on ADD *with* hyperactivity, but only 50 or 60 have addressed ADD *without* hyperactivity. Two researchers who are best-known for studying this disorder are Ben Lahey, Ph.D., a psychology professor at the University of Chicago, and Tom Brown, Ph.D., a Yale psychologist.

Another important contribution to the field has been made by Dr. James Swanson, a professor and researcher at University of California, Irvine, and his colleagues who conducted a "review of the review" of the literature in 1993 on thousands of research articles regarding the effectiveness of medication in treating ADD. Other important physicians and researchers whose work has provided helpful insights include Gabriella Weiss, M.D., Lilly Hechtman, M.D., Paul Wender, M.D., Marcel Kinsbourne, M.D., Melvin Levine, M.D., Edward Hallowell, M.D., John Ratey, M.D., Rachel Gittelman-Klein, M.D., Charles Popper, M.D., Theodore Mandelkorn, M.D., and Michael Gordon, Ph.D. Most of them have made presentations at national conferences and I have had the opportunity to hear them speak.

Two national advocacy organizations have assumed a leadership role advocating for improved services for youth with ADD: CHADD (Children and Adults with Attention Deficit Disorders) and ADDA (National Attention Deficit Disorders Association). CHADD has done a superb job of bringing national experts to their conferences and developing educational materials. Both CHADD and ADDA publish newsletters. Local CHADD chapters have been established in almost every state and are an excellent source of support and education for many parents. Addresses for the national offices are provided in Appendix D.

Parents Need Help and Hope

Raising a teenager with ADD can be an extremely painful and lonely job for a parent. Because ADD is an "invisible disability," most parents of teenagers with ADD feel isolated and receive little support and understanding from others. The teenager looks normal, but may perform erratically at school and seldom does as parents ask. Some family members and friends may be quick to give advice, saying that strict discipline will solve all the teenager's problems.

> **"As a graduate of the U.S. Naval Academy, I thought stern discipline would solve all Steven's problems. Now that I understand ADD, I find myself frustrated that most adults have the same attitude I had toward my son. They feel that these children are lazy and don't care. There are a lot of children in our society who need our understanding. They need to be protected against that type of negative attitude. If all adults had to raise a child with ADD and if they could see the dramatic difference medication can make, we could improve the lives of so many children and families."**

When their teenager struggles, parents experience a great deal of anxiety and self-doubt. Sometimes they wonder if they have been "bad" parents or if they have a "bad" child. If they are informed about typical behaviors that teenagers with ADD exhibit and potential interventions, however, parents are able to anticipate and weather the challenges of raising their child.

It may help to know that most teenagers with ADD make it through this difficult period successfully. During the ages from 17 to 21, many of these teenagers seem to mature and establish a clearer direction for their lives. As they achieve more successes, their self-esteem is bolstered. They appear to settle down and be happier. In addition, many children outgrow the symptoms of ADD or exhibit milder symptoms as they reach adolescence and adulthood. With proper diagnosis and treatment, most teenagers with ADD will grow up to be well-adjusted adults.

Parents Must Advocate for Their Teenager

Since parents know their teenager better than any professionals involved with the family and are committed to their child's success, they make excellent advocates. They know their offspring's strengths and weaknesses, and often know which medications and interventions work best. This knowledge makes parents indispensable as respected partners in the treatment process. It is critical for parents to learn everything they can about ADD. The more parents learn about ADD, the more effective they become at advocating on behalf of their teenager.

Education of teachers, treatment professionals, and other adults who work with teenagers with ADD is also essential if these young people are to succeed in school and grow up to be happy, productive adults. This is because a teenager's ability to cope successfully with ADD depends a great deal on how the teenager and others perceive ADD. Having people who believe in the teenager is essential for successful adjustment.

Many professionals are well informed about ADD and monitor the teenager's response to medications and adjustment at home and school. However, other professionals do not. Until all key professionals become better informed about ADD, *parents may have to take charge of helping educate the professionals and ensuring coordination among them.* This book offers concrete information and suggestions that will enable parents to feel confident enough to take charge of helping their teenager cope successfully with ADD.

Now Let's Start at the Beginning

The most elating experience of my life occurred the day my son was born. Alex was delivered at 1:11 a.m. after a brief three hours of labor. Natural childbirth procedures allowed me to be awake and alert during his birth. When the doctor pronounced the delivery of a healthy baby boy with an APGAR score of 10, I heaved a sigh of relief. Ten fingers and ten toes, they were all there. He was beautiful! No problems.

I promptly rejected the doctor's suggestion that I skip Alex's 6:00 a.m. feeding. I wasn't tired. I was exhilarated! At 30 years of age, I had been waiting for this day for a long time. I lay awake waiting for the nurse to bring him for his scheduled feeding. He arrived. I held the world's most beautiful child while he nursed, savoring the joy this child had brought into my life.

The joy of watching my precocious, happy child crawling undaunted into the ocean as an infant, diving at age two, and water-skiing at age four was rudely interrupted when he entered first grade. For some reason, he could not keep up with his classmates in spite of his high intelligence and good intentions. My sensitive, loving six-year-old child was reduced to tears because he could not quickly finish his classwork and as a result, his teacher thought he was "bad." Our high expectations for him in school were dashed as he struggled to cope with overwhelming academic demands. I knew he was a good child who wanted to do well at school, but was at a loss to understand the contradictions between his ability and poor academic performance. This battle with an undiagnosed adversary—ADD—created a cruel learning environment for the next six years. The major thing my son learned was to hate school. Alex was 12 before we discovered that ADD was the culprit behind his devastating struggles at school.

Our hopes and dreams for our children are so grand when they are born. We dream of school successes, athletic or artistic talents, solid values, leadership skills, and a spiritual strength to sustain them in difficult times. As the years roll by, we watch our child's life unfold. Some teenagers' lives seem to unfold easily in a very logical and orderly fashion. The lives of other teenagers, including many with ADD, are much more difficult and stressful. Nothing seems to come easily.

Upon learning that their child has ADD, some parents are devastated at first. But given time to absorb this information and its positive potential for enabling their child to live a happier and more productive life, most parents are relieved and grateful. At last, you know the reason for your child's puzzling behavior. Now, you can begin to tap into the growing body of knowledge about ADD that you can use to help your child succeed. *Teenagers with ADD*, based as it is upon the research of professionals and the collective wisdom and experience of contributors, should help you begin to understand and appreciate your child's world. It is my fondest hope that what we—the author and contributors—have learned from living with this disorder will make a meaningful difference in your life as you and your family cope with ADD.

CHAPTER ONE

WHAT IS ADD?

"When you have ADD, you don't know what 'normal' attention and concentration are. You just assume that everyone concentrates the same way you do. It's like having a vision problem. You don't realize what the real world looks like or that you have a vision problem until you are tested and get glasses. The same thing is true with ADD. You don't know you have ADD and problems with attention and concentration until you take Ritalin and find out what it's like to be able to concentrate."

— *Alex, age 16*

The ABC's of ADD

Attention Deficit Disorder (ADD) is a neurobiological disorder.* That is, researchers believe that the symptoms of ADD are caused by chemicals in the brain that are not working properly. As a result, many children and teenagers with ADD have problems with attention and learning that may cause significant problems both at home and school. The two most common characteristics in teenagers with ADD are inattention and impulsivity. Although *all* children may be inattentive and impulsive at times, youngsters with ADD behave this way more frequently. In addition, their impulsivity and inattention are more likely to cause serious problems at home and school.

Another hallmark of many teenagers with the disorder is underachievement in school. That is, these students don't perform as well academically as would be expected, given their level of intelligence. For some, but not all, hyperactivity during childhood is also a classic indicator. By adolescence, this hyperactivity has usually subsided, to be replaced by restlessness or sometimes rebelliousness. Beyond these core characteristics, there is great variability in behavior among young people with this disorder. Seldom will two teenagers with ADD behave the same way.

There are two distinctly different types of ADD: (1) ADD with hyperactivity and impulsivity as primary characteristics (ADD/H) and (2) ADD with inattention as the primary characteristic (ADD/I/WO - formerly called ADD without hyperactivity and Undifferentiated ADD). Teenagers with ADD with hyperactivity (ADD/H) may be very energetic, while teenagers with ADD/I/WO may be lethargic. Some teenagers may have both types of ADD. Combined hyperactivity-impulsivity and inattention is also known as Attention-Deficit/Hyperactivity Disorder (ADHD).

It is important to note here that far more is known about *ADHD* than about *ADD/I/WO*, and that more is known about ADHD in *children* than in *teenagers and young adults.* This is because most research conducted to date has been on children with ADHD. Consequently, the implications of this research for adolescents with ADD/I/WO are not always clear. This book therefore uses the terms ADHD and ADD/I/WO to specify studies limited only to youngsters with those types of ADD, and the term ADD to refer to studies that apply to both groups.

---

* As used in this book, the term "ADD" includes all diagnostic categories of attention deficit disorders.

Researchers have estimated that ADD occurs in as few as 1 percent and as many as 20 percent of children under eighteen. Most often, however, it is estimated that ADD affects 3 to 5 percent of all children. Another way of putting this is to say that approximately one to three students in every classroom of thirty students has the disorder. ADD is more common in boys than girls. Again, estimates vary, but different studies have found that ADD is anywhere from three to six times more common in boys than girls.

One of the primary complaints from parents and teachers is that these teenagers have *difficulty following rules and instructions.* The two core characteristics of ADD, inattention and impulsivity, are largely to blame. *Inattention* is most obvious when teenagers with ADD need to sustain attention to dull, boring, repetitive tasks such as schoolwork, homework, or chores. These teenagers prefer high-interest activities that offer a more satisfying, immediate reward. Specific examples of inattention frequently noted by parents and teachers include: doesn't listen, doesn't pay attention, can't concentrate, loses things, can't work alone, doesn't finish tasks, and shifts from one task to another. Parents frequently complain that their teenager doesn't complete his chores. He may start a job but somehow never gets it finished.*

Impulsivity is the second primary characteristic of ADD. Parents and teachers describe impulsivity as follows: responds quickly without waiting for instructions, makes careless errors, doesn't consider consequences, takes risks, carelessly damages possessions, has difficulty delaying gratification, and takes short cuts in work. Sometimes these youngsters, especially those who were hyperactive as children, talk a lot, are bossy, say things without thinking, offend people without realizing it, don't pick up on subtle social cues, and interrupt conversations. Consequently, they may have more *difficulty making and keeping friends. Talking back and arguing* with adults may also be a problem.

Both inattention and impulsivity contribute to *disorganization, difficulty getting started, and failure to complete homework,* which are also common complaints from parents and teachers. Because of these behaviors, these teenagers may appear to be irresponsible, immature, lazy, and rude. Consequently, they experience more criticism, punishment, and rejection from parents and teachers than their peers. As a result, children with ADD may have lower self-esteem as early as first and second grade. Many teenagers with ADD are less mature and may be *developmentally behind* their peers by as much as three or four years. For example, a 15–year-old may act more like a 12–year-old with regard to obeying his parents and completing chores and schoolwork. Often, it is difficult for them to live up to the expectations of their parents and teachers. Problem behaviors resulting from inattention and impulsivity plus suggested intervention strategies are discussed in detail in Chapters 5 through 10.

Although elementary school aged children with ADD also have problems with inattention and impulsivity, the challenges facing teenagers with ADD are more complex. Problems common in younger children—talking excessively, blurting out answers in class, not sitting in their seat, and doing sloppy work—are not the major issues facing middle and high school students. During the teenage years, the risks of school failure, school suspension or expulsion, dropping out of school, substance abuse, pregnancy, speeding tickets, car wrecks, and suicide are greater for these youngsters. Unfortunately, because of their academic struggles, many teenagers develop an aversion to school.

Other behaviors related to ADD also influence their day-to-day performance at home and school. Because teenagers with ADD have difficulty following rules and are impulsive, they are likely to have *conflicts with their parents, teachers, and other authority figures.* The most common conflicts arise when they don't do their class work, homework, or chores. Power struggles between teenagers and parents are common. Dr. Russell Barkley, author of the book *Attention Deficit Hyperactivity Disorder,* reports that 65 percent of these youngsters have problems with *stubbornness, defiance, refusal to obey, temper tantrums, and verbal hostility.* Many chafe for independence from their parents, typically, before

---

*   Since the majority of teenagers with ADD are male, the pronoun "he" is used throughout the book to refer to both males and females with ADD.

they are ready to manage their independence responsibly. Parents have long observed that youngsters with ADD are more difficult to discipline. They simply *do not respond to rewards and punishments* like other youngsters do. This behavior may help explain why they receive more criticism, rejection, and punishment than other children their age.

Low frustration tolerance is also common. Teenagers with ADD seem to respond more emotionally to stressful situations than other teenagers. These teenagers may anger easily, have a "short fuse," and "blow up" over trivial things. Some may be defiant and argumentative with their parents and other authority figures. *Anxiety and depression* may be common, but their importance and impact on the teenager's performance often may be overlooked.

Several researchers report that approximately half of all teenagers with ADD have *sleep disturbances.* They may have trouble falling asleep at night and difficulty waking up each morning. In addition, they may wake up each morning feeling tired. (These sleep disturbances are a separate problem from those caused by taking stimulant medication such as Ritalin too late in the day.) Sleep problems are discussed in more detail in Chapter 6.

Many students with ADD have *major problems at school.* Our educational system is highly structured, and requires students to have organizational skills, a good memory, good listening skills, and the ability to stay on task, follow up, and complete work rapidly. As Dr. Barkley points out, our educational system also requires students to delay gratification for their "rewards." For example, they must work today for a grade (reward) that they will receive in nine weeks, a semester, or a year later. These are all skills that many teenagers with ADD do not have. High school and college settings present the most structured and demanding environments these teenagers will face in their lifetime.

Parents and teachers may be puzzled because teenagers with ADD are bright but *under achieving academically.* Frequently, teachers comment that these teenagers are not doing well in school mainly because they don't pay attention, don't complete class work and homework, forget to do make-up work, make a lot of zeros on daily work, and sometimes, sleep in class. Even when they do their homework, they may forget to turn it in. Students

with ADD have tremendous difficulty getting started on schoolwork and frequently may turn in assignments late. Sometimes teenagers with ADD must be baffled by their own behavior.

❧

"I have always been curious why it is that so many kids feast at the table of knowledge, when all I get is indigestion"
> —*Nick, an intellectually gifted eight-year-old upon learning that he had ADD*

❧

Many teenagers with ADD have *serious learning problems* that are not recognized and probably contribute to their academic underachievement. Approximately 25 percent have specific learning disabilities (SLD)—a special education category in federal law that is used to describe learning problems that are not due to low intelligence. Common learning disabilities in students with ADD include poor listening comprehension, reading comprehension, written expression, and slow math computation. (See the detailed discussion on SLD in Chapter 8.) Other teenagers, possibly as many as 20 to 25 percent, may have serious learning problems which do not meet the criteria for specific learning disabilities and may not be brought to parents' attention by school personnel. Nonetheless, these learning problems may seriously interfere with school performance. Inattention, disorganization, poor memory, and fine motor problems (especially poor handwriting) are common in teenagers with ADD and may also cause problems in school. (Common learning problems and classroom adaptations are listed in Table 10-2 in Chapter 10.) These learning problems may result in poor and sloppy handwriting, slow or low production of written schoolwork, and failure to memorize information such as multiplication tables. Avoidance of written work may soon become a problem.

Uneven academic performance is another common characteristic that is extremely confusing to both parents and teachers. Some days these students can do the work; other days they can't. On the surface, it looks like they can do the work but choose not to. Parents begin hearing, "He can do the work but he just doesn't try." Or, "He isn't living up to his potential." Dr. Barkley believes that this un-

evenness of schoolwork is one of the primary problems of youngsters with ADHD.

⚜

"It is not unusual to hear a teacher say, 'Your son
could do the work, if he would just try. He has a high
IQ.' Parents and teachers often assume, incorrectly,
that intelligence is the only prerequisite for good
grades."

—*Steven Evans, Ph.D., Western Psychiatric
Institute and Clinic, University of Pittsburgh*

⚜

Academically and emotionally, many children
with ADD are able to cope adequately with the demands of elementary school. Some teenagers are
able to succeed with minimal problems even in
high school. However, for many youngsters with
ADD, frustration begins building in fourth and
fifth grades. It increases still more in middle
school, when academic demands are greater. If
their frustrations are not recognized and adjustments made at home and school, parents may be
faced with a very hostile, angry teenager who is
struggling at school.

A few of the more impulsive and aggressive
teenagers may have *problems with law enforcement
agencies.* These "brushes with the law" are usually
minor and are not the result of any malicious or
criminal intent. Instead, they result from poor impulse control, risk taking behavior, and/or failure to
anticipate the consequences of their actions. For
example, teenagers with ADD have been known to
receive speeding tickets, talk back to police offi-
cers, shoplift inexpensive items, sneak out of the
house after city curfew, drink under age, and experiment with drugs. Understandably, parents may
be afraid that this kind of acting out behavior may
become more serious. Fortunately, parents can
often prevent more serious problems by learning to
intervene when their child misbehaves, impose an
appropriate consequence, and continue to believe
in and support their child. Consequences for these
types of misbehavior are discussed in more detail
in Chapters 5, 6, and 7. Obviously, if problems are
serious and potentially life threatening, parents
should seek professional help.

⚜

"One snowy winter evening Cassie and some of her
friends went to a late movie in our old station wagon
nicknamed the 'boat.' On the way home, they pulled
into a large deserted parking lot and on a lark began
driving and sliding in circles on the icy surface. A police officer stopped them and gave my daughter a
ticket. Her response to the police officer was to say,
'Don't you have better things to do than harass perfectly behaving seventeen-year-old girls who are just
doing doughnuts in this parking lot?' The officer
wrote on the ticket that the child was extremely agitated and was insubordinate to the police officer. She
had to go to court and pay a fine."

⚜

"Once when my father, who I believe has undiagnosed ADD, was stopped for speeding, the highway
patrolman sarcastically asked to see his 'pilot's license.' My father promptly handed his real airline pilot's license to the highway patrolman. The patrolman
threw the pilot's license back in the car window, gave
him a warning, and told him to get back home to
Georgia. Once when he was in high school, he took a
cow up to the top floor of the school. Fortunately, he
didn't get caught pulling that prank."

⚜

"When our son was twelve and before ADD was diagnosed, he sneaked out of the house one night. The
police called at three a.m. telling us that he had been
picked up inside the local mall which was about a mile
from our home. He had not done any damage or stolen anything. I know my son. I don't believe he was
up to any malicious mischief. Primarily, I think he enjoyed the daring adventure of sneaking out of the
house. He and a friend had found a door unlocked
and were walking through the mall. They got scared
and ran when a security guard shouted at them. He
had to do community service and we put him on restrictions. Although his actions worried us sick at the
time, he is nineteen now, a freshman in college and
doing well. Just because a teenager has a brush with
the law does not mean he will be a delinquent."

⚜

These teenagers are not "bad, lazy, or unmotivated," as sometimes suggested by parents or
teachers, but are struggling to cope with ADD.

Most of us have known children or teenagers like this, whether they are our own, a relative's, or a friend's child. (Some readers may even recognize themselves in the descriptions of teenagers presented in this book.) It has intrigued me to discover that so many people I talk to about this disorder either have a family member with symptoms of ADD or know a family who has faced this difficulty.

Childhood Characteristics of ADD

Many other books describe ADD in young children in great detail. If your teenager was only recently diagnosed with ADD, however, you may find it helpful to look back on his early childhood and see which of the typical behaviors he had. If you are not yet sure that your teenager has ADD, comparing his behavior as a child to the behavior described here may help you decide whether to pursue a diagnosis. In either case, the information below should help you understand some of the differences between ADD in younger children and ADD in teenagers and young adults.

Classic ADD with Hyperactivity

Frequently, when people think of ADD, they picture Dennis the Menace—a child who is constantly moving and getting into mischief. Children with classic ADD *are* extremely hyperactive at an early age, with some being diagnosed during early infancy. Often parents tell professionals that their child with ADD has been different from their siblings or other children since birth. Some are more active in the womb.

Children with ADD may stand or walk at an early age. Children who are hyperactive learn as young toddlers to "escape" from their cribs, strollers, and playpens. They may be very talkative and may seem to be in constant motion.

✠

"Cassie walked at seven months and it seemed like all hell broke loose. At seven months she weighed eleven pounds. She was tiny and very agile. Nothing was safe!

"We couldn't have anything in our house, no knickknacks. Nothing, nothing could be in her reach. By nine months she had kicked two slats out of her crib. At ten months, our pediatrician recommended putting a mesh roping over the top of her crib because she climbed out every time we put her in. If you have ever seen a tiny nine-month-old swing from the top bar of the crib and drop to the floor, it was quite a sight. We were afraid that she was going to hurt herself."

✠

According to Dr. Barkley, approximately one-third of all children with ADHD may be very hyperactive and be diagnosed during infancy. However, the average age for diagnosis of ADHD is 3 or 4 years of age. Because of their hyperactivity, most children with ADHD are diagnosed before entering school or soon after they enter kindergarten.

✠

"Our daughter was so active that the pediatrician wanted to put her on Ritalin at age two. My husband and I decided to behaviorally manage her behavior instead. However, we may have done it too successfully because when she entered school, educators were reluctant to believe she was hyperactive. They said, 'She doesn't act like the boys. It isn't that she can't sit in her seat. She just seems unable to concentrate. We hate to medicate her.'"

✠

In extreme cases, children with ADHD may sleep only two or three hours a night, driving their parents to exhaustion.

✠

"She would sleep all night once we got her to sleep. The problem was getting her to fall asleep. At first, we would spank her every time she got out of her bed. Our pediatrician recommended that we pick her up, say, 'Bedtime is for sleeping,' and then put her back in her youth bed. We did that for four or five months where we had to sit outside her door and keep putting her back in bed."

✠

Hyperactive children may have trouble sitting still and are constantly in motion—running, jumping, and climbing the unclimbable. Toddlers and nursery school children race from one activity to another. They may become upset and kick things or hit or bite other children if they don't get what they want, when they want it. They may be extremely independent from an early age.

🦋

"Our son always had this, 'No, I'll do it myself,' attitude from the time he was about one year old. When he went to nursery school, the teacher said she had never met a more independent four-year-old."

🦋

When these children enter preschool or elementary school, they may have a very difficult time adjusting and following rules. They can't remain in their seats. They may be aggressive, fighting with other children, biting, or taking their toys away. Day care or school officials may call and ask parents to take their child home because his behavior is out of control.

🦋

"Kaiha was diagnosed with ADD in the first grade. She was so active she couldn't sit still in her seat. She exhibited the classic symptoms. She would blurt out answers in class."

Mild ADHD or ADD/Inattentive

ADD is more than just classic Dennis the Menace hyperactivity. A different picture emerges for children with *mild hyperactivity* or ADD/Inattentive/Without Hyperactivity (*ADD/I/WO*). Parents of children with milder cases of ADHD say that their children were active but not overly active. These children may run and climb but they can sit still long enough to watch TV, play Nintendo, or play with their favorite toys. In addition, children who have ADD/I/WO are sometimes described as underactive or lethargic. Since their symptoms of ADD are not as obvious, diagnosis of these two groups of youngsters is more difficult and may not be made until after they enter school. However, *all children with ADHD or ADD share one characteristic in common—inattention*, which may negatively affect their school performance. Although school adjustment may not be as traumatic initially for these

children as for children with classic ADD with hyperactivity, school may cease to bring joy or a sense of success in the early elementary school years.

Secondary Childhood Characteristics

Researchers have found that many children with ADD also have more *health problems* than children without ADD. Allergies, colds, ear infections, asthma, and upper respiratory infections occur more frequently. As infants, they may have colic, have irregular eating and sleeping patterns, be more fitful and restless, cry easily, and have trouble adjusting to change in routine. Some infants with ADD may be undemonstrative and noncuddlers. Some may have delays in talking or speech problems."

🦋

"From the time our son was born, he had a mind of his own. He was not the kind of child who could be held or cuddled. He resisted being held or cuddled by arching his back to get away from us. If he initiated cuddling, that was okay but it very rarely happened. Mostly he would squirm down out of our reach and do what he wanted to do."

🦋

"Our daughter had colic. I thought we'd never get through that period."

🦋

Children with ADD who are hyperactive tend to have more than their share of *accidents* and visit emergency rooms more often than other children. Researchers found that up to 46 percent of these youngsters may be considered accident-prone, and that 15 percent have had serious accidents such as broken bones, cuts, head injuries, lost teeth, or accidental poisonings. They may get into everything, touch and handle everything they see, climb the unclimbable, get into childproof cabinets and containers, have accidental burns and electrical shocks, or rush into the street or other dangerous situations. Toys and household items may be damaged or broken because parents take their eyes off the child for one moment.

Some children with ADD have trouble with *bladder control*. Toilet training may be delayed and problems with enuresis (bed wetting) or encopresis (soiling) may occur. Sometimes these children are "too busy" to go to the bathroom and may have "accidents." However, research is somewhat contradictory with no clear evidence that this problem occurs more often in youngsters with ADD.

🖏

"Potty training was very difficult for my child. Enuresis continued to be a problem until age ten or eleven."

🖏

Children with ADHD may have *problems making friends and keeping them*. They may be bossy, want their own way, or may not follow rules of fair play. Some youngsters demand to be the center of attention. They may monopolize conversations, talk too loudly, and show off with their friends. Researchers have found that they may be rejected by their playmates within only twenty or thirty minutes. Their playmates may react with aversion, criticism, rejection, counterattack, or withdrawal from their aggression, unpredictability, and disruptiveness.

Then again, there are the *exceptions to the rule*. Some youngsters with ADD don't exhibit any of these secondary characteristics. Others may exhibit only a few characteristics. Perhaps it is because they may have ADD/I/WO or a milder case of hyperactivity.

🖏

"My son who has ADD without hyperactivity (ADD/I/WO) really didn't have very many of the textbook symptoms. He was never hyperactive, his developmental norms were normal, and he never had colic. However, he was inattentive, very adventuresome, and moderately active. He had some sleep problems and as a result never seemed to need as much sleep as other children. Getting him to bed at night or to take a nap was frequently a battle."

🖏

Several excellent books have been written about younger children who are hyperactive. See the Bibliography for a list of reading materials on younger children with ADD.

Diagnostic Criteria for ADD: DSM IV

Often parents, teachers, pediatricians, or others may strongly suspect that a teenager or child has ADD because of behaviors like those described above. The diagnosis of Attention Deficit Disorder is not "official," however, unless the child meets certain criteria developed by the American Psychiatric Association (APA) and published in their *Diagnostic and Statistical Manual of Mental Disorders (DSM)*. The revised third edition of this manual (DSM III-R), which was in effect from 1987 to 1993, contained only two diagnoses of ADD in youngsters: Attention-deficit Hyperactivity Disorder (ADHD) and Undifferentiated Attention-deficit Disorder (ADD). In May of 1994, a new edition (DSM IV) was released. This edition established four categories of ADD in children, teenagers, and adults, including a new term for the condition as a whole: Attention-Deficit/Hyperactivity Disorder (AD/HD).* DSM IV diagnostic criteria are listed in Table 1–1.

In determining whether your child has an attention deficit disorder, a licensed counselor, psychologist, or physician will compare your child's behavior (or your reports of his behavior) with the characteristics listed under each of the types of ADD included in the DSM IV. If he has a sufficient number of the characteristics to a degree that is "maladaptive and inconsistent with developmental level," he will be diagnosed with ADD. Typically, this means the symptoms of ADD are serious enough to interfere with the teenager's ability to

---

* Because the DSM IV criteria are still relatively new at this writing, common abbreviated terms have not yet been established. The author has attempted to select terms for the three categories of ADD that would make sense to a reasonable person: 1) ADHD [combined hyperactive and inattentive]; 2) ADD/I/WO [inattentive, without hyperactivity]; and 3) ADD/H [hyperactive only].

TABLE 1–1

DSM IV Diagnostic Criteria for Attention Deficit Disorders

CRITERIA:

Attention-Deficit/Hyperactivity Disorder

A. Either (1) or (2)
• (1) six (or more) of the following symptoms of **inattention** have persisted for at least 6 months to a degree that is maladaptive and inconsistent with developmental level:

INATTENTION

(a) often fails to give close attention to details or makes careless mistakes in schoolwork, work, or other activities
(b) often has difficulty sustaining attention in tasks or play activities
(c) often does not seem to listen when spoken to directly
(d) often does not follow through on directions and fails to finish schoolwork, chores, or duties in the workplace (not due to oppositional behavior or failure to understand directions)
(e) often has difficulty organizing tasks and activities
(f) often avoids, dislikes, or is reluctant to engage in tasks that require sustained mental effort (such as schoolwork or homework)
(g) often loses things necessary for tasks or activities (e.g., toys, school assignments, pencils, books, or tools)
(h) is often easily distracted by extraneous stimuli
(i) is often forgetful in daily activities

• (2) six (or more) of the following symptoms of **hyperactivity-impulsivity** have persisted for at least six months to a degree that is maladaptive and inconsistent with developmental level:

HYPERACTIVITY

(a) often fidgets with hands or feet or squirms in seat
(b) often leaves seat in classroom or in other situations in which remaining seated is expected
(c) often runs about or climbs excessively in situations in which it is inappropriate (in adolescents or adults, may be limited to subjective feelings of restlessness)
(d) often has difficulty playing or engaging in leisure activities quietly
(e) is often "on the go" or often acts as if "driven by a motor"
(f) often talks excessively

IMPULSIVITY

(g) often blurts out answers before questions have been completed
(h) often has difficulty awaiting turn
(i) often interrupts or intrudes on others (e.g., butts into conversations or games)

[Most of the symptoms in A(2) above describe the behaviors of younger children. Parents may compare their teenager's behavior as a young child with these criteria to determine if ADD/H is also present.]*
B. Some hyperactive-impulsive or inattentive symptoms that caused impairment were present before age 7 years.
C. Some impairment from the symptoms is present in two or more settings
(e.g., at school [or work] and at home).
D. There must be clear evidence of clinically significant impairment in social, academic, or occupational functioning.
E. The symptoms do not occur exclusively during the course of a Pervasive Developmental Disorder, Schizophrenia, or other Psychotic Disorder and are not better accounted for by another mental disorder (e.g., Mood Disorder, Anxiety Disorder, Dissociative Disorder, or a Personality disorder).

POSSIBLE DIAGNOSES:

314.01 Attention-Deficit/Hyperactivity Disorder, Combined Type: if both criteria A(1) and A(2) are met for the past six months.

[Two categories of attention deficit disorders have been established for children who are hyperactive. To make it easier to differentiate between them, the author is using the acronym **ADHD** for ADHD/combined hyperactive-impulsive and inattentive.]*

* Comments in brackets are the author's and are not part of DSM IV.

314.00 Attention-Deficit/Hyperactivity Disorder, Predominately Inattentive Type: if criterion A1 is met but criterion A2 is not met for the past six months.

[Formerly called Undifferentiated ADD or ADD without hyperactivity. ADD inattentive is much more than just a simple case of ADHD without hyperactivity. Inattention is the predominate feature of this disorder. Thus, the term **ADD/I/WO** will be used throughout the book to designate this type of ADD.]

314.01 Attention-Deficit/Hyperactivity Disorder, Predominately Hyperactive-Impulsive Type: if criterion A2 is met but criterion A1 is not met for the past six months.

[A notation of **ADD/H** will be used to indicate hyperactive only].

314.9 Attention-Deficit/Hyperactivity Disorder Not Otherwise Specified: This category is for disorders with prominent symptoms of inattention or hyperactivity-impulsivity that do not meet criteria for Attention-Deficit/Hyperactivity Disorder.

function successfully at home and school. Chapter 2 explains the process of diagnosis in more detail.

Despite a few problems, the DSM IV diagnostic criteria for ADD are an improvement over those in the previous editions. The new criteria describe the inattentive aspects of ADD more accurately and separate them from the hyperactive/impulsive characteristics. The DSM IV also creates a separate category of ADD for children who are hyperactive only, but not inattentive. Another addition to DSM IV requires that the person being diagnosed as having ADD must exhibit symptoms in more than one setting (home and school).

One change in the DSM IV, however, may be problematic: the "H" for hyperactivity is included in the term AD/HD, Predominately Inattentive Type, for diagnosing children who are *not hyperactive*. This diagnostic title, AD/HD, does not accurately describe children with ADD who are *not hyperactive* and will most likely cause confusion among parents, educators, and treatment professionals. Parents and professionals will ask, "How can a teenager have Attention-Deficit/Hyperactivity Disorder and not be hyperactive?" The myth that a youngster has to be hyperactive to have ADD may be perpetuated and problems diagnosing ADD/I/WO will probably continue.

The release of the new DSM IV criteria and recent federal policies from the U.S. Department of Education should promote early identification and treatment of youngsters with ADD. Descriptions of everyday behaviors teenagers with ADD exhibit at home (Chapters 6 and 7) and school (Chapters 8 through 10) should also make it easier for parents

and teachers to identify teenagers with the disorder. Diagnosis of ADD is discussed in detail in Chapter 2.

The Myths Hindering Diagnosis of ADD

Several common myths have sometimes prevented diagnosis and treatment of ADD:

Myth I: All children/teenagers with ADD are hyperactive.

Some professionals and parents still mistakenly believe that a child or teenager with ADD must be hyperactive. They may be unaware that by the teenage years, hyperactivity is usually no longer present and has been replaced by restlessness. In addition, children with milder cases of ADHD may not seem excessively hyperactive. Students who have ADD/I/WO may actually be lethargic. Consequently, teenagers who have ADHD with restlessness or ADD/I/WO may be overlooked.

According to Dr. Barkley's research, ADHD occurs more frequently than ADD/I/WO. Approximately 75 percent of boys with ADD are hyperactive. Among girls with ADD, roughly 60 percent are hyperactive.

⬚

"When I have called some teachers and mentioned that 'John' had ADD, frequently the teacher will say that can't be true. John isn't hyperactive."

—Pediatric Center Staff

Myth II: Hyperactive children/teenagers with ADD can't sit still for ten minutes.

Hyperactive youngsters with ADD do better in one-to-one and novel situations. They can sit still and maintain a conversation with a doctor or other treatment professional during an office visit.

※

"It has been my experience that even the most hyperactive child with ADD can be relatively quiet during a ten-minute evaluation, especially when they are bright. Some physicians and clinicians are still using this criteria to say if they can sit still in my office for that period of time they must not have ADD."

— a school psychologist

※

Myth III: ADD disappears in adolescence and adulthood.

One of the reasons that parents, teachers, and physicians believe that youngsters outgrow ADHD is because their hyperactivity decreases as they reach adolescence. The attention problems often persist, however, and manifest themselves in a different way in teenagers. The hyperactivity appears to be replaced with restlessness, inattentiveness, or sleeping in class. The ADHD teenager who feels "hyper" knows it isn't acceptable to get up and walk around in class, so instead he may tune out mentally or sleep.

Myth IV: Stimulant medications such as Ritalin no longer work when the child reaches adolescence.

Research has shown that stimulant medications are effective in both children and teenagers with ADD in decreasing hyperactivity, impulsivity, negative behaviors, and verbal hostility, while improving attention, concentration, compliance, and completion of schoolwork. See Chapter 4 for more information on medications.

Myth V: ADD will always be diagnosed in childhood.

Unfortunately, ADD is overlooked in a number of teenagers and adults. Most parents and high school personnel have not considered ADD as a potential culprit underlying student underachievement. They presume that ADD, if present, would have been diagnosed in elementary school.

The age of diagnosis may vary depending on the severity and type of ADD. Children who are extremely hyperactive are usually diagnosed early. Children with milder cases of ADHD or those who have ADD/I/WO may not be diagnosed until middle or high school. Teenagers who are extremely bright may compensate for their ADD and elude diagnosis until middle school, high school, or even college. Girls with ADD are also frequently overlooked. They may go undetected until middle or high school because they usually do not exhibit major behavior problems.

Causes of ADD

Until the last few years parents were sometimes singled out as the cause of their child's attentional and behavior problems. They were accused of "bad parenting" and often criticized for failing to discipline their child properly.

Although researchers and medical experts have not yet reached unanimous agreement about the causes of ADD, most would agree that the symptoms of ADD are beyond the child's—and his parents'—control. Parents do *not* cause their children's ADD. As mentioned earlier, there is now evidence that ADD has a biochemical basis. That is, deficiencies in chemical messengers in the brain (neurotransmitters) prevent it from working properly, causing symptoms of ADD.

Having an underlying biochemical problem doesn't mean the teenager is totally at the mercy of chemicals in his brain and is powerless to control his life or impulses. It does mean, however, that he will have to work much harder to pay attention, obey his parents, and complete chores and schoolwork. Teenagers with ADD need to seek appropriate treatment and learn to compensate for having this disorder.

The evidence for a biochemical cause for ADD is based upon research in several areas. First, ADD often seems to be inherited—passed down from one generation to the next. Second, stimulant medications such as Ritalin, which affect neurotransmitters in the central nervous system, reduce symptoms of ADD. Third, the absorption of glucose in the brains of adults with ADHD is lower than in adults without ADHD. This indicates underactivity or underarousal in the brain.

Inherited vs. Noninherited Causes

Parents (or other close relatives) often seem to pass ADD on to their children. Family histories frequently show that a parent (usually the father), or an uncle or grandfather, acted the same way the child with ADD acts. According to Dr. Barkley, approximately *40 percent of all youngsters with ADD have at least one parent who has the condition.* This makes ADD the most often inherited childhood disorder identified in the DSM.

✖

"I suspect that my father, sister, and son all have ADD. My father recently retired after 43 years of elected public service. He was honored this summer at a retirement ceremony after serving 35 years as probate judge. Although Dad was not a good student in school, he graduated from law school when he was in his early thirties. Subsequently, he was elected to the Georgia House of Representatives and later county probate judge. My sister finished her doctorate when she was in her mid-thirties.

"Some of my favorite stories about my Dad reflect his creativity and high energy level. In 1949, when Dad was elected to the Georgia House of Representatives, he gave new meaning to the term campaigning by airplane. Dad and his brother rigged up a public address system in an open cockpit airplane and flew low over houses asking people to vote for him. People were impressed!! He was elected with the highest vote of any of the eight candidates."

✖

When ADD is not inherited, it may be caused by trauma at birth or to the fetus during pregnancy. Consequently, children with fetal alcohol syndrome (FAS) or fetal alcohol effects (FAE) often have symptoms of ADD. So, too, do some children whose mothers abused drugs during their pregnancy. ADD is also common in children with disabilities such as spina bifida, cerebral palsy, Tourette syndrome, and fragile X syndrome.

Research has shown that a significant number of children with thyroid disease also exhibit symptoms of ADHD. In one study, approximately 5 percent of children with ADHD had symptoms of thyroid disease. However, most researchers do not think adequate research is available regarding the thyroid/ADHD link. Thyroid screenings should be done on youngsters who have a depressed rate of growth or swelling of the thyroid gland. The effects of hormone treatment for an underactive thyroid have been contradictory: in some children, ADHD behaviors improve; in others, they worsen. If parents have concerns about potential thyroid problems, they should discuss them with their physician.

Sometimes external factors such as having too much sugar in the diet have been thought to cause ADD. However, research indicates that neither sugar nor artificial sweeteners produces hyperactivity.

Neurotransmitter Deficiencies

Much research into the causes of ADD is presently focused on deficiencies in neurotransmitters in the central nervous system (CNS). The CNS is comprised of the brain and nerves in the spinal cord. It acts as the main control system of the body, directing and coordinating actions. In ADHD, the prefrontal and limbic portions of the brain are believed to be the major sites with neurotransmitter problems. Some researchers believe that ADD/I/WO involves problems in a different section of the brain—the posterior cortical areas of the brain. The major sections of the brain thought to be involved in ADD and the actions each controls are noted in Figure 1.

To understand how deficiencies in neurotransmitters could result in ADD, a brief description of how neurotransmitters are *supposed* to work may be helpful. The human nervous system has billions of nerve cells or neurons that carry messages throughout the body (See Figure 2). These messages might direct a teenager to listen, pay attention when the parent or teacher is talking, remember the assigned task, and stick with the task until it is finished.

Technically speaking, the nerve cells, or neurons, carry impulses (nerve signals) from one end of the cell to the other—from the dendrite to the axon. There is a space between neurons—known as a synapse. Since the axon and dendrites of the next neuron do not touch, messages must cross

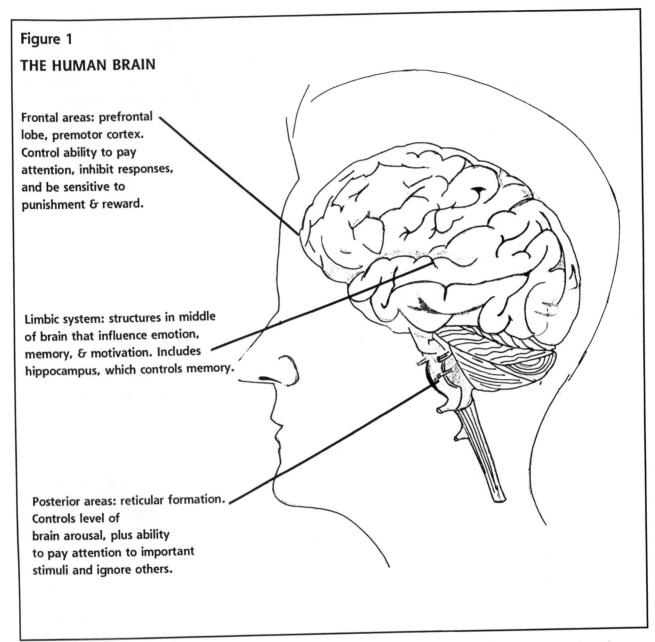

Figure 1

THE HUMAN BRAIN

Frontal areas: prefrontal lobe, premotor cortex. Control ability to pay attention, inhibit responses, and be sensitive to punishment & reward.

Limbic system: structures in middle of brain that influence emotion, memory, & motivation. Includes hippocampus, which controls memory.

Posterior areas: reticular formation. Controls level of brain arousal, plus ability to pay attention to important stimuli and ignore others.

synapse. Neurotransmitters, the chemical messengers of the brain, are released at the synapse to help the message move across to the next neuron.

When ADD is present, it is believed that messages move down the neuron, but stop and don't always cross the synapse to the next one. This disruption is most likely caused by a chemical deficiency in neurotransmitters, which interrupts the normal flow of messages throughout the body. When neurotransmitters do not work properly, youngsters have difficulty paying attention, controlling impulses, suppressing inappropriate responses, and regulating motor activity.

The two primary neurotransmitters thought to be involved in ADD are dopamine and norepinephrine. Another neurotransmitter, serotonin, which is essential for restful sleep and feelings of well-being, is also thought to be involved. When availability of these neurotransmitters is low, inattention, distractibility, aggression, depression, and irritability may result. Researchers speculate that the major problem in ADHD may be with dopamine; in ADD/I/WO, with norepinephrine. Neurotransmitters, their role in ADD, and use of medication to improve their functioning are discussed in detail in Chapter 4.

Figure 2

Diagram of a Neuron

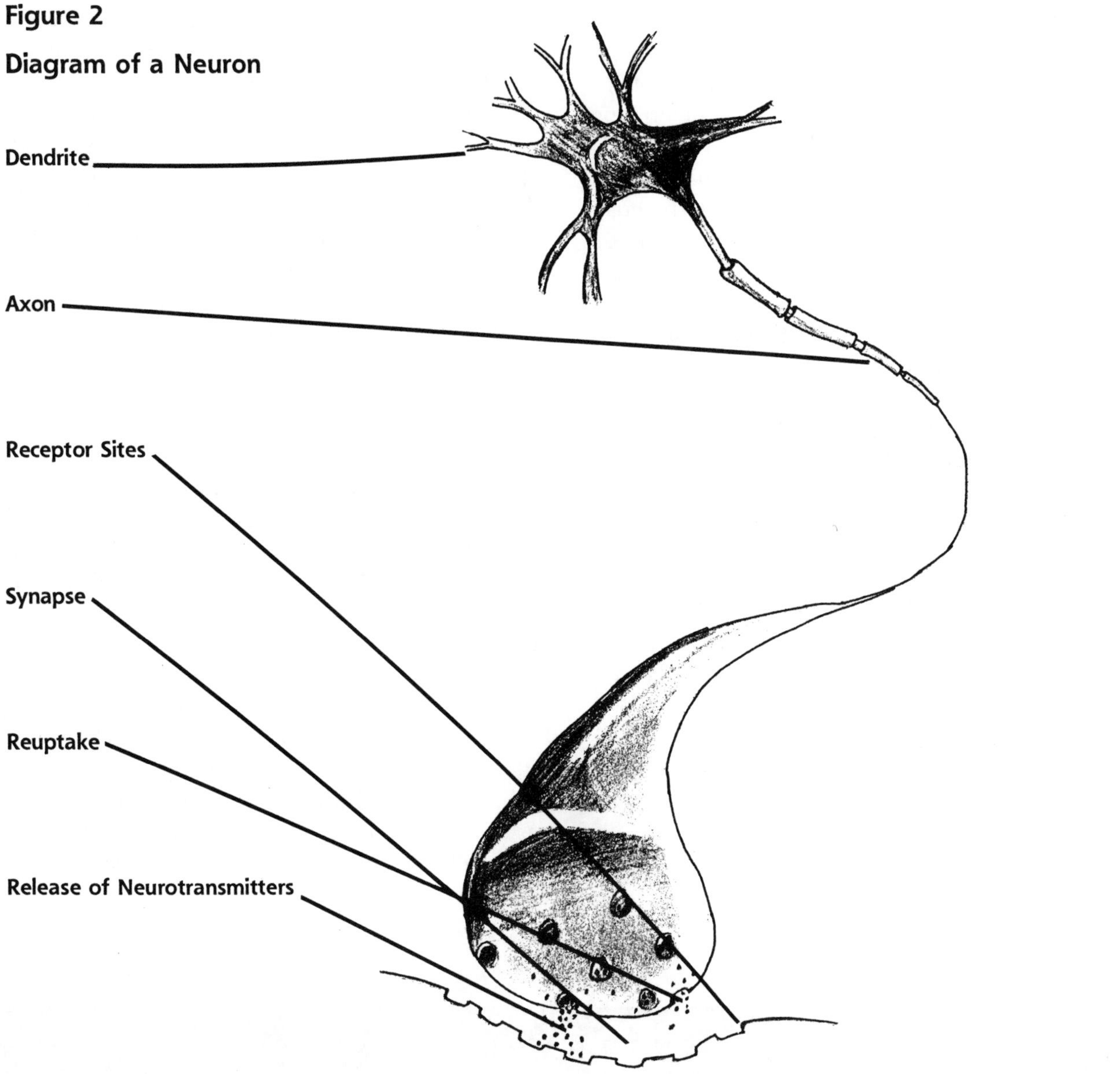

Dendrite

Axon

Receptor Sites

Synapse

Reuptake

Release of Neurotransmitters

The theory linking ADD to a neurotransmitter deficiency is supported by the fact that stimulant medications, such as Ritalin, can often improve symptoms of ADD. These stimulant medications, so called because they stimulate the central nervous system, are known to promote release of dopamine, norepinephrine, and serotonin—the very neurotransmitters that appear to be deficient in children with ADD. (Medications that enhance the functioning of neurotransmitters are discussed in Chapter 4.)

According to Dr. Paul Wender, author of *The Hyperactive Child, Teenager, and Adult,* the production of neurotransmitters increases with age, which would explain why youngsters with ADD seem to outgrow some of their symptoms as they get older.

NIMH Research Points to Biochemical Link with ADD

Exciting studies at the National Institute of Mental Health are shedding new light on the nature and causes of ADD. These studies involve using techniques such as a Positron Emission Tomography (PET) scan. A PET scan is a procedure that is similar to taking a color x-ray of a cross section of the brain to depict its activity levels. These studies have shown underactivity in the prefrontal portions of the brain of adults with ADHD, including the premotor cortex and the superior prefrontal cortex areas. The frontal lobe of the brain controls complex mental processes such as memory, speech, and thought. These areas of the brain are where dopamine and norepinephrine are most involved in transmitting messages.

A landmark study using a PET scan, published in November, 1990 in the *New England Journal of Medicine,* provided the first direct evidence that *ADD has a biochemical basis.* Dr. Alan Zametkin, M.D., a psychiatrist and researcher at the National Institute of Mental Health (NIMH) in Bethesda, Maryland, conducted the PET studies of the brains of adults with ADHD. These studies showed that the rate at which the brain absorbs glucose, its main energy source, is lower in adults with ADHD than in adults without ADHD. The largest reductions in glucose absorption are in the premotor cortex and the superior prefrontal cortex. Figure 3 shows the difference in brain activity between adults with and without ADHD. In the brain on the left (non-ADHD), there are a number of white areas indicating a great deal of brain activity, while there is only one white area in the brain on the right (ADHD).

The PET scan was conducted while the adults completed a simple test which required them to pay attention for 35 minutes. The adults were blindfolded and listened to a series of three tones. They were asked to press a button to indicate which of the three tones was the lowest. Although the significance is not clear, the adults with ADHD scored as well on the test as the adults without ADHD even though there was reduced activity in their brains.

The NIMH research was conducted on adults with ADHD, so the implications for adults with ADD/I/WO are unclear. As discussed earlier, some researchers believe that ADD/I/WO is a different type of attentional disturbance and not a subtype of ADHD. Dr. Barkley, for example, believes that ADHD involves a failure to control motor activities or behaviors (a problem with output of messages from the brain), and ADD/I/WO involves sluggish cognitive processing (a problem with the brain receiving and processing information quickly and accurately.)

Dr. Zametkin's research offers increased reassurance that *the difficulties that youngsters with ADD face are the result of medical problems, not "bad parenting."* Parents cannot cause their teenager's ADD behavior because of the way they raise him. However, as discussed in later chapters, they can help him make a better adjustment at home and school.

Figure 3

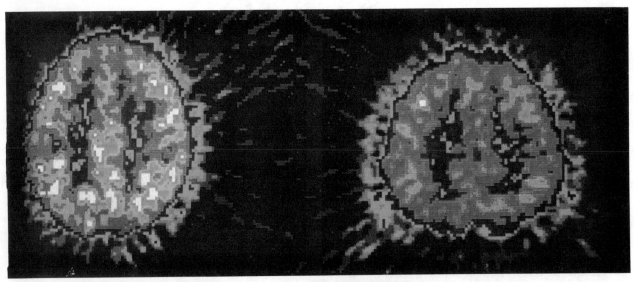

NON-ADHD ADULT　　　　　　　　**ADHD ADULT**

Perhaps Dr. Zametkin's research may also eliminate arguments over whether ADD has psychological or biological roots. Experts who believe solely in a psychological basis for ADD believe that these children can control their behavior without medication. Instead, these experts urge parents to use behavior-modification techniques, family counseling, training in social skills, and educational remediation instead of medication. However, as explained in Chapter 4, medication is a critical cornerstone of treatment for many teenagers, especially those who are struggling at home and at school. Research has shown that stimulant medication is effective in reducing the symptoms of ADD for all but approximately 5 percent of children.

Although current research supports the hypothesis that ADD has a genetic/biological basis, other factors may also influence the teenager's behavior. Dr. Bill Buzogany, a psychiatrist, and Dr. Steven Evans, a psychologist, remind us that many problems parents and teenagers face are the result of an interaction between biochemical, psychological, and social factors.* For example, a student who is impulsive as a result of ADD (biological cause) may act worse if his parents provide no rules or structure, or are hostile, physically abusive, or inconsistent in their discipline (psychological factors). The influence of his friends (social factors) will also have a major impact on his behavior.

Biological, psychological, and social factors must therefore be considered in your teenager's treatment. Medications alone are usually not sufficient to solve every problem related to ADD. Many experts believe that a multi-faceted approach, including medication, academic consultation, classroom adaptations, behavioral programming, and counseling, is best for children with ADD and their families. Treatment methods and parenting skills are discussed in detail in Chapters 4 and 5.

Beyond DSM-IV: What is Current Research Telling Us about ADD?

The leading researchers view ADD from a more scientific and sophisticated perspective than most local treatment professionals and parents. Researchers study ADD intensely to learn more about the scientific reasons for its symptoms. What this means to parents is that as researchers learn more, new and improved techniques for coping with ADD should be developed.

Presently, researchers are fine tuning the descriptions of the primary characteristics of ADD. Dr. Russell Barkley, who is probably the most respected authority on ADHD, has identified five major characteristics of the disorder:

- *lack of persistence of effort* on a task;
- *behavioral impulsivity* (acting before thinking, due to great difficulty delaying a response or delaying gratification);
- *hyperactivity* (hyper responsiveness);
- *failure to follow through* on rules or instructions; and
- *fluctuation in the quality of work* (one of the primary problems in ADHD, according to Dr. Barkley. In his opinion, this variability may actually be useful for diagnosing the disorder.)

An example of persistence of effort should clarify what Dr. Barkley means by this term: when most people listen to a speaker, they pay attention for a few seconds, look away, shift in their seats, and then redirect their attention to the speaker. Teenagers with ADHD cannot do this easily. They must struggle to constantly redirect their attention to the original task—to persist with the activity. Unfortunately, they quickly grow tired of listening and begin looking for something more interesting to do.

Some research challenges a few of our previous assumptions about ADHD. For example, Dr.

---

* Dr. Buzogany is an Associate Professor of Psychiatry at University of Wisconsin Medical School and medical director for an adolescent residential treatment program. Dr. Evans, an Assistant Professor of Psychiatry at Western Psychiatric Institute, University of Pittsburgh, works with teenagers in a program for ADD.

Barkley explains that youngsters with ADHD are not particularly distractible, although they appear to be to the casual observer. When distractions were introduced into research studies, youngsters with ADHD actually did *better* on the tests. That may be why placing a child in an isolated study carrel is not particularly effective. Students with ADHD actually work better when learning is active and the classroom is stimulating. Although these children may appear distractible, they apparently lose interest in their work rapidly and actively begin seeking more interesting stimulation.

Perhaps you wonder why it is important to know about research that may challenge traditional assumptions about the nature of ADD. The reason is that treatment for ADD is based on the perceived causes of the symptoms. If the underlying causes of the symptoms of ADD are different than we originally assumed, then intervention strategies must change, too.

Each Teenager with ADD Is Unique!

Teenagers with ADD do not all act alike or have the same strengths and problems. Symptoms of inattention, impulsivity, and hyperactivity, if present, may vary from mild to severe. Learning problems may also occur in one or more academic areas and may vary from mild to severe. Other problems such as anxiety, depression, and aggression may be present, further contributing to the unique make-up

of the teenager. In addition, teenagers with hyperactivity often have different behaviors from those who have ADD with inattention.

Many factors, including basic personality, intelligence, severity of the ADD, response to medication, learning disabilities, temperament, and family and school support all affect a teenager's ability to adapt successfully. So, too, do outside stresses such as divorce, sexual or physical abuse, family moves, ill health, a death in the family, lack of supervision, lack of family supports, single parenting, remarriage (step-parenting), out-of-home placement, and poverty. Your child's ADD is really only one small part of who he is.

To get an idea of the uniqueness of each teenager with ADD, review the sample profiles of two teenagers included as Table 1–2. These profiles can help you to become more aware of the many factors which influence your teenager's development and to identify areas which you can change. The profiles developed for a teenager with ADHD and one with ADD/I/WO emphasize the differences in their behaviors.

Develop a Profile of Your Teenager

To better understand your teenager with ADD, you may want to develop a profile by completing the blank form (Understanding the Teenager) in Chapter 13. This form identifies a broad spectrum of factors, both positive and negative, which may affect your teenager. Many rating scales focus only on problems, and thus fail to identify strengths (and may inadvertently discourage parents and teenagers). By filling out this form, you can clearly see your teenager's strengths and difficulties, and important areas in which you can make changes. This information can be helpful to both parents and teachers in targeting specific behaviors for improvement.

Remember, however, that the behaviors associated with ADD are not the only ones that influence your teenager's ability to cope successfully with the disorder. Parents and teachers are urged to identify the teenager's positive qualities as noted in Table 3–1 in Chapter 3 and build upon those strengths. Parents are also encouraged to cherish their teenager's strengths and zest for living. The more "positive factors" in a teenager's life and the fewer stresses and hostile interactions, the

Table 1–2

Understanding the Teenager with ADD

NAME: _Student with ADD/I/WO_   AGE: DATE:

By completing this form, parents should gain a better understanding of their teenager's unique characteristics, personality, strengths, difficulties, and how he is different from other teenagers with ADD. In addition to the symptoms of ADD, all the factors listed below also influence the teenager's behavior, self-esteem, and ability to cope successfully with ADD. The severity of behaviors will vary. Please circle words that best describe your teenager.

DIAGNOSIS: Symptoms of ADD may range from mild to severe.

ADD/Hyperactive (ADD/H) mild moderate severe

ADD/Inattentive (ADD/I/WO)
  without Hyperactivity mild moderate (severe)

ADD/Combined (ADHD) mild moderate severe

COEXISTING DIAGNOSIS: ADD frequently coexists with other disorders.

Anxiety	mild	(moderate)	severe
Depression	mild	(moderate)	severe
Oppositional Defiant	mild	(moderate)	severe
Conduct Disorder	mild	moderate	severe
Learning Disability	mild	moderate	severe
Learning Problems	mild	moderate	(severe)
Sleep Disturbance	mild	(moderate)	severe

FACTORS INFLUENCING ADD: Other factors influence a teenager's personality and ability to cope successfully with ADD. These factors may also vary in intensity: mild/moderate/severe. Teenagers with ADHD and ADD/I/WO may be almost exact opposites in some behaviors. Circle the word that describes your teenager's behavior most of the time.

TEMPERAMENT

(calm)/fidgets
(easy going)/aggressive
high energy/(lethargic)
(happy)/depressed
(pleasant)/irritable
(charming)/sullen
class clown/(shy)
relaxed/(anxious)
cautious/daring
(tenacious)/gives up easily
(compliant)/defiant _sometimes_
copes well/(easily frustrated)
(angry outbursts)/calm
(talks a lot)/quiet & low key

GENERAL ISSUES

self esteem: (good)/fair
intelligence: average/(high)
gets along with friends: (yes)/no
inattentive: (yes)/no
impulsive: (yes)/no
disorganized: (yes)/no
loses things: (yes)/no
forgets things: (yes)/no
complies with requests: yes/(no)
will do chores: (yes)/no ← forgets
truthful: (yes)/no
response to medication: good/(fair)
difficulty falling asleep: (yes)/no
difficulty waking up: (yes)/no
restless: (yes)/no
self-centered: (yes)/no
accident prone: (yes)/no
interrupts/butts in: yes/(no)

FAMILY STRESS FACTORS

two parent family: (yes)/no
step-parents: (yes)/no
family understands ADD
  (supportive): (yes)/no
reasonable discipline: (yes)/no
  (not too harsh or lenient)
open communication: (yes)/no
few hostile inteactions between
  teenager and parents: (yes)/no
relatives understand ADD
  (supportive): (yes)/no
family stresses (money, illness,
  divorce, remarriage): (yes)/no
moved to new community: (yes)/no
attending same school: yes/(no)

AREAS OF SUCCESS	POTENTIAL PROBLEM AREAS	MORE SERIOUS PROBLEMS
sports: (yes)/no	defies/disobeys adults: yes/(no)	bullies or threatens others: yes/(no)
computers/Nintendo: yes/no	argues with adults: yes/(no) sometimes	starts fights: yes/(no)
music/art: yes/no	loses temper: (yes)/no	uses weapon to harm others: yes/(no)
religious activities: yes/no	blames others: yes/(no)	physically cruel to others: yes/(no)
hunting/fishing: (yes)/no	intentionally annoys others: yes/(no)	physically cruel to animals: yes/(no)
others:	touchy or easily annoyed: (yes)/no	forces others to have sex: yes/(no)
electronics	angry & resentful: (yes)/no	lies or "cons" others: yes/(no)
wiring stereo	spiteful or vindictive: yes/(no)	steals without confronting: yes/(no)
water skiing	speeding tickets: (yes)/no	(shoplifting, credit card fraud)
drives boat	substance abuse: (yes)/no	robs someone: yes/(no)
motorcycle	sexually active: (yes)/no	sets fires: yes/(no)
lifeguard/swims	skips school: (yes)/no *sometimes*	breaks into houses, cars, etc.: yes/(no)
computer programming	school suspension: (yes)/no	destroys other's property: yes/(no)
	school expulsion: yes/(no)	substance abuse: yes/(no)
	drops out of school: yes/(no)	runs away from home: yes/(no)
	access to weapons: (yes)/no	pregnancy: yes/(no)
		suicide risk: yes/(no)
		car accidents: (yes)/no
		before age 13:
		stays out all night w/o permission:
		yes/(no)
		truant from school: yes/(no)

SCHOOL PERFORMANCE	LEARNING PROBLEMS	SPECIFIC LEARNING DISABILITY
poor handwriting: (yes)/no	poor organizational skills: (yes)/no	Oral Expression: yes/(no)
reading skills: (strong)/weak	poor fine motor coordination:	Listening Comprehension: yes/(no)
writing skills: (strong)/weak	(yes)/no	Written Expression: yes/(no)
can organize themes: yes/(no)	poor memory: (yes)/no	Basic Reading Skills: yes/(no)
vocabulary: (strong)/weak	lacks attention to detail: (yes)/no	Reading Comprehension: yes/(no)
spelling skills: (strong)/weak	poor concentration: (yes)/no	Mathematics Calculation: yes/no **?**
math skills: strong/(weak)	slow reading: (yes)/no	Mathematical Reasoning: yes/(no)
knows multiplication tables: yes/(no)	slow math calculation: (yes)/no	
history/social studies: strong/(weak)	slow writing: (yes)/no	
foreign language skills:	poor reading comprehension:	
strong/(weak)	yes/(no)	
passes all classes: yes/(no)		
failed a grade: yes/(no)	**SCHOOL ENVIRONMENT**	
test anxiety: (yes)/no		
likes to go to school: yes/(no)	school personnel:	
forgets homework assigned: (yes)/no	positive/(hostile)	
forgets make-up work: (yes)/no	flexible/(rigid)	
forgets special projects: (yes)/no	will make adaptions: yes/(no)	
remembers teacher instructions:	use reasonable discipline: yes/(no)	
yes/(no)	special education eligible: yes/(no)	
difficulty getting started: (yes)/no		

Table 1–2

Understanding the Teenager with ADD

NAME: _Student with ADD/H_   AGE: DATE:

By completing this form, parents should gain a better understanding of their teenager's unique characteristics, personality, strengths, difficulties, and how he is different from other teenagers with ADD. In addition to the symptoms of ADD, all the factors listed below also influence the teenager's behavior, self-esteem, and ability to cope successfully with ADD. The severity of behaviors will vary. Please circle words that best describe your teenager.

DIAGNOSIS: Symptoms of ADD may range from mild to severe.

ADD/Hyperactive (ADD/H)   mild   (moderate)   severe
ADD/Inattentive (ADD/I/WO)
   without Hyperactivity   mild   moderate   severe
ADD/Combined (ADHD)   mild   moderate   severe

COEXISTING DIAGNOSIS: ADD frequently coexists with other disorders.

	mild	moderate	severe
Anxiety	mild	moderate	severe
Depression	mild	moderate	severe
Oppositional Defiant	(mild)	moderate	severe
Conduct Disorder	mild	moderate	severe
Learning Disability	mild	moderate	severe
Learning Problems	(mild)	moderate	severe
Sleep Disturbance	mild	moderate	severe

FACTORS INFLUENCING ADD: Other factors influence a teenager's personality and ability to cope successfully with ADD. These factors may also vary in intensity: mild/moderate/severe. Teenagers with ADHD and ADD/I/WO may be almost exact opposites in some behaviors. Circle the word that describes your teenager's behavior most of the time.

TEMPERAMENT

calm/(fidgets)
easy going/(aggressive)
(high energy)/lethargic
(happy)/depressed
(pleasant)/irritable
(charming)/sullen
(class clown)/shy
(relaxed)/anxious
(cautious)/daring
(tenacious)/gives up easily
(compliant)/defiant sometimes
copes well/(easily frustrated)
(angry outbursts)/calm
(talks a lot)/quiet & low key

GENERAL ISSUES

self esteem: good/(fair)
intelligence: average/(high)
gets along with friends: yes/(no)
inattentive:(yes)/no
impulsive:(yes)/no
disorganized:(yes)/no
loses things:(yes)/no
forgets things:(yes)/no
complies with requests:(yes)/no
will do chores:(yes)/no
truthful:(yes)/no
response to medication:(good)/fair
difficulty falling asleep: yes/(no)
difficulty waking up: yes/(no)
restless:(yes)/no
self-centered:(yes)/no
accident prone: yes/(no)
interrupts/butts in:(yes)/no

FAMILY STRESS FACTORS

two parent family:(yes)/no
step-parents:(yes)/no
family understands ADD
  (supportive):(yes)/no
reasonable discipline:(yes)/no
  (not too harsh or lenient)
open communication:(yes)/no
few hostile inteactions between
  teenager and parents:(yes)/no
relatives understand ADD
  (supportive): yes/(no)
family stresses (money, illness,
  divorce, (remarriage):(yes)/no
moved to new community: yes/(no)
attending same school: yes/(no)

AREAS OF SUCCESS	POTENTIAL PROBLEM AREAS	MORE SERIOUS PROBLEMS

sports: yes/no *(yes)*
computers/Nintendo: yes/no *(yes)*
music/art: yes/no *(no)*
religious activities: yes/no *(yes)*
hunting/fishing: yes/no *(yes)*
others:
 	
bow hunting
deer hunting
car mechanic
works on truck
loves war history
life guard
perfect attendance at
school
	defies/disobeys adults: yes/no *(no)*
	argues with adults: yes/no *(yes)*
	loses temper: yes/no *(yes)*
	blames others: yes/no *(yes)*
	intentionally annoys others: yes/no *(no)*
	touchy or easily annoyed: yes/no *(yes)*
	angry & resentful: yes/no *(yes)*
	spiteful or vindictive: yes/no *(no)*
	speeding tickets: yes/no *(yes)*
	substance abuse: yes/no *(no)*
	sexually active: yes/no *(yes)*
	skips school: yes/no *(no)*
	school suspension: yes/no *(no)*
	school expulsion: yes/no *(no)*
	drops out of school: yes/no *(no)*
	access to weapons: yes/no *(yes)*
		bullies or threatens others: yes/no *(no)*
		starts fights: yes/no *(no)*
		uses weapon to harm others: yes/no *(no)*
		physically cruel to others: yes/no *(no)*
		physically cruel to animals: yes/no *(no)*
		forces others to have sex: yes/no *(no)*
		lies or "cons" others: yes/no *(no)*
		steals without confronting: yes/no *(no)*
		   (shoplifting, credit card fraud)
		robs someone: yes/no *(no)*
		sets fires: yes/no *(no)*
		breaks into houses, cars, etc.: yes/no *(no)*
		destroys other's property: yes/no *(no)*
		substance abuse: yes/no *(no)*
		runs away from home: yes/no *(no)*
		pregnancy: yes/no *(no)*
		suicide risk: yes/no *(yes)*
		car accidents: yes/no *(no)*
		
		before age 13:
		stays out all night w/o permission:
		   yes/no *(no)*
		truant from school: yes/no *(no)*

SCHOOL PERFORMANCE	**LEARNING PROBLEMS**	**SPECIFIC LEARNING DISABILITY**

poor handwriting: yes/no *(yes)*
reading skills: strong/weak *(strong)*
writing skills: strong/weak *(no)*
can organize themes: yes/no *(yes)*
vocabulary: strong/weak *(strong)*
spelling skills: strong/weak
math skills: strong/weak *(weak)*
knows multiplication tables: yes/no *(no)*
history/social studies: strong/weak *(strong)*
foreign language skills:
   strong/weak
passes all classes: yes/no *(no)*
failed a grade: yes/no *(no)*
test anxiety: yes/no *(no)*
likes to go to school: yes/no *(no)*
forgets homework assigned: yes/no *(yes)*
forgets make-up work: yes/no *(yes)*
forgets special projects: yes/no *(yes)*
remembers teacher instructions:
   yes/no *(yes)*
difficulty getting started: yes/no *(yes)*
	poor organizational skills: yes/no *(yes)*
	poor fine motor coordination:
	   yes/no *(yes)*
	poor memory: yes/no *(yes)*
	lacks attention to detail: yes/no *(yes)*
	poor concentration: yes/no *(yes)*
	slow reading: yes/no *(no)*
	slow math calculation: yes/no *(yes)*
	slow writing: yes/no *(no)*
	poor reading comprehension:
	   yes/no *(no)*
	
	SCHOOL ENVIRONMENT
	
	school personnel:
	   positive/hostile *(positive)*
	   flexible/rigid *(flexible)*
	   will make adaptions: yes/no N/A
	   use reasonable discipline: yes/no *(yes)*
	special education eligible: yes/no *(no)*
		Oral Expression: yes/no *(no)*
		Listening Comprehension: yes/no *(yes)*
		Written Expression: yes/no *(no)*
		Basic Reading Skills: yes/no *(no)*
		Reading Comprehension: yes/no *(no)*
		Mathematics Calculation: yes/no *(no)*
		Mathematical Reasoning: yes/no *(no)*

more likely he will successfully adjust at home and school. Several chapters explain how parents can forge partnerships with professionals to help capitalize on their teenagers' strengths: issues regarding treatment professionals are discussed in Chapter 4; regarding school personnel, in Chapters 8, 9, and 10.

What Does the Future Hold?

Scenes from Ron Howard's movie *Parenthood* humorously capture the hopes and fears many parents have for their children. In the movie, the father (Steve Martin) daydreams about the future of his 10-year-old son. Will he be a success or a failure? In the first scene, he proudly envisions his grown-up son as the valedictorian of his class delivering the commencement address. In the next scene, his crazed son has barricaded himself atop a tower and is shooting innocent people.

The pain within the child as he struggles to understand himself and find understanding from others is poignantly portrayed in the movie. "Dad, what's wrong with me? Why am I going to see a psychiatrist?" Teenagers with ADD must experience a similarly intense emotional struggle as they try to figure out "What's wrong?" or "Why am I having so much trouble in school?" (missing instructions in class, dealing with seemingly hostile teachers, failing classes, disappointing parents, and becoming angry and having conflicts with authority figures).

Many teenagers with ADD experience an overwhelming sense of despair. Some become so depressed about failures in school and conflicts with parents and teachers that they see no way to succeed in school or life. They may comment that they feel dumb, crazy, and overwhelmed, and sometimes they come to believe that they are "bad." As a result, their ambitions or expectations may plummet. They may give up pursuing positive goals for their future. Much to their parents' dismay, they may select friends who are experiencing similar or even more serious difficulties.

If you have a teenager with ADD, you are probably extremely concerned about his future. Perhaps you worry about whether he will become a productive, well-adjusted adult. You may even secretly fear that he may become a juvenile delinquent.

Since these teenagers seem to take longer to reach their potential and establish themselves as adults, parents have a number of years to "worry and worry some more," as one parent noted.

> "Parents of teenagers without ADD worry. The concerns of parents of teenagers with ADD are greatly magnified!!!"

The Good News

For some parents and teenagers, simply having the diagnosis of ADD is good news. At last, they understand why school and life have been so difficult.

⚜

"I thought a good title for this book would be <u>Good News: Your Teenager Has ADD!!</u> It was a relief for me to find out why Steven had so much difficulty in school and to learn that his problem could be treated."

⚜

As Chapter 4 discusses, behavior improves significantly in the vast majority of youngsters with ADD when given appropriate medication. In addition, 50 percent experience less severe symptoms in adulthood. Many teens mature plus learn to compensate successfully for the symptoms of ADD. Their impulsivity and overactivity decreases, and their ability to sustain attention improves.

In addition to experiencing milder symptoms, adults with ADD learn to compensate for symptoms of ADD by using lists or beepers, or by finding someone such as a secretary to remind them of appointments or due dates. In his book *Driven to Distraction,* Dr. Edward M. Hallowell refers to the person who provides this extra support as a *coach.* According to Dr. Hallowell, a psychiatrist who also has ADHD, a coach may also be needed at home to help deal with the routines of daily living such as remembering to do chores, doing homework, or remembering family events. If adults need coaches, teenagers need them even more. Yet parents are often made to feel guilty about their involvement in their teenager's life. Throughout this book parents are encouraged not to be embarrassed or reluctant to help their teenager when he needs help.

For adults who pursue careers in which ADD presents few if any problems, medication may no longer be needed. A few adults whose symptoms are severe may elect to continue medication or take it only on days requiring more intense concentration. Dr. Hallowell's and Dr. Paul Wender's books offer more information about the continuing impact of ADD on adults.

Career selection is critically important. Parents and professionals need to help these young people match their personalities and skills with an appropriate career. Teenagers with ADD need to find careers in which ADD characteristics are an asset rather than a handicap. Some teenagers who struggled through school may blossom once they graduate. But be prepared. These teenagers may take longer to find themselves and their successful niche in life. Finding a career after high school is discussed in Chapter 12.

Keys to a Good Outcome

As mentioned above, many factors determine how successfully a teenager is able to cope with having ADD. Some of these factors are beyond anybody's control. Fortunately, however, many important factors are within your control. Dr. Gabriella Weiss and Dr. Lily Hechtman, authors of *Hyperactive Children Grown Up*, followed youngsters with ADD for 15 years. They, in addition to Dr. Barkley, have found several factors which make it more likely that a teenager can successfully cope with ADD:

- higher intelligence,
- less severe hyperactivity as a young child,
- emotional stability (less aggression, better tolerance of frustration, fewer emotional blowups),
- an ability to get along reasonably well with peers,
- middle to upper socioeconomic status,
- a nurturing and supportive home,
- emotionally healthy parents (lack of a family history of criminal behavior or serious emotional problems such as substance abuse, alcoholism, or mental illness), and
- positive parenting practices (infrequent hostile parent/teenager interactions).

Clearly, parents play a critical role in helping their teenager cope with ADD. This fact is supported by further observations from Dr. Weiss:

🎋

"When the adults who had been hyperactive were asked what had helped them most to overcome their childhood difficulties, their most common reply was that someone (usually a parent or teacher) had believed in them. . . ."

🎋

Unfortunately, giving your teenager the support he needs is sometimes easier said than done. First, you may not have much quality time to spend with your teenager if both you and your spouse work or if you are a single parent. The little time that is available may be spent on negative interactions—nagging or criticizing him for misbehavior and things not done. In addition, thanks to our hectic lifestyles and the technology boom, teens spend a lot of time in their rooms alone with their Walkman, Nintendo, VCR, and TV.

Dr. Barkley has pinpointed another reason it may be difficult to support your teenager: *sometimes when he misbehaves, he is not very lovable.* Teenagers with ADD tend to be inattentive, impulsive, and less likely to follow instructions. In response, their parents tend to be more commanding, negative, critical, and angry, and to use punishment more often. The teenager's misbehavior and attitudes actually affect his parents' actions and attitudes, and vice versa. Most people recognize that what parents say and do affects their children, but they forget that *children's behavior also is a major influence on their parents' actions.*

Dr. Barkley explains, somewhat tongue in cheek, that an interesting side effect of stimulant medications is that parents and teachers get better. When youngsters with ADD take medication, parents and teachers are less critical, rejecting, and punitive. Since the teenager's behavior improves when he is on medication, it is easier for parents to create the loving, positive, nurturing environment their child needs.

Since conflicts within the family are more common, it is not surprising that marital problems are

also more common. In Dr. Barkley's research, rates of separation and divorce were significantly higher than for other families. Mothers report more depression, self-blame, and social isolation, and lower self-esteem regarding their parenting skills than do other mothers.

Because your teenager's ADD can lead to so many problems within the family, getting proper treatment for his symptoms should be a family priority. See Chapter 4 for indepth information on treatment approaches; Chapter 5 for information on positive parenting practices.

Seeking Help to Ensure Success

With proper diagnosis and treatment, most teenagers with ADD will grow up to be well-adjusted adults. Unfortunately, finding and implementing the "proper" treatment for your child can be a long and complicated process. Because each teenager with ADD is unique, treatment must be tailored to their individual symptoms, strengths, and needs. There is no "one-size-fits-all" plan for treating ADD.

Research regarding effective treatment for ADD is sorely lacking. However, common sense tells us that treatment plans should be aimed at helping teenagers with ADD get along better in all aspects of their life—home, school, and community activities. Treatment is defined broadly to include any activities that help a teenager succeed in life. Keep in mind that many activities—not just taking medication and counseling—can be extremely therapeutic for your teenager. These activities include succeeding in school; mastering sports,

debate, art, modeling, and other skills; and positive relationships between parent and teenager.

Chapter 4 covers treatment for ADD in detail. Briefly, however, components of your child's individualized treatment program will probably include:

- taking medication and fine tuning the proper dosage;
- treating coexisting problems such as anxiety, depression, or sleep disturbance;
- identifying learning problems;
- making adaptations in the classroom or providing special education to help your child succeed at school;
- providing extra support and supervision at home and school (coaching);
- participating in activities to build self-esteem;
- seeking counseling for yourself and/or your teenager;
- attending parent training and parent support groups;
- and last but not least, viewing ADD positively, believing in your teenager, and building on his strengths.

Involving your teenager as a respected partner in the treatment process is very important! Your teenager is probably just as mystified and frustrated by his disorder as you are. Treatment is more likely to be successful if he is working with you rather than against you and sabotaging everything you attempt to do.

Conclusion

To raise your teenager with ADD, you will need to invest more time, energy, and patience than usual. You will need to do more hands-on behavior management and be more involved in making sure your teenager completes schoolwork and chores. Parenting your teenager is not, however, an impossible job or insurmountable challenge. Nor do you have to do it all alone. As later chapters explain, a wide range of professionals and other parents have expertise that can be of tremendous help to you.

After treatment is begun, you may see immediate rewards when your teenager comes home all smiles with passing grades, thanks to identification of learning problems, adaptations to the classroom, and medication. Other rewards may come later when he reaches his late teenage years and looks at you and says, "Thanks for believing in me. I couldn't have done it without you." I can personally attest to how sweet the tears of joy are when you hear these long-awaited comments.

Research into causes and treatment of ADD continues and is producing exciting new information for families. As a result, the professionals who deal with ADD on a daily basis are becoming better informed about the disorder. Just as importantly, we may be on the threshold of major discoveries and breakthroughs about ADD. In short, the future picture for teenagers with ADD and their families has never been more hopeful.

CHAPTER TWO

THE DIAGNOSIS OF ADD

"The school psychologist and doctor who diagnosed ADD were both a godsend!!! Finally, we had found someone who understood, who had a name for the elusive problem we were confronting. At long last we had a diagnosis. The emotional relief that followed was bittersweet. Finally, we had some answers but why had it taken so long to find them? My son and I had been living for twelve years with a disorder for which there had been no name, little sympathy and understanding from family, friends, and school personnel."

✺

Most children with ADD are diagnosed in early childhood or elementary school. By the time they reach adolescence, they have usually been receiving treatment for several years. However, *it is not unusual for teenagers to reach adolescence or even adulthood without having the disorder diagnosed.* Teenagers who are extremely bright or who have ADD/Inattentive/Without Hyperactivity (ADD/I/WO) are more likely to reach adolescence without a diagnosis.

The information in this chapter will help parents determine whether or not their teenager should be referred for a formal evaluation. If ADD has already been diagnosed, this information may help parents identify coexisting problems such as depression or learning problems. It may also help parents identify other children in the family who may have a milder form or a different type of ADD. Some parents may also diagnose themselves with the disorder.

✺

"Because of his hyperactivity, I had known for some time that my nine-year-old son had ADHD. However, after reading this book, I was shocked to realize that my sixteen-year-old daughter exhibits all the symptoms of ADD without hyperactivity. I can't believe I didn't identify it earlier. I feel guilty about all the time we wasted when we could have been treating the ADD. Now I understand why she has struggled in school all these years.

"She has an IQ of 132, but she is failing her sophomore year in high school. As a special education teacher, I feel guilty for all the times I sat her down with a stack of papers and made her practice math facts. She said them, sang them, but just couldn't memorize them."

✺

"Robert's ADD wasn't diagnosed until his senior year in high school. He had problems paying attention in class and remembering assignments. We knew he was smart but he made mostly C's and D's in high school. In kindergarten, he climbed up a bookcase in the classroom, but no one ever mentioned ADD or hyperactivity. After he began taking Ritalin, his grades were mostly A's and B's."

Why ADD Can Go Undiagnosed until Adolescence

Perhaps you think it is unlikely that your teenager has ADD because you believe he would have been diagnosed with the disorder by now if he had it. After all, wouldn't one of his teachers have referred him for an evaluation if he showed signs of having ADD? Or perhaps your child actually *was* evaluated for ADD at one time, but you were told that he didn't fit the criteria. Could it be that your child really is just lazy and disobedient?

There are, in fact, many reasons why ADD may go undiagnosed for years. Just because no one has sought you out with the diagnosis does not mean that you should not have your teenager evaluated (or re-evaluated) for attention deficit disorder. Below are some reasons ADD is frequently overlooked.

Not Every Student with ADD is Hyperactive. As mentioned in Chapter 1, it is a common but erroneous belief that all children with ADD are hyperactive. Youngsters with Attention-Deficit/ Hyperactivity Disorder, Predominately Inattentive Type (ADD/I/WO) may not be diagnosed until middle or high school. They are more difficult to diagnose and frequently may be overlooked, primarily because they do not aggressively act out and cause few, if any, problems during the early school years. In elementary school, their teachers may describe them as well behaved. As teenagers, they tend to have *low energy levels,* rather than hyperactivity, and may even appear lethargic at times. Teenagers with ADD/I/WO are not as talkative as those with hyperactivity. Serious academic problems are more likely to surface in middle and high school when academic tasks increase and become more difficult. Differences between these two types of ADD are discussed in more detail later in this chapter.

❧

"My twelve-year-old son's teacher told me she thought he had ADD. However, I really didn't believe it at first because nothing I read about the disorder seemed to describe my son. The books I read talked about the hyperactive child and my son definitely wasn't hyperactive. Now that I understand more about ADD with inattention problems, I think that he probably has this type of ADD."

❧

No Two Teenagers with ADD Are Alike. Because two teenagers with ADD seldom behave the same way, parents may become confused when trying to determine if their teenager has the disorder. Their teenager may not act like other teenagers who have ADD. Few adolescents exhibit the classic symptom of hyperactivity so severe they can't sit still. Although they may be restless, most teenagers no longer exhibit high levels of hyperactivity. Instead, underachievement, inattention, and impulsivity are considered the hallmark characteristics of teenagers with ADD. As discussed in Chapter 1, Dr. Russell Barkley thinks that lack of persistence of effort on a task, difficulty following through on instructions without supervision, and variability in the amount and quality of work produced over time are also key symptoms of ADD. Beyond these hallmark characteristics, there are wide differences in behavior. The teenager's basic temperament, academic successes, learning problems, sleep disturbances, successes in non-school activities, and the level of family support all contribute to making each teenager with ADD unique. (See Table 1–2 in Chapter 1.)

Students May Be Able to "Get By" Until Middle School or High School. Children with ADD and mild to moderate levels of hyperactivity are often able to keep up with schoolwork when they are in elementary school. This is also true for non-hyperactive children with ADD (ADD/I/WO). Frequently, academic problems do not become obvious until the middle and high school years, when increased academic demands are placed upon them. Students who are intellectually gifted may be overlooked until high school or college. They are so bright they can compensate for their ADD. When students reach middle school or high school, they are expected to accept greater responsibility for completing their schoolwork. Although teenagers with ADD have the intellectual abilities to do the work, they are two to four years behind their friends in the ability to accept responsibility and other measures of maturity. Because of these developmental delays, many students with ADD are unable to accept full responsibility for their schoolwork and need additional supervision and structure from their parents and teachers as they progress through school.

❧

"Students with undiagnosed ADD seem to fall apart in middle school with so much to keep up with. Gaps in

their fund of knowledge from five years of having tuned out in school finally catches up with them. . . ."

—*Pediatric Center Staff*

"Our son's major academic difficulties surfaced in middle school. He was able to pass subjects in elementary school simply because he was so bright. However, in high school, he couldn't pass subjects as easily without studying and turning in homework assignments."

Girls with ADD Are Often Overlooked. As mentioned earlier, girls make up approximately 20 to 25 percent of all teenagers with ADD. Girls who have ADD are less likely to be hyperactive than boys. And according to Yale researchers Bennett A. Shaywitz, M.D., and Sally Shaywitz, M.D., girls with ADD exhibit less physical aggression and loss of control. Because girls are less likely to be discipline problems at school, they are more likely to be overlooked than boys.

Although girls with ADD may not cause as many discipline problems as boys with ADD, the problems they face appear to be just as serious. Girls are more likely to have cognitive and language difficulties, and often have more trouble with social relationships than boys do. The Shaywitzs have found that girls tend to be more fearful, are more likely to be enuretic (bedwetters), and are more likely to be rejected by peers. Some researchers have found that hyperactive girls have more tension and anxiety problems than hyperactive boys.

"I think I spent most of my second grade sitting in a corner for talking too much and not being able to keep my hands to myself. I made good grades academically but made U's in conduct."

—*a female psychologist diagnosed with ADD as an adult*

Clearly, the under-diagnosis of girls with ADD is a serious problem. Because ADD is more prevalent in boys, most parents and teachers don't think to look for it in girls. One speaker at a CHADD conference speculated that the diagnostic criteria

for girls may not be fine-tuned sufficiently to identify the disorder.

Although the reasons are not clear, one researcher found that the number of men and women seeking treatment for ADD in his practice was equal. Perhaps the numbers are equal because women may be more likely to seek treatment than men. On the other hand, perhaps the disorder has been overlooked in females and occurs more often among women than previous research has indicated. Further research is needed on children and teenagers who are treated in their local communities to find out more about the ratio of males and females with ADD plus the ratio of ADHD to ADD/I/WO.

ADD May Be Overlooked During Evaluations. When teachers and parents realize that a teenager is struggling in school, he may be referred for a psychological evaluation. Unfortunately, referral and evaluation provide no guarantee that the ADD will be diagnosed. Sometimes multiple psychological evaluations are conducted, yet ADD is never detected.

"Our son was not diagnosed until his third psychological evaluation. His first evaluation in kindergarten was to determine eligibility for a program for intellectually gifted children. He missed the cut-off score by two points because he couldn't sit still long enough to finish the test. The second evaluation was conducted in the fourth grade because he was underachieving in school. His high IQ score made him eligible for programs for gifted students.

"His ADD was finally diagnosed by accident when he was in the seventh grade. When we moved that year, he had to be retested for the gifted program. We were fortunate that the school psychologist picked up on his ADD and referred us to a physician who specialized in this area."

⚜

Diagnosis of ADD is not a clear-cut process. Teenagers with ADD do not have identical test profiles. Interpreting information obtained during an evaluation is not an exact science and requires good clinical judgment that is developed through experience working with teenagers with ADD.

A study conducted at Yale University showed how frequently diagnosis of ADD is overlooked, especially when hyperactivity is not present. For youngsters with ADD/I/WO, the diagnosis was missed 77 percent of the time when DSM III-R criteria alone were used. Even skilled clinicians overlooked the disorder 50 percent of the time. Although ADD with hyperactivity was correctly diagnosed more frequently, it was still overlooked 40 percent of the time when DSM III-R criteria alone were used and 10 percent of the time when a skilled clinician gave a diagnosis. *If you feel strongly that your teenager has ADD, yet a professional says that ADD is not present, seek a second opinion.* By familiarizing yourself with diagnostic criteria and procedures discussed in this chapter, you can ensure that proper evaluation procedures are used so that all major learning and attentional problems are identified.

Diagnostic Criteria Were Not Developed for Teenagers. The diagnostic criteria for ADD in the DSM III (difficulty staying in seat, difficulty awaiting turn in games, difficulty playing quietly, and blurting out answers), described the behavior of younger children, not teenagers with ADD. Many of these same behaviors are still listed in the DSM IV as diagnostic criteria for ADD/H. However, the new DSM IV criteria for ADD/I/WO more accurately describe the behavior of teenagers with ADD.

The School Might Not Have Recommended an Evaluation. Before 1991, ADD was not considered an eligible "handicapping condition" under federal law. That is, it was not mentioned in federal laws as a disability that might qualify a student for special educational help at public expense. Consequently, some schools were reluctant to diagnose ADD and did not direct school psychologists to screen students for ADD. This means that there are many students who completed elementary school before 1991 who should have been evaluated for ADD but were not. Even though their teenager is in high school, parents may still request an evaluation for ADD under current federal laws and policies. Relevant federal laws are discussed in Chapter 11.

ADD Slips through the Cracks. Students with ADD can easily get lost in large, unresponsive school systems. Especially in urban areas where students move frequently, school personnel may not know students or their parents. In high schools with 1,000 to 2,000–plus students, the teenager is more likely to become a number with no name. In these large schools, teachers may not feel responsible for monitoring the progress of their students or call parents if a student is struggling academically.

⚜

"The high school environment is less structured and teenagers are expected to take full responsibility for completing their schoolwork. Since students change classes every period and have at least six teachers, typically, their teachers do not get to know them as well or understand their disability."

⚜

"A 16–year-old Polish immigrant experienced serious difficulties at school during the 6 years he was in this country. Although his spoken English was quite good, his reading and writing skills were weak. He failed all his classes his first semester in high school, had disciplinary problems at school, was suspended and sent to an alternative school. After passing three of four classes at alternative school, he returned to regular classes, where he failed all his classes the first semester of his sophomore year.

"Obviously, the student was at high risk for dropping out of school. His school had the second highest drop-out rate in the county (18.2%). Yet, no school personnel referred him for evaluation or requested parent teacher conferences. I was appalled and astounded! It didn't take a Ph.D. to figure out this young man needed help. I suggested that the father request a teacher conference.

"Finally, as a concerned friend and professional, I reviewed his school records and wrote up a report for the school requesting an evaluation. The school took little action on the report. When he was not tested by the school, I referred him to a doctor for evaluation for ADD. His ADD and language and academic problems were diagnosed at that time.

"This young man dropped out of high school at age 17. Despite the doctor's and my urging, the school did not develop a meaningful plan to help him cope with his ADD and learning disabilities."

✎

Too many students with ADD are slipping through cracks in the system! It is important that teachers develop a personal interest in their students, regardless of the size of their school. Teachers need to pick up the phone, call the parent, and develop a plan for helping the student.

The First Step to a Diagnosis

There are two ways the evaluation process may be set in motion if there is a suspicion that your teenager has ADD. First, a teacher or other school staff member may recommend that your child be evaluated for ADD. In this case, the school will schedule the evaluation, select the individuals who will conduct the evaluation, and pay all expenses. (They must first obtain your permission, however.) Second, you, as a parent, may decide that you would like your child to be evaluated. You may then either request an evaluation for ADD from your child's school, or find a professional in private practice to conduct the evaluation.

Usually, a reasonable first step is for you to talk with the teacher or call the guidance counselor at your local school and request an evaluation. This way, if a comprehensive evaluation is conducted it will include specific tests required by the school system. In addition, you will not have to pay for the evaluation out of your own pocket.

Schools have the right to determine what constitutes an adequate evaluation for ADD. If they do not believe the student has ADD, they may not do an indepth evaluation. If the school doesn't do a thorough evaluation, parents may wish to seek a private evaluation. If this evaluation confirms a diagnosis of ADD that adversely affects their child's ability to learn, parents may ask the school system to reimburse them for the evaluation. Parents may also prefer to seek a private evaluation if lengthy waiting lists prohibit prompt evaluation by the school. Although there are federally suggested timelines for completing an evaluation and an individualized education plan (IEP), three or four months could pass before the evaluation is completed and adaptations put in place. Timelines vary from state to state, so ask what is mandated by your state. Federal laws are discussed in more detail in Chapter 11.

If you decide to pursue a private evaluation, there are a variety of routes you can take. You might ask members of local CHADD groups to recommend competent treatment professionals who have extensive experience working with ADD. If you live near a university, you can call the psychology or counseling department and ask for names of medical or counseling professionals in the community who specialize in treating ADD. You might also call the local mental health center or the psychological services section of the local school system. A variety of licensed treatment professionals in private practice, for example, psychologist, social worker, or physician, are capable of conducting a proper evaluation. The competence of the individual professional is more important than the field in which he or she is trained. Ultimately, however, if ADD is diagnosed and medications are required, your teenager must be referred to a physician.

A psychological evaluation conducted by a private treatment professional may cost between $500 to $2,000 and may take up to two full days to complete. Insurance policies vary, so you will need to check your coverage. Generally, insurance companies are more likely to pay for evaluations conducted by physicians, state-licensed psychologists with a Ph.D., or sometimes, social workers with a master's degree.

Under DSM IV, the same diagnostic criteria will be used for adults and children. The diagnosis of ADD, Residual Type (RT), which was in DSM III-R, has been deleted from the DSM IV. For adults, a childhood history of symptoms of ADD, with continuing problems into adulthood, will be the primary indicators of the disorder.

A Comprehensive Diagnostic Evaluation for ADD

The components included in your child's diagnostic evaluation for ADD may vary depending on who conducts it. Typically, an evaluation begins with an interview of you and your teenager. The interview should include a discussion of your child's history, his performance at school, and problems your family is experiencing at home. Many skilled professionals have a pretty good idea of whether or not a teenager has ADD after the first interview. Although a diagnosis of ADD may be given after this interview, many professionals conduct a more in-depth evaluation to identify specific learning and behavioral problems, and to rule out other disorders. The evaluation may include personal interviews with you, your teenager, and school personnel; observations of the teenager at home and school; completion of a social history; completion of behavior rating scales by you, your teenager, and his teacher; review of old report cards and school records; completion of formal IQ and academic achievement testing; and a thorough physical examination.

The following section describes how a comprehensive diagnostic evaluation may be conducted. It describes the procedures used at the Pediatric Center, a medical center in Stone Mountain, Georgia, whose staff specialize in treating ADD. The professional(s) conducting your child's evaluation may or may not routinely follow these same procedures. But if there are tests or procedures discussed here that you think would be helpful in evaluating your child, don't hesitate to discuss them with your doctor. If you would like more detailed information about evaluation, Dr. Russell Barkley's book, *Attention-Deficit Hyperactivity Disorder: A Handbook for Diagnosis and Treatment*, devotes eleven chapters to the nature, diagnosis, and assessment of the disorder. In addition, you can refer to Table 2–1 for a summary of the most important points to keep in mind about diagnostic evaluations.

TABLE 2–1
DIAGNOSING ADD

- **ADD cannot be diagnosed on the basis of a single test.**
- **Underachievement** in school should be a red flag signaling parents to evaluate for ADD or other learning problems.
- **The best indicators** of ADD are the diagnostic criteria contained in the DSM IV. The primary behaviors that parents may see include inattention and impulsivity, and for those who have ADHD, hyperactivity in childhood.

    Presence of these behaviors may be identified and confirmed based upon information from:
    —DSM IV diagnostic criteria,
    —the childhood history from the parents,
    —a description of school performance by parents and the teenager,
    —school report cards, e.g., grades and teacher comments,
    —official school records, e.g., standardized academic achievement tests such as the IOWA Test of Basic Skills; Individualized Education Plans (IEP); school psychological evaluations,
    —classroom observations, and
    —teacher reports.
- **Helpful indicators** include formal tests, such as:
    —Behavior rating scales,
    —Academic and intellectual testing to help identify academic strengths and learning problems.
- A thorough **physical examination** should be conducted to rule out other disorders.
- **Coexisting problems** such as learning problems, sleep disturbances, anxiety, depression, defiance, and aggression are common and must be identified and treated. Typically, treatment of ADD in isolation is not sufficient to ensure that a teenager will be successful in school and life. These issues are discussed in detail in subsequent chapters.

An Evaluation for ADD

At the Pediatric Center, a comprehensive diagnostic evaluation and assessment for ADD lasts approximately six to eight hours. Currently, it is conducted by Edward M. Gotlieb, M.D., who is a pediatric and adolescent medicine specialist, plus a nurse, and a licensed clinical counselor. The assessment includes a family interview to obtain a detailed history on the teenager and family; behavioral assessments completed by the youngster, parent, and teachers; administration of an intelligence test; an academic assessment; a physical examination; and sometimes classroom observation. The assessment process is also intended to diagnose or rule out other problems such as learning disabilities, depression, bipolar disorder, conduct disorder, or mental retardation. Typically, since the assessment is conducted through a physician's office, it is at least partially reimbursable by insurance companies.

Developmental/Social History. Staff at the Pediatric Center interview the parents about the teenager's behavior from birth until the present. It is important to determine if the symptoms have been present over a long period of time, or have recently appeared as the result of a specific occurrence. Since ADD is a lifelong problem, teenagers with the condition will have shown some symptoms, possibly mild ones, since early childhood. However, the significance of their problems may not have been clear during the early years. This interview is thorough and may last one and a half to two hours. This history is usually extremely helpful in confirming the diagnosis of ADD.

Birth and developmental milestones are discussed. Some parents feel that their children with ADD have been different from birth. Some report that their children had colic as babies.

❧

"I suspect that even at birth some children with ADD have difficulty eliminating stimuli. They are so bombarded by light, sound, smells, and feelings, they can't tune out stimuli. They are colicky. Many of them are tense, irritable, hard to calm, and hard to comfort infants."

— *Pediatric Center Staff*

❧

Few parents report that their children were extremely hyperactive as small children. *Most parents say their child was active but not overly active.* Parents will frequently comment that their youngster seemed to "tune out" a lot and had to be told over and over again to do or not to do things.

A family medical history is obtained. Any major medical diseases which occur in the family are listed. The interviewer also looks for previous history of family members who have experienced

ADD, severe depression, anxiety, or bipolar disorder. During this interview, it often becomes apparent that other adults in the family have symptoms of ADD. Typically, the father, grandfather, or uncle will be mentioned.

The parent is asked to describe any medical problems the teenager may have had, beginning at the head and working down to the toes. Head trauma? Headaches? Double vision? Ear infections? Some youngsters with ADD have problems with bedwetting, some as late as age 12 or 13.

Parents are also asked to describe their teenager as he is today. How they respond often provides insight into their perception of and relationship with their teenager. Some parents list the positive qualities first and a few negative ones. Other parents list all negatives and can identify few positive characteristics. The interviewer then goes on to ask about living arrangements, important family members, and relationships between members of the family. Questions are asked to better understand interactions within the family. Does the teenager have chores? Who disciplines the teenager? How? What is the biggest problem parents are presently facing with the teenager? Who would he talk to if he had a problem? Who are his friends? Does he get along with his peers?

School History and Performance. The Pediatric Center obtains as much data on the teenager's school years as possible. Parents are asked to bring old report cards and any standardized achievement test scores available. Old report cards and scores on standardized tests usually contain important information about the teenager's past academic performance, as well as teacher comments regarding the teenager's behavior and work habits, and his intellectual ability and academic skill levels.

Parents are asked which school years were better and why. They may say their youngster had a good teacher who took time to modify the school environment to help the teenager stay on task. For example, the teacher may have seated the student near the front of the class, modified assignments, made eye contact when speaking to the teenager, etc. What are the teenager's favorite subjects in school? In what subjects does he receive the best and worst grades? Are there any attendance problems? What are his aspirations for the future? Will he go to college?

Usually, a profile emerges of a teenager who has been an *underachiever in school.* He may be bright but just getting by or failing classes in middle and high school. Approximately a third of the youngsters seen at the Pediatric Center have developed some *school avoidance symptoms.* They may refuse to go to school, skip school, have physical symptoms such as stomach aches and headaches, or fight with their parents about getting up for school each morning.

Review of Permanent School Records. Parents may sign a release of information form so that staff may review the teenager's permanent records at school. The written comments or behavior check lists from elementary school may be especially revealing. Comments such as "needs to use time wisely," "needs to follow directions," "needs to listen," "needs to complete assignments," and "not working up to potential" may be consistently marked through the school years when a student has ADD. Helpful information may also be obtained from old psychological evaluations, IQ tests, and IEPS.

Intelligence Tests. There is no single test available which confirms the diagnosis of ADD, but intelligence tests can be helpful in several ways. They can: (1) determine the general level of a teenager's intellectual ability, (2) identify learning problems, and (3) indicate problems with attention.

One of the most commonly administered intelligence tests is the Weschler Intelligence Scale for Children, third revision (WISC-III). Three Intelligence Quotients (IQ) scores are obtained: a Full Scale IQ score, plus Verbal IQ and Performance IQ scores. The Full Scale IQ is a measure of the student's scores from both the verbal and nonverbal portions of the test. The Verbal subtests measure verbal reasoning, verbal expression, memory and attention and the Performance subtests assess nonverbal reasoning, attention to detail, spatial organization, and hand-eye coordination. An IQ score which falls in a range from 85 to 115 indicates average intelligence. A sample profile of scores obtained on a WISC-R* by a student with ADD is provided in Table 2–2.

The Weschler is made up of ten subtests plus three optional subtests. The actual scores for each subtest (the number of answers correct) are converted to a scale score, which is adjusted for age and allows comparison with other students' scores. These scores are helpful for identifying potential learning problems. Scale scores range from 1 to 19 with a score of 10 falling at the fiftieth percentile or median. If a teenager obtained scale scores of 10 on all his subtests, his Full Scale IQ would be 100. The average range for subtest scale scores is between seven and thirteen. Two thirds of all scores fall in this range. Most teenagers without ADD or learning problems obtain roughly the same scale score on each subtest. Approximately half of the youngsters with ADD, however, have widely varying scores.

Table 2–2
WISC-R SCORES FOR A STUDENT WITH ADD

9–year-old male, ADD
Full Scale IQ: 141

Verbal Subtests (Scale Scores)

Information	13
Similarities	17
Arithmetic	11
Vocabulary	19
Comprehension	16
Digit Span	12

Performance Subtests (Scale Scores)

Picture Completion	17
Picture Arrangement	18
Block Design	14
Object Assembly	17
Coding	7
Mazes	12

⚹

"My son's scale scores ranged from 7 on the Coding subtest to 19 on the Vocabulary subtest. His lowest scores in addition to Coding were Arithmetic—11 and Digit Span—12. His full scale IQ was 141, yet he could not learn his multiplication tables. What a puzzle!"

⚹

---

* The WISC-R was revised and replaced by the WISC-III in 1991.

Table 2–3

FACTOR ANALYSIS OF THE WISC-R

VERBAL COMPREHENSION		PERCEPTUAL ORGANIZATION		DISTRACTIBILITY	
Information	13	Picture Completion	17	Arithmetic	11
Similarities	17	Picture Arrangement	18	Digit Span	12
Vocabulary	19	Block Design	14		23
Comprehension	16	Object Assembly	17	(average 11.5)	
	65		66		
(average 16.3)		(average 16.5)			

PROCESSING SPEED*		ACID TEST	
Coding	7	Arithmetic	11
Symbol Search	-	Coding	7
		Information	13
		Digit Span	12
			43
		(average 10.8)	

* Processing Speed cannot be determined on the WISC–R. Symbol Search is a new subtest on the WISC–III and was not included on WISC–R.

The WISC scale scores may be grouped by several factors to help identify strengths and weaknesses: Verbal Comprehension, Perceptual Organization, Freedom from Distractibility, and Processing Speed. Based upon the WISC scale scores in Table 2–2, scores are provided for each of the four factors shown in Table 2–3 above.

Low scores on certain subtests of the WISC-III (or WISC-R) may indicate ADD or learning problems, although they do not give conclusive proof. WISC-III subtest scale scores which tend to be low in teenagers who have ADD are *A*rithmetic, *C*oding, *I*nformation, and *D*igit Span. This grouping of scale scores is referred to as the *ACID test*. When the averages of the scores on the ACID Test are significantly below the averages on Verbal Comprehension and Perceptual Organization (three or more points), ADD or learning disabilities should be considered as a possible diagnosis. However, just because the ACID profile is not present, does not mean that ADD or learning disabilities can be ruled out.

The average for the ACID Test (10.8) in Table 2–3 is approximately 6 points lower than the average scores on Verbal Comprehension (16) and Perceptual Organization (16.5). This 6 point difference is important and indicates potential ADD and/or learning problems.

Skills assessed by the subtests of the WISC-III may be helpful for identifying learning problems. In assessing learning problems, the evaluator looks at patterns of strengths and weaknesses on the IQ test. Differences of more than 17 points between the Verbal and Performance IQ scores on the WISC-III may indicate learning problems. In addition, discrepancies of five points or more between the individual subtest scale scores may also be characteristic of learning problems. Information from the WISC may be helpful for parents and teachers in selecting classroom adaptations or a teaching approach.

Subtests of the WISC. A brief discussion of the academic implications of low scores on individual subtests of the WISC-III may be helpful. The *Coding* subtest is a timed test requiring the teenager to copy a series of simple symbols. Two experts on ADD/I/WO, Dr. Tom Brown and Dr. Russell Barkley, have found that *youngsters with ADD/I/WO typically make low scale scores on the Coding subtest (7 or lower).* In addition, teenagers who are distractible or write or process materials slowly also make low scores. A low score on the Coding subtest is significant because it indicates that the teenager interprets and writes symbols (words) slowly. From a practical standpoint, the teenager with ADD who has processing and/or fine motor problems will probably read and write slowly, produce less written work, and have trouble completing work on time. Written work is so time consuming, the teenager may give up and not even try to finish his classwork or homework. In addition, he is unlikely to have the time to double check his answers after finishing an assignment or test. Clearly, the teenager has a learning problem that will significantly affect his classroom performance, even though it may not meet special education criteria for a specific learning disability (SLD). Chapter 11 explains how a student with these learning difficulties can qualify for special educational services from the school.

In the *Digit Span subtest* the teenager must remember and repeat an increasing sequence of numbers. The teenager is also asked to repeat numbers in order backwards. Again the inability to concentrate, poor short-term memory, and poor listening comprehension will result in lower scores. In the classroom, the teenager's poor short-term memory may impair his ability to memorize information such as basic math facts, especially multiplication tables, history facts, spelling words, or foreign languages. A student could, however, make a decent score on this subtest and still have memory problems. For example, as noted in Table 2–2, the student obtained a scale score of 12 on Digit Span, yet he could not memorize his multiplication tables. This subtest does not measure memory skills typically used in a real world classroom. In a classroom, the student must memorize facts one day and remember them the next day, week, or month. He must remember homework assignments for several hours. This subtest assesses whether a teenager can remember numbers for a few seconds.

The *Arithmetic subtest* measures increasingly difficult basic math skills. The teenager is asked to respond to math word problems which are read aloud. To solve the problems, the student must hold information about the problem in his head. This subtest may be a better measure of attention and concentration than of mathematical skills. Impulsivity, poor short-term memory, and poor listening comprehension may also interfere with the teenager's ability to do well on this subtest.

Low scores on the *Information subtest* may indicate that the teenager has problems with long-term memory, difficulty retrieving information, or has gaps in knowledge due to his learning problems. These gaps in knowledge may occur as a result of the teenager's inability to pay attention, memorize, or complete work. Low scores on the *Block Design* and *Object Assembly* subtests may indicate poor organizational and analytical skills.

Not all teenagers with ADD will show the usual wide range between highest and lowest scores on the WISC subtests. All of their subtest scores may be within a five-point range of each other. In a one-to-one testing situation with the examiner, some teenagers with ADD are able to stay on task so they score well on an IQ test. The novelty of the testing session may also help the teenager stay on task, thus masking the attentional problems.

In this situation, the evaluator may also observe the manner in which the teenager takes the intelligence test. He or she may observe that the teenager seems quite disorganized while taking the WISC-III, even though his final scores do not reflect that disorganization. Scattered approaches to problem solving also seem to be indicative of ADD. For example, a teenager may show poor problem solving ability and use trial-and-error approaches to complete these subtests. The teenager may have trouble staying on task during the evaluation and may be easily distracted.

☒

"One teenager I tested recently scored pretty well on the WISC-R with low scores on only one of the three 'attentional' subtests. Yet, the teenager had all the classic symptoms of ADD as reported by him, his parents, and teachers. His performance on the sentence completion was revealing. The teenager's handwriting was terrible and he worked very slowly, taking 15 minutes to do 10 sentence completions. Based upon this I would assume, that he would have difficulty completing schoolwork in a timely manner."

— *Pediatric Center Staff*

☒

Some teenagers appear to be hypersensitive during testing situations.

꙰

"I remember testing in a room with a fish aquarium in the corner with an almost silent air pump. The youngster said, 'I can't concentrate in here because of all that noise.'"

— *a School Psychologist*

꙰

Because of their attentional problems and gaps in learning, *it may be difficult to obtain accurate estimates of intelligence for teenagers with ADD.* The IQ test results may reflect an underestimate of the teenager's intelligence, possibly because of related learning problems or difficulty staying focused on the test. Students with ADD/I/WO who write or process slowly may not do well on timed portions of tests. Sometimes these teenagers are conversationally very bright, yet give short, concrete answers, resulting in lower scores on the WISC-III. Teenagers who are hyperactive may want to get the test over with as quickly as possible and impulsively give the first answer that pops into their head. Teenagers who have ADD/I/WO may have problems with slow processing or verbal expression and may give brief answers. Sometimes teenagers with ADD may miss easier questions and answer harder questions correctly. They seem to enjoy a challenge and may take more time to answer tougher questions or solve more difficult problems. Consequently, although ADD doesn't affect intelligence, teenagers with ADD may show an "unevenness" of intellectual development, as reflected by high scores on some subtests and low scores on others.

IQ scores which underestimate a teenager's intelligence can cause problems. Even though the student may be extremely bright, he may not meet eligibility requirements for participation in a program for intellectually gifted students. Most states have a cut-off score for this program somewhere around a Full Scale IQ score of 130 and higher. In addition, some teachers may base their expectations of ability on the inaccurate lower IQ score. Students may not be encouraged to reach their true potential in spite of the learning problems caused by ADD.

Standardized School Achievement Test Scores. Many of these teenagers are bright, yet their performance on standardized tests in school may be erratic. Sometimes these scores may be high and other times they may be low. Sometimes students with ADD make high scores in spite of poor academic performance in school. The discrepancy between high standardized test scores and low grades is confusing to both parents and teachers. They may think that the teenager's biggest problem is that he is just not applying himself or that he is lazy.

꙰

"My son's scores on standardized academic achievement tests in elementary school were usually quite high, in the 90th percentile and above. The discrepancy between his academic performance and high achievement on these tests was extremely puzzling to teachers and reinforced their thinking that he was not trying and could easily do much better class work. My son was learning in the classroom in spite of not completing written assignments."

꙰

"Most standardized tests have bubble sheets where answers are marked. Sometimes, these kids lose their places and mark the wrong item. It may also be important to know which portions of the tests were given in the morning and which ones in the afternoon. You may see a decline later in the day."

— *a School Psychologist*

꙰

Sometimes, a teenager's performance on these tests may be influenced by situations on the day of the test—illness, sleep deprivation, fights with parents, a crisis with a girl or boy friend, school problems, or hunger. Other times, performance may be related to the skills being measured or the nature of the test itself. For example, scores on the math computation, math concepts, and problem solving sections of the Iowa Test of Basic Skills may be low. Sections which measure punctuation, capitalization, or spelling may also be low due to the teenager's lack of attention to detail.

A test profile on the Iowa Test of Basic Skills is provided for the same student whose IQ scores were contained in Table 2–2 as a seventh-grade

Table 2–4   IOWA TEST OF BASIC SKILLS

	GE	NPR-S		NATIONAL PERCENTILE RANK
				LOW 1 ———— 10 — 25 — AVERAGE 50 — 75 — 90 ———— HIGH 99
VOCABULARY	91	80 7		--X--
READING	97	85 7		--X-
SPELLING	89	71 6		--X--
CAPITALIZATION	94	75 6		---X--
PUNCTUATION	107	92 8		--X--
USAGE AND EXPRESSION	106	91 8		--X--
LANGUAGE TOTAL	99	87 7		-X-
VISUAL MATERIALS	98	89 8		--X--
REFERENCE MATERIALS	86	66 6		-X--
WORK-STUDY TOTAL	92	80 7		-X-
MATHEMATICS CONCEPTS	95	84 7		--X--
MATHEMATICS PROBLEMS	86	71 6		--X--
MATHEMATICS COMPUTATION	65	20 3		--X--
MATHEMATICS TOTAL	82	65 6		-X-
BASIC COMPOSITE	90	80 7		-X-
COMPLETE COMPOSITE	92	83 7		-X-
SOCIAL STUDIES	112	92 8		---X--
SCIENCE	128	99 9		--X

GE=GRADE EQUIVALENT NPR-S=NATIONAL PERCENTILE RANK & STANINE

student. The teenager, whose ADD was diagnosed six months earlier, was not doing well academically in school. As expected, the Math Computation score was the lowest score. The Math Total score plus Spelling and Capitalization were also low.

Academic Assessment. Tests such as the Woodcock-Johnson Psychoeducational Battery, Kaufman Test of Educational Achievement, or the Weschler Individual Achievement Test may give important information about the teenager's academic strengths and deficits. The evaluator may find lower scores on sections of these tests which measure math computation skills, since teenagers with ADD tend to have problems with memorization, slow processing, and observing symbol changes in computation. Some teenagers with ADD have never mastered rapid recall of basic math facts, such as simple addition, subtraction, and multiplication. Sometimes the teenager will not notice when the signs on the math problems change from addition to subtraction or from multiplication to division. The teenager may add all the problems, failing to see the change in symbols.

While reading, teenagers with ADD may be visually distracted and see a lot of other words at the same time. Sometimes, they may also skip words, lose their place, or correct errors in their head. Sometimes it helps to slide a ruler down the page as they read each line.

🌿

"Sometimes I will have the youngster read questions aloud in the proofing section of the Woodcock-Johnson even though they are asked to read silently. Teenagers with ADD tend to correct the errors in the sentences as they read them silently. For example, the sentence reads 'Jeff is look for his wallet,' but the teenager reads it silently as 'Jeff is looking for his wallet.' Then they respond incorrectly by saying there was no error in the sentence."

🌿

Behavioral Assessment. Several behavior rating checklists may also be used to assist the treatment professional in diagnosing ADD. The Conners' Behavior Rating Scale, which has a short and longer version, is one of the most commonly used checklists. The Achenbach Child Behavior Checklist (CBCL), which takes longer to administer but also identifies emotional problems such as depression, anxiety, and aggression, may also be completed. Although these tests will identify ADHD, unfortunately ADD/I/WO is unlikely to be picked up. Sometimes the behaviors listed in the DSM IV diagnosis of ADD are used as a checklist.

Staff at the Pediatric Center frequently use the ANSER System (Aggregate Neurobehavioral Student Health and Educational Review) developed by Melvin D. Levine, M.D., University of North Carolina. Three questionnaires are completed, one each by the teenager, parent, and teacher, rating the degree to which the teenager exhibits behaviors associated with ADD. These questionnaires not only identify problem behaviors, but also address the student's academic performance, feelings about himself, positive behaviors he may exhibit, plus current adaptations, tutoring, or counseling provided at school.

Sentence Completion. The teenager may also be asked to answer some open-ended sentence completion items, such as "my mother gets angry when I_____," "I am happy when I_____." This activity provides a sample of handwriting, provides insights about the teenager's feelings and concerns, and shows how rapidly he writes.

Classroom Observations. As part of the evaluation for ADD, staff from the Pediatric Center may observe the teenager's behavior in the classroom. This observation is easier to do when children are in elementary school. Teenagers may be aware that they are being observed and change their normal behavior. Some school psychologists recommend that more than one classroom observation be made if possible. The teenager's ability to stay on task may vary at different times of the day. Usually, they are more productive in the mornings. Teenagers with ADD also have periods when they seem to have greater control over their behavior or may seem less distractible when working on a subject in which they excel.

Interviews with Teachers and Significant Others. Staff obtain as much information as possible from the teenager's teachers, guidance counselor, school psychologist, or other school personnel: academic strengths, potential learning problems, current grades, confirmation of behaviors listed in DSM IV, what classroom adaptations are in place now, and what interventions have worked before.

Identification of Learning Problems. If a teenager is diagnosed with ADD, the next critical diagnostic task is to identify any learning problems and make appropriate adaptations to the classroom. Approximately 25 percent of teenagers with ADD have learning problems that are serious enough to be categorized as a specific learning disability (SLD). SLD is a label that qualifies a student for special education services under federal law. A student may receive the diagnosis of specific learning disability if he has significant learning problems in one or more of these areas: oral expression, listening comprehension, written expression, basic reading skills, reading comprehension, mathematics calculation, and mathematical reasoning. To be eligible for SLD, a student must show a major discrepancy between intellectual ability (IQ) and academic achievement (reading and math grade levels). These issues are discussed in more detail in Chapter 8.

In addition, many teenagers with ADD, possibly an additional 25 percent, have serious learning problems that do not meet SLD eligibility criteria, yet interfere significantly with their ability to learn. Several learning problems are commonly associated with symptoms of ADD: inattention, language expression problems, poor short-term memory, poor concentration in class and during homework, poor fine motor coordination, and poor organizational skills. Some perceptual areas in which teenagers with ADD experience difficulty are related to distinguishing sounds, sights, or direction. Elementary age children with ADD or an accompanying learning disability may not know right from left, may read the word "saw" as "was," or may write letters in a reverse manner—substituting "b" for "d," for example. Common learning problems are discussed in detail in Chapter 10.

Because teenagers with ADD so often have learning problems, a major portion of the evaluation for ADD is aimed at also identifying learning problems. Scores on the WISC and Woodcock-Johnson may give an estimate of intellectual ability plus identify potential learning disabilities.

Even if ADD is being treated, there is no guarantee that the teenager's learning problems are being adequately addressed. Some teachers are not aware of common learning problems associated with ADD. After reading Chapter 10, parents may want to talk with teachers about their teenager's learning problems and which adaptations are currently being made at school. It may help to describe the adaptations that previous teachers have found to be effective.

Physical Examination. A thorough physical examination is conducted at the Pediatric Center. Dr. Gotlieb and his staff attempt to confirm the diagnosis of ADD and to rule out any other medical conditions which might cause symptoms similar to ADD. Medical or mental health conditions which may result in symptoms similar to those seen with ADD are discussed later in the chapter in the section "Identifying and Ruling Out Other Health and Mental Health Problems." A statement from a physician confirming the presence of ADD may be required for eligibility for special education services under the category of "Other Health Impaired."

Appropriate Use of Psychological Evaluations

A psychological evaluation of the type described above can be very helpful for diagnosing ADD. You should use some caution, however, in determining who will do the evaluation and what their evaluation will include. First, the evaluator must be experienced in diagnosing ADD, or the evaluation may not be helpful. Second, the evaluator should not only identify problem areas, but also suggest intervention strategies. Some evaluations provide a diagnosis only, but no constructive advice to the parent and teacher about how to cope with the teenager's problem behaviors. You, as a parent, should be an informed consumer. Feel free to ask what is included in the clinician/doctor's evaluation, how long it will take, and whether or not a written report with recommendations is provided.

During a crisis, parents and teenagers may need immediate help with the most pressing problems. Parents should not be afraid to ask professionals for what they need—for example, help with a crisis now, and an evaluation only after the crisis is resolved.

❧

"Once when my teenager was failing four of six classes, three weeks away from the end of the semester, a private psychologist wanted to conduct an intensive two-day evaluation. At first I agreed. After thinking it over, I called back and canceled the evaluation. I explained that a psychological evaluation including an IQ test had already been done for my son. The psychologist agreed and then suggested that personality tests should be done. I thought about it again, called back and canceled the appointment again.

"I told them I didn't want a nice six-page written evaluation of my teenager. I wanted him to pass all his subjects. Passing all his classes would be much more enhancing for his self-esteem and my peace of mind than a six-page evaluation. I felt the psychologist was not dealing with the immediate problem for which I had asked for help. My son needed to pass his classes.

"My son's ADD had already been identified and was being treated. He did not need further testing."

❧

It may be more helpful to families in crisis if specific behavioral action plans are developed to help the parents and teenager cope with the present situation.

❧

"Teacher conferences were held and make-up assignments to be completed were identified. Some teachers agreed to assign projects for extra credit. A friend, a 'study buddy,' was invited over to study for final exams. My son earned passing grades in five of six classes."

❧

Personality tests such as the Minnesota Multiphasic Personality Inventory (MMPI) are not used as frequently as the other tests described in this section for diagnosing or treating teenagers with ADD. The MMPI identifies more serious mental health problems such as psychosis, thought disorders, and antisocial personality.

Getting the Diagnosis

At the Pediatric Center, staff meet initially to discuss the results of the parent interview and completion of the family history. A second staff meeting is held after the tests and physical examination have been completed. The family then returns for another visit to hear the results of the assessment and recommendations for treatment. A verbal report is given and then a written report is finalized and given to the parents. If parents request, a copy of the report may be sent to the school. No matter where your child receives his diagnostic evaluation, you, too, should be given the results of his evaluation. You may want to request a written copy of the evaluation for future reference and have the opportunity to study the results more thoroughly. You should feel free to ask questions about anything you don't understand. Sometimes, the report will include a lot of jargon. If so, ask what the practical implications of the test results will mean for your teenager's schoolwork. The results of each test battery will probably be written up in the report. If not, you may ask which tests were used and request certain scores such as the subtest scores for the WISC. You may take notes or ask for permission to tape record the session. This may be a period of high anxiety and it is difficult to remember everything that is said in these meetings. If the evaluation makes your teenager eligible for special education services under IDEA, an individualized education plan (IEP) including recommendations for specific academic interventions will have to be developed jointly by your family and the school system.

What Does Your Child's Diagnosis Mean?

As discussed in Chapter 1, there are three major categories of attention deficit disorders listed in the fourth edition of the *Diagnostic and Statistical Manual of Mental Disorders* (DSM IV). This book contains the "official criteria" used in diagnosing attention deficit disorders. So, if your teenager is found to have ADD, the evaluator should tell you which of these types he has:

(1) Attention-Deficit/Hyperactivity Disorder, Predominately Hyperactive-Impulsive Type **[ADD/H]***;

(2) Attention-Deficit/Hyperactivity Disorder, Predominately Inattentive Type (Without Hyperactivity)**[ADD/I/WO]**;

(3) Attention-Deficit/Hyperactivity Disorder, Combined Type (Hyperactive and Inattentive)**[ADHD]**.

You might also hear that your teenager has Attention-Deficit/Hyperactivity Disorder Not Otherwise Specified if he has significant symptoms of inattention or hyperactivity/impulsivity but does not fit all the criteria for one of the types listed above.

The diagnostic criteria for each type of ADD are listed in Chapter 1. This section describes what each of these diagnoses may mean to you and your teenager on a day-to-day basis.

AD/HD, Hyperactive-Impulsive Type (ADD/H). Children with ADD who are extremely hyperactive cannot be overlooked by parents or teachers. Younger hyperactive children with ADD tend to get into everything, have trouble sitting in

their seats or keeping their hands to themselves, and talk a lot in class. As teenagers, these children still have the hallmark characteristics of inattention and impulsivity, but the hyperactivity is usually replaced by restlessness. As a result, parents and treatment professionals must rely on a past history of hyperactivity in childhood to help make a diagnosis.

As mentioned earlier, teenagers with ADD/H and ADHD don't seem to listen, don't obey rules, don't finish tasks, can't concentrate, don't work well independently, and shift from one task to another. They may also have difficulty delaying gratification, difficulty getting along with peers, and disruptive behavior in the classroom. Although they may talk more than their peers in many situations, when asked to respond to specific questions, they talk less. Sometimes they learn to be the class clown or become adept at "charming" the teacher simply as a survival skill that compensates for their academic difficulties. These teenagers are more likely to be aggressive, oppositional, and defiant than teenagers with the inattentive type of ADD (ADD/I/WO). Some may receive an additional diagnosis of Oppositional Defiant Disorder (ODD) or Conduct Disorder (CD). (ODD and CD are discussed in more detail later in the Chapter. Youngsters with mild to moderate hyperactivity may be overlooked until late elementary or middle school. Parents describe them as having been active children but didn't always perceive them as hyperactive.

The majority of children with ADD are hyperactive and diagnosed either as having ADHD or ADD/H: 78 percent of all boys and 63 percent of all girls.

AD/HD, Inattentive Type (ADD/I/WO). This diagnosis was previously known as ADD without hyperactivity and Undifferentiated ADD. Clearly, this disorder is more than just a mild case of ADD minus the hyperactivity. ADD/I/WO has its own distinct set of characteristics.

Three leading researchers on ADD/I/WO, Dr. Ben Lahey, Dr. Tom Brown, and Dr. Russell Barkley, have observed that the behaviors of teen-

---

* Abbreviated terms in brackets are the author's and are not part of the DSM IV.

agers with major inattention problems are different from those who are hyperactive. Dr. Barkley believes that *ADD/I/WO involves problems with focused attention and cognitive processing speed, rather than the problems with sustained attention and impulse control observed in ADHD.* Teenagers with ADD/I/WO have several distinguishing behaviors, with the common thread being slow cognitive functioning even though the teenager may be bright. For a teenager to know that he is bright but that information is somehow trapped inside his brain must be extremely frustrating for him.

Slower cognitive functioning and expressive language problems may contribute to problems at school and home: slow processing of information; slow response to requests; poor memory recall; and slow completion of work. Specific school-related problems include: listening comprehension problems (difficulty following instructions, confusion with verbal directions, difficulty taking notes, difficulty identifying main points); spoken language problems (slow verbal responses, difficulty giving clear answers, avoidance of responding in class); written language problems (slow writing, less written work produced, difficulty getting ideas down on paper, difficulty writing themes, difficulty taking written tests, slow reading, and poor reading comprehension). Getting started and sustaining effort on tasks such as schoolwork is extremely difficult for these teenagers. School issues are discussed in detail in Chapters 8–10.

※

"In our case, Shawn's problems (ADD/I/WO) didn't begin to show up until third grade. At first, it seemed to be the result of an unstructured second grade class combined with two moves. At that time the problem was minor. Shawn was in a very structured first grade class and did exceptionally well.

"In fourth grade his disorganization began to show up: not getting assignments home, wrong book, etc. By fifth grade, his grades really began dropping. By sixth grade it seemed that he couldn't pass tests and needed and received tutoring in testing skills but his grades continued to drop. By ninth grade he was failing. He was diagnosed ADD without hyperactivity when he was fifteen."

※

"My early memories of my son (ADD/I/WO) are of a happy, enthusiastic child eager to tackle any activity or challenge. Kindergarten was a joy for him, primarily because he had a warm, loving teacher. Learning was exciting and fun. The teacher liked him and he was crazy about his teacher.

"My son's difficulties concentrating, listening, following directions, completing assignments, writing and reading more slowly than other children were noticeable in the first grade but did not present major problems. He is intellectually gifted and was able to compensate until middle school, when his major academic problems surfaced. His ADD without hyperactivity was diagnosed when he was twelve."

※

When teenagers can no longer sustain attention to school tasks, they may sit quietly in their seats, tapping their pencils or foot, playing with their hair or paper, staring into space, daydreaming, or sleeping in class rather than exhibiting physically hyperactive behavior. These teenagers may also appear low in energy, apathetic, or unmotivated. They are less active, sometimes slow moving, and less disruptive than teenagers with ADHD. Depression and anxiety may be more common in teenagers with this type of ADD. Family members tend to have a history of learning disabilities and anxiety disorders more often than in families with ADHD.

In contrast to teenagers who have ADHD, teenagers with ADD/I/WO don't seem to have as many problems related to impulsivity (as described in DSM IV) and intrusiveness. They are less likely to be socially aggressive, oppositional, or defiant. They get along better with their peers and don't seem to have problems with social rejection that some teenagers with ADHD have.

Teenagers with ADD/I/WO and ADHD *can* share some characteristics. For instance, learning disabilities are more common in teenagers with ADD than in students without ADD. In addition, teenagers with ADHD and ADD/I/WO may have difficulty delaying gratification. And sleep disturbances are common in both conditions. These teenagers may have difficulty staying awake when they start on their homework. In addition, both may have problems with inattention and failure to complete work, but sometimes this may occur for

Table 2-5

THE BROWN ATTENTION DEFICIT DISORDER SCALE

Scores show how much that feeling or behavior has been a problem within the past month.

0   not at all a problem; never occurs
1   just a little problem; occurs rarely
2   pretty much a problem; occurs a few times in a week
3   very much a problem; occurs almost every day

Activating/Organization	Sustain Attention	Sustain Effort
difficulty getting started	mind drifts off	feels sleepy during day
feels overwhelmed	spaces out when reading	needs extra time on assignments
difficulty setting priorities	easily sidetracked	criticized as lazy
procrastination	needs to re-read	inconsistent work quality
difficulty getting organized	loses main point in reading	information processed slowly
slow to react	gets lost in daydreams	not working to potential
perfectionist	easily distracted	effort fades quickly
hard to wake up	seems out of it	sloppy penmanship
misunderstands directions	appears not to be listening	needs reminder to work
		doesn't finish task

Irritability/Sensitivity	Memory Recall
impatient	forgetful
sensitivity to criticism	forgets intentions
short fused	repeats/restarts in writing
difficulty expressing anger	misplaces words and letters
depressed mood	loses track of belongings
keeps to self socially	difficulty memorizing
(not true for all)	
appears apathetic	

different reasons. More research needs to be done on the differences in learning problems between teenagers with ADHD and ADD/I/WO.

❦

"When my son starts working on his homework, frequently he gets sleepy. His physical appearance changes. His eyes look very heavy, like they have sandbags on them. He has to struggle to stay awake to finish his homework."

❦

An informative article about ADD/I/WO was written by Dr. Tom Brown of Yale University for the CHADD newsletter, Spring/Summer 1993. Based upon his research with teenagers and adults with this disorder, he has developed the Brown Attention Deficit Disorder Scale, a 40 sentence self-report/parent-report checklist. Although there is some overlap with DSM IV, Dr. Brown's Scale includes more behaviors that may be helpful in diagnosing this type of ADD. A brief summary of the five core clusters of symptoms is listed in Table 2–5. Dr. Brown reads each sentence to the teenager and asks him to give a score of from 0 to 3. A score of 50 or more is considered indicative of ADD with inattention problems.

The list of behaviors included in this Scale should remind adults of the challenges some teenagers with ADD/I/WO face in their efforts to master schoolwork. It is sobering to realize that seemingly simple tasks, such as reading, finding the main point, and processing information rapidly, may be extremely difficult for teenagers with this type of ADD. Just getting started on a task, or even simply knowing how and where to begin can be a monumental job. Sometimes parents and teachers overlook just how courageous these teenagers are to continue to tackle academics when the task can be so difficult and overwhelming.

As a result of the revisions to DSM IV, ADD/I/WO *should* be easier to diagnose. The criteria listed describe the disorder much more accurately than in earlier editions of the *Diagnostic and Statistical Manual.* Unfortunately, as mentioned in Chapter 1, difficulties in diagnosis of ADD/I/WO may continue. A reasonable person would expect a teenager diagnosed with Attention-deficit/Hyperactivity Disorder, Inattentive to be hyperactive. As a result, teenagers with this type ADD may continue to be overlooked. Apparently, use of the term AD/HD in DSM IV is intended to mean either Attention-deficit *or* Hyperactivity Disorder.

ꕤ

"I always thought a child had to be hyperactive to be diagnosed as having ADD. Consequently, since my son sat quietly in his desk, I assumed incorrectly that he could not have ADD."

ꕤ

AD/HD, Combined Type, Hyperactive and Inattentive (ADHD). The diagnostic label for this disorder is self-explanatory. The teenager is or was hyperactive and also has significant problems with inattention. He exhibits characteristics which were described in the two preceding sections. Dr. Barkley has found that approximately 30 percent of youngsters with ADD have both ADD/H and ADD/I/WO. A few other researchers estimate that the rate is closer to 50 percent.

AD/HD, Not Otherwise Specified. This diagnosis is given when the teenager has prominent symptoms of inattention or hyperactivity, but does not meet the full criteria for the other categories of attention deficit disorders. For example, the teenager may have fewer than the required six DSM IV symptoms to be diagnosed with ADD/H or ADD/I/WO.

Differences Between ADD/H and ADD/I/WO

Although there are some similarities in behaviors between teenagers with ADD/H and ADD/I/WO, there are also several differences. Many of these differences are noted in the DSM IV criteria in Chapter 1 and in the section on ADD/I/WO above. Table 2–6 summarizes the most important of these differences. Because each teenager with ADD is unique, however, remember that not everyone with ADD/H or ADD/I/WO will have all the behaviors listed.

TABLE 2–6 COMPARISON OF ADD/H AND ADD/I/WO	
ADD/Hyperactive	**ADD/Inattentive/ Without Hyperactivity**
hyperactive	not hyperactive/lethargic
out of seat	sits in seat, daydreaming
talkative	quiet, less talkative
blurts out answers	slow to respond in class
talks and acts before thinking	slow cognitive processing appears confused slow retrieval of information slow writing
memory problems	greater memory problems
poor sustained attention	poor focused attention trouble getting started on homework/chores
responds to stimulant meds	doesn't respond quite as well to meds
class clown	socially withdrawn apathetic
difficulty with friends	gets along better with peers
Not all children with ADD will exhibit the following characteristics. However, when these behaviors do occur, they are more likely to be associated with the type of ADD noted.	
aggressive	anxious
oppositional	less oppositional
defiant	less defiant
conduct disorder	depressed
Behaviors sometimes shared in common:	
poor impulse control (poor regulation of behavior) difficulty delaying gratification or waiting difficulty controlling emotions difficulty using self-talk to control behavior difficulty learning from past mistakes poor sense of time poor self-awareness difficulty planning for future	

Identifying and Ruling Out Other Health and Mental Health Problems

As mentioned above, a good physical should be part of your teenager's diagnostic evaluation for ADD. This is because teenagers may have medical or mental health conditions that coexist with or mimic ADD. For example, several disorders have symptoms similar to ADD. These include lead poisoning, fetal alcohol syndrome, and thyroid problems. And some common health problems, such as anemia and mononucleosis, have symptoms of low energy which may be mistaken for symptoms of ADD/I/WO. ADD cannot be diagnosed as the sole cause of a teenager's behaviors until these conditions are ruled out.

There are other mental health conditions that can occur at the same time as ADD. According to Dr. Lahey, the most common problems that coexist with ADD include *Oppositional Defiant Disorder (ODD) or Conduct Disorder (CD); anxiety or depression; and learning disabilities.* Sleep disturbances may also be present. Others seen less often include obsessive-compulsive disorder, Tourette syndrome, substance abuse, and bipolar disorder.

Diagnosis and treatment of any coexisting disorders is critical. The subtle differences in these disorders need to be identified in order to prescribe the proper medication and treatment regimen. If your teenager's symptoms do not significantly improve with stimulant medications or a combination of stimulants and antidepressants prescribed for ADD, you should work with treatment professionals to rule out these other disorders.

※

"For our family, learning problems, sleep disturbances, and the proper medication regimen and dosages continued to be identified and fine tuned over a six-year period."

※

Depression. Teenagers may experience depression just as adults do. However, the disorder may be overlooked because the symptoms may not always be the same as for adults. Hyperactive children may look and act quite energetic. However, if left alone in a room, they may appear depressed or even fall asleep. In addition, depression in teenagers does not always involve sadness. Milder forms of depression may involve bad moods and less enjoyment of life. Sometimes, aggressive antisocial acts such as those described under Conduct Disorder may result from and actually mask depression. Typically, the antisocial behavior occurs after the symptoms of depression are observed. By treating the depression, antisocial behavior may be reduced.

According to DSM IV, major depression in adults and teenagers involves physical symptoms, including changes in sleep patterns, eating habits, and energy levels. A decrease in both mental and physical energy occurs. Teenagers may comment that nobody loves them. Low motivation, lack of enthusiasm, and reduced enjoyment of life may also be a problem. So, too, may frequent difficulty concentrating, slowed thinking, and indecisiveness. Other symptoms may include: depressed mood, weight loss or gain, agitation, or feelings of worthlessness. A depressed person may complain of memory problems and appear easily distracted. Thoughts of death may also occur.

Researchers do not agree as to whether depression occurs more frequently among ADHD youngsters than among their peers. A NIMH study on this subject being conducted by Dr. Steven Evans of the University of Pittsburgh may eventually provide some insight. When depression *is* present, however, it is more likely to occur in teenagers with ADD/I/WO than in those who are hyperactive.

Sleep Disorders. Sleep disturbances, which are present in half the children with ADD, may cause serious problems. Lack of sleep impairs memory and the ability to concentrate. Sleep deprivation, being deprived of restful sleep, may be the reason 50 percent of these children wake up tired each morning. Sleep problems may be symptoms of both depression and ADD. Sleep issues plus suggested interventions are discussed in detail in Chapter 6.

Family fights over going to bed or waking up are common. The teenager may complain of difficulty falling asleep, waking up during sleep, early morning awakening, or difficulty waking up. Extreme difficulty waking up may also be a symptom of depression. Sometimes, even though a teenager may have slept eight or nine hours, he may wake up feeling groggy and may take an hour or more to really get going. If your teenager is persistently groggy, has stomach aches or headaches, or wakes up in an irritable mood, consider discussing these behaviors with his doctor. It may be difficult to determine whether sleep disturbance is occurring as a result of ADD or depression. Sleep problems related to ADD may be more long-term, however, having been observed for several years. The family history should be reviewed to determine if depression may also be a problem for other family members. Although reasons for the sleep problems may be different, treatment may be the same.

Anxiety Disorders. Some teenagers with ADD may experience excessive anxiety and worry. They can't seem to stop worrying. In addition to worrying, the teenager may feel on edge, tire easily, have difficulty concentrating, be irritable, have muscle tension, or a sleep disturbance. Severe anxiety disorders such as panic disorder and obsessive-compulsive disorder are rare but are discussed briefly.

Researchers do not agree on whether or not anxiety disorders occur any more often among youngsters with ADD than those without ADD. However, when anxiety is present it is more likely to occur among teenagers with ADD/I/WO.

Occasionally, a teenager may become so anxious that he experiences a panic attack. A panic attack may include intense fear, rapid heart beat, chest discomfort, sweating, trembling, shortness of breath, dizziness, nausea, tingling sensations, chills, or feelings of being detached from oneself. The teenager may be afraid of losing control or going crazy. These feelings of panic may occur during stressful situations. Panic disorders are believed to be inherited and are the result of biochemical problems in the brain. Sometimes a bright teenager who has undiagnosed ADD and is underachieving may experience high levels of anxiety and be diagnosed with panic disorder. The anxiety may mask symptoms of ADD, so the ADD remains undiagnosed.

Obsessive Compulsive Disorder (OCD). Rarely, teenagers with ADD may experience obsessive recurring thoughts, impulses, or images even when they try to suppress them. They may then compulsively act upon them. They seem driven to continue repetitive behaviors such as hand washing, counting things, double checking to be certain

that tasks are done (door locked), or rigidly following rules or rituals. Little research has been done on coexisting ADD and OCD. However when a child has both, the issues are complex and make treatment difficult.

☒

"My son has ADHD and obsessive compulsive symptoms. Dealing with OCD behaviors plus ADHD is really complicated and frustrating. We are still trying to determine which is the primary disorder. We can't find a medication that will help with all his symptoms. We've been to so many specialists seeking help, yet still haven't found the help we need. Rituals are a major issue. He has to go to the bathroom the last thing at night before going to bed. He may go several times. He has to wear certain clothes together, sit in certain places in the car and at the table. He has major dietary problems and will not eat many foods. When we find something he can eat, he must eat them in certain ways. Macaroni and cheese may only be eaten with potato chips. Pizza can be ordered only from Dominos. Things must be in order. He has difficulty with new experiences and transitions."

☒

Bipolar Disorder. Bipolar disorder, formerly called manic depression, is a mood disorder which may have alternating periods of high energy (manic moods) and low energy (depression). Adults with the disorder may have as few as four of these episodes of highs and lows per year, while children and adolescents may have changes of mood every few days.

It is sometimes difficult to tell ADHD and bipolar disorder apart, because they share several common characteristics: impulsivity, hyperactivity, high physical energy, and behavioral and emotional ups and downs. The key difference between the disorders seems to be that with ADHD, symptoms such as hyperactivity are consistently present rather than occurring in cycles. Teenagers with bipolar disorder are more likely to look like those with ADHD during the manic phase of bipolar disorder when they are more talkative, have problems sleeping, and are distractible. Dr. Charles Popper, a psychiatrist and psychopharmacologist who serves on CHADD's Professional Advisory Board, has found that a teenager may have both ADD and bipolar disorder.

If a teenager isn't responding well to treatment for ADD, some professionals may wonder whether ADD has been misdiagnosed and bipolar disorder is perhaps the correct diagnosis. However, Dr. Barkley has found that the vast majority of youngsters with ADHD do not meet the criteria for bipolar disorder. Their poor response to treatment may be due simply to a less-than-optimal medication regimen and failure to make adaptations for learning problems.

On the other hand, a few young people who have a bipolar disorder may have been misdiagnosed as having ADD during early childhood. If there is a family history of mood disorders, bipolar disorder, or manic depression, this is an important diagnosis to consider. Bipolar disorders in adolescents can be treated effectively.

An awareness of the symptoms of bipolar disorder may help parents avoid an incorrect diagnosis. Dr. Popper has identified several symptoms of bipolar disorder in teenagers:

1) psychotic symptoms that reflect an impaired thought process with gross distortions in reality. Flight of ideas (a rapid shift from one thought to another) may be observed. Teenagers with ADD may also shift from one topic or idea to another, but they always remain in touch with reality. Delusions, belief in something that is not true, may be present. For example, the teenager may have delusions that he or she is rich or is God.

2) severe temper tantrums that release tremendous physical and emotional energy. These tantrums may last longer than for children who are not bipolar (from 30 minutes up to 2–4 hours), even when they are alone and no audience is present.

3) pronounced irritability, especially in the morning. These youngsters may be rejecting or hostile when they meet people. For example, they may be rejecting or insulting toward a treatment professional during the first few seconds of an interview. They may try to disrupt or get out of the interview or ask when the interview will be over.

4) sleep disturbances. Sleep problems may include difficulty sleeping through the night, or

severe nightmares with explicit gore or images of bodily mutilation.

5) aggression and destructiveness. Teenagers with bipolar disorder may intentionally hit or hurt someone and may relish the fight or power struggle. In contrast, the misbehavior or destructiveness of teenagers with ADHD is often accidental.

6) a pronounced sexual awareness and interest, danger-seeking, giddiness, and loud giggling may be observed, even in the preschool years.

Tourette Syndrome. Tourette syndrome is a genetic disorder that results in both motor and vocal tics. Motor tics involve involuntary muscle movements, such as rapid eye blinking, mouth opening, lip licking, sticking tongue out, grimacing, shoulder shrugging, or stretching movements. These actions are often repetitious and ritualistic. Vocal tics may include throat clearing, grunting, coughing, humming, or spitting. Symptoms wax and wane, sometimes becoming more apparent, and sometimes less. Frequently old symptoms disappear only to be replaced by new ones. Stress, excitement, anxiety, or drinking caffeine can make the symptoms worse.

Tourette syndrome occurs in less than 1 percent of the population. Researchers believe that hypersensitivity to the neurotransmitter dopamine may be the underlying cause of the disorder. *Children with Tourette syndrome also frequently have ADHD.* At the Tourette Clinic at Johns Hopkins University, approximately 80 percent of the patients also have a diagnosis of ADHD. Likewise, Dr. David Comings, M.D., a nationally recognized researcher on Tourette syndrome at the City of Hope Medical Center, has observed that 60–80 percent of his patients with Tourette syndrome also have ADHD. Typically, symptoms of ADHD precede Tourette symptoms by an average of 2.5 years.

Substance Abuse Problems. Dr. Barkley has found that the only substances that teenagers with ADHD are more likely to use than their peers are alcohol and cigarettes. Research regarding drug abuse risk and ADHD is inconclusive. There is some evidence that teenagers with ADHD and Conduct Disorder may be more likely to use drugs. Teenagers with ADHD may experiment with drugs as teenagers, but one study found that as young adults, they do not use drugs any more frequently than their peers. Chapter 7 discusses possible signs of substance abuse, as well as strategies for parents to use in helping to prevent or curtail such abuse.

Seriously Emotionally Disturbed or Emotional and Behavioral Disorders. If your teenager is having serious behavior problems at school, school personnel might tell you that he is Seriously Emotionally Disturbed (SED) or has an Emotional and Behavioral Disorder (EBD). These are special education categories, not medical diagnoses. Chapter 11 covers classroom implications for students who are labeled SED or EBD.

School personnel may recommend placing a student in an EBD classroom if he exhibits aggressive, defiant, and disruptive behavior, even though he may have learning problems which are contributing to his misbehavior. The student may have behaved disruptively enough to have had frequent school suspensions and also be diagnosed as having Oppositional Defiant or Conduct Disorder. (The pros and cons of EBD placement are discussed in Chapter 11.)

Several of my colleagues have collected information about the percentage of youngsters with serious emotional problems who also have a diagnosis of ADD. An eight-year study of 800 youngsters with serious emotional problems was conducted by Dr. Bob Friedman, Dr. Starr Silver, Dr. Krista Kutash, and Dr. Mark Prange at the Florida Mental Health Institute, University of South Florida, Tampa. Dr. Friedman is Professor and Chairman, Department of Child and Family Studies. The youngsters in this study, begun in 1985, had serious emotional problems and were placed in residential treatment facilities or classes for students with emotional or behavior disorders (EBD). Approximately 16 percent of the children in residential care and 8 percent in EBD classes were diagnosed as having ADD.

More recent information reflects even higher percentages of youngsters with both ADD and serious emotional problems. In a study conducted at one site in North Carolina, Dr. Lenore Behar found that 24 percent of children receiving mental health services had ADD. In South Carolina, Paula Finley, director of a statewide program serving youngsters with the most serious emotional problems, reported that approximately 27 percent of the youngsters had ADD. Informally, several of my

colleagues who work with children with serious emotional problems say that approximately one-third of their referrals have ADD.

Oppositional Defiant Disorder (ODD) and Conduct Disorder (CD)

In addition to the mental health conditions discussed above, there are two other conditions that warrant a section of their own because they occur so frequently and cause such worrisome behaviors. These conditions are Oppositional Defiant Disorder (ODD) and Conduct Disorder (CD). Understandably, many parents are concerned when treatment professionals discuss a second diagnosis of ODD or CD. Like a diagnosis of ADD, these labels are shorthand for behaviors that occur in a cluster. The diagnostic criteria given in the DSM IV for ODD and CD are given below.

Oppositional Defiant Disorder (ODD)

Teenagers who are argumentative, hostile, defiant, and refuse to follow rules may be given the diagnosis of Oppositional Defiant Disorder (ODD). To be diagnosed with ODD, four of the following behaviors must be present for a period of six months.

- often loses temper
- often argues with adults
- often actively defies or refuses to comply with adults' requests or rules
- often deliberately annoys people
- often blames others for his or her mistakes or misbehavior
- is often touchy or easily annoyed by others
- is often angry and resentful
- is often spiteful or vindictive

Conduct Disorders (CD)

Teenagers who have more serious behavior problems, such as persistent stealing, lying, setting fires, destroying property, physical cruelty to animals or people, and fighting, are diagnosed with Conduct Disorders. Teenagers with CD consistently violate the rights of others and refuse to comply with rules. Conduct Disorder is one of the most serious diagnoses among the DSM IV classifications. To be diagnosed as having a Conduct Disorder, a teenager must have done at least 3 of the following during the past 12 months with at least one present in the last 6 months:

Aggression to people and animals

1) often bullies, threatens, or intimidates others

2) often initiates physical fights

3) has used a weapon that can cause serious physical harm to others (e.g., a bat, brick, broken bottle, knife, gun)

4) has been physically cruel to people

5) has been physically cruel to animals

6) has stolen while confronting a victim (e.g., mugging, purse snatching, extortion, armed robbery)

7) has forced someone into sexual activity

Destruction of property

8) has deliberately engaged in fire setting with the intention of causing serious damage

9) has deliberately destroyed others' property (other than by firesetting)

Deceitfulness or theft

10) has broken into someone else's house, building, or car

11) often lies to obtain goods or favors or to avoid obligations (i.e., "cons" others)

12) has stolen items of nontrivial value without confronting a victim (e.g., shoplifting, but without breaking and entering; forgery)

Serious violations of rules

13) often stays out at night despite parental prohibitions, beginning before age 13

14) has run away from home overnight at least twice while living in parental or parental surrogate home or once without returning for a lengthy period)

15) often truant from school, beginning before age 13

The more of these behaviors a teenager has and the greater their severity, the more serious the ODD or CD are considered to be. Teenagers with a combination of hyperactivity and Conduct Disorder seem to have the most serious problems and the poorest prognosis. Youngsters with Conduct Disorder are more likely to be expelled from school, be arrested, abuse drugs, and break the law, possibly ending up in jail or a psychiatric treatment facility.

Prevalence and Cause of ODD & CD

Children may begin to show signs of Oppositional Defiant Disorder and Conduct Disorder as early as six or seven years of age. By the time they reach adolescence, approximately 65 percent of teenagers with ADD are also diagnosed with ODD and 45 percent with CD. However, these figures can be somewhat misleading and need further explanation. Many studies of young people with ADD and CD were performed on those with the most severe symptoms who were in psychiatric hospitals or residential treatment facilities, juvenile detention facilities, or jails. These young people tend to have more serious symptoms than teenagers with ADD who have adjusted fairly well and are being treated only by their local physician. As a result, estimates of the frequency of these disorders are probably too high. In the average community, the frequency is probably closer to 30–35 percent for ADD/ODD and 20–25 percent for ADD/CD.

According to Dr. Lahey's research, children who have the most severe problems have high levels of hyperactivity and are diagnosed with ADHD by the age of 2 or 3, ODD symptoms by 4 or 5, and CD symptoms by the age of 8 to 11.

There are several theories about the causes of ODD and CD. Some researchers think the conditions are caused by a disorganized, chaotic, and disturbed family situation. Obviously, some family behaviors, such as abusiveness or constant hostile interactions, play a major role in causing a teenager's problems. Current research, however, also points toward coexisting biochemical problems as a contributing cause. Parents can help avoid problems by taking steps such as those described in Chapters 4 and 5: keeping family life as organized as possible, providing supervision and structure, keeping the teenager busy in activities to build self-esteem, and giving medication, if needed.

Dr. Herb Quay, former chairman of the Department of Psychology at the University of Miami, believes that some youngsters with CD also have a biochemical problem—a deficiency in neurotransmitters. This deficiency results in decreased sensitivity to punishment, making it harder to learn from punishment or rewards. They repeat misbehavior even after being punished. On the surface, it looks as though they are maliciously disobeying or defying their parents and other authority figures.

Recent studies in Canada, California, and Finland have provided additional evidence that there is a biochemical basis for aggression. Researchers were able to increase aggressive behavior in both people and monkeys by reducing the levels of the neurotransmitter serotonin. According to these studies, when the levels of serotonin are low, both people and animals are more impulsive, aggressive, violent, and even suicidal. Apparently, low levels of serotonin may be the result of both inherited and environmental factors. Studies at the National Institutes of Health have identified a faulty gene that makes people predisposed to this problem. In addition, violence or neglect in childhood or excessive alcohol can trigger lower serotonin levels.

To Label or Not to Label?

Sometimes labels such as Conduct Disorder can be harmful to a teenager. For example, some schools may refuse to educate a student with that diagnosis. Plus, labeling is not particularly helpful in treatment. Since treatment professionals have some latitude in selecting a diagnosis, they should therefore be cautious in making a diagnosis as serious as Conduct Disorder. Or as Hippocrates wisely admonished physicians, professionals should try ". . . to help, or at least, to do no harm."

Diagnostic labels alone have no great mystical power. A counselor, doctor, or teacher who learns that a teenager has ADD, ODD, or CD does not automatically know how that teenager acts or how to treat him. *Having an additional label or diagnosis is not as important as identifying specific problem behaviors and developing an intervention to cope with each problem.* If a teenager is aggressive or defiant, plan strategies to cope with those problems. If a teenager is having difficulty sleeping, treat the sleep problems.

There are several reasons for avoiding use of the diagnosis of Conduct Disorder except when the behaviors are very serious: First, as mentioned earlier, some schools may refuse to provide an education for a student who is diagnosed as having a Conduct Disorder and frequently gets into trouble at school. Some schools define Conduct Disorders as social maladjustment, and federal regulations do not require schools to serve students who are socially maladjusted. The bottom line is that the school system will not be responsible for providing an education or any services if the student is expelled for misbehavior, even if misconduct is related to the disorder. This problem is discussed in more detail in Chapter 11.

Second, although it is more convenient to say Conduct Disorder than list 15 behaviors, this label is not particularly helpful to professionals in planning for treatment. Does the teenager have only 3 or all 15 behaviors? Which specific problems cause the most concern? How severe are the behaviors he exhibits? Again, it is more helpful in treatment to identify the specific problem behaviors and develop strategies to reduce the behaviors.

Finally, the label of Conduct Disorder sounds terrible and may be frightening to parents. A parent's imagination can run wild if a diagnosis of CD is given. A self-fulfilling prophesy may come into play here. If all the adults around this teenager think he is bad and cannot benefit from help, they may give up on him. Without intervention, misbehavior may become progressively worse, possibly resulting in illegal activities that land the teenager in jail or a psychiatric hospital.

Ordinarily, a diagnosis of Conduct Disorder is given by a treatment professional rather than school officials. If a private psychological evaluation is completed, parents should review it to decide whether it is helpful or damaging, and whether a copy should be sent to the school system. If you are concerned that a diagnosis of CD will harm your teenager, discuss it with the treatment professional. There are a variety of ways that this can be handled: You may not need to do anything. The diagnosis is confidential information and cannot be released without your permission. If you want a report sent to the school, the treatment professional may choose to address issues that are relevant to your child's functioning in the classroom without giving a diagnosis such as ODD or CD. You could also seek a second opinion.

Usually, a diagnosis of ODD is not as much a cause for concern. Since oppositional behavior is fairly common among teenagers regardless of whether or not they have ADD, a diagnosis of ODD does not carry as much stigma as CD.

This is not to say that parents should stick their heads in the sand and ignore problem behaviors. They need to work with treatment professionals to develop a plan to cope with specific problems.

❧

"My son's therapist seemed irritated and told me that we were dealing with 'more than just ADD.' When I asked her why she thought my son had a Conduct Disorder, she replied that he was sneaky. She seemed surprised when I told her I knew that my son did not meet the criteria for Conduct Disorder."

❧

"Some professionals don't think twice about giving a diagnosis of Oppositional Defiant or Conduct Disorder to teenagers with ADD. I wonder if they would want *their* teenager to be given these diagnoses if he had these same behaviors. I don't think they would. It is a pretty insulting diagnosis for the whole family, particularly if viewed as being caused by a chaotic, disorganized family."

❧

Three worrisome behaviors frequently identified in students with the diagnosis of ODD and CD are anger, aggression, and oppositional behavior. Common treatment strategies for these behaviors include medications and interventions which help reduce frustration and increase compliance at home and school. These strategies are discussed in Chapters 4–10.

Even if your teenager has some behaviors which are characteristic of a Conduct Disorder or Oppositional Defiant Disorder, do not despair and give up. Your teenager's behavior may change and improve over time. A teenager diagnosed as having Conduct Disorder does not necessarily continue to exhibit these problem behaviors forever. As Dr. Gabriella Weiss was quoted earlier in the book, *the key to successfully surviving ADD is to have someone who believes in you,* even during difficult times. True, when your teenager is in a crisis, it may be extremely difficult for you to be positive and to continue to believe in him. Yet even though you may

sometimes have doubts and get pretty discouraged, it may help to *act* as if you believe in your teenager. You can discuss your fears in private with your family or a treatment professional. Thankfully, most crises have a way of "blowing over" fairly soon without irreversible damage. Sometimes a parent's whispered words of hope and self-encouragement may be: "This too shall pass."

Parents as Partners

Two sets of experts must be involved in diagnosis and treatment of ADD: the treatment professionals (pediatricians, clinical psychologists, psychiatrists, teachers, school psychologists, social workers, and/or guidance counselors) and the families (parents and the teenager). Each group has a unique contribution to make to the diagnostic and treatment process.

As a parent, you know your teenager best, having lived with him and with ADD for many years. *You and your teenager should be treated with respect by any professional who is conducting an evaluation for ADD or associated conditions.* Professionals should not make you feel guilty or that you are to blame for your child's behavior. In addition, they should ask for your input as a treatment strategy is developed. They should be open about answering questions you ask about the evaluation, treatment approaches, or medications. Ideally, the treatment professional will identify your teenager's strengths and tap those as part of the treatment plan. If you do not like and respect a professional, consider finding someone else. If your teenager is willing to go to counseling, it is important to select someone he likes and respects.

It is also important for you to treat professionals with respect. A positive parent/teacher partnership is critical. You will need to work closely with school officials to help your teenager succeed at school. Typically, students with ADD need more support from teachers at a time when the system expects more independence and offers less support. Teachers will need to spend more time and energy than usual with your teenager if his educational program is to succeed.

Sometimes parents are so frustrated and angry, they may inadvertently alienate school officials by misdirecting their frustration about ADD toward them. Usually, however, you will be more successful at having your teenager's needs met by working collaboratively *with* school personnel. Occasionally, "being nice" doesn't work and you may have to be more assertive to get the help you need. Legal rights under federal laws are discussed in Chapter 11.

Conclusion

There is still so much to learn about ADD. Although the symptoms that comprise the diagnosis of ADD have been observed since at least the early 1900s, researchers did not make much headway in understanding the disorder until the last several decades. In fact, only a generation ago children with ADD were sometimes diagnosed inappropriately as having minimal brain damage. It was not until 1972 that Dr. Virginia Douglas at McGill University in Montreal first identified the problems with sustained attention and poor impulse control associated with ADD. She noted that hyperactivity was just one of several symptoms of the disorder. And it was not until the publication of DSM III in 1980 that the condition was first labeled Attention-deficit Disorder. Two categories of ADD were included: ADD with and without hyperactivity. Prior to that time, ADD was called Hyperactivity or Hyperkinetic Syndrome.

Proper diagnosis and effective treatment strategies for ADD are still evolving, especially for teenagers. Through additional research, the subtle characteristics and problems related to treatment of ADD should become clearer during the next few years. As with diagnosis and treatment of any fairly new disorder, *you should not assume that all the symptoms related to your teenager's ADD have been identified and are being properly treated.* You must continue to be vigilant in the years after your child is diagnosed to ensure that his needs are being properly met.

CHAPTER THREE

MOVING BEYOND GUILT, ANGER, AND FEAR TO OPTIMISM!

Parenting a teenager with ADD can be compared with riding a roller coaster: there are many highs and lows, laughs and tears, and breathtaking and anxiety-producing experiences. Most parents of teenagers with ADD would give anything for a week that was relatively calm and free of turmoil. However, unsettling highs and lows are likely to be the norm for many families with ADD.

When parents encounter difficulties raising their teenager with ADD, they often have deep feelings of self-doubt, fear, and guilt. *Some parents worry that they have been "bad" parents and have caused their teenager to act the way he does.* Other parents simply believe that they have a "bad" child. Because of their teenager's behavior, parents may experience a wide variety of emotions ranging from embarrassment and depression to anger. All of these feelings are perfectly normal and understandable, under the circumstances. Learning to handle these stressful feelings in a constructive way should make it easier for parents to raise a teenager with ADD.

Despite your teenager's misbehavior and the stressful demands of parenting, you undoubtedly still love your child and want the best in life for him. You may be desperately seeking special guidance to help him succeed, since traditional child rearing techniques don't seem to work as effectively. This book is intended to provide that special guidance. This chapter in particular will help put you in a more positive frame of mind so you can follow that guidance. Its goal is to help parents understand their teenager's behavior, plus their own negative feelings that may have built up over the years, and then to cope with those feelings constructively. By first dealing with your own feelings, you can begin to deal more optimistically with ADD.

The Emotional Impact of ADD

Raising a teenager with ADD can exact a tremendous toll on the family, especially when ADD is more serious and is not being properly treated. Family arguments and fights over homework, skipping school, school failure, and medication refusal can thrust the family into an emotional pressure cooker. With all the stress involved, it is not unusual for parents to feel inadequate and overwhelmed. Researchers have found that *parents of youngsters with ADHD experience more feelings of depression and doubt about their parenting skills.* According to Dr. Russell Barkley, these parents are three times as likely to separate or divorce as parents who do not have children with ADD.

⋙

"In the midst of a major crisis when her son had been suspended from school . . . again, one mother cried, saying, 'I don't want to give up my whole life for this child.' Yet by the next day, after this brief angry outburst, she was back at the job of helping her son cope with the blow-up at school."

⋙

As parents, your whole world may revolve around your teenager with ADD. You may expend tremendous amounts of time and energy worrying, providing needed supervision and support, and occasionally, "rescuing" him. At times, you may become exhausted and depressed. Conflicts with your teenager, your family, or your spouse can contribute to your exhaustion, depression, or feelings of being overwhelmed. So, too, can coping with your own conflicting emotions. The typical conflicts facing families with ADD are discussed below.

Conflicts with Your Teenager

Noncompliance

One of the most common sources of conflict between parents and teenagers is their failure to do as parents ask. *Their inattention, forgetfulness, and sometimes, defiance play a major role in their noncompliance with parental requests.* Many teenagers with ADD are not doing well at school and are disobedient at home. As a result, parents spend a lot of time monitoring school work, nagging about homework and chores, dealing with teachers, and setting limits for their teenager. They grow weary of constantly having to handle these problem behaviors. This is particularly true if the behaviors have not improved with treatment or if the teenager has co-existing problems such as a learning disability.

Although parents know intellectually that their teenager's misbehavior is often related to his symptoms of ADD, this does not make it any easier to cope emotionally with these problems. Even when ADD is a contributing factor, behaviors such as defiance, stubbornness, talking back, and disobedience infuriate most parents. These types of behaviors can be a tremendous source of frustration and embarrassment to parents.

☒

"Parents tell me they are constantly saying 'No!' to their children and teenagers with ADD. These teenagers are constantly testing and pushing parents to their limits. This is so exhausting for everyone!"

☒

"It is so embarrassing when my son talks back to me or disobeys me in front of others. I know other people must think I am a terrible parent. At times, I feel like such a failure."

Emotionality

Teens with ADD often have *low tolerance for frustrating situations* and *intense emotional reactions.* They have great difficulty handling their anger, stress, and disappointment, and therefore approach situations more emotionally than other teenagers do. Their increased emotionality may trigger a strong emotional response from parents, setting in motion a vicious cycle of yelling fights. Typically, if parents respond in a loud, angry manner, the teenager gets even angrier. He then becomes increasingly aggressive and less likely to do as he is asked. The best response for parents is to lower their voice, stay calm, and give the teenager some time and space to cool off. This is easier said than done, however, when the teenager yells, talks back, curses, or cries. Sometimes because parents dread the emotional blow-up, they may avoid confronting their child about his behavior or misbehavior (poor grades, missed curfew, drinking). Since parents know these issues *must* be dealt with eventually, anxiety about the inevitable confrontation builds up and is very stressful.

Crisis Situations

Crises occur far too frequently and often contribute to family friction. Some parents dread receiving "bad news" phone calls about their teenager. If their teenager is out with friends at night, parents start worrying when the phone rings. "Mom, I got a speeding ticket tonight." "I had a wreck." "Dad, I'm at the police station—can you come get me?" "I think I'm pregnant." Other "bad news phone calls" come from school: "Your daughter is not at school today. Where is she?" "Your son is failing chemistry." "Your son was in a fight at school. Please come take him home." Parents long for the time when they receive "no more bad news phone calls."

☒

"I live with a constant underlying feeling of anxiety when my teenage son is out at night during the weekend. I wonder what's going to happen next."

🖾

Some parents have had to face police bringing their teenager home for violating curfew, or judges when accompanying their teen to juvenile court. These trips to court are typically over less-serious issues—speeding tickets, riding a dirt bike on paved roads with no driver's license, violating curfews, minor car wrecks, sneaking out of the house at night, staying out overnight without permission, driving off without paying for $5 worth of gas, and drinking.

Any crisis, major or minor, may throw the whole family into emotional turmoil. *Tremendous emotional energy is required to parent these teenagers when they are in crisis.* It is a perfectly normal reaction for parents to be angry and depressed about the stress their teenager causes. No doubt, the teenager is also angry with himself, and, sometimes, with the whole world.

🖾

"There were times when my daughter was in high school, when I thought, 'I just can't go through another day or another moment.' I would be so tired of having the phone ring and having it be the police department or school saying my kid wasn't at school today."

Daily Friction

Crises aren't the only thing that cause conflicts between parents and their teenager with ADD. *The teenager with ADD has difficulty meeting the seemingly simple demands of daily living.* He doesn't do chores. He seems lazy and appears eager to avoid helping around the house. The yard is never mowed on time. The teenager's room is a disaster zone. The teenager is argumentative and talks back to parents. He stays out late or parents don't know where he is. He may be moody, irritable, and explosive at times. If parents had to deal with just a few of these behaviors on an occasional basis, it wouldn't be terribly stressful. Dealing with one behavior on top of another, however, quickly wears

down even the most patient parent. Yelling battles may be common.

🖾

"Knowing the value of the child and experiencing the love of the child do not keep parents from feeling weary unto tears."

🖾

"By his early teens, all of my son's anger and frustration was directed toward me. We ended in verbal conflicts even over the weather, date, time . . . everything. I would go to work early so we wouldn't have conflicts before school to start both our days on the wrong foot."

🖾

"Although I was a teacher, I didn't want to be my son's teacher at home. I wanted to be his mother. I wanted him to always feel he could come to me about anything. Home was to be a refuge from the world . . . not another battlefield.

"I was always fighting with my son. No matter what I did or how patient and tactful I tried to be, it ended in a loud verbal fight."

Communication Problems

A host of communication problems may strain relationships between parents and teenagers with ADD. According to Dr. Barkley's research, many parents and teenagers with ADHD say mostly negative things to each other. Sometimes parents can't find anything positive to talk about with their teen. *Because of their child's disobedience and defiance, parents may issue more commands and putdowns, plus make more negative comments.* Before parents are educated about ADD, they may assume incorrectly that their teenager is acting maliciously. Many view their teenager as "lazy, stupid, unconcerned, irresponsible, unmotivated, a liar, and/or selfish." And that may be exactly what they tell their teenager. Not surprisingly, arguments can be very heated and intense. Parents and teenagers may begin distancing themselves from each other emotionally if these negative exchanges persist.

🖾

"'You aren't going to amount to anything when you grow up if you don't change.' Parents often say things like this in the heat of anger and later regret it. It is so difficult for parents to maintain their composure when they are angry and frustrated.

"We used to put our son down like this. Fortunately, he seemed to have an insight telling him we were wrong. Parents need to think before they open their mouths.

"The major point I would like to convey to other parents is, don't say degrading things to your child. Don't call your child stupid or a lazy bum. Don't tell him you wish you never had children or that you wish he were never born. I've said some of those things and I'll regret those words until the day I die."

♚

"Don't let siblings say negative things either. It is easy when the sibling is hurt by the child with ADD to lash out in anger. Siblings need a lot of support and information in trying to understand ADD. Patience and understanding are needed for both children."

♚

To add to communication problems, the teenager's perception of family interactions is not always accurate. Often, he sees his parents' rules as unfair and too restrictive. This leads to even more arguments.

As a result of these frequent conflicts, the primary caregiver, usually the mother, may feel more depression, self-blame, and social isolation. Frequently, depression contributes to a vicious cycle of problems. Parents who are depressed are more critical, disapproving, and punishing with their children. Depressed parents are less tolerant, and may consequently see their child's behavior more negatively than it actually is. In addition, depressed parents use inconsistent child management techniques, which undermines their effectiveness. For their part, children of depressed parents are more likely to be aggressive toward their parents.

There *is* some good news about communication between parents and teenagers. As discussed earlier, *communication becomes more positive when the teenager is taking medication*. In addition, conflicts are worst and parenting stress greatest with very young children with ADHD. Conflicts tend to decline in adolescence. Families with children with ADHD always have more conflict than other families, however, regardless of the child's age.

Conflicts within Your Family

ADD has a tremendous impact on the whole family. *Brothers and sisters in particular often feel strong, conflicting emotions.* On the one hand, they feel terribly *sorry* for the struggles their sibling must go through. But on the other hand, they are equally as *angry and resentful* that he messes things up, gets into trouble, embarrasses himself and his family, harasses their friends, and makes his parents angry and depressed. To a large degree, it must seem to them that family life unfairly revolves around their sibling's needs. They may resent their sibling for hogging the lion's share of their parents' time and energy and feel as if they are shortchanged as a result.

Some siblings believe that their parents have a *double standard* for behavior. They often think that the teenager with ADD gets away with more misbehavior than they do. They may second guess and be angry with their parents because the teenager with ADD "isn't punished often enough."

In comparison with a teenager with ADD, the brother or sister may *seem angelic* to parents. In some families, siblings feel they have to be the "model child" to make up for the teenager with ADD.

♚

"My daughter felt guilty that her brother had a disability instead of her. She wished she could have the ADD to relieve her brother's pain for a while. She was always a good student. She was trying to make up for her brother's problems.

"If I had it to do over again, I would be more honest and explain the disorder better. I would give her something to read about ADD. I didn't give her credit for being able to understand what was going on."

♚

For their part, teenagers with ADD are *not particularly sensitive to how their behavior affects others*. They *borrow* things without permission and sometimes *lose or break* them. These behaviors may lead to frequent arguments that escalate into screaming or shoving matches or occasionally fights.

🌿

"My older brother (who has ADD) makes me so angry because he borrows things from me without asking and never returns them. He doesn't respect my property. My irritation level with him on a scale of 1–10 is 12. I've tried everything to get him to stop taking my things. Yelling doesn't work. Asking doesn't work. I threatened to beat him up. I am starting to dislike him. I hate to admit it, but I can't trust him. He's very selfish. He doesn't care about anyone's feelings but his own. He eggs me on and tries to get me mad. He plays with my mind. My parents are tougher on me because of things my brother has done."

🌿

Often, teenagers with ADD don't handle their anger very well. Consequently, they may *take their frustration and anger out on younger siblings*. If the teenager comes home angry because of frustrations at school, he may yell at younger brothers or sisters, boss them around, threaten them, or hit them. The teen's sense of powerlessness or impotence is translated into anger directed at others. Obviously, younger siblings get upset and come crying to parents. Then another battle is set in motion between the parents and the angry teenager.

If more than one family member has ADD, problems may be even more complicated. According to Dr. Barkley, *40 percent of all children with ADHD have at least one parent with the disorder*. In addition, *26 percent of siblings* also have the condition. Obviously, if several family members are inattentive, impulsive, disorganized, and have difficulty handling anger and stress, family life may frequently be in an uproar.

Conflicts with Your Spouse

There is great potential for conflict between parents who are raising a teenager with ADD. *Many mothers and fathers have difficulty agreeing on the best method for disciplining their teenager*. In addition, some parents blame each other for their child's difficulties. Often, one parent is the disciplinarian in the family. Frequently, the "disciplinarian" believes that if only the other parent were less permissive,

their teenager would not have so many problems. Agreeing on appropriate discipline is especially ticklish if one parent does not understand ADD and wants to impose punishment that is too rigid and harsh.

Parents may argue or fight over the teenager's behavior. Sometimes, if one parent is too tough on the teenager, the other parent compensates and is too easy. The "easy" parent may "protect" the teenager from the disciplinarian by covering up his misbehavior. Communication between spouses becomes strained. They talk less, withhold information about misbehavior from each other, or actually lie to cover up for the teenager. Obviously, parents in these situations don't act as a united team in disciplining their teenager. Although this problem is relatively common, it can be emotionally damaging for both the parents and the teenager. Parents may benefit from talking with a licensed treatment professional such as a psychologist or family counselor who can mediate and help them agree on a parenting approach.

Differences in parenting styles may also cause conflict. Generally speaking, mothers talk more, reason more, and are more affectionate with their children. Fathers talk less and take action by using punishment or consequences more quickly. Obviously, these roles can sometimes be reversed.

Sometimes parents' perceptions of their child with ADD is influenced by traditional parental roles. For example, a mother's self-esteem may be closely related to the house, its appearance, and the accomplishments and behavior of her children. As a result, she may be more upset than the father about a dirty room, chores that are not completed, or poor grades. Conversely, many fathers' personal satisfaction is wrapped up in their professional accomplishments at work, so they are bothered less by some things that upset mothers. Of course these generalizations may not apply in every family.

Misunderstandings between spouses can arise if the teenager behaves better with one parent than the other. As researchers have found, this is often the case among *children* with ADHD. (Researchers have yet to study whether the same holds true for teenagers.) Dr. Barkley and Dr. Zentall have each speculated why *children behave better for their fathers*. Dr. Barkley explains that these children respond better to immediate consequences, which fathers are more likely to use. And Dr. Zentall points out that children with ADD do better in novel situations. Typically, children spend more time with their mothers (familiar) and less time with their fathers (novel). In addition, fathers are stronger and physically more intimidating. Children may feel safer expressing their feelings, including anger, with their mothers.

According to Dr. Barkley, some fathers assume that the mother is not an effective parent because their child behaves better with them. As a result, they may believe that their child's problems are not as serious as described by the mother. Some fathers believe that if only the mother was less permissive and used more discipline, the teenager would behave better. A few fathers may even believe that it is the mother, not the child, who needs help. Or the father may think that the mother is overly sensitive to behavior that he sees as being normal in an "all American" boy.

❦

"When my wife and our son's teachers began talking about his problems at school and mentioned ADHD, I was very skeptical. There was nothing wrong with my son. He acts just like I did when I was in school. Later it became clear to me that I also have ADHD."

—Bobby Robbins, director of a
community mental health center

❦

"My husband didn't really say it, but I know he really felt the problems were my fault too. I felt guilty and a failure as a mother. But with me working, there just were not enough hours in the day."

❦

Researchers emphasize that *the child's response to his mother is usually not a negative reflection on her parenting skills.* In his book *Attention Deficit Hyperactivity Disorder*, Dr. Barkley noted that, "It is time for fathers and male professionals to realize that children, especially ADHD children, do show differences in the actual manner in which they respond to their mothers compared to their fathers. This does not necessarily implicate flaws in the mother's caretaking abilities or an excessive sensitivity to normal child behavior" (p. 141). Dr. Barkley also suggests that if fathers and mothers switched daily responsibilities, fathers would most likely experience many of the same problems mothers do. Obviously, the parent who places the most demands on the teenager to complete work will be involved in more conflicts. If the primary caregiver corrects the teenager for everything he does wrong, that person will be involved in a constant battle all day.

Parents need to understand each other's parenting style, as well as their teenager's unique response to each and avoid being judgmental of each other. You can also take heart from the knowledge that research on ADHD has shown that the mother/child relationship improves with age and involves fewer negative interactions.

Parents may need to compromise—talk less and take action—when misbehaver occurs. Or as Michael Gordon, Ph.D., author of several books on ADHD, is often quoted as saying, "Act. Don't Yak." Dr. Gordon, a Professor of Psychiatry and Director of ADHD Clinic, SUNY Center, Syracuse, New York, is also a member of CHADD's Professional Advisory Board. If it is necessary to punish your teenager, talking and reasoning may be done later after a consequence has been imposed. Keep in mind, however, that harsh punishments are not particularly effective and should be avoided. Other problems may arise within a marriage if parents are afraid to go out and leave their teenager at home for fear of the impulsive misbehavior he may get into. Although the teenager doesn't really need a "baby-sitter," his parents may feel that he needs some kind of adult supervision. Unfortunately, if a husband and wife spend little or no time together, they will have trouble nurturing their own relationship. Their limited time together may be spent fighting about their teenager. They begin to think of themselves only in the role of parents, and may lose sight of the common interests and values that originally drew them to one another. Resentment and depression at having no life outside of their family can follow.

Although research on families with *teenagers* with ADD is lacking, it is clear that the parenting approach used with younger children must be modified to be effective with teenagers. Parents must learn more sophisticated strategies, such as those discussed in Chapters 5, 6, and 7.

Your Own Conflicting Emotions

Confusion and Self-Doubt

You may be *bewildered and frustrated* by your teenager's behavior, both before and after the diagnosis of ADD. Your teenager doesn't mind at home and may not be doing well in school. He is angry and defiant. If you have raised other children "successfully," it is especially hard to understand why this teenager is different and more difficult to raise. Punishment worked for the other children. Why doesn't it work for this child?

Your teenager himself is likely at a loss to explain his own behavior. He is probably confused and bewildered because he wants to do well in school and at home but can't seem to follow through on his good intentions. As a teenager or young adult, he may struggle to find his niche in life.

🌿

"I remember a touching conversation at bedtime one evening when Alex was in elementary school. He described his eagerness to turn over a new leaf when the new school year started and made a sincere commitment to make all A's. His ADD hadn't been diagnosed at that time. Without medication, he could not sustain this commitment. He genuinely wanted to do better in school but could not."

🌿

"I truly believe that my daughter Elizabeth really wanted to succeed. I also believe there is a 'fear of trying'—that is, if I don't try and I fail, then it is because I didn't try, not because I'm not smart enough. I believe they have great fear of failure."

🌿

A teenager's bewildering misbehavior may lead parents to doubt their own feelings about the worth of their child. Intuitively, many parents know their teenager is basically a "good child" who wants to do well at home and in school. In the midst of a crisis, however, it is difficult for even the most devoted and loving parent to maintain faith in their teenager's goodness. This is true even if they know that ADD is responsible for a lot of their teenager's struggles.

To add to the self-doubts, other well-meaning adults voice opinions that "a good spanking will straighten the child out" or "the teenager just needs to be disciplined." Because they see no other logical explanation (prior to diagnosis of ADD), some parents believe their teenager is lazy, "doesn't care," and "doesn't try" to complete work or chores. Some classroom teachers make similar comments, reinforcing this idea.

🌿

"It was suggested that Steven be evaluated by a psychologist regarding his performance in school. I felt that would be a terrible waste of money. I thought if he would just apply himself, he would do fine in school. His biggest problem appeared to be that he made way too many zeros in class. I was convinced he was just lazy and was not willing to give up any of his play time to devote to his studies.

"Since Steven has been diagnosed as having ADD, I realize he has much more difficulty concentrating on school work than I had. As a graduate of the U.S. Naval Academy, I thought anyone who tried could discipline themselves to accomplish what I had in school. I have learned so much and have come to understand how difficult school is for teenagers with ADD."

🌿

"A lot of parents think their child is lazy. As a psychologist, I believe there is no such thing as a truly lazy child. They may act lazy outwardly because everyone expects them to act that way. Usually, they get into that because something is wrong. The problem just hasn't been diagnosed."

🌿

"After we held Scott back in the eighth grade and his maturity level was more appropriate to his grade level, things got better, but there was always the 'laziness' issue. No one could explain his behaviors any other way, but I always knew in my heart he was not lazy."

🌿

Unfortunately, *some teenagers come to believe what adults have said about them*—that "they are lazy" and that's why they don't do well in school. Parents are trapped with their offspring in a complicated web of self-doubt, misinformation, and subtle blame. Hopefully, Dr. Alan Zametkin's research at the National Institute of Mental Health (NIMH) gives parents some reassurance that they have not been "bad" parents, nor are their teenagers "bad" children. (See Chapter 1.)

Resentment/Anger

In moments of anger or crisis, some parents may wish their teenager with ADD had never been born. If their child is involved in one serious problem after another—speeding tickets, car wrecks, drinking, and school suspensions—parents may have fantasies of "running away from home" or trading their teenager in for a "newer model" with fewer problems. Anger and resentment are bound to surface when parents get a call from the local police station at 3:00 a.m. to come pick up their son who has sneaked out of the house and violated city curfew hours.

When parents are angry, they may have trouble finding any lovable characteristics about their teenager. They may be so stressed out and depressed that they focus only on the negative behavior of their teenager. Then they must struggle with overpowering feelings of guilt and inadequacy as a parent.

⚜

"I wished we didn't have teenagers. I only wanted babies. I really loved the early years. I felt really good about the ways the babies were developing. I wish I could say that now. I feel like such a failure as a parent."

Guilt

When ADD is diagnosed, especially if the diagnosis is delayed until adolescence, some parents experience overpowering feelings of guilt. They second guess themselves and question why they didn't figure out their teenager's problem earlier. Parents "beat themselves up" and ask themselves a thousand questions. "Why didn't I find this out sooner? Why did I push so hard? Why did I degrade my child so much? I should have known he was ba-

sically a good child. A better parent wouldn't have done the things I've done."

⚜

"I'll regret some of my putdowns until the day I die."

⚜

"Every parent must work through the guilt, particularly those of us with educational and psychological backgrounds!"

⚜

Make peace with yourself and your teenager. You did the best you could with the knowledge and skills you had. Any past negative interactions between you and your teenager were not intentional, nor were they done in a malicious manner. You were simply dealing, as best you could, with your teenager's behavior. Parents need to forgive themselves.

"We have made peace with our son. But, I still haven't completely forgiven myself."

⚜

"After all, for most parents, it is on-the-job training . . . . No course prepares us for parenthood."

⚜

"Our own self-esteem as parents also needs to be worked on. We always did the best we could at the time."

⚜

Sometimes parents get upset with their teenager even after they learn of the implications of ADD. Parents yell or overreact, and then feel very guilty. These feelings are normal. It would take a saint to be a "perfect parent" and always maintain a calm, reasonable exterior when dealing with a teenager with ADD. Some parents may benefit from training to cope with typical behaviors related to ADD. Parent training and support are discussed at the end of this chapter and in Chapter 4.

Inadequacy: "I Don't Have the Answers"

Parenting a teenager with ADD can be a very humbling experience. Typically, parents are aware early in their child's development that this child is different. In their more positive moments, parents see the teenager as a unique and special person. During a crisis, parents may view their teenager as a "pain in the neck" and an unwanted burden. Often, they feel inadequate and overwhelmed. Parents are acutely aware that they don't have all the right answers for raising their teenager with ADD. Furthermore, many of the experts they consult don't have all the answers either. Several parents with professional training in this field echo the difficulties inherent in raising a teenager with ADD:

※

"As the parent of a child with ADD, I have had the humbling experience of living with, loving, and 'sweating bullets' raising a child whose world inside his head was not like the world I knew growing up. I have struggled to understand my son's thoughts and actions, and provide loving but firm support and direction in a world, particularly a structured academic one, which in large measure did not understand him, his disability, or value the very special person he is."

※

"When we who are 'professionals' in this field have trouble, it is a double blow. We feel we should have the answers. If we have difficulty, surely parents without formal training would have even more so."

※

"Despite all my 'expert skills and knowledge of children,' I have experienced strong feelings of inadequacy as a parent and definitely have not felt like an 'expert' raising my own child. There have been too many times I have not had the answers; too many times the professionals to whom I have turned for advice have not had the answers. Too many times I have questioned my own judgment in 'disciplining' my son. Too many times I have felt the disapproval of my son's teachers, principals, and some family members, regarding how I chose to 'discipline' and raise my son."

※

"I fall back on, 'I live with her, know her best, and do the very best I can with the help I receive.'"

Emotional Pain

Although it can be hard to remember during a crisis, parents aren't the only ones who live with the daily stress of ADD. Having ADD is no picnic for the teenager either. If the teenager with ADD had a choice, no doubt he would not choose to have the disorder. It's true that many teenagers with ADD eventually cope successfully with the disorder. Others, however, struggle to find a place in school and in the work world where they can succeed and feel good about themselves. Teenagers with ADD frequently have difficulty verbalizing the pain they feel, but the perceptive parent knows it's there.

※

"Mom, am I going to feel this way all my life? Sometimes, I feel like I am going to die of a heart attack or anxiety."

※

"I feel like I'm always doing something wrong at school."

※

"Dear God, please don't let me have ADD."

※

When teenagers hurt, their parents hurt too. *No pain can be any greater than the pain a parent feels for their teenager in distress.* Parents and teenagers *both* hurt because this world does not understand ADD and has not been particularly kind to many teenagers with the disorder.

※

"There is nothing worse than not being able to help my child, and there is nothing better than seeing her succeed. As parents we hurt when we see our child suffering and we can't fix it. It's very frustrating and depressing. That's why it is so important for us to latch on to the successes and to reinforce those every time we see them.

"I've found myself, at times lately, struggling to find the positive behaviors. While I know they exist, the negative ones that involve peer relationships in particular rip my heart out as I struggle to help her become more mature. I have trouble sometimes sorting

out what is normal (whatever that is) teenager separation struggles and the impulsive, naive behavior that comes from the need for immediate gratification. The scary part is she thinks she's making sound judgments. I love the highs but the lows are the pits."

Worry/Concern for the Future

As discussed in Chapter 1, parents worry a lot about the future. "Will our teenager be able to graduate from high school? Will he find a good job and support himself as an adult?" Because parents worry so much, they may focus most of their energies on their teenager's negative behavior. Some days parents feel tired and overwhelmed just thinking about everything they'll have to go through until their teenager becomes a responsible adult. Since most teenagers cope successfully with ADD, parents probably waste a lot of time worrying unnecessarily.

Perhaps you worry that if your teenager is having trouble succeeding in high school, how can he possibly manage technical school, college, or a job? *Keep in mind that although he is not ready to attend college today,* that is all right. He doesn't have to cope with those demands right now. When your teenager reaches eighteen, he will be older and more mature. In addition, you can help him obtain needed supports and adaptations to succeed in high school, technical school, or college. Issues related to succeeding in school and career options are discussed in Chapter 12.

🖎

"Once adaptations were made in college, my son did better there than he did in high school."

🖎

Sometimes your good intentions (worrying) about helping your teenager succeed in life may backfire. When parents nag, regardless of their good intentions, conflicts with their teenager get worse. Your teenager's school performance won't improve if you nag at him about making good grades for college and preparing for his future job. There will, however, be more animosity between you.

When parents worry too much about tomorrow and the future, they may forget to enjoy their relationship with

their teenager today. Learning to live one day at a time is a difficult lesson for most adults to master. Trying not to worry about problems that may arise next month or next year is easier said than done. You and your teenager should try to maintain a belief in your ability to cope successfully with each problem—when it arises.

Isolation and Loneliness

As if it weren't bad enough to *have* so many conflicts within the family, *parents often have no place to turn for help outside the family.* No one else seems to understand. They feel a tremendous sense of isolation because they assume that no other parent could possibly have gone through the same struggles they face on a daily basis. They have trouble confiding their pain and concerns to other adults who do not have teenagers with ADD. Other parents can't fully understand how difficult these teenagers can be to raise. Sometimes other adults come across judgmentally, sending the message: "Your child wouldn't do these things if only you would discipline him properly." Even grandparents and other relatives don't always understand ADD, are critical of the teenager's behavior, and judgmental of your parenting skills.

🖎

"When my father told my new husband that my son just needed discipline, I was devastated. My feelings were so hurt because my own father thought I was not doing a good job as a parent."

🖎

"Sometimes at midnight on a Friday, I would be hoping that my husband and daughter would both be coming in soon. I would be exhausted from work and would be waiting for my husband to get home from the airport. When a crisis arose, I would be crying and thinking, I don't want this and I don't need this. I bet all of my sisters and brothers-in-law have never had kids who have done all these 'terrible' things."

🖎

Over the years, parents often have difficulty taking a break from the stresses of raising their teenager with ADD. Frequently, babysitters are hard to find. After experiencing a hyperactive youngster, the babysitter may not be willing to come back. Even grandparents or other family members may be reluctant to keep these youngsters overnight, for a weekend, or a week in the summer. When these problems arise, seek a creative solution—hire two or more babysitters, perhaps.

Sometimes even professionals fail to give parents the support they need. Parents can't always find the services their teenager needs, or don't know where to request help. It is very difficult to find someone who understands the full implications of having ADD and can work effectively with the disorder. When other adults don't understand the disorder or provide support, parenting a teenager with ADD can be an extremely lonely job.

Special Parenting Issues

Unique Issues for Single Parents

Divorce is a fact of life in the world today and may have a negative impact on many teenagers with ADD. The exploding divorce rate (almost 50 percent) has resulted in approximately 40–50 percent of all teenagers living with a single parent, typically their mother. Adolescence alone is a difficult adjustment period for many young people. If the teenager has ADD plus parents who are divorcing, it is an extremely stressful time in his life.

Single parents face a special challenge raising a teenager with ADD. Although researchers aren't certain why, children with ADD who live with a single parent are more aggressive than those living in a two-parent family. Having the sole responsibility of raising a teenager with this disorder is an exhausting job, especially if no family members live nearby to provide support and help. This doesn't mean single parents cannot be good parents. However, the job of raising a teenager with ADD is usually easier when two parents work together and give each other some relief from the stress. Two-parent families who move a lot and have no relatives nearby also miss the extra support an extended family can provide.

Single parents who begin dating again after divorce or the death of their spouse face a difficult situation. Frequently, the people they date do not understand the teenager or ADD. Consequently, they think that increased discipline will solve all problems. These "significant others" face major conflicts and disappointments if they are rigid or expect the teenager to respond to traditional discipline and instantaneously obey their requests.

❦

"People I dated during my ten years as a single parent would try to tell me what to do to 'straighten Lewis out.' They just believed it was my fault because I was a single parent."

❦

The mother-son or father-daughter relationship may be extremely intense and difficult during this period for several reasons. First, the teenage male with ADD is becoming a man and that means behaving like men do. He wants to be the male head of the household in his father's absence. Consequently, the son may feel threatened by men dating his mother. He may be possessive for fear the man may take his mother away from him. Competition with the "other man" for his mother's attention is likely to occur. Similar problems may occur if the daughter has ADD and her father is dating or decides to remarry.

In addition, the teenager with ADD may act like his father did and some of the problems the divorced parents had may be played out between the mother and the son. If the divorce is recent, then the teenager may struggle with depression and anger as well as with ADD.

Conflicts between the parent and "significant other" about child-rearing practices and discipline of the teenager with ADD are almost certain to arise. If a long-term relationship develops, educating the friend about symptoms and treatment of ADD is important. A good first step is often to provide some reading materials about teenagers with ADD. Start out with something brief and easy to read. Attending CHADD meetings together may also be helpful. It helps to make a special effort to include the teenager in activities with the two adults. Scheduling special alone time with just the parent and teenager is also helpful. These two steps should make the teenager less anxious and more accepting of the new person in his parent's life. Remember, it takes a very special and understanding person to cope with a teenager with ADD, especially when the teenager is not his own.

The Complexities of Second Marriages

Second marriages present complex issues for all families. When a child has ADD, the pressures on stepfamilies are compounded. You should be aware of the factors that make stepparenting difficult for all families, as well as the unique ways ADD can affect stepfamilies.

First, being a member of two families can become very *complicated*. The teenager may have as many as "four" parents, plus extra grandparents with whom he must interact. Parents may or may not agree on common child management strategies. Each family's ability to maintain consistent family rules and consequences for misbehavior varies. This could be a nightmare for the teenager with ADD who needs structure, routine, and consistency. Remembering which rules apply in which family is extremely hard.

Second, making decisions about *living arrangements* may be difficult. Since most children of divorce live with their mothers, the typical stepfamily consists of the teenager, his mother, a stepfather, and sometimes other siblings or stepchildren. Frequently, the teenager spends alternating weekends with the absent parent, most often, the natural father. However, if parents have joint custody, the teenager may live alternating weeks with each parent. In this situation, it is difficult for the teenager to make transitions such as moving back and forth between families. Usually, the "weekend parent" spends less time with the teenager, has fewer conflicts, and may be tempted to just have fun with the teenager. He or she doesn't want to be the "bad guy" and may ignore the need for routine, structure, and consequences.

On a more practical level, can you imagine what havoc a teenager's ADD-related disorganization and forgetfulness can cause when living arrangements are divided? Now they have two homes where they can lose or leave things. If they need the math book, homework, or computer, it is probably going to be at the wrong house.

Third, the teenager's natural *loyalty* to biological parents may result in strong conflicting feelings. The teenager may think subconsciously, "If I like and have fun with my stepfather (stepmother) that means I am not loyal to my real father (mother)." The teenager may fear that the stepparent is trying to replace his natural parent. Stepparents have to carve out their own special relationship with the teenager and make it clear that they are not trying to take the absent parent's place.

Fourth, the teenager and the parent with whom he lives are sometimes extremely close and develop a very special relationship. When a stepparent enters the relationship, their time must now be shared among three people, not just two. Initially, feelings of *displacement* are common among teenagers. Sometimes, the son (daughter) who has been the man (woman) of the house is resentful, jealous, or frightened that he or she is being replaced by the new spouse. These feelings increase the potential for family conflict.

Fifth, the stepparent's *role in parenting* is seldom clearly defined. Children are unlikely to accept parenting or discipline from a stepparent until trust and a relationship have been established. According to research, being a stepmother is the more difficult role—perhaps, in part, because of our society's negative attitude toward "the wicked stepmother." Often the teenager feels the stepparent hasn't earned the right to intervene or discipline until their relationship is solidified. The teenager may say, "You're not my father (mother). You can't tell me what to do." As a result, the biological parent may make decisions about most of the disciplinary actions. Unfortunately, developing trust between stepparent and teenager takes time, perhaps years. You can't force or rush it. The biological parent must make a special effort to involve the new stepparent in decision making and to present a united front to the teenager. Sixth, stepparents may consciously or subconsciously attribute a teenager's misbehavior to poor parenting. This spoken or unspoken *criticism or blame* results in the biological parent feeling hurt and defensive. The biological parent then finds herself (himself) frequently trapped between the stepparent and the child. This creates tremendous stress. Most natural parents want to build a cohesive parenting team with the new stepparent. However, this is difficult, especially if the stepparent does not fully understand ADD.

Finally, most biological parents are *naturally protective* of their teenager, particularly with their new spouse or people they are dating. Feeling guilty about the divorce and their child's "loss" of a parent contributes to this protectiveness. Plus, parents are even more protective when a child has a disability. Parents often work to keep their interactions positive and to avoid conflict. Although they do set limits, they may ignore more misbehavior than the average parent. Other adults may not understand this.

Obviously, many of the typical problems associated with stepparenting are magnified because of the teenager's symptoms of ADD. The "invisible" nature of ADD—inattention, disorganization, learning disabilities, sleep disturbances—makes it difficult for most stepparents to understand its profound impact on the teenager's day-to-day behavior. Some stepparents perceive the teenager as lazy and his misbehavior as malicious and intentional, further adding to family conflict.

Natural parents are often extremely embarrassed by their teenager's misbehavior. Even though they know better, they may sometimes feel as if their teenager's misbehavior is a negative reflection on their parenting skills. They may reluctantly withhold information from the stepparent simply to avoid conflict.

🌿

"Although I know I shouldn't withhold things from my husband about my son, I have done it before. It is so embarrassing to tell him some things that my son has done. Occasionally, when I don't tell my husband something, I feel very guilty. But otherwise if I told him everything, a huge fight would erupt between us. Sometimes, I deal with the problem myself and impose a consequence when necessary."

🌿

New stepparents usually feel overwhelmed when they inherit a son or daughter with ADD. Some stepfathers or stepmothers who are disciplinarians believe that their strong influence and discipline will solve the teenager's problems. This is more likely to be true if the new parent has other children who don't have ADD and are easier to raise, or if they have no children at all. Yet, unless the teenager is receiving proper treatment and the stepparent is educated about ADD, problems are likely to become worse, not better.

🌿

"I can remember as a young treatment professional I gave other parents 'great advice.' I had all the right answers until I had a child with ADD. Then when I became a stepmother, I had to learn how to deal with the unique characteristics of a stepson with ADHD."

🌿

Occasionally, both parents bring children with ADD to a marriage. These parents may be more understanding of the behavior associated with ADD. However, parenting a second child—a stepchild with ADD—is still very difficult. Unfortunately, it is usually easier for parents to be tolerant of *their* teenager's behavior than the stepchild's.

🌿

"Our marriage and parenting experiences were unique. We both had sons with ADD from previous marriages. We were much more understanding of each other because we each had struggled to cope with the disorder. In many ways we were extremely lucky. A parent who does not have a teenager with ADD can't understand the challenges of raising one."

🌿

"I know I was more tolerant of my own child's ADD behaviors than I was of my stepson's. I made a special effort to treat them equally, but it was terribly difficult. I feel guilty about it, but unfortunately, I think it's a pretty common parental reaction. The age difference was also a factor. His son was older and I felt he should have been more responsible. Later, when my son reached the same age and did the same things, I realized I should have been more understanding of my stepson. At that time we were not aware of their developmental delays and related impact on their maturity level and ability to accept responsibility. Unfortunately, our oldest son didn't have the benefit of our new knowledge when he was in high school."

🌿

Conflicts over the teenager's behavior may put a serious strain on the marriage. Ideally, the couple should not wait until the relationship deteriorates, but seek counseling early from a treatment professional who specializes in working with families with ADD.

Just looking at data about all remarriages is scary, and not just in families with ADD. About 50 percent of remarriages end in divorce. The primary reason these marriages fail is due to conflict over children. Stepfamilies coping with ADD are clearly in double jeopardy, since conflict over these children is inevitable. The remarriages that have the greatest risk of failing are those in which the father has children and marries someone who does not have children. However, the family unit is strengthened and more closely bonded when the new parents have another child. The arrival of a baby strengthens the relationship between the siblings.

The simple passage of time plays a major role in cementing relationships in stepfamilies. Some research has shown that "blended families," as second marriages involving children are sometimes called, take approximately five years to bond and feel like true family members.

⚥

"We have been married eight years now. The early years in our marriage were very difficult. Our teenage sons, both of whom have ADD, are now young adults. My husband and I have fewer conflicts with them and are closer not only to our own sons but stepsons too."

Coping: Is the Glass Half Empty, or Half Full?

"It has been my experience as a parent, school teacher, school psychologist, and counselor that most teenagers are good, and our job as parents and teachers is to 'Catch them being good' and praise them for what they do correctly. I prefer to view the glass as being half full, rather than half empty. I praise my teenage son for remembering to mow the yard even though he forgot to feed the dog."

⚥

A risk inherent in writing a book about Attention Deficit Disorder is that the teenager's negative characteristics are discussed in such detail that they inadvertently overshadow his strengths. The main reason problem behaviors are discussed in detail is to help parents and professionals recognize the symptoms of ADD and coexisting problems, to

---

Table 3–1
IDENTIFY THE TEENAGER'S STRENGTHS
INDIVIDUALIZED TREATMENT PLANNING: "DO WHATEVER IT TAKES"

NAME: Tom   AGE: 17   GRADE: 12th

STRENGTHS

HOME/COMMUNITY
- Intelligent
- Creative
- Caring/kind hearted/helps others
- Fast swimmer/lifeguard
- Daring/will try most anything once
- Easy going nature
- Good with electronics/wiring stereos
- Complies with requests
- Pursues interesting hobbies, scuba diving, flying an airplane, photography
- Sensitive
- Willing to take medication
- Trying to understand ADD and himself better
- Tall and handsome
- Good caring for young children

SCHOOL
- Intelligent
- Creative
- Good with computers
- Good with hands; did well in shop class
- Complies with most rules/not a discipline problem
- Allows parent to monitor and prompt when assignments are due
- Writes great creative stories
- Kept class snake during summer/helpful
- Great vocabulary
- Has ability to get algebra answers correct even when he doesn't do the problems right

begin treatment as early as possible, and to help parents cope with their own feelings of doubt and anger. As Chapter 4 explains, treatment including counseling, behavior management, classroom adaptations, educational planning, and medication may help many of these teenagers cope with most social and academic problems.

The key to coping emotionally with ADD, however, is not to focus on all your teenager's irritating and demanding behaviors. Instead, *you must look beyond the negative behaviors and latch onto his strengths.* You must ask one critical question: "Are we going to dwell on our teenager's deficits, or build on his strengths?"

Discover Your Teenager's Strengths

Teenagers with ADD have many strengths. Often, they are delightfully entertaining and charming. Most teenagers with hyperactivity have boundless energy. Some teenagers also seem to be especially creative. Many have an amazing zest for living and unflinchingly tackle new and exciting adventures. When properly channelled, a teenager's daring and risk-taking behavior can be a real asset. Someone must be willing to tackle daring careers such as fighter pilot, firefighter, or astronaut. Parenting a teenager with ADD is never, ever boring. Something exciting is always going on with these teenagers, whether it is some new project they have undertaken or a problem they have experienced. Frequently, they will be the first to volunteer to try new things. As teenagers and young adults they have ventured off to Europe alone and climbed the Himalayas.

"Even though our son did not do well in school, his skills with electronics are amazing at times. He wired his car so each car door pops open when he mashes a button on his key ring. His car is modified so that there are no external door handles. It is somewhat comical when he takes his car in to have the oil changed. The mechanics can't figure out how to open his car door."

The teenagers with ADD I know have diverse interests, have excelled in academic and non-academic areas, and include two state championship wrestlers, an excellent bow hunter, a competitive swimmer, a college football player, a college wrestler, a stand-up comedian, an artist, a horse woman, a computer and electronics whiz, a scuba diver, life guards, a skateboarder, car mechanics, merit scholars, and perhaps a budding poet. . . .

There's this thing called A.D.D.
That's not a drug or something growing in a tree,
But an attention deficit that's been affecting me.
Before I couldn't sit and learn
Because my thoughts were all in a churn.
Even if the teacher screamed right in my ear,
My A.D.D. wouldn't let me hear.
My grades are up and my spirits are high
'Cause I gave Ritalin just one single try.
Now I've found a part of life I'd never seen,
So I've started all over and wiped my slate clean.

—Written by Lee, age 16, a state champion wrestler

Successful adults with ADD who survived their difficult childhood are found in all walks of life. A few of these adults did well in school, but many were either mediocre or very poor students.

One thing that may help you view your teenager in a more positive light is to identify his strengths and help him develop them as fully as possible. Generally, *parents who help their teenager build on his strengths experience many joys parenting their child.* The strengths of one teenager with ADD have been identified and are listed in Table 3–1. A blank form is provided in Chapter 13 to help you identify your teenager's strengths.

Reframe Your Perceptions of ADD

Dr. Sydney Zentall has a refreshingly creative way of looking at youngsters with ADD. She suggests that we *reframe* the way we look at the characteristics of youngsters with this disorder. For example, she explains that bossiness may be viewed as "leadership." Qualities that are not endearing in school settings may well be highly valued in the adult business world. Members of the

Gwinnett County, Georgia CHADD chapter have added to Dr. Zentall's list of positive aspects of the teenager with ADD:

- bossiness—"leadership" (albeit carried too far)
- hyperactivity—"energetic," "unlimited energy," able to conduct ten projects at the same time, work long hours.
- strong-willed—"tenacious"
- stubborn—"persistent"
- poor handwriting—"maybe they'll be a doctor one day"
- day dreamers—"creative, innovative, imaginative"
- question authority—"independent, free thinker, make own decisions"
- daring—"risk-taker, willing to try new things"
- argumentative—"persuasive, maybe attorney material"
- laziness—"laid back/Type B personalities live longer
- instigator—"initiator/innovative"
- manipulative—"delegates/gets others to do the job"
- failure to follow directions verbatim—"creative thinking"

Some teenagers have clearly defined strengths that do not need to be reframed.

🎜

"Teenagers, especially those with ADD without hyperactivity (predominately inattentive), tend to be sensitive. They are sensitive to the needs of others, show personal warmth and affection, are kindhearted, and show remorse when they have done something wrong. However, being sensitive can also be a double-edged sword. When someone is unkind or critical, the sensitive teenager also feels the pain very intensely."

— *Bob Friedman, Ph.D., Chairman, Department of Child and Family Studies, University of South Florida*

🎜

Another issue to keep in mind is that the *desirability of certain behaviors changes over time.* Behaviors parents and teachers worry about now may not present problems in adulthood. For example, hyperac-

tivity (high energy) and failure to follow teacher instructions verbatim (creative thinking) are not particularly valued in students in school, but may be highly valued among adults in the work force. Daring behavior is required for some careers. Compliance is valued in students, but adults who are too compliant may be completely dominated by a spouse or supervisor.

🎜

"I heard Dr. Zentall make a wonderful presentation at a national CHADD conference. During her talk, she told us that she has ADHD. I loved her comments about ADD: 'I like my ADD friends best! They are more fun. They talk about more interesting things and go more interesting places. I have four offices and usually have about ten projects going at one time.' Talk about reframing ADD. I came away feeling a little jealous that I didn't have it."

🎜

"When I was attending a wedding recently, I saw a sign in the church parking lot that reserved a space for the 'physically challenged'. . . not the physically handicapped. I liked the notion of our children being considered 'emotionally challenged,' 'emotionally challenging,' or perhaps as Karl Dennis, Director of Kaleidoscope in Chicago, is fond of saying, 'emotionally unique.'"

Believe in Your Teenager and Yourself

Short of purchasing a bulletproof vest, parents must develop certain armaments for coping with their teenager during crises. *Believing that you and your teenager will cope with whatever crisis arises is probably the most important armament you will need.* Parents must believe in the "goodness" of their teenager. More importantly, parents and professionals should work together to help the teenager believe in himself again. Conveying positive messages to your teenager about his worth as your son or daughter and as a human being is extremely important! Often your teenager's self-esteem is battered because of repeated failures in school and frequent negative interactions with parents and teachers.

As you convey your expectations to your teenager, it is important to be aware of a concept known as a *"self-fulfilling prophesy."* That is, if you convey by word and action that you expect your teenager to be responsible, he will usually rise to your expectations. A positive self-fulfilling prophesy is a powerful influence: if parents believe their teenager is "good" and will succeed in life, then he probably will. Unfortunately, the opposite is also true. If a parent thinks his teenager is "bad" and treats him as though he is "bad," he will probably have more trouble succeeding.

Somehow, it is easier to believe in the "goodness" of your child or teenager if you know he exhibits inappropriate behavior because of a medical problem—ADD. Your teenager may feel better about himself too when he realizes that he has ADD and isn't just being "lazy or bad." Of course, he must also learn that he still has to work to compensate for problems caused by ADD.

Do You Have ADD? Should You Seek Help?

As Chapter 1 discusses, many parents of children with ADD have ADD themselves. Parents with ADD may be disorganized and have difficulty being consistent in their approach to child management. If you suspect you may have ADD, pursuing a diagnosis can be helpful. *Medication helps some parents be more organized and more consistent, handle their frustration better, and cope more effectively with their teenager and his crises.* See Chapter 4 for further discussion on this issue.

In some respects, there are actually some advantages to being a parent with ADD. Parents with ADD who have successfully coped with the disorder view ADD more positively. "My son acts just like I did—I did okay and so will he." They can empathize with the challenges their child faces. Sharing their own personal experiences may be beneficial to their teenager. The teenager may be more inclined to listen to what his parent says, because he knows his parent has dealt with similar problems. These parents also understand their teenager's pain, as one parent explains:

🦋

"I've been through so much pain in my life and I can see how so much of it is directly attributable to my ADD. This is such a mixed blessing—on one hand, I see how handicapping ADD is. But on the other hand,

I realize that those of us who are touched with this extra dimensions to our souls are the dreamers and poets and gentle spirits—way down deep. If we didn't have the ability to tune out and to forget and to try again, I truly believe we would lose our minds. Those of us without hyperactivity in the physical sense make up for it by being emotionally hyperactive.

"Since my ADD was diagnosed and I began taking Ritalin, my life has been so much better. After I got home from buying groceries one night at 10:30, I started to clean up my kitchen so I could put the groceries away. I was so thrilled that I could stay organized to start and finish this process. I even washed the kitchen trash can. I was standing there KNOWING how to clean the can. I began to cry. I wonder if anyone could possibly understand that my life is so unproductive and so disorganized that in all the fifteen years I've been a wife, I have never washed my kitchen trash can? I have bought new ones when the old one was too gross to use. This morning I'm embarrassed. In the past washing out the can was never even a THOUGHT."

🦋

"We can punish ourselves better than anyone else could ever dream of. The guilt, self-doubt, recrimination . . . the perfection we hold up as our role model. It's no wonder we don't try sometimes."

🦋

"Taking Ritalin is like having a conversion experience. Like a day when it hits you with overpowering certainty that there is a God. I am going to be okay. Really and truly okay."

—Amber, mother of three children with ADD and herself diagnosed within the last six months as having ADD

Maintain a Strong Sense of Humor

A good sense of humor is critical for parents of teenagers with ADD. Crises will happen and parents must learn to roll with the punches. Humor is healing! Parents need to learn to laugh at themselves and their teenager's crises. Typically, parents can allow their sense of humor to surface once the crisis is safely over. Remember, however, to laugh *with* your teenager, rather than *at* him. There is a difference and your teenager will sense if you are laughing at him.

🦋

"In response to questions about how her teenager was doing, one mother commented that he had not raped, robbed, or pillaged that week."

🦋

"How is your son doing? Well, he hasn't gotten any speeding tickets this week."

🦋

"My son is on the six-year plan for college."

🦋

"One night I was called to come pick up my daughter at the police station because she and a friend had attempted to 'borrow' a 200–pound concrete deer and put it in the back of their Honda. They were going to put it in another friend's yard as a joke. The policeman could hardly keep from laughing when he turned them over to me. We had to go to court. We can laugh about some of these things now, but they certainly weren't funny at the time."

Weather Each Crisis As It Comes

Teenagers with ADD often do well for awhile and then exhibit problem behaviors at home or at school. Crises may erupt daily, weekly, or monthly, or, if parents are lucky, only once every six months or so. One important lesson for parents to learn is *not to overreact when their child experiences one of the typical bumps associated with being a teenager who has ADD.* In moments of crisis, the teenager's problems may appear exaggerated and overblown. Problem behaviors such as sneaking out of the house at night, speeding tickets, or having a party while parents are out-of-town are definitely inappropriate, but they do not mean the teenager will be a delinquent. Address the problem, impose a consequence if appropriate, and nudge the teenager back on the "straight and narrow path." Then be prepared for the next "mini-crisis." *Learning to live one day at a time is critical.*

Keep ADD in Perspective

Sometimes in the middle of a crisis, parents have to put things in perspective by stepping back and asking themselves, "What is the worst thing that could happen to my teenager?" The ultimate answer is death. Your teenager could die in a car wreck, accident, or suicide attempt. The next worst thing might include involvement in violent criminal acts such as murder, armed robbery, or rape. If your teenager truly is in danger of one of these calamities, you should, of course, take immediate action. (See Chapters 4 and 7.) But if the current crisis is something along the lines of failing to complete homework, talking back, or staying out too late, you may need to re-evaluate your reaction. By identifying truly "bad behaviors or horrible events," you may be able to place minor crises in perspective. *Remember, a teenager's life includes a much larger picture than just twelve years in school.*

🦋

"Just last week, a 12–year-old student at my son's school hanged himself, because he received a mid-term warning about his bad grades at school. Apparently, he was really upset, especially because his mother was a teacher."

🦋

Many youngsters with ADD have rough teenage years. Parents have to develop a tough hide and learn not to be surprised by anything. They have to respond by thinking, "Oh well, my teenager is having a crisis, but in the long run, he is going to grow up to be okay." The major issue here is to deal with each problem as it arises and continue to love and support your teenager. You must believe that you and your teenager will handle each crisis as it comes up, and that ultimately, there will be a happy ending.

🦋

"The belief that we will handle whatever crisis arises is what gets me through and keeps me going."

🦋

Good Grades Are Not the Final Measure of a Person's Success

According to Robert Brooks, Ph.D., author of *The Self-Esteem Teacher* and member of CHADD's Professional Advisory Board, research has shown that *good grades are not a predictor of success in life*. Many people, some famous and some not, did not do well in school. Thomas Edison was constantly in trouble as a child and was removed from school. Winston Churchill was hyperactive. Albert Einstein was kicked out of school because he failed some classes.

Cher and Bruce Jenner have learning disabilities and did not do well in school. Sylvester Stallone was a very poor student. His father and teachers called him dumb. His father's favorite remark to Stallone was that his "brain was dormant." Although Stallone's creative abilities were not appreciated, he went on to write and star in *Rambo* and *Rocky*. Although some may question the artistic content of his movies, their financial success cannot be denied. A former Florida governor tells of being asked to leave two kindergartens because of his active, aggressive behavior.

For most parents, *the ultimate goal is for their teenager to become a happy adult and a contributing member of society*. Successes help build a teenager's self-esteem and his ability to cope with life. For some teenagers with ADD, school is difficult and successes are few and far between. Areas outside of school may offer greater opportunities for success. Early on, the families of teenagers with ADD should concentrate on helping their youngster succeed in non-school activities to compensate for any negative experiences at school.

Be Grateful for Small Favors

Although most parents of teenagers with ADD may never be able to brag about their child's Merit Scholarship or straight A's, there are other things to brag about. Teenagers with ADD have excelled in wrestling, swimming, football, art, dance, music, comedy, acting, hunting, fishing, scouting, sewing, and religious activities.

You should take great pride in each of your teenager's accomplishments. You can show your pride in a variety of ways: framing pictures of athletic teams, dance recitals, or debate competition and prominently displaying them; submitting photos to the local hometown newspaper; enlarging a photograph to poster size of him in some activity; sending pictures to grandparents; bragging to friends in front of the teenager; displaying ribbons and awards or things the teenager made; or videotaping his activities. With each accomplishment, your child takes another step toward overcoming a disability and becoming a successful adult.

❦

"The thing I have seen in my daughter from age 18 to 24 was that she assumed more and more responsibility for her own actions. While she has gone to India, Thailand, Nepal, and the Himalayas all by herself, she has really had to search her own soul to be independent. Although we have paid her college tuition and room and board, she has been financially responsible for her other expenses since she was 18."

❦

Frequently, parents of teenagers with ADD learn to be thankful for small favors: their teenager didn't fail any classes this grading period, didn't receive a speeding ticket this week, or even though he received a speeding ticket, it was not a ticket for Driving Under the Influence of alcohol or drugs (DUI).

Beginning to See the Rewards

Some parents who were involved in developing this book have teenagers who are now in their early twenties. Their comments are extremely encouraging.

❦

"Steven's first year in college was extremely difficult. He dropped out, worked for a year, and then went back to school. His ADD was diagnosed when he was twenty years old and he started taking Ritalin when he went back to college. He made two A's, a B, and a C last semester. He even qualified for the 'good student' discount for our car insurance. He graduated from college last year and has a wonderful job. He has so much energy he sometimes works twelve-hour days. We are so proud of him."

⚘

"Teenagers with ADD can and usually do grow up and do okay. My daughters, who are in their early twenties, have made me feel like it was all worthwhile by saying things like, 'How did you do it, Mom?', and 'Thanks for hanging in there, Mom,' or 'For my next adventure, I think I'll try Australia.'"

Join Local and National Advocates

One final coping method that many parents swear by is to join a group of other parents of children with ADD. At first, parents may seek this companionship to reassure themselves that they are not alone in their parenting struggles. They are able to trade war stories and share their emotions, and get the support and advice that parents of "typical" teenagers could never give them. Later, as parents learn more about ADD and treatment methods, they may be motivated to work together for changes that will help their teenager and other teenagers like him. That is, parents may be drawn into *advocacy*—speaking up on behalf of their teenager for improvements in services, public attitudes, and laws.

As awareness of ADD has increased in the last few years, parents of children and teenagers with ADD are emerging at the local, state, and national levels as influential advocates on behalf of their children. These advocacy groups now provide support to parents of children with ADD through local support groups, training materials, national conferences, and efforts to influence policy makers.

CHADD (Children and Adults with Attention Deficit Disorders) is the largest national ADD advocacy group. CHADD has numerous chapters in every state and publishes an informative newsletter. Through local CHADD support groups, parents offer mutual support and the opportunity to talk with other parents of children with ADD. In 1994, 3,000 parents and professionals from across the country attended the annual CHADD conference in New York to hear the latest research and treatment strategies for ADD. Hearing keynote speakers who have ADD and who are also leading researchers in the field is *inspirational*. Several leading researchers and physicians who have ADD are also quoted in this book: Dr. Sydney Zentall, Dr. Ben Lahey, and Dr. Theodore Mandelkorn. Dr. Edward Hallowell and Dr. John Ratey, authors of *Driven to Distraction*, also have the disorder. Children and teenagers with ADD do grow up to be successful, productive adults. ADD can be treated effectively!

Through the leadership of Harvey Parker, Fran Gilman, Sandra Thomas, Mary Fowler, Bonnie Fell, and Wade Horn, CHADD has helped shape federal educational policies affecting youngsters with ADD. This group, in collaboration with others, orchestrated a massive grass-roots campaign to obtain federally mandated educational help for students with ADD. This campaign culminated in the *U.S. Department of Education issuing a major policy memo (9/91) regarding the special needs and supports required by youngsters with ADD at school.* See Chapter 11 for more information about this policy memo.

Another national ADD advocacy organization is the Attention Deficit Disorders Association (*ADDA*). The oldest advocacy group, the ADDA also has numerous local chapters which provide parent support and serve as educational resources. The leadership of ADDA worked actively with CHADD to obtain the US DOE policy memo. Some teenagers with ADD also have serious emotional problems. Their parents may not find all the help they need from CHADD or ADDA parent support groups. Several advocacy groups are active on behalf of children and teenagers with a broader range of emotional problems: Federation of Families for Children's Mental Health, Mental Health Association (MHA), and the Alliance for the Mentally Ill (AMI). These organizations work to help improve services for children with serious emotional problems, including those who also have ADD. If your teenager's problems are more serious, you should find out which of these organizations are active in your community and what support they provide. Your local mental health center should have a phone number for these organizations. These groups frequently have information about more intensive treatment services that are available. Based upon this information, you can decide if it would be beneficial to join.

The Federation of Families for Children's Mental Health is a parent-run organization focused on the needs of children and adolescents with emotional, behavioral, or mental disorders and their families. It has local chapters in many states. This organization advocates for treating families with respect and involving them in the therapeutic process as equal partners and as experts on the needs of their children. Keeping families together by providing treatment at home is another of their key principles. The Federation, under the leadership of Barbara Huff, Naomi Karp, and Al Duchnowski, Ph.D., advocates nationally for delivery of individualized services which build on the strengths of families. The *National Mental Health Association* spearheaded an initiative in 1992 which has resulted in a significant expansion of funding to develop services for children with serious emotional problems. The Alliance for the Mentally Ill (AMI), through their children's division, *AMI CAN*, has also increased its commitment to providing services to these children. You may want to become involved with one or more of these organizations if your child has more serious emotional problems, or if you are interested in local and state level advocacy for policy changes that affect youngsters with ADD. In some communities, you may find chapters of these organizations, but not of CHADD or ADDA.

Addresses and phone numbers for the national offices of each of these organizations are listed in the Appendix. Contact the national office for the location of the chapter nearest you.

Conclusion

The road to successfully raising your teenager with ADD may be bumpy! You should expect crises on a fairly regular basis. Try not to become discouraged, however, and cope with each crisis, one day at a time, as it arises. Reframe your child's behavior in more positive terms and build on his strengths. It is also important to remember that you don't have to do it all alone. Other parents and professionals experienced in working with teenagers with ADD can offer you invaluable support and advice. Although coping may be difficult at first, eventually you will become an expert "crisis counselor" through on-the-job training.

CHAPTER FOUR

TREATMENT OF ADD

Many people think that treatment for ADD involves only medication and counseling. This view, however, is unnecessarily narrow. Treatment should actually be defined more broadly to include any activity that has a positive therapeutic effect on the child or teenager. Treatment strategies may include parent training, a parent support group, behavior management, medication, and counseling for the teenager or family. *Many other activities can also be extremely therapeutic, even though they aren't traditionally considered "treatment."* These activities involve doing well at school, succeeding at a sport or hobby, doing fun things with parents or family, maintaining positive relationships with friends, or having a girlfriend or boyfriend who is a positive influence.

The ideal treatment plan for any teenager with ADD will be tailored to his individual needs and be comprehensive—designed to help him succeed at home, at school, and in the community.

✄

"My son's girlfriend was the most therapeutic thing in his life during his senior year in high school. She was a tremendous positive influence on him regarding schoolwork, going to church, staying out of trouble, and treating me with respect. She had a greater impact on his life than any counseling session."

✄

Treatment of teenagers with ADD is not easy, yet very little has been written to guide parents and professionals through this difficult time. If treatment procedures for teenagers were clearcut, there would be as many books on the subject as there are about treatment of children. Teenagers are in transition from childhood to adulthood, which is a factor that complicates treatment. Roles are changing for both the teenager and the parents. The parents' job is to teach the teenager how to make responsible decisions, help him move toward independence, and to begin "letting go of their reins" controlling the teenager's life. Unfortunately, *the teenager's developmental delays in maturity and problems with inattention and impulsivity lengthen and complicate this transition.* As a parent, you must learn to alternate between sometimes giving encouragement, asking how you can help, and teaching new skills, and at other times, applying pressure or initiating consequences. This chapter offers suggestions for treatment based upon the best available research, plus the professional and personal experiences of several of my colleagues.

Traditionally, parents and teenagers are expected to take somewhat passive roles in treatment and to do as the professionals tell them. In contrast, *this book is intended to empower the family to use their unique strengths in helping their teenager cope with ADD.* Most parents have a fierce commitment to helping their own flesh and blood that professionals can never match. The parent's insights, commitment, and love are often the greatest treatment asset a teenager has working in his favor. After all, as a parent, you know your teenager best. Often, you know which parenting and teaching strategies work best with him and which ones are ineffective.

This book encourages you to take an active role in coordinating your teenager's treatment needs by working with professionals to develop an *individualized treatment plan.* This treatment plan should be built on your teenager's unique strengths, identify problem areas and needs, and include interventions tailor-made for your family. Guidelines to help you develop this type of treat-

TABLE 4–1 INDIVIDUALIZED TREATMENT PLAN

Utilizing a quilt pattern, an individualized treatment plan for a seventeen year old teenager is displayed below. Although the procedure for developing a treatment plan is explained throughout the book, Chapter 13 contains more details about specific plan development. To help in development of the treatment plan, parents are encouraged to gather information about their teenager and complete the forms in Chapter 13:

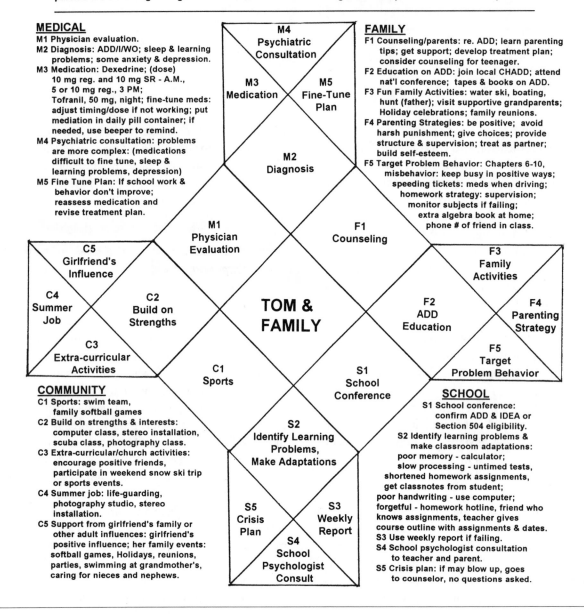

MEDICAL
M1 Physician evaluation.
M2 Diagnosis: ADD/I/WO; sleep & learning problems; some anxiety & depression.
M3 Medication: Dexedrine; (dose) 10 mg reg. and 10 mg SR - A.M., 5 or 10 mg reg., 3 PM; Tofranil, 50 mg, night; fine-tune meds: adjust timing/dose if not working; put mediation in daily pill container; if needed, use beeper to remind.
M4 Psychiatric consultation: problems are more complex: (medications difficult to fine tune, sleep & learning problems, depression)
M5 Fine Tune Plan: If school work & behavior don't improve; reassess medication and revise treatment plan.

FAMILY
F1 Counseling/parents: re. ADD; learn parenting tips; get support; develop treatment plan; consider counseling for teenager.
F2 Education on ADD: join local CHADD; attend nat'l conference; tapes & books on ADD.
F3 Fun Family Activities: water ski, boating, hunt (father); visit supportive grandparents; Holiday celebrations; family reunions.
F4 Parenting Strategies: be positive; avoid harsh punishment; give choices; provide structure & supervision; treat as partner; build self-esteem.
F5 Target Problem Behavior: Chapters 6-10, misbehavior: keep busy in positive ways; speeding tickets: meds when driving; homework strategy: supervision; monitor subjects if failing; extra algebra book at home; phone # of friend in class.

COMMUNITY
C1 Sports: swim team, family softball games
C2 Build on strengths & interests: computer class, stereo installation, scuba class, photography class.
C3 Extra-curricular/church activities: encourage positive friends, participate in weekend snow ski trip or sports events.
C4 Summer job: life-guarding, photography studio, stereo installation.
C5 Support from girlfriend's family or other adult influences: girlfriend's positive influence; her family events: softball games, Holidays, reunions, parties, swimming at grandmother's, caring for nieces and nephews.

SCHOOL
S1 School conference: confirm ADD & IDEA or Section 504 eligibility.
S2 Identify learning problems & make classroom adaptations: poor memory - calculator; slow processing - untimed tests, shortened homework assignments, get classnotes from student; poor handwriting - use computer; forgetful - homework hotline, friend who knows assignments, teacher gives course outline with assignments & dates.
S3 Use weekly report if failing.
S4 School psychologist consultation to teacher and parent.
S5 Crisis plan: if may blow up, goes to counselor, no questions asked.

ment plan are provided throughout this chapter and in Chapter 13. For more information on this treatment approach, consult the monograph *Individualized Services in a System of Care* (Stroul, Lourie, Katz-Leavy, and Dendy, 1992; see Reading List). This type of individualized, needs-based approach to planning and providing treatment has been dubbed "Wraparound" by my colleagues Karl Dennis, Dr. Lenore Behar, and Dr. John VanDenBerg.

When I make presentations about individualized treatment and Wraparound to parents and professionals, I frequently use an analogy, describing a treasured quilt my grandmother hand made for me. Symbolically, a quilt conveys feelings of warmth and tender loving care. A quilt may also be physically wrapped around someone to provide real comfort and warmth. Sewn together into one square, the whole quilt becomes much stronger than its individual pieces. These same principles apply to an individualized treatment plan. A comprehensive treatment plan covering all the important aspects of a teenager's life is more effective than a plan that touches only one or two parts such as medication and counseling.

Although quilting is a dying art, I am continuing a family tradition by making a quilt for my son. As shown in Table 4–1, I have used the design for my son's quilt to help parents visualize the important concepts of individualized treatment and Wraparound.

Principles Guiding Treatment

Several philosophical themes underlie the treatment suggestions woven throughout this book. Briefly, these themes include the importance of reframing ADD in a positive light, building on your teenager's strengths, ignoring minor misbehavior, using positive interventions more frequently than negative ones, avoiding harsh punishment, treating your teenager as a respected partner in the treatment process, giving choices, using logical consequences, ensuring success at school and in the community, and believing in your teenager.

The treatment approach must also take into consideration the current theories about the biochemical basis of ADD. *Medication may be necessary to help neurotransmitters function properly*, making it easier for your teenager to pay attention and comply with requests. In addition, common characteristics of ADD, such as impulsivity, inattention, difficulty following rules, decreased sensitivity to punishment and rewards, and rapid loss of interest in rewards and consequences, will all play a major role in the treatment strategies chosen. For example, finding effective rewards and consequences is difficult. When you find a technique that works, it will quickly lose its effectiveness. Rewards and consequences must be changed more frequently.

※

"Parenting techniques that work today may not work tomorrow. Parents must develop a large repertoire of disciplinary techniques. If one fails, go to the next one, and the next one. When that stops working, start through the list again."

—*Kathleen Allen, MS, Pediatric Center*

※

"I have found that interventions are effective for about three weeks. Parents and teachers may anticipate the need to change strategies at the time."

—*Claudia Dickerson, Ph.D., a school psychologist*

※

Strategies for Individualized Treatment

As mentioned earlier, intervention strategies for ADD may include parent training, support groups, behavioral interventions, medication, adaptations at school, skills training, and possibly some counseling for the parents or teenager. You may elect to use some or all of these strategies, depending on the severity of your teenager's problems and his specific needs.

Identifying your teenager's treatment needs may be compared to peeling layers from an onion. . . . You and the professionals should continue to examine layer after layer, until all the core problems are uncovered and the services necessary for your child's success at home and school are provided. Each teenager's treatment needs will be different. For some, medication and behavior management are all that are needed to help improve behavior and school performance.

The first step in the treatment process is to *review the results* of your teenager's evaluation and decide their implications for treatment. Information in Chapter 2 may help you better understand your teenager's evaluation. You can also discuss the evaluation results with your physician, licensed clinician psychologist, a school psychologist, or guidance counselor. Ask these professionals their opinions about the best intervention strategies for your child. Remember, however, that you have the right to accept or reject any proposed treatment interventions. If you disagree with the recommendations, discuss alternatives with your treatment professional. If you cannot agree on a treatment approach, look for another professional who shares your treatment philosophy and in whom you have more confidence.

Behavioral Interventions

The first intervention most parents try with children is behavior management, or *behavior modification* as it is also known. Behavior management programs use several techniques, including positive reinforcement; "shaping" or teaching desired behavior; withholding rewards or privileges; and punishment to change a child's behavior. Effective use of these techniques plus suggestions for how to use punishment are discussed in Chapter 5. *Although behavior management is one of the best strategies parents can use, even it has some limitations.* First, since teenagers with ADD don't learn from rewards and punishment as easily as other children, these techniques are slightly less effective. Second, behavior management techniques that were effective during childhood do not work as well with teenagers. Many teenagers have been on behavioral programs since they were children and are sick of "charts and stars." As teenagers, they may rebel against what they perceive as being constantly manipulated.

For most teenagers, positive reinforcement and logical consequences, with some modifications, continue to work pretty well. Examples of positive reinforcement include praise ("good job"), affection (a pat on the back or hug), privileges (TV, phone, Nintendo, movies, concerts, sports), and material things (stereo equipment, clothes, money).

If you are interested in trying a behavioral program, you might tell your teenager he can earn certain privileges or possessions by doing something you want (completing homework, cleaning up his room, finishing a chore). Strong rewards, especially money, are usually effective. Positive reinforcement should be tried first. If this technique doesn't seem to work for you, then ask for help from a treatment professional to make certain you are using it correctly. You may be advised to try pairing frequent positive reinforcement with occasional negative consequences. Examples of negative consequences for misbehavior include withholding privileges such as those listed above or placing the teenager on restrictions for a period of time. Dr. Russell Barkley is quick to point out, however, that punishment alone is usually ineffective.

Behavior management may be all that is needed for some teenagers, especially if the symptoms of ADD are mild and are not interfering with their ability to function at home and school.

Parent Training and Support Groups

At the same time you are seeking treatment for your teenager, you may also want to seek guidance and support for yourself. As you have probably already observed, *traditional approaches to discipline don't seem to make lasting changes in the behavior of youngsters with ADD.* Learning additional and more creative ways to channel your teenager's energy and cope with misbehavior can be a lifesaver. It is also unrealistic to assume that an outside treatment professional will be able to solve all of your teenager's problems for the family. Parent training classes may be especially helpful in introducing you to behavior management and other effective parenting techniques. Short classes (lasting perhaps eight weeks) are offered by many groups: schools, mental health centers, religious groups, the Federation of Families, CHADD, and ADDA chapters.

Educational and support groups that meet on an ongoing basis are additional resources you may want to use. You might attend CHADD, ADDA, or Federation meetings to educate yourself more fully about ADD and seek support from parents who have faced similar challenges. You may find it reassuring to learn that you are not alone. Many of these groups have monthly programs and offer educational materials such as handouts and newsletters. This information may also help educate other family members or school personnel about ADD. See Chapter 3 for more information on parent groups.

Sometimes parents who also have ADD elect to meet together as a separate group. For many parents, their diagnosis of ADD is still relatively new. They are eager to learn about the disorder and better understand its impact on their lives. Parents with ADD may have powerful feelings to deal with regarding their own personal struggles, and discussing them with other adults with ADD may be helpful.

Medication

If behavioral interventions alone don't work, then medication may be needed. *Medication is the cornerstone of the treatment program for the majority of teenagers with ADD.* However, medication alone is not a panacea for all of a teenager's problems. It is one part of a comprehensive treatment plan.

The first medication dosage prescribed may not meet the teenager's needs. For optimal results, some *"tinkering and fine tuning"* must be done with medication types and dosages. Most doctors start out with lower dosages of medications and increase them gradually until the parent and teenager feel that the best results have been attained. If stimulant medication alone does not result in a significant improvement in schoolwork and behavior, the doctor may consider prescribing a different stimulant medication or combination of medications such as a stimulant and antidepressant. Medical interventions are discussed in detail in the next section of this chapter.

Adaptations at School

The importance of making adaptations at school is critical and cannot be emphasized enough! If a teenager has untreated learning problems, a vicious cycle of school failure, conflicts with adults, and lower self-esteem may occur.

Classroom adaptations should be made to accommodate any learning problems identified during the evaluation. For example, a teenager with short-term memory problems who cannot memorize multiplication tables may be allowed to use a calculator. A student who has slow cognitive processing (slow reading and writing) may be given shortened homework assignments or extended time for tests. Adaptations might also include changing the parts of the school environment that contribute to a teenager's difficulties. For instance, it might help to switch to a classroom teacher who is more understanding of students with ADD or to schedule difficult academic classes earlier in the day. Identification of learning problems plus appropriate classroom adaptations are discussed in detail in Chapter 10. Chapter 11 explains the federal laws requiring schools to make adaptations for students with ADD.

Skills Training

Since teenagers with ADD have trouble with social, organizational, and study skills, it seems logical that training in these skills should help. The research to date, however, shows that this isn't a particularly effective treatment, at least for *children* with ADHD. Perhaps as children with ADD reach adolescence and abstract thinking improves, their ability to learn from skills training classes may carry over into real-life situations. Surely, this training wouldn't hurt your teenager and perhaps he can learn a few new things to help him be more organized. You may be able to find a class or group that focuses on an area where your teenager is especially weak: for example, communication, organization, getting along with peers, anger control, study habits, time management, and test taking. Check with the high school guidance counselor, mental health center, or your doctor to see what groups are offered.

Counseling

At some point in your teenager's treatment, you may want to seek counseling for yourself, your family, and or/your teenager. Counseling is just one strategy that may be used in conjunction with other interventions as part of a comprehensive treatment plan.

The ideal counselor for your family is a treatment professional who believes in a "wellness model" and builds on the strengths of your family. This is in contrast to an "illness model," which focuses only on identifying problems, diagnosing an "illness," and placing blame on the teenager and parents. Your teenager should not be viewed as "bad or lazy," nor should his attention difficulties or behavior problems be viewed as the result of inadequate parenting. Local parent organizations such as CHADD, ADDA, or the Federation of Families are excellent resources for finding professionals who specialize in treating ADD.

🦋

"I knew our doctor was exceptional when I learned that he employed a counselor in his office specifically to help parents and their teenagers learn new coping skills and to handle the stress caused by ADD. His staff have participated in specialized training regard-

ing treatment of ADD. They were so helpful in educating me about ADD and treating my son.

"For my family, the environment that best matched the "wellness" philosophy was having our medical doctor treat our sons. One of the major advantages has been that our sons are 'treated' at a doctor's office rather than in a psychologist's or psychiatrist's office. That has been a more acceptable (normal and less stigmatizing) option to our boys. It is not unusual for teenagers to have an annual physical plus have their medication monitored and academic progress reviewed at the same time.

"Our medical doctor was extremely sympathetic and supportive. Dr. Ed, as he is affectionately known to his patients, has always been there for us when we needed him. When my son balked at talking with a 'shrink,' Dr. Ed spent an hour talking with us about the best way to handle our crisis. Dr. Ed has held our hands and loved us through a crisis on more than one occasion."

⚲

Sometimes when a teenager is having adjustment problems related to ADD, the typical reaction is to send him to a psychologist or doctor to be "fixed." In the process a message may be sent to the teenager that something is seriously wrong with him and that he, alone, needs help. Since teenagers are very sensitive to the subtle messages parents and professionals give, care must be taken to avoid making them think they are "defective or sick" or that their problems are more severe than they are.

Counseling for Parents. Once your teenager has been evaluated and a diagnosis has been made, you may want to seek counseling on your own to learn new parenting skills. If problems are less serious, most parents can learn effective methods for coping with their teenager's misbehavior. Eventually, your teenager may need to talk with the counselor or doctor, but the least intrusive method should be tried first. For the best results, the problem may require the involvement of the whole family—parents, the teenager with ADD, and other siblings. Educated parents and teenagers are critical for effective treatment.

Counseling for Your Teenager. Even if problems are mild, someone—parents, the physician, teacher or counselor—needs to educate the

teenager about ADD. In one or two sessions, the physician or counselor should be able to help the teenager grasp the basics of ADD and how it affects his behavior, to reframe the positive elements of his ADD, to explain that he can cope with and compensate for ADD, and to assure him that a lot of successful people have ADD. Initially, your teenager may rebel at the suggestion of being sent to a counselor, psychologist, doctor, or psychiatrist. He may resent counseling and make comments such as "Mom, I don't want to go see your shrink." Even if your teenager is resistant, you can usually talk him into meeting with his doctor or a counselor—at least once. If problems are serious—aggression, suicidal risk, depression, substance abuse—you should bring your teenager in for counseling or a psychiatric evaluation, especially to help determine the best medication regimen.

Although teenagers may resist counseling in the beginning, they often come to perceive their counseling sessions as very positive. You may need to shop around to find a person who is well matched for your teenager. The counselor must be someone your teenager likes and trusts. If the first one doesn't work out, try another professional. Again, other parents are an excellent referral source for finding effective treatment professionals.

⚲

"The summer before her senior year Cassie wasn't sure of anything in her life; what she wanted to do, her boyfriend, nothing. She would get angry with us as we tried to talk with her about what she wanted to do. We suggested that she needed an objective third person to talk to.

"'Your Dad and I think that maybe you need to have somebody in your corner; your own person who isn't going to be talking to your Dad and me or anybody else but you. You can process who you are, what you want to do, and how you want to get there.' For an entire year, Cassie went to see the psychologist once every week or every other week. That was some of the best money we ever spent. It helped her work through independence versus dependence issues.

"She went through the whole thing where she said, 'I don't want to go see a shrink; I don't want anyone to know; I'm not sick.' We said, 'Those things are all true, but you're obviously in distress about what you want to do and you don't want to talk to us about it.' It only took two visits for Cassie to decide that this was a good thing. The psychologist seldom called us. If I called and said how is it going, she would say, 'Fine,' and that would be the end of the conversation.

"The psychologist was very good about saying, 'Lots of people have learning disabilities or ADD and they have gone on to lead successful lives. You just have to figure out what you want to do and how you want to do it. You don't have to have all the answers when you are eighteen years old.'"

❈

"One good thing my son knows is that it is okay to get help when you need it. He saw his Dad get help (from AA and a psychologist) and me getting some positive results from therapy."

❈

Effective counseling for complicated problems may require more than the traditional one hour of therapy a week. Other treatment options such as intensive in-home services, self-contained special education classes at school, day treatment, intensive summer programs, or as a last resort, placement in a residential treatment program may be necessary and are discussed later in this chapter.

Ongoing Assessment

Your teenager's treatment plan should include an ongoing assessment of his functioning. Are his grades improving? Is he complying with your requests more often?

If your teenager continues to struggle even after treatment has begun, you need to reassess and possibly revise his treatment plan. If his school performance doesn't improve so that he is passing all his subjects, then you and the professionals may need to change your current strategy. Reassessing and fine tuning both medication and the treatment plan are critical. Several actions could be taken:

1) identify any learning problems he may have that are described in Chapter 10;

2) in partnership with school personnel, develop a plan to meet the academic needs of your teenager at home and school, and/or

3) reassess the effectiveness of his present medication regimen.

If problems continue at school, the reasons may be fairly simple. *First, the most appropriate medication(s) or dosage may not have been found for your teenager.* As a result, problems with attention and completion of schoolwork may not have improved as much as possible. A change in the present medication dosage may be warranted or you may need to try other medications. *Second, your teenager may have serious learning problems that were overlooked in the preliminary evaluation.* Many teenagers with ADD have significant learning problems that do not meet school criteria for a Specific Learning Disability. Yet these learning problems have a significant impact on their school performance, preventing them from achieving their full academic potential. Seven learning problems common in teenagers with ADD are discussed in Chapter 10. These learning problems may be minimized with the proper classroom adaptations.

When more serious problems such as aggression, agitation, explosiveness, or depression continue, despite treatment, counseling or different medications may be helpful. A licensed clinical psychologist, doctor, or psychiatrist should be able to make appropriate treatment suggestions. Medications effective in treating aggression or depression are discussed in the next section.

Medical Treatment

Research has shown that *most youngsters with ADD benefit from low levels of stimulant medication.* These medications, which are so called because they stimulate activity in the *central nervous system (CNS)*, help students concentrate better, remember more information, and complete schoolwork. Stimulant medications are especially helpful as students advance in school and the number and difficulty of assignments increases.

If a teenager continues to struggle at home and school, the benefits of medication usually seem to outweigh any risks. The decision to use medications, however, has to be a personal decision made by the teenager and family involved.

Some parents and professionals are enthusiastic supporters of using stimulant medications. Indeed, they are concerned about the "side effects" of not giving medication when it is needed. According to Jerry M. Weiner, M.D., former President, American Academy of Child and Adolescent Psychiatry, the risks of not treating ADD include "school failure, rejection by peers and family turmoil, all of which can lead to developmental delays and psychiatric complications stemming from low self-esteem and frustration." It is true that some children with ADD may appear to cope successfully in elementary school. However, there is a risk that they may be just "getting by" without medication and may be developing significant gaps in academic knowledge.

To explain the need to prescribe medication for treatment, some researchers compare ADD with a visual disability. Just as people who cannot see well need glasses to help correct their vision, people with ADD may need medication to help neurotransmitters work properly plus adaptations at school to help compensate for their learning problems.

Naturally, some parents have reservations about giving medication to their teenager unless they are convinced that it is absolutely necessary for school performance and behavior to improve. Reasons for concern include: 1) Negative publicity about Ritalin, the primary medication prescribed for ADD; 2) Difficulty believing their teenager's problem is a biochemical one, treatable by medication; 3) Fear of immediate or long-term side effects of the medication; 4) Guilt—are we "taking the easy way out"? 5) Worry about possible addiction to medication.

⧉

"One parent who struggled with this decision finally said, 'I've decided I'm not copping out by using medication.'"

⧉

The information in the next section should address these concerns and help you make an informed decision about seeking medical treatment. Obviously, if your teenager is adjusting successfully at home and school, he will not need medication.

Why Treat ADD with Medication?

As discussed in Chapter 1, a 1990 study by Dr. Alan Zametkin established a biochemical link to attention deficit disorder. Researchers believe that ADD is a neurobiological problem caused by neurotransmitters that are not working properly. Because ADD has a biochemical basis, medication is frequently prescribed to enhance the functioning of neurotransmitters, the chemical messengers of the brain. The medications most commonly prescribed for ADD all affect the production or absorption of neurotransmitters.

The role neurotransmitters play in ADD is still not entirely understood. Since the human brain produces infinitesimally small amounts of neurotransmitters, it has been almost impossible to study them in humans. What information we do have about neurotransmitters has come primarily from animal studies. However, according to neurologist Marcel Kinsbourne, M.D., a professor at Tufts University, researchers can speculate how neurotransmitters influence human behavior based upon these studies. Although the information presented in Table 4–2 is somewhat simplified, it gives a general understanding of how neurotransmitters influence the behavior of youngsters with ADD. *The three neurotransmitters most commonly associated with ADD are norepinephrine, dopamine, and serotonin.*

Based upon a teenager's behavior, the doctor may speculate which neurotransmitters may be causing major problems. The doctor can then prescribe the appropriate medication to increase or decrease a neurotransmitter. According to present theories, stimulant medications are believed to increase production of norepinephrine, dopamine, and serotonin. Specifically, Ritalin™ increases dopamine and to some degree norepinephrine, while Dexedrine™ increases all three. Cylert™ increases production of dopamine only. Clonidine™ reduces norepinephrine and increases serotonin, and thus may be helpful for reducing aggression and behavior problems. Antidepressants such as Tofranil™ and Prozac™ can be useful in improving symptoms of depression, irritability, and impulsivity by decreasing norepinephrine and increasing serotonin.

Table 4–2
NEUROTRANSMITTERS AND RELATED BEHAVIORS

Dopamine	High Level Undistracted Works intensely on tasks	Low Level Inattentive Distractible, moves from one thing to another Difficulty completing job Difficulty thinking ahead Difficulty delaying response Cognitive impulsivity
Norepinephrine	Thrill seeker Seeks new activities Impulsive aggression	Indifferent Depressed Planned aggression
Serotonin	Satisfaction Sense of well being Focus on one thing Helps with sleep	Dissatisfaction/Irritability Aggression to self/others Impulsivity Difficulty sleeping Fire setting Obsessive compulsive Suicide risk

What Is the Best Medical Treatment for Your Teenager?

All of us—teenagers, parents, and professionals—would like the medical information about ADD to be crystal clear. We would like to know the exact cause of ADD, the best medications, proper medication levels, and treatment outcomes. Unfortunately, medical treatment is not that simple. Response to medication varies with each child and teenager. ADD must be treated by conducting an ongoing assessment of the teenager's response to medication and making appropriate adjustments to the medication and other aspects of the treatment plan.

If you want more information on specific medications than is provided here, talk with your physician. You may also ask your pharmacist for a package insert describing the medication, precautions, adverse reactions, and dosage. Some states require pharmacies to provide a more concise description along with the medication. To stay abreast of the latest medical information, you might also want to read articles on medication in various CHADD publications: *CHADDER BOX* (newsletter), *ATTENTION* (magazine), or *CHADD Facts* (educational series).

Please remember that the information about medications provided here is not intended to re-place the expert advice of your medical doctor. No changes should be made in your teenager's prescribed level of medication without a doctor's approval.

Stimulant Medications

Stimulants are considered the medication of first choice for improving a child's attention, and thus for treating ADD. These central nervous system (CNS) stimulants appear to affect neurotransmitters, enabling teenagers with ADD to stay on task, concentrate, produce more schoolwork, behave less aggressively, be less disruptive, and have more stable moods. Ritalin and Dexedrine are the two most commonly used stimulant medications.

Ritalin has been found to be effective with approximately 70 to 80 percent of children with ADHD. When children who do not respond to Ritalin are given Dexedrine or Cylert, the *effectiveness rate for stimulant medications jumps to 96 percent.* That means that the vast majority of children with ADHD respond well to one of the commonly used stimulant medications. Although stimulant medication response in teenagers has not been thoroughly studied, teenagers do not seem to respond quite as well as children. Some teenagers may respond better to Ritalin and others to Dexedrine. If a teenager has only a marginally positive response or has negative side effects with Ritalin, the physician may try Dexedrine.

According to Dr. Barkley, some children with ADD are more likely to benefit from stimulant medications than others. For example, he has found that children whose inattention is related to restlessness or hyperactivity respond well to these medications. In other words, stimulant medication seems to work slightly more effectively with youngsters who have ADHD as opposed to ADD/I/WO. And the better the mother-child relationship is, the better the response to medication.

Researchers emphasize that the ideal dosage of stimulant medication depends on the child's or teenager's individual response. Although different physicians prefer different medications, the key issue is the teenager's response to the medication and a careful assessment of its effectiveness. Usual dosages for specific medications are discussed in the sections below.

✂

"When Steven was a senior in college he took Ritalin (5 mg), once a day, only when he went to chemistry class."

✂

Manufacture and prescription of stimulant medications are carefully controlled by the federal government. Recently, this has resulted in some shortages late in the year. Some states have regulations governing these medications that allow physicians to write a prescription for only a one-month supply. Each subsequent prescription must be written and cannot be phoned in to a pharmacy. Some physicians feel this rigid monitoring is not warranted and should be changed. CHADD and the American Academy of Neurology have petitioned the Drug Enforcement Administration (DEA) to ease regulations on Ritalin. This petition is also supported by numerous organizations, including the American Psychiatric Association, the American Academy of Child and Adolescent Psychiatry, and the American Academy of Pediatrics.

Ritalin and Dexedrine

Ritalin (methylphenidate) is by far the most commonly prescribed and most often researched stimulant medication. However, the limited research available on Dexedrine (dextroamphetamine) shows that it appears to work as well as Ritalin. The physician preference for Ritalin may be due to greater name recognition through research studies and pharmaceutical marketing. Physicians may also be reluctant to prescribe Dexedrine due to negative attention generated in earlier years when it was viewed as a street drug and diet pill.

✂

"As an undiagnosed college student with ADHD, I took diet pills for a weight problem and found that I began making better grades. Somehow I accidently stumbled on to the right treatment of my ADHD. Now twenty years later, when my son was diagnosed with ADHD, I realize I have it too."

✂

Most physicians typically prescribe Ritalin as the stimulant medication of first choice. If the response is not positive, Dexedrine is then tried. Although Ritalin and Dexedrine may produce similar results in patients, the medications have a slightly different chemical mechanism and act on neurotransmitters in a different way. Ritalin primarily increases the activity of dopamine, and, to some degree, norepinephrine. Dexedrine increases dopamine, norepinephrine, and serotonin.

Information about the effectiveness of Dexedrine is largely anecdotal—that is, based upon reports of individuals who are taking it rather than upon formal research. Edward M. Hallowell, M.D., and John Ratey, M.D., in their book, *Driven to Distraction*, report that their patients who have switched from Ritalin to Dexedrine describe Dexedrine as a "softer" medication. Some patients say that Dexedrine makes their brain feel alert without making them feel "driven" or that their body is in "overdrive," as Ritalin sometimes does. One of their patients described Dexedrine as "caffeineless" Ritalin.

Regular tablets of both Ritalin and Dexedrine work in a very predictable manner for most teenagers. Typically, the effect of the medication is observed in approximately 15–30 minutes. Its peak effectiveness is maintained for approximately two hours and rapidly declines across the next two hours. Drug effectiveness may be longer or shorter, since individual responses to the medication vary.

Sustained-release (SR) tablets or capsules act somewhat differently than regular tablets. SR medications are absorbed more slowly, reaching peak effect within about one to three hours, and lasting longer—four to eight hours. Simplistically, the assumption is that approximately half of the stimulant medication is released immediately and the remaining half is released two or three hours later. When a sustained-release medication is needed, Dexedrine appears to have some advantages over Ritalin. Dexedrine seems to last longer, be more potent, release medication more evenly throughout the day, and has a greater variety of doses from which to select.

Ritalin SR does not appear to be as effective as a regular tablet of Ritalin. The Ritalin SR appears to provide only 5–8 milligrams (mg) of medication,

Table 4–3 Most Commonly Prescribed Stimulant Medications		
DOSAGE	EFFECTIVE	MAXIMUM DOSE
RITALIN (methylphenidate)		
5, 10, 20 mg (tablets)	lasts 3–4 hrs; begins working in 30 mins.	60 mg maximum daily dose 10 mg typical single dose
20 mg SR (tablets) (sustained release) (only 5–8 mg meds actually released)	last 4–6 hrs; begins working in 1 to 3 hrs	
DEXEDRINE [(dextroamphetamine); twice as potent as Ritalin]		
5 mg (tablets)	lasts 3–4 hrs; begins working in 30 mins.	40 mg maximum daily dose 5 mg typical single dose
5, 10, 15 mg SR (capsules)	lasts 6–8 hrs; begins working in 1 to 3 hrs	

side effects are minimal, most physicians are cautious and don't want to cause any unwanted side effects, such as sedation, by overmedicating.

Dr. Theodore Mandelkorn, who specializes in treating youngsters with ADD, prescribes Ritalin SR in conjunction with regular Ritalin. He has found that combining regular and SR Ritalin tends to smooth out the peaks and valleys of taking only regular tablets. Given in combination, the positive effect of Ritalin may be prolonged to five or six hours.

Dr. Steven Evans and Dr. William Pelham, who are psychologists and researchers at Western Psychiatric Institute, University of Pittsburgh, conducted a study to determine which dosages of Ritalin were most effective for a group of junior high school students. They found that an average single dose of approximately 10 mg is as effective as higher dosages when all factors were taken into consideration. There is, however, a great deal of variability in how adolescents respond to medication, so each teenager should be evaluated individually.

Previously, physicians prescribed the dosage for stimulants based upon the child's weight (milligrams of Ritalin per kilogram of weight). However, this formula may not be as helpful for teenagers. Sometimes younger children are on higher dosages of Ritalin than teenagers. In addition, teenagers who have ADD/I/WO may respond better to a slightly lower dosage of medication than hyperactive teenagers.

You, your teenager, and your physician must decide how frequently to take medication. Some families decide to use medication very sparingly, perhaps due to fear of side effects or the cost of the medication. For example, the teenager may take the mediation only while he is at school. However, when a teenager takes medicine only once a day, his parents do not have the opportunity to have more pleasant interactions with him when his concentration and attention are better. Also, if a lot of homework has been assigned, the teenager may have difficulty completing assignments or remembering what he studied. Family arguments may erupt, and may eventually damage the par-

instead of the anticipated 20 mg. Plus it may take up to three hours to act. A higher dosage may be required to get the same effect as a 10 mg Ritalin tablet. According to an article in the *Journal of Child and Adolescent Psychopharmacology* (Spring 1990), "In general, Ritalin SR is not more helpful and is more expensive" (than regular Ritalin tablets). Some youngsters also develop a tolerance to Ritalin SR, so it is not as effective after a few months. No research is available on tolerance to Dexedrine SR. Each of these medications is discussed in subsequent sections. A summary of forms, dosages, and effectiveness is displayed in Table 4–3.

Medication Forms and Dosages for Ritalin. The most commonly prescribed forms of Ritalin are 5, 10, and 20 mg tablets, plus 20 mg sustained-release (SR) tablets. Some physicians consider 60 mg daily as a maximum total dosage for Ritalin. In Dr. Barkley's clinic, teenagers are rarely prescribed more than 30 to 40 mg daily. Some teenagers may require 40 to 60 mg daily; for others, 10 to 15 mg may suffice. If the Ritalin (10 mg) seems to wear off fairly quickly, the teenager may need to take medication two to four times a day: at approximately 7:00 a.m., 10:30 a.m., and 2:00 p.m. If a dose is needed later in the day, a smaller one (5 mg) may be taken around 5:00 p.m. The teenager should be taking the lowest possible amount of medication, as few times daily as needed to function successfully. Although research has shown that

ent/teenager relationship if they continue long-term.

❧

"Lewis has a learning disability in addition to ADD and I don't often see positive effects of the medication because he takes Ritalin during school hours and skips evenings and weekends."

❧

Medication Forms and Dosages for Dexedrine. Dexedrine is available in 5 mg tablets and 5, 10, and 15 mg sustained-release (SR) capsules. Total daily dosages may range from 2.5 mg to 40 mg. Dexedrine dosages are more potent than equal quantities of Ritalin. Five (5) mg of Dexedrine is comparable to 10 mg of Ritalin.

As mentioned earler, Dexedrine SR seems to have several *advantages* over Ritalin SR for some teenagers. It is reported to last longer—six to eight hours, thus eliminating the need for administering a dose at school. Dexedrine SR is also taken in capsule form, in comparison with Ritalin SR tablets. Capsules seem to give a more accurate and even release of medication throughout the day. Plus, unlike Ritalin SR, Dexedrine SR delivers the full dosage stated. Having the greater variety of sizes—5, 10, 15 mg SR—to choose from as a physician determines the proper dosage is better than being limited to only one size Ritalin SR—20 mg.

Parents should be aware that Dexedrine SR, just like Ritalin SR, may take one to three hours to be effective. Parents and teenagers should take this delayed effect into consideration when determining when to take the medication prior to class. For example, if a Dexedrine SR is taken at 7:00, it may not be effective until 9:00 or 10:00. Parents could also talk with their physician about combining a regular 5 mg tablet and a SR capsule to give more uniform dosing throughout the day.

Typically, Dexedrine is prescribed for teenagers who have not done well on Ritalin and vice versa. Other physicians prefer to try Dexedrine before they prescribe Ritalin. According to anecdotal reports, some psychiatrists have found Dexedrine more effective for their adolescent patients.

Although Dexedrine is considered as effective as Ritalin and is cheaper, it is not as widely known. Sometimes Dexedrine may be more difficult to find due to distribution problems. If your doctor prescribes Dexedrine, talk with your pharmacist in advance to make certain it will be available when you need it. Your family pharmacist can order Dexedrine for you.

Cylert

If other stimulant medications are not effective, Cylert (magnesium pemoline) may be prescribed for ADD. Cylert tends to be the stimulant medication of last choice because it must be more closely monitored and can have more negative side effects. Few research studies have been conducted on Cylert's effectiveness. Since it tends to be prescribed for those who have not responded well to either Ritalin or Dexedrine, the limited available research may be negatively biased and somewhat contradictory. Different studies report positive response rates to Cylert ranging from 50 to a very respectable 75 percent. Dosages of Cylert include 37.5 and 75 mg tablets. Cylert takes longer to reach peak effectiveness than the other two stimulants. Although it is generally thought to last all day, Dr. Mandelkorn reports that it usually lasts only 6–8 hours. If your teenager is prescribed Cylert, he will require more careful monitoring, as the medication may cause liver damage.

Adderall

Adderall™ is a new stimulant medication that is similar to Ritalin and Dexedrine. Because it is new, little research has been done on its effectiveness. Adderall contains a combination of dextroamphetamine and amphetamine. Doctors tend to try a new medication like Adderall when maximum results have not been obtained with Ritalin or Dexedrine. Word-of-mouth communication indicates that some youngsters have responded favorably to the medication. A typical dose of Adderall, which is made in 10 and 20 mg tablets, ranges from 5 to 60 mg per day.

Generic Stimulant Medications

According to many physicians, generic forms of stimulant medications such as methylphenidate do not work as well as brand names (Ritalin). Other physicians report that generic brands work effectively. Remember, medication response varies according to the individual, so some children may respond better than others to generic medications.

Unique Aspects of Stimulants

There are a few unusual facts about stimulants you should know. For example, *chewing Ritalin SR* instead of swallowing it may result in an unpredictably high blood level of the medication and toxic side effects. This, however, is unlikely to occur since the pill has a bitter taste, and teenagers should know better than to chew the medication. In addition, Dr. Charles Popper recommends that patients not take stimulant medication with *aspirin or acidic foods* (citrus fruit or orange juice), since they prevent absorption of the medication.

If your teenager is prescribed an antidepressant, be aware that *stimulants may change the metabolism of the antidepressant.* As a result, he may need a lower dose of the antidepressant when he is taking both medications.

At a national CHADD conference, one speaker noted that a small number of children may have an adverse reaction to taking 5 mg tablets of Ritalin. The children became more active and agitated, possibly because of an *allergic reaction to the yellow dye* contained in 5 mg Ritalin tablets. The 10 and 20 mg tablets of Ritalin do not contain yellow dye. Thus, if your youngster had a bad reaction to Ritalin as a child, the yellow dye may have caused the problem rather than the Ritalin. As a teenager, he may respond well to 10 or 20 mg tablets of Ritalin.

Side Effects of Stimulant Medications

Stimulant medications such as Ritalin and Dexedrine have unfairly received some bad press over the years. Because of lack of accurate information, parents are understandably fearful of side effects. The truth is, Ritalin has been studied carefully for the last 20 to 30 years and has few side effects. Ritalin and Dexedrine are similar; they are in the same class of medication—central nervous system stimulants. Although Dexedrine has not been studied as often, researchers seem to think it is as safe as Ritalin.

The two most commonly mentioned side effects for both Ritalin and Dexedrine are *loss of appetite* and *sleep problems. Irritability* and *weight loss* are the next most often reported symptoms. Approximately half of the children in one study who took Ritalin for ADHD exhibited mild symptoms including loss of appetite, insomnia, anxiousness, nervousness, irritability, and/or proneness to crying. One-third reported mild headaches and stomachaches. Many of these side effects decline within one to two weeks after starting on medication. Mild increases in blood pressure and heart rate may also occur. Youngsters with ADD may also seem to lose their spontaneity if the dosage is too high. In one study, researchers found that adolescents had fewer negative side effects than children.

Some teenagers have serious *sleep problems* that may interfere with their ability to function at school. If they take medication too late in the day, they may have trouble falling asleep and thus will be tired the next day at school. For other teenagers, the sleep disturbance may actually be a symptom of ADD rather than a result of taking the medication. These teenagers had sleep problems before they ever began taking stimulant medications. To avoid sleep difficulties and possible rebound effect (see below), some physicians prescribe a lower dose of Ritalin in the late afternoon but suggest taking it no later than 5 or 6 p.m. Suggestions for dealing with sleep disturbances are provided in Chapter 6.

Some physicians recommend that medication be taken at mealtime or just afterwards so that it will not suppress appetite.

Rarely, stimulant medications may delay a youngster's *growth rate,* but these medications do not permanently stunt growth. According to research, when growth is delayed, it is only a temporary problem. Studies have shown that youngsters on stimulants whose growth initially appeared slow, gained normal rates of growth (height) over a three- or four-year period. If you are concerned that your child is experiencing growth problems, perhaps unrelated to stimulant medications, you should talk with your doctor to see if referral to a specialist is warranted.

Since Cylert is prescribed less often, side effects are not as well documented. It may cause some *allergic skin rashes.* Rarely, teenagers on Cylert may lick or bite their lips or fingernails or pick at their finger tips. Reducing the medication seems to eliminate the problem. Youngsters who are on Cylert must have liver function blood tests every six months, as the medication may cause damage to the liver in about 3 percent of people who take it.

If your teenager has a mood disorder or bipolar disorder in addition to ADD, stimulant medications may make his symptoms worse. He may become angrier, more impulsive, more hyperactive, and more difficult to manage. Sometimes stimulants seem to help at first when the initial diagnosis of ADD is made. Later, stimulants may stop working or may make things worse. The need for careful, regular assessment of the medication's effectiveness is obvious. Diagnostic criteria for bipolar disorder in teenagers are provided in Chapter 2.

Stimulant medications may also cause an *increase in tics* if your teenager has a tic disorder and ADD. Sometimes when a child begins taking stimulant medications such as Ritalin, his tics may get worse. When the stimulant medication is discontinued, the tics usually disappear. Most physicians urge a cautious approach to prescribing stimulants for combined ADHD and tics. Sometimes Clonidine or tricyclic antidepressants (see below) may be prescribed instead. See Chapter 2 for additional information on tics and Tourette Syndrome. Two additional resources on Tourette Syndrome include *Tourette Syndrome and Human Behavior* by David E. Comings, M.D., and *Children With Tourette Syndrome: A Parent's Guide,* edited by Tracy Haerle.

Rebound Effect

Approximately one-third of youngsters on medication experience something called a "rebound effect" as they are coming off their medication. For half an hour or two, as the level of stimulant medication falls, the teenager may be irritable or aggressive and his activity level and restlessness may increase. He may have mood changes, and actually have more ADD symptoms than usual. This problem is usually observed late in the afternoon or early evening. From the teenager's perspective, it must be extremely unsettling to have the ability to concentrate and stay on task for several hours and then lose it when the medication wears off.

For youngsters who experience the rebound effect, the severity of the problem varies from day to day. According to Dr. Barkley, the problem is rarely severe enough to have to stop medication. To reduce the rebound effect, some physicians suggest that a smaller dose be added later in the afternoon to alleviate the peaks and valleys of Ritalin. Sometimes the last dose of the day (early afternoon) may be reduced. For example, if your teenager takes 10 mg Ritalin twice a day, morning and noon, he may take a third smaller dose, 5 mg, later in the afternoon around four or five.

"Medication Holidays"

Some doctors recommend "medication holidays" during the weekends or summer. A doctor may recommend a "holiday" just to be safe, thus avoiding any unusual long-term side effects unique to a specific child. "Holidays" may also be recommended if the medication is prescribed primarily for problems at school. At a minimum, medication may be discontinued periodically over a period of years to ensure that symptoms are still present and medication is still needed. Since stimulant medications wear off after a few hours, however, most parents can easily see on a daily basis whether or not the symptoms of ADD are still present. Some doctors *oppose* these "holidays" because of the potential damage to self-esteem and concern for safety. A teenager's inattention and impulsivity can sometimes lead him into danger if he is driving or going out with friends. Parents and physicians may also elect to continue medication year round if problems are occurring at both home and school. As a parent, you must weigh the pros and cons in making this important decision.

❧

"Our son did not take medication in the evenings, weekends, or summers. Our approach to medication use was extremely conservative because of our initial fears about giving medication. In retrospect, it appears we made a mistake.

"Being the conservative parent I am and wanting to minimize the amount of medication he took, I did not give him medicine in the afternoon or evening when he did his homework. What I realize, in retrospect, is that the effects of Ritalin had worn off totally by the time he started his homework in the evening. It is no wonder we continued to have so many battles over homework. Our son's behavior at home and performance at school improved significantly when we increased his medication levels and began giving him medication in the late afternoon before he did his homework. He seemed to concentrate better and remember more of his studies. We had fewer fights over homework."

❧

One reason *not* to give your teenager a "medication holiday" is for fear that he will become addicted to stimulant medications. Researchers have not found problems with addiction or drug dependence to stimulant medications in later life. In reality, many youngsters don't like to take medication and would rather avoid it if possible. See Chapter 7 for more information on substance use and abuse among teenagers with ADD.

Impact of Stimulant Medication on School Performance

Dr. James Swanson and his colleagues at University of California, Irvine ADD Center, recently conducted a comprehensive "review of a review" of the literature on the use of stimulant medications with children with ADHD. That is, they reviewed the findings of research studies published in the last 50 years and attempted to reach some general conclusions. Personally reviewing between 8,000–10,000 studies on ADHD would be impossible, so Dr. Swanson and his associates also analyzed the

summaries of reviews of literature previously conducted by leading researchers such as Dr. Barkley. According to this research, stimulant medication results in the following changes in behavior in youngsters with ADD:

- Increased attention and concentration;
- Increased compliance and effort on tasks;
- Increased amount and accuracy of schoolwork produced;
- Decreased activity levels;
- Decreased impulsivity;
- Decreased negative behaviors in social interactions;
- Decreased physical and verbal hostility.

In their study discussed earlier, Dr. Evans and Dr. Pelham found that stimulant medication helped most teenagers improve their performance on quizzes and tests, improved attention, and decreased disruptive behavior. Quiz and test scores rose from an average of D minus to B or B minus. In addition, teacher ratings improved.

Informal parent observations back up the results of scientific studies:

❧

"Our sons began doing better in school and their interpersonal relationships improved when they began taking medication."

❧

Memory improved . . .

"Shawn's memory has improved so much since he has been on medication it really blows my mind. He remembers to do his chores and to bring his laundry down to be washed. He never could do this before. It's like the difference between night and day."

❧

Can study longer . . .

"The most amazing observation to me was the day I saw Steven sit down at a desk and study for over three hours. That was shortly after he was put on Ritalin as a sophomore in college. Before, it would have been rare for him to spend even fifteen minutes studying."

❧

Less daydreaming . . .

"I called one family to ask how the medication was working at school. The child said, 'I tried and tried to daydream and I couldn't.'"

—*Pediatric Center Staff*

⧉

Homework is no longer a battle . . .

"When my teenage son is having academic difficulties, I tend to monitor his schoolwork very closely including completion of homework. Until the last few months when he started taking Ritalin in the evening, I had never had the opportunity to work with him when he didn't have difficulty concentrating and completing his homework. The evening study periods seem much more productive and pleasant now that he is on the medication."

⧉

Grades improve . . .

"Lewis's grades are much improved since starting on Ritalin. No F's this semester. He even had his second A this year. Quite an achievement!"

⧉

Improved driving, perhaps. . . .

"Will was complaining about taking Ritalin. 'When I drive, I don't think about anything else but driving.'"

⧉

Sometimes, teenagers are smarter and know themselves better than adults.

"My son always told me it didn't do him any good to study for tests because he couldn't remember what he studied. I was somewhat skeptical of his comments until I was talking with a psychologist who specializes in working with ADD patients. The doctor told me of a twenty-year-old diagnosed as having ADD and placed on Ritalin. The young man commented that, thanks to Ritalin, for the first time in his life he could remember what he studied for tests."

Antidepressant Medications

Antidepressants may be prescribed for ADD instead of, or in combination with, stimulants. Ap-proximately 70 to 80 percent of youngsters with ADHD respond favorably to these medications. As the name implies, these medications are primarily used to combat depression in adults. Antidepressants, however, are also effective in treating other problems, such as anxiety, ADD, bedwetting, and Tourette syndrome. These medications are prescribed to treat ADD because they, like stimulant medications, improve the functioning of neuro-transmitters. These medications affect the activity of the neurotransmitters norepinephrine and serotonin, which can improve the symptoms of both ADD and depression.

For most teenagers with ADD, *antidepressants are considered a medication of second choice.* Antidepressants can help reduce inattention and hyperactivity, but they are not as effective as stimulant medications. Antidepressants are especially helpful, however, for teenagers who are anxious, depressed, or aggressive, or are experiencing emotional highs and lows. These medications may help level off mood swings. Antidepressants may also help treat sleep problems. For some teenagers, antidepressants may be equally as important as stimulant medications. According to Dr. Tom Brown, some teenagers and adults who have ADD/I/WO respond better when treated with a combination of antidepressants and stimulants.

One advantage of antidepressants is that they have a *longer-lasting effect* than stimulants. Teenagers can take medicine at night and benefit from the medication all day long, not just three or four hours. It may, however, take two to four weeks for the medication to achieve full therapeutic effect. This is because antidepressants build up in the bloodstream over time.

A few words of caution about antidepressants: it can be dangerous to take these medications at the same time or within two weeks of taking Monoamine Oxidase Inhibitors (MAO) antidepressants such as Nardil™, Parnate™, or Marplan™. Blood pressure may rise, resulting in headaches, severe convulsive seizures, or high fevers. On rare occasions, the reaction may be severe enough to be fatal.

If your teenager is prescribed an antidepressant, you should work closely with your physician to monitor its use. First, drinking alcohol while taking antidepressants could cause serious problems since the medication intensifies the depressant effects of alcohol. As a result, a teenager may get drunk more easily or have an accidental overdose. If a teenager is depressed and consumes excessive alcohol, he might be more prone to consider or attempt suicide. Second, an overdose of an antidepressant could be fatal. Parents should keep these medications in a safe place. You might consider placing your teenager's medication in a pill container, so that he will have access to only a week's supply at one time.

Two types of antidepressants are used to treat ADD: (1) *tricyclic antidepressants* (Tofranil and Norpramin), so called because of the structure of the chemical compounds; and (2) *Selective Serotonin Reuptake Inhibitors (SSRI's)* such as Prozac, Paxil, and Zoloft. SSRI's are so named because they increase levels of the neurotransmitter serotonin. Typically, after being released into the synapse, serotonin is reabsorbed back into the axon from which it came (reuptake). These medications inhibit the reuptake of serotonin, allowing it to remain active longer in the synapse.

Tofranil and Norpramin

Tricyclics are the most commonly prescribed antidepressants for treating teenagers with ADD. The two tricyclics most often used are Tofranil™ (imipramine) and Norpramin™ (desipramine). Pamelor™ (nortriptyline) is another tricyclic that is sometimes used. Tricyclic antidepressants may also help youngsters who have depression and conduct disorder problems such as those described in Chapter 2. This may be because the *aggressive, antisocial behavior associated with a conduct disorder may actually mask an underlying depression.* Treating the depression with an antidepressant may result in a reduction of aggressive, impulsive behavior. Tricyclics may also have the side benefit of reducing sleep problems in some teenagers who are taking these medications for depression and anxiety. They may wake up more easily and be able to fall asleep earlier. Perhaps the quality of their sleep is also improved. Specifically, Tofranil appears to increase serotonin, which is essential for sleep. (See Chapter 6 for more information on sleep problems.) Tofranil has also been used effectively to treat enuresis (bed wetting) for years.

Commonly prescribed dosages of Tofranil and Norpramin include 10, 25, and 50 mg tablets. In-itially, physicians start with low doses of 10–25 mg and raise them slowly as needed. A maximum daily dosage of less than 100 mg per day should be effective.

The *side effects* of these medications in teenagers with ADD have not been studied as carefully as those of stimulant medications. Reported side effects include dry mouth, dizziness or lightheadedness, constipation, increases in blood pressure and rapid or irregular heart rate, appetite increases, nervousness, headache, sleep problems, and/or nausea. Because of the possible effects on the heart, physicians should request an EKG to make certain the teenager doesn't have any preexisting heart problems. According to Dr. Barkley, evidence is building that Norpramin has fewer negative side effects, such as less sedation, dry mouth, and constipation, than Tofranil. However, Tofranil may do more to improve sleep.

Prozac, Zoloft, and Paxil

The most commonly prescribed SSRI's include Prozac™ (fluoxetine), Zoloft™, (sertraline), and Paxil™ (paroxetine). Prozac has received mixed reviews in treatment of teenagers with ADD: some doctors have found it effective and others have not. In a study by Dr. Tom Brown, teenagers and adults with ADD/I/WO responded favorably to a combination of Ritalin and Prozac. One advantage with Prozac and the SSRI's is that they, unlike stimulants, have very little effect on heart rhythm. A typical initial dose may be a 20 mg capsule taken in the morning. This amount of medication may be enough to treat depression effectively.

Side effects of SSRI's include headaches, anxiety, nervousness, insomnia, sexual dysfunction, nausea, and/or diarrhea. Since little research has been done on the effectiveness of these three medications in treating ADD in comparison with other antidepressants, they're not prescribed as often as tricyclic antidepressants.

Newer Antidepressants

When better known antidepressants such as Tofranil don't work, doctors may try newer medications. Occasionally, *Welbutrin*™ (bupropion), *Ludiomil*™ (maprotiline), and *Effexor*™ (venlafaxine) have been prescribed for treating ADD. Research, however, is lacking on their effectiveness. Dr. Martha Little, an Atlanta psychiatrist and pharmacist, explains that physicians select medications to meet specific needs of a youngster. That is, they may choose a medication because it may also treat a coexisting problem such as anxiety or aggression. For example, *Busbar*™ (busiprone) has been prescribed for ADD and anxiety. Sometimes medications may be avoided because of potential damaging side effects. Welbutrin would not be prescribed for anyone who has had a head injury such as a concussion, since the medication lowers the threshold for seizures.

Of course, all these medications have to meet safety standards and cannot be manufactured without proper research and approval by the Drug Enforcement Administration (DEA). As with all medications, parents must monitor any disturbing changes in their teenager's behavior and discuss them with the physician.

Other Medications for Treating ADD

Clonidine

Clonidine™ (catapres) is sometimes used as an alternative medication for more difficult-to-treat teenagers with ADD. When used alone or in combination with Ritalin, it can be effective in helping teenagers with *severe hyperactivity or aggressiveness*. In addition, it may reduce anxiety and restlessness. Occasionally, it is prescribed to treat serious *sleep disturbances* associated with ADD. Furthermore, psychiatrist Robert Hunt, ADD Center Director at Vanderbilt University, has found that this medication helps control *oppositional behavior, anger, aggression, cruelty, destructiveness, explosiveness, frustration, and obsessive-compulsive behavior*. (This drug was first used to treat high blood pressure in adults.)

Clonidine is also the medication of choice for treating Tourette Syndrome. Sometimes Clonidine and a low dose of stimulant medication may be combined to treat ADHD and tics. As discussed in an earlier section on stimulant medications, prescribing stimulants for tic disorders should be approached with caution.

Clonidine is available in .1, .2, and .3 mg tablets, plus skin patches in three doses. The skin patches may be cut in half, if necessary. Patches last 5–6 days, but may result in skin irritation. Skin irritation may be minimized by putting the patch in different places. Tablets are short acting, 4–6 hours. The primary side effect is tiredness, or sedation, which may occur if the dosage is raised too quickly. Dizziness and dry mouth may also occur. Sometimes Clonidine increases, rather than decreases, negative behaviors in youngsters with ADD. These youngsters should discontinue the medication.

According to Dr. Hunt, Tenex™, a new medication that is similar to Clonidine, has fewer side effects (less sedation).

Lithium

Occasionally, other medications may not be effective in treating a teenager with ADD whose aggression, impulsivity, or explosiveness are of serious concern to parents and physicians. In these instances, Lithonate™ (lithium carbonate)—a mood stabilizing medication—may be prescribed. This medication is primarily used to treat bipolar disorders. Although little research has been done specifically on treating ADD with this medication, general research has shown that *lithium is effective for reducing aggression*. It also helps level off a teenager's emotions, especially when there are mood swings or intense anger. Lithium affects neurotransmitters by reducing levels of norepinephrine and increasing serotonin.

Lithium is available as Lithonate capsules and Lithotabs in 300 mg capsules and tablets. A few psychiatrists who have used lithium to treat teenagers with ADD (but no symptoms of bipolar disorder), report that the therapeutic range—the level of lithium required to be effective—is lower than for adults with bipolar disorders. For adults with bipolar disorders, the lithium must be maintained within a therapeutic range of 0.8 to 1.4 milliequivalents per liter (mEq/L) total body water. Between 0.4 and 0.6 mEq/L may be effective for teenagers with ADD. Once the initial therapeutic range has been reached, teenagers may be maintained on a lower dosage.

One of the major *side effects* of lithium is potential damage to the kidneys if the medication exceeds the therapeutic range. To avoid potential problems, blood tests must be done regularly. This can be a source of conflict, as some teenagers are adamantly opposed to monthly or quarterly blood tests. When lithium levels are higher, other side effects may include slowed intellectual functioning, poor memory, acne, hand tremor, increased thirst, and increased urination. Many teenagers with ADD already have a problem with short-term memory, and lithium may make it worse. To minimize these side effects, teenagers may be maintained on a lower dosage, such as 300 mg Lithonate (one capsule), morning and evening, once a therapeutic level has been reached.

In *Driven to Distraction*, Dr. Hallowell and Dr. Ratey discuss *other mood stabilizing medications* that may be used with young adults with ADD. Medications discussed include Depakote™ (valproic acid) and Tegretol™ (carbamazepine), which may help control outbursts of rage, tantrums, or violent behavior that sometimes accompany ADD. Dr. Hallowell and Dr. Ratey also explain that beta-blockers Corgard™ (nadolol) and Inderal™ (propranodol) can reduce explosiveness. In addition, he mentions Anafranil™ (clomipramine) as helpful in treating obsessive-compulsive disorder when it coexists with ADD.

Medication Combinations

Sometimes a teenager with ADD is prescribed stimulant medications but continues to struggle at home or at school due to aggressiveness, moodiness, or impulsivity. This presents a real dilemma for the teenager, parents, and physician. As discussed in the preceding paragraphs, a combination of medications may then be tried. However, many family physicians or pediatricians are cautious about trying medication combinations, as no research is available about the long-term effects of these combinations. Most physicians won't recommend medication combinations unless they are critical to treat complex problems.

If your teenager is continuing to struggle and a combination of medications seems warranted for your teenager, you may want to consult a psychiatrist. Psychiatrists prescribe antidepressants and other medications such as Clonidine and lithium more frequently than other physicians do, and may

be more familiar with their action and effectiveness in treating ADD. A psychiatrist may be able to help you determine the proper medication regimen and to obtain the most up-to-date information on effective medication combinations for treating ADD.

The Right Medication and Dosage

Two critical issues are at the heart of effective medical treatment for ADD: *(1) determining which medication works best for the teenager, and then (2) determining the proper dose and frequency of medication.* Most family doctors start with a very conservative level of medication and increase it until the family feels that the teenager is doing better at home and school. Most often, medication dosages are determined by reports from the teenager, parents, and teachers.

Usually, when a teenager with ADD starts on medication, his parents call and give the physician a report on how the medication is working after the first week or two. The parents may also consult with teachers about the effectiveness of medication at school. The teenager himself may or may not be able to accurately gauge the medication's effectiveness. When parents ask if the medication helps, many teenagers say they can't tell for certain.

Assess Medication Effectiveness

One parent's assessment of the effectiveness of their teenager's medication is displayed in Table 4–4. Obviously, with a daily dosage of only 20 mg Ritalin SR, the teenager's medication was not effective. Ultimately, the doctor prescribed 40 mg Ritalin SR, 10 mg Ritalin (a.m.), and 50 mg of Tofranil at night to help level off mood swings and help with sleep.

Completing the blank form in Chapter 13 may help you assess your teenager's response to medication. When medication is working properly, you should observe improvements in behavior. For example, positive improvements may include having less hyperactivity, paying attention better, completing homework, improving grades, obeying par-

Table 4–4

ASSESS MEDICATION EFFECTIVENESS AT HOME AND SCHOOL— INDIVIDUALIZED TREATMENT PLANNING: "DO WHATEVER IT TAKES."

NAME: _Tom_   AGE: _17_   HEIGHT & WEIGHT: _6'; 157 lbs_

MEDICATION HISTORY: List medication(s) currently being taken, dosage, frequency and describe how effective it is. Circle the number that describes the effectiveness of the medication.

Medication/Dosage/Frequency	Not Effective				Very Effective
1. _Dexedrine / 10 mg SR / 7 a.m._	1	2	3	4	(5)
10 mg reg. / 7 a.m. (5mg-3p.m)	1	2	3	4	(5)
2. _Tofranil / 50 mg / 10 p.m._	1	2	3	4	(5)
	1	2	3	4	5
3. _Ritalin / 20 mg SR / 7 a.m._	1	(2)	3	4	5
(previous medication)	1	2	3	4	5

EFFECTIVENESS OF MEDICATION: When medication is working properly and learning problems have been identified, most of the problem behaviors described below should decrease and academic performance should improve. Remember that it will take time to "fine-tune" the medication regimen. Even small adjustments such as changing the time of day or increasing the amount of medication may make a major difference in your teenager's behavior at home and school. Circle the correct number (1 if you strongly agree and 5 if you strongly disagree). Parents should ask teachers to complete this form to determine if behavior is improving at school.

When my teenager takes medication, s/he:

	Strongly Disagree	Disagree	Neutral	Agree	Strongly Agree	Comments (Optional)
1. Makes better grades	1	2	3	(4)	5	
2. Passes subjects	1	2	3	4	(5)	
3. Finishes homework	1	2	3	(4)	5	
4. Finishes classwork	1	2	3	(4)	5	
5. Pays attention in class	1	2	3	(4)	5	
6. Participates in class	1	2	3	(4)	5	
7. Obeys school rules	1	2	3	(4)	5	
8. Gets along with friends	1	2	3	4	(5)	
9. Stays awake in class	1	2	3	(4)	5	
10. Wakes up easily	1	2	3	(4)	5	
11. Listens when adults talk	1	2	3	(4)	5	
12. Obeys adults	1	2	3	(4)	5	
13. Is easily distracted	1	(2)	3	4	5	
14. Is forgetful	1	2	(3)	4	5	
15. Is irritable	1	(2)	3	4	5	
16. Is aggressive	(1)	2	3	4	5	
17. Is impulsive	1	(2)	3	4	5	
18. Talks back to adults	(1)	2	3	4	5	
19. Is easily frustrated	1	(2)	3	4	5	
20. Is hyperactive	1	2	3	4	5 _N/A_	

Comments:_____

_____

If problems are continuing at school, one logical area to explore further is identification of learning problems and making appropriate classroom adaptations. Even if the teenager is doing okay academically, the current medication may need to be changed or adjusted if sleep disturbances, irritability, or aggression continue to be problems.

ents more often, and having fewer family arguments. You should also look for, and report, any negative side effects, such as loss of appetite, sleep problems, sedation, irritability, or headaches.

At first, the dose may be too low for you and your teenager to observe any changes. At this point, your physician may recommend a modest increase in the dose—from 5 to 10 mg, for example. Your physician will continue to increase the prescribed dosage until your teenager reports maximum benefits.

Fine Tune Medication

Trial-and-error fine tuning is the name of the game for determining the proper medication and dose for each teenager. Dr. Hallowell and Dr. Ratey suggest that families not come to the conclusion too quickly that "medication isn't working." It may take weeks or months to find the best dosing schedule, since each teenager responds differently to medication. Medication needs may also change over time as the teenager grows older and faces new demands in school or on the job. Remember, a medication that previously appeared to be ineffective may work a few months or years later.

❧

"Our son did not respond well to Dexedrine when he was in high school. Now, a few years later, he prefers Dexedrine. In retrospect, my guess is that when we switched from Ritalin to Dexedrine, we gave him a dose that was too high. As a result, he was agitated and had trouble sleeping. In addition, he was in the middle of a personal crisis when we made the medication change. Now that we know more about Dexedrine and have him on an appropriate dose, it is working effectively."

❧

Usually, subjective reports from the teenager, parents, and teachers about the medication's effectiveness are all that is needed to find the proper dosage. If your teenager's problems are more complex and he isn't responding well to the medication, however, a more formal assessment of medication response should be done. This assessment can help determine which medication is most effective and to fine tune exact dosages and times for administering.

One way to obtain objective information is to complete Table 4–4 both before and after your teenager begins to take medication. Or you make

also take the diagnostic criteria in the DSM IV listed in Chapter 1 and give your teenager a rating from 1 to 5 for each one. A score of 1 means that the behavior is not a problem and 5 means that it is a major problem. For example, if you rate your child as 5 on "fails to finish schoolwork" before medication is administered, and give him a score of 2 after medication, improvement has been documented. The same rating can be done for "always on the go" or "talks excessively." If only marginal improvement is noted, your doctor may decide to increase the medication.

Another way to fine tune your teenager's medication regimen is to seek a *formal medication assessment* from a treatment professional who specializes in ADD. Specialized programs for ADD at universities or hospitals may also have the capacity to carefully monitor medication through behavior rating scales and observations. When medication dose and type are working effectively, formal rating scales, such as the Child Behavior Checklist (CBCL), typically reflect a reduction in inappropriate behavior. CHADD, your treatment professional, the local mental health center, school psychological services, or a university operated program for ADD may be able to refer you to someone who can perform this type of assessment.

❧

"As our family knows from first-hand experience, determining the proper level of medication is critical since a teenager's medication level could be too low and thus be ineffective. It has only been within the last six months that adequate levels of medication have been established for our 16–year-old son. Initially, our son's academic progress was limited perhaps because the medication levels were not properly adjusted and the medication (20 mg Ritalin SR taken once a day) was effective only four to six hours. As we learned later, the Ritalin SR provided only 5–7 mg and he wasn't receiving enough medication."

❧

Timing of Medication is Critical

Timing issues related to medication are very important. How long does the medication last? How long does it take to kick in? When does it reach peak effectiveness? Table 4–5 shows this information for a typical high school student.

When your teenager has problems with misbehavior or failing classes, it is a good idea to see when these problems occurred compared to periods of medication effectiveness. Medication wearing off may be a major contribution to problems.

If you look for patterns of misbehavior or class failure, you may find that this teenager is failing English and Government. He may also be a behavior problem in those classes and on the school bus.

Table 4–5 CHARTING EFFECTIVENESS OF MEDICATION			
Time	Meds (10 mg Ritalin)	Classes	Meds Status
7:00 AM	Wake up		
7:30	Take medicine		
8:00	Meds are working		
8:30	Meds peak	Algebra class	good
9:00			
9:30		History class	
10:00			
10:30		English	not good
11:00	Meds gone		
11:30		American Gov.	gone
12:00 PM			
12:30	Lunch/take meds		
1:00	Are working		
1:30	Peak	Biology	good
2:00			
2:30		PE	
3:00			
3:30		Bus home	not good
4:00	Gone		
5:00			
6:00	Take Meds (5 mg Ritalin)		
6:30	Take effect	Homework	good

The Teenager: A Respected Member of the Treatment Team

Including your teenager as a truly respected member of the treatment team and involving him in all major decisions affecting his life is critical. It may be easier to treat your teenager with respect if you are aware of your own feelings and subtle attitudes about ADD.

If you, as a parent, think that your teenager is maliciously misbehaving and intentionally failing to do schoolwork, then a logical response is to believe that he will get better *only* if you force him to do things or punish him. On the other hand, if you believe that he wants to do well but is struggling to cope with ADD, then you will convey a different attitude. You will be positive, provide support and guidance, and if needed, suggest he consider taking medication. When appropriate, you will impose consequences for misbehavior. You will enlist his help in solving his own problems: "I believe you are doing your best, but ADD is making school difficult for you. I truly believe in your heart you want to follow rules and do well in school. What do you think you need to do to solve _____? How can I help you?" If he has no suggestions, then you may suggest something like, "Completing your homework is essential for passing your classes. Let's develop a plan for making certain your homework is

done every night." *You will help teach him needed skills rather than just punish him for his lack of skills—disorganization, slow processing, poor time management, or impulsive comments and actions.*

ADD, however, cannot be used as an *excuse* for misbehavior or school failure. Rather, it is a mitigating factor that helps explain why your teenager has trouble doing as adults ask and completing schoolwork. The teenager must still accept the consequences of his actions and learn to cope with and compensate for the symptoms of ADD. These issues are discussed in more detail in Chapter 5.

Helping Your Teenager Take Charge of His Medical Treatment

It is important to explain to your teenager how the medication helps him. He shouldn't expect medication to be a miracle cure, but should understand both its benefits and limitations. He needs to understand that *he is still going to have to make a conscious effort to improve his organizational skills and schoolwork.* He must learn to compensate for having ADD. You may want to enlist the help of doctors, other treatment professionals, or a CHADD training session for teenagers to help explain to your teenager what medication can and can't do.

❦

"One child with ADD was talking about his 'smart pill.' I told him, 'It isn't a smart pill. You are your smart pill. This medicine simply allows you the opportunity to make choices that are more appropriate and allows you to be more successful. You can choose to complete your work or choose not to complete your work regardless of whether you have taken your Ritalin. Ritalin may make it easier for you, but in the long run, it is still your choice.'"

—*Kathleen Allen, MS, Pediatric Center*

Taking Medication Regularly

Many teenagers don't mind taking their medication regularly because they can tell that it improves their ability to concentrate. It feels good to be able to concentrate and make better grades in school.

❦

"Over the past three years, our teenage son and his friends have come to feel special because they have ADD. When one of them becomes too talkative or spaces out, they remind each other to take their medication. They even have a chant, 'Take your medicine!' that they sing to each other. Since four or five of the boys take Ritalin, they are not embarrassed to take medicine."

❦

One of the major problems with medication is that teenagers with ADD have difficulty remembering to take it! But then, most adults would have difficulty remembering to take medication three times a day, every day, forever. Keep in mind, too, that these teenagers are forgetful by nature.

You may need to help your teenager devise a system to remember to take his medicine. For example, you may place pills in a weekly container and put them somewhere he will be certain to see them—by his breakfast plate or bathroom sink. If medicine is placed in a weekly container, you can tell at a glance whether or not he has remembered to take it. Or if you are away from home, beep him as a reminder. Your teen could also set an alarm on his watch, ask to be prompted by teachers, or simply take Dexedrine SR so he doesn't have to remember to take medication at school.

Try not to nag. Teenagers quickly tire of having adults constantly asking, "Did you take your medicine?" This constant questioning may lead to medication becoming the focal point of a power struggle between you and your child.

❦

"We put our son's medication and vitamins in one of the pill boxes that are marked for each day of the week. I fill it up each week and put it on the sink by his toothbrush. When he was in middle school and early high school years, I put it by his plate at breakfast. He also has a pill box about the size of a half dollar to carry Ritalin to school. I can glance at his pill box and know whether or not he has taken his Ritalin. This process is nice because now I don't have to nag him by asking if he took his medicine. I can see for myself. If he has taken it, I don't say anything. He doesn't even know I double checked it."

❦

"Sometimes when we are out of town, I call our son and leave a code on his beeper to remind him to take his medication."

Medication at School

School personnel should be told that your teenager has ADD and is taking medication. If he has just started medication, a different dosage, or new medication, the classroom teacher can give feedback regarding its effectiveness. The school nurse may need to be involved if a dose is given at school. Some students don't mind going to the school clinic to take their medicine—in fact, there may be several other students there taking their medication too. If going to the clinic embarrasses your child, a more discreet schedule can be arranged, such as dropping by the office or clinic on their way to lunch or another time when it may be less obvious to their friends.

Although most schools don't allow students to carry medications on them, some students do anyway and take their medication unobserved by any teachers. With their natural tendency to be defiant and question authority, teenagers may perceive school rules about prohibiting carrying medication as ridiculous. Although they may take their medication as needed, they may get into trouble with school officials if they are caught taking it on their own. As a parent, you should familiarize yourself with school rules about medication management and the consequences for breaking them. If punishment is stiff and your teenager may be suspended, find another way to get him to take medication at school. Or switch to a sustained-release medication.

❧

"My son always took his medication on his own in high school. He had it in his pocket, never flaunted it, and took it with his lunch."

Medication Refusal

Refusal to take medication may become a problem for some during adolescence. Some teenagers *don't like to be different from their friends* and don't want to take medication at school. *Denial* may also play a role in medication refusal. "If I take medication that means I have a problem. There's nothing wrong with me. I don't have ADD." Others *don't like the way it makes them feel.* They may feel like they are missing out on things and that life isn't as much fun. (See quotes from teenager below.) Most often, teenagers with ADD *simply forget* to take their medication. If you mistakenly assume the worst, that your teenager is refusing the medication, rather than just forgetting it, a power struggle may develop inadvertently. Taking medication may unnecessarily become the focal point of a major power struggle between you and your teenager.

❧

"I started taking Ritalin the summer before third grade. It helped me pay attention but it didn't help me learn my multiplication tables. I thought I was taking Ritalin to help me do better in math. At first I didn't mind, but then I noticed Ritalin took away the

fun. **When I wasn't on medication I was a chatterbox at school. I wasn't disruptive or hyperactive. I was just talkative. In seventh grade, I finally had a teacher agree with me. He liked me better when I didn't take my medication. I was such a loner when I was on it. It was like I wasn't able to feel loose and fun and silly. I started giving my pills away. Sometimes my friends would act like me because they took my pills."**

—a 19–year-old female

❧

"Another college-age teenager reported he didn't take his afternoon dose when he knew he was going out to drink beer. He was afraid of the interaction between medication and alcohol."

❧

It is probably wise not to force your teenager to take medication. If he is refusing to take his medication, ask why he has reservations about taking it. Ask whether medication helps him concentrate at school and make better grades. Listen to his response and see if changes can be made to accommodate his concerns. Sometimes teenagers are embarrassed to take Ritalin at school since they may not want other students to know they are on medication. As mentioned earlier, use of sustained-release forms of stimulant medications (Dexedrine), or as in the case of Ritalin, SR in combination with regular strength, may eliminate the need for taking medication at school. Sometimes, as described above, teenagers don't feel like themselves when they are on medication. Lowering the dosage may remedy this problem.

If you reach an impasse, convey the message that you respect your teenager's judgment. You might say: "When you are ready and need medication, the doctor and I will be glad to help you." Ask if there is anything else that you or the doctor can do. If your teenager continues to struggle, periodically ask if he thinks he should try medication again. He may decide to try meds again but being so forgetful, may never remember to ask you to get his prescription refilled. Usually, when things get bad enough, a teenager with ADD will ask for help. If your family can't resolve problems regarding medication, talk with your physician to see if he can work through this problem with your teenager.

Occasionally, not taking medicine may pose a *safety risk*. In these instances, you may want to insist that your teenager take it. For example, you might say, "You must take medication when you drive the car."

Should Parents with ADD Seek Treatment/Medication?

Approximately 40 percent of teenagers with ADD have a least one parent who has symptoms of ADD. If you are one of these parents, you must consider whether your own symptoms are serious enough to consider taking medication. For example, do you have difficulty monitoring your teenager's behavior and consistently using management techniques? As noted earlier, stimulant medications are highly effective with adults.

In one case study conducted by Dr. Evans, Dr. Pelham, and others, a parent of a child with ADHD agreed to participate in treatment for her own symptoms of the disorder. The mother had trouble monitoring her child's behavior, couldn't use child management techniques consistently, had difficulty getting things accomplished at home, had difficulty staying on task in counseling sessions, and frequently fidgeted. She was given 15 mg of Ritalin at 7:00 and 11:30 a.m. and 10 mg at 3:30 p.m. each day. This reduced the severity of her own symptoms, and she was able to improve her child management skills. This mother's symptoms were considered severe both as a child and as an adult.

Parents must make the judgment call about seeking treatment. If your symptoms are keeping you from functioning successfully as an adult, you may wish to talk with a physician about your symptoms of ADD. If you decide to seek treatment, your biggest problem may be finding a physician who is willing to treat you. How you approach the subject with your physician may depend on your relationship with him. If you both agree that you have the symptoms of ADD and they are interfering with your ability to work, he may be willing to give you a trial on stimulant medication. If you think your physician may be skeptical, you may need to come armed with information such as a copy of the new DSM IV criteria with your charac-teristics checked off, reports from early school years, a letter from your parents describing your childhood behavior, old report cards with teacher comments documenting underachievement in school, or old psychological reports.

✻

"After being treated for depression for several years, I realized that I have ADD. I couldn't get organized enough to get my work done. As a result I was always depressed."

Other Treatment Options

Several treatment options beyond the services discussed in the previous sections are available. They include *respite, intensive in-home services, day treatment, after school programs, summer treatment programs, and 24–hour residential treatment.* Unfortunately, these services are usually either hard to find or extremely expensive. They can, however, be a lifesaver for families in crisis or for a teenager who has more serious emotional problems. The majority of these treatment options can be provided in conjunction with other basic services while the teenager is still living at home. Other critical interventions such as techniques for behavior management and building self-esteem are discussed in subsequent chapters. Parents can find out about the availability of these services through their local mental health center, school psychological services office, psychiatric hospital, or university ADD program. If services are not available, you may be able to create some of them yourself. For example, find and train a coach to help your teenager stay organized.

Some people incorrectly assume that intensive services are synonymous with 24–hour residential care. If intensive individualized services are "wrapped around" a teenager and his family, however, residential treatment can usually be avoided, even when emotional problems are serious. The services described in this chapter constitute an effective range of comprehensive services for children with serious emotional problems. Development of these services has been promoted nationally by the Child and Adolescent Services System Program (CASSP), Center for Mental Health Services.

Respite. When raising a teenager with ADD gets too emotionally demanding, parents need time away to recharge their energies. Getting a babysitter for a night out is one form of respite. Sending the teenager on a supervised trip with friends or relatives also provides respite for parents. Sometimes parents have trouble getting babysitters or chaperons because other adults don't know how to cope with youngsters with ADD. Parents in this predicament may be able to benefit from formal respite care. Respite care may be offered by mental health centers for their clients whose children have serious emotional problems. These centers may have trained paid staff who can stay with the teenager while parents go out. The teenager may stay in his own home or may go somewhere else for the respite care. Respite care is often one of the greatest needs parents have, but is seldom available. You could ask your local CHADD chapter to offer training for babysitters or chaperons of youngsters with ADD.

Intensive In-home Services. "Intensive In-home" services are appropriate to use when a family is in crisis and the teenager's problems are considered serious enough to warrant residential treatment. This in-home crisis service is extremely effective in diffusing family emergencies, thus preventing a residential placement. Unfortunately, few intensive in-home services are accessible to the average family. Your local mental health center will know if this service is available in your community.

Homebuilders, one of the first intensive in-home programs, was developed in 1974, in Tacoma, Washington. In this program, a counselor has only two to four clients at one time and will spend up to twenty hours a week with one family, if needed. The primary goal of the program is to prevent children from being removed from their home. The intervention is intensive, highly effective, and brief, lasting only six weeks. During the last fifteen years, this program has been replicated in most states across the country. In Florida, the program is called Intensive Crisis Counseling Program (ICCP); in West Virginia, Family Services Network. Many of these programs are operated by local community mental health centers.

Day Treatment/Partial Hospitalization. In some communities, day treatment or partial hospitalization programs are available for teenagers with ADD who are experiencing serious emotional problems. These programs typically offer services that include academic instruction; individual, group, and family counseling; behavior management; medication evaluation/monitoring; and psychiatric evaluation and follow-up. Program staff also usually identify learning problems and provide special academic tutoring or adaptations.

The teenager lives at home, while attending school at the day treatment program. Programs may be jointly operated by a local school and mental health center and located at either site. Programs with greater medical involvement may be offered through a psychiatric hospital and housed in the hospital. Sometimes insurance coverage is available for this partial hospitalization service.

After School Programs. A few organizations around the country have begun offering specialized after school services for children or teenagers with ADD. The services are similar to those offered in day treatment programs, except that they are held for only two or three hours each day after school. Programs may include academic interventions, recreational activities, and/or counseling. At one such program, the Western Psychiatric Institute and Clinic (WPIC), University of Pittsburgh, teenagers attend the program from 3:30 in the afternoon until 6:30, up to five days a week.

Summer Treatment Programs. Some organizations that specialize in treating youngsters with ADD have developed intensive summer programs—for example, WPIC at the University of

Pittsburgh, and Emory University in Atlanta. Teenagers are taught new social skills and competencies through participation in recreational activities, academic interventions, and counseling. This service is typically expensive, but some insurance policies cover it.

Residential Treatment. As a last resort, teenagers with ADD and more serious problems are sometimes placed in 24–hour residential care. Residential care may be offered through several types of programs: *group homes, specialized foster care homes (a foster home with trained parents plus mental health support), residential treatment facilities, or psychiatric in-patient hospitals.* The decision to place must be made very carefully in conjunction with the teenager's doctor and/or counselor. Residential treatment is considered primarily when a teenager presents a danger to himself or others. Residential care may also be provided when the teenager is engaging in self-defeating behaviors such as substance abuse. Costs vary, but in-patient psychiatric hospitalization is usually the most expensive residential service, ranging from $500 to $1,000 a day.

The purpose of in-patient hospital programs is to help the teenager find the right medication regimen to stabilize his moods and reduce aggression, explosiveness, or depression. Services usually include individual, group, and family counseling; psychiatric evaluation; and medication monitoring. The in-patient program may also continue the teenager's education through day treatment. The student attends a special school program during the day, but comes back to the unit at night. Or the day treatment program may be located at the hospital. The length of stay may vary from a few days to several months. Often these programs have locked units in which the teenager may be placed.

You should consider residential care only if other interventions have not worked or if your teenager is a danger to himself or others. Do not allow yourself to be pressured by the aggressive advertising campaigns of private psychiatric in-patient facilities, suggesting hospitalization of teenagers who are depressed or out of control. These campaigns are made to play on parents' fears. National data reflect that psychiatric in-patient hospitals and residential treatment placements for children and teenagers with emotional problems are over-used. In testimony before congressional committees in 1988, Ira Schwartz of the University of Michigan stated that placement of teenagers in psychiatric residential treatment facilities had increased approximately 450 percent over a five-year period. He also found that two-thirds of all placements of teenagers in these psychiatric facilities were inappropriate. Furthermore, the length of stay in these facilities was linked to insurance coverage, rather than to the severity of the teenager's diagnosis.

Inappropriate placements result in parents shouldering an unnecessary financial burden *without any guarantee it will help their teenager.* In addition, teenagers with ADD may be exposed to others who have more serious emotional problems and may learn new inappropriate behaviors or develop close relationships with other teenagers who aren't coping very well. Worst of all, the teenager's self-esteem is unnecessarily damaged, leaving him to believe that he is emotionally "sick" or crazy. If your teenager is placed in a residential treatment facility, you should monitor your child's length of stay in the hospital and work with your local doctor and counselor toward an early return home.

❧

"One teenager with ADD was placed in a residential 'rehab' treatment program when he was fifteen. He met a girl there who became his girlfriend. Within six months she was pregnant and they got married. At age sixteen, he dropped out of school and went to work to support his family. They were divorced within a year."

❧

Sometimes the only services available to a family during a crisis are at either extreme of a continuum—either one hour of counseling or placement in a residential facility. During a crisis, one hour of counseling may not be sufficient to help a family resolve their problems, but a residential placement may not really be needed. If you are ever in such a situation, remember, the key to deciding whether residential placement is appropriate is whether your teenager poses a danger to himself or others. Otherwise, seek services that will support you and your teenager at home during the crisis.

Conclusion

Unfortunately, the treatment for teenagers with ADD is never cut and dried. To begin with, most research on effective treatment for ADD has been done on *children* with ADD, not teenagers. And even with this age group, not nearly enough research has been done to understand the many complex issues that contribute to the success or failure of treatment. Second, each teenager with ADD is a unique individual with his own complex treatment needs. What works for one teenager is not necessarily going to work for another. Clearly, every treatment strategy described in this chapter is not appropriate for all teenagers with ADD. This broad overview of treatment options, however, should help you and your teenager determine which options seem to fit your family's needs.

As a parent, you should keep in mind the factors that are *predictors of a positive outcome* for ADD. *Many factors are beyond your control, but you should attempt to change any negative factors that are under your influence.* Factors related to positive outcomes discussed in Chapter 1 include: a nurturing supportive home, emotionally healthy parents, positive parenting practices (infrequent hostile parent/teen interactions), positive friends, emotional stability with less aggression and fewer emotional blow-ups, higher intelligence, less severe hyperactivity, and middle to upper socioeconomic status.

Ensuring that an *individualized treatment plan* is developed for your teenager is also critical. Common sense tells us that a treatment plan should help the teenager succeed in all aspects of his life—home, school, and community activities. Involving your teenager as a respected partner in the treatment process is also crucial. Obviously, he is more likely to follow a treatment plan that he helped develop.

In summary, key elements of an individualized treatment plan include:

- *taking medication(s)* to enhance the functioning of neurotransmitters believed to be linked to symptoms of ADD;

- *finding the right medical doctor* (treatment professional) who understands ADD and can prescribe appropriate medications as needed;
- *reframing ADD* in a positive light and building on your teenager's strengths;
- *treating coexisting problems* such as anxiety, depression, conduct disorder, sleep disturbances, or learning problems;
- *implementing specialized instruction, classroom adaptations,* or special education to fit the unique learning needs and strengths of an individual student, thus ensuring success at school;
- *providing classroom consultation* to teachers, if needed, by school psychologists or private treatment professionals;
- *providing a "coach"* to help the teenager with academics, chores, or social events;
- *ensuring completion of homework* through a regular homework routine, plus parental monitoring;
- participating in activities to *build self-esteem and confidence*;
- *attending parent training classes* to learn about common problems of teenagers with ADD, new parenting skills for coping with ADD, how to oversee the teenager's treatment, and to receive support from other parents who have teenagers with the same problems;
- *seeking counseling (parents)* to receive one-to-one guidance from a treatment professional and deal with any feelings of anger and self-doubt;
- *seeking counseling (teenager)* to help him better understand himself ADD, and his behavior, and to learn ways to cope with the disorder; and
- *finding other services* such as respite, day treatment, and residential care, if needed.

So when does your involvement ever stop? Most likely, you will need to monitor and fine tune your teenager's treatment plan on an on-going basis through high school and possibly into college. With a little luck, someone else, perhaps a girlfriend, will become his "coach" and you may be relegated to assistant coach status. The big picture goals you hope your teenager achieves may include success in school, happiness at home, responsible behavior, good friends, and a zest for living. If he is doing well in these areas, then your treatment plan must be working. As your teenager matures and he gains confidence in his ability to manage his own life, your involvement and supervision gradually decline. Thankfully, many treatment and support resources are now available so you won't have to tackle this job uninformed and alone.

CHAPTER FIVE

RAISING A HEALTHY, WELL-ADJUSTED TEENAGER

Parents of teenagers with ADD often have questions about the "right" way to raise their son or daughter. Should we be strong disciplinarians or should we be more democratic? Are we being too strict or too lenient? If our teenager repeats misbehavior, should punishment be more severe? Does nagging help? How can we use positive reinforcement to help him avoid misbehavior? When punishment is necessary, what are some good strategies to use?

Because teenagers with ADD are more difficult to discipline, parents may second guess themselves and question their own effectiveness. If parents assume they are doing something wrong, they may resort, unsuccessfully, to increasingly harsh punishment. Although parents typically receive a lot of advice from other well-meaning adults, *there is no "magic formula" or "right way" to raise a teenager with ADD*. A variety of parenting approaches may be used effectively. As a parent, you must decide which techniques work best with your teenager.

❧

"My sister and brother-in-law think they have all the answers. From their perspective, my son just needs to be disciplined. They cannot begin to understand what it is like to raise a youngster with ADD. They think their child is an angel because of their superior parenting skills. I'd like to see them do any better with a child with ADD than I have."

❧

Parents have raised children successfully for generations without the benefit of special training. Although parent training can be helpful, it does not appear to be the critical element for helping teenagers cope successfully with ADD. *Ongoing positive support for your teenager, plus medication when needed, seem to be more important than the parenting approach you use*. As discussed earlier, Dr. Gabrielle Weiss believes a major key to coping with ADD is having an adult who loves and believes in the teenager. This does not mean that love alone cures all problems nor that parents should let their teenager run wild. Common sense tells us that these teenagers need support, structure, supervision, and encouragement. The challenge for parents is to achieve a balance between positive feedback for good behavior and negative consequences for inappropriate behavior. Parents must learn to impose reasonable consequences, at appropriate intervals, without obliterating their teenager's self-esteem.

Frequently your teenager's misbehavior is related to his symptoms of ADD—impulsively talking back, losing things, being late, being forgetful, breaking things, difficulty sitting still, not listening, difficulty getting started on schoolwork, and last minute planning. You should remember that *punishment alone is not going to make these behaviors go away*. Punishment will not produce more neurotransmitters to help improve your child's attention, compliance with requests, and ability to finish tasks. In fact, major problems may occur if you take a punitive, punishing approach to parenting. Over a period of years, children who are exposed each week to hundreds of negative interactions with adults will begin to develop negative, aggressive behavior.

The expression "different strokes for different folks" is especially true when it comes to raising children with ADD. Some teenagers are more sensitive and may respond quickly to a raised voice or dirty look. Others will require more intense parental intervention. Most teenagers with ADD, however, respond better to stronger, more meaningful rewards and punishment. This punishment does not have to be harsh to be effective. In fact, harsh punishment may only make problems worse.

As discussed in earlier chapters, raising teenagers with ADD can be extremely challenging because *many of them don't respond to traditional punishment and rewards the same as teens without ADD.* They don't seem to learn from their mistakes, be deterred by punishment, or motivated by rewards as easily as teenagers without ADD. These factors, combined with their impulsivity and sometimes daring behavior, may make them a handful for parents to manage. If parents place them on restrictions, they will turn around the next week and repeat the same misbehavior. Much to parents' dismay, when an effective consequence is found, it doesn't work very long.

Deep down inside, *most children and teenagers with ADD want to please their parents and teachers, want to do well in school, and actually feel better when they do as adults ask.* It is highly unlikely that a teenager gets up every morning and makes a pledge to see how miserable he can make his parents' day. Sometimes after years of failure, however, teenagers may become so discouraged and depressed that they no longer care about adult approval. Ideally, parents will seek help before problems reach such crisis proportions.

If traditional "child rearing" methods are working effectively with your teenager, then you should continue your current methods of parenting. However, if your family is experiencing problems, you may want to try some of the suggestions given here. Techniques discussed in this chapter will work for most teenagers, including teenagers with ADD.

The Big "D's": Democracy and Discipline

The authoritarian child rearing methods used by past generations don't work quite as well with the teenagers of today. Parenting techniques tend to be more democratic now, and teenagers are both "seen and heard." Teenagers are taught to be independent, speak out, and make their own decisions. Yet, when we as parents make a request, we expect the opposite—we want them to obey immediately and without question. Striking a reasonable balance between democratic principles and discipline in child-rearing is challenging.

"How can you help your teenager grow up to be a responsible, happy, productive adult?" There is no right or wrong answer for this question. Generally speaking, however, you will be more successful if you and your teenager can work together toward this goal. During the early years of adolescence, you will want to increasingly involve your teenager as a respected partner in the treatment process. You must try to help him understand the impact of ADD on his life, recognize his strengths and limitations, build his self-esteem, accept increasing levels of responsibility, gain some sense of control over his life, and feel confident that he can cope with whatever problems arise.

As your child reaches the teenage years, you must learn alternative ways of dealing with problems, since the time will come when physical punishment no longer works and behavior management loses much of its effectiveness. Spanking a 6'2", 180-pound 16-year-old isn't particularly feasible or effective. Nor will a teenager be motivated by charts and stars.

There *are* several strategies, however, that should help make your job as a parent easier. These include behavior management, positive reinforcement, logical consequences, and medication management. Other helpful techniques such as ignoring minor misbehavior, active listening, negotiating, giving choices, and following Grandma's rule are also discussed in this chapter.

For additional practical and humorous insights into coping with teenagers, see Dr. Thomas W. Phelan's book, *Surviving Your Teenagers*. Having raised two teenagers, one of whom has ADHD, Dr. Phelan gives advice based upon experience, not just theory. He suggests four steps for coping with a teenager: doing nothing, consulting with the teenager, negotiating a compromise or settlement, and taking charge when problems are very serious.

Guiding Principles for Parent/Teenager Interactions

This section discusses a dozen key principles to bear in mind when parenting and communicating with teenagers with ADD. These principles are especially important if your teenager is struggling and his self-esteem is fragile.

Give Unconditional Positive Regard

One critical step in coping successfully with ADD is for you to give your teenager what treatment professionals commonly refer to as *"unconditional positive regard."* This simply means that you should make every effort to love your teenager, just as he is, with all his special strengths and faults. He needs to know that you, his parents, believe in him and will be there when he needs you. Remember: as Dr. Weiss explains, believing in your teenager and supporting him through the good times and the rough times are the foundation for successfully coping with ADD. Although this is all so much easier said than done, several suggestions are provided below.

Reframe Your Perception of ADD. Reframing your perception of ADD and your teenager's behavior in a more positive light can help you give him unconditional positive regard. As discussed in Chapter 3, viewing the cup as half full (looking at strengths), rather than half empty (looking at problems) is important. These teenagers aren't 'bad,' nor are their parents 'bad' parents. You should also try to understand that many characteristics that are bothersome in teenagers may serve adults well. High energy, persuasiveness, tenacity, risk-taking, creativity, and independence are characteristics that may help your child be successful in his chosen career.

Keep a Disability Perspective. Sometimes it is hard to accept and remember that *ADD is* a disability for some youngsters with ADD.

〽

"Even though our family has been struggling with this disorder for eight years, sometimes I still forget that ADD is a disability. Developmentally these teenagers

are behind. If a child couldn't read because of a visual disability, parents wouldn't be angry. They would say, 'Put on your glasses when you study.' In a parallel situation, we, as parents, should avoid getting angry with a teenager because of misbehavior related to ADD. We should have our teenager take his medicine, make adaptations at school, and work with him to succeed."

〽

Enjoy Your Teenager. Parents and their teenagers need to laugh together and have fun. By doing this, a solid base of positive memories is built that will stand the teenager in good stead when he faces difficult times. Can you remember the last time you had a really good side-splitting laugh with your teenager? If it has been so long you can't remember, find something humorous to share, even if it is just a good comedy movie. You might also suggest a "special event" for just the two of you, such as eating dinner out or an activity of the teenager's choice.

It is especially important to share activities that are fun and pleasant if your teenager is doing poorly in school. Active participation may be better than spectator activities. Many teenagers with ADD have trouble sitting for very long and may lose interest in watching a football or baseball game. Play tennis or basketball, ride bikes, or jog together. Swim or water ski as a family. Some fathers and sons enjoy hunting, fishing, or playing golf together. Mothers and daughters may enjoy shopping, a make-over at a local department store, or tennis. The whole family may enjoy putt-putt golf or going to a movie. Table games such as Trivial Pursuit, Pictionary, or card games may be fun for families to share. Other hobbies such as art, music, and cooking may also be shared by family members. Make sure that the activity is fun for your teenager too. If Mom and Dad are the only ones having fun throwing the baseball, this is not the best activity for a positive interaction.

Don't avoid activities in which your teenager is more skilled than you are. Go ahead and play basketball with him, even though you are out-of-shape and your teenager may win. He may even get to teach you a thing or two. Hopefully, you can laugh at yourself. Your teenager's ego could probably use the boost.

Above all, remember that the purpose of the special time is to have fun and build a stronger bond of trust between the two of you. *Avoid the temptation to nag or discuss problems once you have your teenager "corralled."* Try to avoid these negative discussions unless the teen insists. Enjoy this time together.

Nurture with Touch. Human touch is extremely healing and nurturing. Yet as children move into adolescence, touching occurs less frequently. Sometimes play wrestling or touch football are nice activities within the family to "legally allow" touching. Massage or back rubs can be very relaxing, nurturing activities. Don't be afraid to hug your teenager and tell him you love him.

Treat Your Teenager as an Equal Partner in the Treatment Process

Involve your teenager in decision making as frequently as possible! For example, talk with him about best medication dosages and how frequently he needs to take it. "Does your 10 mg of Ritalin seem to be working effectively? Does it help you concentrate better? What time do you think you should take your medication at school? Can you feel it when your medication wears off?"

Likewise, involve your teenager in trying to solve school- related problems or homework issues. You might begin by stating the obvious: "Sometimes you have trouble getting your homework done, and as a result you are failing algebra. I feel like you want to do well at school. How can we solve this problem together? How can I help you?" Or, regarding curfew, "What time is a reasonable curfew on Saturday night—12:00 or 12:30?"

The level of your child's involvement and degree of autonomy will depend on his age. Obviously, an eighteen-year-old is capable of handling more freedom and making more responsible decisions than a thirteen-year-old. By treating your teenager as part of the solution rather than just the problem, you convey a message of respect and that you are partners working together to solve difficult problems.

Give Choices. Learning to make choices is an important part of growing up and becoming inde-

pendent. Giving your teenager choices shows you respect him and his opinions, plus allows him to have more control over his environment. In addition, researchers have found that teenagers who have choices at school are more compliant, less aggressive, and produce more work.

When possible, give your teenager choices about the things he does. "What time is a good bedtime for you?" If you think he may give an outrageous reply, such as 1:00 a.m., then suggest two more reasonable options. "Which is better—11:00 or 11:30?" You can maintain some control by limiting choices to only two or three. Even when limited choices are given, teenagers feel a greater sense of control over their lives. "What time do you want to start on your homework? Seven or seven thirty?" If he does suggest outrageous starting times, don't lecture him about it—just ignore it and repeat the choices. Or you can use humor without sarcasm—"Bedtime at 1:00 a.m.? Not!! Nice try."

Set Reasonable Expectations. Because teenagers with ADD act younger than their age and may also have learning problems, parents may expect more of a teenager than he is capable of producing. Keep in mind that most of these teenagers are as much as *30 percent behind their peers developmentally* (two to four years). This means that they seem less mature in their ability to accept responsibility, complete chores and homework, follow rules, or deal with their emotions. A sixteen-year-old may act more like a thirteen-year-old.

⚹

"It is difficult not knowing where to set expectations— not too high or too low. My frustration comes in trying to mold Lewis into just a 'normal teenager' and not taking into account his ADD and learning disability."

⚹

Negotiate/Consider Compromise. When less serious problems come up, you might try to reach a satisfactory compromise with your teenager. Dr. Phelan suggests asking for a time to discuss the issue and to deal with only one problem at a time. For example, "When is a good time for us to talk about your room? or smoking? or coming in late?" Once the time is set, find a quiet place to talk, briefly discuss the problem, and ask if he has any ideas for solving the problem. After he explains his thoughts, then state your concerns.

"Win-win" situations—where everyone gets something out of the deal—are best. Your teenager is more likely to follow through on a solution that he has helped develop. Solutions may include: a dirty room - close the door during the week and clean up on Fridays; being late - give a later curfew (if appropriate), give 15 minutes leeway, have your teenager call if he is going to be late, have him set his watch alarm to go off fifteen minutes before he is due home, or allow a later curfew on special occasions. Since these teenagers have problems with awareness of time, they are more likely to lose track of time and be late. If they are running late, they may speed home. Most parents would prefer that their teenager get home a few minutes late rather than have a car accident as a result of speeding.

Depersonalize Problems. Sometimes it helps to take away the personal or blaming elements of a problem. Rather than criticize your teenager, you might reframe the problem by depersonalizing it and discussing it in terms of the typical behavior of teenagers with ADD. For example, "Sometimes teenagers with ADD have trouble being aware of time, so they come home late." "Sometimes teenagers with ADD have trouble . . . getting started on their homework . . . remembering to take their medicine . . . saying things impulsively that they don't mean. Do you think this is true for you sometimes?" Listen to your teenager's response, then ask: "What can we do to solve this problem? How can I help you cope with this problem?" Try to have this discussion at a time when you can control your anger. For example, don't wait until your teenager comes home late for the third night in a row and then confront him as soon as he walks in the door: "You always come home late and I'm sick of it. Don't you know what time it is?"

Most parents slip into a pattern of nagging about misbehavior, even though it doesn't help change the teenager's behavior. If you have been nagging your teenager for years about something, maybe it's time to try a different approach like the ones suggested above.

Assume Good Intentions. As parents, it is easy to assume the worst intentions. "My son was late on purpose. He is intentionally lying about homework. He doesn't care if he fails his classes." Sometimes, however, it helps to approach problems by assuming that your teenager has good intentions. By avoiding a hostile confrontation, you avoid making your teenager defensive. Your teenager may then be more willing to work with you to find solutions to problems. "I feel like you are willing to come home on time but you lose track of time." "I believe in my heart that you really want to make good grades in school. I know it's difficult for you. I'm willing to help you. Let's work together."

Maintain Good Communications

Maintaining open communication with your teenager is critically important. If the only parent/teenager communication is negative (about misbehavior), your teenager may begin avoiding you. Once this happens, your relationship may deteriorate further. Below are some guidelines to help keep information flowing freely in both directions.

Listen When Your Teenager Talks. In the rare event your teenager wants to talk to you, you must be ready to listen. Parents must take advantage of these rare and fleeting times when the teenager is in the mood to talk.

❧

"Maybe once or twice a month my son will come into a room where I am working, flop down in a chair or on the floor, and start talking. Typically, whatever I am working on, I stop and set it aside. This talkative streak may last ten or fifteen minutes. Then this window of opportunity closes, until two or three weeks later when he is in the mood to talk again. I have learned that I need to make myself available when he is in the mood to talk."

❧

If it really is a terrible time to talk because of a major conflict—an important meeting at work and you're 15 minutes late already—set up a specific time to talk later. If necessary, call him from work after the meeting. If it is a crisis for your teenager, take at least five minutes to listen briefly, hug him, and tell him you're sorry he's hurting, you love him, and together you'll work it out. One creative solution may be to continue the conversation on the car phone. Obviously, if it is a serious crisis, you should stay with your teenager and contact your treatment professional for advice.

Learning to listen without being judgmental is an important skill to master.

▨

"My son has always told me everything both good and bad that he has ever done. Some of the things he tells me are a little embarrassing. In some ways I wish I didn't know when he has had a beer to drink or that he always carries a condom. Although I would prefer that he not drink or engage in a sexual relationship, I feel good that he tells me everything. Our communication is strong."

▨

The technique of active listening, described below, can help you learn to listen without judging who is right or wrong or taking sides.

Use Active Listening. Active listening is a technique that may help you defuse your teenager's anger. When he is talking about things that interest him or potential areas of conflict between the two of you, you should listen and try to understand his viewpoint first. You then restate what he said to confirm that you have heard him correctly.

For example, your teenager may come home and tell you that a teacher yelled at him in front of the whole class. You might respond by saying, "I'm really sorry your teacher yelled at you today." You can also make supportive comments. "I know it isn't fun to have a teacher yell at you. That can really be embarrassing. I always hated when my teacher did that." Don't take sides with anyone, just listen and reflect your teenager's feelings back to him.

If your teenager says he is angry with his teacher and she isn't fair, you might reflect: "I know you must have felt really angry. I didn't like it when my teachers weren't fair." He may say she gave him a zero because he forgot and left his homework at home. You may respond by saying, "I'm sorry she gave you a zero. Is there anything I can do to help?" You are trying to defuse anger rather than confront, criticize, or blame. He needs someone to listen while he blows off steam in a healthy way. Your child is upset enough with himself and his teacher without you placing blame too.

You can talk later about how to address the homework problem and avoid conflict with his teacher when he is calmer and less agitated.

Give "I" Messages. One technique that may keep communication more positive is to give what are known as "I" messages instead of "you" messages. "You" messages tend to be negative and blaming and frequently put the teenager on the defensive. "You didn't do your homework. You aren't being responsible." It is better to state how you feel about a certain problem—"I am very unhappy that your homework was not turned in on time. I get very angry and upset. I would like for you to help me solve this problem." Your teenager is more likely to work with you if he is not feeling defensive.

Smooth Ruffled Feathers. Teenagers with ADD have difficulty coping with stressful situations, yet frequently seem to find themselves in crises. As a result, parents and teachers may find themselves interacting with a teenager who is angry and argumentative. Sometimes adults can ignore the hostile questions or comments and calmly state the job that needs to be done. If your teenager refuses to do as requested, sometimes it is helpful to wade through the anger and hostility and address the real issue that may be underlying a particular incident. Smoothing ruffled feathers rather than meeting hostility with a hostile response may be effective, as described in the following example. Otherwise, a hostile response typically results in even more anger and fighting.

▨

"My son advised me that he was not going to school today. I ignored most of his comments and avoided arguing with him. I told him his jeans were clean and were in the dryer. I knew he was angry because of a fight with his girlfriend the night before. Mistakenly, he thought he would feel better if he could draw me into an argument with him. He changed tactics and asked, 'Why will it hurt me to miss one day of school?'

"I sat and looked at him for a few moments trying to figure out what was going on behind the anger. Finally, I remembered the fight and said, 'I'm sorry you've been having such a rough time lately. Fighting with your girlfriend hurts.' I did not try to explain to him why he should go to school. I walked

off. Within a few minutes, he started his shower in preparation for going to school."

⚏

"Sometimes when my son erupts in a hostile manner, I will say, 'This really isn't like you to act this way. Is something wrong?' I learned this lesson one day when I was teaching school and was confronted by a hostile fourteen-year-old. I gave this same response. Much to my surprise, the student calmed down and apologized. He told me that the teacher in his previous class had yelled at him and embarrassed him. He was angry with his teacher but was taking it out on me."

⚏

If you make comments aimed at smoothing ruffled feathers, you must genuinely mean them. If you say, "I'm sorry you've been having a rough time lately," in a sarcastic manner or give a hostile look, your teenager will pick it up instantly. The whole purpose of being understanding and supportive will be defeated.

Encourage Expression of Feelings. It is important to encourage your teenager to be aware of his feelings and to express them. Many teenagers with ADD experience painful emotions which they often suppress. They have difficulty being in touch with these feelings or expressing them.

⚏

"My teenage son came home one Saturday night and he had drunk a few beers. Although I was concerned about his drinking, I just listened to him as he talked. He began to open up and talked about his deepest feelings, pains, and fears. He cried as he told me that sometimes he felt like he was going crazy. He hated school and felt stupid at times. Sometimes he wished he were dead. My heart was breaking. I listened and hugged him close. I told him, 'Those feelings are not unusual for teenagers with ADD. A lot of people worry about going crazy. Those feelings are a part of growing up. When I was younger, I wondered if I was going crazy. All of us act a little crazy at times. I love you and I'll always be here for you.' I didn't want to close the door on our communication by confronting him at that moment about his drinking. I dealt with the drinking issue later when things were calmer."

⚏

As a parent, you should not be afraid to tell your teenager about personal things that make you happy or sad. When you are upset, your child may learn from comforting you and listening to your concerns.

⚏

"I remember being really upset and crying about some problem I was having at work. I wasn't afraid for my teenage son to see me crying. He sat down beside me, hugged me, and told me not to worry, everything was going to turn out okay. It sounded just like something I would say to him. I think it was good for him to feel like he was strong and was able to help me."

⚏

Another way to encourage expression of feelings is to ask questions when your teenager tells you about emotional experiences. For example, if he is telling about a teacher who has embarrassed him in class, ask him, "How did you feel when she did that?" Avoid pressuring him by peppering him with questions. Don't rush him for an answer. It's okay to have periods of silence which give him time to think and formulate his response. Remember, he may need more time to express his emotions. You may need to suggest possible feelings: "Were you embarrassed?" (listen) Or, "Were your feeling hurt?" (listen) "Did you feel angry?" (listen) "Those are pretty normal feelings. I'm sorry this was such a painful experience for you."

Teach by Example. The section above recommends teaching your teenager by example how to express his own feelings. You can also show him through your actions how to respect others' feelings, handle conflict, and accept each other for who you are. For example, you can show your teenager that you always love *him* even though you may not love his *behavior* at times. When you are patient, you teach your teenager to be patient. If you handle your anger about less serious issues by discussing them and reaching a compromise (or exercising, or counting to ten), your child will learn to handle his anger in a healthy way. The converse is also true. If you are impatient, your teenager will learn to be impatient. If you are untrusting and hostile, you are teaching your teenager to be the same way.

Avoid Subconscious Negative Messages. Most messages parents give to their children are direct and the result of conscious decisions. For example, if they are angry because their child didn't complete his homework, they may tell him they are angry and put him on restrictions. But parents may also send indirect negative messages that are made subconsciously. Parents may not even be aware they are sending them. These messages are subtle and harder to detect and describe. But children and teenagers can be extremely perceptive: they know if parents and teachers approve of them, if adults trust them, or if adults think they're bad. The teenager will perceive the parent's or teacher's true feelings when the nonverbal messages don't match the verbal messages adults convey. Even though you don't *tell* your child you think he's bad, you can convey this message through disapproving looks, frowns, negative comments, and lack of positive comments or touch. You need to monitor yourself to see whether you are sending subtle negative messages that may be damaging to your teenager.

Understand Factors Influencing Behavior

There are certain situations in which teenagers with ADD seem to function better. Being aware of these situations should be helpful to you and his teachers in interacting with him. (Table 5-1).

Table 5–1 COMPARISON OF BEHAVIOR IN DIFFERENT SETTINGS	
BETTER	**WORSE**
One to one setting	Group setting
Novelty situations	Familiar
High interest activities	Low interest activities
Immediate consequences	Delayed consequences
Supervised settings	Unsupervised settings
Morning	Later in the day

In addition, some research in school settings has indicated that giving choices, even limited choices, is more effective than giving commands. Giving choices helps reduce aggression and increase compliance.

Provide Structure and Supervision/Be a Coach

Most teenagers with ADD will need more structure and supervision than their friends without ADD, and they will need it for a longer period of time. There are a variety of ways you can provide this structure, depending on your teenager's age, sense of responsibility, and independence.

Establish a Daily Routine. Having a set time to get up, go to bed, eat, and study each day adds needed structure to your child's life. Since these teenagers have major problems with organization, awareness of time, and time management, having a schedule and routine will help them cope better with responsibilities in life (schoolwork and chores). Involve your teenager in making decisions about his daily routine. Specific suggestions for establishing routines regarding homework are discussed in Chapter 9.

Develop Rules and Consequences. You and your teenager may jointly develop a few basic rules which address the issues that are most important to the family. Rules should be clearly stated. Consequences for breaking them should also be known in advance. For example, "You can't go out on Friday until your homework is completed." (See Chapter 9 for more information regarding homework.) "If you get a speeding ticket, you will have to pay the fine and you will not be able to drive for a week." Try to involve your teenager in selecting the consequence. If he suggests a consequence that is too easy or too harsh, you may need to suggest more reasonable consequences.

Develop a Contract. A contract can be developed in which you, your child, and/or teachers clearly define expectations and consequences and rewards for appropriate and inappropriate behavior. Contracts seem to work better if your teenager helps write it and chooses positive and negative consequences. It is important to build in more positive consequences so your teenager will want to uphold his end of the bargain. A sample contract is provided in Appendix A. Feel free to modify/simplify this contract to meet your needs. A contract alone is seldom enough to bring about major changes in behavior, but at least it does spell out expectations and consequences.

Schedule Chores. It helps to have regularly scheduled chores so that your teenager knows that the yard must be mowed every other Friday and the garbage taken out each Tuesday. He knows what is expected, when, and can't say "but I already made other plans." If he needs a reminder, remind him the day before. If he didn't mow the yard Thursday, then remind him Friday afternoon when he gets home from school. When Friday evening rolls around and he still hasn't mowed the yard, you must "be cool." Don't nag him to mow the yard—wait until he comes to you and wants to go out. Remind him that he may go out when the yard has been mowed.

Sometimes this approach will work for only a short while. It may develop into a power struggle in which your teenager proves that he can out wait you. For example, he may refuse to mow the lawn and then contentedly stay home on Friday night. Sometimes you can extend the consequence for not doing a chore to the next day: "When you mow the yard, you may play football with your friends." If you try this approach for a few weeks and it doesn't work, then try another intervention.

🦋

"Waiting and being cool is so difficult for me. Sometimes I slip and start nagging at him to mow the yard. Usually, a fight erupts and we both end up feeling terrible. When I can do it, it is so much nicer to look at my son and calmly and sympathetically say, 'I think it's a great idea for you to go to the movies. When you finish the yard, you may go.'"

🦋

Give Advance Notice and Time Frames. "Do it now because I said to do it" is not as effective with this generation of teenagers. Try to give your teenager advance notice and a time frame for doing something. "I am leaving for work at 8:00. If you are ready, you can ride with me instead of riding the bus." "If you want to wear something on Monday, it needs to be in the laundry room by Saturday morning." Simply giving advance notice is not going to create any magic, however. Occasionally, your teenager is still going to forget what you told him. It may help him remember things if you

remind him the next morning that you are leaving at 8:00, or write responsibilities on a calendar or Post-it note.

Link Responsible Behavior to Privileges. For many teenagers, driving a car is one of the most important privileges in their lives. This privilege gives the parent tremendous leverage. Parents frequently link being responsible with having the privilege of driving in discussions with their teenager. Students who are responsible complete their homework, help around the house, don't get speeding tickets, and drive responsibly. Consequently, if your teenager brings home failing grades (because he isn't trying), doesn't do his chores, gets speeding tickets, or doesn't come home on time, he may not be allowed to drive for awhile. For example, he can drive when his chores are completed or he brings home a weekly report that indicates that all work was turned in to his teachers.

If your teenager is really trying but not earning passing grades, you should have him evaluated for learning problems and request appropriate classroom adaptations. If a student is doing his best on his schoolwork, punishment is not appropriate.

🦋

"As my son approached age sixteen and would soon obtain his driver's license, we talked more and more about the importance of being responsible. I have told him that if he is not responsible about his schoolwork then that makes me wonder if he can be responsible while driving a car. Being allowed to drive is a powerful incentive for him to do as we ask. Driving is probably the most important privilege my teenager has."

🦋

Set Limits/State Expectations. If an issue is serious, you can set limits and state your expectations without first consulting your teenager. For example, if you know or suspect that your sixteen-year-old is planning to do something inappropriate, you might say, "Staying at a motel overnight for a New Year's Eve party is not acceptable to me. I expect you to be home by one o'clock." Or, "Cursing at me is not acceptable. I expect you to talk to me with respect." If your teenager is defiant, state your expectations (I expect you to . . .), and walk away. If you stay and argue, the situation

will probably escalate. If your teenager disobeys you, follow through with a reasonable consequence.

Provide Supervision/Be a Coach. You will have to provide supervision to ensure completion of most jobs, including chores and homework. Supervision of social activities is also important. You need to know where your teenager is, what he is doing, and with whom. How much supervision should you provide a teenager with ADD? The answer is pretty simple: as much supervision as he needs to succeed. Teenagers who act responsibly will be given more freedom and less supervision. The amount of supervision needed will vary. Some young people may need to receive support and some supervision from parents (with the teenager's permission) even in college. This is discussed in more detail in Chapter 12.

This need for supervision or "coaching" can be a major source of conflict between parents and teachers and between the parents themselves. Typically, teenagers follow certain developmental norms. For example, by age 16, most teenagers are responsible for completing their homework, passing their classes, and scheduling and remembering to take make-up exams. Parents will frequently hear teachers say (and it is true) that teenagers have to learn to be responsible for completing their work, remembering to get homework assignments, and remembering to bring home weekly reports. However, teachers and parents sometimes forget to take into consideration that many teenagers with ADD are developmentally behind their peers by two to four years.

Most professionals still do not comprehend how difficult being responsible can be for teenag-

ers with ADD. Parents need to help teach, provide supervision, and "coach" while teenagers are learning to accept more responsibility and follow up on their work. Your teenager *will* master most of these important skills, but not as quickly as adults would like.

🙣

"I struggled with myself regarding how involved I should be with my son. As a former teacher and school psychologist, I felt I was more involved than I should be in his schoolwork. When I didn't provide supervision, he would fail a class or two. He really seemed sorry and wanted to do better at school. Even after he had to go to summer school and it was a very negative experience, he still did not take full responsibility for doing his schoolwork. The hassles and embarrassment of school failure and summer school were too far removed in time to motivate him to complete his schoolwork. I had to stay involved and monitor his homework on a daily or weekly basis or he would fail. I didn't see any valuable lessons to be learned from continuing to let him fail classes. After I started monitoring his schoolwork closely, he began passing all his classes."

🙣

If your teenager is in danger of failing any classes, you may have to monitor homework on a daily basis. You shouldn't wait until the end of the semester to get involved. Specific suggestions for ensuring that homework is done are given in Chapters 8 and 9.

Encourage Your Teenager to Do as Much as Possible for Himself. Although it may be easier and faster for you to do things yourself, it is critically important to encourage your teenager to take as much responsibility as possible for doing his chores and schoolwork and for solving his own problems. You should continually lead him to take the next step in accepting complete responsibility for these activities. If he gets a speeding ticket, he must earn the money to pay for it. He should go to the police department or court, if needed, and handle the details of paying for the ticket. Don't be surprised, however, if you have to remind him when the ticket is due or go with him to court the first time to understand the procedure.

🙣

"Our pediatrician's motto was, 'Never do for Cooper what he can do for himself.'"

🖌

"As a parent, I am an advocate for my son. When I have worked myself out of a job, I will have been a successful parent and advocate. I don't want to be so involved in helping my son succeed in community activities or at school. I continue to decrease my involvement and encourage my son to increasingly accept more responsibility for his future."

Look for the Good/Be Positive

In *The ADHD Report* of April 1993, Dr. Barkley discusses several principles of behavior management for parents to keep in mind when interacting with youngsters with ADD. For example, Dr. Barkley has observed that *children with ADD need positive feedback (reinforcement) more often* than other children do. These basic principles are discussed below. More specific suggestions for improving school performance are included in Chapters 8 through 10.

Provide Feedback Immediately. Teenagers with ADD are governed by what is going on *right now*—today or this week—not some goal or consequence in the distant future. Feedback that is delayed (such as grades at the end of the six weeks) is not particularly effective in motivating a teenager to do a good job. Feedback may need to be given daily or weekly. For example, if you pay your teenager for chores such as mowing the yard, paying immediately after the yard is mowed is more effective than paying at the end of the week. Likewise, you should praise your teenager each day for completing chores or homework.

Provide Feedback More Often. Teenagers with ADD need feedback more often than other teenagers. When teens receive positive feedback more frequently, they tend to do better. Unfortunately, they usually receive more negative feedback than their friends since they are more likely to break rules than teenagers without ADD. Minor misbehavior may be ignored. If important rules are broken, a reprimand or mild punishment may be needed. (See sections below on avoiding negatives, ignoring minor misbehavior, and proper use of punishment.)

Provide Positive Feedback Before Negatives. If you want to change a behavior, don't just punish the problem behavior. Try to find a positive way to change behavior. Incentives may work. "If you mow the yard by Friday (on time), I'll let you stay out thirty minutes later Saturday night (or pay you a five dollar bonus)." Chances are, eliminating the fight over the chore is worth five dollars, plus you may be planning to give him extra money anyway. "If you finish your homework on time, I'll let you stay up thirty minutes later (or I'll let you play Nintendo for thirty minutes before you go to bed)." But remember: unless the incentive is important to your teenager, he will not work to earn it.

Also try telling your teenager what you want him to do, rather than what you don't want him to do. Typically, parents say something like, "I'm sick and tired of you coming in late every Friday and Saturday night." Instead, it may be more effective to say, "I want you to come home by 12:00 or call me if you are going to be later than fifteen minutes." Another example may be, "I want you to start your homework each night by 7:00 or 7:30." Then set up the necessary structure and supervision to ensure he does his homework each day. Give positive feedback or rewards when he completes his homework or does as you ask.

Use Strong, Meaningful Rewards and Consequences. Many teenagers with ADD do not seem to be as sensitive to rewards and punishment, nor to learn as readily from them, as teenagers without ADD. They do not respond very well to traditional rewards and punishment, so typical parent responses such as praise or negative comments alone may not work very effectively. You may find that stronger reinforcers are more effective. Examples of positive reinforcers include praise ("Congratulations. You passed your test"), verbal and nonverbal approval (smiles or head nods), affection (pat on the back or hugs), privileges (driving, TV, phone, Nintendo, movies, concerts, sports), and material things (stereo equipment, Nintendo game cartridges, clothes, or money). Money is usually an especially effective reward for teenagers with ADD if you are willing to pay them to complete certain tasks. Some parents think it is a great idea. They believe that adults receive a pay check for work they do at the office. Why shouldn't teens be paid for some of their work efforts? Other parents, however, feel guilty or irritated that they have to "resort" to using material rewards with their teenager. They argue that a teenager should contribute to the family without being paid. Some parents prefer that teenagers do certain chores to earn their allowance. Unfortunately, due to the nature of ADD, consequences *must* be stronger and more meaningful in order to work effectively. You must make the judgment call. Many parents avoid paying their teenager for completion of homework unless he is in danger of failing his classes.

Table 5-2 BEHAVIOR CHART							
TASK	M	T	W	Th	F	S	S
Completes homework							
Gets up on time for school							
Mows yard (Fri. only)							
Takes trash out (Tues. only)							
Cleans up room (Fri. only)							
Discusses disagreements in reasonable calm manner							

▧

"When I was a single parent, I had to pay someone to mow the yard or do other chores. When my son was old enough to mow the yard, I decided to pay him for the job. That allowed him to earn some extra spending money, which I would have given him anyway, and helped me out at the same time."

▧

Rewards must be something your teenager really likes. "When you finish your homework, you can play Nintendo." Or, if he can wait a whole week for a reward, "You can go to the movies Friday night when you bring home the note from your teacher saying all your schoolwork for the week has been completed."

Use Behavioral Charts. Behavioral charts come in many shapes and sizes. A basic behavioral chart consists of a list of several behaviors that parents want their teenager to do. The teenager may receive checks each day he does them. Parents may specify that once a certain number of checks (points) have been earned, the teenager may have a desired reward—a compact disk, a movie, a skiing trip, money. Desired behavior should be stated in positive terms instead of negative. For example, "discusses disagreements in reasonable way," instead of "doesn't scream and blow up."

Usually, behavioral charts work best with younger children. However, they may still work for middle school students if parents provide a reward that is really important to the youngster. Quite honestly, behavioral programs can be difficult to

implement consistently, especially if parents also have ADD.

By the time your child reaches adolescence, he may feel as though he has been on behavioral programs all his life.

▧

"One teenager with ADD whose mother is a psychologist called the rewards, 'Kibbles and Bits,' after the dog food. He must have felt like a 'trained laboratory animal.'"

▧

Be as Consistent as Possible. One of the basic principles of behavior management is to be as consistent as possible with both rewards and punishment. Your teenager will know what to expect if he behaves a certain way. To put it very simply, he will understand that "good things happen when I behave and unpleasant things happen when I don't."

Once you and your spouse agree on a reasonable consequence, you should try to use it consistently each time. For example, your teenager *cannot* go to the movies or to the mall on Friday night until all his homework is completed. Of course, being consistent is especially difficult if one or both parents also have ADD. Realistically, you should be as consistent as possible, but not lose any sleep over it. A parent would have to be a robot to be consistent 100 percent of the time. Also remember that if a consequence just isn't working or if you decide it is too harsh, you can change it.

Increase Positive Interactions. Although teenagers with ADD need more positive feedback, they are more likely to receive negative feedback because of their misbehavior. It is easy for parents of teenagers with ADD to fall into a trap of having mostly negative interactions with their son or daughter. Negative interactions are emotionally draining for everyone involved. Constant criticism is damaging and may drive a wedge between you and your teenager. You may even reach a point where you have difficulty seeing your teenager's good qualities.

Try to increase positive interactions with your teenager. The world in which we live can be such a negative place. Human nature is such that people complain when something is wrong but say very little when things are done right. It will not be easy for you to change to a more positive way of interacting. Ideally, you should try to get the rate of positive comments and interactions to between 50 and 75 percent. Even if this feels a little phony at first, it will get easier and more sincere with practice.

You may wish to "listen and observe" your own behavior toward your teenager for a day. Count how often you make positive statements. Can you find good reasons to smile at your child, make positive comments, or hug and kiss him? "You did a great job cleaning up your room." "Boy, you must be proud of the 87 you made on your biology test. That's great! Keep up the good work." "The yard looks great. Thanks for mowing it."

In contrast, how many negative statements do you make? "You've got to study; you can't watch TV all evening." "Your handwriting is so messy." "You aren't trying." "You've failed the test." "Don't leave your clothes on the floor. You're such a slob." "You did a terrible job cleaning up the kitchen." "You did a sloppy job of making up your bed."

Are your interactions mostly positive or negative? One of my former teachers, Dr. Charles Madsen, a psychology professor at Florida State University, coined the term "catch the child being good." Parents need to "catch their teenager being good" and brag about the things he does well. If schoolwork has been a major problem and your teenager starts working on his homework without being asked, give him a pat on the shoulder, a smile, or thanks immediately.

Parents should give praise sincerely and in moderation. Find some part of the job to praise. According to Dr. Dale Carter, Director of Psychological Services for Gwinnett County Schools, if praise is too flowery, the child may reject it. Many of these children are very perceptive. If parents praise schoolwork as perfect and the teenager recognizes that it is not, he may not respond positively to his parent's praise.

Remember that there are plenty of people in the world who are willing to tear your teenager down by telling him he is bad or wrong. Few people are willing to spend the extra time and energy required to be positive and build your teenager's self-esteem. It will take a strong conscious effort from both parents to become more positive.

Try Grandma's Rule. "Grandma's Rule" teaches a valuable lesson: "First we work and then we play." "When your schoolwork is completed for this week, you can go to the movies or the mall" (or the activity of his choice). Treatment professionals refer to this behavior management technique as the "Premack Principle."

Verbally, you encourage your teenager throughout the week. Tell him that you know he wants to do well and is trying hard. Check up on him at the end of the week and give him a lot of praise if all the work is done. If his work is done, he gets to do the activity of his choice. If he didn't do all the work, tell him you're sorry—he can go to the movies (or wherever) when his work is finished. Hopefully he'll finish it as soon as possible so he can go. You can be sympathetic and supportive and don't have to be angry, scream, or yell. Exceptions to this consequence, such as when the amount of homework is impossible to complete, are discussed in Chapter 9. If this isn't an effective approach for your teenager, modifications, such as switching to a daily report from the teacher, may be needed.

Start at Your Teenager's Present Level. Avoid putting more pressure on your teenager than he can handle. You need to work with him at his present level of functioning. As mentioned earlier, many teenagers with ADD may be behind developmentally in their ability to accept full responsibility for their schoolwork and chores at home. Since the ultimate goal for a parent is to help their child become an independent, responsible adult, you need to help your teenager accept increasing levels of responsibility. To do so, you will need to peri-

Table 5-3
SHAPING BEHAVIOR
(Successive Approximation)

Goal: To complete homework assignments; ultimately to complete homework independently (know correct assignments and have the right books). Move from Point A to Point B by mastering one step at a time. Each step represents growth and progress toward achieving these goals.

A. Beginning Point: No Homework Done.

  1. Parents get him started; supervise whole time.
  2. Parents get him started; monitor occasionally. Prompt, "You're getting sidetracked," if needed.
  3. Parents get him started; he finishes.
  4. Parent sets timer; he starts homework by self; if he doesn't start, parents prompt after 15 min.; he finishes.
  5. Starts and finishes homework by self; no intervention by parents.

B. Target Behavior: COMPLETES HOMEWORK INDEPENDENTLY.

A. Beginning Point: Doesn't Know Assignments/Doesn't Bring Books Home

  1. He won't write down homework assignments; tells parents he doesn't have homework or that it is completed; even if not true.
  2. He forgets to write down assignments most of the time.
  Parents ask teacher to write down assignments for week at a time; keep extra set of books at home.
  3. He makes effort to write down assignments but often forgets.
  Parents ask teacher homework assignment pattern (Algebra homework four nights a week, tests every two weeks); get phone number for friend in each class in which he forgets assignments.
  4. He remembers to write down assignments sometimes; early afternoon or evening, parents ask if he knows homework; if he forgot, take or send back to school to get books and assignments; or remind him to call friend to get assignments.
  5. He remembers right assignments and books most of time; takes responsibility for calling a friend if needed.
  6. Teenager writes down assignments; brings home right books. Parents don't need to monitor.

B. Target Behavior: KNOWS ASSIGNMENTS/HAS BOOKS.

odically reassess his progress. As he masters one behavior or task, then you can guide him to the next developmentally appropriate step. These new skills will help him move toward accepting increased responsibility and independence.

Unfortunately, parents can't always teach their children everything they need to know. Sometimes they must learn lessons the hard way, by experiencing the consequences of their actions.

"Shape" Behavior. One behavior management technique, called "shaping" behavior, is to praise effort and completion of a job that comes close to meeting your expectations. As described in the two preceding sections, the parent starts at the teenager's present skill level and teaches him skills that move him toward the desired skill.

An example of "shaping" to improve completion of homework is provided in Table 5-3. The teenager, a junior in high school, is in danger of failing a class. If prompted, the teenager is willing to do the homework but he loses track of time and

has trouble getting started on his own. The parent sets the kitchen timer to ring at 7:00 p.m. and then checks on him periodically to make certain he hasn't gotten sidetracked. If he has gotten off task, the parent simply reminds him he needs to get back to his homework. The irritating behavior—getting sidetracked—is a symptom of ADD; so parents don't yell or punish, they just prompt him to get back to work. Typically, once he gets started he is responsible enough to finish the work on his own.

Learning to see growth in mastery of small steps and to be happy with your teenager's progress is important. Many teenagers with ADD may need some "coaching" all their lives, and if that is what it takes for them to successfully cope with ADD, what is wrong with that? For example, your teenager may never progress beyond step 4 (parents prompt to start) while he is in high school.

Praise the Part of the Job That Is Well Done. Sometimes you may inadvertently undermine positive efforts from your teenager. Most teenagers with ADD are not going to do chores as well as adults. They are forgetful by nature and may not pay attention to details. For example, your teenager may mow the yard but forget a section by the porch. The natural response is to complain about the part he forgot. It is more helpful, however, if you do not spend 15 minutes complaining about the section that he missed. Is the glass half full or half empty? Compliment him on the 95 percent of the yard he finished.

After a job is finished, thank him for a job well done. For example, after he has mowed the yard, stand on the porch with him and look over the job he did. Then point out a couple of positive things you noticed or tell him how you feel. "Boy, the yard looks great." "I think our home is the prettiest one in the neighborhood, especially right after you mow our yard." "You did a nice job mowing around the flower bed." If he ran over the flowers, say nothing now. Maybe next time, point out where the flowers are and ask him to be careful. Show him how to mow around the flower bed, if necessary. Damaged flowers can be replanted. Damaged self-esteem is much harder to rebuild.

Sometimes parents can anticipate where problems may arise and discuss them in advance. "The grass is growing into the flower bed and it's hard to tell them apart. Let me mow a strip the first time to show you how to do it."

Identify Antecedent Behavior. Sometimes it helps to identify what is known as antecedent behavior—what happened just prior to misbehavior that may have triggered the teenager's response. For example, a teenager who has trouble handling change may always misbehave when a substitute teacher unexpectedly takes over a class. Once the antecedent or "trigger" behavior has been identified, you may know how to intervene to prevent the misbehavior. (See suggestions in next section.)

Change the Environment. *If you can't change the teenager, change the environment.* Or, if you are already trying to get your teenager to change several behaviors and another troublesome behavior arises, you may want to change the environment instead of the behavior. For instance, if your teenager always comes home late, try beeping him 15 minutes before he is due home or setting his watch to go off 15 minutes before he should leave. Or, as described above, if a teenager misbehaves whenever there is a substitute, the environment could be changed by letting him go to his former resource room class for one period when a substitute is teaching. Another option would be to place a teacher's aide in the classroom when a substitute is present. Obviously, if you can, solve this problem more simply—talk to him and help him practice how to act when a substitute is present.

Build Self-Esteem

Positive self-esteem is critical for a teenager to succeed in school and in life. Dr. Robert Brooks, Harvard Medical School faculty member, author of *The Self-esteem Teacher,* and member of CHADD's Professional Advisory Board, reports that children who have strong self-esteem are more likely to succeed in school, to be highly motivated, to stick with a task, and to believe that they have control over their ability to succeed. A teenager who fails repeatedly and does not receive positive messages from his teachers and parents will have difficulty developing strong self-esteem.

A teenager's self-esteem is built by the successes he achieves at home, at school, and in the community; the skills he builds and the level of competence he feels; and through positive interactions with and positive feedback from the significant people in his life. Helping your teenager find areas in which he can succeed is one of the greatest challenges facing you as a parent. One way to develop a plan to build self-esteem is displayed in Table 5-4. You can complete this same information on the blank form in Chapter 13. Parents need to provide their teenager with the opportunity to master skills, experience success, and feel that he is a special person. The major environments in which a teenager lives and works are his home, school, community, and, for some, a religious environment. You can help create a home environment that makes building self-esteem easier, plus take actions that make other environments more positive.

Build on Your Teenager's Strengths. Dr. Brooks uses the term "Islands of Competence" to describe the special strengths or skills in which each teenager takes great pride. Parents need to help teenagers identify and build on their strengths. The strengths of one teenager are listed as an example in Table 3-1 in Chapter 3. Remember to reframe some of the characteristics pre-

Table 5-4
BUILDING SELF-ESTEEM
INDIVIDUALIZED TREATMENT PLANNING: "DO WHATEVER IT TAKES"

NAME: _Tom_ _____ AGE: _17_ DATE: _9/95_

<u>IDENTIFY INTERESTS:</u> Encourage your teenager to pursue his interests. Give him the opportunity to participate in activities that make him feel special. Build on strengths listed in Table 3-1. List interests or talents such as sports, art, music that skills could be developed further through special training.

* _Swimming_	* _outdoor activities_
* _diving_	* _stereo equipment_
* _electronics_	* _modifying his car_
* _shooting rifle_	*

<u>PARTICIPATE IN ACTIVITIES TO BUILD SELF-ESTEEM:</u> Parents may arrange for their teenager to participate in a variety of activities: a summer computer class, art classes, scuba diving class, modeling, boy or girl scouts, acting in school plays, hunting, fishing, motorcycle racing, water or snow skiing, canoeing, baseball/football/wrestling teams, tennis or golf lessons, summer sports camps, gymnastics, karate, or cheerleading camp. Religious activities should also be considered if appropriate: summer camps, Bible school, singing in a choir, public speaking on programs, or activity retreats (snow skiing, camping). Let the teenager select those activities he likes best. If he has no special interests, parents may sign him up for variety of activities and see what skills emerge as strengths.

* _Scuba diving_	* _Camping_
* _diving or swim team_	* _water skiing_
* _life guarding job_	* _install stereo equipment_
* _Computer class_	* _work on car/install alarm_
* _hunting_	* _Huntsville, AL, Space Camp_

viously viewed as negative and list them as strengths.

List Strengths. Many teenagers with ADD receive so much criticism that they may actually begin to believe that they are lazy and unmotivated. If you ask them to list their strengths, their self-esteem may be so low they may not recognize their own assets. One way for parents to approach this is to say something like this:

"I was reading this book about ADD and I came across this form that parents should complete. According to the directions I am supposed to write down all your strengths that I see at home and at school. This is the list I started. Can you think of any I've missed? (wait for a response) According to the book, sometimes teenagers with ADD don't always realize how many skills and tal-

ents they really have. The other interesting thing the book said is that talents you have, such as high energy (creativity, outgoing personality, or whatever skill is applicable to your teenager), may not be appreciated in school but are very valuable in adults. Oh yes, I just thought of another skill you have. You are really good at...."

Using the blank form (Identifying Strengths) in Chapter 13, you can list the strengths your teenager has in several areas—home, family, school, academic classes, church, community, sports, social interactions, hobbies, personality, appearance, skills, and interest areas. You could save one or two talents to add to the list while sitting with your teenager. Your teenager should be impressed with the long list you have compiled. Your teenager may want to keep a copy and read it on days when he is feeling down.

Encourage Pursuit of Interests. Encourage your teenager to pursue interests and activities that he enjoys. Seeking non-traditional activities which involve smaller groups and one-on-one or small group instruction may give your child a better chance to succeed. For example, you might arrange for lessons in music, ballet, modeling, boy or girl scouts, tennis, racquetball, scuba diving, or water skiing. If needed, you may be able to seek financial assistance from the school counselor or county social services agency, which may have flexible funds available to pay for such services. Some YMCAs may offer scholarships if contacted by a school counselor or treatment professional.

Group activities and recreational sports such as football, basketball, Boy Scouts, or Girl Scouts may be difficult for your teenager. He may not be able to stay with the group while instructions are given, as his mind is a thousand miles away. There are always exceptions to the rule, however. If your teenager expresses a strong interest in trying a particular activity, he may have the motivation to succeed. One option to help them succeed is to take medication, if needed, before participating in the activity.

Select Sports Carefully. Some teenagers with ADD are excellent athletes and will excel in almost any sport. Many, however, are more likely to succeed in sports which require large muscle coordination (swimming, soccer, gymnastics, karate, and wrestling). Sports which require greater hand-eye coordination (basketball and baseball) may be more difficult for them.

❧

"When Robert played Little League baseball, he sat down in the outfield once and began pulling up grass. Another time I looked up and he was trying to catch a grasshopper that was hopping through the outfield. My son is an excellent athlete but he had difficulty with Little League baseball."

❧

Sometimes giving a teenager medication when he participates in sports may help his concentration and performance. This option may not be for everyone, but some parents find it is a helpful solution.

❧

"Baseball is very important to Andrew, but he couldn't concentrate during the game. We decided to give him his Ritalin just before game time. He played so well he won the game ball. He was thrilled. He didn't have any trouble going to sleep because he had so much exercise."

❧

Physical activities that require self-discipline and repetition of a skill, such as swimming strokes, wrestling, martial arts, or gymnastics, may help increase a teenager's self-esteem, self-discipline, and frustration tolerance. This knowledge may be carried over to less interesting situations in ways the teenager can understand. For example, if your teenager seems frustrated when he is memorizing foreign language vocabulary or multiplication tables, you can remind him how important practice is in mastering any skill, whether it is wrestling and gymnastics or academic skills.

Provide Support in Religious Environments. Religious institutions tend to have structured environments similar to schools in which teenagers are expected to sit quietly in their seats, listen to instructions, absorb and understand what is said to them, and follow directions.

In addition, Sunday school teachers and religious leaders may be even less prepared than teachers to deal with problem behaviors in a positive, loving manner. As a result, a teenager's experiences in religious settings may be as negative as his school experiences. What some people fail to realize is that if a teenager is constantly criticized and forced to sit still in a religious setting, he may be learning to hate church or synagogue, religion, and God.

❧

"I once had a church member sitting near me turn and tell me in a hostile and disapproving manner that I needed to make my six-year-old son sit still and listen to the preacher. Angry and hurt at the lack of understanding this person showed, I moved my son to the back pew for the remainder of the service. My

son didn't want to be in church anyway. If I constantly fussed at him for not sitting still, then the only messages he would receive about church and God would be negative ones. He would not receive any positive, loving messages about religion."

⬗

Clearly, any religious staff who interact with your teenager need training regarding ADD. Parents may invite interested staff to attend local CHADD training. It may help to familiarize them with some of the strategies in this chapter, as well as in Chapters 8 and 9.

Match with Good Coaches or Leaders. Some teenagers with ADD can participate in sports or group activities without any extra supports. Others have great difficulty participating successfully in group activities. Finding supportive, charismatic coaches, scout leaders, or religious or activity leaders is critical. It will take a special adult leader to have the patience and skill to bring out the best in your teenager. Leaders who know how to use positive reinforcement to motivate students are especially effective.

If the leaders are receptive, give them tips on interacting with your teenager. Talk to the leader "off the record," and ask him or her to use this information discreetly and not do anything to embarrass your child in front of his teammates. If possible, discuss this with your teenager before you talk to the coach. As a parent you may volunteer to become one of the coaches for the team to help provide the support and supervision your teenager needs or to model how to act for other coaches.

Make the School Environment More Positive. There are many steps you can take to help make the school environment a place where your teenager with ADD can succeed. Chapters 8, 9, and 10 provide suggestions about consistent completion of homework, identification of specific learning and behavior problems, and adaptations to the school program that can be made under federal law. Chapter 11 offers suggestions regarding relevant federal laws and policies that affect students with ADD. Chapter 12 contains guidance for teenagers who have graduated from high school and are making career decisions or are considering college.

Teach New Skills

One approach is to teach your teenager skills, such as problem solving, time management and anger control, that he lacks. This job will not be easy. It will take lots of time and patience!! Don't expect them to learn the new skill the first time you teach it. Practice, practice, practice will be the key. Watch for *teachable moments*—times when he brings up an important issue or things come up naturally in conversations with friends or on TV. If he asks your help solving a problem, discuss his options as explained in the next section. If he asks questions about sex or drugs, be prepared to answer the question then. Obviously with his short attention span, discussions must be brief. Learning to speak in "sound bites"—brief memorable quotes that capture the essence of an issue—is difficult but necessary.

Teach Problem Solving. Teaching a teenager how to solve his own problems is one of the best gifts a parent can give. A teenager who can handle his own affairs will have stronger self-esteem.

To teach problem solving, begin by asking your teenager questions about possible solutions for resolving a problem and helping him identify pros and cons of each option. You or your teenager should write down his options, plus the advantages and disadvantages of each. Visually being able to see his choices should be helpful. Teenagers who write or process slowly will avoid writing the pros and cons themselves, since it will be a very time-consuming process. In this case, you may write the information for your child. Keep this process as brief as possible, since it will be difficult to keep your child's attention for more than fifteen to thirty minutes.

Next say: "We've discussed your options. Now, what is your plan for solving your problem with . . . homework completion (coming home on time)? As long as you have a plan, I will leave you alone to solve it. Is there anything I need to do to help you?" This allows your teenager to assume ownership and responsibility for handling his own problems. Again, he is more likely to follow up on a plan that he selected. Let him attempt to solve the problem on his own, if that's what he wants to do. The plan may include a limited role for you, his parents—perhaps reminding him when to start on homework. If it is unsuccessful, then you can discuss different options with your teenager.

Teach Time Management. To help your teenager improve his management of time, you might help him develop a schedule for a day or week at a time. Use a weekly schedule with the hours marked to help make the abstract concept of time management more concrete and visual. Then show your teenager how to schedule backward to finish a project on time. For example, if a report on the atomic bomb is due Friday, you might begin by asking your teenager these questions: "How long do you think it will take you to finish it? Do you need to develop an outline (or write a draft)? Are there pictures, models to be built, or library books or articles that you must get?"

Depending on your teenager's age and skill level, the schedule may look something like this: Monday after school, visit the library. Read a summary about the atomic bomb from an encyclopedia. Check out two books on the bomb. Photocopy two magazine articles about the topic. (References—two books and two magazine articles—are required.) Begin reading and highlighting important information. Tuesday continue reading the material. Develop an outline. Wednesday write a draft. Thursday write the final draft of the report.

Follow a similar process in scheduling chores and leisure time. For example, if your teenager is supposed to mow the yard, plus wants to visit his girlfriend Saturday afternoon, discuss the schedule with him. "What time do you want to go see Tonya? How long does it usually take you to mow the yard? How long will you need to take a shower and get dressed? What time do you think you need to get up and start mowing the yard?" Time management for college students is more complicated and will be discussed in more detail in Chapter 12.

Teach Techniques for Dealing with Anger. Your teenager can do several things to learn to handle his angry feelings better. You may say something like this. "Sometimes it's harder for teenagers with ADD to handle anger in a reasonable way without blowing up. Being angry is okay. Anger is a normal feeling but you need to learn to handle it in a healthy and safe way. There are *several things you can do when you are angry*: 1) take three deep breaths; 2) hit something such as a pillow, punching bag, or hammer a nail; 3) do some strenu-

ous exercise such as running or swimming; 4) talk to someone such as a friend, teacher, parent or counselor; 5) do something fun such as watch a movie or play a video game to take your mind off the problem; or if you can, 6) look at the humorous side of the situation. Sometimes *you can avoid conflict* with another person who is angry with you by talking calmly, walking away, or if you are at fault, apologize. To *diffuse a tense situation*, you can use humor, stall for time (let's talk about this later when we're calmer), or try to negotiate a compromise."

You may ask your teenager which one of these suggestions might work best for him. You may also help him identify those situations which are most likely to cause him to get upset. After an emotional outburst, you might discuss how he could handle this in the future if the same situation occurs again. Sometimes guidance counselors may offer groups regarding anger control and conflict resolution at school.

Keep in mind, however, that low frustration tolerance and impulsivity will contribute to emotional blow ups even when these youngsters truly wish to stay calm. Medication can be helpful. But the reality is that these emotional outbursts will be a problem for some teenagers with ADD.

Teach How To Do the Job Properly. Sometimes it is a good idea to begin teaching your teenager to do certain basic skills by doing them together, or "modeling" the proper behavior. For instance, when teaching him to make his bed properly, show him how to do it. Don't expect perfection in all areas overnight. Praise him for the portions he does well. Talk and enjoy the interaction as much as possible. Set reasonable standards. Perhaps the bedspread isn't going to be smooth or on the bed straight, but at least it is pulled up. As you continue to teach, over time your teenager will come closer and closer to meeting your standards.

Avoid Negative Interactions

Sometimes a simple "No" from parents is sufficient to set limits for a young person with ADD. At the other extreme, some teenagers with ADD are very strong willed, impulsive, and frustrated. They seem to be constantly butting heads with their parents. As you undoubtedly know very well, teenagers with ADD do things that are extremely irritating to parents. If you chose to do so, you could spend your whole day correcting your child's behavior. Several techniques may help parents avoid negative interactions. For example, ignore minor misbehavior and save reprimands for more serious problems. Or, if you can't change your teenager's behavior, you can always change your own behavior.

Ignore Minor Misbehavior. Because many teenagers with ADD misbehave frequently, many parents make a conscious decision to address only the most important misbehavior rather than respond to each wrongdoing. Ignoring minor misbehavior is a more effective teaching tool than using constant criticism. If parents comment negatively on everything that teenagers with ADD do wrong, they will be exhausted and hostile from all their negative thoughts and comments. In addition, the teenager's self-esteem will suffer. However, if you decide your teenager's behavior is inappropriate and should not be ignored, you should use a negative consequence immediately. Consequences should be reasonable and not harsh.

🐾

"I try to be somewhat laid back about most minor rule infractions. More intense punishment should be reserved for more serious infractions. The things I worry about most involve imminent risk of death or permanent injury. I try not to get 'bent out of shape,' yell and scream, and have major confrontations with my son about his dirty room, dirty clothes, curfew missed by a few minutes, or other less important rule infractions. He faces the logical consequences of the rule infractions but not a ranting and raving mother.

🐾

"Part of my reason for this approach is purely selfish. I don't want to be a screaming lunatic, get upset, feel hostile, raise my blood pressure, and shorten my life span over the trivial things in life."

🐾

Talk about Behavior, Not the Person.
When your teenager gets into trouble, talk about the behavior that was unacceptable, not his personality, values, or ability. You can give your teenager the message that he is a good person even if you are not pleased with his behavior. You might say, "I am very unhappy that you came home late (didn't do your homework). That is not acceptable. You must come home on time or call and let me know you are on your way home (do your homework every night)." Avoid character assassinations, such as, "You're lazy." "You're intentionally being defiant." "You're stupid." "You're just not trying." "You don't care." "You're bad." "You'll never amount to anything." Then develop a plan to ensure that the problem behavior will not occur again.

If your teenager is off-task, try prompting him by making a simple statement about the behavior: "You're getting sidetracked." Don't fuss about not doing homework (finishing a chore) or say anything negative about him ("you're lazy"). Discuss this issue with him before the problem occurs and ask him if you can prompt him when he is off task. "Teenagers with ADD frequently get sidetracked. Is it okay with you if I remind you when you need to get back to work? My cue will be to say, 'You're getting sidetracked.'"

Avoid Power Struggles. When parents give orders to try to make their teenager to do something, a power struggle may develop. Avoiding these power struggles is important. It is extremely difficulty to "win" power struggles with teenagers. If parents try to prove that they are totally in control, the teenager may work equally as hard to prove that parents can't control him. The battle may escalate and erupt into a major power struggle. By winning the battle, you may lose the war. You may win on a specific issue, but overall, family problems may only get worse. If serious conflicts build over time, worst case scenarios may include having your teenager run way or move out and live with undesirable friends.

It is an intellectual challenge to talk with a teenager with ADD and get him to do what you want him to do. Sometimes you may be tempted to say, "You'll do it now, because I said do it." Or, "I forbid you to . . ." This authoritarian approach is difficult to use with teenagers with ADD without making every interaction a major confrontation. *Some of these teenagers are extremely strong-willed, stubborn, impulsive, and frustrated.* If a parent says "no," it is like waving a red flag in front of a bull. The teenager will be determined to do the forbidden activity. If you make a big deal about any issue, such as telling your teenager not to date or run around with certain people, he may embrace the challenge and show you he will do what he wants to do. If the problem is serious and compromise is not appropriate, you can take charge and impose consequences for misbehavior. Possible solutions are discussed in the next section on effective punishment. To avoid a power struggle, you may find it helpful to learn effective ways to say "no" indirectly.

✄

"When Cassie became a teenager, we had to learn not to react to anything she said. If she saw a reaction that meant we might not approve, she was bound and determined to do that very thing. We had to respond intellectually instead of emotionally."

✄

Avoid Badgering. Avoid badgering your teenager about past misdeeds. What's done is done. Focus on the future. Word requests positively. "From here on out, I want you to . . . come home on time . . . complete all your homework assignments." Then come up with a plan to make sure this happens.

Avoid Nagging, Lecturing, and Arguing. Dr. Phelan's four "Cardinal Sins," which parents should avoid at all costs, are real gems.

(1) *Avoid nagging.* Nagging usually doesn't work and only causes friction.

(2) *Avoid lecturing.* The transfer of words of great wisdom from the parent to the teenager doesn't work in these one-sided conversations. "Transplants of insights" from the parent to the teenager, regardless of how well-meaning, don't result in a change of behavior.

(3) *Avoid arguing* with your teenager. Rarely is anyone ever argued into submission. If your teenager continues to argue, you can change your own behavior by refusing to argue. Remember that it takes two people to have an argument. State your bottom line position—"You can't stay out all night. I'll let you stay out an hour later, but I *expect* you to be home by 1 o'clock"—then walk away.

(4) *Avoid spontaneous discussions* about problems. These discussions typically increase irritability and decrease cooperation. Schedule a time to talk to your teenager about issues such as his chemistry project due after Christmas.

As Dr. Phelan reminds parents, *"Your level of aggravation is not always an accurate measure of the seriousness of the problem."* Sometimes because of "emotional dumping or displacement," parents transfer feelings from one situation to another without even being aware of it. Anger over a fight with the boss may be misdirected at the spouse, the teenager, or the dog. Anger at the other parent may occasionally be misdirected at the teenager.

When serious problems arise, parents must take charge. Specific problems such as substance abuse, sexual acting out, pregnancy, truancy, aggression, defiance, and guns are discussed in detail in Chapter 7.

Redirect Interests/Avoid Saying "No" Directly. Parents can often distract a young child from misbehaving by getting him to substitute another activity for the misbehavior. The same strategy may work with teenagers with ADD. For example, if your teenager is picking on his younger siblings, you may redirect his interests by asking him to show you his latest Nintendo video game. You ignore the conflict and never ask him to stop harassing his brother. Likewise, if your teenager is spending time with friends who are a negative influence, you might encourage participation in events with other friends. For instance, if your family plans to attend a sports event or go on vacation and take someone else along, you might suggest two or three friends for your teenager to choose from. You do not criticize the unacceptable friends.

You can learn effective ways to get around saying "no" directly: use tact, redirect your teen's interests, suggest substituting another activity, or buy time for things to cool off by saying, "I don't know. Let me think about this." If you later decide that you don't want your teenager to participate in the activity, you can always suggest a different activity. For example, if you find out that the party your teenager wants to attend is unsupervised, you might suggest that he go see a new movie with a friend instead. Occasionally, reverse psychology may work. For middle school students, say something like, "only very mature and responsible teenagers can mow the yard. I'm not certain you're old enough. Do you think you're ready to accept that level of responsibility?"

Tap Their Forgetfulness. Although it is somewhat embarrassing to mention, occasionally parents may take advantage of their teenager's natural forgetfulness to avoid a confrontation. For instance, if your teenager is nagging you about doing something you don't want him to do—buy a new game cartridge, go to a party—occasionally, you can buy time by saying, "Let me think about it." Your teenager may get busy and forget about his request.

Punish Wisely

When punishment is necessary, you may try these tips. One parenting philosophy parents may want to read more about is described by Rudolph Driekurs, M.D., in his book, *Children: The Challenge* (1964). Dr. Driekurs proposes using logical or natural consequences when a youngster misbehaves or fails to comply with rules. When a "logical consequences" approach is used, the parent allows the teenager to *experience the logical consequences of his actions rather than impose an arbitrary punishment*. The consequence is the result of his actions.

Although the use of logical consequences has many positive aspects, it also has some drawbacks. One major problem is that sometimes natural consequences do not occur quickly enough to be effective. For example, waiting to impose consequences or give rewards until the end of the nine-week grading period is too long for many teenagers with ADD. They have trouble sustaining commitment over a long period of time. Ultimately, they may feel they can't win anyway and may give up. You may therefore have to make some modifications to ensure immediate consequences when using this approach. The definition of "immediate" will vary from teenager to teenager. Some will need daily feedback and others will respond to weekly consequences, such as a weekly report from school.

❧

"A colleague laughingly commented that Driekurs must not have worked with any teenagers with ADD. If he had, he would have entitled his book <u>Children with ADD: The Real Challenge</u>."

❧

Impose Consequences Consistently and Immediately. Consequences for misbehavior for teenagers with ADD need to be consistent, immediate, and reasonable. When possible, consequences should be a natural result of the

teenager's actions. Logical consequences plus positive support may help parents work effectively with their teenager. This process treats the teenager with respect and shows him an immediate cause-and-effect relationship, which tends to be more effective.

If possible, let the logical consequences of your teenager's behavior occur rather than punishing him or putting him on extended restrictions. Admittedly, sometimes it is difficult to think up the most appropriate logical consequence for an action, but the effort is usually worthwhile. Here are some examples of using logical consequences:

• The logical consequence for not making a bed is sleeping in an unmade bed.

• If your teenager doesn't pick his clothes up off the floor and put them in the clothes hamper, he will not have clean clothes. He will have to wash his own clothes or wear them dirty. You can be very sympathetic that he doesn't have clean clothes to wear without yelling and getting upset.

• If your teenager isn't ready to leave for school on time, he will have to get dressed in the car on the way to school.

• If he is too sick to go to school, he will need to stay in bed most of the day. Obviously, he must be too sick to go out with friends that evening.

• If your teenager leaves his games or clothes all over the house, you might put them in the "lost and found" box, which may be put away for a few days.

• If your teenager comes home fifteen minutes late, have him come home fifteen minutes earlier the next night. Some parents may choose to ignore it if their teenager is only ten or fifteen minutes late.

• The logical consequence of failing a class is that your teenager must attend summer school and give up a more leisurely, fun summer. Another logical consequence is that he may not have enough credits to remain with his peers as sophomores or juniors. He may be placed in a homeroom with younger students.

Unfortunately, attending summer school may not always be an effective consequence for teenagers with ADD. This consequence is too far removed in time from his failure to complete class work during the regular school year.

This consequence may also be punishment for the parents because of the imposition of having to drive their teenager to and from class. The cost of summer school is also a negative factor, plus family vacation plans may be interrupted.

✎

"At first my son said that attending summer school was 'no big deal, because all you had to do was show up and you would pass.' He learned the lesson the hard way. He went to summer school and had to work very hard for three hours each day for six weeks."

✎

• The logical consequence of not making passing grades in high school is that your teenager many not be able to get into the college of his choice.

✎

"I am happy if my son makes passing grades. As he approaches his junior year in high school, I have advised him that he needs to bring his grades up his junior and senior years. Otherwise, he will be unable to get into some universities that he might like to attend. The logical consequence of his action is that he may be rejected at a university that he likes. Unfortunately, these natural consequences are too far removed from the present to have a great impact.

"Within the last month, he has expressed concern about the bad grades he has made in the past and talks about improving his grades next year. It is so satisfying to hear him talk this way. However, his grades may be too low to get him in any large universities."

✎

• The logical consequences of receiving speeding tickets is to pay the fine plus any increases in insurance rates. In addition the teenager's driver's license may be suspended.

Unfortunately, delayed consequences may again be a problem. Car insurance rates may not go up for a year and it may take a year or two for a teenager to accumulate enough points to have his driver's license suspended.

Consequences Should Be Brief and Reasonable. For maximum effectiveness, negative consequences should be brief and occur as soon as possible after the problem behavior occurs. When logical consequences or punishments are too restrictive or severe, teenagers with ADD may become terribly angry and resentful. They may become even more aggressive as a result of harsh and unpredictable punishment. In addition, high levels of hostility and power struggles between the parent and teenager are likely. *Sometimes when a power struggle erupts, the teenager focuses energy on getting even with his parents rather than on learning from his mistakes.* The goal, however, is for your teenager to see the consequence as a logical result of his action, rather than as an action you imposed as a punishment.

Some professionals suggest that a teenager be allowed to face the logical consequences of his actions without any parental intervention, regardless of how severe the consequences. For example, if a teenager doesn't do his homework, he will fail all his classes.

Sometimes this approach may be detrimental and unreasonable for a teenager who is having serious academic problems. *It may be better to intervene and monitor his schoolwork on a daily basis, rather than allow him to experience logical consequences that are too harsh* (failing all his classes). Otherwise, the teenager may experience so much failure that he feels overwhelmed. *Remember: teenagers with ADD are more easily discouraged.* "Digging himself out of the hole he's in" will seem impossible. He may not pass to the next grade level and would then be put in the embarrassing position of being in a homeroom with younger students. He may give up, fail more classes, and possibly drop out of school. It is okay for parents to intervene and assist the teenager with his schoolwork. Until a teenager gets hooked on succeeding in school, he will need more encouragement and support than other students.

Don't Make Consequences Too Restrictive. As a general rule, try to make consequences the least restrictive and intrusive as possible. For example, youngsters with ADD have an impaired sense of time. Sending a young child to his room for 15 to 20 minutes seems to be as effective as sending him to his room for hours. In fact in his book *1-2-3 Magic*, Dr. Phelan recommends placing children in time out or sending them to their room for one minute for each year of their age—15 minutes for a 15 year old. Depending upon the misbehavior, parents may elect to send them to their room for 30 minutes to an hour. Remember, however, a teenager's resentment will build and he will focus on getting even when punishment is too harsh.

Except when serious offenses occur, putting a teenager on restrictions for one day or a weekend seems to work as well as putting him on restrictions for a whole week, month, or grading period. Teenagers with ADD appear to remember only that they were punished, not really how long the punishment lasted. In addition, lengthy restrictions are also punishment for the parents, and are less likely to be consistently enforced.

Examples of restrictions that may work with your teenager include: no TV, no phone, no Nintendo, no dating, or no driving, for one to three days, one to four weeks, or for the most serious offenses, a couple of months. The restrictions you choose should depend on the severity of the behavior. For example, restrictions for drinking and driving typically will be much more severe than for having a party while parents are gone or receiving a speeding ticket.

Continue Some Consequences without Increasing Harshness. For some offenses, you may want to repeat the same consequences over and over, even though they don't seem to stop the problem behavior. For example, you may want to continue having your teenager pay for his speeding tickets and taking away driving privileges for a week or more, even though he may receive additional tickets. Remember, even when consequences are imposed, teenagers with ADD sometimes repeat the same behavior. Switching to a harsher punishment may not solve the problem either. The consequences *will* sink in eventually, but it may take three years or loss of your teenager's driver's license.

You should use your own judgement based upon the severity of the problem and risk of danger. For instance, if he gets speeding tickets for going 45 mph in a 30 zone or 65 mph in a 55 zone, you might continue the same punishment. (Speeding tickets are discussed in more detail in Chapter 7.) Sometimes harsher punishments are unavoidable:

⚘

"Our son fell in love with motorcycles at age 14. We bought him a dirt bike hoping that it would be an incentive to improve his grades. Typical incentives did not seem to motivate him. He brought his grades up until we bought the bike and then his grades began to slip again.

"He rode his dirt bike (motorcycle) on a paved street and was given a ticket by a policeman. He was driving without a driver's license and no insurance. Dirt bikes are not street legal and are not intended for riding on paved streets. Thankfully, he was not speeding and he was wearing his helmet. Nonetheless, the bike was impounded (he wasn't old enough to drive it home) and we had to appear in juvenile court. The bike was stored and he could not ride it for a month. This was a pretty stiff consequence but riding on the street was dangerous.

"Our son was told not to ride on the streets again or his bike would possibly be sold or taken to a North Georgia farm where he would have plenty of room to ride. He loved that bike . . . but he rode it again on a paved road and was given another ticket. The bike was moved to North Georgia and placed off limits for three months."

⚘

Give A Second Chance. If your teenager breaks your trust and doesn't handle freedom responsibly, discipline him with a logical consequence. A few weeks later, give him a second chance. Teenagers with ADD must be given numerous additional chances to prove they are responsible until they learn the lesson and can behave appropriately.

Don't be afraid to take a humane approach to parenting. Your teenager is going to make mistakes. One of my colleagues says, "They deserve an occasional 'gimme' also known as 'give me a break.'" Your teenager can learn from a mistake without always having to be punished. Teaching new skills is an alternative to punishment. When my colleague teaches parenting classes, one of the major goals is to help parents remember what it was like to be a teenager. One of the first activities parents do is tell one really stupid thing they did in high school that their parents still don't know about.

Weather Each Crisis as It Comes

One important lesson for you to learn is not to overreact when your teenager experiences the typical bumps associated with having ADD. *In moments of crisis, his problems may appear exaggerated and overblown.* Address the problem, impose a consequence if appropriate, and nudge him back on the "straight and narrow path." Then be prepared for the next "mini-crisis." Don't be surprised if you have a crisis a day, a week, or a month. If you are lucky, you may experience a crisis only once every six months or so. Learning to live one day at a time is critical.

It is important not to overreact and assume, incorrectly, that your teenager is going to be a delinquent. It may help you keep problem behaviors in perspective if you are aware how common they are among teens with ADD. Common problem behaviors of teenagers with ADD and indicators of more serious problems are discussed in Chapters 6 and 7. Some of the tips below may also help you keep your emotions under control.

Manage Your Frustration and Anger. When a teenager with ADD is difficult to manage, his parents may become frustrated, embarrassed, or just plain furious. You should try not to lose your cool, but remember you are dealing with a child with a disability. Dr. Barkley's advice is helpful: "*ADHD children cannot always help behaving in the ways they do: the caregivers can.*"

Some parents become so angry with their teenager that they tell him he is lazy, stupid, bad, or will never amount to anything, or that they wish he had never been born. Other parents may become so enraged that they slap or hit their teenager. Most often, parents don't really mean to react this way, but are very frustrated because they do not understand what is going on with the teenager. The teenager already feels negatively about himself, so angry parental outbursts only add to his self-doubts and damaged self-esteem.

Do you feel angry toward your teenager? Being angry and frustrated with someone who has caused you a lot of grief is a pretty normal reaction. Sometimes parents feel guilty for having these angry feelings. The first step in the process of coping with your anger in a healthy way is to admit to yourself that you have these feelings and then deal with them. Sometimes admitting feelings and talking about them to someone you trust (your spouse, friend, or treatment professional) helps to diffuse and diminish the anger. Holding all the angry feelings inside usually makes things worse.

State Facts and Consequences. When your teenager breaks a rule, calmly state the facts and what the consequences will be. "You haven't finished all your homework this week. When you finish it, you can go to the movies." Avoid placing blame and being angry with him. Be brief. At this particular moment, the less talk the better. Later, when things are calmer, a more reasonable conversation may be held to discuss how to avoid the problem in the future.

Don't Say Things You'll Regret Later. Avoid saying things in the heat of anger that you will regret later. Count to ten. Leave the room, but try to avoid screaming and blowing up.

When Frustration Builds, Take a Break. If you and your teenager are working together on chores or a homework assignment that is particularly frustrating, try taking a break to allow things to cool off. The break may help both of you clear your heads and allow you to tackle the problem with renewed energy. You might comment, "We're both tired, this material is really difficult, and I'm feeling frustrated. I'm being impatient with you and I don't mean to be. Let's take a break." By labeling your feelings, you are also helping your child be aware of his feelings.

⚜

"Now that my son is in college, I am delighted that I am starting to hear some of my comments about feelings being repeated. Sometimes I help him with subjects such as Spanish that require memorization. During a review for final exams, he commented: 'We're both a little impatient because we're uptight about my final exam. It is not going to help me for you to get angry with me. I'm doing the best I can. I'll just be thinking about you being angry when I go into my final rather than thinking about the test. Let's take a break and I'll call you back in a few minutes.'"

⚜

Remove Yourself from Conflict/Give Yourself Time to Cool Off. Avoid overreacting when your teenager disobeys you or gets into trouble. If you are enraged, you might say, "This is

not acceptable. I am very angry. I want to think about what you did and what your consequence will be. Then I'll come talk with you in a few minutes." Then leave: perhaps go into the bedroom or bathroom to regain your "cool." When you calmly walk away, your teenager no longer has an audience. He may also benefit from having time to cool off and rethink his behavior.

If Your Teenager Blows Up, Stay Calm and Lower Your Voice. Especially if your teenager has learning problems, the chances of him becoming frustrated over schoolwork and blowing up are very likely. When this occurs, if you can, stay calm and lower your voice. "I know this is difficult and you are frustrated. Let's take a break." Researchers have found that loud emotional responses from adults result in students becoming more aggressive and producing less schoolwork.

Nurture Yourself.

Being the parent of a teenager with ADD can be very stressful. As Chapter 1 discusses, parents with children who have ADD are much more likely to divorce. Fighting over these teenagers can lead to serious problems in a relationship.

Parents must take care of themselves both individually and as a couple. *People who are loved and nurtured have more energy to give love and support to others.* Parents that experience marital stress and depression perceive their children more negatively than they are and act more negatively toward them. Emotionally bankrupt parents won't have much

love to give to their teenagers. You and your spouse should try to schedule a night out regularly and make certain you do things to have fun together. Do something nice for yourself occasionally. Go to a movie. Go out to eat. Buy something new. Have a massage.

Talk with Your Spouse or a Friend. Sometimes you can diffuse your anger by talking with your spouse, another friend, or relative. You can let off steam and regain your composure. If you and your spouse don't agree on discipline, however, your anger may only escalate if you talk with each other. In this situation, you may need to talk to someone who is not emotionally involved in the problem. Step-parents in particular may first need to talk with a friend to let off steam so that they can talk with the teenager's natural parent in a reasonable way. Usually, natural parents have more tolerance for their teenager's behaviors than step-parents do.

Exercise May Help. When you are anxious or upset with your teenager, try jogging, going for a walk in the neighborhood, or walking on a treadmill. Exercise is a natural way to reduce tension and make you feel better. This may also give you some time to develop your strategy and cool off.

Seek Professional Help. Sometimes talking about your feelings with a treatment professional can help. The professional you choose should be able to offer you two sources of help. First, he or she should help you reduce some of your anger toward your child by talking about frustrating issues. The professional can also help you learn to avoid conveying anger inappropriately to your teenager. Secondly, you can learn new skills for coping with your teenager with ADD and the stresses on your family and marriage.

In choosing a counselor, look for someone who understands ADD and the related parenting frustrations. Local parent support groups such as CHADD may be able to help you find someone who has a good understanding about ADD.

Practice Forgiveness. Dr. Barkley's last piece of advice for parents is powerfully compassionate. He encourages parents at the end of each day to forgive their teenager, to forgive others who have misunderstood their child, and, last but not least, to forgive themselves for less than perfect parenting.

Table 5–5
GUIDING PRINCIPLES FOR PARENT/TEENAGER INTERACTIONS

These guiding principles for interacting with your teenager should help improve communications within the family plus interactions around specific issues such as chores and homework.

1. Give unconditional positive regard
- Reframe your perception of ADD
- Keep a disability perspective
- Enjoy your teenager
- Nurture with touch

2. Treat your teenager as an equal partner
- Give choices
- Set reasonable expectations
- Negotiate/consider compromise
- Depersonalize problems
- Assume good intentions

3. Maintain good communications
- Listen when your teenager talks
- Listen without being judgmental
- Use active listening
- Give "I" messages
- Smooth ruffled feathers
- Encourage expression of feelings
- Teach by example
- Avoid subconscious negative messages

4. Understand factors influencing behavior

5. Provide structure and supervision/Be a coach
- Establish a daily routine
- Develop rules and consequences
- Develop a contract
- Schedule chores
- Give advance notice and time frames
- Link responsible behavior to privileges
- Set limits/state expectations
- Provide supervision/be a coach
- Encourage to do as much for himself as possible

6. Look for the good/Be positive
- Provide feedback immediately
- Provide feedback more often
- Provide positive feedback before negatives
- Use strong, meaningful rewards and consequences
- Use behavioral charts
- Be as consistent as possible
- Increase positive interactions
- Try grandma's rule/"first we work and then we play"
- Start at your teenager's present level
- Shape behavior
- Praise part of job well done
- Identify antecedent behavior
- Change the environment

7. Help build self-esteem
- Build on your teenager's strengths
- List strengths
- Encourage pursuit of interests
- Select sports carefully
- Provide support in religious environments
- Match with good coaches or leaders
- Make the school environment more positive

8. Teach new skills
- Teach problem solving
- Teach time management
- Teach techniques for dealing with anger
- Teach how to do job properly

9. Avoid negatives
- Ignore minor misbehavior
- Avoid character assassinations/talk about behavior not the person
- Avoid power struggles
- Avoid badgering
- Avoid nagging, lecturing, and arguing
- Redirect interests/avoid saying no directly
- Tap their forgetfulness

10. Punish wisely
- Use logical consequences
- Impose consequences consistently and immediately
- Use brief and reasonable consequences
- Don't make consequences too restrictive
- Continue some consequences without escalating harshness

11. Weather each crisis as it occurs
- Manage your frustration and anger
- State facts and consequences
- Don't say things you'll regret later
- When frustration builds, take a break
- Remove yourself from conflict/cool off
- If the teenager blows up, stay calm, lower your voice

12. Nurture yourself
- Talk with your spouse or a friend
- Exercise
- Seek professional help
- Practice forgiveness

CHAPTER SIX

COMMON BEHAVIORS OF TEENAGERS WITH ADD

"It seemed like I was always in trouble with my parents. Since third grade I felt like I had been grounded my whole life. I forgot my chores a lot. If Dad asked me to bring my dirty clothes to be washed, I forgot to do it. I would forget to clean my room. I felt like my parents didn't trust me. Sometimes I didn't always tell them the truth because I knew they didn't trust me anyway."

—*Shawn, describing life prior to diagnosis of ADD when he was 15*

┊

"When I'm not on my medicine, I drive real bad. I forget to stop at red lights and sometimes I stop at green lights."

—*a 16–year-old male*

┊

"Punishment at the time given seems to devastate Lewis but consequences are soon forgotten."

—*a parent*

┊

"Sometimes I have trouble getting to sleep at night. I always have so many things I want to do, like work on my car, stereo system, Nintendo, or on anything electronic. I get busy and can't get to bed on time."

— *Alex, age 16*

┊

Clearly, being the parent of a teenager with ADD is not an easy job. Your child's impulsivity, in-attention, and other classic symptoms of ADD can be very challenging. In addition, these symptoms may result in troublesome behaviors that are not listed in the official DSM IV diagnostic criteria. For example, many teenagers with ADD act younger than they are, are forgetful, argue or talk back, are hard to wake up, have a messy room, don't learn from discipline, get speeding tickets, or act without thinking of the consequences of their actions. When these behaviors occur, parents are sometimes bewildered and angry.

Since the DSM IV tells only part of the story about ADD, this chapter describes what it is like to live with a teenager with ADD on a day-to-day basis at home. (For information on common *school*-related behaviors, see Chapters 8, 9, and 10.) Depending on the severity of his symptoms and the presence of other coexisting problems, your teenager may have some or many of these characteristics. This chapter offers brief suggestions for coping with these problems, with the goal of helping parents and professionals treat the disorder more effectively. This information should also help parents anticipate and possibly avoid some problems. An easy-to-reference chart of common behaviors and solutions is provided at the end of the chapter (Table 6–1).

A primary reason for describing these ADD behaviors is so that parents will realize how common they are. If your teenager misbehaves, you may be less likely to overreact and believe that the behavior is a sign of laziness, intentional defiance, or budding delinquency. It may also be reassuring to you and your teenager to realize you are not alone. Parents are often surprised and relieved to learn that teenagers with ADD act so much alike. They assumed their teenager was the only one who behaved in such an irritating manner.

※

"When I talked with other parents at our CHADD group, I was amazed at how similar our sons' problems were. It's nice to know other teenagers with ADD do the same things."

※

As a parent of a teenager with ADD, you can find plenty of problem behaviors to criticize. However, you will be worn out physically and emotionally if you correct every misbehavior. You must pick your battles carefully, use reprimands sparingly, and deal assertively with misbehavior which could harm your teenager or others. Even though your teenager has many of the behaviors described in this chapter, you may be more successful if you pick one or two behaviors that are most disturbing and work on improving those. (See the example described in Table 6–2 at the end of the chapter.) You can't solve all problems overnight. Plus, punishment is not going to make those behaviors that are a direct result of ADD—disorganization, forgetfulness, lack of awareness of time—disappear. Your teenager *can* learn to compensate for these problems as he gets older, but it will take time.

Independence and Freedom

Independence and freedom are a high priority for teenagers with ADD. One parent described it as "irresponsible independence." They believe they have perfect, responsible judgment. Frequently, however, they want more freedom than parents believe they are ready to handle. They don't want anyone to tell them what to do. Dr. Sydney Zentall explains that these youngsters seem to have a greater need to be in control than their peers.

※

"Cassie had been to Nepal twice and climbed the Himalayas by the time she was twenty-two."

※

"Alex, at age sixteen, was adamant about going to Panama City, Florida, unchaperoned, with a group of his friends for a week during Spring break. He didn't have a clue why I objected."

※

"These teenagers want so much freedom. Sometimes, they can't seem to set limits for themselves. They need external limits but balk against them. Instinctively, they know they need limits but resist them anyway."

※

Encourage Independence/Trust Your Teenager. Try to give your teenager as much freedom as you feel he can cope with successfully. Give him numerous opportunities to make his own decisions. Sometimes, this means trusting him, even though you are ambivalent and anxious and may not feel he deserves your trust. You are conveying an important message to your teenager: "I trust you."

Be Observant. You should be discreetly observant and intervene when your teenager isn't handling his independence well. It may be necessary to regroup and take away privileges, but extend them again later to give him a second chance. For example, you go out of town for the weekend. You give permission for a friend to spend the night to keep your son company. No one else is allowed to be there. Later you find out he had a party at the house. You put him on restrictions for a weekend. A month later you go out of town again but make it clear, no partying. You give him a choice of staying by himself with one friend or having another adult stay with him. If he breaks his word and has a party, the next time you are out of town an adult will have to stay with him.

Consider Compromise. Perhaps you can structure the proposed activity so that your teenager is more likely to handle the independence successfully. For example, a brave parent may volunteer to accompany a group of teenagers to the beach for a Spring Break weekend. This is considered a "win-win" situation. Through this compromise, both the parent and the teenager are happy. The teen is allowed to go to the beach with friends and the parent is along to provide some level of supervision.

Offer An Attractive Alternative. If your teenager wants to participate in a forbidden activity, try presenting an alternative. Bear in mind that any activity offered as a substitute must interest your child and provide sufficient freedom. For example, suppose you discover that your child and some friends have rented a motel room for a New Year's party. After telling your child you do not approve, you may offer to let him have a party in your basement with unobtrusive adult supervision. Or, as described below, you might offer to take him and several friends to the lake.

You should also anticipate that major events such as a prom or New Year's Eve will spark your teenager's need to do something different and exciting. It may help to propose an interesting activity *before* your child has ideas of his own. Having an overnight party where the teenagers can stay up all night and play pool, Nintendo, or cards, or watch movies may be appealing to them. Other parents may be willing to help supervise the event.

🌿

"On prom night, we offered to feed our son and his friends breakfast at 2:00 a.m."

🌿

"To celebrate New Year's we took fourteen teenagers to the lake to spend the night. They stayed up all night, watching movies and playing pool. The next day they went for boat rides, and one brave soul put on a wet suit and went water skiing."

Disobedience/Conflict with Parents and Teachers

Teenagers with ADD don't always do as their parents and teachers ask them to do. On the surface, this may look like intentional defiance. Most often, however, their failure to comply with requests is inadvertent.

There are a variety of reasons they may not comply with adult requests. Sometimes they simply forget what was asked of them. Other times they may disobey their parents and teachers because they weren't listening and didn't hear instructions. Their immaturity and impulsivity may also contribute to this problem. They have trouble focusing on one activity, so they move from one activity to another. Sometimes they become wrapped up in other activities, totally losing track of time. The next thing they know, it's 9:30 p.m. and they haven't started on their homework yet. They tend to avoid unpleasant jobs and keep putting off or forgetting to mow the yard. Conflicts may be heightened because teenagers with ADD often seem oblivious to rewards and punishments aimed at changing their behavior. In addition, frustration over other issues such as undiagnosed learning problems or school failure may surface through angry, defiant confrontations with parents over seemingly minor things.

State Rules Clearly. Rules and responsibilities must be clearly stated. Sometimes it helps to post them in writing.

Develop Rules Jointly. Teenagers with ADD may be more likely to remember and comply with rules they help develop. A few, simply stated rules are usually better.

Teenagers with ADD Act Younger

Teenagers with ADD may act younger than they are. According to Dr. Russell Barkley, their social development is approximately 30 percent behind their peers. In addition, if they have learning problems, their communication skills may be somewhat impaired. For example, many teenagers with ADD may have trouble following and remembering lengthy explanations or requests (listening comprehension) or finding the right words to answer quickly or in an organized manner (verbal expression). These learning problems must be extremely frustrating to teenagers since their intelligence is usually not affected and they may be very bright. (See the discussion on learning problems in Chapter 10.)

Your teenager may want the privileges "due a person of his age," yet may not handle them very maturely. Sometimes, you may be deeply disappointed or even infuriated because your child is not as responsible as someone his age should be. But this behavior is part of having ADD.

Adjust Expectations. Parents and teachers should adjust expectations for the teen with ADD to a more appropriate age level. Don't be surprised when your 16–year-old continues to forget chores, procrastinates about homework, repeatedly comes home late, leaves his room and the garage a mess, and argues and talks back. Don't take this misbehavior personally. Most likely, the teenager is not intentionally trying to make you miserable. As discussed in Chapter 5, the symptoms of ADD are the underlying cause of many of these problems.

Ask His Help Solving Problems. Even though your 16–year-old acts like he is 13, try some of the suggestions in the preceding chapter that treat him as a respected partner in the treatment process—ask his help in problem solving, teach him the desired behavior, or if needed, impose a reasonable consequence without a verbal fight or character assassination. Remembering your child's actual maturity level, yet treating him without condescending and with the respect due a 16–year-old, requires a delicate balancing act.

Expect Impulsive Behavior

Impulsivity is one of the major characteristics of teenagers with ADD. If a thought crosses their mind, they may act on it. If they think it, they'll probably say it. Or stated another way, "In one ear and out the mouth." According to psychologist Dr. Robert Brooks of Harvard Medical School, a teenager with ADD is more likely to say, "Ready. *Fire!* Aim," rather than the traditional sequence. You can also add an "Oops!!" to the end of this sequence, since they often say or do things they wish they could take back. They have a terrible time keeping secrets. They live for the moment, and delaying gratification is very difficult for them. They want to open their Christmas or birthday presents early. If they earn money, they want to spend it. Being untruthful may also be a manifestation of their impulsivity.

🦋

"I was driving down a winding mountain road when Steven, who was sitting in the back seat, suddenly threw his blanket over my eyes and I couldn't see a thing. He was only eight and had heard me say I could drive this road blindfolded. Oh well . . . that is what I said."

🦋

"At age 15, Robert, who had only a learner's permit and had to be accompanied by an adult, took several friends in the family car to McDonald's without his

parents' permission. In the excitement, he locked the only key in the car. He had to call his father to come get him."

🦋

"When I was eight, my Dad told me what he bought Mother for her birthday. I got excited and told her. Dad was so angry, he spanked me."

🦋

Anticipate When Impulsiveness May Cause Problems. Often you can anticipate when difficulties will arise because of your teenager's impulsiveness and plan an appropriate intervention. If he is so excited he can't wait, buy a small gift for him to open the night before Christmas or his birthday. If he is working and earning money, talk with him in advance about putting the money in a savings account. Don't tell him secrets you don't want known.

Avoid Tempting Your Teenager to Act Impulsively. If possible, provide supervision after school or keep your teenager busy with constructive extracurricular activities such as sports. If you suspect that he may be driving the car without permission, simply put the car keys away so he can't find them. Or note the mileage on the odometer to see if it is driven while you are gone. If he drives it, you have several options. Don't say anything, but put the car keys away so he is not tempted to take the family car out for a drive. Or say, "I know you drove the car without permission. Don't do it again. You can't drive the car by yourself until you are 16." Or you make the preceding comment, plus put the teenager on restrictions for a day or weekend.

Medication May Be Helpful. As Chapter 4 explains, medication helps reduce impulsive behavior for most teenagers with ADD. They are less likely to blurt out comments or act impulsively.

Difficulty Paying Attention

Teenagers with ADD don't seem to pay attention when parents talk to them. As noted earlier, problems with listening comprehension contribute to their difficulty paying attention. Dr. Brooks describes children with ADD as viewing the world through a wide-angle lens. They seem to pay attention to everything at once and have trouble selecting what is most important and should receive their attention. For example, they enjoy the thrill of driving and handling the car while being oblivious to their speed. Because they may be speeding, playing with the car radio, or aren't paying attention to an approaching car or a road hazard, they are more likely to have accidents.

Although they have trouble paying attention in many situations, teenagers with ADD can sometimes "over focus"—concentrate on a single activity for hours. Activities such as Nintendo or computer games that are high interest or have a more intense one-on-one interaction can often hold their attention for hours. Their ability to over focus may be misleading to adults. Parents/teachers may believe the teenager is deliberately not paying attention in other situations.

For more information on listening problems, see the section below and Chapter 10. Chapter 7 covers more serious problems related to inattention such as car wrecks.

Are You Listening to Me?

Trying to talk with a teenager with ADD can be an exercise in frustration. While the parent is talking, the teenager may look around, continue to watch TV or work on the computer, or walk away from the parent in mid-sentence. One of the questions parents most often ask is, "Are you listening to me?" Since the teenager doesn't appear to be listening or "showing proper respect," parents can't help being irritated.

〰

"When I tried to talk to Alex when he was growing up, I wondered if he was listening to me. Getting his undivided attention was almost impossible unless he was on medication. Eye contact was usually brief and I always had the feeling that he was not listening. He always looked as though he was ready to leave, had more important things to listen to, or wanted to be doing something else. This occurred whether I was scolding him for something he did wrong or even bragging on him for the good things he did."

〰

"When Lewis (age 16) is on his medication, he will actually stand still long enough to listen to what I say. He can carry on a conversation and seems more mature. He seems like he is three years older."

〰

"Lots of times when I wanted to talk to Steven when he was in elementary school, he seemed preoccupied and wanting to do something else. Sometimes I had to tell him, 'Steven, come over here right now. Stand right here and stay there until I finish.' Otherwise he would walk away while I was still talking to him."

〰

Make Eye Contact/Use Touch. Sometimes, getting your teenager's undivided attention is the hardest part about talking with him. You may not have to use all these steps to get his attention, but here are a few suggestions: Stand or sit in front of him (close proximity). Then gently place your hand on his shoulder or knee (touch). Say his name (sound), and then begin talking. Usually, the teenager will make eye contact with you. Avoid turning this interaction into an unpleasant power struggle. Even if he won't look at you, you most likely have his attention. Keep your comments brief and leave.

Keep Instructions Brief. Many of these teenagers cannot remember more than two or three things at a time and will have trouble picking the important points from a parent's lengthy "sermon." The teenager very quickly "tunes out" and begins thinking about other things. When giving instructions, keep them brief and to the point. "Robert, please do two things before you go out tonight. First, clean your room, and second, tell me when it is finished so I can check it out."

Avoid Preaching. Sometimes, it is tempting to take this opportunity to preach: "Your room is like a pig sty. You never clean your room. You'd walk knee deep in garbage before you'd clean it up." Avoid preaching. Most likely, you'll be wasting your time and energy. You may also be tempted to talk about things that have to be done tomorrow or next week: "Remember you've got to work on your chemistry project tomorrow." By this time, your teenager has already "tuned out" and his mind is miles away. As explained in Chapter 10, many of these teenagers have learning problems (inattention, listening comprehension, and memory problems) which make it more difficult for them to understand and follow directions.

🐾

"When giving instructions to their teenager, parents should make eye contact first. Stating tasks numerically may help.

"Every detail must be stated: 1, 2, 3. Don't assume it will be done if it's not stated every time—i.e., '1. Go to the store.; 2. Don't go anywhere else.; 3. Come straight home.'"

🐾

Write Instructions Down. As a reminder, either you or your teenager may write down brief instructions.

Accept His Listening Style. Sometimes, teenagers do hear what you are saying even though they appear not to listen. You may elect to ignore your teenager's restlessness and apparent inattention and accept his unique listening style under certain conditions. For example, if he continues to play Nintendo and can repeat your instructions, then he may not need to look at you or write down instructions. However, if he does not follow through with instructions or does not answer questions, then try the suggestions above.

Forgetfulness/Doesn't Do Chores

Having to constantly remind your teenager to do his chores can be a major frustration. Actually, forgetfulness and inattention sometimes combine to cause problems with compliance. Sometimes forgetfulness can give the appearance of intentional disobedience. In reality, the teenager may not be paying attention, hears only a portion of the instructions, fails to recognize the key words of instruction in the sermon about a dirty room ("clean your room"), or procrastinates and then forgets what he was supposed to do.

Make a Written List. Making lists of chores or other responsibilities such as a doctor's appointment may provide a helpful reminder for your teenager. Try putting "Post-it" notes in a conspicuous place as a reminder. A note may be placed on the bathroom mirror, door to his room, top of his books, or jacket. A reminder placed on the steering wheel of the car he drives may help him remember

to turn in the note for his excused absence or to ask about make-up work.

🐾

"Now that he is a teenager, sometimes I make a list of things he has to do before he can go out with friends. He can't remember all his chores if I just tell him. It's better to make a list."

🐾

"The most wonderful thing happened last week. I walked into my son's room and saw a list of 'things to do' that he had written. I think that must be the first list he has ever made for himself. He's eighteen now and a freshman in college. I was elated!"

🐾

Quite frankly, it would be nice to tell your teenager with ADD to do something only once and have him remember to do it. However, don't hold your breath. You will need to remind him frequently if tasks are to be completed.

Help Get Started/Show How to Do. You may help your teenager get started on his chores. You may also have to do some chores with him to show him how they should be done or how to get organized to complete a job. For example, when cleaning the garage, have your teenager pick up the largest things and put them away. Next concentrate in one area, maybe one-fourth of the garage, until it is all cleaned up.

Ask What Would Help. On one of your more patient days, talk with your teenager about chores. "You haven't cleaned up the garage yet. Is there a problem? Do you need some help?" As you talk with him, you may realize he feels overwhelmed, doesn't know where to start, and has trouble making himself begin the job.

Their ability to concentrate and pay attention to high interest activities combined with their poor memory contributes to some interesting contradictory behavior.

🐾

"Frequently, they can't remember their chores or other requests. They may forget to feed the dog, take the garbage out, mow the yard, or bring down their laundry. They may not remember their homework assignments. They forget major semester pro-

jects that are due after the Christmas holidays. . . . But they can remember every verse to every rock and roll or rap song."

🖋

"Getting started and finishing classwork and homework is especially difficult for these teenagers . . . but they can play Nintendo for hours."

Disorganization/Losing Things

Many teenagers with ADD are disorganized in their personal lives and at school. They lose things such as clothes, shoes, jewelry, games, books, or tools. Messy rooms are another manifestation of their disorganization. They take electronic devices apart and somehow never manage to put them back together. The garage, like their room, is usually a wreck and tools are never put back in their place. Some teenagers seem to live out of their cars. Missing clothes, books, homework, and tools may be found in their cars. Strategies for dealing with disorganization at home are discussed below; for disorganization at school, see Chapters 8, 9, and 10.

🖋

"My husband is the most patient person I know, but the one thing that drives him crazy is the constant mess in our garage. Tools are strewn all across the garage from when our son has worked on his car. When he cleans out his car, he sets papers and clothes on the floor. He never puts the trash in the can or puts his cleaning supplies back on the shelf after he washes his car. We have had water hoses run over and ruined because they were left in the driveway after the car was washed. We can never find the hammer or screwdriver when we need it. We must have bought hundreds of screwdrivers over the years and they always disappear. About once every six months we all go down and clean out the garage."

🖋

"Even as a high school student, my son has lost coats, clothes, shoes, and his high school senior ring. He stays overnight with friends and leaves his clothes. He doesn't even remember they are missing, let alone where he left them."

🖋

Put His Name on Possessions. Put your teenager's name on his clothing and books with a magic marker or on other possessions with an engraver.

Purchase Less Expensive Items. Until your teenager is older and more responsible with possessions, you might want to purchase less expensive items of clothing or other possessions. If losing things is a frequent occurrence, you might have your teenager buy replacement items himself or do without. You may also have him visit the school "Lost and Found" to look for his things.

Help Your Teen Be Organized. You will probably spend a lot of time helping your teenager with organization. Encourage him to have a specific place for his belongings. School books are placed on his desk. Nintendo games are placed in a special rack. When homework is finished, follow a routine for getting all books and assignments together and ready for school the next morning as suggested in Chapter 9. You can help by providing storage areas that will help your teenager be organized—plenty of shelves, a desk, stack baskets with labels for schoolwork. As Chapter 5 discusses, you should also be teaching time management constantly.

Serve as a Coach. As noted earlier, Dr. Hallowell (*Driven to Distraction*) suggests that coaches are helpful, even for adults, to improve organization and give reminders about important responsibilities. Parents often serve in this role as a coach for their teenager.

List Steps for a Clean Room. Don't assume your teenager knows what you mean when you say "Clean your room." To him, it may mean pushing everything under the bed or in the closet. Make a list of key activities: make up bed, hang up clothes, pick up things off floor, put them in closet, and vacuum. Most likely, your teenager is not going to make up a bed as well as an adult. You may have to show him how to do it. For starters, just pulling up the bedspread may be a great improvement.

Help with Cleaning/Organizing. You may want to work with your teenager to straighten the room/garage on a weekly or monthly basis as you teach him how to keep things in order. Make this learning opportunity as pleasant as possible. Listen to music, talk about hobbies or his plans for the evening. In the process, your teenager learns that everything has a place. If clothes or games are put away in their proper place, they can be found the next time the teenager wants them.

⚶

"I keep thinking that the logical consequence of never being able to find anything in his room will hit him one day. So far, it hasn't worked. He still doesn't clean up his room. Occasionally, I remind him that if his room were clean he would be able to find things. I state it matter-of-factly, not sarcastically."

⚶

Close the Bedroom Door. You may elect to close the door to your teenager's room so you don't have to look at the mess. Teenagers with ADD give their parents plenty of other reasons to be angry. You must pick your battles and decide which behaviors are most important to try to change. You may decide to save your reprimands for other issues.

Lack of Awareness of Time

Teenagers with ADD are often late for meals or family events because they lose track of time. They also have difficulty guessing how long it will take to finish a task. For example, if they are getting ready to go somewhere, they may not allow enough time to get dressed, plus they may not check ahead to see if all the clothes they need are ready.

⚶

"I had a brunch to celebrate the high school graduation of six teenagers who had ADD. As you can guess, they were late. A car broke down. They forgot to call me and tell me. But I had already anticipated all the scenarios of what could go wrong. I didn't start cooking the eggs until they arrived at my house. They were two hours late, but I didn't get upset. Fortunately, my husband and I have learned to be very flexible. I enjoy them and their enthusiasm! Life is never dull when they are around."

⚶

Set a Wristwatch Alarm for Key Times. Your teenager can set his alarm for two or three important events that he must remember: time to

leave for school, time to take medicine, time to do homework, time to get ready for bed, or time to leave a friend's home, a party, a dance, etc. With the alarm set, he can relax and enjoy himself without worrying that he will be late. You may need to remind him to set the alarm before he leaves the house. Some wrist alarms will go off each day at the same time without being reset.

Rent or Buy a Beeper. This idea might not be for everyone, but it solved one family's problems of having their son lose track of time and come home late.

⚶

"We finally bought our son a beeper so that we could find him when we needed him. Dinner time seemed to sneak up on him. He would be somewhere and lose track of time. He wouldn't be home when we were ready to eat. Now I beep him about 15 minutes before dinner and he is home on time. If he is running late coming home from a date, I may beep him to remind him of the time. Sometimes when we are out of town, we beep him with a code, '1974,' which is his birth year, to remind him to take his medication."

⚶

Teach Awareness of Time. Time management is discussed in Chapter 5. (College students, also see Chapter 12).

Difficulty Planning Ahead

Teenagers with ADD may have trouble planning ahead when it comes to schoolwork or social or family events. They prefer to do things on the spur of the moment. Trying to get them to make a commitment to participate in a future activity may be very difficult.

Teach Planning and Time Management. You will need to actively work with your teenager to help him get in the habit of planning ahead. You may, for example, include him when planning for family activities. As discussed in Chapter 5, using a weekly calendar to help with time management plus making a "to do" list may be helpful. Plan backward from the final day and estimate time required for each step. For example, help your teenager write on the calendar the individual steps involved in planning for a trip: e.g., May 15, leave for Florida; May 14, pack; May 13, select clothes to take on trip; make sure they're clean; May 10, get traveler's checks, buy swimsuit; May 1, last day to bring in permission slip and deposit.

More Difficult to Discipline

Traditional punishment doesn't seem to work as effectively with teenagers who have ADD. They don't seem to learn from their mistakes or parental punishment as easily as most teenagers do. Some parents will say that their teenager doesn't respond to discipline. No matter what the parent does, it never seems to make a lasting difference. The teenager will repeat the misbehavior. Or he may repeatedly do something dangerous. Sometimes, these young people don't seem to make a connection between their misbehavior and consequences.

✍

"When I'm not on Ritalin, I forget why I was grounded and feel like my parents are just being mean to me. It doesn't connect in my mind that I really did something wrong. Punishment doesn't work a lot of times because it doesn't connect in my mind."

—a sixteen-year-old

✍

"Cassie never seemed to learn from experience like other children. If a parent says to a young child, 'Stove hot!', most children learn if they touch it just once. But Cassie had to touch the stove each and every time to find out the one time when it was hot."

✍

Because traditional punishment doesn't seem to work, parents may resort to using harsher discipline than they feel should be necessary. The teenager's behavior is exasperating at times and it is easy for parents to lose control of their emotions.

As explained in Chapter 1, many experts believe that biochemical deficiencies are to blame for the difficulty teens with ADD have following rules and their reduced sensitivity to rewards and pun-

ishment. A key point to remember is that *most of their misbehavior is not malicious, intentional defiance of parents or other authority figures or a flagrant disregard of the rules.*

These factors should influence how you discipline your teenager. If symptoms of ADD appear to be the major reason for the problem—coming home late—you may decide not to punish but to teach your teenager a system for remembering to come home or simply beep him 15 minutes before he is due home. You should avoid frequent hostile interactions with your teenager since it may result in even more serious problems later on.

✍

"Steven always loved his bicycle when he was in elementary and middle school. Whenever he received low grades, we put his bicycle up in the attic for the next six-week grading period. The bicycle was in the attic more often than not. He really seemed sorry that his grades were low and promised to work hard to bring them up. He would bring his grades up and get his bicycle out of the attic. Next six weeks, the bicycle was back up in the attic."

✍

"No punishment was ever effective! Shawn got to the point that he didn't care when we punished him. As a young child when we took away his toys, he'd play with toothpicks, or make shadows with his fingers.

"At first, grounding Shawn seemed to work, but eventually he got to the point that he would say, 'I'll be grounded the rest of my life—but it won't make any difference.'"

✍

"Punishment at the time given seems to devastate Lewis, but consequences are soon forgotten. If he is on restrictions, it seems like he falls asleep if he slows down. Lewis says he wishes 'he could be in a coma' so that time would go faster."

✍

"When he was eight or nine, Alex told me somewhat apologetically, 'I'm sorry Mom, but when you punish me, it just doesn't seem to work.'"

✍

Many times the teenager seems genuinely sorry when he does something wrong, but has trouble maintaining his good intentions.

✥

"Our sons would appear extremely remorseful about something they did wrong, such as not doing homework, would make a commitment to do better, but could not maintain their good intentions. They sincerely wanted to do better but had great difficulty following through on their promises."

✥

Since some teenagers act out impulsively without forethought or planning, they are more likely to get caught by parents or the police. Dr. Robert Brooks describes this as "malice without thought" as opposed to "malice with aforethought."

✥

"My son may be the only person in the country to have received a ticket for bridge jumping. He and several friends were jumping from a bridge that is under the jurisdiction of the federal government. He was the only one to get caught and get a ticket."

✥

Some parents may find it difficult to decide which disciplinary style works best for their teenager. A number of different behavior management strategies *may* be helpful. Refer to Chapter 5 for a detailed discussion of these strategies.

Low Frustration Tolerance/Emotionality

Many teenagers with ADD become frustrated easily and respond more emotionally than other teenagers. Often they may seem irritable or moody, especially when they are not on medication. Sometimes their moods are pleasant and at other times hostile. Most are oppositional (65 percent), arguing with their parents and teachers over the smallest issues. Parents are never quite certain what mood to expect when they greet their teenager.

✥

"Teenager males with ADD seem to have a bad case of testosterone poisoning (testosterone is a male hormone)."

—a humorous observation from a nurse who specializes in working with teenagers with ADD

✥

Teens with ADD may respond to stress with angry temper outbursts and aggression. Anger may be directed at their peers, parents, or inanimate objects. Sometimes, when a teenager does something wrong, rather than apologize or accept a punishment, he gets defensive and becomes angry at the person correcting him. They don't always seem to understand what they have done wrong or why their parents are punishing them. Dr. Steven Evans and his colleagues have found that these teenagers also have a distorted sense of fairness. They blame some of their anger on "unfair" actions by their parents and others. Often this anger is directed more at parents than at other adults. Paradoxically, they may direct their anger at the person they love the most and with whom they feel safest.

✥

"My son has gotten so angry he punched a hole in the wall in the garage. I guess that's better than hitting another person."

✥

"My son broke his hand twice in one month when he punched a locker at school. He was failing all his classes and was extremely frustrated. Thank goodness he didn't hit another teenager or adult."

✥

"I got a call to come pick up my son from middle school. He was so frustrated that he hit the brick wall in his room and his knuckles were bleeding. I suggested to teachers that when something like this happens again to try to find out why he is frustrated. He incorrectly assumed that he was going to be punished for earlier misbehavior and would not be allowed to attend the school dance."

✥

Many teenagers with ADD seem extremely sensitive to criticism or disapproval from their parents or teachers. They have a tremendous fear of being embarrassed. Some of them overreact or are overly sensitive to crises in their lives. If they fail a test or a teacher embarrasses them in class, they become very upset. They may become distraught if they break up with a girlfriend or boyfriend or receive a speeding ticket. Their reaction seems more intense than would generally be expected for teenagers. They may also become anxious or depressed.

🎗

"My son went up after class to ask his teacher if there was any homework assigned. The teacher must have forgotten about his ADD because he gave him a look like 'you must be stupid' or 'where have you been for the last hour?' Now my son is very reluctant to approach the teacher to ask him anything. He is very sensitive and hates to look foolish."

🎗

Your teenager may also be experiencing the normal adjustments related to adolescent hormonal changes. During these years, most teenagers feel different. At times, they may feel extremely lonely and isolated, even in a crowd. They are seeking answers to difficult questions: "Who am I? What are my values? What do I have to do to be accepted by my peers? Am I attractive to members of the opposite sex?" In addition to the usual stress of growing up, teenagers must find their ADD and heightened emotionality even more puzzling and frustrating. They wonder if they are the only one who has felt this confused. They may also wonder if they are going crazy or if they are bad.

Sometimes it is very hard for parents to cope with their teenager's emotionality and "talking back." Parents get weary of being the adult and trying to stay calm and keep family interactions peaceful. Ignoring minor blow-ups or using "active listening" is difficult to do in highly charged emotional situations.

Listen/Be Supportive. Most teenagers seem sensitive during their adolescent years, but teens with ADD seem even more so. Treating your teenager with respect is important. He is learning from his parents and family and will model your behavior. If you are patient and listen, your teenager will learn to be patient and listen. You can be supportive by encouraging your teenager, bragging about things he does well, helping him develop strategies

for coping with his schoolwork, and being his advocate with his teachers. Refer to Chapter 5 for a detailed discussion on active listening and teaching problem-solving skills plus anger control. Medications discussed in Chapter 4 may also help reduce anger, frustration, and aggression.

Verbal Fights/Arguing

Parents often complain that their teenager with ADD argues, talks back to them, uses profanity, and treats them disrespectfully. Family fights may erupt when parents press the teenager to complete homework assignments or try to discipline him for misbehavior.

Teenagers are struggling to grow up. As they discover who they are, they experiment with different clothes, haircuts, earrings, actions, and/or profanity. Sometimes they try to shock parents to get an angry reaction and draw them into a power struggle. Being a parent and not responding angrily in return is not easy.

Overlook Minor Infractions. If the misbehavior is minor or you suspect your teenager is intentionally trying to get a rise out of you, you may ignore the behavior.

Walk away from Conflict. Sometimes you may respond to profanity by calmly telling your teenager, "I know you are upset, but cursing is not acceptable around me. I will not stay here and listen to you talk that way. I will come back later and we will talk when you have calmed down (if he is agitated) or when you can talk without cursing." Then leave the room. Ten or fifteen minutes later, come back and resume the earlier conversation.

Give Your Teen Space When Angry. These teenagers seem to need time alone when they are angry or have had an emotional blow-up. Otherwise, they are more likely to say or do something impulsively that they later regret and that may only make matters worse.

🎗

"Elizabeth says, 'Mother, you don't give me enough space when I'm upset and you make it worse.' I think she is right. But my overwhelming need to fix it and help her out of her pain sometimes makes things worse. It is hard for parents to hit the fine line."

🎗

"Once when my 16–year-old son and his girlfriend broke up, he became extremely angry and depressed. I was so worried about him. He wanted to ride around in his car and think about things for awhile. I agreed to let him drive around if he would take his medicine before he left and call me every hour for the next two hours so that I would know he was okay. Before he left, he seemed calmer, so I felt comfortable letting him drive. By midnight, he was feeling better and came home."

🦓

Impose a Consequence. If you find profanity deeply offensive, you may choose to send your teenager to his room or place him on restrictions. Some teenagers will accept their consequences without question. With others, this situation may escalate into a power struggle, resulting in a battle that is worse than the initial confrontation over the profanity. As mentioned before, you must pick your battles carefully. The family situation will be incredibly hostile if teenagers with ADD are corrected for everything they do wrong.

Adjust Medication. In a few instances, irritability may occur because of hypersensitivity to stimulant medication or a dosage that is too high. You must be alert and monitor your teenager's response to medication. You should also be aware that as stimulant medication is wearing off, some youngsters experience a "rebound effect" (See Chapter 4). They may be more active or more irritable as the medication level drops. As a result, they may be more argumentative or grouchy during this period.

Consult your doctor if you think a medication adjustment may be in order. The doctor may lower the current medication dosage or consider switching to another medication, such as Tofranil or Clonidine, if aggression or defiance become major problems. See Chapter 4 for more details.

Difficulty Accepting Responsibility for Their Actions

Sometimes teenagers with ADD have trouble admitting they have done something wrong. They may blame someone or something else for their actions. "It was my teacher's (friend's) fault." Sometimes they also have trouble saying they are sorry.

Deal with the Problem Behavior. Deal with the problem behavior rather than trying to assess your child's degree of guilt or accept excuses. If a pattern of problems develops, you and your teenager may set consequences for specific misbehaviors, such as skipping school:

"You skipped school. That is not acceptable. I don't care if Mike (your ride home) left school at lunchtime. You didn't have to go with him. You should have called me to come get you. You have to be responsible for your behavior. You made the decision to leave. You can't blame anyone else. I am really sorry to have to do this, but you knew the consequences for skipping school. You won't be able to go out Friday night and you will have to make up work you missed at school."

I Hate to Say It, But . . . They Don't Always Tell the Truth

Teenagers with ADD don't always tell the truth. For instance, they may say that they don't have any homework at night, when in fact they do. Many times, they have honestly forgotten something and are not lying. Other times, lying is prompted by impulsivity and a desire to avoid punishment or unpleasant work, especially homework. Regardless of the reason, they appear to be lying intentionally. Dr. Thomas W. Phelan captured just how common this problem is in a clever article entitled, "The Truth about Lying and ADD."

Parents often cringe at the thought that their teenager would lie to them. Most parents believe that honesty is a very important value to teach their offspring. Although lying is a worrisome behavior, parents should avoid overreacting. Typically, as teenagers mature and achieve more successes at school and home, they are more likely to be truthful.

If You Know the Answer, Don't Ask. Don't create opportunities for your teenager to lie. If you know for a fact that your teenager did something wrong, don't ask him if he committed the misdeed. For example, avoid asking if he finished his homework if you know he hasn't done it. This is not the time to "test his honesty." If you observed the misbehavior firsthand, you should state the facts you know, and simply impose consequences without badgering or yelling . . . as much as possible.

"You know your curfew is 12:30 on weekends and I heard you come in at 1:30. You didn't call and let me know where you were or if anything was wrong. You'll have to come in an hour earlier tonight. Call me if you're going to be late so I won't worry."

"You hit your brother first when he wouldn't give you the remote control. That behavior is not acceptable. Now, both of you have to sit on the couch 15 minutes. I'll tell you when your time is up. Maybe next time you will remember to take turns and come up with a better solution than fighting."

"Your history questions have to be done each Tuesday night. It's 7:15 and time for you to get started."

Eliminate Some Punishment. If you believe that your child is lying to avoid punishment for a behavior such as not finishing homework, Dr. Sydney Zentall suggests that you eliminate the punishment.

Develop a Plan to Solve the Problem. Of course, you must develop a plan to deal with the problem that your teen has been lying about—for example, not completing homework. You may need to teach your teenager new skills or supervise his homework more closely. Homework assignments may need to be modified or adaptations made for class work. Specific suggestions for facilitating completion of homework are discussed in detail in Chapter 9.

Impose a Consequence. You may decide to impose an appropriate consequence if your teenager has been dishonest.

※

"You told me you were going to spend the night with John and then told John's parent's that you were staying here. Then you both stayed out all night and partied. That kind of behavior is not acceptable. I am putting you on restrictions this weekend."

Difficulty Participating in Family Events

Taking teenagers with ADD out to eat, to church, to sports events, or to public events where they are required to sit still for an hour or more may be extremely difficult. Because of their restless nature, they are often ready to get up and walk around after about half an hour or so.

Keep Outings Simple. Don't ask your teenager to do more than he is capable of doing. Keep family outings simple without demands to "perform" as a perfect angel. For example, at a large family Thanksgiving meal, perhaps the young people may eat at a separate table from adults so that "bad manners" or restlessness are less noticeable. If the family event was previously a negative experience because your teenager was not accepted or was put down by other cousins, don't make him attend the family lunch. Perhaps he can drop by briefly but plead having other plans, such as eating with his girlfriend's family. Or he may bring a friend with him so he has someone around whom he enjoys.

Keep Outings Brief. Brief outings may be better. If possible, provide a "safety release valve" that will allow your teenager to get up and move around. You might allow him to sit in the car and listen to the radio after the restaurant meal is over and the adults want to sit around and talk.

Find Creative Solutions. If sitting still in concerts or church is a problem, providing an outlet for restlessness may be more difficult. Some teenagers may be interested in helping with the nursery at church or may find interesting church materials to read during the service. If your teenager is not interested in going with the family to an activity such as the Nutcracker ballet, then it may be better not to take him.

Medication May Help. Remember, too, that teenagers on medication can usually sit still and participate more fully in family activities.

Difficulty Participating in Sports

Inattention and distractibility may make it harder for teenagers with ADD to take part in organized sports and physical education classes. They may have difficulty listening to the coach's instructions, following the rules, staying calm when frustrated, watching the ball, or keeping up with what is happening in the game. In addition, 50 percent of teenagers with ADD have poor motor coordination. As a result, they may be awkward and clumsy.

Although finding a sport that your teenager enjoys can be difficult, it is definitely worthwhile. Exercising is a good way to reduce stress, plus it may help reduce levels of hyperactivity or restlessness. It is also good for the heart, helps people sleep better, and increases the production of neurotransmitters.

Pursue Gross Motor Sports. Some teenagers with ADD may have problems with hand-eye coordination. Catching or hitting a ball that is thrown to them is a highly challenging skill. Comparatively speaking, their gross motor skills may be better. Consequently, they are usually more successful in activities such as swimming, soccer, or track, which require large muscle coordination. Both swimming and soccer have the added benefit of requiring a lot of physical energy, which is good for these teenagers. Wrestling and karate may also be sports in which they excel, and, at the same time, develop self-discipline.

Baseball can be a more demanding sport for some teenagers with ADD, since it requires concentration and good hand-eye coordination to hit or catch a ball. Players must spend long periods waiting—to take their turn at bat or for a ball to be hit or thrown to them. Since playing a position in the outfield is less demanding, many children with ADD are assigned to play those positions.

❧

"My son played baseball when he was in elementary school. He would get distracted by other things during the game and forget to watch the ball. One day he was standing in right field having a great time throwing dirt in the air. He had filled his pockets with dirt when his team had come in to bat. So now that he had nothing better to do, he was throwing the dirt in the air. I prayed that the batter wouldn't hit the ball to him while he was throwing dirt."

❧

"One day when my son was playing baseball, a train came by. He was playing in the outfield. He turned around and was absorbed watching the train, totally oblivious to the batter."

❧

Play a Position That Requires Full Attention. Sports positions such as pitcher, catcher, or quarterback, which involve higher activity levels, are more likely to hold the teenager's attention and focus. On the other hand, playing goalie on a soccer team would *not* be such a good idea, as it requires waiting and paying attention to prevent a score.

❧

"My son played catcher in baseball. That was the only way he could pay attention. He was so busy catching and throwing the ball, he had to concentrate."

❧

Consider Medication. Most parents are pretty conservative about giving medication, especially late in the afternoon, for fear of disrupting the teenager's sleep. However, some teenagers take medication just before game time. The medication improves their concentration and ability to focus on the game. Since they also have a good physical workout, the medicine usually doesn't interfere with sleep.

❧

"Andrew cannot concentrate well enough to play baseball without taking his medication. Otherwise he would be daydreaming or be distracted the whole game. The first time he took medication, he played a great game. They gave him the game ball because he played so well."

❧

"Robert and Lee are both state high school championship wrestlers in their weight class. Neither one of them takes Ritalin when they are wrestling, but they do when they play football."

❧

"Will says he can concentrate better and his golf game improves by a few strokes when he takes Ritalin."

Restlessness/Easily Bored

As children with ADD reach adolescence, their hyperactivity declines. Their hyperactivity may be replaced by feelings of restlessness or sometimes rebelliousness. Both hyperactive and non-hyperactive teenagers may appear restless and complain of being bored and having nothing to do. *Most teenagers with ADD want to be doing something or be going somewhere constantly.* They are often not satisfied with staying home. Parents may find it helpful to recognize and accept this need as much as possible.

Encourage Involvement in Community Activities. If your teen's time is unstructured, he will find something to get into, and it may be behavior that is undesirable or dangerous. You should encourage your child to take part in structured positive activities. Involvement in physical activities or organized sports, for example, helps teenagers release pent-up energy in positive ways. You might also encourage your child to join the YMCA or religious groups and participate in "overnight" parties or weekend activities such as ski trips. Sometimes, the YMCA sponsors overnight events during which the teenagers are "locked in" and supervised, yet get to stay up all night and be with friends. Volunteer work may interest some teenagers.

Plan Interesting Family Outings. Schedule family events that allow your teenager to be very active. Visit a science or activity-oriented learning museum, or go hiking, canoeing, camping out, or to an amusement park. Ask your teenager for suggestions. Planning a family vacation around the teenager's interests is another option—visiting Civil War battlefields or the Space Center in Florida.

Encourage Hobbies and Interests. Many teenagers with ADD pursue unusual hobbies, interests, or pets. As discussed in earlier chapters, these youngsters are drawn to novel and exciting activities.

✍

"In middle school, our son volunteered to keep the school snake for the summer. He fell in love with the snake and we ended up buying one for him. He loved to take it to school and show it to other students. One day when he brought the snakes home in a shoe box he forgot to put them back in their aquarium. They got loose in the house. The older lady who had watched him after school for five years quit on the spot when I told her two snakes were loose in the house. My dog found one snake in the closet but we never did find the other one."

✍

"My teenage son has pursued interests in photography, a blow dart gun, scuba diving, and flying lessons. He was not especially interested in team sports."

✍

You can help your teen discover his interests by exposing him to a variety of team sports and other activities. Most of us, teenagers included, like to do those activities which we do well. *Play to his strengths.* If he is a strong swimmer, a swim or diving team, scuba diving, or life guarding may be interest areas to consider. If he is good with computers or Nintendo, consider a summer computer class. If he is interested in space flight, engineering, and computers, the Space Camp in Huntsville, Alabama, offers exciting activities for teenagers.

If your teenager constantly complains of boredom and seems at a loss as to what to do, you could discuss options and then let him pick one out. Sometimes the options may be very simple—inviting a friend over to play Nintendo or watch movies or go swimming. Encourage him to be responsible for finding something to do. But occasionally, he may need help selecting an activity.

Make Special Plans for Holidays. Arranging for your teenager to participate in structured activities during the holidays may help him avoid boredom, plus make the time pass more quickly. Some religious groups may help needy families or put on plays or have parties. The YMCA may have a program of activities when school is out but parents are still working. Some older teenagers may want to get a part-time job during the holidays.

Material Possessions Are Important

Youngsters with ADD have an intense interest in acquiring material possessions, according to Dr. Melvin D. Levine, a professor at the University of North Carolina School of Medicine. Many of these teenagers have difficulty feeling satisfied with their activities or possessions. They constantly want something else or something different. They may be bored with their presents a few days after

Christmas and want something else to play with or something else to do. On the surface, this behavior appears to reflect a teenager's lack of appreciation for his parents' generosity. But it is more likely related to his symptoms of ADD—short attention span, restlessness, and need for new and different stimulation.

Allow Your Child to Earn Money. If your teenager is interested in material possessions, you can use that knowledge to your advantage. Depending upon his age, help him get a job during summers or holidays or allow him to do extra chores around the house to earn money. Your child may also respond to money as a reward for appropriate behavior or completion of tasks.

Plan for Holidays or Birthdays. Holidays and birthdays are times when the importance of material possessions to teenagers with ADD is very obvious. They may become upset if they have only two or three presents to open. You may try buying a number of less expensive Christmas or birthday gifts instead of two or three expensive items. If your teenager is bored after gifts are opened, he may want to visit friends or relatives and enjoy trying out their new gifts too.

Teach to Express Gratitude. Although all adolescents must be taught good manners and expression of appreciation, teaching teenagers with ADD takes a lot of patience and repetition. You may tactfully prompt your teenager to say thank you for gifts from his other parent or grandparents. Sometimes you may need to dial the grandparents' phone number and hand the phone to your teenager to say thank you.

Self-Centered

Some teenagers with ADD appear somewhat self-centered. Because of their difficulty delaying gratification, impulsivity, forgetfulness, and need to acquire material possessions, they may overlook the needs of others. For example, they may forget to buy gifts for birthdays or holidays. Sometimes they seem unaware of others' misery or problems because they are too wrapped up in themselves. They may say something that hurts someone's feelings without even realizing the significance of what they said. Over time, teenagers with ADD become less self-centered, but they must be taught to be thoughtful of others.

🦋

"I remember one Christmas when my son was in high school, he forgot to buy me a Christmas present. We are very close and I know he loves me. But Christmas Eve came, all the stores were closed, and he was horrified that he had forgotten me. I had an apropos gift for him to give me, an intricately carved wooden plaque that had the inscription, 'Love bears all things.' I had reminded him to buy gifts for all the other family members, but no one had double-checked to make certain that he had bought one for me."

🦋

"Now that my son has a girlfriend, he is much better about remembering when gifts should be purchased. I am pleased that he will buy her a rose occasionally, for no special reason. It makes me feel good for him to be thoughtful of those he loves."

🦋

Sometimes teens with ADD may exhibit the exact opposite behavior also. They may be generous to a fault. They may literally give a friend the shirt off their backs or lend them more money than they can afford. Sometimes they give away their parent's money. One teenager gave her parent's ATM bank card to a needy friend to withdraw 20 dollars.

Remind of Special Occasions. Remind your teenager about upcoming gift-giving occasions. So often during the holidays he is thinking of what he wants and does not give much thought to what he will buy other family members. One way to teach him to think of others is to discuss his holiday gift list. You might also invite him to go shopping with you, or encourage him to go with his girlfriend or another friend when he shops. Finally, you may need to double check just before the occasion to ensure a gift was purchased.

Encourage to Do Things for Others. Encourage your teenager to volunteer during the holidays to help gather food for less fortunate families, to write a brief personal letter to distant grandparents complete with pictures of himself, or to sing Christmas carols in a nursing home.

Breaking Things or Having Accidents

Sometimes in their excitement, teenagers with ADD may break things. Typically, it isn't malicious destruction. They act impulsively without considering consequences, plus they don't pay attention to what they are doing. Some may also have poor motor skills that contribute to their accidents.

☙

"One large athletic teenager with ADD who has visited our home has broken a chair, our son's bed, a boat paddle, and a door, and has dented the top of our car."

☙

Since they don't anticipate consequences, they may not take good care of their possessions. For example, they may run a battery-operated car through water without a thought that this may ruin the toy. Eye glasses may be left on the floor, then accidently stepped on and broken.

Handle Accidents Philosophically. One way to approach this issue is to remember that accidents are bound to happen and not a lot can be done to avoid them. Broken objects can be replaced; "broken self-esteem" is extremely hard to repair. Parents inadvertently damage their teenager's self-esteem when they constantly tell him: "You're a real a klutz." "You don't ever use your head." "I can't believe you were so stupid to leave your glasses on the floor." You may think things like this, but try not to say it or show him how you feel.

Treat Your Teenager as You Would an Adult. Imagine how you would handle an accident involving an adult. How would a mother handle a situation if the father broke an object or spilled tea? Most likely, the father would apologize. The mother would bite her lip and tell him it was okay. It was just an accident. Why not handle a teenager's accident the same way we would adult accidents? If he spills a glass of tea, calmly help him clean up the mess without making a big issue of the accident. If similar accidents happen often, take some precautions—for example, move the glass away from the edge of the table or set the glass further away from the plate.

Discuss Your Teenager's Physical Strength. If your teenager is strong and prone to break things, sit down and have a talk with him about his strength and the need for more caution.

Put Expensive Possessions Away. Keeping more expensive family possessions away from your teenager is also a possibility. Do not be too obvious about doing this, though, or he will sense your lack of trust. Avoid telling him that he is clumsy or that he will probably break the object if he uses it. If possible, try to subtly divert him to another activity or object. If he is on medication, he may be less impulsive and less likely to break things.

Our Daring Little Darlings/Broken Bones

As mentioned above, teenagers with ADD frequently act without thinking of the consequences of their behavior. Many teenagers, even some without hyperactivity, seek excitement, and the more daring the activity, the better they like it. Such daring activities may result in injuries or broken bones. Inattention probably plays a major role in causing their accidents. That trait, together with impulsiveness and an inability to anticipate consequences of their actions, frequently means that teenagers with ADD don't avoid dangerous situations.

☙

"Alex had five broken bones in a three-year period (ages 13–16). He broke his leg twice—once while riding a dirt bike (motorcycle) and once when jumping off railroad tracks. My husband and I were both out of town on business when he broke his leg the first time. The doctor couldn't administer medical treatment until the hospital finally contacted us for consent. After that, we wrote up a notarized letter giving medical consent for treatment for him to carry in his wallet."

☙

"One of Lewis's and Alex's favorite summer activities is riding their bicycle off a ramp into the lake . . . also known as 'lake jumping.' They built a four-foot ramp on the end of our boat dock. They ride their bicycle down the hill, across the dock, up the ramp, and into the lake. Their 'flight' takes them 25 feet in the air

and about 20 feet out into the lake. The first ramp they built was only two feet high. It wasn't challenging enough, so they began diving over the handlebars in midair. To escalate the challenge, they began doing one and a half somersaults over the handlebars. Some of their friends with ADD are more cautious and don't want to even try lake jumping."

🦋

"Shortly after our son took his first snow skiing lesson, we told him not to go down the 'expert slope' just behind our cabin until he was more experienced. He quickly replied that he went down the slope the day before."

🦋

Climbing is a favorite pastime for many children with ADD and may continue into adolescence. Their lack of fear probably plays a role in this behavior.

🦋

"A neighbor called telling me to come quickly because Cassie, at age four and a half, had climbed to the top of the gas well in their back yard. Her husband wouldn't even climb it because he is afraid of heights. Sure enough, it was three stories high and there she

was sitting on top taking her shoes off. She has always done these risky, chance-taking kinds of things. She has never, ever given it a second thought that this might be dangerous or she might be hurt."

🦋

"Once my son wanted to help me clean the pine needles off our roof. At first I refused to let him go on the roof. However, his stubborn independence won me over. I was afraid that as a single parent I was being overprotective, so I gave in. I stood near the lower portion of the roof just in case he fell off. He slipped on the pine needles, and to my horror started sliding off the roof. I was running around near the edge of the roof, blindly guessing where he would slide off, and trying to position myself to catch him before he hit the ground. Thankfully, there was a happy ending. He slid off feet first. I caught him as he fell and we both lay on the ground laughing."

🦋

"When my son was in high school, I found out he had climbed a radio tower one night so that he could take a time-release photograph of the cars driving in the city. It made a beautiful picture but scared me to death."

🦋

"When Damian was seven, he climbed up the side of a two-story building to get a ball the children had accidentally thrown there. The building had spaces between the blocks that were large enough to put his feet in and hold on to. Once he got on top of the building and threw the ball down, he realized he couldn't climb back down. He jumped into a nearby tree and climbed down."

🦋

Some of the "stunts they pull" are humorous but harrowing. Because they are inattentive or do not anticipate consequences of their actions, they seem unaware of their surroundings or potentially dangerous situations.

🦋

"When he was young, Lewis vacuumed all the water out of the toilet one day. He used a regular vacuum cleaner. I was just grateful that he didn't get electrocuted."

🦓

"Alex has always been a strong swimmer, so taking scuba diving lessons when he was in high school was a natural choice for him. After lessons were completed, he went to Panama City, Florida, for his final check-out dive. He and a partner were diving around a sunken ship. Alex was so excited he was breathing deeply and forgot to check his air supply. He ran out of air! He calmly tapped his partner on the shoulder, indicating his predicament, and they shared the air 'octopus' as they ascended to the surface. His partner was more nervous than Alex was. Most likely he had forgotten to take his medicine before the dive."

🦓

Regardless of their age, some youngsters with ADD seem to know no fear.

🦓

"At age two, Travis was sitting near me on his 'Big Wheel.' He said, 'Mommy, bye, bye!' Then he smiled and plunged down the basement stairs on the Big Wheel."

🦓

"When Alex was two, he climbed up on the diving board and dove in the water. He had seen another child dive, so he tried it. His Dad taught him to water ski when he was four years old."

🦓

"My son put a decal on his car that says 'No Fear!!' It seems to convey his attitude about life."

🦓

Encourage Safe, Stimulating Activities. Although there are no easy answers to reducing accidents, guide your teenager into satisfying activities which are not as risky. For example, wind surfing, sailing, and water or snow skiing have a high excitement level, but are somewhat safer than hang gliding, cave diving, bridge jumping, or riding motorcycles. Trying to teach about the dangers of certain activities may help some but probably not a lot.

🦓

"The world needs people who are daring; people who are brave enough to land jets on the decks of aircraft carriers or rescue others from danger. I could never do these kinds of things, but my son certainly could."

🦓

Monitor the Danger Level of Activities. While accepting your child's need for challenging activities, you can also monitor the danger level. If it is too dangerous, you may need to take charge and state limits as described below.

🦓

"The original ramp for lake jumping was almost five feet high and had a slope that was nearly vertical. We watched the boys jump one time and made them cut the ramp down to four feet and decrease the slope."

🦓

Provide Supervision. Providing closer supervision sounds like a great answer. But providing close supervision for teenagers is not very easy. Your teenager may impulsively participate in dangerous activities such as scuba diving alone, bungee jumping, or bridge jumping and never tell you. Still, it doesn't hurt to try to keep tabs on your child's activities. Subtlety is best if you don't want your teenager to feel as though he is experiencing an inquisition. You can find out a lot about your teenager's plans if you just listen to casual conversations between him and his friends. Remember, though, if you "eavesdrop" and intervene too often, your teenager may become more secretive but continue to pursue daring activities.

Negotiate a Compromise. If you don't approve of his plans, talk with him about it. Negotiate a reduced level of danger, substitute another activity, or tell him he can't go. Of course, even if you say no, your teenager may go ahead and do it anyway without telling you. If you can negotiate a safer compromise, you may be better off. For example, he can go scuba diving but only if he takes a partner with him.

Ask Others for Help. If your teenager is taking lessons or classes to learn an exciting hobby such as scuba diving, you may need to talk confidentially to instructors to make them aware of the symptoms of ADD plus the importance of taking medication. Discuss this with your teenager first and get his permission to talk to his instructors. If your child's class takes a trip, you may make the trip contingent upon having the instructor discreetly check to see if he takes his medication. A responsible sibling or friend may also keep an eye on your teenager and make sure he doesn't do anything too dangerous.

Difficulty Sleeping

Researchers have found that approximately half of all youngsters with ADD have problems related to sleep. These problems occur twice as often in children with ADD as in other children. They may have problems falling asleep, waking up, or both. Half also report that they feel tired when they wake up, but others appear to need less sleep. They may also have frequent night waking, nightmares, or restless sleep in which they move all around in the bed.

Researchers are not yet sure why teenagers with ADD have these problems. It may be, however, that their biochemical problems and reactions to stressful situations make it difficult to fall asleep and to get a truly restful night's sleep. Serotonin, which is essential for sleep, is thought to be low in children with ADD. It is also possible they get distracted by one activity after another, which prevents them from getting into bed and falling asleep. Sometimes teenagers with ADD feel as though they can't turn their brains off when it is time for bed. They think, and think, and think. They hear every sound and creak the house makes.

⚝

"Our 'night owl' son with ADD has periods when he has difficulty sleeping. Occasionally, he can't fall asleep before two or three o'clock in the morning. Sometimes these sleepless periods seem to be related to stressful events such as receiving failing grades, speeding tickets, car accidents, and loss of money.

"As a young child, my son didn't need as much sleep as other children. He didn't always need naps. When he was eight or nine, he sometimes stayed up later than I did on Friday nights. I went to sleep at 11:00 or 12:00 because I was exhausted from work and he would still be watching TV."

⚝

"Our daughter has always kept late hours from infancy. Sometimes I'd fall asleep rocking her and she'd be awake in my arms!"

⚝

Establish a Reasonable Time for Bed. Discuss and set a reasonable bedtime with your teenager. "I've observed that you need at least seven hours sleep or you are tired and have trouble getting up. That means that if you get up at 7:00, you must get in bed no later than midnight. What time do you think is a good bedtime?"

⚝

"Because of the early starting time for high school, we realized that getting ready for bed beginning at 11:00 p.m. was too late. Our son was getting up at 5:45 a.m. so he could shower in the morning and wash his hair. He was attempting to function at school with only six hours sleep. Most people can't function very well on less than seven or eight hours sleep. We encouraged him to start getting ready for bed at 10:00 or 10:30 p.m."

⚝

Prompt to Get Ready for Bed. Establishing a time to begin getting ready for bed may help, too. Because your teenager is easily distracted, it may take longer to prepare for bed. You may have him set an alarm or verbally prompt him when to start getting ready for bed.

Establish a Bedtime Routine. Establishing a night time routine that begins a half hour to an hour before bed may be helpful. For example, your teenager may wish to take a shower at the same time each evening and read or listen to music for awhile before turning out the light. Taking a warm shower actually helps many teenagers relax. He might also eat an apple, cookies, or other snack and drink a glass of milk. Your teenager may need to avoid soft drinks with caffeine near bedtime, but soft drinks don't seem to interfere with sleep for many teenagers. Other activities that have a calming effect on your child such as reading can also be incorporated into his routine.

⚝

"Our son wanted to stay up extremely late on the weekends and had difficulty getting to sleep Sunday night. Our doctor suggested going to bed at a reasonable hour even on weekends plus establishing a bedtime routine. He pointed out that it is important to establish a more consistent sleep schedule throughout the whole week, including the weekend. Midnight or one o'clock would have been acceptable, but our son liked to stay up until four or five in the morning on the weekends. His schedule was terribly out of balance."

❦

Don't Start Projects after a Set Time. Come to an agreement that your teenager will not start any projects until his homework is finished. No projects will be started within an hour of bedtime on school nights.

❦

"Our son loses track of time and the first thing he knows, it's 11 o'clock and he hasn't done his homework. Or he gets sidetracked wiring his stereo system and suddenly it's two o'clock in the morning. He is impulsive and starts wiring his stereo system at 10:30 p.m. He doesn't think ahead and figure out how long it will take or if he can finish it by bedtime. He is so intensely wrapped up in the project, he will work on it until it is finished regardless of the time. 'Just give me 15 more minutes.' Meanwhile, an hour later, he still hasn't finished."

❦

Compromise May Be Necessary during a Crisis. Sometimes during a crisis or unusual situation, you may need to work out a compromise with your teenager. An example of an unusual situation which required a compromise is discussed in the following paragraphs. You can't go wrong by applying good common sense in these situations.

❦

"During one particularly difficult sleepless period when our son couldn't fall asleep before three o'clock in the morning during the school week, I let him go back to sleep and go to school after second period. Realistically, I knew that if he went to school at 7:30, his school day would be wasted anyway. He could not think clearly, would probably sleep through class,

would be grouchy, might fail a test, and perhaps have cross words with a teacher.

"I wouldn't want to make this a habit, but I felt the circumstances warranted this unusual approach. We worked as quickly as possible to change his 'environment' to normalize his sleep schedule. He drank milk, ate cookies, took a warm shower near bedtime. Sometimes I would give him a facial massage to help him relax. Our son decided to take his medication (Tofranil) earlier—10:00 p.m. rather than 11:00, take a shower, and maybe watch TV or listen to tapes just before bedtime."

❦

Encourage Exercise. In addition to following a bedtime routine, physical exercise earlier in the day is also helpful. Teenagers tend to sleep better when they exercise. Avoid exercise too late in the evening, however, or it may actually interfere with sleep.

Confer with a Physician. Some teenagers have difficulty sleeping because of the effect of stimulant medication. If sleep problems arise *after* your child begins taking medication, talk with his doctor. It may help to adjust the time at which the medication is administered, reduce the amount of the afternoon dosage, or, if necessary, try another stimulant medication. Sometimes it helps to take medication earlier in the day. Together, you and the physician can determine the latest hour (between three or six o'clock in the afternoon, for example) that your teenager can take medication and not disrupt his sleep pattern.

Some physicians suggest using antihistamines such as Benadryl™ to help teenagers fall asleep more easily. Sometimes small doses of Clonidine™ (.05 to .1 mg, 1 to 2 hours before bedtime) are prescribed for teenagers who are having serious sleep problems. Although Clonidine is usually prescribed to help reduce anger or aggression, one side benefit is that it also helps some teenagers fall asleep more easily. Some teenagers who take Tofranil™ also report falling asleep and waking up more easily.

Trouble Waking Up

Extreme difficulty waking up may also be indicative of a sleep disturbance. Many parents hate waking up their teenager with ADD because it is such a terrible battle. The teenager will say and do things that he may not remember later. Parents and teenagers may scream at each other, starting off the day on a terribly negative note. If parents are busy trying to get ready for work, it is a major hassle to keep checking on the teenager to make certain he has gotten up. Parents may arrive at work feeling frustrated and angry. By the time the teenager gets to school he may be so angry he may snap at other people. Sometimes it may be difficult to determine if the ADD or depression is responsible for the sleep problems.

❦

"One of the most common complaints we get from our patients at the Pediatric Center is the battle that parents face trying to get their kids up for school."

—*Pediatric Center staff*

❦

"Waking up our 16–year-old son to go to school each morning is a battle. I hate it. You can shake him, yell at him and you can't wake him up. He can sleep through alarms, loud music, and lights on in the room. Finally, he will talk to you, promise to get up, and then fall back asleep. Later he will have no memory of what he said or did."

❦

Buy an Alarm Clock. Try buying your teenager an alarm clock and telling him he is responsible for getting up and going to school on his own. If he oversleeps, then he will have to go to school late and will miss some of his classes. If he enjoys going to school, then he will be upset that he didn't get up on time and will try harder to wake up. This idea probably won't work if he dislikes school.

❦

"Lewis sleeps like a dead person. He is so hard to wake up, it is incredible. He will talk to you and not remember a word he has said half an hour later. Somehow, he has learned to get up on his own when his alarm goes off. He is a senior and enjoys school."

❦

Connect Lights and TV to a Timer. If an alarm clock doesn't work, try connecting the lights and TV to a 24–hour electric timer, such as the ones people use when they're away on vacation. When the timer reaches a set time, lights and the TV will turn on. The novelty may work for awhile.

Try Positive Incentives. If your teenager hates school and is doing poorly, he would probably be happy to stay in bed half the day. Other measures must be tried. Try positive incentives first. "The fights we have every morning about your getting up for school upset me and my day starts out on a bad note. If you will get up on time for five days each week, I'll rent you an extra video game or movie Friday night . . . or I'll pay you a dollar for each day you get up on time." If these ideas don't work and he claims illness, you may say, "If you are sick and don't feel like going to school today, then you need to stay in bed so you'll feel better tomorrow." Or, "I expect you to go to school every day and be on time. If you don't go today, then you can't have the car and go out tonight." The impact of sleep disturbances on school performance is also discussed in Chapter 9.

Consider Medication as a Last Resort. If major fights are erupting each morning and everything else has failed, consider discussing medication with your child's physician.

❦

"Both Ritalin and Tofranil were prescribed as the best medication regimen to meet our son's needs. One of the side benefits is that he has been easier to wake up since he began taking 50 milligrams of Tofranil at bedtime. The second morning after he began taking the medication, he opened his eyes when I turned on the bathroom light. I was shocked. It is wonderful to be able to wake him up without having a major yelling, screaming family fight."

❦

Look for Other Causes. Sometimes ADD alone is not to blame for a teenager's sleep difficulties. A good physical examination can pinpoint any health problems that may be causing sleep problems. If life is not going well at home and school, your child may also be depressed. If he is depressed or anxious, he may not be getting truly restful sleep. If this is a major problem, you should talk with a mental health professional or physician.

For more information on depression, see Chapters 2 (diagnosis) and 4 (use of antidepressants).

Mornings May Be Difficult

The morning routine of getting dressed for school may be a nightmare because of a sleep disturbance or distractibility. Teenagers with ADD start getting ready, then get sidetracked on something more interesting than getting dressed. If mornings are a terrible battle, develop a plan to change whatever is bothering you. Otherwise, if your teenager misses the bus occasionally, drive him to school when he gets ready.

Allow Enough Time. If your teenager is slow moving each morning, you may need to build in 15 extra minutes for him to wake up and become alert enough to get ready.

Use Logical Consequences. If he misses the bus frequently, you can try a couple of approaches. For example, talk with him and ask his help in solving this problem. "These battles each morning really bother me. Please help me come up with a solution to solve this problem. You need to get up on time to ride the bus." Or, subtract his late time from some event he really likes. For example, he loses 15 minutes Nintendo time or his curfew is backed up by 15 minutes. Or if he lives close enough and especially likes school, he can walk even though he will be really late. Don't try this approach if he has a very low frustration tolerance and you suspect that he will blow up and have even more serious problems at school.

Leave On Time/Dress in Car. If your teenager rides to school with you, plan to leave for work/school at a set time and tell him in advance. If he isn't ready, he has to dress in the car. You may tell him, "I am leaving for work at 8:00. If you are not ready to leave at 8:00, you will have to take your clothes and get dressed in the car." It may help to warn him ten minutes before you are ready to leave. Finally, say, "I am ready now and I am going to the car." After he has to dress in the car a couple of times, he will probably make a greater effort to be ready for school on time.

Take Away Driving Privileges. If being late is a major problem for a high school student who is driving himself to school, one logical consequence is to take away his driving privileges. Remember, immediate consequences work best. "If you are late to school today, you cannot drive to school tomorrow." Or to state the same concept in a positive way, "Each day you leave for school on time you earn the privilege of driving your car to school the next day. Otherwise, if you are late, you cannot drive to school the next day." It shouldn't take too long to change this behavior, unless depression or sleep disturbances are a major problem. If these problems are severe, medical treatment may be required.

Get Ready the Night Before. Your teenager could take a shower the night before and lay his clothes out in preparation for the next morning. However, night time showers may not work for some teenagers, since they need their morning shower to wake up and function at school.

One exasperated parent decided to avoid the battle with her younger child with ADD by dressing him in a wrinkle-free jogging suit the night before when he was tired and easier to manage. The child slept in his clothes. Although this is a somewhat humorous solution, the main benefit is that the angry morning battles were avoided and both parents and child could go to work and school in a more pleasant mood. If you can handle the thought of sending your child to school in wrinkled clothes, this is really a pretty clever solution. This is an excellent example of changing the environment when you can't change the child.

Give Medication Immediately. If mornings are really a battle, one fairly simple solution is to give medication as soon as your teenager wakes up. You could wake him up a few minutes early, give him his medication, and let him stay in bed a little longer. Once the medication becomes effective—in 15–30 minutes—it may be easier for him to get up and get dressed. One drawback is that he may not be hungry at breakfast.

Birds of a Feather Flock Together

Subconsciously, teenagers with ADD may seek out friends who also have ADD and act the same way they do. This may occur more often in urban areas where families are more likely to move and teenagers are less likely to have childhood friends with whom they have grown up. If your teenager has friends from early childhood, they are more likely to include a broader range of personality types, not just other teens with ADD.

"Several of our youngest son's friends 'hang out' at our home. We observed that a few of his friends seemed to exhibit characteristics of ADD. At first I couldn't explain this phenomenon and wondered if I was projecting these behaviors on everyone else.

"It was not my imagination. At least five of my son's teenage friends have ADD diagnoses confirmed by a physician. I suspect they tend to be drawn to each other because they exhibit similar behavior, are having difficulty at school, and feel more comfortable with other teenagers who are more like themselves."

"I think part of the attraction is that they are very bright and have many varied interests. None of them do very well at school. Therefore, they don't care about grades. They don't see grades as being a measure of their intelligence or worth."

If your teenager only makes friends who have ADD, it will be important for all of them to be diagnosed and treated. Having friends who have ADD in itself is not bad. However, if his friends have severe cases of ADD and are always doing reckless things, this could be dangerous.

Refer Other Teenagers for Treatment. As a matter of self-defense, you may consider referring other teenagers you suspect of having ADD for treatment. Otherwise, several very impulsive, daring teenagers who are doing poorly in school may

be influencing each other to try new and daring adventures.

If your teenager suspects that one of his friends has ADD, he could talk with him about the characteristics of the disorder. Your child may describe his own behavior and how ADD was diagnosed. He may also explain how much better things are going now that he is being treated for ADD. If he has a good relationship with his friend, he may show him a list of behaviors from DSM IV that are characteristic of ADD and ask, "Does this sound like you?"

You may be able to help your teenager educate other parents. If you also suspect that one of your teenager's friends has ADD, be tactful in raising the issue with the friend and his parents. You might tell the parents what a difference treatment has made in your teenager's life. If the other parents volunteer that their teenager isn't doing well in school, you may offer them materials to read about ADD. If the parents and their teenager seem interested, discuss the issue in more detail. However, if the other parents are reluctant to talk about ADD, drop the subject. Sometimes you can be very helpful by simply planting a seed for parents to think about. After they have had some time to think things over, they may come to the same conclusion about ADD. Some parents may think outside intervention is meddlesome. Common friends or authority figures such as school personnel, doctors, or religious leaders may be willing to bring up the issue if other parents are unwilling to listen to you.

Encourage Other Friendships. Consider encouraging your teenager to associate with a variety of friends, including some who don't have ADD. You might invite different friends to do things with your teenager—spend the night, go to amusement parks, or participate in sports.

Teenagers with and without Hyperactivity

Although teenagers who have ADD/H or ADD/I/WO share many common characteristics, they may also show some distinctly different attributes. Teenagers with ADD/I/WO may have problems with lethargy, daydreaming, spaciness, or lack of awareness. Teenagers with ADD/H may be attention seekers, intrusive, or have more difficulty making and keeping friends.

Lethargy

Many teenagers who have ADD/I/WO seem sluggish or lethargic. They may also be more likely to become depressed than teenagers with ADD/H. They tend to prefer sedentary activities such as watching TV or playing video games to physically strenuous activity. Even though they may be lethargic, restlessness may also be present and should be channelled into positive activities. Sometimes aggression may also surface as the result of the teenager's frustration or depression. The impact of lethargy or depression on school performance is discussed in Chapter 9.

Encourage Pursuit of Physical Activities. If your teenager enjoys any physical activities, encourage him to participate in them. Physical activity will help relieve depression, direct his energies in positive endeavors, and may also help build his self-esteem if he excels in a sport. As discussed earlier, individual sports such as karate, gymnastics, swimming, or wrestling may hold greater interest for some teenagers than traditional team sports. Skills required for team sports such as social interactions, team play, and sensitivity to cues from teammates are not always strengths of these teenagers. Plus, they like novelty, and individual sports may allow more individuality. If you expose your teenager to enough activities, you will usually find one in which he excels. For example, horseback riding, riflery, modeling, motor cycle racing, or scuba diving are less traditional activities that your teenager may like.

Consult Your Physician. A change in medication may help if lethargy is a major problem. If your teenager has ADD/I/WO, Dexedrine or Ritalin may improve both his attention and energy level. Stimulant medications affect one or more neurotransmitters—norepinephrine, dopamine, and/or, to a lesser degree, serotonin. Serotonin is essential for sleep, plus a sense of well-being. If your teenager with ADD/I/WO is also depressed, has emotional ups and downs, or is aggressive, medications such as Tofranil, which also increase serotonin, may also be prescribed. See Chapter 4 for more information on medications.

Get a Physical. A good physical examination is important to rule out other health problems that may be causing the lethargy. For example, anemia or mononucleosis may cause reduced energy or depressive symptoms. Teenagers with ADD seem more prone to have allergies, which may also contribute to feelings of low energy.

The Absent-Minded Professor

Some teenagers who have ADD/I/WO may have a spacey or "absent-minded professor" quality to their personality. Daydreaming in class is common. They may become confused easily and lack awareness of their surroundings, instructions, or consequences. They may get lost when they are driving or have trouble following travel directions. When they are shopping, they could unthinkingly put a small item—an audio tape or toy—in their pocket or purse and forget to pay for it. If observed by store security, they could be stopped for shoplifting.

🖎

"My son was driving home from college and totally missed his exit off the interstate. If his roommate hadn't been watching, they would have ended up in another state. He has driven that route hundreds of times but was oblivious to road signs."

🖎

"A college student with ADD was told that if he had a 90 average for the semester, he didn't have to take a final exam. He didn't take the exam because he thought his average was 90, but it was actually 87. He remembered taking only two tests and receiving grades of 90 on each. He had forgotten that he had a third exam and had made 80."

🖎

Help With Organization. See the earlier section on "disorganization" plus Chapter 9 for tips on planning ahead with regard to schoolwork.

Anticipate Problems/Make Adjustments. If getting lost is a problem, mark the route on the map and review it with him. Or encourage him to take a friend with him who can help follow the map.

Medication May Help. Medication may help improve your teenager's ability to pay attention and plan ahead. See Chapter 4.

Slow Processing

Slow cognitive processing is more likely to be characteristic of teenagers with ADD/I/WO. This can have a major impact on school performance. As discussed in detail in Chapter 10, they may read and write very slowly. They may feel overwhelmed by their schoolwork. They may also have problems understanding instructions from parents and, as a result, may not do chores correctly.

Make Adaptations. As discussed in this chapter, you should keep this problem in mind when you talk with your teenager. For example, keep instructions brief and write them down. Adaptations may also be needed at school. See the suggestions in Chapter 10 on written homework assignments, note takers, or shortened assignments.

Attention Seekers

Many teenagers who have ADD with hyperactivity (ADHD or ADD/H) love to be the center of attention. They may monopolize the conversation at dinner or family outings or be the class clown.

Because they like attention, if a new fad comes along they will probably try it. Teenage boys may go through a stage where they want to wear their hair long or cut it into a mohawk style. Sometimes conflicts also erupt over clothing and jewelry teenagers want to wear. One fad, which most fathers have trouble accepting, is for their teenage son to wear an earring.

Give Opportunities to Be Center Stage. Provide opportunities for your teenager to be the center of attention. At dinner, ask him to tell about school or a recent special activity such as a deer hunting trip. Praise his successes and recognize his accomplishments. After he has told of his adventures, draw siblings into the conversation. Each should have a turn to share their joys and successes.

Encourage Pursuit of Activities That Give Recognition. Encourage your teenager to purse activities which allow him public success and recognition. For example, he may enjoy activities like theater, music, debate team, or stand-up comedy.

You can help your teenager find out if these activities are offered at school, YMCA, or through other community groups.

Discuss Inappropriate Attention Seeking. Occasionally, your teenager may alienate teachers and/or lose friends because of inappropriate attention seeking. Try discussing this situation with him. "Sometimes teenagers with ADD become the class clown and some teachers don't like that. Your history teacher, Mrs. Smith, is less than thrilled with your behavior. On the other hand, Mrs. Duncan enjoys your entertainment. Can you clean up your act and cut out the clowning in Mrs. Smith's room? One of the lessons we all have to learn in life is to adjust our behavior to the situation."

Ignore Some Behavior. If possible, ignore attention-getting behavior such as long hair, mohawk haircuts, or earrings. Or develop a compromise— ask your teenager to take out his earring when he visits his grandfather. These behaviors usually run their course and disappear. Frequently, teenagers reach an age when they decide on their own to cut their hair or take out their earring. Sometimes their behavior also changes when they learn that long hair and earrings don't make a good impression at most job interviews.

Intrusiveness

Sometimes teenagers with ADD, especially with hyperactivity, have difficulty understanding boundaries of space and communication. They may intrude on parents who are trying to spend time alone, go into their parents' room, and get into others' possessions without permission. They may also interrupt others when they are talking.

Set Boundaries. Obviously, the more rules you have, the more rules there are to break. There is no need to declare a room off limits unless your teenager is causing problems because he is getting into things that don't belong to him.

One potential area of conflict is when your teenager borrows things from his brother or sister and breaks them or never returns them. If this happens, you may decide to make certain areas "off limits." Tell him which room is off limits and ask him to leave if you find him in the room. If necessary, put him on restrictions or have him pay for lost or damaged items. To avoid potential accidents, keep fragile, expensive items such as a video camera in your space and not in "shared spaces."

Teach Your Teenager to Wait. If your teenager interrupts people who are talking, teach him to wait until the conversation is finished and he is recognized. If he interrupts *you,* you can try ignoring him. However, teenagers with ADD may be pretty difficult to ignore. It will probably work better to explain, "I am talking with someone right now. I'll be finished in a minute and I can listen to you then." Later, explain the procedure you want him to follow. "When I am talking on the phone, I don't like to be interrupted unless it is urgent. Please tap me on the shoulder. When I get off the phone, I will come find you or I will pause and talk with you briefly."

Difficulty Relating to Others

As discussed in Chapter 1, teenagers with ADD, especially with hyperactivity, may have trouble finding and keeping friends. Some teens may have difficulty establishing close relationships because they have trouble focusing or concentrating long enough to communicate with their friends. Many teenagers with ADD also appear to miss social cues in their communication with others. They may say something harsh or blunt and have no clue that they have insulted someone or hurt their feelings. Sometimes they miss the meaning behind subtle facial expressions or body language and may not accurately interpret others' reactions to them. They may interrupt others and monopolize conversations. They may be aggressive and bossy.

✳

"I make new friends and then I lose them. I get in trouble. And people don't want to play with me when they say they would. And people call me names and make faces at me when I am looking the other way. People say things behind my back."

—*an eight-year-old with ADD*

✳

"Our sons with ADD are different in the way they relate to others. One is an extrovert and the other tends to be more introverted."

✳

Invite His Friends on Outings. Try placing your teenager in the center of activities by being the parent who is willing to take several teenagers on fun outings. You may allow your child to invite one or two friends to go along on a special activity such as going to an amusement park or to the lake to swim, water ski, or drive a boat.

Provide Tips on Relating to Friends. If your teenager is receptive, you or a teacher or counselor may give him hints on how to interact successfully with his friends. Identify one or two major behaviors that cause trouble with his friends and work on those. Be gentle, subtle, and loving. Don't blast the teenager as he learns new skills. For example, avoid putdowns: "You're a loud mouth. You're so bossy. You talk too much."

Wait for a Teachable Moment. If he complains that no one likes him or he doesn't have any friends, listen to him talk. Then say, "Sometimes teenagers with ADD have trouble getting along with friends. Would you like some tips on getting along better with others?" If he says "yes," offer a suggestion about behaviors that may be turning people off: "When someone else is talking, they like other people to listen to them. Try not to interrupt your friends." Other possible issues include: "Most people like to hear themselves talk. Give everyone a chance to talk. Don't monopolize the conversation." "Try talking less and listening more." "Most people don't like to listen to a person who brags all the time. If you are proud of something, tell your best friend or someone in our family." In addition, some schools offer social skills groups that may benefit your teenager.

Coach His Team. Depending on your relationship with your teenager, you may want to sponsor/coach an athletic team, scout troop, or religious group. A major question is "Does your teenager want you to help coach the team or will it be an embarrassment?" There may be some advantages to being a parent/coach—you know your teenager's strengths, his strongest and weakest skills, and how ADD affects his playing ability. As a result, you may be a more patient and effective coach. On the other hand, some parents may be more impatient with their own child than someone else's. Do what works best for your family.

Medication May Help. Medication often seems to help reduce impulsivity and other behav-

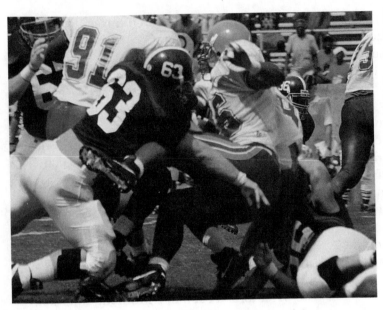

iors that can be offensive to other teenagers and coaches.

Encourage Having Friends in Addition to Girlfriends (Boyfriends). Some teenagers with ADD have intense, short-term girlfriend (boyfriend) relationships with members of the opposite sex. Relationships may last for a couple of weeks or a month at most. Others may have long-term relationships based on an unhealthy dependency that doesn't seem good for them.

For some, a girlfriend may be a very positive influence. If she is a good student, his schoolwork may improve. She may share your role as "coach" in reminding him of homework assignments. So even though they are dependent on each other, the relationship may be good for your teenager. You should use common sense in looking at relationships. If the benefits are primarily positive, don't intervene.

If your son is too dependent on a girlfriend, you may have to let the relationship take its natural course. Trying to force a couple to break up seldom works. One thing you can do is to encourage your teenager to do things with other friends as well as with his girlfriend. Also, let him make as many decisions as possible about things that affect

his life. Hopefully, as he makes more and more decisions on his own, he will become increasingly independent.

Conclusion

Living day-to-day with ADD can be very trying for parents. Forgotten chores, unfinished homework, chronic lateness, and repeating the same misbehavior are enough to give parents gray hair or ulcers. For best results, target one or two problem areas and work on those. Select interventions based upon your family's unique needs. Remember, too, that consequences may be effective for only a limited time; when one intervention ceases to work, you will need to try another one. The easy-reference guides at the ends of Chapters 5 through 10 can help you select interventions appropriate for specific behavior and school problems.

One last thought: it is easy for outsiders to have all the answers—to tell you how to properly discipline your teenager with ADD. However, most professionals will acknowledge that it is easier said than done. Outsiders don't live with your teenager 24 hours a day; you do. Parents can only do so much, and regardless of how "perfect" your parenting is, crises will inevitably occur. When parents blow up and "lose their cool," they tend to "beat themselves up" for their lack of parenting skills. It is far better to simply do your best, learn new parenting techniques, and be forgiving of yourself and your teenager.

TABLE 6–1
COMMON BEHAVIORS OF TEENAGERS WITH ADD
EASY REFERENCE GUIDE

A summary of the common behaviors, plus possible interventions, discussed in this chapter is provided. Most teenagers with ADD will have some but not all of these behaviors. More information on particular behaviors and interventions can be found on the pages noted below. As you become more familiar with using these strategies, you will find that you can often use them to handle more than one problem situation.

CHALLENGING BEHAVIORS	POSSIBLE INTERVENTIONS
• Seek independence and freedom	• Encourage independence • Trust until proven not trustworthy • Be observant of activities & friends • Consider compromise • Set up win-win situations • Offer an attractive alternative
• Disobey/Conflict with adults	• State rules clearly • Involve in developing rules • Write down rules/post them
• Act younger	• Adjust expectations • Ask his help in solving problems • Teach desired behavior • Impose consequence if necessary
• Act impulsive	• Anticipate problems • Avoid tempting teenager • Consider medication
• Difficulty paying attention/ don't seem to listen	• Make eye contact/use touch • Keep instructions brief and simple • Avoid preaching • Write instructions down • Accept his listening style
• Forgetful/Don't do chores	• Make a written list • Use "post-it" notes • Help get started/show how to do • Ask his help
• Disorganized/lose things/ have messy rooms	• Put name on possessions • Purchase less expensive things • Assist in being organized • Serve as a coach • List steps for clean room • Help clean room/garage • Close door to messy room
• Lack awareness of time/ they're late	• Use wrist watch alarm • Rent or buy a beeper • Teach awareness of time

CHALLENGING BEHAVIORS	POSSIBLE INTERVENTIONS
• Difficulty planning ahead	• Teach planning • Teach time management
• Difficult to discipline	• Use positive reinforcement • Use logical consequences • Reward or punish immediately • Be consistent • Create new consequences/rewards • Use behavioral charts • Use rewards/may include money • Try "Grandma's Rule" • Avoid power struggles • Redirect interests • Give second and third chances
• Low frustration tolerance/ irritable/emotional	• Listen/be supportive • Use active listening • Teach problem solving skills • Teach anger control
• Argue/talk back	• Ignore minor infractions • Walk away from conflict • Give space and time to cool off • Impose a consequence • Adjust medication
• Don't accept responsibility for actions	• Deal with problem behavior
• Dishonest	• If you know answer, don't ask • Eliminate some punishment • Develop plan to deal with problem • Impose a consequence
• Difficulty with family events	• Keep outings simple/reduce demands • Keep outings brief • Look for creative solutions • Medication may help
• Difficulty participating in sports	• Play large muscle sports • Play an active position • Consider medication
• Restless/easily bored	• Get involved in activities and sports • Plan interesting family outings • Encourage hobbies & interests • Make special plans for Holidays

CHALLENGING BEHAVIORS	POSSIBLE INTERVENTIONS
• Seek material possessions	• Allow to earn money • Plan for Holidays or birthdays • Purchase fewer, less expensive gifts • Express gratitude
• Self-centered	• Remind of special occasions • Invite to shop with you • Encourage to do things for others
• Break things or have accidents	• Handle accidents philosophically • Treat as would an adult • Discuss physical strength • Put expensive possessions away
• Daring/have accidents/ climb the unclimbable/ do harrowing stunts/ break bones	• Encourage safe stimulating activities • Monitor level of danger • Provide supervision • Negotiate compromise • Ask others for help
• Sleep disturbances/ can't fall asleep	• Establish reasonable bedtime • Prompt to get ready for bed • Establish bedtime routine • Don't start projects after set time • Consider compromise during crisis • Encourage exercise • Consider medication/confer with Dr.
• Can't wake up	• Buy alarm clock • Connect lights and TV to timer • Try positive incentives • Consider medication as last resort • Look for other causes

• Difficult morning routine	• Allow enough time
	• Use logical consequences;
	  walk to school;
	  leave on time/dress in car;
	  give 10 minute warning;
	  take away driving privileges
	• Get things ready night before
	• Give meds immediately upon waking

• Birds of a feather, flock together	• Refer friends for treatment • Approach other parents with tact • Tell of treatment benefits • Encourage other friendships

Behaviors Unique to Teenagers with ADD With and Without Hyperactivity:

ADD/I/WO

- Lethargy/apathy
  - Encourage physical activity
  - Consult physician
  - Get physical exam
  - Check for depression/meds if needed

- Absent-minded/spacey
  - See suggestions re: organization
  - Anticipate problems/make adjustments
  - Medication may help

- Slow processing
  - Make adaptations
  - See suggestions for school (Chapt. 10)

ADD/H or ADHD

- Attention seekers
  - Give opportunities to be center stage
  - Participate in activities allowing recognition
  - Discuss inappropriate attention
  - Ignore some behavior

- Intrusive
  - Set boundaries
  - Identify parent's & sibling's space
  - Impose consequences
  - Teach to wait

- Difficulty relating to others
  - Invite his friends on outings
  - Provide tips on relating to friends
  - Wait for teachable moment
  - Coach his team
  - Medication may help
  - Encourage having friends in addition to girlfriends

Table 6-2
IDENTIFYING CHALLENGING BEHAVIORS
INDIVIDUALIZED TREATMENT PLANNING: "DO WHATEVER IT TAKES"

NAME_____ AGE_____ GRADE_____

Identify two or three challenging behaviors both at home and school and select intervention strategies. Information in Chapters 5-9 should be helpful in completion of this form.

CHALLENGING BEHAVIORS

AT HOME/SCHOOL	INTERVENTION/COMMENTS
• Difficulty getting up for school; mornings were battlefield: slept through lights, TV, radio, and yelling; couldn't remember having early morning arguments.	• Get him to start getting ready for bed earlier. • Give him his own alarm clock. • Because he had ADD/I/WO, Dr. prescribed Tofranil; wonderful side benefit was he woke up more easily.
• Didn't remember homework assignments; didn't complete homework	• Get phone numbers for student in his classes he is in danger of failing. Call them to find out assignments. • Send back to school when he forgets books. If school locked, borrow book from another student. If this doesn't work, borrow extra algebra book and keep it at home. • Use weekly report. Must bring home good weekly report to go out Friday night. Must finish any incomplete work before going out.
• Received speeding tickets	• Take car away for a week. • He will pay for tickets. • Identify days and times at high risk for speeding tickets. • Will try Dexedrine at 6:00 p.m. Friday and Saturday when he is driving.

CHAPTER SEVEN

WHEN TEENAGERS CONTINUE TO STRUGGLE

Many teenagers do well at home and school after their ADD is diagnosed and treated. Often, using suggestions such as those given in Chapters 4, 5, and 6 is enough to help parents bring their behavior within manageable limits. Some adolescents, however, continue to struggle. Perhaps learning problems have not been properly treated, the best medications have not yet been identified, or outside stresses are compounding the problem. For whatever reason, the teenager is unsuccessful and unhappy, and as a result of his pain, lashes out at the world. He may make poor decisions that endanger himself or others.

More serious behaviors that parents may worry about the most include *defiance, aggression, excessive drinking or drug usage, speeding tickets, car wrecks, sexual acting out or pregnancy, shoplifting, running away from home, a suicide attempt, purchase of a handgun, or brushes with the law.* Most parents hope they will never have to deal with any of these stressful problems. However, since teenagers with ADD have a tendency to be impulsive and daring and fail to anticipate the consequences of their actions, you may be faced with some of these problems.

"My son and a friend sneaked out of the house one night to go buy cigarettes. Since they were out after the local curfew, a police officer brought them home."

"My son's friend, who is really a great kid, was picked up for attempted shoplifting. He was at a local store with some friends who suggested they take some things. Impulsively, he did. He had to go to juvenile court and participate in a community service program. There have been no more problems with shoplifting."

"I know at least three teenagers with ADD who were pregnant or got a girl pregnant when they were in high school."

"A couple of teenagers with ADD I know ran away from home for a few days at a time. Things were going badly at home and school. Eventually they came home."

"One mother told me about her daughter's suicide attempt. Her teenaged daughter's ADD was not diagnosed until she was placed in a psychiatric hospital after the suicide attempt. This poor mother felt so guilty because she didn't recognize the ADD and had taken the school's side when the girl had not been doing well in school."

If your child is undergoing any of the difficulties described in this chapter, you are probably experiencing a wide range of feelings. You may be frightened, and justifiably so, for your teenager's life and safety. You may be angry that your teenager is making your life so difficult. You may feel powerless because it seems as though you have very little control over your teenager. Feelings of isolation are also common since you may face this frightening time alone. Besides handling your misbehaving teenager, you may also find yourself grappling with a punitive world governed by school administrators, police, probation staff, and juvenile court judges who may blame you for your teenager's problems. You may feel helpless, overwhelmed, and depressed because you can't find the assistance you need.

🖋

"I remember being so frightened for my son. His judgment during the teenage years was not the best. He was angry at the world and ever so daring. I was so afraid that something terrible might happen to him and that he would die or that he would impulsively do something stupid and end up in jail. Because he was in high school prior to the release of the DOE memo requiring special services for students with ADD, no formal accommodations were made at school for his learning problems. Finally, when the proper accommodations were made in college, he began to succeed academically. Next we found the right medication combination and he was so much happier and on an even keel emotionally."

Behaviors That Worry Parents Most

Teenagers of today face challenges that their parents never had to confront. Illegal drugs, guns, and AIDS are just some of the dangers young people must evade on their way to adulthood. It is not an easy time to grow up, and for that matter, not an easy time to be a parent—especially of a teenager with ADD. No parent encourages their teenager to smoke, use drugs, get drunk, or engage in premarital sex. Yet many parents are faced with teenagers who are doing these things.

Table 7–1 YOUTH RISK BEHAVIOR SURVEY ALL CHILDREN AGES 12 TO 21 PERCENTAGE WHO ENGAGED IN HEALTH-RISK BEHAVIORS CDC–1992

BEHAVIOR	AGE GROUP (YEARS)		
	12–13	14–17	18–21
Smoked cigarettes	29.9	58.0	76.9
Current cigarette use	07.7	25.4	37.6
Drank alcohol	28.0	65.6	86.7
Occasional heavy drinking	04.3	21.0	39.7
Smoked marijuana	03.4	20.4	45.8
Used cocaine	00.4	2.5	11.4
Rode with a drinking driver	11.3	21.7	34.5
Used seat belts	31.6	33.5	36.1
Involved in a fight	49.0	43.8	29.4
Carried a weapon	12.6	17.1	13.6
Had sexual intercourse	*	43.4	81.7
with more than 4 partners	*	13.3	41.3
Used a condom	*	58.5	36.9
Used birth control	*	18.2	34.8

*Children in this age group were not asked this question

FIVE LEADING CAUSES OF DEATH AMONG YOUNG PEOPLE (15–24)

Accidental Death	15,278 (11,664 from car wrecks)
Homicide	8,159 (6,714 with guns)
Suicide	4,751 (3,109 with guns)
Cancer	1,814
Heart Disease	990

To help parents put these problems in perspective, statistics are included from studies by the Centers for Disease Control and Prevention (CDC) in Atlanta. Things have changed a lot since we were children. Many teenagers of today engage in more risky behaviors at an earlier age than we did. It should help parents to compare their teenager's behavior with "typical" adolescent behavior. As you can see from the CDC study above, experimenting with cigarettes, alcohol, drugs, and sex is fairly common among teenagers of today.

Sometimes these problems are linked to each other. For example, a teenager who drinks excessively may also be more sexually active, have a car wreck, or attempt suicide. The importance of one condition—depression—in these high risk behaviors is sometimes overlooked. As discussed in Chapter 4, some researchers believe that acting out behaviors such as delinquency, sexual promiscuity, alcohol, and drugs are actually symptoms of depression. This is significant. *By treating the depression, some of these problems may disappear.*

Unfortunately, there are no easy answers for resolving most of these behavior problems among teenagers with ADD. Generally speaking, keeping your teenager busy with activities, helping him succeed in school, giving him a sense of hope, providing supervision, and seeking treatment for ADD and coexisting problems such as depression and sleep disturbances should be helpful and also strengthen self-esteem. Teenagers with high self-esteem are more confident, less likely to be pressured into doing things they don't want to do, and better able to withstand disappointments.

The suggestions given below are offered as broad guidelines only. If your teenager is having serious problems, you should talk with a treatment professional to develop a strategy for coping with these issues. Licensed counselors, social workers, physicians, psychologists, or psychiatrists—especially those who specialize in treating ADD—should be able to help your family.

Defiance and Aggression

Teenagers who are very aggressive and defiant may be diagnosed with an emotional or behavioral disorder in addition to ADD. The conditions that teenagers with ADD are most commonly diagnosed with are Oppositional Defiant Disorder (ODD) and Conduct Disorder (CD). Diagnostic criteria for ODD and CD are discussed in detail in Chapter 2. According to the CDC study, fighting, one form of aggression, is common among all high school students. Approximately 40 to 45 percent had been in a fight in the preceding 12 months. Teenagers of today are sometimes frightened for their own safety. As a result, they, foolishly, may carry a weapon to school (17 percent). Weapons are discussed later in this chapter.

At school, students with serious problems of aggression and defiance may be placed in special education classes for students with emotional and behavior disorders (EBD). See Chapter 11 for more details about special education classes and alternative interventions. For detailed suggestions for coping with anger, defiance, and aggression, see

Chapters 4 through 6. One key intervention is worth restating here: a second medication such as Tofranil or Clonidine may help reduce aggression and defiance.

Substance Abuse

It is not clear whether teenagers with ADD are more likely than other teenagers to use illegal substances. Research done from two different perspectives—on children with ADHD and separately on substance abusers—sheds some light on this topic. *ADHD alone does not appear to put a teenager at risk for drug use. However, ADHD in combination with high levels of aggression and hyperactivity does.*

Based upon an eight-year follow-up study, Dr. Russell Barkley found that alcohol and drug use was not significantly higher among teenagers with only ADHD than other teens. However, they were twice as likely to smoke cigarettes as their peers. In Dr. Barkley's study, 50 percent of teenagers with ADHD said they smoked cigarettes regularly as compared with only 27 percent of teenagers without ADHD. The incidence of substance use among teenagers with ADHD was as follows: 40 percent have used alcohol, 17 percent have used marijuana, and only 4 percent have used cocaine. Not surprisingly, Dr. Barkley found that teenagers with both ADHD and Conduct Disorder (extremely aggressive and defiant) were much more likely to drink and smoke cigarettes and marijuana than teenagers with ADHD only. Dr. Barkley also found that teenagers in large cities were more likely to use drugs than those in rural areas.

Dr. Rachel Gittleman-Klein, Director of Psychology, New York State Psychiatric Institute, obtained similar results. In 1985, she found that teenagers with both ADHD and Conduct Disorder were more likely to experiment with alcohol and marijuana, plus were more likely to try hallucinogens such as LSD or PCP. On a positive note, however, Dr. Gittleman-Klein found that people with ADHD were no more likely than their peers to use drugs once they reached young adulthood.

Ari Russell, Director of GUIDE, a Gwinnett County, Georgia, drug prevention program, offers helpful information on substance abuse in general. She explains that researchers have identified two predictors of future substance abuse. In rank order, they are: First, hanging out with friends who use drugs, and second, being aggressive and hyperactive. Aggression and hyperactivity alone do not necessarily cause substance abuse problems. However, if not properly treated, school failure, defiance, and an increase in aggression may occur. Ultimately, substance abuse may become a problem. Implications for us as parents are: (1) we should be aware of our child's friends and subtly influence their choice of companions as much as possible, and (2) we should ensure that serious aggression and hyperactivity are properly treated and brought under control.

Some teens with ADD may experiment with substances occasionally, while others may abuse them (use them to excess). Those who abuse substances usually do so because they have low self-esteem and misguidedly think it helps them cope with the stresses of life. Teenagers don't abuse drugs to intentionally punish their family.

If a teenager becomes addicted, he may not be able to stop even if he wants to. And begging or telling him to stop is not going to work. Addiction may be both physical (the body craves the substance and experiences withdrawal symptoms) and psychological (the teen thinks he needs the drug to function normally).

Addiction problems cause a range of contradictory feelings for parents: fear, rage, depression, and self-blame. Teenagers who are addicted need more love, understanding, and support at a time that is most difficult for a family to give it. Parents may be so upset that they don't have any emotional energy left to give their teenager. If so, Al-Anon or other groups can offer family members information and support regarding substance abuse problems.

Some experts think that teenagers with ADD may use alcohol or drugs to "self-medicate" to deal with school failure, hostile fights with parents, and anger directed at themselves. Drugs help ease the pain of coping with the disorder. This may be especially true when ADD is undiagnosed or not properly treated.

Convey a Sense of Concern and Trust. It is important to convey a sense of concern and trust. For example, "I think it is important for you to have information about the effects of drug use. I think once you have that information you will make responsible decisions. Some drugs like cocaine are highly addictive and can kill you. I love you and don't want anything bad to happen to you.

Please stay away from drugs. If you have any questions about drugs, ask me. I may not know the answers but I'll find out for you."

Avoid Scare Tactics. Sometimes we describe the side effects and dangers of drugs in hopes of scaring our teenagers away from them. Be cautious when using this approach. Keep in mind that side effects of drugs that alarm us, as parents, may not scare our teenagers. For example, a teenager may not worry much about an increased heart rate from using cocaine. In addition, if you exaggerate the negative effects of drugs or alcohol, you lose credibility with your teenager.

Make certain your information is accurate, so your child will trust your advice. Try contacting your local drug prevention program first. Librarians, high school guidance counselors, or mental health center staff may also help you find appropriate materials on a variety of substances. The Drug Free School Coordinator in each local school system should also be a helpful resource.

The next section covers a few key points about the substances teenagers most often abuse. For more information, contact:

National Clearinghouse for Alcohol
and Drug Information
(Rockville, MD) 1–800–729–6686

U.S. Department of Education
(Washington, DC) 1–800–624–0100

Al-Anon/Alateen Family Group
(New York City) 1–800–344–2666

National Crime Prevention Council (NCPC)
(Washington, DC) 1–202–466–NCPC

Educate about Drugs and Alcohol. Educate your teenager about the effects of drugs. The better informed he is, the more likely he will steer clear of drugs. Since most children experiment with substances at young ages, the importance of early education is clear. In one study of high school students in general, the average age for first smoking cigarettes was 11, for drinking alcohol, 12, and for smoking marijuana, 13.

Alcohol, marijuana, cocaine, and heroin are probably the most common drugs that come to mind when substance abuse is mentioned. Sometimes we tend to forget that other substances such as *nicotine* in cigarettes are also highly addictive. Smoking is a very serious form of substance abuse, but it is a legal one.

Use of *inhalants* can also be a problem among teenagers, since they are readily available at home. Inhalants such as gasoline, aerosol sprays, airplane glue, nail polish remover, lighter fluid, and sprays for water-proofing fabrics may also be used to get high. Inhaling too much may result in blurred vision and hallucinations or even permanently damage the brain. Inhalants can also be deadly.

One of the most dangerous drugs, *cocaine*, poses special risks of addiction and possibly death. Parents should learn more about the drug and share that information with their teenager. Two points you may want to make include: "Cocaine damages your heart. The heart muscles lose their elasticity, possibly causing a heart attack. Second, cocaine permanently alters your brain chemistry. The full implications of this are not clear, but it seems to make it harder for teenagers to be happy doing normal things. They may have to take illicit drugs in order to feel good."

Cocaine comes in two major forms: a white powder, which is snorted through the nose, and crack cocaine, a more potent form, which is smoked. To your teenager, you might say, "Did you know that some experts believe that three of four first-time users will become instantly addicted to crack cocaine? The 'high' from cocaine doesn't last very long, only fifteen minutes or so, and then the user 'crashes' and becomes depressed. When you stop taking the drug, you have withdrawal symptoms that include severe depression and craving for the drug." Withdrawal from crack cocaine may also cause shakiness, extreme anxiety, and fatigue.

Additional side effects of cocaine include rapid heart beat, possible high blood pressure, respiratory problems, plus decreased appetite. Over time, the highs don't last as long. A tolerance to the drug may develop and more cocaine is needed to get high. John Belushi, the well-known comedian and actor, died of a cocaine and heroine overdose and Len Bias, a star basketball player, died from a heart attack triggered by cocaine.

Heroin is also extremely dangerous, but fortunately most teenagers seem to know this and avoid the drug. Withdrawal from heroin is very painful. Ultimately, people don't take heroin to get high but take it to keep from experiencing the terrible symptoms of withdrawal.

Marijuana or "pot" causes a psychological dependence—that is, smokers may feel as if they need to smoke it to feel good. Although it has not traditionally been thought of as being physically addictive, some substance abuse experts now believe differently. The marijuana cigarettes, or "joints," smoked today are significantly stronger than were smoked during the 1960s and 1970s, and sometimes cause addiction problems. Only one "hit" or puff can make a teenager high for two to six hours, according to Katie Evans, author of several books on substance abuse and director of a treatment clinic in Beaverton, Oregon. Since many parents grew up during the 1960s and 70s, they may have a fairly tolerant attitude toward smoking marijuana. However, the more potent "pot" may pose problems for our teenagers.

Smoking marijuana can impair coordination, leading to accidents. Furthermore, smoking pot is actually more damaging to the lungs than smoking cigarettes. Marijuana impairs memory, reasoning, attention, and coordination. In one test of short-term memory, Ms. Evans names three objects such as cup, plate, and fork and asks the teenager to remember them five minutes later. Many marijuana smokers are unable to remember these three simple items. Because short-term memory is already a problem for many teenagers with ADD, the additional memory loss from smoking pot may cause problems at school.

Of course, teens with ADD may argue that their memory was terrible before they began smoking marijuana. And, they may be right. However, it can't hurt to mention the memory problems associated with frequent "pot" smoking. Sometimes by just planting a seed of information, parents may make a difference in their teenager's behavior. The teen may be more observant of his own behavior and if his memory gets worse, he may stop smoking "pot."

Stimulants such as Ritalin are listed among drugs which may be abused in a brochure published by The U.S. Department of Education. This brochure, "Growing Up Drug Free: A Parent's Guide to Prevention," gives descriptions and illustrations of the major substances, along with their common nicknames. Despite the information given in the brochure, several leading researchers on ADD have stated that they have *never* seen cases of abuse of stimulant medications. Actually, most teenagers with ADD would prefer not to take their medication. However, my conversations with substance abuse treatment specialists have led me to conclude that *abuse of stimulants may occur, but it is very rare.* Teenagers who abuse stimulants may hoard them and then binge—taking one after another so that they don't sleep and are even more hyperactive and aggressive. They may also give or sell them to others.

Their intentions for giving Ritalin to a friend may be positive. For example, these teenagers are pretty good at identifying other teenagers who also have ADD. As a result, they may occasionally give Ritalin to "help" a friend with suspected ADD study and do better in school. If your teenager wants to help his friends, make sure he knows that the best way to do so is to send his friends in for treatment.

Alcohol is the substance used most often by teenagers. A major concern about alcohol is that it greatly impairs the ability to drive. In fact, alcohol-related accidents are the leading cause of death among 15- to 24-year-olds, according to the Department of Health and Human Services. Facts about alcohol that you might want your teenager to know include:

- one 12-ounce beer has as much alcohol as a 1.5-ounce shot of whiskey, a 5-ounce glass of wine, or a 12-ounce wine cooler.
- you'll get drunk quicker when drinking on an empty stomach; food slows the absorption of alcohol.
- it takes about two hours for the effects of the alcohol in one drink to wear off; you can't make it leave the body any faster.

Use Fact Sheets: Fact sheets about the effects of alcohol and drugs are available from the sources listed earlier in this section. You could give your teenager a fact sheet and say, "I would prefer that you wait until you are twenty-one if you are going to drink. However, there are some things you should know about alcohol. Look over this fact sheet. (Mention one or two facts). Let me know if you have any questions."

Use Teachable Moments. Throughout the year, you may find a few "teachable moments" to comment about substance use. TV programs, newspaper articles, or things that happen to your teen's friends may offer a springboard for discussion. "I read in the paper about a teenager at your high school who was injured in a car wreck caused by his friend who was driving drunk. Did you know them?" Pose hypothetical situations and ask how your teenager would handle them. "What would you have done? What would you do if you were riding with a friend who was drinking and driving?"

Don't Teach the Wrong Information. Potentially, there is a down side to drug education. Don't inadvertently teach your teenager how to use drugs. For example, don't name specific inhalants such as airplane glue or water repellents. Or don't talk about different ways to snort or smoke cocaine. Of course, your teenager may be exposed to much of this information from friends and the media.

Avoid Mixing Alcohol and Medication. A couple of things make it very difficult to determine the impact of taking stimulants and drinking. First, according to Dr. Theodore Mandelkorn, a Washington physician and member of CHADD's Professional Advisory Board, there is no research on the medical risks of mixing Ritalin and alcohol. Actually, if teenagers drink at night, stimulant medications are typically no longer in the blood stream. However, drinking excessively may result in increased impulsivity and risk taking, whether or not the teenager is taking medication. This, in turn, could lead your teenager into dangerous situations. Some teenagers are afraid of mixing their medications and alcohol, so they may give up their Ritalin rather than alcohol.

✖

"In college I wouldn't take my afternoon dose of Ritalin when I knew I was going to party and drink at night. Unfortunately, my grades suffered."

✖

Clearly, *excessive drinking in combination with antidepressants is dangerous* because the effect of alcohol is intensified. One drink (or one marijuana cigarette) plus an antidepressant may produce the effects of two or three drinks. The combination of higher dosages of antidepressants, such as Tofranil, and excessive alcohol have the greatest potential for causing an accidental overdose. An overdose may result in an irregular heart beat, or the heart may actually stop beating, resulting in death.

Parental Dilemmas about Substance Use. Many parents who drink alcohol socially may face a dilemma when deciding how to handle the problem of teenage drinking. Your teenager sees you drinking and thinks it is okay for him to drink too. Some parents may even view under-age experimentation with alcohol as an age-old "rite of passage." Once your child reaches legal drinking age, it will be up to him to decide about using alcohol responsibly. Obviously, until that time, the best advice for parents is not to encourage your teenager to drink.

You may not be able to give logical answers to all your teenager's questions about using substances. Some questions our clever children ask between the ages of 18 and 21 are very difficult to answer. They point out inconsistencies in adult rules and regulations. "How come we are old enough to serve in the army at age eighteen and possibly die for our country but we can't drink?"

If your teenager is determined to drink alcohol, *he will*, regardless of his age and what you do. If he has to sneak off somewhere to drink, the consequences may be even worse. He may end up driving home under the influence of alcohol. Some parents prefer that their teenager drink at home, if he is going to drink. Parents can monitor their child's consumption and make certain he doesn't drive. In some states, including Georgia and Florida, it is legal for teenagers to drink under the direct supervision of their parents in their own home. However, it is illegal for anyone else's child to drink there.

〽

"We locked up our liquor in a cabinet when our son was in high school. That did not really stop him from drinking. For our son, having our liquor locked up became a challenge. Sometime later he told us that he took the hinges off the cabinet door. I don't think he really drank that much but he couldn't resist the challenge of showing us that we couldn't control his behavior by locking the cabinet."

〽

"During the ages from 16 to 18, we have let our son have an occasional beer or glass of wine at home, provided he doesn't drive afterwards. We have an occasional social drink and are trying to teach our son that if he is going to drink to do it responsibly and in moderation. I believe it takes away the glamorous appeal of a forbidden activity and avoids unnecessary power struggles."

〽

According to Ari Russell, teenagers who are allowed to drink *regularly* at home are more likely to believe they can drink everywhere else too. She notes that successful lawsuits have been won against host parents who allowed under-age teenagers to drink, even at social functions such as wedding receptions.

Absolutely No Drinking and Driving. Approximately 60 percent of all teenage drivers (not just those with ADD) who die in car accidents have been drinking. The youngest drivers, age 16, are responsible for 40 percent of all teenage car accidents involving alcohol.

Make it clear that drinking and driving will not be tolerated. Driving privileges will be taken away for two to four weeks or more. Typically, two weeks is an eternity for a teenager, especially one with ADD. Include a statement about the consequences of drinking and driving if you draw up a contract regarding rules for driving. Contracts are discussed in Chapter 5, plus the next section on driving. A model contract is provided in Appendix A.

Provide Supervision. Knowing where your teenager is and with whom is important. If he is going to a party, is it supervised? Ask your teenager if adults will be present and tell him you will need to confirm it. If necessary, call and talk with the parents who will be chaperoning. "Hello. I'm Robert's mother. He said he has been invited to a party at your house. I was just calling to make certain that you or another adult will be supervising the party."

Curfews are still appropriate for high school students. Curfews should be reasonable and not too different from the majority of your child's friends. Obviously, older teens will be allowed to have slightly later curfews. The main issue is not to allow your child to stay out all night without any supervision. Late curfew may be allowed on special occasions.Greet your teenager and his friends in a positive manner when they return home. In addition to listening to their adventures for the evening (if they are in a talkative mood), you can see for yourself if they are drinking or using drugs.

Tactfully Influence Selection of Friends. If you suspect that some of his friends are abusing drugs, encourage your teenager to do things with other friends who are not. Tactfully steering him away from friends who are a bad influence will be more effective than a volatile confrontation.

Try the indirect approach first. If that is not successful try a more direct one. "I've heard that your friend John uses drugs pretty heavily. If you hang around with him, your friends will think you are using drugs too. Your other friends may start to avoid you. Drugs are serious business. It's illegal, plus penalties are stiff. If drugs are ever sold on our property, technically our house or car could be seized and sold by law enforcement. We cannot allow drug use in our house." See if he will agree to stop seeing this friend for a while, maybe two weeks. During that time, try to get him interested in other friends or activities.

⚭

"Our son was shunned by one of his friends because he was hanging out with someone who used drugs. He learned that if you hang out with drug users, other people automatically assume you are also using drugs. He asked a friend to spend the night and was told he couldn't because he was going out of town. Well, as luck would have it, we ran into him at the mall the next day. The truth came out that he was avoiding my son because of possible drug use. In a way we were very lucky. It made a big impression on my son."

⚭

Sadly enough, these teenagers are sometimes rejected by the very friends you would like them to have. They then turn to less desirable friends to find acceptance and approval. To guard against this happening, keep him busy. For example, let him go to a parent's office and help after school. Sign him up for after school sports or classes. Suggest that one or two friends join him for special activities.

Watch for Signs of Substance Use and Abuse. Some parents believe that if their teenager is using drugs he will act like a monster. Usually, this is not true. Teenagers who are experimenting with substances will not have all the characteristics of substance abuse and thus can often hide their symptoms from parents.

There are some general signs to watch out for. When a teenager has been drinking, you can smell alcohol on his breath, he may stagger, slur his speech, or be more talkative. Drug use may be more difficult to detect than alcohol use. When your teenager is on marijuana or cocaine, he may be more talkative or laugh excessively. With marijuana, his eyes may be red and look a little glassy. When marijuana is being smoked, it has a distinctive smell like burnt rope. LSD may cause the pupils to dilate.

Many parents have never seen some of these drugs and wouldn't recognize them if they found them. You need to know what these substances look like. For example, one drug education instructor uses a small chunk of Ivory soap to show what crack cocaine looks like. Tiny $\frac{1}{8}$ inch squares of paper, some plain and others with innocent looking blue stars or dots, may actually be "hits" of LSD. These squares are placed on the tongue and the LSD is absorbed into the body. The "hits" are usually kept in plastic bags or cellophane. The pictures and descriptions in "Growing Up Drug Free" are very helpful also.

Be aware of potential abuse of inhalants and keep them stored away. Or at least pay attention to how frequently they are used. Do the cans quickly become empty? Do you find them on the floor in your child's room? You may also notice drug paraphernalia such as a glass pipe for smoking cocaine, a "roach" clip (tweezers) for holding a marijuana cigarette, or cigarette papers for rolling marijuana "joints."

Watch for the *signs of substance abuse* (alcohol and drugs) listed in Table 7–2. These signs may be more likely to surface when things are not going well at school.

How You Can Help

If you suspect your teenager has a substance abuse problem, DHHS suggests the following:

Table 7–2
WARNING SIGNS OF SUBSTANCE ABUSE

- an abrupt change in mood or attitude
- excessive or giddy laughter
- sudden and continuing decline in school attendance or a drop in grades
- sudden and continuing resistance to discipline at home or in school
- impaired relationships with family members or friends
- avoiding parents and going straight to room at night
- slurred speech
- unusual temper flare-ups; irritability
- increased borrowing of money from parents or friends
- stealing from home, school, or work
- heightened secrecy about actions and possessions
- associating with a new group of friends, especially with those who use drugs
- frequent phone calls late at night or from strangers

According to the U.S. Department of Health and Human Services (DHHS), Substance Abuse Administration, specific <u>symptoms of a drinking problem</u> include:

- inability to control drinking; frequently getting drunk even though they decide not to
- using alcohol to escape problems
- changing from typical reserved personality to the "life of the party"
- a change in personality; Dr. Jekyll to Mr. Hyde
- a high tolerance level; drinking others under the table
- blackouts; don't remember what happened when they drink
- problems at work or school because of drinking
- family members expressing concern about drinking

- don't be judgmental or preachy; remember, alcoholism and drug abuse are diseases
- be willing to listen
- voice your concerns about his drinking or drug use; but don't do it when he is under the influence
- offer your help; get educational materials; attend AA or Narcotics Anonymous (NA) meetings
- be encouraging and positive if he tries to stop drinking or using drugs

Find an Approach That Works for Your Teen. If your teenager is abusing substances, you can try one of several approaches. As discussed in Chapter 5, your teenager is going to make mistakes. Your main goal is for him to learn from his mistakes and to stop inappropriate behaviors. Sometimes different approaches are needed. If it is a first offense, you might try talking to him first. The simplified message, in your own words, should be: "Using drugs is not acceptable. Please stop. I love you and am afraid of what will happen to you if you become addicted to drugs. How can I help you?"

Next, try using restrictions or loss of privileges (driving) to try to change his behavior. Remember, reasonable consequences are most effective. If restrictions are too harsh, your teenager's reaction may be volatile and the conflict may get worse. He may drink even more to get back at you (or to drown his sorrow). If he is out of control, you should seek professional treatment.

Should You Consider Drug Testing? If your teenager is experiencing serious problems, you might consider having a drug test done to see if drugs may be a factor in his misbehavior. There are pros and cons to testing. The primary advantage to testing is that it will confirm the presence of most drugs. Also, if your teenager adamantly denies drug use and refuses treatment, a positive drug test may give you some leverage to push him into treatment. Then you can say with certainty, "You are using drugs. Your grades have dropped and I believe you need help."

One drawback is that a teenager may be using drugs and the test may not pick it up. Ask the doctor what drugs will be identified by the test. Alcohol is excreted from the body rapidly and will not show up in most of these tests. Many people believe that LSD does not show up in drug tests. However LSD can be identified if the urine sample is handled properly. Evidence of cocaine use may only be present in the body for 24–48 hours. Marijuana is easier to pick up, since traces are present in the body for approximately two to four weeks.

🎋

"My son had a urine test for drugs as part of his annual physical exam. The test came back negative, but he later told me he had used LSD. Initially I felt guilty because I had 'wrongly suspected' my son. Boy, did I feel stupid when I realized he had been using LSD and I didn't even know it."

🎋

The worst part of having your teenager take a drug test is that it may further damage your relationship with him. One option is to simply ask him if he is using drugs. He may say, "yes," thus saving you the time and expense of a drug test, plus preserving some element of trust in the relationship.

In deciding whether or not to seek drug testing, ask yourself a few important questions: First, what is the purpose of a drug test? Second, how will it help my teenager? And third, what will I do after I obtain the test results? The American Academy of Pediatrics issued a policy statement in 1989 opposing random drug testing of teenagers. If you can take action without the results of a drug test, try that approach first. If you suspect serious drug use, you can seek treatment from a substance abuse counselor without ever having your teenager undergo testing. Later, as part of their evaluation and treatment, they may do a physical examination, including a urine test, for drug use.

Sometimes a teenager will tell his counselor whether or not he is using drugs. If he is 18 or older, federal and state confidentiality laws forbid the counselor from sharing this information with anyone else, including you. Even though your curiosity may kill you, the good news is that he *is* in treatment.

Seek Professional Help. If your teenager cannot function well at home, school, or work because of substance abuse, seek professional help. But be prepared for any solutions to take time. If your teenager is addicted, there are no quick, easy answers. Some treatment professionals specialize in treating alcohol or drug problems. Contact your local drug prevention or treatment programs, mental health center, AA group, or hospital to ask for the names of professionals effective in treating substance abuse problems in teenagers.

Some drug treatment programs offer effective outpatient services, which include counseling, psychological assessments, and drug testing. The counselor may first give the teenager the opportunity to tell his parents about his drug use. Or the counselor will tell them. The drug testing keeps him honest with his counselor and family.

If problems are serious and your teenager is in denial about his addiction, counselors known as "intervention specialists" can meet with your family to assist you in confronting him. According to Bruce Hoopes, director of a substance abuse program, family members and friends rehearse in advance what each will say when they confront the teenager. Or the teenager may be placed in an inpatient detoxification program for three to five days to ensure that all drugs or alcohol are out of his system. Outpatient counseling can be effective when the whole family is involved. Residential treatment programs may also be available, but are expensive and may not be covered by insurance. Any good residential program will involve the whole family. Otherwise, the teenager will return home to face the same set of circumstances that contributed to his substance abuse problems.

Participating in AA or NA groups may be helpful. Unfortunately, you may have trouble finding a group specifically for adolescents. You might also encounter philosophical differences over treatment of ADD. Many members of AA and NA believe that alcohol and substance abuse should be treated without any medication. Since teenagers with ADD benefit from stimulant medication, this may well be a major point of disagreement between your family and these organizations. Even if you ultimately decide not to send your teenager to AA or NA, however, you may still choose to attend Al-Anon for family support.

Driving/Speeding Tickets and Car Accidents

Because of their impulsiveness, daring, and difficulty anticipating the consequences of their actions, children with ADD may attempt to drive a car long before they are old enough, sometimes as early as age two or three. Never leave a child with ADD alone in a car with the motor running, even if you are going into a store for only a few minutes. Keep car keys away from them.

❧

"Michael, our two-year-old son, found our car keys and tried to drive our car. He put the keys in the ignition and began turning the steering wheel back and forth. He turned the ignition just enough for the car to slip in gear. The car rolled backward down the driveway and hit a tree. Try explaining to your car insurance agent that the driver of the wrecked car was your two-year-old son."

❧

"My wife left Steven, our three-year-old, in the car for a few minutes while she ran into a friend's house to drop something off. While she was inside, he began turning the steering wheel pretending to drive. The car slipped into gear and rolled down a long hill, finally stopping when it hit a pecan tree."

❧

When teenagers with ADD are old enough to drive legally, they may also be more likely to get speeding tickets or have car accidents. In a survey of 16– to 22–year-olds, Dr. Barkley found that *teenagers with ADHD had almost four times as many traffic citations as non-ADHD teenagers.* Speeding was the most frequent traffic citation. Some of the more daring teenagers may also sneak the car out for a drive before they get their driver's license.

❧

"Both of our sons have received numerous speeding tickets. Their lack of awareness and concentration, impulsiveness, and daring nature seem to result in their being oblivious to speed limits. When they drive they don't seem to be aware of speed limits or how fast they are driving. Frequently, they don't see the police sitting with their radar guns until it is too late. One police officer reported that he had his blue lights on and was chasing another speeding car, when our son passed him at an even faster rate of speed. The first six months our son was driving, he was stopped seven times for speeding and 'totaled' his car. Obviously, I worry about him a lot."

❧

"I'm waiting for the speeding ticket and praying it doesn't come. I remind my daughter every time we ride together to curb her speed."

❧

Because teenagers with ADD have more difficulty concentrating and paying attention, they may be more likely to have car accidents than teenagers who don't have the disorder. According to Dr. Barkley's survey, *teenagers with ADHD had almost four times as many car wrecks and were more than seven times as likely to have had a second accident.* They were more than four times as likely to be at fault in the accident. Inattention was the most common reason given for the accident. Their impulsiveness and attraction to exciting, daring things also play a role. Unfortunately, risk-taking behavior in an automobile can be fatal.

❧

"Our daughter was explaining about the two broken headlights on her new car. 'Dad, the light was green. But the truck didn't go.'"

❧

"Our son has had two major wrecks in the three years he has been driving. He was driving about thirty miles an hour when he hit a solid brick mail box in our neighborhood and totaled the car. His medication hadn't taken effect yet. He leaned down to pick up something from the floorboard and hit the mailbox. His second wreck occurred during a terrible rain storm. He hydroplaned across three lanes of traffic, barely missing an eighteen-wheel truck and struck the guardrail head-on. He had on his seatbelt and walked away without a scratch. The good Lord was watching over him that day. We were lucky."

❧

"When our son was 18, his driver's license was suspended because he received so many speeding tickets. He was devastated! He took a defensive driving course and his license was returned. Hopefully, he has learned an important lesson."

🦓

Again, I emphasize, not all teenagers with ADD are alike. Some teenagers with this disorder are very cautious drivers and do not speed. However, they still may have problems paying attention to stop lights and concentrating on their driving unless they are on their medication.

🦓

"Shawn has his learner's permit. Before his ADD was diagnosed we were so worried about his concentration that we wouldn't let him get his learner's permit until he was 16, even though he was eligible at age 15. When he hasn't taken his medicine, he'll stop at green lights, go through red lights, weave from side to side of the road. With the medicine, he is a very good driver.

🦓

"Sometimes Shawn starts driving too soon before his medicine has taken effect. We have to remind him to be careful and wait until the car is stopped to turn the radio off or on, turn up the volume, or change stations."

🦓

Send to Driver Training. Some states require that teenagers take driver education training or a defensive driving course before they can be licensed. If this is not required in your state, consider sending your child for training anyway. Specialized training should be very informative and help improve your teen's driving skills. Some insurance companies discount their premiums for teenagers who have completed such training.

Develop a Contract for Driving. You may want to develop a contract clearly stating rules for driving. A model contract is included in Appendix A. Include statements about your teenager's responsibilities: seat belt use, maintenance, who will pay for gas and insurance, few or no friends riding with them, who else may drive your car, and when to call for help. Getting your child to fulfill the con-

tract can be difficult; frequent reminders may be needed. For example, although wearing a seatbelt is critical, only about a third of all high school drivers wear them. Students Against Driving Drunk (SADD) have developed a "Contract for Life" that both the parents and teenager sign. These paragraphs are included in the model contract:

"Teenager: I agree to call you for advice and/or transportation at any hour, from any place, if I am ever in a situation where I have been drinking or a friend or date who is driving me has been drinking."

"Parent: I agree to come and get you at any hour, any place, no questions asked and no arguments at that time, or I will pay for a taxi to bring you home safely. I expect we would discuss this issue at a later time."

If your teen is responsible and you don't think he will use too much gas when driving, you may not need to set limits on miles driven. However, if gas use is excessive or you anticipate that it could be, you might give a monthly gas allowance. If he exceeds the allowance, he or his friends must pay for gas themselves.

Gradually Increase Driving Privileges. After several teenage car-related deaths, a Gwinnett County (Georgia) task force published an excellent handbook for teenage drivers. Ari Russell, a task force member, suggests the following procedure for gradually increasing driving privileges: As the teen moves from a learner's permit to a driver's license and drives responsibly, gradually increase his driving privileges. You might allow him to drive only during the day during good weather for a couple of months. If there are no problems, he graduates to driving some at night, in good weather. Next he moves to driving during the day in bad weather, first with a parent and then on his own. He can then drive at night in bad weather. This provides more practice time to gain experience driving in increasingly difficult situations.

Purchase a Slow "Tank." If you buy a car for your teenager, consider a larger, heavier car that offers more protection in the event of an accident. For some teenagers, a pickup truck may be the perfect choice. Instead of having six or eight people crammed into a car for the teenaged driver to impress, only one or two passengers can ride in the cab. Purchasing a car with a four- or six-cylinder engine may also decrease the risk of speeding. Some cars with smaller engines, however, can achieve a high rate of speed very quickly.

Dealing with Speeding Tickets

If speeding tickets become a problem, here are several strategies to try:

Identify the High Risk Time of Day. Determine whether your teenager receives speeding tickets during the same time period. Then develop a plan to deal with the problem. For example, consider letting his girlfriend drive during this time or have him take medication when driving.

※

"We warned our son that his 'danger zone' (getting tickets) was between 10:00 p.m. and midnight on Friday and Saturday nights when his medication had worn off. We encouraged him to let his girlfriend drive during those hours."

※

Take Medication When Driving. If you anticipate a problem with accidents or speeding tickets, or if your teenager has already received several tickets, ask your physician about having him take medication (Ritalin or Dexedrine) at 6:00 or 7:00 in the evening when he drives on the weekend. Ritalin taken at 7:00 should wear off by 11:00 or so. This runs counter to the general medical advice not to take medication too late in the day to avoid sleep problems. However, most teenagers stay up late on weekends anyway so sleep difficulties caused by taking Ritalin may not be a major problem. Medication should help improve your child's concentration and reduce his impulsiveness. Having a driver who is more alert and aware of his speed may be worth the risk of a mild sleep problem.

※

"Our son is taking 10 mg. Ritalin around seven o'clock on Friday and Saturday nights. It's still too early to tell how much this will help him, but his girlfriend tells us he is driving more slowly."

※

Use Logical Consequences. Tell your teenager in advance what the consequences for speeding tickets will be and stick to it. "If you get a speeding ticket, you will have to pay for it." Or, you may elect to take driving privileges away for a week or two, or a month.

If your child accumulates many tickets, you should reassess the consequences you are using. Logical consequences that sound good but aren't necessarily effective include: (1) "You will have to pay for any increases in our insurance premiums." Sometimes insurance companies check drivers' records only once a year. Up to a year could pass before your teenager experiences any consequences. Consequences are more effective if they occur soon after an offense. (2) "The State will take away your license if you accumulate a certain number of points for speeding tickets." Again, two years may pass before your child's driver's license is suspended. By that time, he may have matured significantly, outgrown some of his impulsive behavior, and become a fairly responsible driver. These real-life consequences certainly are acceptable, but others may need to be used earlier before your child's driving record reaches a crisis level.

Ride with a Police Officer. One set of parents elected to use a somewhat unusual approach. They allowed their teenager to ride on duty with a police officer so he could see the dangers of speeding from another perspective. Although this arrangement can be a good learning experience, it is also potentially dangerous for the teenager. Liability issues may also make most police departments reluctant to allow teenagers to ride on duty with them.

※

"Our son was stopped twice in one week for speeding by the same police officer. The officer was very kind and came to our home to talk to us. We suggested that our son ride on patrol with him one night. We hoped he would see the potential danger of speeding. My son established a good rapport with the officer and saw him as a human being, not just a man in a uniform. He developed a new respect for the police. Previously, he was negative toward them because he had been stopped for speeding several times. He really seemed to want to curb his speed.

ᘳ

"Things got a little too exciting while they were on patrol. They were the first car on the scene to investigate a stabbing at a local fast food restaurant."

ᘳ

Have Your Teenager Pay for His Own Insurance. If your teenager has to pay for part or all of his own insurance, he will definitely experience the natural consequences of getting speeding tickets or having accidents. If he gets several tickets, he may not be able to afford the insurance. If you pay for his insurance, consider having him pay for any rate increases. Also, remind him that once he is out of school he will have to pay for his own insurance.

Insurance May Be Canceled or Be Cost Prohibitive. If your teenager has a major accident, plus has received several speeding tickets, insurance costs may be prohibitive. Insurance companies may cancel the family's insurance or continue the policy for the parents while refusing to reinsure the teenager. If this happens, insurance coverage may be purchased from a high-risk pool, but will be more expensive. Quotes from a high risk pool for adequate insurance coverage to protect the parents' assets in the event of a lawsuit may range from $1,500 to $15,000 a year. Discussing the potential consequences of a poor driving record for you and your teenager in advance may be of some help.

ᘳ

"We were notified that our insurance company would no longer provide automobile insurance coverage for our son because he had so many speeding tickets. We were able to obtain coverage for our son (liability:

$50,000 per person, $100,000 per accident) in a high-risk pool for approximately $3,000 annually."

ᘳ

Check Tire Size and Speedometer. If your teenager doesn't think he was speeding when he was given a ticket, he may be right. Have the speedometer checked; it may not be accurate. Some teenagers with ADD love to customize their cars and trucks. Sometimes they buy oversized tires. Larger tires will cause the speedometer to read incorrectly, so the teenager will actually be driving faster than the speedometer shows. An authorized speedometer repair service can fix any problems with the speedometer and issue a statement about any speedometer error.

Appeal the Speeding Ticket. If you or your child obtains a certified statement from the repair service, you can usually appeal a speeding ticket in traffic court. The judge's response will vary. He may dismiss the ticket or allow the teenager to plead guilty to a lower rate of speed. Pleading guilty to a lower rate of speed may eliminate the addition of any points to his driving record. But he will still probably have to pay a fine.

Plead Nolo Contendere. Sometimes a teenager cited for a traffic violation may plead *nolo contendere* in court, which means, "I agree to pay the fine, but I am not pleading guilty." In some states, if a nolo plea is entered, no points are added to the driving record. If you believe your teenager's driving skills are improving and he should be allowed to drive, you may want to consider this option.

Take a Defensive Driving Course. In some states, a teenager may take a defensive driving course and have the number of points on his driving record reduced.

Sexual Behavior

The sexual behavior of teenagers with ADD may be influenced by their impulsivity, tendency to take risks, or excessive alcohol or drug use. They may be more likely to experiment sexually, and therefore more likely to contract a venereal disease or get pregnant. Some may have sexual intercourse indiscriminately with multiple partners. When drugs or alcohol are combined with these characteristics, girls with ADD may be more likely to put themselves in dangerous situations which could result in rape or assault. Rape brings not only the emotional trauma of the rape itself but also the risk of AIDS.

According to a study by the CDC, 43.4 percent of all high school students have engaged in sexual intercourse. Sixteen percent had sexual intercourse for the first time before age 13. Presumably, with their impulsivity, teenagers with ADD have even higher rates of sexual activity.

🦋

"I was shocked when my son told me he was only 12 years old the first time he engaged in sex with a girl."

🦋

It is your responsibility to ensure that your teenager receives appropriate sex education. You should not assume that someone else will teach your child what he needs to know about sexual relationships. The emergence of AIDS is forcing us as parents to change the way we approach sex education with our children, especially impulsive teenagers with ADD. Being sexually active in this day and age can be deadly. We can no longer permit our children to learn about sex from their friends and through experimentation.

Discuss Values Related to Sexual Relationships. If you have a comfortable relationship with your teenager, discuss important elements of sexual relationships with him. Basic anatomical differences between men and women are often taught in biology or science classes. However, other important issues must be addressed at home or through classes: love, commitment, making decisions, responsible relationships, sexual intercourse, birth control, protection from disease, and pregnancy. Sometimes it is nice to have spontaneous discussions on these topics. Again, teachable moments are important. For example, if there is a TV program, newspaper article, or a class discussion, ask how he feels about the topic. This is also your opportunity to share your values regarding sexual relationships.

Any discussion should be a two-way open exchange of information. Listen to your teenager's opinions. If you disagree, avoid arguing or putting him down. His ideas may change with time, but for now may be different from yours. Briefly, explain the reason for your beliefs. You may well be influencing his thinking, although he may not show it at the time.

Avoid Tempting Your Teenager. You and your teenager may develop rules for having a girlfriend (boyfriend) come for a visit. For example, your teen cannot be home alone with his girlfriend. When you are home, however, his friends are always welcome. Know where your teenager is going and whether or not the activity will be supervised.

Avoid Overreacting. If you come home and find your teenager involved in heavy kissing and petting, don't jump to the conclusion that he or she has had sexual intercourse. Try not to overreact and attack the teen ("You're promiscuous. You'd have sex with anything that moves."). If you do so and impose a harsh punishment, the teenager may respond just as angrily. He may think, "Since my mother already thinks I'm having sex, I may as well go ahead and do it." A more helpful approach may be an open discussion and an agreement on rules regarding being at home without parental supervision.

Teach Your Teen It's Okay to Say No. Knowing the reasons why teenagers have sex may help you prepare your child to say no to sexual activity. "You may be pressured by your friends to be sexually active before you are ready. You might get a lot of peer pressure ('Everyone is doing it'). Or you might want to be popular or be curious about what it's like. Someone might use guilt ('I've spent a lot of money on you') or make threats ('I won't date you anymore unless you have sex with me'). Or you might feel you have to prove you're not gay. You may even feel as if you need to rebel against Dad and me because we're too strict. Anticipate these pressures and try to figure out in advance how you will respond to them. If you like, I'll help you figure out what to say."

Emphasize that it is okay to say no. Explain that people may try to pressure him into being sexually active by bragging about their own "manly" conquests, calling him names, saying he must be gay, or daring him. According to Dr. Marion Howard, author of *How to Help your Teenager Postpone Sexual Involvement,* there are several steps your teenager may take: 1) Make a direct statement. "No. I don't want to do that." 2) Turn the pressure around by asking, "Why are you trying to pressure me into doing something I don't want to do?" 3) Put them on the defensive by saying "You're making me angry by pressuring me to do something I don't want to do." 4) If the pressure continues, leave or ask to be taken home.

Provide Sex Education. Sexual behavior is such an emotionally charged issue, each family will approach it differently. You should select an approach to teaching about sexual issues that you feel comfortable with and that is consistent with your values.

The young people of today are having sex at a younger age and may be more sexually active than we suspect. Since teens with ADD may experiment early, most will need information early in their teenage years. Actually, the foundation of sex education really begins well before the teenage years. During adolescence, more specific information about sexual intercourse, birth control, and protection from disease may be provided. However, if you have a teenager and are just now getting started teaching sex education, that's okay too. Better now than never.

Arrange for a Sex Education Class. Children and teenagers are often embarrassed to talk about sex with their parents. So they may be more receptive to taking a class at their church, synagogue, or school. Even then, they may feel more comfortable if they are allowed to write down their questions rather than ask them aloud. If your teen does attend a class, you should still provide reading material at home, including a reference book, and be available to answer questions.

The availability of good sex education programs varies across the country. Some areas are conservative and offer only cursory sex education. Some existing programs place an emphasis on responsible decision-making skills, including identifying choices, weighing decisions, and evaluating outcomes. Other programs have older teens talk with younger ones to help them withstand peer pressure to have sex. These teens serve as role models who are attractive and popular yet are not sexually active.

Provide Reading Materials. Make reference materials available to your teenager. This way your teenager can look things up in a book without having to ask you questions. *Changing Bodies, Changing Lives* by Ruth Bell is one factual, non-judgmental source of information regarding a wide range of sexual issues. Dr. Howard's book on postponing sexual

involvement, plus *Be Smart About Sex: Facts for Young People,* by Hal and Jean Fiedler, may also be helpful. You may also suggest that your teenager write down any questions he may have and give them to you. This may be a less embarrassing way to handle sensitive sexual questions.

Local churches, synagogues, chapters of the Red Cross, AIDS organizations, Planned Parenthood, or health departments have information and materials to help educate about sexual issues. Your local library is also an excellent resource.

Talk with Your Teen about the Impact of Pregnancy. You may want to talk with your teenager about the responsibilities of being a parent. Since teens with ADD tend to think in concrete terms rather than abstract ones, discuss the impact in specific details. Look for a teachable moment when the issue of pregnancy comes up. You might ask, "How would your life change if your girlfriend (or you) were pregnant?" After he responds, share a few more ideas. For example, "Have you also thought that babies require a lot of time and love? You don't sleep very well because they wake up every 3–4 hours at night. Babies are totally helpless. You have to feed them, give them a bath, change their diapers, put on their clothes, and take them to the doctor. You can't go out at night without getting a babysitter. Babies are expensive too. The hospital and doctor costs of having a baby range from $3,000 to $10,000, or even more. You have to buy them clothes, diapers, food, medicine, and pay for child care."

For boys you could also say, "If your girlfriend gets pregnant, you may have to pay $100 to $200 a month child support." For girls, "Your body changes, you can't wear your clothes, your friends may avoid being with you, and you can't go out unless you find a babysitter. Having a child is wonderful, but you will be able to handle it better when you are older, in love, married, and you and your husband want children."

⚜

"One teenage father with ADD had to pay 25 dollars a week child support while he was in high school. After he graduated from high school, he had to pay fifty dollars a week. Two hundred dollars a month is a lot for a teenager to have to earn. He had to work while he went to college to pay child support."

Consider Birth Control. If you learn that your teenager is sexually active, you will have to struggle with the decision of whether to assist in obtaining birth control supplies. Although this may be in conflict with your family values, the alternatives—pregnancy or AIDS—are frightening. If your daughter does take birth control pills, she will probably need help remembering to take them.

Educate about the Risks of Unprotected Sex. The risk of sexually transmitted diseases (STDs), especially AIDS, poses tremendous health risks for anyone who is sexually active. Presently, slightly less than 1 percent of the population has AIDS. It is the sixth leading cause of death among teenagers. However, this low percentage rate is misleading, since a teenager who is exposed to AIDS when he is 13 will not show symptoms for 8 to 10 years, at age 21 or 22. Other diseases such as syphilis, gonorrhea, genital warts, herpes, and chlamydia can cause serious problems. Most of these diseases show symptoms and respond to treatment. However, chlamydia does not have any symptoms and, untreated, can cause infertility. Herpes cannot be cured, but is not fatal.

Some AIDS information you may want to share with your teenager includes: "AIDS is caused by the human immunodeficiency virus, HIV, which weakens the immune system. As a result, the body is unable to fight off disease and infection. AIDS is spread through the exchange of body fluids (blood, semen, vaginal secretions, saliva, tears, urine). The two most common ways the virus is passed from one person to another is unprotected sexual intercourse, both vaginal and anal, and blood on shared needles used for illegal drugs. You can't get AIDS from coughs, shaking hands, or toilet seats. People who have AIDS don't show symptoms for several years so you can't tell by just looking at someone whether or not they have AIDS. Furthermore, a person may not even know he has AIDS, and may unknowingly give it to you. Anyone can get AIDS even if it's their first time to have sex."

"AIDS can strike anyone regardless of age or wealth. Remember how stunned everyone was to learn that Magic Johnson, one of the greatest basketball players of all times, had the HIV virus. Although he had not developed any obvious symptoms of AIDS, he retired from playing basketball."

The CDC has a toll-free telephone hot-line to answer your questions about AIDS: 1–800–342–AIDS.

Suicide Risk

According to the CDC, suicide is the third leading cause of death among young people between the ages of 15 and 24. Among teenagers ages 15 to 19, approximately 1 in 9,000, or .01 percent, commit suicide each year.

One study found that the number of youngsters with ADHD who *attempted* suicide (10 percent) was higher than for youngsters without the disorder. (In this study, none of the children without ADHD attempted suicide.) As discussed in Chapter 1, research statistics on ADHD tend to be higher since they are collected on children with more serious problems. However, if even a 5 percent rate is accurate, the high risk of suicide for children with ADD is of serious concern.

Suicidal thoughts and planning among all high school students are alarmingly common. Approximately 60–65 percent have thought about committing suicide. Twenty-five percent have actually gone so far as to develop a plan. Although girls attempt suicide five or six times more often than males, more boys die as a result of their attempts. Boys tend to use more lethal methods, such as guns, to attempt suicide. However, suicides rates among females are starting to change since girls are also using more lethal methods. White male teens, primarily from middle to upper-middle class families, are responsible for 78 percent of all teenage suicides.

Teenage suicides have tripled in the last two decades. We must ask ourselves why? Perhaps our achievement-oriented, highly competitive society has contributed to this grim statistic. Failure and lack of achievement is very painful for adolescents with ADD. Even when they appear indifferent, most want to succeed. Some teenagers with ADD may develop feelings of hopelessness about their ability to succeed. They may think, "If I'm having such a difficult time passing high school classes, how can I ever succeed in college or life?"

Key stress factors which may lead a teenager to consider suicide include: depression, feeling alienated from the family, loss of a parent (death or divorce), feelings of hopelessness about the future, feelings of worthlessness, and employment problems. Other factors that may trigger an attempt include: loneliness, breaking up with a girlfriend or boyfriend, a fight with parents, pressure to succeed at school, receiving bad grades, failure in academics or athletics, not getting accepted into college, poor health, or physical awkwardness. Teenagers who consider suicide tend to have low self-esteem and feel unworthy, abandoned, and unloved. They are deeply angry with themselves and those around them. Their depression manifested through delinquency, drug addiction, and alcoholism may actually be a "cry for help" and an indicator of suicidal risk.

Other factors may also contribute to suicidal risk. Nearly half of all adolescent suicide victims used drugs or alcohol just before they died. Some teenagers may seem to have a "death wish" by drinking excessively and speeding. The availability of guns also increases the risk of suicide. Suicides are five times more likely to occur in homes where guns are present. Teenagers who are gay are at greater risk for a suicide attempt. While only 10 percent of all teens are gay, they account for 30 percent of adolescent suicides. For girls, a very stressful time is at the end of their first sexual relationship.

To add to these risks, teenagers with ADD tend to be more emotional and impulsive. Their impulsivity, risk-taking behavior, and failure to recognize the consequences of their actions may also increase the risk of having a suicide attempt or serious accident.

Suicide is a very difficult, emotional topic to discuss. No parent wants to think that his teenager might attempt suicide. You must be alert, however, and watch for signs of serious depression or comments that your child wishes he were dead or wants to kill himself. Most people who are considering suicide give warnings about their intentions. A list of warning signals is provided in Table 7–3.

Any comment by a teenager that he is going to kill himself should be taken seriously. It is also critical to know that someone who has been depressed for a long time but suddenly no longer seems depressed may have decided to commit suicide. The sudden mood change may be a warning sign that such a decision has been made.

Frequently, teenagers are undecided about living or dying. In some ways it is a form of Russian Roulette. They leave it up to fate or others to save them. Asking questions and providing supervision,

---

Table 7–3

WARNING SIGNS OF SUICIDE RISK*

- Direct and indirect statements ("I wish I were dead")
- Severe depression (despondency, loss of zest, weight loss)
- Changes in eating or sleeping habits
- Apathy about school, job, interests
- Dramatic drop in grades; hobbies and sports, once important, are ignored
- Withdrawal from friends, family, and social activities
- Giving away prized possessions
- Increased use of alcohol or other drugs
- Experience of recent loss (death of family member, break-up with girlfriend or boyfriend, moving away from friends, poor health, loss of respect)
- Preoccupation with death
- Unusual purchase (gun, knife, rope)
- Making final arrangements (for adults): wills, funeral plans, insurance changes
- Previous suicide attempts

* *Information regarding suicide is summarized from the Channing L. Bete Co. booklet, "What Is Suicide?" and from "The Alarming Rise in Teenage Suicide," by Mary Ann O'Roark, McCall's, January 1992.*

when warning signals are observed, could save their lives.

Ask about Suicidal Thoughts. "You seem really stressed out. Are you okay? Tell me what's going on." If you are concerned, ask your teenager straight out, "Are you considering suicide?" Or "Are you thinking of harming yourself?"

Listening Is Critical. Listen to what he has to say. Assure him that you love him and that you will help him work through this difficult time. Listening and responding to him in a loving way are the two most important things you can do. Don't argue, criticize, or make him feel guilty. Offer support but don't make judgmental comments. Don't say, "Things are not as bad as you think." Or, "Things could be worse." If you listen to what he has to say, often he will tell you why he wants to commit suicide. You won't have to ask. If he won't talk or denies he is considering suicide, talk in confidence with one of his friends. Ask if they have observed any of the warning signs of suicide.

Show Concern and Affection. Don't be afraid to show your teenager love and affection during this time. Hug him, pat him on the shoulder, hold his hand if it seems appropriate. Tell him you love him and that you will always be there when he needs you. Don't be afraid to cry and laugh together.

❧

"Once my teenaged son was very depressed and I feared a suicide attempt. We talked and cried together. I told him how much I loved him and how sad my world would be if something happened to him."

❧

Take Action to Reduce Depression. Depression, a key factor in suicidal risk, sometimes occurs when people feel they have no control over their lives. One way to combat depression is to identify one or two critical areas of concern to your teenager and develop a plan to resolve them. Ask him what you can do to help. Then develop a plan together. For example, if he is upset about failing a course at school, plan to work with him or get a tutor to bring up his grades. If he has broken up with his girlfriend, would it help for him to talk with his best friend, take a special trip (supervised, of course), or work on a special hobby? Buying a new computer game or going on a trip may help him keep his mind on more positive things. By taking action, your teenager will begin to feel he has some control over his life and future. He also gains experience coping with disappointments in life and problem solving.

Talk with him about the need to see a treatment professional and the possibility that medication such as an antidepressant may help him feel normal again. If your teenager is resistant, explain how the antidepressant works. "When depression is present, the neurotransmitter serotonin is low. Antidepressant medications help increase production of serotonin, and can therefore help you feel better." More information on antidepressants is provided in Chapter 4.

Remove Weapons and Medications from the Home. Remove any potentially lethal weapons and medications from the house. As mentioned earlier, the risk of suicide increases significantly when guns are available in the home. Antidepressant medications in large quantities also pose the risk of a fatal overdose.

Seek Professional Help. If your teenager admits he is considering suicide or shows the warning signs, call a psychiatrist or psychologist immediately to discuss the risk. If your teenager has already developed a detailed plan for suicide, seek help as quickly as possible. The psychiatrist or psychologist can decide whether your child should be brought in for an assessment. If it is an emergency and you don't have a psychiatrist or psychologist, call your local community mental health center (CMHC) or hospital emergency room. These staff have received crisis training and know how to deal with potential suicide attempts.

Provide Supervision. If you think your teenager is extremely depressed, keep him busy and provide supervision and companionship. While you are deciding if you should seek professional help, make certain he does not spend a lot of time alone. You may need to explain your concerns to his brother, sister, or friend and enlist their help keeping him busy.

Supervision will still be needed even after a suicidal teenager begins to feel better. Some research has shown that many suicides occur within three months after a person starts to feel better. By that time, he may have found the energy to carry out a suicide plan.

Weapons

In today's world, many teenagers—whether or not they have ADD—seem to be enamored with guns and other weapons. Guns in the schools have become a national crisis. One in 18 high school students (5.5 percent) has actually carried a gun for protection or self-defense. Nightly news programs tell of teenagers being shot at school over trivial issues that were resolved through fist fights a generation earlier. Guns are easily accessible to young people today, and some teenagers feel they need them for protection. Some teenagers are also drawn to knives or novel weapons such as oriental nun chakus or brass knuckles. For some teenagers, impulsivity and risk-taking behaviors may make the combination of weapons and ADD extremely dangerous, not only for others, but the teenager himself.

When guns are used for hunting, the dangers of accidents or playing with guns may not be as great. In some parts of the country, interest in guns is a family matter, since hunting is a major activity for teenagers and their fathers. Often children are carefully trained in the proper use and care of guns starting at a young age. However, they will still need close supervision when guns are used because of their impulsiveness.

Remove Guns from Home. If you are concerned about your teenager's impulsivity, aggression, or risk of suicide, remove all guns from the house. Storing them at a friend's or relative's house would be ideal. If you keep guns in the car, chances are the teenager can still get to them.

Lock Up Guns. You may decide to leave guns in your home if you feel that your teenager is responsible and that impulsivity and aggression are not problems. The guns should be locked up, however, and only the parents should have a key.

Provide Safety Training. If your teenager is determined to be involved with guns, you may offer him the opportunity to participate in gun safety classes, hunting trips, or visits to shooting ranges so he can learn the proper way to shoot guns. This may also satisfy his need to have and shoot a gun in a safer, structured environment. You could take him to a firing range so that he can practice his marksmanship. If you let him participate in a "forbidden" activity under safe, supervised conditions,

some of the appeal of the forbidden may be removed.

Set Limits. If a discussion of gun ownership comes up, make it clear to your teenager that he will not be allowed to have a handgun until he is legally old enough to buy one. Legal age for owning handguns is 21 in many states. However, teenagers can legally own shotguns or rifles. If you think your teenager will take it as a personal challenge to go out and buy a gun, don't bring this issue up spontaneously. Discuss it naturally when the issue comes up on TV or in the newspaper.

Take Guns Away. If you find a handgun, either lock it away in a safe place or give it to the police. You should first find out, however, what the police will do. Will they press charges against your child, attempt to find the person who sold the gun, or accept the gun with no questions asked? If you have a family friend who is a policeman, an attorney, or judge, you may ask them how these matters will be handled. Or you could make an anonymous phone call. However, chances are that all calls to the police can be traced. For most teenagers, this may be their only involvement with guns. However, if your teenager buys another gun, repeat the same action. Take it away and lock it up or otherwise dispose of it.

⚜

"I couldn't believe my wonderful son had bought a gun. I was terrified and felt totally incompetent. I stood facing him crying and yelling at the same time. 'I will not let you have a gun. I am afraid you will get killed or hurt someone else and be in jail for the rest of your life. I love you too much to let you have a gun.'"

⚜

If he flies into a terrible rage when he discovers you have taken his gun, leave his presence and let him cool off. If you are afraid for your physical safety, leave the house. You should talk with your treatment professional about how to handle issues with guns.

Discuss the Issue with Your Teenager. Afterwards, you need to talk with your teenager. Make it clear he will not be allowed to have a handgun in your home under any circumstances. It is illegal and dangerous. "I love you too much to let you have a handgun. I am not going to take a chance that you will get killed with it or accidently hurt someone else. Most people who are shot at home are killed with their own gun."

You could also say, "I assume you feel you have a good reason for getting a gun. Why don't you tell me about it?" If he has a valid reason for concern, help him find another way to solve the problem.

※

"One teenager who bought a gun had been beaten up on two occasions by a bully at school. These attacks were unprovoked and his fears justifiable. His parents decided to help reduce their teenager's fears by making school officials aware of the other student's aggressiveness. It turned out that the boy had been expelled from school and was hanging out illegally on school grounds. In addition, they offered to sign him up for a self-defense course, plus gave him mace to carry in his car."

Brushes with the Law

Teenagers with ADD may occasionally get in trouble with school officials, law enforcement agencies, or courts. They may be suspended from school, given a ticket, taken home, or arrested. Usually, their misbehavior is not malicious but done impulsively without thought of consequences. Nonetheless, these problems worry their parents sick.

Thinking back about all the teenagers with ADD I have known, I can remember several examples of impulsive, hair-brained, and sometimes dangerous behavior:

- getting stopped for speeding and impulsively arguing with the police officer.
- driving the family car alone before they were old enough to have a driver's license and being stopped by police.
- driving a car into a mailbox while picking something up out of the floorboard.
- sneaking out of the house at night and being brought home for breaking curfew.
- being arrested for public drunkenness.
- having a loud party at the home of a teenager whose parents are out of town; having police called.

- jumping off a bridge and getting a ticket for trespassing.
- being dared to take an item in a store and being arrested for shoplifting.
- getting a girlfriend pregnant and being ordered by the court to pay child support.
- being caught with drugs or a weapon at school.
- being arrested for possession of a gun.
- fighting at school; police were called.
- being given a ticket for water skiing after sunset.
- running away from home and stealing money to buy food to eat.
- drinking underage and being caught by police.
- drinking a beer, driving into a mailbox, and receiving a DUI.
- drinking too much and being raped; pressing charges; AIDS testing.
- making an unsuccessful suicide attempt.

Be Aware of Factors Contributing to Delinquency. Perhaps you fear that your teenager may become involved in malicious delinquent acts such as vandalism, burglary, or assault. If so, you may find information from Dr. Scott Henggeler, professor at the Medical University of South Carolina, helpful in understanding development of delinquent behavior. Dr. Henggeler explains that the number one predictor of delinquent behavior is having "deviant" friends who are breaking the law. Not surprisingly, delinquency is also linked with substance abuse. Clearly, friends who are using drugs or are delinquent present a major problem for your teenager. Just as clearly, it is important for you to subtly encourage your teen to make friends with others who can be a positive influence.

Other factors which Dr. Henggeler notes as contributing to delinquency include: parents with problems such as alcoholism, drug abuse, or mental illness; poor family relations, including a lack of love in the family; lack of supervision and structure; and poor performance at school. Another interesting tidbit of information is that the peak time for juvenile crime is 3:00 p.m., right after school.

Impose Consequences But Don't Overreact. Obviously, behaviors such as those listed above are totally inappropriate. When they occur, we are embarrassed and horrified that this may mean our teenager will be a "juvenile delinquent." Even though some of these offenses are very serious, it does not mean that the teenager cannot grow up to be a productive adult. Dr. Henggeler notes that nationally, 70 percent of first-time offenders have no further brushes with the law. I don't want to understate the seriousness of these problems, but I urge parents not to give up on their teenager. You should continue to believe in your teenager, while addressing each problem as it comes up.

Avoid Court Involvement. Sometimes parents feel so overwhelmed that they petition the court to help control their teenager's behavior. However, sending a teenager to juvenile court is not going to magically make him behave. Usually, the court imposes a consequence—community service, a fine, a curfew, or a loss of privileges. The court may also place the teenager on probation and monitor his behavior. What most courts can't do, however, is provide treatment.

My cousin, Judge Billy Shaw Abney, Walker County, Georgia, is a juvenile court judge with over 30 years experience. He believes that in 95 percent of the families who come before his court in this rural county, the parents are more concerned than anyone else. If the court stays out of the picture and gives parents a chance, most parents correct the problem at home. He reports that only 17 percent of the children seen in his court return a second time. Judge Abney has serious reservations about locking them up with other delinquent youngsters. Research shows that being with other delinquents only teaches someone how to be a better delinquent.

Juvenile court records of delinquency can come back to haunt a teenager as an adult. For example, a teenager may not be accepted into or may be released from the military if he has a court record, even though very minor. Although in many states juvenile records are confidential, the military and other organizations may ask the teenager to sign a release that allows access to his records.

Intervene Early/Provide Supervision and Structure. During his twenty years in Newton County Juvenile Court (Georgia), Judge Virgil

Costly has seen many parents who didn't spend enough quality time with their children. He has observed that parents may see problem behaviors early but don't intervene. They don't seem to know how to help their child.

According to Judge Costly, keeping teenagers involved in activities or providing supervision after school is critical. Parents may have to make adjustments in their activities and lifestyle to provide adequate supervision for their child. Sending the teenager to a psychologist an hour a week and expecting that to solve all the problems is not a realistic solution. Parents need to work together with their teenager to come up with solutions to their family's problems. Parents may also have to look at their own behavior to see if they are doing anything that may be contributing to their child's behavior.

Prepare for Court. If your teenager has broken the law and must go to juvenile court, the following information may be helpful. Most state laws give juvenile court judges greater latitude in dealing with teenagers under 18, allowing them to take into consideration the "foolishness of youth." Typically, an attorney will not be needed except for the most serious charges.

You will need to help your teenager present his case. Court may be difficult for him if he has verbal expression or processing problems. Most judges are not aware that many of these youngsters have difficulty organizing their thoughts and expressing themselves clearly. Teenagers who process information slowly may have little to say or respond slowly, which may come across as insolence or lack of remorse. They may appear confused at times.

Conservative dress—no wild tee shirts with profanity—plus a decent haircut will make a more favorable impression on most judges. Leaving the earring at home may also be a good idea. Encourage your teenager to speak respectfully to the judge and look him in the eye when talking. Be certain he takes his medicine before he goes to court so he can listen and pay attention.

You may help him think ahead and practice what he will say. When you and your teenager are allowed to speak, make brief but methodical comments. By watching the people ahead of you in court, you may get a better feel for how to speak to the judge. Your teenager will probably speak first and admit or deny the allegations, mention if it is his first offense, describe consequences already imposed by parents, and express his regret. You will also probably have the opportunity to speak and may mention anything your teenager left out: your teenager's good character, his ADD and impulsiveness, his good grades (if true), community activities (religious or sports), this one-time lapse in good judgment (if true), consequences already imposed, and the amount of structure and supervision usually provided.

Don't make a lot of excuses, but if the judge seems receptive, mention extenuating circumstances (medication had worn off, change in medication, death of relative, undiagnosed learning disabilities, or new undesirable friends); explain disciplinary steps you have already taken; mention a counselor or doctor you are already working with; and give additional suggestions. If the judge is interested, give information about ADD. Or preface remarks with a comment such as, "I know that his ADD (or his medication wearing off) is no excuse for his misbehavior (shoplifting), but it does contribute to this problem. He has signed up for karate class after school and we are encouraging him to spend more time with different friends (or giving him an afternoon dose of medicine to reduce impulsiveness) to correct this problem."

Judge Costly asks parents to tell him how they have handled past misbehavior, what consequences worked, and what suggestions they may have. This is more helpful than a parent blaming their child, saying he is bad, "throwing up their hands in defeat," and saying they have no idea what to do. Court-imposed consequences are often tailored to suit each child or offense and may include things like having to ride the school bus instead of riding with parents or driving themselves, volunteering at the animal shelter, picking up aluminum cans, or reading specific books and doing a book report.

Seek Treatment. Even if the court gets involved, the underlying problems will be there until your teenager receives proper treatment. If you are lucky, the judge will understand this. Judge Costly, for example, sees his role as helping parents find an effective treatment source. In his county, the local mental health center has assigned a counselor to his court. You may seek counseling for yourself as you learn to use consequences, find activities to build your teen's self-esteem, help him find a more positive peer group, or improve family communica-

tion skills. Or seek treatment for your teen, if depression or suicide are a risk.

Seek Help from the Court. Ultimately, if your teenager is totally out of control and a potential danger to himself or others, you may have no other choice but to ask the court to be involved. Sometimes courts can be helpful by mandating that your teenager and your family seek treatment. If you decide you need help from the court, call your local county juvenile court for advice.

Be Positive/Expect Good Things. Judge Abney believes that a self-fulfilling prophecy is a major factor in helping youngsters who get into trouble with the law. They will act as we expect them to act. No child leaves his court without hearing something positive from the judge. Children make mistakes and should not have to pay for them for the rest of their lives. In his thirty-plus years as a judge, he has seen youngsters in his court who have broken the law and grown up to be highly respected leaders in the community.

Skipping School/Dropping Out/Suspension

Students who enjoy and are succeeding in school don't have problems with truancy. However, some students with ADD experience so much failure in school that they begin to skip classes. School becomes so aversive, they don't want to go. According to Dr. Barkley, approximately 21 percent of teenagers with ADD repeatedly skip school. They also have a high risk of dropping out of school (35 percent) or being suspended (45 percent).

Make Adaptations at School. After learning problems have been identified, it is crucial to make adaptations to help your teenager succeed at school. School-related problems and adaptations are discussed in detail in Chapters 8, 9, and 10.

Running Away

A few teenagers with ADD become so unhappy, angry, and depressed that they run away to escape their pain and ease their frustration. Dr. Barkley's study found that running away from home (twice or more) was a significant problem for only 5 percent of teenagers with ADHD. When they do run away, the length of time they are gone varies from a few hours to several days or weeks.

Parents need to watch for potential problems—breaking up with a girlfriend, school failure, or family fights—and try to help their teenager cope with the crisis before the situation gets so painful that he runs away to avoid it.

Maintain Open Communication. If possible, keep lines of communication open with your teenager during the period of time he is away from home. Avoid arguing or threatening him during telephone conversations. The most important thing is to get him back home, safe and sound.

Try to Find Your Teen. Ask some of his friends to help you find him. They may know where he is staying. If he is missing for several days or you suspect he is in danger, call the police. Some police will begin looking immediately. But others won't take any action for several days until it is clear that your teenager has run away.

File a Petition. Sometimes, parents file a petition with the court to have their child declared unruly or ungovernable. Depending upon your teenager, this may or may not be helpful. Court involvement gives the parent some legal leverage to enforce certain rules such as curfews or school attendance. However, on the down side, if a teen still refuses to comply, he may become further entangled in the legal system. One parent who did this expressed deep regret because now every time her daughter does something, even minor, she sinks further into the bureaucracy. The mother has now lost custody of her teenager. Probation staff, against the recommendations of mental health professionals and wishes of the parent, are attempting to remove her from home and place her in a residential treatment program.

Seek Professional Help First Rather Than Court Involvement. If you still have a fairly decent relationship with your teenager, seek counseling first before court action. The reasons for avoiding court involvement are discussed in the preceding sections. A treatment professional may be able to help you and your family work out a solution to this conflict. If possible, seek help from a treatment professional or family friend who is also respected by your teenager.

Seek Other Successes. In addition to addressing the specific problems described in this chapter, you can also help resolve these issues indirectly. One of the best ways to do this is by helping your teen achieve some sense of normalcy, self-esteem, and joy by getting him involved in special activities—computer class, karate, or whatever his interests are. Chapter 5 contains more information on helping your teenager find other successes.

Conclusion

Helping a teenager navigate the troubles described in this chapter can be exhausting and stressful. You may shed many tears and spend many sleepless nights worrying. At times, you may wonder whether there is really anything useful that you, as a parent, can do. The answer is "yes." You can show your teenager you believe in him by supporting his success at home, at school, and in the community. As discussed in earlier chapters, helping your teenager get involved in activities he likes and can excel in is one excellent support strategy. A teenager who is doing well in school, sports, or other community activities is less likely to become involved with drugs, have need of a handgun, or otherwise get into trouble.

It is important to avoid power struggles if your child has any of the problems described in this chapter. The forbidden has tremendous appeal for teenagers with ADD. If you make a big deal about any issue, your teenager may embrace the challenge and show you he will do what he wants to do. As discussed in Chapters 8, 9, and 10, it is also critical to help your child succeed in school. Often teenagers with ADD have serious learning problems that have been overlooked by school personnel. Students who are succeeding at school are happier and less likely to get into trouble.

Finally, do not hesitate to seek professional help for yourself when your teenager is experiencing serious problems. You may learn new skills that enable you to help your teenager cope with this difficult time in his life.

Table 7-4

PROBLEM BEHAVIORS OF TEENAGERS WITH ADD
EASY REFERENCE GUIDE

A summary of the behaviors discussed in this chapter, as well as helpful interventions, is provided below.

Your teenager may have some but not all of these behaviors. Use common sense in dealing with these issues. If your teenager's problems are serious and these interventions are not working, SEEK PROFESSIONAL HELP. Find a counselor, social worker, physician, psychiatrist, or psychologist who understands ADD and works well with your family.

CHALLENGING BEHAVIORS	POSSIBLE INTERVENTIONS
• Defiance & Aggression	• Criteria for ODD/CD (Chapter 2)
	• Treatment (Chapter 4)
	• Anger control (Chapter 5)
	• Strategies for special education or regular class (Chapter 10)
• Substance abuse	• Convey concern and trust
	• Avoid scare tactics
	• Educate about substances
	• Provide an overview
	• Utilize fact sheets
	• Use teachable moments
	• Avoid mixing alcohol/drugs and meds
	• Parental dilemmas
	• Absolutely no drinking and driving
	• Develop a contract for driving
	• Provide supervision
	• Influence selection of friends
	• Watch for signs of substance abuse
	• How you can help
	• Find what works for your teen
	• Impose consequences
	• Should you use drug testing?
	• Seek professional help
• Speeding Tickets/ Accidents	• Send to driver training
	• Develop a contract for driving
	• Gradually increase driving time
	• Purchase a slow tank
	• Identify high risk time for tickets
	• Let others drive
	• Take medication when driving
	• Use logical consequences
	• Pay for tickets
	• Ride with police officer
	• Have teen pay for insurance
	• Insurance may be canceled
	• Check tire size/speedometer
	• Appeal speeding ticket

- Plead nolo contendere
- Take defensive driving course

- Sexual Behavior
  - Discuss values re: sexual matters
  - Avoid tempting your teen
  - Avoid overreacting
  - Teach it's okay to say no
  - Provide sex education
  - Arrange for sex education class
  - Provide reading materials
  - Talk about impact of pregnancy
  - Consider birth control
  - Educate about AIDS/unprotected sex

- Suicide Risk
  - Watch for warning signs of suicide
  - Ask about suicidal thoughts
  - Listen to teen
  - Show concern/affection
  - Take action to reduce depression
  - Remove weapons/medications from home
  - Seek professional help
  - Provide supervision

- Weapons
  - Remove guns from home
  - Lock up guns
  - Provide safety training
  - Set limits
  - Take guns away
  - Discuss weapons with your teen
  - Address his fears

- Brushes with the Law
  - Be aware of factors contributing to deliquency
  - Promote positive friends
  - Impose consequences but don't overreact
  - Avoid court involvement
  - Intervene early/provide supervision & structure
  - Prepare for court
  - Seek help from court
  - Seek treatment
  - Be positive/expect good things

- Skipping School/ Dropping Out/Suspension
  - Identify learning problems
  - Make adaptations at school
  - See Chapters 8, 9, & 10

- Running Away
  - Maintain open communication
  - Try to find your teen
  - Seek professional help rather than court involvement
  - Seek other successes

CHAPTER EIGHT

THE PARENT'S ROLE IN ELIMINATING ACADEMIC AGONY

"The memories of those early school years came flooding back as I read your book, and tears sometimes filled my eyes. Scott's kindergarten teacher loved him but she told us at his graduation that he marched to the beat of a different drummer and he would have a difficult time with school. Truer words were never spoken.

"It was the beginning of 12 years of agony for us all. How Scott survived with a desire to go on to college is a miracle. His ADD was not diagnosed until he was eighteen."

For many teenagers with an attention deficit disorder, attending school is truly academic agony. As many parents might expect, the teenager's inattention and impulsivity usually make it more difficult for him to succeed in middle and high school. Another debilitating, often hidden factor may also have a profound impact on his school performance: *unidentified and untreated learning problems such as slow reading, writing, or math computation, and poor memory.* In turn, frustration with learning problems may lead to behavior problems. Indeed, coping with the academic frustration that sometimes accompanies ADD can be emotionally upsetting to the whole family. All these factors, plus the defiance and anger of some teenagers with ADD, may make the teenage school years exasperating for all concerned.

For most teens with ADD, medical treatment and academic interventions are critical for success in school. If ADD remains undiagnosed or improperly treated, some teenagers will achieve only marginal successes at school. Others may suffer through years of failure, discouragement, and underachievement in school, hating the hours they are "trapped" in classrooms. They may become extremely discouraged and eventually drop out of school. There is little or no joy in learning for these teenagers.

Obviously, many of these problems at school can contribute to problems at home. This chapter discusses typical school-related problems, including homework hassles and school failure, and suggests ways to deal with them. It also presents research data about common learning and behavior problems.

As discussed in Chapter 4, if your teenager continues to struggle even after treatment has begun, reassessing his academic needs should be a top priority. Specifically, 1) have your teenager evaluated for learning problems, as described in Chapter 10, and 2) in partnership with school personnel, develop a plan to meet the academic needs of your teenager at home (Chapters 8 and 9) and school (Chapter 10).

The Educational Endurance Test

For some of these teenagers, school represents an unpleasant educational endurance test. It is as if they are forced into "careers" (school) for 12 years which many strongly dislike and in which they have difficulty succeeding. Most adults avoid or quit unpleasant endurance tests. Adults usually do not enter careers or participate in sports they hate or in which they cannot excel. Teenagers do not have the same luxury where school is concerned, however.

⚋

"By the time Cassie got to high school, we knew that even with medication she was not going to be an academically brilliant performer. She had often expressed that school was painful for her. It was the worst part of her day and the worst part of her week. Most of Cassie's school life the only thing she felt she excelled in was art."

⚋

"Even though he was very bright, most of Alex's school experiences have been negative. As a result, he hates school. He attends school because it is statutorily required and thankfully because he is a teenager and girls are now a major interest. The few joys he has gained from school are the social interactions with friends, physical education, computer, and industrial shop classes."

Reason for Concern

Researchers have confirmed what parents already knew: there are good reasons to be concerned about their teenager's potential academic problems. The key word here is *potential*. The information shared in this chapter is intended to alert parents to *possible* problems their teenager may face. It is not intended to frighten you, but to make you aware that many school-related problems can be avoided through early intervention.

Most adolescents with ADHD are ill prepared for high school, according to Dr. Gabriella Weiss, a Canadian researcher who has done long-term studies on ADHD. For many, learning disabilities and ADD together add up to significant problems at school.

Learning Disabilities

You may hear a number of different names for learning problems: learning disability (LD), specific learning disability (SLD), learning disorder,

learning deficits, etc. The meaning of these labels is basically the same. For a variety of reasons, the student has more trouble learning than his peers, even though he has average or above average intelligence.

The criteria used in determining whether a student has SLD are spelled out in a federal law called the Individuals with Disabilities Education Act (IDEA). These criteria are somewhat different than those the American Psychiatric Association has established for LD in the *Diagnostic and Statistical Manual (DSM)*.

If your child has learning disabilities, the label he is given—SLD or something else—matters for only one reason. If he is labeled as having SLD, he can automatically qualify for special education services under as the Individuals with Disabilities Education Act (IDEA). If he is considered to have a learning disability, but not SLD, the process of qualifying for special education services is not usually as cut and dried. There are, however, federal laws and policy memos that can be used to help him obtain special education services. See Chapter 11 for more information.

Specific Learning Disabilities (SLD). According to Dr. Russell Barkley, the number of students with ADHD and specific learning disabilities is probably between 20 to 25 percent. Under the Individuals with Disabilities Education Act, SLD is defined as *a significant discrepancy between a student's intelligence and his academic achievement.* A student may have a specific learning disability in one or more of seven academic areas: Oral Expression, Listening Comprehension, Written Expression, Basic Reading Skills, Reading Comprehension, Mathematics Calculation, or Mathematical Reasoning. Exactly how a student is determined to have SLD varies from state to state. In general, however, evaluators look for a *major discrepancy between ability and achievement.* A student is usually considered to have a major discrepancy if he receives a standardized achievement score that is a significant number of points lower than his cognitive ability (IQ) score. The point spread may need to be 20 points or higher, but varies from state to state.

Learning Disorders. The categories and eligibility criteria for learning disabilities included in DSM-IV are different from federal education criteria. The DSM includes the following Learning Disorders: Reading Disorder, Mathematics Disorder,

Disorder of Written Expression, and Learning Disorder Not Otherwise Specified. Students may meet criteria for these learning disabilities, but not SLD. No research is available about the number of teenagers who fall into this group. My best guesstimate is that perhaps 25 to 30 percent of middle and high school students with ADD have serious problems due to either a learning disorder or the characteristics of ADD. This is over and above the 25 percent diagnosed as having SLD.

Children with ADD share several common learning problems which are discussed in detail in Chapter 10. Briefly, researchers estimate that approximately one third of teenagers with ADHD have serious reading, spelling, and/or math disabilities. They tend to receive lower grades and have lower test scores on standardized achievement tests. Math computation is often a major problem for teenagers with ADD, probably because of their slow calculation of math problems. In addition, some have expressive language deficits. That is, they have difficulty organizing their thoughts and expressing themselves clearly when speaking or writing. Academically they may have trouble answering questions orally in class, writing a theme, or completing a test. Cognitive processing—reading, writing, and following verbal instructions—may be slow. Approximately half have listening comprehension problems, which means they have trouble following teacher lectures, taking notes, and understanding directions.

On top of everything, teenagers with ADD often have fine motor deficits, resulting in illegible handwriting. About half of these teenagers also have poor motor coordination. They may not do well in P.E. classes or sports. Frequently, teenagers with ADD have a combination of these learning problems.

Dyslexia is another term that is used to described serious learning problems in reading. However, it is not an official diagnostic category under federal SLD or DSM IV criteria. Other terms which may be used less frequently include: Dysgraphia, a form of dyslexia, in which the student has trouble understanding and writing words. Dyscalculia describes serious problems in solving math problems. The specific label used is not as important as identifying specific learning problems and making needed classroom adaptations.

Inattention and Impulsivity

The characteristics of ADD—inattention and impulsivity—can also adversely affect schoolwork. Teens with ADD may have trouble listening in class, daydream, forget homework, and take shortcuts in schoolwork. Their disorganization and difficulty getting started also make completion of schoolwork very hard. Several other factors which may affect schoolwork are discussed in more detail at the end of this chapter: hyperactivity, uneven academic effort, difficulty maintaining effort, sleep disturbance, lethargy, emotionality, low frustration tolerance, defiance, aggression, depression, anxiety, medication wearing off, and other medical problems.

School Failure

With all the potential academic problems these youngsters face, it should come as no surprise that teenagers with ADD are more likely to fail a grade or drop out of school. Also not surprisingly, they have lower self-esteem than other students. According to a study on teenagers with ADHD and ADD/I/WO by Dr. Barkley, approximately 30 percent of these teenagers had failed a grade. This rate was three times higher than for teenagers in a control group who did not have ADD. When students with ADHD and ADD/I/WO within the study were compared, teenagers with ADD/I/WO were more likely to repeat a grade than those with ADHD. Being retained a grade is very serious, as students who fail a grade are more likely to drop out of school.

Estimates of school drop-out rates vary, reaching as high as 30 percent. Jane Knitzer, a national child advocate and author of *At the Schoolhouse Door*, quotes drop-out rates of 48 percent for a broader group of children with serious emotional disturbances who were placed in classes for students with emotional or behavioral disorders (EBD). Students placed in EBD classes have the highest drop-out rate of all special education categories.

"Behavior Problems"

These teenagers are more likely to get into trouble at school by misbehaving, being defiant, or skipping school. In one study, Dr. Barkley found that they have significant problems with "stubbornness, defiance, refusal to obey, temper tantrums, and verbal hostility toward others." They may impulsively talk back to teachers or say things before they think.

Because of their behavior, students with ADD are ten times more likely to be suspended from school and seven times more likely to be expelled. Of the teenagers with ADHD in Dr. Barkley's study, 46 percent had been suspended and 11 percent expelled. On average, these teenagers had been suspended from school four times. According to Dr. Barkley, rates of truancy were reported at 21 percent.

Keeping Statistics in Perspective

Now that every parent's worst nightmare has been described, a word of caution about research studies may alleviate some anxiety. Most of these studies have been done on a narrowly selected group of youngsters with ADHD (a "clinical sample") who were referred to a clinic for treatment due to more serious problems. Consequently, the results of these studies are skewed negatively when compared to studies that would be conducted on youngsters with ADD who have adjusted fairly well and are receiving services primarily through their local pediatrician or adolescent medicine specialist (a "community or epidemiologically derived sample"). A community sample study by Dr. N. M. Lambert confirms that youngsters served in traditional settings do not have as serious problems as those in clinical samples. These youngsters had less than half the academic problems, antisocial behavior, and ADHD symptoms in adolescence of those in clinical samples.

Parents often look to research studies to help anticipate their teenager's behavior. Obviously, it is important to keep study results in perspective, especially those that are negatively skewed. Otherwise, parents may give up or expect the worst and get it (a negative self-fulfilling prophesy).

Having read this far, some parents may be feeling overwhelmed at the childrearing task that lies ahead. Other parents may be somewhat relieved to know that their adolescent is not so different from others with ADD. A third group of parents may consider themselves extremely lucky because their teenager has had only minor problems. Regardless, don't be discouraged by what may happen in the future. Some teenagers with ADD do extremely well in school. And if yours does not, you are educating yourself now so you can take steps early to avoid potential academic pitfalls.

Success in School Is Critical

Teenagers with ADD must succeed in school if they are to build strong self-esteem and become healthy, productive adults. The more academic successes a teenager achieves, the more likely his problem behaviors will decline significantly. If you must make a choice between working on problem behaviors or academic problems, Dr. Sydney Zentall strongly recommends you *address the academic problems first*. Teenagers who are successful and happy in school are less likely to be angry and aggressive toward teachers and other students.

✉

"One of the most therapeutic things that can happen to a child or teenager is to succeed in school!!!"

Parents Must Pave the Way

Because of the potential for academic problems, parents must be *actively involved* to ensure school success. If your child's problems are less serious, he may be able to succeed academically with adaptations at school and minimal involvement from you. If he continues to struggle, you will have to be *his advocate* at school to ensure appropriate adaptations and supports are provided. Frequent communication between you and the school may be necessary. Even when adaptations are made, you may still need to be your teenager's *academic tutor or coach*. When your teenager forgets to follow up on a specific task, you may have to remind him. You may have to talk directly with the teacher to find out if he is failing a class or to discuss adaptations. Sometimes you may be much more involved in schoolwork than you would wish.

One major question you will need to resolve is, how willing and capable are you of helping your teenager succeed academically? This is a hard decision to make, since other well-meaning adults may tell you that you are overprotective, over-involved with your teenager's schoolwork, or co-dependent. It may be a no-win situation. You may be criticized for not being involved enough! Yet if you don't get involved, your teenager may fail his classes. This could lead to even worse problems such as dropping out of school or running away.

Having a *coach* to help with academic and other activities can be extremely helpful. Some parents will be able to serve as a coach and others will have to find someone else to do this job. If you or your spouse have ADD and problems with disorganization and inattention, it will, of course, be difficult for you to monitor progress and help your teenager be more organized. This is not often discussed, but 40 percent of all youngsters with ADD have at least one parent with the disorder. As discussed in Chapter 3, you might consider getting treatment for yourself so you can help your child. Even if it is hard, you may have to help your teenager, especially if no one else is available. You and your spouse could also work as a team, sharing responsibility for helping your teenager with his schoolwork. As an adult with ADD, you can also help your child by sharing tips you have learned for compensating for your own ADD.

If your teenager's problems are more complex, you must take charge and coordinate an individualized treatment plan with key professionals. This may be the case if your child has serious learning disabilities, depression, or aggression, or is not on a proper medication regimen. As discussed in Chapter 4, it would be nice if you could schedule a meeting and invite all key people—physician, treatment professional, teachers—who are involved to develop a treatment plan. In reality, you may have to do it piecemeal. If necessary, you may have to meet separately with school officials to develop the educational portion of the treatment plan.

Frequently, parents are told that their teenager with ADD should take full responsibility for his schoolwork and experience the negative consequences of not doing so. If your teenager can manage an adequate level of organization, that is wonderful! However, if he is extremely disorganized and doing poorly academically, you should not feel guilty about helping him succeed in school.

Reading this chapter and Chapters 9 and 10 should help you learn to work more effectively with your teenager on his schoolwork. If your teenager is struggling at school, you must understand his learning problems, his learning style, needed adaptations for homework and school, and ways to maximize his strengths to teach him most effectively. Once you understand his educational needs, you can share specific suggestions with teachers who may not know much about individualizing educational services for teenagers with ADD. You can also use many of these same teaching strategies when helping your child with his homework. In addition, you should familiarize yourself with the federal statutes and policies—IDEA and Section 504—that guarantee a free appropriate public education (Chapter 11).

General Strategies for Ending Academic Agony

A major strategy for ending academic agony is to *approach educational problem solving more creatively.* Sometimes it is easy for adults to lose sight of the real purpose of education—to help students learn—and get caught up in the educational process. We fail to ask important questions, such as "What practical application does this learning have to the teenager's life? How much of real life is spent doing this activity?" We cling to outdated traditional methods of instruction. Every child must sit in one seat, read from the same book, and complete the same assignments with the same number of problems. They must memorize multiplication tables even though most adults use calculators.

The method a child uses to learn should not be so important. Providing each child with individualized instruction that meets his special needs is the critical issue. Many students with ADD need creative adaptations to the classroom to help them learn. *So, if you can't change the child, change the environment.* Some adaptations, such as a daily report, may be needed only for a short period until the student masters key skills. Other adaptations, such as untimed tests, may be needed throughout a student's school career. Use common sense when developing adaptations. If your teenager can't learn his multiplication tables, then let him use a calculator.

Although learning problems make school difficult, teenagers with ADD know that they must still master academic skills. They don't want teachers to lower expectations, but to make adjustments to the classroom that will "level the playing field." In the words of Dr. Sydney Zentall: "Don't change the destination but just the route by which the student gets there." These students want and deserve an equal chance to succeed in school.

Another critical element is "working smart" as a parent. Use the parenting approaches which have a greater chance of working effectively with a teenager with ADD. The guiding principles for parent/teenager interactions discussed in Chapter 5 will make your interactions around schoolwork easier. So, too, will the five strategies discussed below.

1. Give Your Teenager Choices

Dr. Sydney Zentall has observed that these youngsters have a high need for control. One reason may be that they feel as if they have very little control over their grades and most events at school. Giving them choices gives them a sense of control and ownership in completion of their schoolwork. According to Dr. Zentall, youngsters who are given choices pay attention better, complete more schoolwork, and are less disruptive and aggressive in the classroom. They also work longer and are more likely to do as adults ask.

It is probably best to limit your child's choices to two or three options. You might give him choices about assignments to be completed, time for starting, length of work sessions, or rewards for completion of work. If he has trouble selecting one, talk through his choices with him. "You like the ocean and scuba diving. Maybe it would be more interesting for you to write a theme about coral reefs." Or flip a coin or pick an assignment for him. Dr. Zentall tells about one student with ADD who was given a choice of five different projects to complete. He decided to do them all.

2. Start at His Present Level

By starting at his present level, you can avoid putting more pressure on your teenager than he can handle. Remember that he may be behind developmentally in his ability to accept full responsibility for his schoolwork and chores at home. Since the ultimate goal for a parent is to help their child to become an independent, responsible adult, you need to help your teenager accept increasing levels of responsibility. As he masters one behavior or task, then you can lead him to the next developmentally appropriate step. This technique is known as "shaping" behavior and is discussed in Chapter 5.

⚭

"My son passed all his classes his sophomore year in high school. His sophomore year was an improvement over his freshmen year, when he failed 3 of 12 classes. He started out the school year with no intervention from me. After his midterm report, we identified those classes which he was in danger of failing, and weekly reports were introduced for those subjects. Once his grades were passing for a grading period, weekly reports were dropped."

⚭

3. Work in Partnership with Your Teenager

A third essential element is including your teenager as a respected partner in the process of pursuing his academic success. *It is important to give your teenager the message that he is a good person even if you are not pleased with him because he is not doing his schoolwork.* Separate the unacceptable behavior from the child. Make statements about the behavior, such as, "I'm not happy you didn't complete your homework last night," but not about your teenager's personality. Praise his effort to complete tasks.

⚭

"When I left on a business trip and we were anxiously awaiting my son's progress reports, I left a message taped to the Coca Cola cans in the refrigerator that read: 'Hope you did well on your report card today. But just remember I love you because of the neat person you are, not because of the grades you make. If you have any problems, we'll work them out together.' Yes, there is life after graduation from school

and my son's self- esteem is more important than making straight A's."

≋

Avoid character assassinations of your teenager when he has difficulty with schoolwork. Don't say: "You're lazy"; "You just don't care"; "You're bad"; "You'll never amount to anything." Continue to work with him so that he experiences success at school and it comes naturally for you to give him approval for completing his schoolwork.

Involve your teenager in the decision-making process regarding school issues. This way, you convey a message of respect and indicate that you are partners working together to solve difficult school problems. One way to involve your teenager is to ask his opinions on the problems and solutions: "Why do you think you are failing Algebra? Have you received a lot of zeros for homework? How can I help you?" Some of these teenagers have listening comprehension problems and may not be able to quickly articulate an answer. Give your child time to respond. If he has no answer, try prompting him by asking, "Does it seem like _____ (not completing homework) is the biggest problem?" If he has no suggestions, say, "Why don't we try _____ (working on Algebra every night) for a few weeks?" Then ask him or the teacher if he is completing more homework.

Your teenager may recognize his need for help and willingly accept your assistance. Or he may not want too much assistance because he doesn't want to be different from his friends. A few teenagers may be very hostile and reject any parental involvement. If this happens, talk with the teacher to see if adaptations can be made at school. That may be enough to help your teenager succeed at school. If not, have the other parent (dad) or a relative talk with the teenager to see if he will accept help from them.

If your teenager acts responsibly and is willing to work with you on a plan to improve performance in school, you should involve him in all the decision making. Encourage him to assume as much responsibility for schoolwork as possible, depending on his ability and learning problems. Dixie Jordan, Family Advocate at PACER Center in Minneapolis, recommends actually *putting the student in charge of their own learning.*" If, however, he is failing

classes and is defiantly refusing to complete schoolwork, you may need to talk with a treatment professional about ways to reduce the conflict. For example, you may have to make privileges such as driving contingent upon your teenager completing his homework. "You can drive the car to school tomorrow (next week) if you do your homework tonight (each night this week)."

Unfortunately, Dr. Zentall has found that *students with ADD are less likely to ask for help.* Many of them have experienced so much failure and negative feedback from teachers, they may understandably be reluctant to approach their teachers. They may fear that the teacher will not listen to them or believe them about the learning problems they are having. Requesting a teacher conference which includes your teenager may document the problems and empower him to ask teachers for assistance. Furthermore, by asking his opinion during the conference, you can show the teacher how to treat him as a respected partner.

There may also be other reasons why teenagers have difficulty asking for help. They may forget to ask later (memory problems), be embarrassed (afraid the teacher answered the question when they weren't listening), have trouble waiting for a response, and/or be unwilling to wait until after school to ask the question (impulsivity and difficulty waiting).

Below are some additional examples of ways to discuss school-related problems in ways that respect your child as an individual. Bear in mind, however, that you may need to intervene earlier than in the examples below. For example, if your teenager usually makes borderline grades and is at risk for failing a class, you may have to intervene after only two or three weeks and find out what his class average is.

"John, as long as you are being responsible about your homework and are passing all of your classes, I will not intervene in your evening study routine.

(A few weeks later) "You got a mid-term academic warning that you are in danger of failing algebra. According to this note, you have not been turning in your homework. I know you want to do well in school. I also know school is harder for you because of your ADD. What do you think is causing the problem? Maybe we can make some accommodations at school that will help us solve the prob-

lem. How can I help you get more organized to complete your work? Do you need for me to work with you to set up a study routine? (If the answer is no.) I'll give you one week to try your ideas first. If you are responsible and turn in homework, I won't intervene.

(Later still, homework is not being turned in) "You haven't been turning in your homework in algebra and are still failing the class. Let's work together to set up a study routine. What are your ideas? I have a few suggestions too." (Implement a strategy. Give choices as described earlier.)

The values behind these statements convey several important messages from the parent:

- I believe you want to do well in school.
- I know you are not intentionally being non-compliant.
- I respect your opinion.
- I want you to be involved in deciding how to solve the problem.
- I believe you can handle your homework problem.
- I know sometimes ADD makes school harder for you, but together we will figure out and solve the problems.
- You may need help from me for awhile, but ultimately, you'll take charge of your homework routine again.
- Things may be difficult, but I'll work with you. Together, we can make it.

This approach may be difficult for many parents because we have been conditioned to assume that if a student doesn't do well in school, it is because he doesn't want to, doesn't care, or isn't trying. If your teenager is discouraged or depressed, he probably acts like he doesn't care. But his attitude will usually change for the better when you intervene and his grades improve. Sometimes it is hard for adults to believe that their teenager wants to do well—and instead they assume they have to *make* their teenager do well in school. Unfortunately, some parents approach this situation with a baseball bat instead of mutual respect and decision making.

4. Use Legal Leverage to Obtain Needed Services

In September 1991, the U.S. Department of Education (DOE) issued a policy memo that can help end your teenager's academic agony. Basically, the memo clarifies that children with ADD who experience *"limited alertness which adversely affects educational performance"* are eligible for extra supports and adaptations to the regular classroom environment. This memo also provides suggestions for making classroom adaptations under two major federal laws—IDEA and Section 504. (These two federal laws, plus the policy memo, are discussed in detail in Chapter 11. A copy of the September 1991 US DOE policy memo is included in Appendix B.)

Because system change comes extremely slowly, local school systems may not have issued guidelines for implementing the DOE memo. In some school systems, adequate staff training regarding ADD may not have been made available. Knowledge of the educational rights and possible classroom adaptations for students with ADD is not widespread among rank-and-file teachers and some mid-level administrators. You may therefore have to help educate teachers about ADD.

5. Work in Partnership with the School

Working in partnership with the school to identify learning problems and implement adaptations at school is crucial. If learning problems are serious, teachers or parents must work together to help the teenager succeed. Specific suggestions for working effectively with school officials are provided in the next section. Parents and teachers need to be familiar with common learning problems, effective teaching strategies, and possible adaptations teachers can make in the regular classroom. This information is discussed in Chapter 10 and summarized in Table 10–2.

Following the strategies outlined above won't guarantee that interactions between you and your teenager will always be pleasant. But then, what teenager always gets along with his parents? The key is to remember that there is no single method that works with teenagers with ADD who are struggling academically. You will have to alternately push and pull your teenager, use reason and logical consequences, try behavioral interventions, treat him with respect, give him choices, and involve him in the decision-making process as much as possible. You must try one intervention and when that stops working, shift to another. Eventually, you *will* see the light at the end of the tunnel. Between the ages of 17 and 21, life usually seems to improve and be on more of an even keel for these teenagers with ADD.

Working <u>with</u> School Officials

If your teenager is struggling at school, the parent-teacher partnership will be critical for his academic success. Parents and teachers must communicate on a regular basis, perhaps daily or weekly, to ensure that the student succeeds at school. Usually, the teacher must monitor the teenager's work more carefully, plus make adaptations in the classroom. At home, parents must ensure that homework is completed and returned to school. Parents must also double check to see that missed assignments and tests are made up. Otherwise, the student may find himself facing academic failure.

Coping with ADD in the Classroom Isn't Easy. Sometimes parents struggle just trying to cope with one child with ADD. Can you imagine having a classroom of 25 students, 3 or 4 of whom have ADD? Most parents readily acknowledge that teaching children and teenagers with more serious cases of ADD is not easy. The troubling things these students do can be infuriating to teachers.

Sometimes, students with ADD do not make it easy for teachers to like them.

Because of lack of knowledge and training about this disorder, some teachers see the actions of teenagers with ADD as willful disobedience, disrespect, and laziness. The teacher's disdain may show in subtle ways, many times without the full awareness of the teacher—through dirty looks, sarcasm, negative comments, and lack of positive approval. Such negative attitudes from teachers can spell "academic agony" for teenagers with ADD. Teachers who are educated about ADD can be more understanding and are more likely to make classroom adaptations to help the teenager succeed.

When teachers do not understand a teenager's attention and learning problems, they may make comments that are extremely damaging to the teenager's self esteem. "Your son is lazy." "He never listens." "He doesn't try." A teenager hearing these negative comments will begin to believe these things about himself and may begin to label himself inaccurately. "I'm lazy." "I don't care." "I guess I don't try hard enough."

▓

"One high school teacher who does not understand ADD has been very negative and insensitive with students in front of the whole class. She has made comments such as, 'Your mother may baby you, but I'm not going to baby you.' And to a student with ADD and SLD, 'If you can't understand how to work this math problem, then you need to go to the resource room (learning disabilities classroom).'"

▓

Occasionally, a teacher may go to the opposite extreme and be too accommodating for students with ADD. A balance is needed to firmly encourage the teenager as he masters needed skills in a supportive, positive environment.

▓

"Cassie's teachers learned very quickly that she was talented in art. She helped with classroom decorations, bulletin boards, and plays. She also tells about being assigned ten-page term papers which required an outline, rough draft, correcting it, second draft, and then turning in the final report. She always felt

overwhelmed by the vastness of these projects. So she would go to the teacher and cry, saying, 'This is really hard for me. Maybe I could do an art project instead.'

"This was a double-edged sword for Cassie. It allowed her to get out of the work. She now says she had to work doubly hard in college. But it also really built her ego to feel that she was that good in art. She received many awards for her art in high school. She was well known for her art work and displayed her art work in local shows at museums and malls. It was her salvation.

"Cassie has ambivalent feelings toward teachers. On one hand, she really loved getting out of things, but she can't decide if it was good or bad. She would have liked for mainstream teachers to say 'Oh, you have disabilities, let's figure out how to work with them.'"

🕱

Fortunately, there is no reason to believe that you will not be able to forge a harmonious partnership with your child's teachers. Schools are a microcosm of our society. Many excellent, dedicated teachers are working in school systems across the country. If your teenager gets one of these "jewels," he will have a very positive school year. His success at school will likely spill over into other aspects of his life, making the whole family happier.

In developing a plan to improve your teenager's academic performance, you should meet with teachers and other involved professionals, such as the school psychologist, the guidance counselor, or the social worker. Generally, it is best to develop the least complicated plan which will require the fewest changes to the normal classroom routine and still allow your child to succeed. Remember, most adolescents with ADD have problems with memory and organization. The more complicated the plan and the more your teenager has to remember, the more likely the plan will fail. Your teenager and your family could become even more frustrated with a complicated, burdensome plan.

Suggestions for Making School More Positive

Several key strategies for making school more positive are discussed below. You may wish to check off each step as you complete it.

____Educate school personnel about ADD

____Educate yourself about school system philosophy and policies

____Request teacher assignment

____Request change in teachers

____Schedule a school conference

____Notify school officials that your teenager has ADD

____Treat teachers with respect

____Build rapport with school before a crisis

____Find the "voice of reason"

____Work through guidance counselor

____Know provisions of IDEA, Part B, Section 504, and the September 1991, US DOE Memo

____Identify learning problems/complete blank form in Chapter 13

____Identify adaptations needed at school

____Seek adaptations in regular classes

____Request formal evaluation for special education services

____Participate in development of Individualized Educational Program (IEP)

____Develop a contingency plan for crises

____Provide assistance with homework

____Phase out interventions over time

____Be knowledgeable: sound knowledgeable!

____Express appreciation!

Educate School Personnel about ADD. Some teachers are very knowledgeable about ADD and are making appropriate adaptations. Sometimes, however, parents may need to educate teachers and other school officials about the disorder. If possible, give brief, one-page summaries on various aspects of dealing with ADD to teachers and school personnel who may not understand the disorder. Several "ADD fact sheets" are available from CHADD. In addition, you might photocopy relevant sections of this book and give them to teachers. You may also find it helpful to give them a four-page summary entitled "ADD: Impact on School Performance," which I developed for parents to give their child's teachers (Appendix C).

Another option is for local parent support groups to talk to the superintendent or board of education members about jointly sponsoring a county-wide workshop on ADD. Parents, teenagers, clinicians, and educators could all be on the program. Topics may include characteristics of ADD, their impact on school performance, identification of common learning problems in students with ADD, classroom adaptations, tips for coping with ADD at school (impulsivity, disorganization, forgetfulness, and poor memory), and tips for parents on helping at home.

Educate Yourself about School System Philosophy and Policies. It may also be helpful for you to understand the educational philosophy endorsed by the superintendent and board of education. Call the superintendent's office and ask for a copy of the school system's mission statement and student handbook. Frequently these documents contain comments about what services and accomplishments will be provided for "all children." For example, the policy may include a statement about providing individualized education to help a child reach his maximum potential. Usually, the county or system-wide policy will include rules for students, special education guidelines, disciplinary actions, and suspensions. Any or all of this information might support your request for services or adaptations.

Request Teacher Assignment. Teenagers with ADD are more likely to be successful with a teacher who is patient, firm but supportive, flexible, and respectful to students. Students with ADD also tend to do better in a class if they like the teacher. If your adolescent is struggling, don't be afraid to request teachers who are more flexible and work well with students who have learning problems. It is often a good idea to request a specific teacher two to four months prior to the beginning of a new school year. Find out exactly when class assignments are made. The principal may not grant a request for a specific teacher by name, but you could say, "He will do best in a classroom with a teacher who is supportive and flexible like Mrs. Smith." Work with the school counselor to avoid having your teenager assigned to teachers who may be rigid or inflexible.

Request a Change in Teachers. If your teenager is placed in a teacher's class a second grading period, and you know it will be a negative experience, *ask for a class assignment change*. If your request is not sufficient, ask your child's psychologist or physician for a letter making the same request.

🦓

"I once requested a class change for my son because he was scheduled to have the same teacher for a second semester in algebra. This teacher was very negative and had a personality conflict with my son. The straw that broke the camel's back was when she said very angrily to my son in front of other students, 'Your mother may overprotect you, but I'm not going to.' The principal would not make this change on the basis of my request alone. However, he accepted the same request from my son's doctor. The doctor submitted a two-sentence request written on a prescription pad."

🦓

Schedule a School Conference. Schedule a meeting with school officials to notify them about your child's diagnosis of ADD. Try to schedule the meeting before school begins, or as soon as possible after school starts. Don't wait until mid-term when parents are notified of failing grades. As one parent explains, "Be proactive, not reactive." Involved parents who are willing to work with the school will get a lot more cooperation than parents who don't seem to care that their child has difficulties.

Notify School Officials That Your Teenager Has ADD. If your teenager needs extra help, *it is critical to have the disorder documented in writing in school records and/or in the Individualized Educational Program (IEP)*. (See Chapter 11 for information on IEPs.) If ADD hasn't already been documented with school officials, *ask your physician/psychologist for a letter* confirming the diagnosis and take it to the meeting with you. The letter should include the diagnosis of ADD, academic or intelligence test results, identification of any learning problems, and suggestions for classroom adaptations. Once ADD has been documented at school, you have more options available:

Option 1: If your teenager has *occasional minor problems* at school, just dropping by his teachers' rooms at the first Parent Teacher Association (PTA) meeting may be enough. Advise the teachers of your teenager's ADD and assure them that he wants to do well in school. Ask the teachers to call if there are any problems.

Option 2: If your adolescent *needs extra help* but has no major problems at school, ask school officials for needed classroom adaptations described in this chapter.

Option 3: If he is *experiencing significant difficulty* (in danger of failing classes or suspension/expulsion because of behavioral problems) or you *anticipate serious problems* in making the transition to middle or high school, consider requesting services under the federal laws discussed in Chapter 11. Ask for needed classroom adaptations. You may also request a meeting with a variety of school personnel, sometimes called a student support team, to discuss your teenager's needs and what can be done to help him succeed at school.

Option 4: If your child is *eligible for special education*, make additional adaptations to the regular class or have him participate in special education classes. (See Chapter 11.)

Treat Teachers with Respect. Respecting teachers and treating them with tact is always important. Teachers are human just like we are: they want to be competent in their jobs and they fear failure. Initial discussions with the teacher may center around your teenager and his learning problems. Give the school a chance to tell you what they can offer based upon the issues you identify. If the school year is in progress, find out what interventions the teacher is currently using or has tried previously. If appropriate suggestions are not made, you might tactfully introduce some new ideas. For example, show the teacher selected passages of this book and say, "Do you think any of these ideas might be helpful to correct . . . (problem)." In the past, my son has had difficulty with . . . ." "Other teachers have found it effective to. . . ." Or, "Here is some material that you may find helpful." Teachers are very busy, so give them a few pages of material at a time. Otherwise, it may go unread.

Build Rapport with the School Before a Crisis. Building a positive working relationship with school personnel before a crisis arises is a good strategy. Some parents volunteer at school to help classroom teachers or in the school clinic. Volunteering to serve as an officer of the PTA or work on PTA projects is another way to build strong relationships with the school. Being present at school in a neutral or positive role will increase the odds that teachers will be more positive with your teenager and work with you if there are problems. If you need help, you will be talking with school officials you know rather than strangers. Most teenagers don't want their parents visiting them at high school, so casual visits are not very practical.

Find the "Voice of Reason." If your teenager has an uncooperative teacher who doesn't understand ADD, or if you have problems with one school official (the teacher, the vice principal in charge of discipline), you should look for another school official who may be helpful and supportive.

Parents can usually find at least one *Voice of Reason* at school. This educator can see the good beneath the adolescent's sometimes aggravating and frustrating behavior and is willing to work as an ally with the parents and teenager. This may be a person who understands ADD or who simply realizes that teenagers have different learning styles. The Voice of Reason may be a teacher, former teacher, principal, guidance counselor, school psychologist, social worker, or special education teacher.

Work through the Guidance Counselor. Since students have several teachers in high school, it may be easier for you to work through the guidance counselor. These counselors can advise all teachers of your teenager's learning deficits and needed supports and adaptations. And teachers could also notify the guidance office first if problems arise, although some teachers call parents directly. However, if your teen is having problems in only one or two classes, you may prefer to work directly with the teachers.

Know Provisions of IDEA (Part B), Section 504, and the September 1991, US DOE Memo. If your child needs special services or adaptations in the classroom, it is essential to know what he is entitled to under the law. These issues are discussed in detail in Chapter 11.

Identify Learning Problems. Make sure you know your child's areas of learning problems and can discuss what they mean in practical terms with him, the teacher, or counselor. For example, having poor fine motor coordination may have several implications: 1) your teenager's writing may be small and illegible; 2) he may write slowly; 3) he may prefer to print rather than write cursive; 4) he may not produce as much written material; 5) he may not be able to take notes fast enough to follow the teacher; and 6) he may avoid writing (completing schoolwork, for example).

You can identify problem areas by reviewing old report cards, including grades and teacher comments, and standardized achievement tests such as the IOWA, and by observing your child while he is working on homework. Discussions with a trusted former teacher or a school psychologist should help you confirm your assessment or correct any errors. Once polished and corrected, this information will be invaluable in subsequent school years.

Identify Adaptations Needed at School. Once your teenager's learning problems have been identified, adaptations can be made to the regular classroom program. For example, a teenager who has poor fine motor coordination and writes or processes material slowly may need extra time on tests and assignments. He may not be able to finish an algebra test within the one-hour time limit. A teenager with ADD who has a math or short-term memory problem may need to use a calculator for math homework and tests.

It is important to ask your child what supports he needs to succeed in school. Most students will not ask for or accept more support than they need. They don't like to be different from their peers. Some may be reluctant to accept any extra support or classroom adaptations even if they need help.

- *Tailor-make Intervention Strategies and Adaptations:* The intervention must be tailored to fit the personality and academic needs of your child. This concept, known as individualized treatment planning, is discussed in detail in Chapters 4 and 10.

- *Select Appropriate Interventions/Adaptations:* Novelty, interactive learning activities, positive reinforcement, and patience during school and homework sessions will be extremely helpful. *Positive incentives should be tried before negative consequences.* To avoid unnecessary involvement or too much control, you may decide to intervene only if your teenager is struggling academically or in danger of failing classes. *Select the least intrusive interventions* that will enable him to succeed in school.

The first line of attack may be common behavioral interventions (as discussed in Chapter 5) or changes in the school environment. Next, you can list learning deficits and adaptations on the blank form in Chapter 13. To help you complete the form, a profile of one teenager's learning problems and classroom adaptations is provided in Table 10–1.

Seek Adaptations in Regular Classes. Most adolescents with ADD can be served effectively in their regular classroom through adaptations to their present instructional program. In most cases, there is no magic academic benefit associated with being in a special education class. Most adaptations that are provided in a special education class can just as easily be provided in regular classes. Under Section 504 (see Chapter 11), schools must make adaptations in the classroom for students with ADD even without special education eligibility. Few teenagers with ADD will need to be placed in special education classes.

Whether or not your child is eligible for special education services under federal law, other supportive services may be available. The level and quality of services varies from one school system to the next, but may include:

1. *Supportive services from counselors, school social workers, and school psychologists,* who will work with the student, parents, and classroom teachers to develop a plan for coping with ADD.

2. The parent may *request a psychological evaluation* from the school if the student appears to have a learning disability or is not achieving up to his intellectual potential.

3. The school may offer *tutoring* each day after school in specific subjects. Call and find out if it is available.

4. The guidance counselors may have *groups to teach various skills,* including study and social skills.

5. Some schools have students who serve as *peer tutors* for other students.

6. School psychologists can help you develop *behavior modification programs* for helping your child complete homework assignments. *Cognitive training,* including techniques for self-monitoring, may be effective for some teens. That is, the teen is taught to check up on his own behavior such as completion of homework. If the teenager is organized enough and can remember, self-monitoring is a good idea.

7. An *outside "expert"* (physician, psychologist, or counselor) or a *child advocate within the school system* may be helpful in bringing about classroom

or policy changes regarding services that your teenager needs. School officials will sometimes listen to outside experts or their peers when they won't listen to parents.

🦋

"I have found it helpful to have a 'professional' attend school conferences to help educate school personnel. Information I presented to teachers, school psychologists, and/or guidance counselors was sometimes considered suspect since I was 'just the student's parent' and might be 'making excuses for my son.'"

🦋

If help is not forthcoming from the school, you may *hire a private psychologist* to go into the school to help your teenager. The psychologist may observe your teenager, consult with the teacher, make recommendations, or go to the classroom on a regular basis. To control costs, a classroom or behavioral

aid may be trained to help in the classroom instead of a psychologist. You may also *hire a private tutor* to help with specific academic deficiencies, teach study skills and organizational skills, and help your child keep up with assignments. The tutor may talk periodically with the teacher to be aware of daily assignments or academic problems that need work.

Request Formal Evaluation for Special Education Services. Adolescents whose academic and/or behavioral problems are more serious may be eligible for special education services. Special education services available through IDEA may be provided in regular, resource (part-time), or self-contained classes. If your child is in danger of failing classes, request an evaluation before a major crisis erupts. The evaluation process may take two or three months to complete. The pros and cons of seeking eligibility for special education services are discussed in Chapter 11.

Participate in Development of the IEP. If your teenager receives special education services, remember that federal guidelines provide that *parents and their teenager should be involved as equal participants* in deciding what should be contained in the IEP. (See Chapter 11.) Information in Chapter 10 will help ensure that learning problems and appropriate adaptations are included in the IEP and implemented.

Develop a Contingency Plan for Crises. Develop a plan for the year, including contingency plans for handling crises or infractions of school rules. *Federal guidelines require the school to develop a plan for dealing with problem behaviors that are related to a child's disability.* In other words, behaviors that frequently get your child in trouble must be identified and a plan developed to deal with them. It is important to identify what happened immediately prior to his misbehavior (antecedent behavior) that may have contributed to the problem. For example, your child may have serious problems with changes in routine, such as having a substitute teacher or going on a field trip. Forgetting medication or medication wearing off (antecedent) is a common cause of crises at school. Leaving some extra medication at school (intervention) would be wise. You can call the school and notify the school nurse so that your teenager will be discreetly given his medication (not called to the office over the intercom).

Provide Assistance with Homework. Since non-completion of homework may be one of the major reasons for school failure, Chapter 9 offers suggestions for helping teenagers with ADD complete their homework.

Phase Out Interventions Over Time. One of the ultimate goals is for adolescents with ADD to *take full responsibility for schoolwork.* However, teenagers with this disorder will take longer to achieve full independence. As noted earlier, these youngsters are developmentally about 30 percent behind teenagers without ADD.

The types of academic assistance most teenagers with ADD require can be phased out over time. For example, your teenager may no longer need weekly reports, homework reminders from teachers, or graph paper for math problems when he begins turning in all his assignments. However, some adaptations, such as untimed tests, written homework assignments, or modified assignments may need to be continued throughout his school career.

Be Knowledgeable: Sound Knowledgeable! Expect the best and reflect it in comments! Be positive with school personnel and avoid hostile confrontations. For example, in discussions with school personnel, you might say, "As you know, students with ADD often have short-term memory problems and difficulty in math. But extended test time, reduced homework assignments, and using a calculator can help. These special supports were suggested in the September 16 Policy memo from the US DOE. I think it's great that these adaptations can be provided in the regular classroom setting. My son would really benefit from these services."

Express Appreciation! If teachers or school personnel have gone out of their way to help your teenager, don't forget to express appreciation. Writing letters or personally thanking the principal, superintendent, or school board for the work of outstanding teachers or school administrators will be helpful. If appropriate, say "Thanks" at the end of conferences or at the end of the school year. Teachers talk to each other, and the reputations of you and your teenager will be enhanced. If confrontations occur in the future, school personnel may have heard positive things about you and may be more willing to work with you.

Conclusion

Unfortunately, working with educators to find the best way to teach your teenager is not something you do once and never have to do again. As parents of children with ADD, in many respects, we are "trail blazers." The best practices for teaching children with ADD are still being discovered. Because you "live and breathe" ADD, you may be better informed about ADD than many teachers. Most likely, you will have to work with each new teacher as your child progresses through school. Other children or your younger children with ADD will benefit from laying this educational groundwork. The suggestions in Chapters 8 through 11 should make this process a little easier. During those years when you have excellent teachers, enjoy your good fortune. For there will be other years when you must find the patience to educate and forgive the few skeptical and uninformed teachers you will undoubtedly run across.

CHAPTER NINE

WORKING ON THE HOME FRONT

"I can picture my son sitting at the kitchen table, starting his homework while I cleaned up the dishes after dinner. 'Starting' his homework is probably not a very accurate description. Typically, the scenario played out like this: 'It's time to start your homework.' 'Okay Mom, I'll be right there.'

"Ten minutes later, he has not yet begun writing. Then he has to go to his room twice. The first trip is for his book. Next he has to return because he forgot his pencil. He cannot resist stopping to watch his snake crawling under a rock in the corner of the aquarium. Another delay occurs because he doesn't remember his homework assignment and has to call a friend. Now I heave a sigh of relief because the first part of the battle has been won. I have him at the kitchen table ready to begin.

"He is tapping the table with his pencil and looking out the patio door at the dog drinking water. Patiently, at first, I say, 'Dear, it's time to get started.' Fifteen minutes later, one problem has been completed. Impatiently, I stop doing the dishes, walk to the table, put my finger on a specific line on his paper and scream, 'Right here, right now, put your pencil on the paper and start writing.' He works hard for a few minutes and then is distracted by something else. This process continues throughout the next hour with both he and I feeling increasingly angry and frustrated."

Failure to complete homework is one of the biggest sources of conflict between parents and their teenager with ADD. Parents often get so angry and upset that they completely lose their patience with their child. Parents from across the country have expressed similar concerns about their teenagers and their homework: they're disorganized, don't have the right books or don't remember their assignments, put off getting started, argue, refuse to complete their work, yell, or accuse their parents of nagging. Or parents may hear two of their more famous lines: "No, I don't have any homework." Or, "I finished it all at school."

You and your teenager may face many challenges as he attempts to succeed in school. As discussed in Chapter 8, you should give yourself permission to do whatever it takes to help your teenager succeed at school. If your child is struggling academically, you should not feel guilty about helping him. Once a routine of successful school performance is achieved, you will be able to reduce your day-to-day involvement. The key is for your teenager to accept increasing levels of responsibility for his schoolwork.

This chapter discusses common school-related problems that parents and teenagers can work on together at home to resolve. They include: battles over homework, forgotten assignments, books, and weekly notes; failure to complete homework; getting too many zeros; failing classes; sleep problems; and school avoidance. A summary of intervention strategies is provided in Table 9–2 at the end of the chapter.

The Bloody Homework Battles

If your teenager with ADD takes full responsibility for his schoolwork, you are lucky. Many parents, however, are forced to regularly check that their teenager has completed his homework, especially if he is in danger of failing classes. Because homework sessions can be extremely exasperating, many parents dread evenings and the looming battles over homework.

Sometimes, anger and frustration over homework battles lead to a great deal of guilt and depression for both the parents and the teenager. If parents aren't careful, love for their teenager may become conditional, contingent upon good academic performance. Inadvertently, parents may send the message, "I love you *only* when you do well in school."

🙚

"We reached a point where our interactions were a constant battleground over his academic work. In my frustration and anger, I would lose my cool and find myself screaming. I would guiltily think to myself, 'I am a well-trained, compassionate professional. I should know how to deal more effectively with my own child.' Without realizing it, my unspoken message to my son was that my love and approval were contingent upon his school performance. The subtle messages I had been unwittingly giving my son were: 'You are not okay. You are not 'good' unless you complete all your homework. We don't like you when you do not complete your homework.'

"When I came to that realization, I began changing ways I interacted with my son and the kinds of statements I made to him."

🙚

Avoiding bloody battles over homework is important. If homework becomes a constant battleground, your teenager may come to associate learning with negative experiences that are to be avoided at all costs, along with *you*, the "slave driver" who is forcing him to do all this "stupid schoolwork." Although the reactions of both you and your teenager are understandable, allowing battles over school to continue can damage the parent-child relationship. Frequent hostile interactions may cause even worse behavior problems. The best way to end the fighting is to ensure that learning problems are identified, adaptations are made in the classroom, and if appropriate, medication is taken during homework sessions.

If you end up having tremendous battles with your teen when you try to help with homework, re-cruit someone else for the job—your spouse, a friend or relative, or a paid professional. If you are working, you may even find an adult who can help on two levels: supervising your teen after school and also helping with his homework.

Parents grow weary of hearing themselves constantly repeat statements and questions about schoolwork: "What is your homework in math? Your math teacher always puts the math assignments on the board. Write them down every day! Do you have your math book? You don't have it? Well, let's get in the car and go back to school and get it." Sorry, but repetition, ad nauseam, goes with the ADD territory.

Avoiding Bloody Homework Battles

The following suggestions will help you provide structure for your teenager when he is doing homework. These suggestions are summarized at the end of the chapter in an easy reference chart.

Take Medication When Doing Homework. If your child is having great difficulty completing his schoolwork, consider having him take medication during this period. Frequently, by the time he begins working on homework, all the effects of the stimulant medication have worn off. You and your teenager need to determine the latest time in the afternoon that stimulant medication can be taken without interfering with his ability to fall asleep. For example, if he takes regular Ritalin at five p.m., the medication will wear off by approximately nine o'clock, so homework must be complete before then.

🙚

"My son always told me that it didn't help him improve his grade to study for a test. Initially, I doubted what he said. However, since he began taking Ritalin when he studies at night, his memory of what he has studied for the test has increased and his test grades have improved."

🙚

"A psychologist related a story about a 20-year-old man who was having difficulty finding direction in his life. The young man was diagnosed by the psychologist as having ADD and was subsequently placed on Ritalin. The young man said that for the first time in

his life he could remember what he had studied when he took a test."

<hr>

"A few days after a big fight over homework, I found myself reflecting on the conflict between my son and me. This *can't* be normal. Something is clearly wrong and I don't know exactly what it is. He wants to do well in school but something is going on internally that is making school extremely difficult for him. I reasoned, if he could get started and complete his work promptly, he would, simply to avoid years of ranting and raving by an enraged mother.

"My son's ADD was diagnosed a few years later. Since we were reluctant to give him stimulant medication during the evening, problems with homework completion continued into high school. If I had it to do over again, I would definitely let him take medication while he worked on homework in the evenings."

<hr>

Set a Specific Time to Do Homework Each Evening. Many teenagers with ADD have poor organizational skills and seem to lack awareness of time. *Getting started is frequently the biggest challenge.* The opening vignette in this chapter is typical of many youngsters with ADD—especially before diagnosis of ADD and use of stimulant medications during homework sessions. Usually, these teenagers can also benefit from the structure of having a set time to start homework each evening.

Involve your teenager in selecting his starting time for homework. For example, you might ask if he would like to start his homework at 7:00 or 7:30. He may set 7:00 as the starting time. Wait and see if he starts his homework on his own. Ideally, he will begin when 7:00 arrives. If he doesn't start his assignment by a set time, then remind him to get started. If he doesn't know what his assignments are, let him call a friend or have him look it up on his weekly assignment sheet.

Set an Alarm to Announce Homework Time. A wristwatch with an alarm function may be a wise investment. The teenager (or parent) can set his wristwatch, a kitchen timer, or alarm clock to announce when it is time to start homework. The digital timer on the microwave can also be used as an alarm. The alarm ring announces it is

time to start, not the parent. Your teenager may enjoy the novelty, at least for awhile. Let him select which alarm system to use.

Minimize Distractions. Find a place to study that is relatively free from distractions. The kitchen table or a desk may be a good choice, unless there are objects on them that divert your child's interest from his schoolwork. If the desk in his room is covered with papers and other items, it may not be the best place to study. However, as long as he is completing his work, give him a choice of study location.

Find a "Study Buddy"/Establish a "Study Circle." Your teenager might ask a teenager in the neighborhood or a good friend who is in the same class to study with him. Afterwards, the teenagers can spend time together on recreational activities. This "study buddy" system works best if the other teenager doesn't have ADD and remembers the homework assignments. If his friend has ADD, you'll just have to provide a little more supervision. If your teenager may find the terms offensive, don't use the label "study buddy" or "study circle."

When two teenagers study together, they often review the material verbally. If your child has learning difficulties, this can be very helpful, as the more senses he uses when doing his homework, the more likely he is to learn the material. Instead of just reading and writing his assignments silently, he will also be discussing them out loud.

<hr>

"Kristin was telling me that she has a 'Study Circle' of friends with whom she studies. She thinks it has helped her make better grades."

<hr>

Call a Friend to Confirm Homework Assignments. Sometimes parents set up a daily routine of asking their child what his assignments are for any subject he is in danger of failing. If he can't remember the assignment, then he should have phone numbers of other students in his class to call for the assignment. Be sure to obtain phone numbers for other students early in the grading period. Otherwise, your teenager may need a number and he won't remember last names or addresses.

Call School Homework Hot-line. Find out whether the school has a "homework or tutoring hot-line" that students or parents may call to find out homework assignments or to receive assistance in a specific subject.

Use a Color-Coded Monthly Calendar. Mary Kay Clyburn, a learning disabilities teacher, suggests having teenagers with ADD keep a monthly calendar, perhaps hanging on the wall. This calendar could be color coded for tests, quizzes, and projects, with reminders for when to start preparing for a test. For example, if a test is scheduled for Friday, write a reminder on the calendar to begin studying a couple of days before the test. Otherwise, your teenager may not think about it until Friday morning.

Divide Homework into Smaller Segments. Some students become overwhelmed by the length of an assignment or test. Breaking the assignment into shorter segments can make it seem more manageable. You or a teacher might cut a worksheet into sections. Your child can give you each section as he completes it and pick up the next worksheet or assignment. This allows him to get up and walk, again releasing some of his energy and giving him a little break. For assignments in a textbook, you might ask him to complete one-fourth of it and bring it to you when he is finished. Then you give him the next portion of the assignment. Sometimes using a timer may add more interest for younger teenagers. Ask him to see how many problems he can complete before the timer goes off in ten minutes. Some teens may enjoy this "game." Other teens may think it's stupid.

Let Your Child Use a Computer. Since many of these teenagers have problems with verbal expression, slow processing, and poor fine motor skills, writing assignments may be time-consuming and laborious. If your family has a computer, it will be extremely helpful for completion of homework. Plus, having a copy of all completed work is wonderful insurance for teenagers with ADD, who often lose their schoolwork before it is ever turned in to the teacher.

Have Your Teenager Dictate Themes or Reports. As an alternative to using a computer, he could dictate a theme or report to you to type. Afterwards, you can give him the rough draft to edit and correct. Even for math, you can write the problems down as your child explains what needs to be done. This might be helpful if your child has major visual motor problems or finds math so aversive

that he refuses to do any math problems. Later, you and your child can alternate writing the math problems. Ultimately, you are "shaping" your teenager's behavior by moving him toward completing all his work on his own.

✳

"My daughter has to write a major term paper and was told she would have to handwrite it or if typed, must type it herself. My question is, what are we grading and teaching here: writing or typing?"

✳

The fine motor problems and slow processing some students have affect their typing skill and speed.

✳

"My son took typing, which I assumed would be a fairly easy A . . . wrong. His typing was so slow, he really struggled just to get a C in the class. Because of slow processing skills, it took him so much longer to finish his typing assignments than other students."

✳

Use White Noise or Play the Radio. If your teenager is too easily distracted by other noises, "white noise" in the background may help block out distractions and help him concentrate on studying. You might purchase an audio tape with sound from the ocean. Some students use fans or hair dryers to provide a background noise.

Some teenagers and adults with ADD say they can study better when the radio is playing. One adult with ADD said it helped her stay on task by keeping her from daydreaming. She always likes to do two or three things at a time.

✳

"Beth has always preferred to do homework while listening to the radio and sometimes while watching television. She tells me that she can concentrate better when she studies. This was especially true before her ADD was diagnosed and she started taking medication. Although I cannot study this way, my daughter seems to be able to do so. Usually, if she turns the TV on while studying, I suggest she watch a program that does not involve a plot or story line she needs to follow."

🖎

"Cooper always said he could study better when listening to the radio or TV. He seemed to need some background noise."

🖎

Find Out the Routine of Homework Assignments. Many teachers establish daily and weekly routines for assigning homework. If your teenager often forgets homework assignments or tests, find out what these routines are. For example, one section of history questions may be assigned for homework each night, Monday through Thursday. The "Bio-quiz" questions at the end of the biology chapter may always be assigned weekly. It may take two weeks to complete one chapter. So expect a test every two weeks. These teenagers forget homework assignments and when tests are scheduled. By learning assignment routines, it will be easier to monitor your child's completion of homework. (Biology questions are assigned Tuesday and Thursday.) "Your biology questions are due tomorrow—it's time to start work on them." (An algebra test is scheduled every two weeks.) "You're supposed to have an algebra test tomorrow. You should study tonight."

Find Out When Special Projects Are Due. Teenagers with ADD frequently forget special assignments. This can be an academic disaster, since the project usually represents a major grade. If you know that your teenager frequently forgets these projects, ask teachers at the beginning of the semester about any major projects and due dates. This can be accomplished at the first PTA meeting of the year when you have a chance to meet all of your child's teachers.

Ask the Teacher for Written Homework Assignments. Teenagers with ADD often forget to copy assignments from the board. It is extremely helpful for teachers to give assignments and due dates in writing on either a weekly or monthly basis. That way, parents know in advance what their teenager's assignments are. Your teenager could ask the teacher for these assignments on a weekly basis. If he forgets, *you* can get the homework assignments from the teacher.

Ask the Teacher to Get Another Student to Remind of Assignments. If the teacher is too busy to remind or check to see if homework assignments have been written down, ask her to pair your teenager with another student who can do this job. Of course, this must be handled tactfully to avoid embarrassing your child. The student selected should be someone who is acceptable to your teenager. The reminder should be handled discreetly.

Ask the Teacher to Modify Assignments. Teenagers with ADD often struggle and spend too much time on homework due to slow reading and writing, poor organization skills, or poor memory. They may need modified assignments such as completing every second or third math problem. The teacher can assign half the problems but still cover the same number of concepts. If your child writes very slowly, he might be allowed to photocopy pages of textbooks in subjects such as history, science, or government. He can fill in the blanks with answers to questions, highlight important facts, or highlight answers to questions. The most important thing is for him to learn the information. There is no need to ask him to write the whole question plus the answer.

If a teacher is reluctant to reduce the amount of homework, you may need to build a case for this adaptation. The research data described in this book about common learning problems and adaptations will be helpful. So, too, should the US DOE policy letter discussed in Chapter 11. It may also be helpful to understand the school system's philosophy about giving homework. After you have presented the reasons adaptations are needed, you might ask, "What is the purpose of the homework? I assume it is to learn concepts. If the purpose is to practice concepts learned at school, couldn't my son still master these concepts by doing every other problem?"

Use Daily or Weekly Reports. Under a weekly report system, your child brings home a signed note from his teachers that describes his academic progress that week. The report may indicate whether all homework was completed. What were test and daily grades? This system may be limited to only those subjects which your teenager is failing or in danger of failing. You might make participation in a weekend activity that he likes contingent upon bringing home a satisfactory "weekly report." The teacher may send the report home each week, fax the note home or to your office, or have the school secretary call. Or if teach-

Table 9–1 DAILY/WEEKLY REPORT

NAME:				DATE:	
PERIOD			(CLASS)		

	M	T	W	T	F
homework turned in					
classwork					
grades					

Comments:

Unfinished assignments (Optional):

Teacher Signature:

or you can make it even more simple:

SCHOOL REPORT

NAME:_____ DATE:_____
CLASS:_____ TEACHER SIGNATURE:_____
Comments:

---

ers are willing, they can call each day and leave a message on the answering machine.

Some schools have developed their own weekly report forms. If your school has not, you can design your own. A sample report is provided in Table 9–1. Anything you can do to make the process quick and easy will be greatly appreciated by teachers. They are also more likely to follow up on your request. Keep things simple: decide what information you need (test grades, completion of homework) and include that on the form. You may request the teacher's signature rather than initials. Of course, no student would ever think of forging a teacher's initials, but just in case, it's harder to copy a name than initials.

⚜

"I found that I didn't need to demand A's or B's or passing grades on all his work in order for him to go to the mall. All I had to ask for was completion of all his assignments. Because he was so bright, if he did his schoolwork, then he passed the tests and made good grades on daily assignments."

⚜

If your teenager is struggling and the weekly report isn't effective, then try a daily report. These reports indicate the student's daily completion of schoolwork and may be sent home for awhile until the teenager begins to consistently complete home- and schoolwork on a daily basis. A daily report may include the homework assignment, any uncompleted classwork which must be done that night, or any grades for the day—so you can praise him for his good work. Then you can drop back to a weekly report and eventually eliminate both reports.

Limit Time Spent on Homework. Homework, when completed and done correctly, may take forever for some teenagers with ADD, especially if they have learning problems such as poor memory, slow reading or writing, a written language deficit, poor reading comprehension, or poor organizational skills. A teenager with a memorization problem will have trouble working basic math calculations quickly. Consequently, math homework assignments may be very time-consuming. While a student who works quickly can complete the assignment in 30 minutes, a teenager with ADD may take an hour. If homework takes too long, the student may soon avoid and hate doing homework.

⚜

"As a junior in high school, my son spent two to three hours at least three nights a week on homework. He worked so slowly, it took him forever to finish his work. Prior to starting on medication he could never have worked that long. We probably should have had the amount of homework reduced so that he could finish one assignment in an hour. He understood the math concepts but he just couldn't produce the volume of work necessary.

"You cannot rush our son who has ADD but is not hyperactive. Even though he is very bright, he processes things slowly, reads slowly, works slowly, writes slowly, and has only one speed—slow. Great patience is needed to work with him."

⚜

How much time should be spent on homework? Although there is no exact answer to this question, high school students should generally be able to finish most homework assignments in each subject in an hour or less. If it consistently takes longer than one hour in a subject even when your child is working steadily, discuss modification of the homework assignment with the teacher. This is especially important if he has homework in several subjects and is working for hours each night. An average high school student doesn't spend more than one to two hours total on homework each night. If homework takes more than two hours almost every night, parents will need to work with teachers, guidance counselor, their treatment professional, or physician to develop a plan to modify homework assignments. Sometimes having your treatment professional or physician write a letter requesting an adaptation may help.

On rare occasions, you may elect to limit time spent on homework even if your teenager has not finished the assignment. Sometimes if a student is not on medication, or is upset, angry, in crisis, or struggling with a difficult assignment, he may not be able to concentrate. Rather than have him sit for hours staring at a book, you may stop battling an impossible situation. He probably won't be very productive anyway if more than two hours is required for homework. If you limit his homework, send a note to the teacher asking for a delay or modification of the assignment so that he won't get into trouble at school.

Watch Out for Hasty Errors. If left unsupervised, some students with ADD may rush through homework assignments. Completing homework is such an unpleasant ordeal, some teenagers want to get it over with as quickly as possible. It doesn't matter to them if it is finished or if it is correct.

🎗

"Steven (ADHD) had difficulty working more than fifteen minutes on homework. He would come out of his room talking about how hard he had been working and my husband and I would just look at each other with questioning glances. Later during discussions with my doctor, our son's comments began to make sense. Since it is so difficult for him to concentrate and stay on task, he has to work harder than the average student. Fifteen minutes study time must take tremendous energy for these teenagers and must seem like an eternity."

🎗

"Elizabeth tends to rush through her work because she hates the struggle."

🎗

If your child has a tendency to rush through homework, you may have to review it when he is finished. You can mark mistakes and then have him correct his errors. If you don't know much about the subject yourself, you may only be able to check to see if he has at least answered all the questions. Sometimes answers are found in the back of the book. Or have your son work with a friend and they can double check each other's answers.

Use Suggestions from Chapter Five. A few suggestions from Chapter Five about effective ways to interact with your teenager will make homework sessions more positive.

• When frustration builds during homework sessions, take a break to allow things to cool off.

• If your teenager blows up, stay calm and lower your voice. A loud emotional response may result in your child becoming more aggressive and producing less schoolwork.

Give Time to Unwind Before Bedtime. Your teenager may need time to unwind after the harrowing homework battles. He may want to take a bath, get ready for bed, and have a few minutes to himself.

Teach Your Teenager That School and Homework Must Be Done, Either Now or Later. Sometimes students may learn the wrong lesson. If they don't complete their school or homework, they learn they will receive a zero but, ultimately, never have to do the work.

🎗

"What my son had learned regarding homework was that if you don't do the work when it is due, you will never have to do it."

🎗

To correct this problem, tell your teenager he must make up any schoolwork he doesn't complete during the week. The work must be done even if it is late and he will receive partial or no credit. You will need to review the weekly report to see what work your child missed. Then you can calmly tell him that when the schoolwork is done, he can go to the mall, or do whatever activity he likes. If he finishes the schoolwork at 7:00 p.m. Friday night, let him go to the mall. The lesson learned speaks for itself and you have no need to preach, nag, or punish. Your teenager will learn that he has to do the work regardless. So he may as well do the work when it is assigned.

Of course, you must use common sense when using this approach. When you implement this strategy, start with a clean slate and tell the teenager "We will start next weekend, so please do your homework all week so you can go out Friday night." This intervention will be easier to monitor if only one or two subjects are involved. Your child would probably be overwhelmed if homework from all classes had to be finished before he could participate in any weekend activities. You may need to start with only one or two of his most important subjects. If the work missed is in classes where the teacher will not give any credit for late work, you might ask him just to do a few problems that will ensure that concepts are mastered for the next test.

Forgetting to Bring Home the Weekly Report

Remembering to get the weekly report signed and bringing it home, seemingly simple tasks, are two major hurdles for students with ADD. Use common sense in monitoring the weekly report. If your teenager is failing a class but homework and class work grades have improved, don't have a heart attack if he forgets the weekly note. Of course you must get the report on Friday to determine if he has earned the right to go out on Friday and Saturday nights. Remember, to be effective, feedback must be immediate, not delayed. The teenager who forgets a note is in "hot water" twice: First for not doing the work and second, for not bringing home the note. Obviously, even if your teenager finished his homework but forgot to bring the note home, positive interactions did not increase. Instead, negative interactions increased even though the teenager completed his schoolwork.

⚿

"Until recently, I had always been blessed with an excellent memory. I was unsympathetic to those who did not remember things and assumed my memory was better because I chose to be that way. During a recent illness, my memory was affected. Plus, I must reluctantly admit that perhaps, the aging process may also be having some effect on my memory. I totally forgot a teacher conference I had scheduled for the next day. For the first time in my life, I can identify with my son and his forgetfulness. Being forgetful isn't any fun and it is embarrassing."

⚿

Take or Send Back to School for Note. If necessary, take him back to school to get the note or call the teacher. If your teenager continues to forget to bring the weekly report home even though he experiences the logical consequences of not going to the mall or not playing ball, adjust the plan. For example, you might switch to a daily report and check to see that he completes his work each day. Or have the teacher or school secretary call or fax the information to you. Or with her permission, call the teacher at home. All of us forget things, not just teenagers.

Teach Key Skills First/Let Others Slide. Your teenager can't learn every skill you want him to learn overnight. The most important issue or skills must be identified and taught first. Right now, the most important issue may be the academic one—completion of homework. After he learns to finish his work consistently, you can work on other issues, such as remembering to bring his weekly report home. In truth, he may never consistently remember to bring the report home each Friday. But the major issue—completion of homework—should improve.

Making Too Many Zeros

Many students with ADD make good grades if, and when, they complete and turn in school assignments. Often, however, they have a terrible time remembering to complete and turn in their homework. Consequently, they may have lots of zeros averaged into their grades. This is a common complaint from parents. Zeros on homework, major projects, or missed make-up tests may result in the youngster failing a class.

Monitor for Zeros in Subjects in Danger of Failing. If your child is receiving a lot of zeros and is in danger of failing a class, consider monitoring his progress through daily or weekly reports, homework checks, or a telephone conference with the teacher. Because these teenagers are forgetful, you might also double check to see if make-up assignments and tests are completed after absences.

※

"The grades Shawn receives for completed work are usually pretty good. But he has gotten more zeros than I can count. I remember once when Shawn was in the fifth grade, he had to turn in a composition at the end of each week. One week he spent two and a half hours and wrote a beautiful paper . . . on the wrong topic. When he realized that it was the wrong subject, he just threw his composition away.

"His teacher sent a note home indicating he received a zero. I wrote back and said I hope she had praised him for the report he wrote even though it was on the wrong topic. She wrote back and said, 'What report?' She never even saw the paper.

"If he received a 90, he seemed to take a vacation. He wouldn't do any work for a few days and he would get a few zeros. He never seemed to understand that zeros bring your grades down significantly."

※

"They may also forget the teacher's rules, for example, if you are absent the day before the test and come in on test day, you must take the test anyway. When my daughter's out sick, the last thing she does is organize herself before she goes back to school. The thought of what will we be doing at school never enters her head. She is concentrating on getting her body to school."

※

Ask Teachers to Be Flexible in Grading and Turning in Make-up Work. Sometimes students with ADD forget to do their homework, or complete it but forget to turn it in. Or because of their listening comprehension problems, they may do an assignment incorrectly. Teachers can be most helpful if they are willing to work with your child and allow some flexibility in completion of assignments and determining grades. Ideally, his teachers will allow him to turn in work late for full

or at least partial credit so he doesn't get so many zeros.

※

"One mother told me of her son's beautiful work drawing a timeline of major history events. He spent hours on the project. The teacher gave the student a failing grade because he put approximate dates rather than exact dates. Since his ADD and listening comprehension problems resulted in not completing the assignment correctly, the teacher should have been willing to be more flexible in grading. The teacher should also ensure that the teenager is clear on future assignments."

※

Understandably, high school teachers are trying to instill a sense of greater responsibility in teenagers. They set deadlines and expect them to be met. However, many students with ADD have weak organization skills, poor memory, poor work habits, and knowledge gaps to overcome. Plus, they don't learn from negative consequences (failing a test or class) like other students do. They may feel badly about failing but even their good intentions will not always change their behavior. This is a major difference that may be difficult for you to understand and accept.

Depending on your teenager's confidence and how positive and receptive the teacher is, the teenager himself may ask to turn in work late. If the teacher is negative, you or the guidance counselor may have more success explaining the issue and asking them to cut the child some slack.

Flexibility in turning work in late should be used sparingly for a limited time. You must work with your teenager to improve completion of his homework so that he seldom receives zeros. Once your teenager begins to turn in assignments regularly, he may become hooked on success. The adaptations can then be phased out over time.

Have Your Child Average His Grades. Asking your child to average his current grades may make him more aware of what grade he is earning for the grading period. In addition, to teach him how damaging zeroes can be, you might ask him to determine how many 100's are required to bring a zero up to a passing grade. Or, more realistically, how many grades of 85 does it take to bring one zero grade up to a passing score? The answer: 5 grades of 85 are required.

Failing Some Classes

Because of the factors discussed in previous sections (learning problems, forgetfulness, failure to do homework, and averaging zeros) teenagers with ADD may fail a class. Due to their lack of awareness, some students may not even realize that they are failing. They may be shocked when they fail or receive a low grade.

Discuss the Full Impact of Failing a Class. Teenagers with ADD often don't understand the full ramifications of failing eighth grade (having to stay behind when peers leave for high school) or failing subjects in high school (not being in a home-room or classes with friends of the same age, being ineligible for extracurricular activities, having to attend summer school, or not graduating with class-mates). Discussing these consequences of school failure may impress your child with the importance of maintaining passing grades. On the other hand, because of his ADD, even understanding the implications of failing may not influence his behavior.

🖋

"Alex failed a class his freshman year in high school with a grade of 69. Seventy was passing. He had no idea that he was failing the class. He made 87 on the final exam but forgot to make up two tests that he missed. Consequently, two zeros were averaged in with his test grades. If the educational goal was to teach students the material, my son met that goal by passing the final exam with an 87. However, the secondary goal of being organized and completing and turning in all homework was not met.

"He was allowed to make up the missed tests, but still failed the class by one point. The teacher didn't like him and didn't want to let him make up the tests. Higher ranking administrators authorized the make-up tests. I wouldn't be surprised if the teacher gave my son a 'ringer' test (for advanced classes). The teacher wasn't willing to give him a break."

🖋

"Due to 'no pass, no play' legislation in our state, our son couldn't swim on the swim team. He was the fast-est swimmer on the team. Swimming was one of the things in which he excelled. School was a terrible experience for him. He needed to swim. He needed to be successful."

🖋

Monitor Progress If Your Teenager Is Struggling. To help your child avoid failing a class, monitor progress early in the quarter, after two or three weeks, so you can intervene if necessary. You can call teachers to find out how he is doing, or check the midterm academic progress reports the school sends home. You may also ask teachers to write weekly progress reports, as described earlier in this chapter.

🖋

"When my son started high school, I decided to let him tackle his classes on his own and did not monitor his school progress. He received notices mid-term that he was in danger of failing some of his classes. He ended up failing two classes and had to attend summer school.

"I learned two lessons. First, I needed to monitor his academic progress more closely, even though he was in high school, and make certain he did his homework. Teachers began sending home weekly reports regarding completion of homework. Weekend privileges were contingent upon completion of homework. Second, the logical consequence of having to attend summer school was not especially effective. The consequence (summer school) was too far removed in time from the misbehavior (failing a class)."

🖋

Help Your Teenager Graph His Grades. Helping your teenager chart daily grades on graph paper may give him the visual aid he needs to realize what the grades actually mean. You can encourage him to decrease the distance between the high and low points of his grades on the graph. If necessary, quizzes, tests, and daily grades may be color coded to show him the specific areas needing improvement. Your child can visually observe improvements in his grades and this provides concrete positive feedback.

Find Innovative Ways to Make Up Credits Needed for Graduation. If your teenager has failed some classes, he may not have enough credits to graduate with his friends. If so, you may be able to find an innovative way to help him make up needed credits. Graduating with friends is critically important to many teenagers and they are willing to work hard to accomplish this goal. Typical ways to do this include taking additional credits during the regular school semester, attending summer school, or attending alternative public high school at night. Some public high schools may have a modified semester system for night school in which a student can earn a full semester's credit in eight weeks by attending class eight hours a week. An educational consultant found an innovative way to help her teenager with ADD graduate on time by earning the dreaded science and algebra credits through a correspondence class.

If your teenager has poor organizational skills, you may have to take the initiative to make arrangements for these courses. But your child has the hardest job: she has to do the class work.

〰

"Katie lacked two semesters of physical science to graduate from high school with her classmates. She desperately wanted to finish and walk at graduation with her friends. I did a lot of research and found out that she could earn high school graduation requirements through a correspondence program offered at a university in another state. The critical requirement was that the course content had to meet the credit requirements established by the state. I was so proud of my daughter—in addition to her regular high school classes, she completed both classes. Each class required eight weeks to finish. Staff at the University of Texas said they had never done anything like this before but they were willing to work with us. It was wonderful to have the cooperation of all those involved to help her graduate with her class. I had to do all the leg work required, including linking with the University and the State Department of Education, but she did all her own schoolwork."

— *Joan Maril, Educational Consultant*

〰

The University of Nebraska has offered correspondence courses for earning credits toward high school graduation for years. This service was started years

ago to help youngsters who lived and worked on isolated farms and ranches across the state."

— *John Clark, Nebraska Department of Education*

〰

If you or your teenager are interested in pursuing correspondence courses, check with the nearest state university and their Section 504 coordinator to determine if such courses are offered. You may call your state department of education and ask for the coordinator of special education or Section 504. Be persistent, since several telephone calls may be required to track down the necessary information.

Avoiding School

Because school is such a negative experience, some teenagers with ADD may not want to attend. For these teenagers, the emotional trauma of having to go to school may be enough to make them physically sick some mornings. When they get up, their stomachs may be upset, their heads and muscles may ache. Others may not have physical symptoms but are emotionally fed up with school. They may skip school rather than face failure in an unpleasant learning environment.

〰

"Our daughter attended school regularly, in part because I knew I had to make her go even if she said she didn't feel well. I had to have the 'temperature' rule for missing school."

〰

"Although our daughter didn't have allergies, as a high school student, she developed severe muscle spasms. I'm sure it was from anxiety. Once we even had to go to physical therapy."

〰

For some, school avoidance may not be a conscious action but reflect anxiety about attending school and a desire to avoid a negative experience. As adults, we should understand this feeling, since most of us avoid things we do not do well.

If students with ADD miss a lot of school, they often fall behind academically. Because of their lack of organization and follow-through, they may not complete make-up work. This puts them in danger of failing classes. Frequently, a sense of despair overwhelms them when they get behind in their schoolwork. They see no way out of their predicament. Doing regular homework plus make-up work seems like an impossible task. They fear they can't possibly catch up on their schoolwork and pass the class. They may give up.

Set a Standard for Attending School. You must take care not to allow a major problem with school attendance to develop. It is important to set standards and limits for the circumstances under which you will allow your teenager to stay at home. For example, you might let him stay home from school if he has a fever. Make it clear that if he misses school, you expect him to turn in make-up assignments. You may call or go by school the day he is absent and ask for assignments. If he is feeling better by evening, he can work on assignments then. Most of the time you don't need to be this compulsive unless your teenager gets behind easily and has trouble catching up with assignments or is failing a class.

Some teenagers with ADD may simply refuse to go to school. Obviously, it is difficult to physically make an older teenager go to school. If you find the "fever" rule no longer works, you may have to try the strategies below to resolve the problem.

Have a Physical Examination. A good physical exam should be conducted to rule out any medical problems or allergies. According to Dr. Nadine M. Lambert and Dr. Carolyn Hartsough, approximately one-third to one-half of youngsters with ADHD have chronic health problems such as recurring upper respiratory infections, allergies, or asthma. During certain seasons, sinus drainage and infections may make some teenagers feel nauseated each morning before school. Headaches may be a problem too.

🔏

"Allergies were a major problem for my son and contributed to poor behavior and frequent illnesses starting at four months of age. He was tested for cystic fibrosis at fifteen months. The red dye in medication made things much worse."

🔏

If your teenager has problems with allergies or respiratory infections, seek medical help. The typical over-the-counter antihistamines and decongestants may also help.

If no other medical problems are found, but week after week your teenager complains of being sick or frequently wants to stay home, you need to take other steps. These could include developing a comprehensive strategy to increase successes and make school less aversive, working on solving sleep problems, or adjusting present medications. You may also need to use logical consequences, as described below.

Work on Resolving Sleep Disturbances. Sometimes sleep disturbances play a role in school avoidance. As mentioned earlier, teenagers with ADD may have problems falling asleep and/or waking up. Since over half of these teenagers wake up feeling tired, they may not feel like going to school. The potential for sleep disturbances to undermine a student's school performance is obvious. If a student attends class with less than six or seven hours of sleep, he is not going to have a particularly productive day at school.

🔏

"Since high school classes start at 7:20 a.m., staying awake all day in class with only four or five hours sleep is very difficult. This presents a real dilemma for our son and his teachers. Most teachers aren't aware of his sleep problem. All they see is a student who sleeps through their class. Understandably, most teachers don't feel much sympathy for this behavior unless they are aware of the sleep disturbance problem.

"The alarm goes off, I turn the TV and lights on, and yell but my son can still sleep through all the noise. Thirty minutes later he can't even remember that we had an ugly exchange of words."

🔏

Since many teachers may not realize how common sleep disturbances are for these youngsters, you should explain this problem to them. Teachers need to be aware that teenagers with sleep disturbances may be coming to school exhausted. Also explain that if your child fights with you about getting up, he may feel as though he has been through a major war before ever arriving at school.

He may be in an extremely hostile mood or may sleep through classes. Suggestions for reducing sleep-related problems are provided in Chapter 6.

Use Logical Consequences. If your teenager refuses to go to school, try using logical consequences. "If you are sick, you stay home all day with no company." You might also take him to the doctor, and if he is not sick, then back to school.

▨

"We had a rule that if Cooper stayed home from school he couldn't leave the house that day or have company. 'If you are sick enough to stay home you won't feel well enough to do these other things.' Our pediatrician also helped by saying, 'If you are sick enough to leave school, come straight to my office. If I can't find anything wrong, then you go right back to school.' It worked! He only tested us twice."

▨

Hopefully, you can find a positive solution to school attendance problems. If necessary, however, you may need to make privileges such as driving the car contingent upon school attendance. "When you don't go to school, you can't drive the car."

Seek Professional Help. If school avoidance is a major problem for your teenager, you may need to work with the classroom teacher, school counselor, or school psychologist to improve the school environment. Although there is no official diagnostic category, this pattern of school avoidance or refusal in children is sometimes called a school phobia.

Consider Medication. As a last resort, some doctors prescribe medications such as antidepressants that increase levels of the neurotransmitter serotonin, which is essential for sleep. This medication may enable the teenager to get more restful sleep, wake up more easily each morning, and feel more alert. See Chapter 4 for more information.

Make School More Positive. If your teenager is avoiding school, there is probably a good reason. For example, he may be failing classes because he has learning problems. As Chapter 10 discusses, there are many adaptations that can be made in the classroom that will make school more positive.

Of course, there are always exceptions. Some teenagers with ADD love to go to school. Most teenagers with ADD who like school say they love to visit with their friends. Favorite classes are usually non-academic ones such as P.E., art, music, drama, and shop.

▨

"Lewis has always loved school. He loves to socialize. He never missed much school."

▨

"We never had any problem getting Shawn to go to school. He liked being with his friends. Even in elementary school, he'd tell me the only good thing about school was lunch and gym."

Uneven Academic Performance

Teachers and parents often notice great variability in homework, test grades, and class performance. Students with ADD can do the work one day but not the next. Because of this unevenness, teachers may comment that "the teenager could do the work if he just wanted to." These behaviors may be viewed as "laziness" and are a source of puzzlement and frustration for both parents and teachers.

The person who finds the answer to helping students with ADD produce consistent levels of schoolwork will become rich and famous. In the meantime, parents should let teachers know that uneven school performance is a hallmark characteristic of ADD.

School Problems Related to Specific ADD Symptoms

Hyperactivity

By adolescence, very few children with ADD are extremely hyperactive. Typically, most parents will be dealing with restlessness instead of hyperactivity. If your child *is* still hyperactive, however, his hyperactivity may affect his ability to complete homework.

Accept His Study Style. If your teenager literally can't sit still, Dr. Zentall advises not worrying about appearances. As long as his work is completed, let him choose how and where he sits. Let him sit on his feet, lie on the bed or floor, etc.

Give Study Breaks. Most people, not just students with ADD, work more effectively when they take breaks every 30 minutes or so. Breaks may need to be more frequent—every 20 minutes—for students with ADD. During his five- or ten-minute break, he might listen to music, play with the dog, or eat a snack.

Reward Completion of Work. After he has finished one subject, you might give him a break as a reward. For instance, after he has completed homework in one subject, he can play Nintendo for 20 minutes, take a bath, or watch TV. This approach may not work if it is too late in the evening, medication has worn off, and your teenager cannot refocus on his remaining homework.

Consider Medication. The obvious suggestion is to have your teenager take medication just before working on his homework.

Lethargy

Some teenagers with ADD daydream, yawn a lot, appear bored, or even sleep in class or while doing homework. Attempts to concentrate seem to take tremendous energy: they tire easily. Schoolwork seems to wear them out mentally even though they may work for only 15 minutes to half an hour without completing very much material.

Although lethargy can be a problem for both teenagers with and without hyperactivity, it is more common in those who have ADD/I/WO. Dr. Thomas E. Brown, a Yale psychologist who specializes in treating this type of ADD, describes three major problems for these teenagers: getting started, sustaining energy on a task, and being depressed in addition to having ADD. These teenagers often feel drowsy when they work on tasks even when they have had a good night of sleep. Dr. Brown believes that some appear to be borderline narcoleptics. Although they may not meet diagnostic criteria for narcolepsy, some do report "microsleep"—dozing at long stoplights or while listening to long lectures.

⚹

"Frequently, when my son (ADD/I/WO) sits down to start his homework, he gets very sleepy. His physical

appearance actually changes. His eyelids look heavy and he can hardly keep his eyes open. He has also told me he has to fight off sleep sometimes when he drives. Apparently, he has dozed off a few times while driving. I wonder if he drives fast to provide enough stimulation to keep himself awake."

⚹

Have a Physical Examination. If your teenager is lethargic, a good medical check-up is critical to rule out other illnesses.

⚹

"Our son frequently seemed tired and looked anemic. We had him checked for mononucleosis. The last blood test the doctor ordered showed that he had an iron deficiency. Sometimes because of the teenager's impulsivity and disorganization they don't always eat a balanced diet. They eat snack foods and don't want to eat the healthy meal offered at dinner. They may even forget to eat.

"Our son began taking ferrous gluconate, an iron supplement that is more easily absorbed by the body, and began to look and feel better. He also takes vitamins along with his Ritalin. He seems to have more energy and doesn't seem to be sick as often. We had his blood level checked again later and found it was too high. He cut back on the iron and began taking it every other day."

⚹

Check Lab Results. Be sure to discuss the results of any laboratory tests with the doctor's staff. Ask if there is anything you need to follow up on.

⚹

"Sometimes it is a good idea to follow up on blood or other laboratory test results. The doctor's office was supposed to call us and tell us if there were any problems with the blood test. As a precaution, I called and asked for a report on the blood tests. The doctor's staff had accidentally overlooked the low iron problem. If I hadn't called and asked about the test we would not have picked up the iron deficiency."

⚹

Consider Vitamins. Giving your teenager vitamins may also help him shake off his lethargy. Sometimes teenagers with ADD do not have good

and often feel overwhelmed. They get discouraged and give up easily. Not surprisingly, they are more likely than other teenagers to believe the negative things adults say about them. Hostile feelings emerge and by the time a teenager reaches middle and high school, he may exhibit a tough, "I don't care" veneer to cover years of discouragement and failure. Loving, patient parents and teachers can penetrate that veneer and help these teenagers lead happy, productive lives.

🦋

eating habits. They may forget to eat regularly, plus stimulant medications curb their appetite. Vitamin supplements may ensure they receive all necessary vitamins and minerals.

Encourage Exercise. Exercise can also be extremely helpful. Not only can it help hyperactive teenagers release extra pent-up energy, but it can also give depressed teenagers more energy. Exercise may help them sleep better. In addition, increased athletic skills bring enhanced self-esteem.

Consider Medication. Even if the check-up does not uncover any health problems, medication may be helpful if depression is present or sleep disturbances are contributing to lethargy. Dr. Brown believes that youngsters with ADD/I/WO may benefit from a combination of stimulants and antidepressants. Antidepressants such as Tofranil and Zoloft, prescribed for teenagers with ADD, are discussed in Chapter 4.

Depression, Anxiety, Hostility, and Self-Doubt

After a few years in school, teenagers with ADD may show signs of depression or anxiety. They may have tremendous feelings of self-doubt

"It took only a few months, not years, for my son to become dejected, depressed, and hostile. By the time he reached the second grade, a referral was made for placement in a class for students with emotional problems. We would not give permission for him to participate."

🦋

"Last year, I suspected that one of my son's friends had ADD and referred him to a physician. The teenager was tested and my suspicions confirmed. When I asked the teenager why he thought he had done so poorly in school he said, 'I just thought I was lazy.' He had begun to believe what the adults in his life were saying about him."

🦋

There are many ways parents can help their teenager with ADD feel better about himself. A few are noted below. See the section on building self-esteem in Chapter 5 for more information about pursuing successes outside of school.

Help Your Teenager Succeed in School and Other Environments. Building your teenager's self-esteem through success in school and other settings is critical. Identifying learning deficits, asking for adaptations to the school day, or doing whatever it takes to keep him on track in school is critical. Participation in sports activities may present additional opportunities for achieving successes.

Don't Pressure about Grades. Teenagers with ADD seem very sensitive to pressure and may give up more easily than other students. If you tell your teenager that he has to keep an A or B average, it may make him very anxious. If he is doing his best, but is just getting by with C's and D's, he will be extremely frustrated if you demand that he do better. Particularly if your teenager was older when ADD was discovered, he has experienced a lot of failure at school. He may be terrified of more failure. If he thinks a goal is too difficult to reach, he may not even try to accomplish it.

⚥

"I have not demanded that my teenager obtain certain grades. Although I was a straight-A student in high school and had an A average in college, having my son make straight A's is not that important to me. Having him feel good about himself is much more important. Of course, it would be nice if our son made higher grades, but we are pleased that he has passed all his subjects and improved his grades his sophomore year in high school. He failed three of twelve classes his freshman year.

"The major expectation we have of our son is that he pass all his subjects. Our son is bright enough so that he will pass his high school classes if he does his homework. Requiring completion of homework on a daily or weekly basis is critical for him to obtain passing grades."

⚥

Avoid Challenging/Provide Support. Sometimes it is tempting for parents to challenge their teenager to *prove* that he can do better academically. Many teenagers with ADD, however, will feel overwhelmed with the challenge and may give up completely. The failure further compounds their damaged self-esteem. Most teenagers with ADD respond better to encouragement and support from the family and school.

⚥

"I remember once when my son was doing very poorly in school and I challenged him to prove to me that he could do better. The challenge didn't work. He got really discouraged and gave up."

⚥

Treat Anxiety or Depression. As discussed in Chapter 4, consider medication for treating anxiety or depression.

Defiance/Emotionality/Low Frustration Tolerance

Teenagers with ADD may become upset more easily than other adolescents. As mentioned earlier, over 65 percent of them have significant problems with stubbornness, defiance, refusal to obey, temper tantrums, and verbal hostility toward others. Oppositional behavior is common in many teenagers with ADD. For some adolescents, frustration has been building for years while they have been struggling unsuccessfully in school. They may be overly sensitive to criticism and failure. Parents may see angry temper outbursts, aggression, or what appears to be defiance. These behaviors are more likely to occur as medication is wearing off later in the day. Several suggestions for coping with these problems are discussed in this chapter and Chapter 5: listen, be supportive, use active listening, give choices, teach problem solving skills, teach anger management, lower your voice, overlook minor infractions, and give your teenager space and time to cool off.

Conclusion

In a CHADD conference presentation entitled "Help Me, I'm Losing My Child," Dr. Barkley tells of a distraught mother who came to him for help because her son had started withdrawing emotionally from her. Through her intensive efforts, her son's grades had improved significantly. However, she was devastated when she realized that he was intentionally avoiding her. The spontaneous joy and love in their relationship was dying. Fortunately for them, it was not too late to rebuild their former relationship.

For your family, too, academic success at any cost may not be worth it. Driving a teenager with ADD to achieve high grades is usually not realistic. The high grades become grades that you, the parent, have earned, not the teenager. You need to keep your lifetime relationship with your child in perspective. If your interventions are too intense, controlling, and negative for too long, you risk damaging your parent-child bond and doing irreparable harm to your relationship. Ideally, you will be able to forge a cooperative partnership with your teenager and avoid a protracted, hostile power struggle. Love and accept your teenager for who he is, not for his grades or his accomplishments.

Table 9–2

ELIMINATING ACADEMIC AGONY

This table lists suggestions for parents to try at home that should help the teenager improve his performance with homework and at school.

AVOIDING BLOODY HOMEWORK BATTLES
- Take medication when doing homework
- Set a specific time to do homework each evening
- Set an alarm to announce homework time
- Find a place to study with minimal distractions
- Find a "study buddy"/establish a "study circle"
- Call a friend to confirm homework assignments
- Call school "homework hot-line"
- Use color-coded monthly calendar
- Divide homework into smaller segments
- Allow student to use a computer
- Allow student to dictate themes or reports
- Use white noise or play a radio
- Find out the routine of homework assignments
- Find out when special projects are due
- Ask teacher for written homework assignments
- Ask teacher to get another student to remind of assignments
- Ask teacher to modify assignments
- Use daily or weekly reports (sample forms)
- Limit time spent on homework
- Watch for hasty errors
- Use behavior management suggestions from Chapter 5
- Give time to unwind before bedtime
- Teach your teenager that schoolwork will be done, now or later

FORGETTING THE WEEKLY REPORT
- Take or send back to school to get report
- Teach key skills first (academics)/let others slide
- Work on remembering the report later

MAKING TOO MANY ZEROS
- Monitor zeros in subjects in danger of failing
- Double check homework and make-up assignments
- Ask teachers for flexibility in grading and turning in make-up work
- Have the teenager average his grades

FAILING CLASSES
- Discuss full impact of failing a class
- Monitor progress if struggling
- Use weekly reports
- Help your teenager graph his grades
- Make up credits for graduation

AVOIDING SCHOOL
- Set a standard for attending school/Do you have a fever?

- **Have a physical exam**
- **Work on resolving sleep disturbances**
- **Use logical consequences/if sick, stay home all day or take to doctor, return to school if okay**
- **Seek professional help**
- **Consider medication**
- **Make school more positive/help succeed**

UNEVEN ACADEMIC PERFORMANCE
- **Advise teacher of this ADD characteristic**
- **Use suggestions in this chapter for improving homework completion**

MEDICATION WEARING OFF AT SCHOOL (CHAPTER 10)
- **Schedule key academics at times when medication is working**
- **If problems arise at school, ask when medication was taken**
- **Adjust medication schedule or dose**
- **Ask if he took his medication**

SCHOOL PROBLEMS RELATED TO SYMPTOMS OF ADD

Hyperactivity
- Accept his study style
- Give study breaks
- Reward completion of work
- Consider medication when doing homework
- Provide opportunity to be center of attention; theater, debate team, or school clubs
- Shorten school day for brief time, if in danger of suspension
- Schedule two P.E. classes
- Assign two seats at school
- Assign activities that allow movement

Lethargy
- Have a physical exam
- Check lab results
- Consider vitamins
- Encourage exercise
- Consider medication
- Work on solving sleep disturbance (Chapter 6)

Depression, Anxiety, Hostility, and Self-doubt
- Help succeed in school and community
- Don't pressure about grades
- Avoid challenging to prove themselves, provide support
- Treat anxiety or depression

Defiance/Emotionality/Low Frustration Tolerance
- Listen, be supportive
- Use active listening
- Give choices
- Teach problem solving
- Teach anger management
- Lower voice
- Overlook minor infractions
- Give time and space to cool off

CHAPTER TEN

SUCCESS, NOT JUST SURVIVAL IN SCHOOL

"The most painful vignette for me to recall about Alex's school experience occurred when he was in the first grade. He had just received his first progress report in school and I eagerly asked to see it. As I read the report, he began crying and said, 'Please don't read my report card. My teacher thinks I'm bad.' As I listened to my child's distressed plea, we both cried. Tears flooded my eyes. The first hint of the academic agony ahead had surfaced.

"Alex could not read or understand the passing grades and positive words written on his first-grade report card. But at the young age of six he was extremely perceptive about his teacher's negative attitude toward him. He was right—the teacher thought he was 'bad.' Alex struggled through six difficult and bewildering years of school until a school psychologist diagnosed ADD when he was twelve."

❦

Although children with ADD may start school with great expectations and willingness to do their work, their inattention, impulsivity, and learning problems can make it difficult for them to do well academically. Over the years, the struggle to succeed at school may quickly become an overwhelming challenge. Unless parents and teachers intervene—both at home and at school—teenagers with ADD may give up trying to succeed in school. Chapters 8 and 9 discussed interventions parents may try at home; this chapter covers interventions and adaptations to try at school.

The challenge of educating students with ADD was summed up by Dr. Russell Barkley during a keynote address at a national CHADD conference. As a result of their ADD, "These youngsters,

unlike other teenagers, do not have a natural love of learning, the desire to be the best, to master a skill, or make the highest grades in the class." Even though students with ADD may be bright, parents and teachers need to use a variety of techniques at home and school to help them succeed academically.

COMMON LEARNING PROBLEMS AND CLASSROOM ADAPTATIONS

As discussed in Chapter 8, learning problems are common among teenagers with ADD. Several characteristics commonly associated with ADD contribute to problems at school. The most common symptoms that cause problems include inattention, distractibility, impulsivity, and hyperactivity. There are also a variety of other factors that can affect academic achievement: uneven school performance, difficulty maintaining effort, sleep disturbance, lethargy, emotionality, low frustration tolerance, defiance, aggression, depression, anxiety, or medication wearing off. Chapter 9 covered strategies for dealing with these problems at home; this chapter offers strategies for dealing with them in the classroom. As a parent, you may also find these strategies useful in managing problems with homework.

Further compounding their academic difficulties, approximately one-third of all teenagers with ADD have one or more of these learning problems:

- Language deficits (poor listening comprehension; poor verbal expression; poor reading comprehension)
- Poor organizational skills
- Poor memory
- Poor fine motor skills

Failure to make adaptations for learning problems may be one of the major reasons why some students who are being treated for ADD continue to do poorly in school. The purpose for providing the information in this chapter is for you to identify your teenager's learning problems and ask for appropriate classroom adaptations. As discussed in Chapter 9, one of the most helpful things you can do is ask the teacher to make adaptations to the classroom or modify assignments to help compensate for their learning problems. Table 10–1 shows the learning problems, behaviors observed, and classroom adaptations and interventions identified for one teenager with ADD. This sample plan for classroom adaptations may help you as you develop a plan for your teenager. Blank forms are provided in Chapter 13.

If your teenager continues to struggle at school, consider sharing adaptations suggested in this chapter with teachers. A summary of common learning problems, plus adaptations, is included in an easy to reference chart (Table 10–2) at the end of this chapter. You may find it helpful to skim over the chart before reading this chapter. This will give you an overview of the range of learning problems and types of classroom adaptations.

Inattention/Distractibility

Inattention can cause major problems at home and in the classroom. Students may have trouble staying "on-task" to complete schoolwork and homework. They may be distracted by things in the room or by their own internal thoughts and may not be listening to instructions. They may forget to take home the necessary books, or lose or misplace their homework, notebooks, or notes.

Sometimes behaviors caused by inattention or forgetfulness can be mistaken for defiance. For example, a teenager who forgets to do his schoolwork or chores or to stay after school for detention may seem to be acting defiantly. These kinds of misun-

derstandings can obviously lead to conflicts at home and at school.

Dr. Sydney Zentall, professor of special education at Purdue University, is one of the few educational researchers who has studied techniques for teaching students with ADD. She prefers to describe students with ADD as having an "attentional bias" instead of an attentional deficit. Students with ADD seek out tasks that are high interest, new, or presented in a different way. Problems with inattention are more likely to occur when the material being learned is uninteresting, familiar, and repetitive. Unfortunately, this describes so much of traditional schoolwork.

If your teenager has a great deal of trouble paying attention in class, teachers may be more effective by varying the way they present information in class. Use of novelty, color, and active learning help these students learn more easily. Stimulant medications such as Ritalin or Dexedrine can also improve your teenager's ability to pay attention. Numerous suggestions are provided in subsequent sections to help reduce problems with inattention and distractibility.

Difficulty Completing Work

A major complaint from parents and teachers is that students with ADD have trouble completing their class- or homework. They get distracted by things that they find much more interesting than schoolwork. They focus on people talking in the hall or the air conditioning unit turning on instead of on their work. They impulsively move from one task to another. Many have difficulty concentrating when they read school material. Some suggestions for dealing with these problems are outlined below. You will also find helpful suggestions in the subsequent sections on listening deficits, daydreaming, and difficulty following directions. These are often the reasons a student with ADD has difficulty starting and finishing his work. Additional suggestions for helping teenagers complete homework are included in Chapter 9 in the section on "The Bloody Homework Battles."

Give Frequent Positive Feedback. Positive feedback is important for teenagers with ADD, yet some of these teenagers have trouble doing things that generate positive feedback. Parents and teachers should try to "catch them being good" as fre-

---

TABLE 10–1

LEARNING PROBLEMS AND SCHOOL ADAPTATIONS
INDIVIDUALIZED PLANNING: "DO WHATEVER IT TAKES"

NAME: Tom   AGE: 17   GRADE: 12th

LEARNING PROBLEM	BEHAVIOR OBSERVED	ADAPTATIONS
• Poor short term memory	• Can't memorize multiplication tables	• Use a calculator for class work, homework, and tests
• Slow Cognitive Processing (in addition to poor fine motor coordination)	• Writes very slowly • Takes class notes very slowly • Takes twice as long to complete school work • Takes twice as long to complete tests • Doesn't have time to double check answers	• Obtain guided lecture notes from teacher; get copy of another student's notes • Modify class and homework assignments; every 3rd algebra problem • Give extended time for tests • Use calculator to do problems and to check homework answers
• Poor Written Language Expression	• Difficulty organizing thoughts • Difficulty writing themes, recognizing main topics	• Develop outline for theme before writing theme in class • Teach to write 5 paragraph theme • Allow to use computer at home and school
• Poor Organizational Skills	• Difficulty getting started/ maintenance of effort/ finishing assignments	• Provide prompt from parent or teacher; provide positive reinforcement when working
• Poor Listening Comprehension	• Difficulty following multi-step verbal instructions from teachers and parents	• Provide written list of chores or class and homework assignments • Keep instructions brief and simple
• Inattention (in addition to poor memory)	• Difficulty paying attention in class • Difficulty studying • Forgets homework assignments	• Touch desk or shoulder • Sit near the front of class • Get assignments in writing • Do homework with a friend • Make certain meds are taken

---

quently as possible. Watch for opportunities to praise your teenager for staying on task, working hard, paying attention, completing assignments, and following rules. Dr. Russell Barkley has found that positive reinforcement must be given more frequently and must be stronger for teenagers who have ADD. Using touch, hugs, or praise increases the effectiveness of positive reinforcement. Sugges-

tions for using behavior management effectively are discussed in Chapter 5.

Use Weekly Reports. Use of weekly reports is discussed in detail in Chapter 9.

Provide a Reward for Completion of Work. Make participation in fun activities on the weekend contingent upon receiving a satisfactory "weekly report." If desired, you can provide a small daily reward when classwork is finished or homework turned in: 30 extra minutes on Nintendo, delayed bedtime by 30 minutes to an hour, or extra time on the phone. Remember, immediate rewards (daily or weekly) are more effective.

Take Medication When Doing School-work. As discussed in Chapter 4, taking stimulant medication (Ritalin or Dexedrine) has been found to help reduce impulsivity, improve concentration, and increase accuracy and amount of work completed. As secondary benefits of taking medication, students are better able to monitor and control their own behaviors; try harder and do as they are asked; are less physically and verbally hostile; have fewer negative behaviors; and are less physically active.

Difficulty Getting Started

Getting started on schoolwork can be extremely difficult for teenagers with ADD. Instead, they may be talking to friends, doodling, looking out the window, reading a car magazine (even during class), or thinking about what they are going to do after school.

Since teenagers with ADD have such great difficulty getting started on schoolwork, they may need to be monitored during the starting period. Remember, transition periods such as beginnings and changing from one activity to another are difficult for these teenagers. Monitoring and prompting may be done unobtrusively with minimum embarrassment to the teenager.

Use a Cue to Get Attention. Teachers can get your teenager's attention without calling out his name or otherwise embarrassing him when he is not working. When the teacher notices that your child has not started working, he could walk near your child's desk and place a hand on his shoulder or desk. This cue should be discussed in advance with your teenager so he knows it means it is time to get started.

Tuning Out and Daydreaming

Another common complaint from teachers is that teenagers with ADD don't seem to pay attention in class. When they do listen, their attention span may be short. Since they pay attention only briefly, they may have difficulty following instruc-

tions. Some students also may have learning deficits related to poor memory or listening comprehension, which can further compound their problems following teacher directions.

❦

"Sometimes they don't realize they are off-task until the teacher calls on them. Then anxiety grips them."

❦

"Are you listening to me?" is a question frequently asked by parents and teachers alike. Many times, students with ADD don't seem to be listening, even in one-to-one settings. This characteristic of teenagers with ADD is one of the more aggravating ones since the parent or teacher is never certain if the message has been heard or will be acted upon. This issue was discussed in Chapter 6 because it is also a common problem at home. The discussion of "poor listening comprehension" skills in the next section may also help adults understand why students with ADD don't always know what is said to them or follow directions.

An "absent-minded professor" quality, as reflected in a lack of awareness of time, grades, or assignments, or a lack of attention to detail, may also be observed, especially in children with ADD/I/WO. Teenagers with ADD/I/WO may sit, daydreaming in a world all their own. They may seem confused or appear to be "in a fog." Teenagers with ADD are also described as bored or restless, regardless of whether or not they were hyperactive as children. While daydreaming, they may fidget, tap their foot, drum their fingers on the desk, tap their pencil, or stare into space.

❦

"I was a daydreamer in school. Through college, my daydreaming usually dealt with hunting. In high school, it dealt with cars and girls. In middle school, I daydreamed about bicycles. I was also a doodler. I still doodle a lot.

"The best way I can describe how Ritalin affects me and my daydreaming is by telling this story. When I am sitting in class and my stomach starts growling, before I started taking Ritalin, I would sit there and think, 'When I get home, I'll have me a ham sandwich, with mayonnaise and mustard, two slices of cheese, lettuce, some Fritos, and I'm gonna watch TV.' I visually built the sandwich in my mind. Then I

would realize I had just missed 30 minutes worth of notes. Ritalin keeps me focused."

— *Steven*

Use High Interest Teaching Aids. Using computers or high interest teaching methods helps keep students with ADD more focused.

Use a Multisensory Approach. Teenagers with ADD respond well to a multisensory approach. That is, they may learn better if information is not presented to just one of their senses (passively listening to the teacher lecture or reading silently to themselves). They do better when they can learn through a combination of auditory, visual, kinesthetic, or tactile approaches. They benefit from opportunities for "hands on" experiences, using films, slides, videos, experiments, and concrete manipulatives. They do better if teachers highlight the key parts of their instructions—write key words in a different color, underline or star key directions, or change voice inflection.

Make Eye Contact. Teachers should try to make eye contact with students with ADD when giving assignments. This technique will work for most teenagers but not all. Sometimes they can look right at the teacher and never hear a word she says.

Seat Away from Distractions. It may help to seat your teenager away from major distractions such as windows, doors, air conditioning units, a bubbling aquarium, or talking students. He might be seated near the front of the class to reduce distractions and enable him to pay attention to the teacher. Seating him near someone who is attentive, organized, and generally on task may help set a good example for him.

Realistically, a high school student may be horrified if you move him to the front of the room near the teacher's desk, especially if other students are seated in alphabetical order. Teenagers don't want to be singled out as different. The key is to talk with the teenager in advance and ask his input. If he is passing, the seating assignment should be his choice or the same as for other students. If he is struggling and is agreeable, the teacher may find a discreet way to seat him near the front.

Cue/Use a Private Signal. Teachers can establish a signal with your teenager to indicate they are about to call on him. For instance, they could call on a student near him. Or say, "John, I am going to call on you next. Be thinking about this question." This gives him time to collect his thoughts. There is no need to embarrass him by calling on him when he is not listening.

Cue Prior to an Important Announcement. When making an announcement about homework or a test, teachers might start off with an attention-getting statement such as, "Listen carefully. This is important! or Write this down. It will be on the test." Or they might make a noise by tapping their desk or clapping their hands to get the student's attention.

Keep Instructions Brief and Simple. Keeping verbal instructions simple—two or three steps at a time—plus stating them numerically may help. "Number 1. Do all odd problems on page 29. Number 2. Correct the problems you missed on your last test." Once assignments are made, the parent or teacher should state clearly that a new topic is being addressed before going on to the next subject.

Divide Work into Smaller Segments. As discussed in the preceding chapter, some teenagers with ADD may become overwhelmed by the length of an assignment or test. Dividing work into smaller segments may help the student complete the assignment.

Schedule Short Work Periods. Shorter work periods interspersed with brief breaks help students with ADD be more productive. The breaks may be used for checking work for errors or for activities that allow students to legitimately get out of their seats. Most high school classes offer some change in activity. For instance, the teacher may lecture for half the period and then have students work on an assignment.

Find Activities to Allow Movement. If your teenager with ADD is extremely restless or is still hyperactive, he will need these breaks to release pent-up energy and channel his energy into positive activities. His teachers might let him pass out or collect papers, clean the board and erasers, feed class pets, water plants, or deliver or pick up messages from the office.

Lack of Attention to Detail

Students with ADD make what appear to be "careless errors" in their work and on tests. Typically, they don't double check their homework or tests for mistakes. Even if they do double check, they may still overlook the error. Sometimes when working math problems, they don't notice changes in signs. For example, they may add all the problems, never noticing the change from addition to subtraction. They may overlook errors in spelling, capitalization, grammar, and punctuation. They may not do well on tests that use bubble sheets, since they may lose their place and mark the answer sheet incorrectly.

Use Color as an Aid to Learning. Dr. Zentall has found that using color adds an element of novelty which is effective in teaching these students. Usually, a skill is taught first and then color is used to increase the student's awareness of potential problems. For example, if a student doesn't notice sign changes in math (+ or -), a highlighter could be used to mark all math signs on a homework assignment or test. Or if he consistently misses a letter in spelling words, such as putting the "i" before "e" in "their," highlight the correct information in color. Changes in verbs in foreign languages can also be marked with color: hablar - to speak; (hablo, hablas, habla. In addition, color can be used to highlight material that may be overlooked. For instance, the student may be asked to highlight directions for homework or a test.

Have the Student Read Material/Test Aloud. Researchers have confirmed what one counselor learned from experience: some teenagers overlook grammatical errors when they read silently. The counselor found that if students read the material aloud, they find the errors more easily. If your teenager is having problems in English, he could read his homework answers aloud and record them on tape. For example, sentences which require selection of proper subject-verb agreement, plural vs. singular, or verb tense could be recorded. Or read the material aloud to another student, who writes down the answers.

Occasionally, a student may do better when he takes tests orally. If this is true for your teenager, the school can find someone to be a "reader" for the test and record your teenager's answers.

Modify Grading System. If grammar or spelling errors are a major problem, the teacher could provide two grades on the written material, one for content and the other for grammar or spelling. The student can improve his grade by correcting grammatical or spelling errors and turning the work back in to the teacher. As the student's grammar improves, the teacher may return to a more traditional grading system.

Double Check Answers. As discussed in Chapter 9, have your teenager double check his answers. If he works too slowly or has processing problems, another student or parent may double check answers and then have the teenager correct the errors. Eventually, if assignments are modified (shortened) or untimed tests are given, he will have time to check his own work.

Lack of Awareness of Grades

Some students with ADD have no idea whether they are passing their classes or failing. School grading seems to be a complete mystery. They may make high grades on all their tests but forget to turn in homework, not complete class work, and fail the class. They remember the high test grades and are baffled by the failing grade. They feel confused and may decide that regardless of how hard they try, they are going to fail anyway. Or, they may start off a new grading period with the best intentions and sincere promises of making better grades. Then their grades begin to slide and it is a struggle to pull out passing grades by the end of the period.

🦋

"We referred to this period as 'The Agony and Ecstasy.' The teenager starts off good, goes downhill fast, and then you have to race like crazy the last week to get A's to bring F's up to C's."

🦋

Some teenagers with ADD are oblivious to their past academic performances. When a grading period is over, they do not seem to remember that they barely squeaked through the class, thanks to their parents pushing them. They only remember that they passed the class.

Factors such as inattention, poor organization, and poor memory probably play a role in their lack of awareness of grades.

If in Danger of Failing, Monitor Schoolwork. If your teenager is in danger of failing, you, the teacher and your son might jointly develop a plan to monitor school grades or homework completion on a weekly basis. He could keep a running tally of grades or periodically ask the teacher about his grade average and bring this information home to you.

Obtain Factual Information Regarding Grades. Don't take for granted that your teenager knows what a passing grade is. Find out actual grades or requirements by asking the teacher or by reading written information sent home by the teacher. You may also ask the teacher how final grades are obtained. Some grades such as test scores may be weighted more heavily than homework. For example, grades on homework may be 70 percent of the final grade and test scores only 30 percent.

"My son was depressed recently because he made a 59 on his first pre-calculus test in college. He was talking about dropping the class because he was doing so poorly. He assume that 70 was passing in college just as it was in high school. He seemed pleasantly surprised that 60 was a D. He was feeling overwhelmed without fully knowing all the facts."

Graph Grades. Ask that the teacher send home your teenager's grades at regular intervals. Graph his grades, as described in Chapter 9. Of course if the grading system is complex, this may

not tell you if he's passing or failing, but you can see a trend in his grades.

Impulsivity

Acting or speaking impulsively may cause problems at home and school. Some teenagers with ADD have great difficulty controlling their inappropriate behavior. They begin schoolwork without waiting for instructions, make "careless errors" in their work, take "short cuts" in homework, interrupt others, talk back to teachers and parents, and impulsively break rules. Usually, they are not acting maliciously but simply act before thinking of the consequences. Delaying gratification is extremely difficulty for them. Unfortunately, as Dr. Barkley points out, success in most school systems is based upon the ability to delay gratification: students must wait nine weeks for a grade; earn credits to graduate from high school four years later; do schoolwork to get a job years later.

Getting into Trouble at School

Impulsive behavior is probably one of the major reasons that teenagers with ADD get into trouble. Noncompliance, forgetfulness, lack of awareness of school rules, and academic frustration also contribute to their problems. Examples of behaviors that make school administrators angry and sometimes lose their temper include: talking back to teachers, walking out of class without permission, refusing to do as asked, skipping school, smoking in the restroom, carrying a knife to school, or getting into fights. As noted earlier, approximately half the students with ADHD in one study had been suspended and approximately 10 percent expelled.

Help Succeed Academically. Although there are no easy answers for solving these problems, teenagers who are succeeding academically are less likely to get into trouble at school. You can help your teenager succeed in school by ensuring that learning deficits are identified and appropriate classroom adaptations are made.

Keep Rules Simple/State Clearly. Keep rules at home and school simple and clearly stated. Ask for a copy of the school's student handbook so you are familiar with the rules. If teachers have rules for their classroom, it helps if they put them in writing. For example, make-up work must be turned in within a week of an absence. If you have a copy of the rules at home, you will know how to help your teenager follow them.

Remind of Consequences in Advance. Teenagers should be reminded of the consequences of various rule infractions in advance, especially those rules they are more likely to break. For example, carrying a knife, even a small one, may result in suspension from school.

Notify School Officials of Potential Problems. Parents can often predict which events will upset their teenager and cause problems at school. If you know that your teenager is going to school upset and could possibly get into an explosive situation, you might suggest he talk with the guidance counselor first thing that morning. You could also call the counselor and say, "John broke up with his girlfriend and is really upset. Can you talk to him? I'm afraid he may be planning to fight her new boyfriend."

Take Medication When at School. When a teenager is taking stimulant medication, he is less impulsive, more attentive, and less likely to act out. Additional medications might also be prescribed for teenagers who have greater problems with emotionality and aggressiveness and are in danger of suspension from school (Clonidine, Tofranil, Prozac, Zoloft, and Lithium). See Chapter 4 for an in-depth discussion of medications.

Shorten the School Day. If your teenager may be on the verge of being suspended or expelled, you might consider a shortened school day. For example, your teenager could go home after lunch each day for a few days until the crisis is resolved. If he misses academic classes, check to see what the assignments are. With the teachers' permission, he can work on them when he gets home. Certain times of the year are more difficult than others. Most students are keyed up just before Christmas and at the end of the school year. At those times, students with ADD may be even more rambunctious and get into trouble or be suspended.

Request a Classroom Aide. Classroom aides can provide assistance for teenagers who have more serious academic or behavioral problems. Students who are eligible for special education services under IDEA are more likely to get this service. The aide could be assigned to a classroom for a limited period of time. To avoid embarrassment, other students would not have to know that the aide was assigned to a specific student. He could work with one or two other students at the same time. Jody Lubrecht, Ph.D., a children's consultant with the Idaho Department of Mental Health, has written about an innovative program in Idaho, known as "classroom companions." The program uses this concept to provide the equivalent of day treatment services to youngsters who have serious emotional problems.

❧

"One school system was refusing to take a student in special education on a class field trip because she needed one-on-one supervision. Under IDEA and Section 504, however, the school must meet the student's needs. The parents were unable to go along on the field trip, so they talked with school personnel. Arrangements were made for someone to accompany the teenager on the trip."

Impulsive Learning Styles

Teenagers with ADD may also have impulsive learning styles. Often, they may start assignments without first reading the instructions or examples. They may select the first answer on multiple choice tests. They don't seem to read the other choices carefully. Rushing through homework and not double checking their work are also common occurrences.

Sometimes, impulsivity associated with ADD may be the cause of a teenager's learning problems. For example, a younger student with an impulsive reading style may see the first letter of a word, "c," and then assume the word is anything that starts with a "c."

Review Instructions with the Teenager. You or your child's teachers could review instructions for assignments with your teenager. Ask him to read and repeat the instructions aloud. Or have him discuss the instructions with another student in the class.

Highlight Instructions. You or the teacher can have your teenager highlight key words in the instructions before starting assignments. Tell him, for example, "Read the directions for your English assignment and mark the key words with a yellow highlighter." Then check to make certain he did it right.

Mark Out Wrong Answers on Multiple Choice Tests. Dr. Zentall recommends having students with ADD mark out the wrong answers first. By allowing the student to mark wrong answers first, he can meet his need to mark something immediately. On multiple choice tests, this may help avoid his giving impulsive wrong answers. Ask your teenager if he thinks this idea will help.

Allow Time for Double Checking Answers. Students who are impulsive or process information slowly may not double check answers. If extended time is allowed on tests, he may actually have enough time to double check answers.

🖎

"My son came home from college excited because he made a 93 on his algebra exam. He exclaimed, 'For the first time, I double checked my answers.' He had extended time on tests and he had time to double check his answers. He corrected two or three errors he had made and earned an A on the test. He was so proud of himself."

Language Deficits

Three language-processing problems are common among teenagers with ADD: difficulties with *listening comprehension, spoken language production, and written language production.* Although the reasons for these problems are not fully understood, the brain must have difficulty translating symbols (letters of the alphabet) into words, interpreting words seen and heard, identifying corresponding meanings, and then giving a verbal or written response.

Poor Listening Comprehension*

Teenagers with ADD may have trouble understanding spoken messages due to auditory language processing deficits. They may appear confused by verbal instructions and have difficulty following them. Dr. Zentall explains that they have even more problems listening and comprehending if irrelevant details or lengthy descriptions are added or if interesting conversations of others compete for their attention. If instructions (homework assignments or chore requests) are imbedded within a much longer discussion, the teenager may not "hear" (selectively pick out) the instructions. In addition, students with ADD may have trouble learning foreign languages, especially if the primary method of instruction is verbal and given in the foreign language itself.

For most of us, listening seems like such a simple task. However, Dr. Zentall reminds us that listening is a complex skill that "requires the ability to select out and attend to a message while ignoring competing information."

Difficulty Understanding Instructions

If an assignment has many steps or is given during the context of a general discussion, students with ADD may not understand and may miss the assignment totally. They have difficulty following several instructions at one time and may become confused. Many are too embarrassed or shy to ask questions to clarify their confusion or misunderstanding.

Keep Instructions Brief and Simple. The practical implications of poor listening comprehension are significant: teachers should avoid lengthy verbal discussions (lecturing) about homework assignments or problem behaviors. The teenager will quickly get lost and "tune out" during these discussions.

State Instructions Clearly. Make sure teachers give clear instructions. Numbering the directions may help. "First, do all odd problems on page 37. Second, do all five-word problems on page 38."

Use a Cue to Get Their Attention. This technique is discussed earlier in this chapter.

Difficulty Following Instructions

Teenagers with ADD may have trouble following verbal instructions given in class due to audi-

---

* Asterisks are used to indicate the seven categories of Specific Learning Disabilities (SLD) recognized under the Individuals with Disabilities Education Act (IDEA). See Chapter 11 for more information on IDEA.

tory processing problems. They may miss assignments and never "hear" the teacher when an assignment is made. Even when assignments are written on the chalkboard, they may not see them or remember to copy them down. **Ask the Student to Repeat Instructions.** Parents or teachers may ask students to paraphrase the instructions.

Write Instructions on "Post It" Notes. Teachers may write instructions or assignments on "Post it" notes and put them on the child's desk. He may never see the assignment on the board but he is more likely to see the "Post it" note. The teacher may number and simplify the assignment. For example, "1. Do odd problems on page 27. 2. Swap papers with a neighbor and check answers. 3. Put your finished paper on my desk."

Difficulty Learning Foreign Languages

Teenagers with ADD have enough trouble paying attention when the teacher speaks English. It is easy to imagine how much harder the subject may be if the teacher speaks nothing but a foreign language during class. Besides auditory processing problems, inattention and memorization problems also contribute to difficulty with foreign languages.

🦋

"My son told me that after the first day of class the teacher spoke nothing but Spanish. In addition, his language labs required good listening comprehension since he had to listen to tapes in Spanish. He got lost when he listened to tapes because they speak too rapidly. Fortunately, they allowed him to exempt the auditory tapes and use a computer program instead. Since he is a visual learner, he found the computer more helpful."

🦋

Use Tips on Memorization. Suggestions for improving memorization are provided in subsequent sections.

Ask for Adaptations. If your teenager has listening comprehension problems and is a visual learner, request that tests be presented in writing rather than orally. You could also ask whether a computer instructional program is available.

If All Else Fails, Seek a Waiver. If your teenager has major problems with listening comprehension and memorization, some subjects, such as

a foreign language, may be extremely difficult for him to pass. He may make his best effort and still fail the class. Because his ability to learn is adversely affected by ADD and his learning problems, you may be able to use the laws described in Chapter 11 to exempt the class as a requirement for high school or college graduation. Don't wait until your child has failed the class to intervene. If he is unable to achieve passing grades after intensive intervention, the evidence should be pretty clear that he will be unable to pass it.

🦋

"My son's counselor in college said that his language problems were so serious, he would never be able to learn a foreign language. She requested an exemption from having to take the class. Another class was substituted instead."

🦋

A few parents of high school students have been successful in obtaining a waiver, but this is still a new experience for most school systems. So be forewarned that obtaining a waiver will probably be time-consuming and require you to do a lot of paperwork.

🦋

"Jason transferred from a private to a public school, having taken three years of Spanish. We were told that he would have to take one more year of Spanish, since two years of credit taken prior to ninth grade wouldn't transfer. Because my son has short-term memory problems, foreign languages are extremely difficult for him. We thought we would have to request a waiver to solve this problem. However, when we contacted the State Department of Education we discovered that we could accomplish our goal without a waiver. The wording of the transcript letter from the private school was the key. The state official told us the key elements that had to be included in the letter for Jason to receive proper credit."

— Jamie Hartman, CHADD
Chapter Coordinator, Macon, GA

🦋

You may want to wait to discuss this option with your teenager, since school officials may not want or know how to arrange for a waiver. In addition, your teenager may be tempted to give up too soon on a subject that he is capable of mastering.

Poor Notetaking

Students with ADD may have trouble taking notes in class because of poor listening comprehension, difficulty picking out main points, inattention, poor fine motor coordination, or slow processing (slow listening comprehension and writing). Because notetaking requires such intense concentration for them, they may avoid this difficult task. Dr. Steven Evans and his colleagues found that students who were taught improved notetaking skills increased their comprehension, made better grades on daily assignments, and were less disruptive.

Obtain a Copy of a Classmate's or Teacher's Lecture Notes. Your child might be able to obtain copies of lecture notes from another student, or perhaps the teacher may be willing to provide a copy of his notes. This way, he can concentrate on what the teacher is saying, and not have to take notes, listen, and keep up with the lecture. According to one study on ADD, students' comprehension improves when they are given the notes, even though they don't actually take the notes themselves.

Obtain Guided Lecture Notes from the Teacher. Some teachers give guided lecture notes for each class. Guided lecture notes basically summarize the critical information being presented. Key words and concepts are presented and serve as an excellent document to study for tests. The student may also write notes on the paper while the teacher is lecturing.

Use NCR or Carbon Paper. Another student can easily make a copy of his notes by using carbon paper. Non carbon replica (NCR) paper, a chemically treated paper, can also be used to make a duplicate copy of notes. The paper is available with lines and the two sheets are attached at the top. It is easier to use and is not as messy as carbon paper. Although it may be expensive to purchase from an office supply store, a larger school system with an in-house print shop can make their own.

Record Class Lectures on Tape. Recording the teacher's lecture on tape is a great idea if your teenager is willing to do it. But it doesn't work for all teenagers. They have trouble concentrating long enough to listen to the lecture the first time. Listening to it twice may be torture.

Cue Student When Important Points Are Made. See earlier discussion.

Spoken Language (Oral Expression*) Problems

Some teenagers with ADD are extremely verbal and love making speeches in public, but others really dread it. In fact, about one-third to one-half of all teenagers with ADD have problems with expressive language. This is about two or three times the rate for teenagers without ADD. Interestingly enough, Dr. Barkley and Dr. Zentall have both observed that teenagers with ADHD are more likely than their peers to talk during spontaneous conversations, but less likely to talk when asked to respond to a specific request. Responding to a question or statement requires more organization and careful thought. Again, slow cognitive processing may contribute to this problem.

🦋

"When my daughter tells me about something that has happened, the story comes out all jumbled up. She can't organize her thoughts to tell the story in logical order."

🦋

"My son was frightened to death of having to make a presentation in front of the class. He would take an F on his report rather than speak in front of his classmates."

🦋

Be Positive and Supportive. Many teenagers with ADD need more help and understanding than other students. By being supportive, the teacher creates a positive learning environment in which students are not afraid to ask questions or make mistakes. Teachers can help by praising correct answers or efforts to answer a question, giving students time to think of their answer and respond, and avoiding criticism or put-downs.

Difficulty Articulating Clear Answers

Teenagers with ADD may have trouble organizing their thoughts and expressing them in a logical, sequential order. This can show up in two ways. First, some youngsters talk nonstop and have trouble giving brief, concise answers. Second, youngsters who are slow at processing information need more time to think before responding to questions. This problem increases if the student is nervous, self-conscious, or anxious about his answer. "My son has difficulty sorting out what's important, so he says it all. Rather than give the main idea, he painstakingly repeats every detail."

Teach Mechanics of Outlining and Sequencing. With time and practice, students with ADD can often learn to express themselves more clearly. They can practice telling about events in a story in sequential order. What happened first? Next, and so on? If your teenager has to make an oral presentation, help him outline the speech.

Avoids Responding in Class

Students who have problems with verbal expression may be less likely to raise their hands and volunteer to answer questions in class. They may avoid making presentations to the whole class. Sometimes these students are afraid to ask for help or to ask a teacher to repeat information. They are afraid that they will "look dumb."

◪

"I don't like to raise my hand in class and ask questions. I am afraid that my mind was drifting off and I may look dumb. I'm afraid to ask a teacher a question if it isn't clear. I feel like I shouldn't ask questions about things she has already said. It would be redundant."

—Robert

◪

Make the Teacher Aware of the Problem. Sometimes a portion of the grade is based upon class participation. It might help to make the teacher aware of the reasons why your teenager doesn't actively participate in class. Perhaps the teacher will agree not to penalize his grade for lack of class participation.

Cue/Alert Student Prior to Being Called Upon. As discussed earlier, teachers could cue the teenager prior to calling on him. State the question and give him time to think about the answer. The teacher may also assign specific problems (questions) to each student and say, "In a few minutes, I want each of you to tell me how to do your problem."

Slow Recall of Facts

Even when students with ADD are able to memorize material such as multiplication tables or history facts, their recall of information may be slower. Youngsters who have ADD/I/WO usually have the most difficulty with slow retrieval of stored information. Some medications, such as Lithium at higher doses, may also slow the ability to recall facts quickly.

Give More Time to Respond. Teachers may need to give your teenager more time to think when asking him to respond orally to questions in class. They might also call on another student and then come back to him. Giving notice before calling on him will also give him time to think through his answer.

◪

"I'm not stupid. I knew the answer but the teacher didn't give me enough time to think about my answer."

◪

Provide Less Threatening Opportunities to Speak Publicly. You and your child's teachers can devise less threatening opportunities for him to practice public speaking—through school clubs, debate team, theater groups, boy scouts or girl scouts, church or synagogue, or at family events or holiday programs.

Written Language Problems

Teenagers with ADD may have trouble 1) *writing their own ideas down on paper*, or 2) comprehending (*reading*) what someone else has written. Reasons may include: slow cognitive processing, poor organizational skills, inattention, slow recall of information, poor fine motor coordination, distractibility, poor concentration, and avoidance of unpleasant tasks. On a positive note, Dr. Zentall notes that some teenagers with ADD write more creative stories. At school, difficulty with written language can lead to the following problems:

1. Writes slowly on assignments: Because of the problems described in the preceding paragraphs, these teenagers may work very slowly on their homework, schoolwork, and tests. Some students may take twice as long to complete written assignments.

2. Produces less written work: Slow processing may mean that a student produces less written work and reads less material. Obviously, students with ADD require more time for completing written and reading assignments.

3. Has difficulty writing themes, reports, and tests: These teenagers may have difficulty organizing and expressing their thoughts (written expression*) in a clear, orderly manner as required for writing English compositions or reports.

Use a Computer. If your teenager has illegible handwriting and writes slowly or laboriously, ask the teacher if a computer is available for him to use when writing compositions at school. Hopefully, in the not-too-distant future, most schools will have laptop computers that students with learning problems may check out and use in class to take notes or write compositions.

Teach Strategies for Theme Writing. Sometimes organizational problems improve if students with ADD learn the standard format for writing a five paragraph theme: an introductory and closing paragraph plus three body paragraphs. Ideally, your child will be given a copy of the theme writing guidelines to take home so you can work with him on these skills.

Use Note Cards for Main Ideas. Another strategy that can help with written language problems is to have the teenager write main ideas on 3 x 5 cards. He can then rearrange the cards in proper sequence before writing the report. He can refer to the cards as he writes his paper, or if appropriate, use them later to study for an exam. Summarizing key points on one card from each page he reads may help with reading comprehension.

Use an Alternative to Writing. If your teenager finds writing more difficult than public speaking, it may be helpful if he is allowed to 1) make oral presentations, or 2) record homework on a tape recorder for assignments other than written English compositions.

Modify the Test. As discussed earlier, some students with ADD have difficulty taking a test that is presented verbally. For example, in foreign languages, words or sentences may be read aloud for the students to translate. If auditory processing or listening comprehension is a problem, ask that the test be modified so that the same phrases or words are presented to your teenager in writing.

Provide a Reader for Tests. If your teenager has difficulty reading or responding in writing on tests, the teacher or a student could read the test questions aloud and let him respond orally.

🦋

"I would go over the test with Cassie and find that she knew much of the material. She would say, 'I didn't even see that question on the test—no wonder I didn't answer it.' Sometimes she gave ridiculous answers to questions. When we looked over the questions, we would look at each other in disbelief. Then she would give the correct answer. Finally, I asked for someone to read the test to her since she seemed to do far better when asked questions verbally.

"It was constantly a struggle to have mainstream teachers remember to have a reader lined up for each test. Frequently we ran into mainstream teachers who were adamantly opposed to 'babying' kids with SLD. One teacher said there is nothing wrong with this kid that a little bit of hard work won't cure. I think he was just a mainstream 'hard liner' who felt these children didn't have any problems."

🦋

Modify the Assignment. Talk to the teachers about ways of avoiding unnecessary writing. If your child writes very slowly, he could photocopy pages of textbooks in subjects such as history, science, or government. He could then highlight important facts, or highlight answers to questions. He could also just fill in the blanks with answers to questions. There is no need to ask him to write the whole question plus the answer.

Poor Reading Comprehension*

Some students with ADD have difficulty comprehending and remembering what they have read. Although these teenagers may not have difficulty with vocabulary words, Dr. Zentall explains that they may have trouble comprehending long passages. Other researchers have found that when youngsters with ADHD read silently, they are more likely to make errors and have poorer comprehension since they tend to skip words, phrases, or lines. Several factors combine to make reading comprehension difficult for teenagers with ADD, including inattention, distractibility, memory problems, impulsivity, and losing their place on the page.

Slide a Bookmark Down the Page. Your child can slide a ruler or bookmark down the page as he reads so that he doesn't lose his place.

Allow Him to Use Published Book Summaries. Commercially available book summaries such as *Cliff Notes* provide a brief synopsis of the plot, description of characters, and chapter summaries. These may be a helpful supplementary aid for students who have reading comprehension problems.

Use "Talking Books." "Talking Books," books recorded on audiotape cassettes, are a wonderful study aid for students, both at home and school. The student reads a book while the same material is played on a tape recorder. Two national organizations, "Talking Books" and "Recordings for the Blind," tape record many books, including textbooks. The accompanying book may be obtained from the school or local library. Most schools have access to this resource. Parents also may obtain this free service independent of the school system.

"Reading" books on tape helps a teenager with ADD in several ways:

- The teenager sees and hears the words at the same time. Using two senses (visual and auditory) is often recommended for teaching students with learning problems more effectively.
- By involving two senses, the teenager is less likely to be distracted.
- The tape may be played at variable speeds: faster speeds may help increase reading speed; the slower speed accommodates the slow reader or foreign language practice.
- The teenager is less likely to go back and re-read words when the tape is playing.

❧

"Since my high school age son has started reading books on tape, he has completed a book a week for the last three months. These books were required reading for graduation from his private school."

❧

The novelty of "reading" books on tape should hold the teenager's interest . . . at least for awhile. Books on tape may be helpful for students of all ages, elementary school through college. Textbooks on tape may be especially helpful for students in high school or college. Recordings for the Blind is the only organization to provide *textbooks* on tape.

Although these organizations were originally established for people who are blind, services have been expanded to include people who have learning disabilities. Teenagers whose ADD adversely affects their ability to learn are eligible to use these services. An application must be completed by a physician or other professional to certify the presence of a specific learning disability or ADD. Applications are available from most local libraries or directly from these organizations.

Several special services are provided free by "Talking Books":

- A special cassette player which will play 4-track $15/16$ ips (inches per second) cassettes is available from most local libraries or directly from the organization. The cassette player has a variable speed control.
- Books from classics to current best sellers, plus magazines are available. Catalogs of books on tape are available.
- Tapes are mailed free of charge in special plastic cases directly to your home. Once the teenager has finished with the tape, the mailing label on the plastic case is turned over and free return postage is provided.

For more information, please contact your local library or:

Talking Books (service is free)
National Library Service for the Blind and
Physically Handicapped

Library of Congress
Washington, DC 20542
1–800–424–9100

Recording for the Blind & Dyslexic
(a one-time membership fee of $25–$35)
20 Roszel Road
Princeton, NJ 08540
1–800–221–4792

Check Out Audiotapes of Books from the Library. Many classic books which are required reading for high school students are available on tape from school or public libraries. Students can read the story while listening to it on tape.

Use a Kurzweil Personal Reader. Many public libraries and universities have a Kurzweil Personal Reader. This is a machine that can perform two functions at the same time: read aloud from any book placed on its scanner and record it on audiotape. Selections of various voices (male, female, child) and rates of speed are available on the machine. Parents, teachers, or the teenager himself could take a textbook and make an audiotape of the page, chapter, or book.

Strategies for Strengthening Language Deficits

This section offers suggestions that can help with any of the language deficits covered above, including problems with speaking, reading, or writing.

Seat away from Distractions/Keep Instructions Brief and Simple. Both these suggestions are discussed in the earlier section on "Tuning Out and Daydreaming."

Ask Teacher to Make Adaptations or Modify Assignments. Numerous suggestions were provided throughout this section for adaptations (use of calculator, untimed tests) or modifications (shortened homework assignments).

Allow to Be a Peer Tutor. Dr. Zentall suggests having the student with ADD tutor a younger student or a student who is not doing well academically. According to Dr. Zentall, the student who is tutoring learns more than the student being tutored.

Allow More Time for Completion of Work. If students with ADD work slowly, they may need extra time to complete assignments and tests. Untimed tests would be an appropriate adaptation for many of these teenagers. If needed, request this adaptation for your teenager.

Identify Learning Style/Teach to Strengths. Talk with a teacher or school psychologist to identify your teenager's *learning style*. That is, through what senses does your child learn best? Some children are visual learners and learn better when they can see printed materials. Others are stronger auditory learners and learn more effectively when they hear academic material. Students should be taught in a manner that builds on the strength of their learning style.

Information about your teenager's learning style is vital for planning academic interventions. Sometimes, because of inattention, memory problems, and listening comprehension difficulties, teenagers with ADD have trouble with auditory learning. That is, they may have great difficulty learning from a teacher's lecture or verbal directions. Adding a visual component—with written handouts or written directions—may help. It may also help for teachers and parents to incorporate touch into their instruction with computers or concrete objects such as blocks or cards.

If you think about how you learned to read, you may have a better understanding of how a learning style can affect your ability to learn. For example, some parents learned to read primarily through visual means; memorizing words and using flash cards to say, "See Spot run." Years later, reading was taught almost exclusively through a phonics approach. Students who were primarily visual learners had difficulty learning to read with a phonics approach. Eventually, educators realized that reading (and other subjects) could be taught more effectively if students used two or three senses.

Use Computer-Aided Instruction. If your teenager reads slowly, has listening comprehension problems, or is inattentive, computer-aided instructions may be an excellent resource. Computer programs may be available for certain academic subjects, such as foreign languages, algebra, or social studies courses. Check with the teacher or school librarian to see what is available.

Poor Organizational Skills/Disorganized

On the surface, teenagers with ADD may appear to be "lazy students" who don't want to do schoolwork. In reality, their poor organizational skills make it extremely difficult for them to get started and finish assignments. Language deficits are also likely to contribute to their poor organization. If a teenager doesn't understand instructions correctly, then he won't follow through on assignments. Learning to be organized is one of the most difficult challenges facing teenagers with ADD.

Disorganization is reflected in both: 1) disorganization related to schoolwork and chores, and 2) a lack of awareness of time. Organizing materials and keeping a notebook containing assignments in sequential order border on being impossible tasks for these teenagers. Yet many students are required to do this in their high school classes.

❧

"A high school biology teacher required that each student keep a notebook containing all homework, class work, and tests in sequential order. A cover sheet with three columns had to be kept noting the date, the assignment/test, plus the grade. Teenagers with ADD don't have a prayer in a class like that."

❧

Seek a Structured Classroom. Students with ADD perform better when teachers provide a positive and structured classroom. External order and structure provide a sense of security that students who lack self-control need. Having a routine helps students know the class procedure and what is expected of them. If the teenager forgets his book, he knows where he to find an extra book to borrow. Students with ADD have more trouble in open pods in which several classes are clustered in one open area.

Providing structure is not the same thing as being rigid. When a teenager is struggling, having a teacher who will work with you and allow some flexibility is wonderful. For example, occasionally letting a student turn an assignment in late is very helpful and may make the difference in his passing or failing a class.

Establish a Routine. Teenagers with ADD seem to respond better if their parents and teachers can help them establish a routine. For example, algebra homework might be assigned four nights a week, with tests every two weeks. Homework must be turned in every day at the end of the period, and always placed in the same box. Homework assignments are always written on the board in the same place.

Find a Tutor/Academic Coach. Teenagers with ADD may or may not need tutors for academic purposes. Often, however, they need an "academic coach" to help them learn how to be organized, learn how to study, and to monitor completion of schoolwork and due dates for assignments. This assistance could be split among several adults or peers. For instance, a teacher or guidance counselor may be able to teach organizational skills to your teenager. Another student, rather than a teacher, could help monitor assignments.

The school may also be able to provide tutoring if needed. If not, consider hiring a tutor to teach study and organizational skills to your teenager or try teaching him yourself. If monitoring your teenager's homework becomes a bloody battle almost every night, find someone else to do this job. Finding a tutor who is familiar with or willing to learn the unique aspects of tutoring a student with ADD is important.

❧

"In some ways our son's broken leg was a blessing in disguise. The school system assigned a 'homebound' teacher, who came to see him three times a week. She was the most patient woman I have ever met. She sat with him, waiting patiently, while he figured out which assignments were due when and developed an outline for the assignments due for her next visit. She taught him how to study and be better organized."

❧

Keep an Assignment Notebook. Your teenager knows that he *should* write down his assignments each day. Either you or a teacher can check that he has written them down. This is a great idea if your teenager can remember to write assignments down or keep up with the notebook. An alternative is for the teacher or another student to write down homework assignments. If he still has trouble keeping up with homework assignments, additional suggestions are provided in Chapter 9.

Develop an Organizational Notebook. Consider helping your teenager put together an organizational notebook. The notebook includes a plastic Gladlock type pouch (not zipper) for pencils; an assignment book; a daily assignment sheet between sections; color-coded dividers for each subject; special dividers with pockets called binder jackets, for handouts; and a grade sheet after each jacket—all of which are placed in a three-ring binder. The binder jacket for teacher handouts opens inward toward the rings so papers cannot fall out and get lost. Daily assignment sheets may be initialed by the teacher if necessary.

You and the teacher will have to work with your teenager to see that the notebook is kept up-to-date. You may have to check the notebook weekly or even daily at first. Develop a system that works best for you. If it is too complicated, simplify the process so it works for your teenager.

Dr. Edna Copeland, an Atlanta psychologist who specializes in treating ADD, initially proposed using this type of notebook. Others, including Joan Maril, an educational consultant, have further refined this idea.

Make Lists/Use "Post-it" Notes. Students with ADD are often absent-minded and apt to lose or forget things like homework, books, pencils, and paper. Teenagers, their parents, or teachers may place "Post-it" notes in conspicuous places to remind the student about schoolwork, staying after school, chores, sports events, bringing home a specific book, etc. As discussed in Chapter 9, the school notebook, bathroom mirror, bedroom door, refrigerator, or car steering wheel may be good places to put notes.

Procrastination

Many teenagers procrastinate when it is time to do schoolwork and chores. They do not start work on assigned reports or projects until the last possible moment. Generally speaking, schoolwork is unpleasant, so they avoid it as long as possible. Poor organization, forgetfulness, lack of time awareness, and distractibility may also contribute to procrastination.

Prompt Regarding Assignments and Due Dates. Prompting from you or from teachers may help your teenager remember due dates on reports, themes, or projects. Try writing a reminder for a class project on a "Post-it" note and sticking it in his notebook. Also review the monthly calendar with him on a regular basis and bring special projects to his attention. "Your science project is due next week. When do you want to start?"

Ask your teenager what method of prompting he prefers. If he gets angry when you remind him, discuss the problem. "Sometimes you forget assignments. What is the best way for me to remind you?"

Difficulty Managing and Being Aware of Time

Teenagers with ADD have difficulty managing time, knowing where they need to be at a certain time, or anticipating how much time is needed to complete a task. According to Dr. Zentall, they actually have an altered awareness of time. Time creeps along slowly for them unless they are interested in a task.

Make the Teacher Aware of the Problem. Tell teachers about your teenager's problems with awareness of time. For example, tell them that your teenager may underestimate how long it will take to complete a complex project. Or that altered awareness of time, combined with forgetfulness, can cause problems such as forgetting to do the class project or to stop by after school for a scheduled meeting with the teacher. Asking teachers to give written reminders about upcoming tests, appointments, or projects may help.

Set a Wrist Watch Alarm for Key Times. Your teenager can set his alarm for important events that he must remember: time to leave for school, time to take medicine, time to stay after school and meet with a teacher. With the alarm set, he can relax and enjoy himself without worrying that he will forget something.

Teach Awareness of Time. Parents and teachers can work together to teach the concept of time management and awareness. You can teach the teenager to develop time lines for completion of a project. Chapter 5 provides specific suggestions for teaching time management techniques such as scheduling action steps a week ahead in preparation for completing a major class project.

Difficulty Being Prepared to Do Schoolwork

Teens with ADD have difficulty gathering together everything they need to complete school and homework assignments—the right book, paper, rulers, pens, correct assignment, and due dates. Completed papers are lost or crumpled in the bottom of the locker. Or the assignment is left on the kitchen table where he worked on it last night.

Request Flexibility from Teachers. If your teenager is having problems with organization, teachers may help by being flexible and shaping his behavior as he masters this skill. For example, the teacher may tell him in advance where he can find a pencil or book if he forgets to bring one. If necessary, buy a pack of pencils and give it to the teacher. "Shaping" is discussed in Chapter 5.

Turn In Completed Work Before Leaving School. Sometimes students finish class work, but the teacher postpones collecting assignments. To keep him from losing his work, the teacher may keep a folder or box at a designated place in her room and have him turn in finished class work each day before he leaves.

Lost Possessions

Because of their disorganization and forgetfulness, teenagers with ADD regularly lose possessions—schoolwork, homework, assignments, books, pencils, coats, games, and tools. Notes from the teacher don't always make it home.

Make Teachers Aware of the Problem. Let teachers know that a tendency to lose things is one of the diagnostic criteria for having ADD. Tell them what steps you have taken to help with this problem. For example, double checking that homework is placed in his notebook after it is finished and checking through his notebook for notes from the teacher. You should probably ask permission to look through the notebook for assignments or notes from the teacher. Do this when your teenager is present so that he doesn't feel that you are sneaking around spying on him.

Put Name on Possessions. It may help to put your teenager's name on books, notebooks, papers, coats, and gym clothes.

Check Lost and Found. When possessions are missing, have your teenager check the lost and found at school.

Messy Desks and Notebook

These teenagers may also be very messy. Their desks and school lockers may be crammed to overflowing with papers and books. At home, their room may be a wreck and they may have trouble finding their possessions when they want them.

🖋

"His locker at school looks like a squirrel's nest. There are papers stuffed in his locker and his notebook. He may have his completed homework in his notebook and never even find it. A month's supply of dirty gym clothes may also still be in the locker."

🖋

Clean Out Locker or Notebook Periodically. You or your child's teachers may need to supervise the periodic cleaning out of his notebook, desk, or locker. Often, his notebook is so messy, he can't find important papers. After cleaning out his notebook, he can put current assignments in the proper section of his notebook. Be sure to hang onto old papers. Otherwise, you may find out that you have thrown away assignments your teenager completed but failed to turn in. If grades are missing and the teacher will accept homework late, find the completed papers and turn them in.

🖋

"Bart would do his homework and forget to turn it in. Days later we would find out that he was missing some grades. The teacher never received the homework. We would usually find it in his bookbag and turn it in then."

Poor Memory

Many teenagers with ADD have difficulty memorizing information. Often they are described as having a poor short-term memory. Students who have ADD/I/WO may have more serious memory problems than teenagers with ADD/H.

Researchers speculate that some people with ADD may not actually have a memory deficiency. Instead, they may have trouble with memorization due to poor strategies for memorizing, poor complex problem-solving strategies, difficulty focusing attention, and poor organizational skills. Dr. Zentall reports that students with ADD make fewer auditory memory errors when teachers use visual cues in addition to verbal instruction. That is, they can remember information (spelling words) the teacher *says* when they also *see* it (spelling flash cards). The implication from all this research is that teenagers with ADD can memorize information more easily if they learn special techniques and are given assistance from others.

Teenagers with ADD who have serious memory problems are at significant disadvantage in school. Students who are good at memorizing usually make better grades. It is therefore critically important to make adaptations for memory problems.

❧

"Shawn had trouble memorizing, but we thought it was because he didn't care and couldn't see any reason why he would need it. If he didn't like the teacher, or if he couldn't see an immediate useful application for the information, he wouldn't even try to memorize. If he really liked the teacher, then he would make a real effort to learn something—but his memory was very short-lived."

❧

Subjects which require rote memorization of isolated facts such as math, algebra, spelling, history, and foreign languages can be especially difficult. This section covers suggestions for dealing with problems with rote memorization. Math in particular presents one of the biggest challenges and is addressed in the next section.

Use Flash Cards or Tapes. You, the teacher, or another student can use flash cards when helping your teenager memorize vocabulary, foreign languages, or algebra formulas. He will *say* the words plus *see* them printed. Using these two senses increases the likelihood he will remember the material. Vocabulary words or foreign languages on audio tape may also be helpful. However, if your

teenager is a visual learner or has an auditory processing problem, auditory tapes should only be used in conjunction with visual materials.

Use Color to Highlight Information Being Memorized. As discussed in the earlier section on "Attention to Detail," color can be used to highlight common errors that are made when memorizing.

Use Word Associations. When memorizing vocabulary words, your teenager can think of another word that reminds him of the new word or draw a mental picture of the word in his mind. "What do you think of when I say *obese?* Think fat." You could also use the word in a brief phrase: "*plausible* lie"; "*volatile* temper"; "*prolific* writer or rabbits."

Use Mnemonics. Using mnemonics, a student figures out a way of thinking about facts or concepts that will help him remember them more easily. Often, mnemonics involves taking the first letter of words to be memorized and forming another word or sentence with those letters. For instance, music students are often taught the sentence "**E**very **g**ood **b**oy **d**oes **f**ine" to help them remember the notes on the lines of the treble clef. This technique can be especially helpful when memorizing information in subjects such as history, geography, biology, or chemistry. For example, the five main kinds of substances in chemistry are **m**ixtures, **e**lements, **s**olutions, **s**uspensions, and **c**ompounds. The mnemonic term, MESSC (messy), may help the student remember the substances.

Use Spell Check Aid. If your teenager has trouble remembering spellings, have him use a hand-held spell checker, spell check on a computer, or a dictionary to double check spelling words.

Ask Teachers Not to Count Off for Spelling. If spelling is a significant problem, ask teachers not to count off for spelling in non-spelling classes. Or at a minimum, perhaps they will agree to give your teenager two grades—one for content and the other for spelling. They could allow him to correct misspelled words and turn the paper back in for additional credit.

If All Else Fails, Seek a Waiver. Seeking a waiver to exempt certain classes is discussed in Chapter 9.

Weak Math Skills/Can't Memorize Multiplication Tables

Many teenagers with ADD appear to have serious weaknesses in their math skills. Two major problems are relevant here: *memorization difficulties and slow math calculation* (processing).*

Memorizing basic math facts and recalling them quickly is a critical skill. Memorization of simple addition and subtraction facts such as 5 + 7 = 12 or 3 + 6 = 9 enables a student to complete complex math problems more quickly. Teachers in elementary school drill children to increase their speed working these basic math problems. Yet, some teenagers are unable to memorize and recall basic math facts even with intensive practice sessions. According to Dr. Zentall, youngsters with ADD have a *slower speed of calculating math problems* than other children with comparable intelligence. Poor memorization skills, slow computation, and inattention may make it extremely difficult for teenagers to develop a solid foundation of basic math facts upon which to build more complex math concepts.

When a student enters middle school without mastering the multiplication tables, he will work math problems more slowly and will not be able to finish his assignments quickly. As a result, he may be penalized unfairly. He may know the math concepts but work so slowly that he cannot finish assignments in class. In addition, if teachers insist that he continue trying to memorize multiplication tables, valuable time will be taken away from the major class objective: learning more advanced math functions.

⚹

"Our son has great difficulty memorizing anything even though he is extremely bright. Although he passed high school algebra and geometry, he still has not memorized his multiplication tables.

"My son and I spent hours drilling on multiplication tables, which he promptly seemed to forget the next day. This process continued for weeks. I battled my own ambivalent feelings about my son's ability to remember and memorize things. Was he not trying? Did he not care? Was he just being lazy? Couldn't he try harder? Finally, I realized he <u>was</u> doing his best. He could not memorize things very easily.

"Because the ability to memorize had been one of my greatest strengths in school, it was even more difficult to accept my son's disability in this area. I didn't fully appreciate that the ability to memorize was a God-given gift."

⚹

If your teenager cannot memorize multiplication tables, it is not the end of the world. Most adults use a calculator when they need to multiply. In fact, a good question to ask about material that must be memorized is, "Do adults in the real world use this information frequently?" Most adults use calculators to balance their checkbooks, and spell- and grammar-check functions on the word processor to correct letters they are writing.

One school principal commented that classroom accommodations "should be encouraged . . . just like glasses, hearing aids, or other devices that are needed for a disability. Anything that makes life easier is fair game!" Even organizations such as The College Entrance Examination Board recognize the practical use of calculators and now allow students to use calculators when taking the SAT.

Use a Calculator/Multiplication Chart. Perhaps when your teenager reaches middle school, teachers will allow him to use a calculator or multiplication chart while working math problems. This will enable him to do assignments more rapidly. He can also work on mastering each new math concept as it is presented without being slowed down by not knowing multiplication tables. And he may actually learn some of the tables from punching the numbers into the calculator.

⚹

"Cassie's math disability is described in her IEP as 'the inability to retain math facts over time.' She wonders why no teachers in either SLD or mainstream classrooms ever said, 'That's not a problem. She knows the process. She can get an answer with a calculator. Let's just go on from there.' Yet they knew that was her disability when it was apparent even after fifth grade that she couldn't memorize her multiplication tables."

⚹

Ask the Teacher to Modify Assignments. If your teenager processes slowly or has difficulty with math, his math teachers may be willing to assign all odd number problems or every third problem for homework. This ensures that he knows the math concepts but doesn't burden him with lengthy homework assignments. If your teenager cannot complete his math assignment in an hour or less, consider asking his teacher to modify the class or homework assignment. The teacher can discuss this reduced assignment privately with your teenager so other students are not aware it is occurring.

❦

"Thank goodness teachers are willing to shorten math assignments. Otherwise, my son would have been up half the night working on math that others could finish in an hour.

"Stephen can do long division in his head but fouls up on paper because he can't line the numbers up correctly. His teacher agreed to let him give the answer without showing all his work as long as he continues to get the answers correct."

❦

Reward Accuracy/Reduce Work. You might also suggest that the teacher reward your teenager by reducing the work assignment if he completes his work accurately. For example, if he completes two problems correctly, he doesn't have to do the next two. He can check his answers in the back of the book or the teacher's answer book.

If your child is *required* to memorize multiplication tables, here are some suggestions that may help. These suggestions may also help him memorize material for other classes. In general, incorporating several elements in the teaching process will be helpful: novelty, color, manipulatives (things to handle), and use of multiple senses (visual, auditory, tactile).

Use Flash Cards. Using flash cards with multiplication facts may help your teenager learn them more easily. Work on one set of tables (4 X ?) at a time until he has mastered them. Take turns holding up the flash card. If he answers correctly, he gets to keep the card. Otherwise he hands cards to you that he hasn't yet memorized. If he always misses 4 x 8, then highlight 32 in color to draw attention to the number he needs to remember.

Next, review the cards he missed the first time through. The review continues until he has collected all the cards for the fours multiplication tables. It is easier to hold your teenager's attention if he actively participates in handing flash cards back and forth between you. This is an especially good technique since several senses are involved. That is, he sees the numbers, says them aloud, hears you state the correct answer, and is then handed a card.

Use Math Shortcut. You can teach the teenager to figure out the nines multiplication table by counting on his fingers. Have him hold his hands out in front of him and spread his fingers. For 9 x 7, count from left to right until you reach the seventh finger. Hold that finger down and then count the remaining fingers on either side to obtain the correct answer. (There are six fingers to the left and three fingers to the right, or 63).

Use Other Teaching Aids. There are video tapes and computer software programs that can help with learning multiplication tables. A software program is especially good since it will give immediate feedback regarding correct and incorrect responses. To find out more about available computer programs, check with the classroom teacher, the school library, community library, or local computer stores.

Difficulty with Multi-step Math

Many teenagers with ADD have problems with the multi-step math which is involved in algebra and other advanced math classes. They want to take short cuts. They like to do much of the work in their heads, skip steps, and never write everything down on paper. Sometimes they write their numbers and problems very small, all on one line. As result, they make "careless" errors. It is also difficult to follow what they have done because their writing is so poor and so small. If they write slowly, they may skip steps because they are afraid they will not have enough time to finish the assignment. Poor memory, short attention span, and organizational skills also contribute to problems in this area.

Write Problems Correctly. You or the teacher can demonstrate how to write the problem, spacing it correctly on the paper. It may be helpful for you to "talk through" the problem, step by step. Have him write on one line for each step of the math problem. Since this is a basic concept, take care to do it tactfully and not embarrass him by making him appear stupid in front of other students or friends. It may be best to show him how to do this in private after school.

Use Graph Paper. Your child could write out his math problems on graph paper to ensure proper spacing of numbers. Only one number may be placed in each square of the graph paper. After a few practices, he should be able to work on regular notebook paper.

Modify the Assignment. If homework assignments are not too long, your teenager may be more inclined to write down all the steps required for completing each problem. Talk to the teacher about the possibility of having your teenager complete only every other or every third problem, as suggested earlier.

Use Choral Response to Memorize. Stating math facts in quotable "sound bites" or singsong chants may help your teenager remember key steps: "What you do to one side of the equation, you have to do to the other side." Dr. Zentall recommends using good old-fashioned group choral response as an effective way to help students memorize. Have students repeat aloud words or multiplication tables after the teacher. Parents can use this technique at home too.

Forgetfulness

Forgetfulness in these teenagers is one of their more exasperating characteristics. Many teenagers have a terrible time remembering: 1) class- and homework assignments; 2) to bring home the correct book; 3) to complete homework; 4) to take it to school; and 5) to turn it in.

Sometimes their homework makes it to their school locker but never makes it to the classroom. Sometimes they can't remember if they turned in the assignment. If they miss a test, they forget to request a make-up exam, even though their grade may be lowered significantly. They forget to complete major class projects. They may forget something so basic as writing their name on their paper. Poor organizational skills and listening comprehension, in addition to memory problems, contribute to their apparent forgetfulness.

⚘

"**If my son needs help, I am going to help him without feeling guilty. If he is able to learn the material but forgets his book, or the page number, or can't organize a semester's worth of information to study for a final exam, are we supposed to let him fail? What are we grading: the subject or organizational skills? I'll take an F in organization and a C in Math any day!**"

⚘

"**A 12-year-old girl with ADD called our office in a rage. A teacher had given her a zero on a test because she had forgotten to put her name on her paper. The child's actual test score was 91. A call to the teacher revealed that she did not give her a zero but gave her credit for the 91. The child never remembered to put her name on the paper even after repeated reminders by the teacher. The poor exasperated teacher had hoped to scare her into putting her name on future papers.**"

⚘

Talk to the Teacher about This Problem. Make teachers aware that your teenager is forgetful due to his ADD. Ask them to call if problems related to forgetfulness arise. You, your child, and teachers may jointly be able to develop a plan to solve the problem.

Keep an Assignment Book. As mentioned earlier, an assignment book may be helpful.

Check to See If Assignments Are Written. If your teenager is extremely forgetful, the teacher or another student may check his assignment sheet each day to see if he has remembered to write down the assignments. This daily repetition should teach him to make note of assignments. When he gets in the habit of keeping up with his work, teachers will no longer need to provide this much supervision.

Have Another Student Prompt about Homework. Dr. Zentall suggests having the teacher ask another student who sits nearby to discreetly discuss with the teenager with ADD what the assignment is for the class or evening.

Ask Teacher for Written Homework Assignments. As noted in Chapter 9, it is helpful when teachers give homework assignments in writing for a week or month at a time, especially when students are in danger of failing.

Use Daily or Weekly Reports. If your teenager forgets to complete and turn in homework assignments, a system can be worked out with teachers to monitor and correct this problem. Weekly or daily reports may be used for awhile if your child forgets to complete and turn in his schoolwork. (See Chapter 9 for information on using daily reports.) The teacher could include two things on the daily report: homework assignments for the next class, plus a grade for homework turned in that day.

Monitor Make-up Work. If your child is really struggling just to pass a class, the academic coach (you, your spouse, a friend, or tutor you have hired) may help him monitor when make-up work is due and remind him to complete it.

Buy a Name Stamp. If your teenager forgets to put his name on his papers, consider buying an inexpensive stamp with his name on it. He can stamp his name in advance on several sheets of notebook paper in his folder. This may work since teenagers with ADD respond better to novel situations.

Use Other Suggestions from Chapter 9. Several helpful suggestions given in Chapter 9 include: get two sets of books, keep one set at home; allow flexibility in turning in assignments late for full or partial credit; find out routine of homework being assigned (Algebra problems each night except Friday - test every two weeks).

Poor Fine Motor Coordination

Fine motor coordination problems are common in teenagers with ADD and may result in poor handwriting, avoidance of writing, and low output of written work (homework or classwork).

Poor Handwriting

Teachers may complain that your teenager's writing is hardly legible. Like many teenagers with ADD, he may prefer to print rather than write in cursive. In addition, he may write very slowly and produce less written work.

✹

"Both of our sons had very poor handwriting. One son wrote extremely small letters and numbers and he also wrote very slowly. Homework took forever to complete. Both boys preferred printing their schoolwork rather than writing in cursive even as late as middle and high school grades.

"Alex's writing was not very good, plus he wrote very slowly. His first grade teacher made him write his whole name, Alexander. By the time he laboriously finished writing his name, the rest of the class had almost finished the assignment. Finally, I was able to convince the teacher that it was okay for him to write "Alex" and not the sixteen letters which comprised his first and last names."

✹

"Our daughter writes very small. Letter formation is not neat or smooth, but she doesn't seem to care."

✹

Accept Poor Handwriting and Printing. Urge teachers to allow your child to print his schoolwork as long as it is legible. Ask them to accept his writing as is, as long as it is his best effort, without badgering or subtracting points from his overall grade.

Use a Computer. See earlier discussion.

Modify Assignments and Tests. As discussed earlier, if your teenager writes and processes information slowly, suggest that he be allowed untimed tests. Another common adaptation is to shorten written assignments. For example, completing every third algebra problem or photocopying questions from the biology book and underlining or highlighting the answers on the page, rather than writing questions and answers.

Do Not Ask to Write Sentences as Punishment. Writing 500 sentences such as "I will not talk back to my teacher" for punishment is inappropriate for youngsters who have fine motor coordination problems. Writing sentences is a cruel and unreasonable punishment.

✹

"My son had to write 500 sentences in high school because he didn't do his homework. He forgot to do the sentences and the teacher added another 100 sentences for each day he was late. He writes so slowly. This was a terrible punishment. He truly didn't think

he would ever finish writing. I finally helped him finish his sentences."

Difficulty Completing Board Work

Some students with ADD have difficulty completing board work. They may have difficulty looking back and forth from the chalk board to their paper, keeping their place, and completing the assignment. Poor fine motor coordination and slow processing skills may contribute to this problem.

Minimize Board Work. If this is a problem, reducing the amount of work students are expected to copy from the chalk board should help. Ask the teacher to give your teenager a written copy of the material on the board.

Poor Motor Coordination

Some teenagers with ADD have trouble participating successfully in physical education classes. Approximately half of these youngsters have poor motor coordination. Poor concentration and distractibility may also be problems in P.E. classes and organized sports. Teenagers may have trouble staying with the group and paying attention when the teacher is talking. In addition, they can have difficulty with the transitions and rule changes that are so often a part of sports. For example, at the beginning of P.E. class, they might be allowed to be loud and active, but then suddenly they have to change (transition) to quietly listening to the teacher. In addition, teenagers with ADD may not have the social skills required for cooperative interactions in P.E. classes and sports.

Participate in Sports Where Success Is More Likely. Remember, about 50 percent of teenagers with ADD have *good* motor coordination. Those who do have problems, however, may have some difficulty with hand-eye coordination. Since their gross motor skills may be stronger, they may do well in sports such as swimming, soccer, karate, or wrestling. They may not do as well playing baseball, basketball, tennis, or racquetball. (See the discussion of sports in Chapters 5 and 6.)

Work with Guidance Counselor in Scheduling P.E. Classes. To help make P.E. class a more positive experience, check with the guidance counselor to see which sports are taught when.

Your teenager can then sign up for P.E. when sports like soccer or wrestling are taught.

Help with Transitions. Sometimes the teacher can help with transitions, by standing near the student as class starts and roll is taken. The teacher's presence or a touch on the shoulder may remind him to be quiet. When P.E. is over, the teacher may have another student walk with him back to class.

Give Student a Job Helping the Teacher. Sometimes the teacher may tap a student's high energy by giving him a job during class. For example, handing out towels or giving out or taking in equipment may be jobs he would be willing to do. Having a job will keep the teenager busy and out of trouble, plus help him feel successful in P.E. class, even if he is not athletic.

Other Factors Affecting Completion of Schoolwork

Although these issues were discussed in earlier chapters, a brief discussion about their impact on school performance is provided in this section. Remember, too, that some teenagers with ADD also meet criteria for depression, anxiety disorder, oppositional defiant disorder, or conduct disorder. These co-existing diagnoses are also discussed in Chapters 2, 4, and 7.

Hyperactivity

As discussed earlier, most teenagers are restless, rather than hyperactive, in the classroom. Teenagers who still have hyperactive tendencies may talk loudly, interrupt others, or monopolize conversations. They may act out to draw attention to themselves. They may enjoy being the center of attention or the class clown. When not on medication, hyperactive teenagers may wait for the exact moment to deliver a classic line that sends the whole class into peals of laughter.

Provide Opportunities to Be Center of Attention. Encourage your teenager to participate in activities such as theater or debate team that allow him to act or speak and be the center of attention.

Shorten the School Day. As discussed earlier, if the teenager is struggling and on the verge of being suspended, a short-term strategy may be to attend school half a day.

Schedule Two Periods of P.E. If hyperactivity is severe, particularly with younger children, try scheduling two periods of physical education. Of course, consider this option only if it is something the teenager enjoys and it won't interfere with satisfying graduation requirements.

Assign Two Seats. If you have a younger teen with severe hyperactivity, you could ask teachers to assign two seats on opposite sides of the room. When he feels that he must move around, he may move from one desk to another.

Assign Activities That Allow Movement. See the discussion in the earlier section on "Tuning Out and Daydreaming."

Accept His Style of Studying. Some of these youngsters need to move when they are studying or at least take a little break from sitting. As long as they can finish their work and don't disrupt the rest of the class, let them sit, stand, or move as needed. Some students can do two things at one time.

❦

"Cooper got off to a great start in first grade but was struggling in second. Finally, he came home one day and said, 'I think I know what's wrong with my teacher. She doesn't understand that I can dance and learn at the same time.'"

Medication Wears Off

Major problems can arise at school when medication wears off. The teenager can't concentrate on academics and is more likely to make impulsive decisions that get him into trouble. The most commonly prescribed stimulant medication, Ritalin (regular), loses its effectiveness within approximately three hours. This means that the medication has usually worn off well before lunch. Fine tuning the proper medication dosage and timing is very important. See the discussion of medications in Chapter 4.

Schedule Key Academics at Times When Medication Is Working. Schedule important academic classes or classes in which your teenager has the most trouble paying attention for times when medication has its maximum effect. This is usually early morning, or, if a noon dose is taken, right after lunch.

If Problems Arise, Ask When Medication Was Taken. If your teenager is not doing well academically or misbehaves only during one or two classes, you need to discuss this with teachers. Identify the time of day the problems are occurring. If it is either late in the morning or afternoon, the medication may have worn off. If this is an ongoing problem, you may decide to try a longer-lasting medication or change the time the medication is administered.

Adjust Medication Schedule or Dose. Your teenager may be able to take medications at a different time, or you may consider switching to sustained release Dexedrine. Since Dexedrine SR lasts longer, the need for a midday dose will be eliminated.

Ask If He Took His Medication. If the teenager appears inattentive only on rare occasions, the teacher may discreetly check to see if he forgot his medication that morning. As suggested earlier, it may help to leave some Ritalin or Dexedrine at school so that if he forgets his medication, he can go to the office and take it.

Other Symptom-Related Problems

A variety of other symptoms of ADD can also lead to problems in school. These symptoms, plus suggestions for dealing with problems, are discussed in more detail in Chapter 9. It is important to make sure that whenever any of these problems crop up, the teacher knows that they are all part of having ADD—your child is not just deliberately misbehaving.

Uneven Academic Performance. Teachers will see great variability in homework, test grades, and class performance. This variability may continue to be a problem for many teenagers with ADD even when they are taking medication.

Lethargy. Teenagers with ADD may daydream, yawn a lot, appear bored, or even sleep while in class. Schoolwork seems to wear them out mentally. Lethargy is usually a greater problem for teenagers with ADD/I/WO.

Sleep Disturbances. The potential for sleep disturbances to undermine a student's school performance is obvious. Sleep deprivation may result in irritability, poor concentration, poor memory,

TABLE 10–2

COMMON LEARNING PROBLEMS OF TEENAGERS WITH ATTENTION DEFICIT DISORDER

ADAPTATIONS FOR HOME AND SCHOOL

Common learning problems, the behavior observed, and possible classroom adaptations are presented below. Your teenager may be experiencing some but not all of these learning problems. The adaptations listed in the last column may be used for more than one behavior listed below. Plus, two or three adaptations may be used for one problem behavior. So appropriate adaptations don't always line up exactly with the problem behavior observed. To help improve homework completion see Chapter 9. If your teenager doesn't know how to study or is disorganized, someone must act as an "academic coach."

LEARNING PROBLEMS	BEHAVIOR OBSERVED	ADAPTATIONS
• INATTENTION POOR CONCENTRATION DISTRACTIBILITY	• Difficulty completing work (Changes from one task to another) (Forgets assignments or books; See secion on Memory below and Chapter 9.)	• Give frequent positive feedback • Provide more supervision/check homework • Use weekly report • Provide reward for completing work • Take medication when doing school work • Study with a friend
	• Difficulty getting started (Starts and stops work) • Tuning out and daydreaming (Difficulty paying attention in class) (Easily distracted) (Doesn't seem to listen)	• Monitor getting started • Use cue to get attention • Use high interest material, interactive learning • Use multisensory approach • Make eye contact • Seat away from distractions • Cue/use private signal system • Cue prior to important announcement • Keep instructions brief and simple • Divide work into smaller segments • Schedule short work period • Find activity to allow movement • Use color as aid to learning • Encourage to double check answers • Highlight signs in color until student becomes aware & no longer needs cue
	• Lack of attention to detail (Make apparent "careless errors";) (Don't notice changes in math signs (+, -, x); e.g., add all problems regardless of sign) (Has trouble finding errors in grammar, punctuation, capitalization, and spelling)	• Highlight potential errors in color • Have student read material aloud • Modify grading system • If never double checks answers on tests (too tired or too much homework), parent highlights error & teenager corrects
	• Lack of awareness of grades (Don't know when failing)	• Monitor school work • Obtain information about grades • Graph or average grades
• IMPULSIVITY	• Getting into trouble at school (Noncompliance, forgetfulness, talks back to teachers, walk out of	• Help succeed academically • Keep rules simple; state clearly • Remind of consequences of

LEARNING PROBLEMS	BEHAVIOR OBSERVED	ADAPTATIONS
	class, defiance, skips school, smokes at school, fights, carries a weapon to school, speaks and acts without thinking)	breaking rules • Notify school of potential problems • Take medication at school • Request a classroom aide • Review instructions with teen • Highlight instructions • Mark out wrong answers on multiple choice test • Allow time to double check answers • At home, double check answers with teen
	• Impulsive learning style (Starts without reading directions, rushes through homework, doesn't double check work)	

• LANGUAGE DEFICITS: SLOW PROCESSING (Listening, speaking, reading, or writing)

LEARNING PROBLEMS	BEHAVIOR OBSERVED	ADAPTATIONS
LISTENING COMPREHENSION	• Difficulty understanding instructions (Lose main point in instructions) (Confused with verbal directions)	• Keep instructions brief and simple • State directions clearly; "Number 1. Do all odd problem. Number 2. Do all five problems on the next page." • Use cue to get attention
	• Difficulty following verbal instructions (Don't always "hear" instructions	• Ask student to repeat instructions • Write instructions on post-it notes
	• Difficulty learning foreign language	• Use tips on memorization • Ask for adaptations, e.g., all written tests, not verbally administered • Seek waiver to exempt
	• Difficulty taking good notes (Takes notes very slowly)	• Get copy of notes from student or teacher • Use NCR paper or carbon paper
	(Difficulty identifying main points) (Difficulty taking notes and listening to teacher at same time)	• Get guided lecture notes from teacher • Record lecture on tape • Cue for important points; Teacher may say; "This is a major point".
SPOKEN LANGUAGE	• Difficulty giving articulating clear answers (Trouble giving brief clear answers) (Slow cognitive processing) • Avoids responding in class • Slow recall of facts Reluctant to raise hand or answer questions) (Problems with memorization)	• Be positive/supportive • Make teacher aware of problem • Give notice prior to calling on • Give more time to respond • Teach outlining and sequencing • Provide less threatening situation to speak publicly
WRITTEN LANGUAGE	• Writes slowly, takes longer to complete • Produces less written work • Difficulty writing themes, reports, & tests	• Use computer; a laptop for school • Use computer aided instruction • Teach strategies for theme writing •Teacher models skill, i.e., brainstorming ideas

LEARNING PROBLEMS	BEHAVIOR OBSERVED	ADAPTATIONS
	(Difficulty organizing thoughts and ideas in compositions/themes) (Difficulty taking good notes) (Difficulty taking written tests; may take twice as long; may have difficulty understanding questions and expressing and organizing answers)	• Use alternatives to writing, e.g., tape record in non-English classes • Use note cards for main ideas • Modify the test/untimed • Provide a reader for tests • Modify the assignment
READING COMPREHENSION	• Poor reading comprehension • Can't remember what he reads (Difficulty reading; stops and starts over; slow reading, loses place, skips words)	• Slide a paper or ruler down page • Use published book summaries • Use <u>Talking Books</u> at home & school • Check audio or video tapes from library • Use Kurzweil Personal Reader • Seat away from distractions • Keep instructions brief and simple • Ask teacher to make adaptations or modify assignments • Allow to do peer tutoring • Allow more time for doing work & tests • Identify learning style/teach to strengths
• ORGANIZATIONAL SKILLS	• Disorganized (Appears lazy, difficulty getting started and finishing school work, doesn't understand directions, forgets assignments, or to turn in papers; see Memory below) • Procrastination • Difficulty managing and being aware of time (Altered sense of time; forget & are late for appointments) • Difficulty being prepared to do school work • Lost possessions, e.g., homework, books clothes • Messy desk, notebooks, & lockers (Can't find homework, books)	• Seek a structured classroom • Establish routine • Find a tutor or academic coach • Keep assignment notebook • Develop an organizational notebook • Make lists/use post-it notes • Prompt on assignments • Make teacher aware of problem • Set wrist watch alarm or beeper • Teach awareness of time; time management • Request flexibility from teachers • Turn in work before leaving school • Make teacher aware of problem • Put homework in same place each night • Put names on possessions • Check lost and found at school • Look for lost papers • Don't throw away completed papers
• MEMORY	• Difficulty memorizing • Difficulty with rote memorization (Difficulty with subjects requiring memorization; spelling, history, algebra, & foreign languages)	• Teach strategies for memorizing • Use flash cards or tapes • Use color to highlight error • Use word associations • Use mnemonics • Use spell check or dictionary • Don't count off grade for spelling • Seek a waiver

LEARNING PROBLEMS	BEHAVIOR OBSERVED	ADAPTATIONS
	• Weak math skills • Can't memorize multiplication tables (Poor basic math skills; slow recall of basic addition, subtraction, multiplication division math facts) • Difficulty with multi-step math (Take short cuts, do math in head, skip steps, don't write work down, write small, make "careless errors")	• Give chart with multiplication tables • Allow use of calculator • Ask teacher to modify assignments • Reward accuracy/reduce work • Use flash cards • Use math short cut • Use other teaching aids • Write problems correctly • Use graph paper • Modify assignments, reduce amount of homework • Use choral response to memorize
FORGETFULNESS	• Forgets to bring home assignments, work sheets, books, etc. (Forgets homework assignments) (Forgets or can't find books, pencils, paper, folders, report covers) (Forgets to do homework & make-up work) (Forgets to bring work to school), (Forgets to turn in) (Forgets to put name on paper)	• Work with teacher; See Chapt 9, Homework • Keep assignment book • Check; assignments written down • Have student prompt about homework • Ask teacher for written weekly assignments • Call friend to confirm homework when teenager can't remember • Ask about homework assignment routine • If pick up at school, ck assignments & books • Keep extra supplies at home • Get two sets of books, keep one at home; • Parent prompts: See Chapter 9 , Homework • Monitor make-up work • Put school work in same place each night • Allow flexibility in turning work in late • Buy a name stamp

• FINE MOTOR SKILLS
  FINE MOTOR AND
  LANGUAGE DEFICITS
	• Poor handwriting, illegible
	(Avoids writing, writes slowly, produces less written work, prints instead of cursive)
	
	• Difficulty doing board work
		• Accept poor handwriting & printing
		• Allow to use a computer
		• Modify assignments; shorten, give untimed tests
		• See section on language deficits
		• Do not write sentences as punishment
		• Minimize board work; give written copy

MOTOR COORDINATION	• Poor coordination	• Select PE classes where can succeed: e.g. swimming, soccer, wrestling • Work with counselor to schedule best PE • Help with transitions to and from PE class • Give job to help teacher

and possibly falling asleep in class. Suggestions for dealing with sleep disturbances are provided in Chapter 6.

Depression, Anxiety, Hostility, and Self-doubt. Teenagers with ADD may be depressed or anxious and may experience feelings of self-doubt. Hostile feelings may emerge by middle and high school. See Chapters 4, 7, and 9 for a discussion of these issues.

Emotionality, Defiance, or Aggression. Since oppositional behavior is common in many teenagers with ADD, they may get into trouble for impulsively talking back to teachers or administrators. They may get upset and end up fighting at school. Suggestions for coping with problems of defiance are discussed in Chapters 4 and 7.

Medical Problems. Teenagers with ADD may be ill or absent from school due to other medical problems, such as recurring upper respiratory infections, allergies, or asthma. See Chapter 4.

Exceptions to the Rule

Not all teenagers with ADD do poorly in school. Some are outstanding students even without medication. For example, half of the major speakers at a recent national CHADD conference identified themselves as having ADD. These speakers included professionals with Ph.D.'s and M.D.'s. Most likely, these adults were extremely bright, learned to compensate for their inattentiveness, had milder cases of ADD, and were able to do well in academic settings in spite of their disability. As mentioned previously, children and teenagers with ADD *can* learn to compensate and find ways to succeed.

❧

"As a child I was chronically in trouble. I received straight A's in all my classes and U's in conduct. I lived in the corner when I was in the second grade. I smuggled books in under my clothes so I would have something to read. When I got in trouble, I gave my teacher 'drop dead looks.' In the third and fourth grades I would lose my temper and get paddled at school. I was chronically on restrictions at home. My ADD wasn't diagnosed until graduate school when academic demands became so much greater." - a female psychologist with ADD

Conclusion

This book recommends many possible interventions so you can choose which procedures work best with your teenager. You are not expected to use all of these strategies. Use as few interventions as are needed to help your teenager succeed. If you try to use too many strategies,  you and your teenager may get caught up in a colossal power struggle. You both will be worn out and your teenager will be well on his way to hating school and you. As a parent, I personally avoided implementing any major strategies unless my son was in danger of failing classes or his self-esteem was being damaged because of his poor grades. Of course, if your teenager expresses a desire to make better grades, you should work with him to make any adaptations that might help.

Use common sense in deciding when and how to use adaptations. For example, younger children need to practice multiplication tables with their peers when they are first introduced in elementary school. In later grades, if it becomes obvious that your teenager cannot memorize multiplication tables, then allow him to use a calculator or a sheet with all multiplication tables listed on them.

Ask your teenager for input about adaptations. Remember, he may feel uncomfortable or embarrassed when adaptations are made in class. Be sure to handle adaptations as discreetly as possible. Ideally, only your teenager and his teacher should know about the change. He could, for example, be tested in another room so that other students are not aware that he is using a calculator or taking an untimed test.

Periodically reassess the adaptations being used to see if any can be eliminated. Bear in mind, however, that some adaptations may be needed throughout your teenager's high school and college career. The underlying goal is to teach your teenager increased self-reliance, independence, and strategies for compensating for the challenging symptoms of ADD. As your teenager assumes more responsibility for his schoolwork and other activities of daily living, you will want to continually reduce your involvement in his life.

Identifying Common Learning Problems and Making Adaptations in the Classroom

Common learning problems of students with ADD, the practical implication of the problem upon the student's ability to learn, and suggested intervention strategies and classroom adaptations are displayed in the chart on pages 252–55. Although these issues are complex, the information is listed as simply as possible.

Although common behaviors at school may be listed under only one category, remember that the problem may be the result of more than one learning problem. Also remember that the same intervention may be helpful in dealing with more than one learning deficit area or symptom of ADD. For example, using a calculator can be helpful for both memory and slow processing problems.

Identify which learning problems your teenager may be experiencing and possible adaptations. Then discuss this information with a teacher or treatment professional whom you trust to see if they agree with your initial assessment.

CHAPTER ELEVEN

LEGAL LEVERAGE FOR PURSUING ACADEMIC SUCCESS

For several decades, federal laws have guaranteed special educational services for students with a variety of disabilities. Until very recently, however, it has been extremely difficult to use these laws for the benefit of students with ADD. Consequently, many parents have had trouble getting schools to accommodate the special learning needs of their children with ADD in the classroom. Fortunately, this situation is beginning to change, thanks to official decisions of the U.S. Department of Education (DOE), Office for Civil Rights (OCR), and the U.S. Supreme Court. Now many families of students with ADD can use legal leverage to get schools to make changes that will help their teenager with ADD succeed academically.

This chapter includes information on the two federal laws that can be used to obtain special educational assistance for your child, as well as on the official interpretations that make the laws more relevant to students with ADD. It also covers the pros and cons of pursuing special education eligibility for your teenager, and specific suggestions for working with the school system to ensure his academic success.

IMPORTANT FEDERAL LAWS

Two federal laws play a crucial role in ensuring that students with ADD achieve academic success: the Individuals with Disabilities Education Act (**IDEA, Part B**) and the Vocational Rehabilitation Act Amendments of 1973 (**Section 504**). These laws require that public schools provide a free appropriate education to all children, regardless of their disability. The full impact of a third law, the Americans with Disabilities Act (ADA) of 1990 is not yet known. However, ADA appears to extend Section 504 protections to children attending private but not parochial schools. If your teenager with ADD has academic or behavior problems that make it difficult for him to succeed in the classroom, it is important for you to learn how these laws may help him.

Individuals with Disabilities Education Act (IDEA)

The Individuals with Disabilities Education Act (IDEA), or Public Law 101–476 (1990), is the new name for the Education for All Handicapped Children Act (Public Law 94–142) of 1975. Under this law, the federal government provides funding to the states so they can develop and maintain quality special education programs. To qualify for these funds, states must guarantee students with special needs a variety of services and rights. The sections below explain the most important provisions of IDEA.

1. A Free Appropriate Public Education

Under IDEA, children with disabilities are guaranteed a "free appropriate public education" (*FAPE*). "Free" and "public" mean that if the school system is unable to provide an appropriate education for your child, then they must pay for his education, even if it must be provided in a private school or residential school. What constitutes an "appropriate" program will be determined by you, your child, and a group of educators. This information will be written down in an *Individualized Education Program* (IEP).

2. Involvement of Parents in Educational Decisions

Parents must be equal partners in the process of developing an educational plan for their adolescent. At first, you may feel intimidated by this process. Usually, however, parents know their child best and have learned over the years which intervention strategies are most effective. Dixie Jordan, Pacer Center, Minneapolis, who attends many IEP meetings with parents and is also the mother of a son with ADHD, has wisely observed that parents may "not always know what will work with their adolescent, but they certainly know what has *not* worked." You can also educate yourself by reading books like this and talking with other parents or teachers so that you feel confident enough to be an active participant. You have valuable insights and advice to offer the education professionals—don't be afraid to speak up.

3. Nondiscriminatory Evaluations and Assessments

Only students with certain disabilities or levels of impairment are eligible for services under IDEA. Before a student can begin receiving special services or accommodations, he must be formally evaluated by the school system to determine whether he qualifies. Follow-up assessments are also needed on a regular basis to identify problem areas that should be addressed in the IEP. When evaluating a child, schools must ensure that:

- Parents are given a written notice before their child is tested;
- Parents give consent prior to testing, for first-time assessment;
- Parents may refuse assessment (in writing) if they believe it is not needed;

- Parents give their consent before the child is placed in special education;
- The student's records are kept confidential;
- Parents are allowed access to student records;
- Evaluations are conducted by multidisciplinary teams—that is, by a group of people who each have expertise in different areas (including someone knowledgeable about ADD);
- Evaluations are non-discriminatory or culture (bias) free evaluations;
- If any of the above rights have been violated, parents have a right to an impartial due process hearing by a person who is objective and who is not directly involved in the case (see below); and
- Parents may request an independent evaluation, at no cost, if they disagree with school evaluation results.

The school system has the right to determine what constitutes their evaluation. They decide how extensive the assessment should be and which, if any, tests should be given. They may do the evaluation in phases. When ADD is suspected, the first phase may consist only of 1) a classroom observation by a school psychologist, 2) a review of current school records, 3) a teacher conference, and 4) possibly an interview with the parents. It might not include any formal testing. If school staff suspect ADD, a permission form will be mailed home for the parents to sign authorizing an evaluation.

A typical *test battery* may include an *academic assessment* (Woodcock Johnson or the Kaufman Test of Educational Abilities), an *intellectual assessment* (Weschler Intelligence Scale for Children - WISC), or a *behavior rating scale*. After the evaluation is completed, parents will be invited to a meeting to discuss the results. If the student is determined to be eligible for special education, an IEP will be developed jointly by the parents and school. (See below.)

There are two potential areas of conflict between parents and school personnel regarding evaluations: 1) timing (how soon can it be done), and 2) adequacy of the evaluation. When the issue of an evaluation surfaces, it is usually in the midst of a crisis—your child is not doing well at school. You want the evaluation done yesterday. But school officials may have a backlog of children awaiting evaluation. If school personnel cannot do an evaluation within a "reasonable" amount of time, they must contract with an outside agency to complete the assessment. Although federal policy does not spell out what is "reasonable," some states have written policies giving specific timelines. Otherwise, federal authorities usually consider 60 days reasonable. The 60 days begin the day parents sign a permission slip for testing and end the day the evaluation is complete. If the school is not planning to do their evaluation within a reasonable time, request an evaluation by an outside expert.

If you disagree with the results of the school's evaluation—perhaps because you believe it is inadequate (no IQ or academic achievement tests were given) or inaccurate—you may seek private testing. For example, if the school system did not use DSM IV criteria, ADD/I/WO may well be overlooked. If you request another evaluation, the school district is responsible for arranging and paying for it—unless they believe it is unnecessary. If the school disagrees, they must request a due process hearing to deny your request. Since a due process hearing generally costs much more than a complete evaluation, most schools are unlikely to take this route. *If parents want an independent evaluation paid for at public expense, they should make the request in writing to the school system.* The school may have an approved list of qualified professionals from which the parent may chose.

If the school refuses to pay or is moving too slowly to suit you, you may seek testing on your own. If results from independent testing help in determining school services needed, the school system *may* have to reimburse you for testing. Don't count on this, however, since the legal process of securing payment for the testing may be expensive and time consuming. In addition, if testing is not done by an approved school evaluator, you may not be reimbursed. Another potential problem with private evaluations is that they may not include the same tests required by the school system.

4. An Individualized Education Program (IEP)

At the heart of each student's educational program is the Individualized Education Program (IEP). The IEP is developed at a meeting between parents and school personnel, where they *jointly* decide "what the child's needs are, what services will be provided to meet those needs, and what the anticipated outcomes may be." Once the child is evaluated, the school has up to 30 days to hold an IEP meeting. Then, with the parent's consent, services can begin immediately. A full reevaluation must be conducted every three years.

This section includes the actual IEP for a 13–year-old with ADD who was also experiencing behavior problems at school (Table 11–1). Many IEPs are brief (1–3 pages) as you will see from the one included in Table 11–1. This teenager's IEP is compared with the framework of federally required elements of an IEP. Verbatim quotes from his IEP are placed in quotation marks and italics. This IEP does not address the student's learning problems, nor does it have an adequate plan for coping with his behavior problems. (During the past year and a half, his "school disciplinary record" contained 34 entries that included fighting, profanity, refusing to obey teachers, and yelling or cursing at teachers.) Based upon input from his mother, a *revised IEP* designed to better meet his needs is displayed in Table 11–5.

Elements of an IEP

The six federally mandated components of an IEP are underlined and shown in Table 11–1. Suggestions for helpful information that may be included in each component were given by special educators and NICHCY, the National Information Center for Children and Youth with Disabilities.

IEP Meetings/Scheduling/Participants. Meetings to develop an IEP must be scheduled at times that are convenient for *both* parents and school officials. If the time scheduled for an IEP is not convenient for you (it may cause you to lose a half day's pay or work, for instance), ask to reschedule. Everyone who has a contribution to make should be present and have a chance to give his input.

At a minimum, *four participants* should be invited to develop the IEP: you, your teenager, the special education teacher, and a representative of the school who is qualified to provide or supervise special education services. Ideally, others will be invited at the discretion of you or the school: the

Table 11–1

_____ COUNTY (GA) PUBLIC SCHOOLS

INDIVIDUALIZED EDUCATION PROGRAM: (Actual IEP with Comments)

| Student | Morris | Sex | M | Age | 14 | Grade | 7 |

1. "a statement of the child's present levels of educational performance." [In this section, parents and teachers identify the problems the IEP should address. For example: "has difficulty when substitute teacher is present; reads and writes slowly; has problems with memorization. *All* behaviors or academic skills of concern should be listed in this section.]***

A. *Academics:* The teenager's "test scores indicate that he functions above average in reading decoding and math skills. He functions on grade level in reading comprehension. (His) written expression skills were average . . ."

B. *Social Skills/Behavior:* He "has difficulty with self-control and compliance. He has been in several arguments with his peers which on many occasions has led to fights. (He) at times blurts out inappropriate verbalizations during class time which disrupts the class. When (he) is angry he becomes very defiant and belligerent."

[If a child has problem behaviors that interfere with his ability to function at school, sometimes a school may develop an optional document, known as a *behavior management plan.* Sometimes, this plan is written primarily for the school's benefit. Consequences for misbehavior are determined before a crisis occurs. Parents can use this document to their advantage by requesting modifications in traditional punishment such as "in-school" suspension instead of "at-home" suspension. This document should be used to teach desired behavior rather than simply punish the child.]

C. *Has an Individualized Behavior Management Plan been written:* "Yes"

[This teenager's behavior plan is two pages long and includes a restatement of his problem behaviors. The plan describes the student's problem behavior, previous attempts to deal with the misbehavior and the results, a list of behaviors needing improvement, effective positive reinforcers for this student, and separate checklists of consequences for minor and more serious misbehaviors. Three specific behaviors are identified as needing improvement.]

Behaviors which this behavioral plan will attempt to improve:

"1. Inappropriate comments to teachers and peers
 2. Disrespect for authority figures
 3. Peer relations"

[The statement of present performance and the behavior management plan for this teenager could be better. Punishments and rewards are discussed but no effort is made to teach him needed skills or to make adaptations to his academic program.]

D. *Tests used:* "Kaufman Test of Educational Achievement; Woodcock Johnson Written Language Test."

E. *What are his academic and behavioral strengths and needs?*

Strengths: "academics"

Weaknesses: "self-control, peer relations, inappropriate verbalization, self-concept"

[The behavior problems identified for this student are correct, but could be explained in more detail. For instance, what is meant by self-control? *When* does he lose self-control, *how* does he act out, *where* does this occur, *what* may have triggered the problem, and *how* do school officials usually handle the problem?]

[Although the school listed only *behavior* problems, the teenager also has *academic* problems with slow cognitive processing (reading, writing, and listening comprehension), poor fine motor skills, poor short-term memory, and a sleep disturbance. Obviously, frustration from undiagnosed academic problems may contribute to this child's misbehavior. The fact that the teenager is very bright and some academic skills are on grade level indicates a *discrepancy* between his intellectual ability and his academic achievement.]

[Only one strength was identified in contrast to four weaknesses. This plan does not build on strengths. Parents should come prepared to suggest strengths to add to the IEP.]

2. a statement of "annual goals and short-term instructional objectives" for each area in which the student is experiencing difficulties. [Goals must be written for the student to accomplish by the end of the school year. Generally speaking, goals are broadly stated; objectives are more specific, can be measured, and may be limited to a shorter period of time such as a grading period.]

---

* *Information in brackets is provided by the author and is not a part of the sample IEP. Actual wording of the IEP is noted in italics.*

[Your child's annual goals and short-term objectives should address the major stumbling blocks that are preventing your child from doing well in school. Beautiful, measurable objectives can be written but if they aren't relevant to your child, they are worthless. According to NICHCY, objectives "are measurable, intermediate steps . . . based upon a logical breakdown of the major components of the annual goals and can serve as milestones for measuring progress toward meeting the goals."]

A. Annual Goals: In this sample IEP, long-term goals are implied, but not stated: to improve self-control and compliance—to reduce inappropriate behaviors such as profanity, fighting, talking back to teachers.

B. Short-term Objectives in the IEP included:

1. *(Child)* *"will make appropriate comments to the teacher."*
2. *"will use socially acceptable language at school."*
3. *"will demonstrate appropriate behavior when angry."*
4. *"will make appropriate comments to peers appropriate to situation."*
5. *"will improve his self-perception."*
6. *"will be able to handle conflicts with others without arguing, yelling, hitting, etc."*

[Although these objectives are reasonable, they do not address all the important issues. For example, no objectives were developed for academic problems. If you find yourself in a similar situation, speak up.]

[Although the method by which the child will learn these skills does not have to be stated in the IEP, you should ask how the objectives will be accomplished. This information will then be included in the minutes of the meeting.]

3. "a statement of specific educational services to be provided to the child and the extent to which the child will participate in regular educational programs." ["Educational services" includes both special education and related services. "Special education" is instruction individually tailored to meet a student's unique learning needs. It is usually provided by teachers with special training and expertise in meeting the needs of students with learning difficulties. It may be provided inside or outside of the regular classroom. Your teenager's IEP should also indicate where the services will be provided, if adaptations will be made in the regular classroom, or if some services will be offered in a part-time resource or self-contained classroom.]

A. *Recommended Special Education Program(s):* *"Emotionally Handicapped program, 30 minutes a week."*

[In this case, it appears the school hoped to solve the teenager's problems by sending him to special education class for 30 minutes each week. Since learning problems were not identified, classroom adaptations such as untimed tests, use of calculator, modified homework assignments, and giving instructions in writing were not addressed.]

[The IEP must also list any *"related services"* which are necessary for the student to succeed in school: counseling, parent counseling and training, psychological services, social work services, audiology, speech therapy, physical therapy, occupational therapy, or assistive technology. Before you attend your child's IEP meeting, *you should decide on your own what services might benefit your child and why.* You could say, "My son could benefit from some training on anger control. Could the guidance counselor or someone work with him to help him develop those skills?"]

B. *Recommended Related Services:* *"none"*

[With all the apparent needs this child and his family have, related services such as counseling would have been very helpful.]

4. the "projected dates for initiation of services and the anticipated duration." [This section includes the beginning date for each special education and related service your child is to receive, as well as how long he is expected to receive the service.]

A. *"8/23/93: one school year"*

[Some students may need a summer program to keep from falling behind academically or to improve their behavior at school. This may be an opportunity to discuss the need for year-round programming. For some students with ADD, however, the last thing they need is to attend summer school.]

5. "appropriate objective criteria and evaluation procedures and schedules for determining whether the short term instructional objectives are being achieved." [This section of the IEP lists what specific tests or other measures are to be used to determine if the IEP is working.]

A. *"daily chart, teacher observation"*

[The use of a daily chart or teacher observation could objectively evaluate whether or not five of the six objectives are achieved. However, measuring improved self-esteem will be difficult without using a formal test.]

---

6. an individualized transition plan (ITP). [A transition plan *must* be developed when a student turns 16 and may be completed as early as age 14.]

   A. *[Since the teenager is not yet 16, a transition plan was not developed.]*
      [This plan must help the student make the transition from high school to "post secondary education, vocational training, integrated employment (including supported employment), continuing and adult education, adult services, independent living or community participation." Activities should be based upon "the individual student's needs taking into account the student's preferences and interests, and shall include instruction, community experiences, the development of employment and other post-school adult living objectives, and when appropriate, acquisition of daily living skills, and functional vocational evaluation."]

---

school psychologist, a former teacher, or the guidance counselor. If it is the first IEP, obviously, a person who is knowledgeable about the evaluation *must* attend. Parents have a right to invite their teenager, a friend, an advocate or other person (such as private therapist or school personnel) to attend and participate in development of the IEP. Parents may want someone to go with them to supply professional expertise or simply moral support. For transition IEPs, representatives from vocational school or Vocational Rehabilitation services must be invited.

Developing the IEP. A completed IEP should *not* be presented for your approval before there has been a full discussion of your child's needs and the services to be provided. You may find that in actual practice, a *draft IEP* has been developed to serve as a springboard for discussion at the meeting. You are encouraged to begin developing an IEP for your child before the meeting. Using information in this book plus your child's old reports cards, previous evaluations, and standardized tests, you can identify potential learning problems and needed adaptations. Do not hesitate to ask that the IEP be changed to better meet your teenager's needs.

I have tremendous admiration for the parent of the 13–year–old boy described in this chapter. She developed an IEP for her son and was an extraordinary advocate on his behalf. Information that she gathered is the basis for the IEP revisions she requested (Table 11–5). Her experiences as described below are inspiring!

༄

"Our local CHADD chapter provided training encouraging us as parents to begin developing an IEP for our child. When I presented my papers to the teachers, THEY were excited. They began asking me questions about what I thought about this modification in his

schoolwork, or if I thought ___ was good way to handle another situation. All of a sudden they were learning from ME about my child, and I was not presenting from a position of weakness. Suggestions I made for dealing with substitute teachers were incorporated in the plan.

"Be nice but be assertive. Go in there and ask for whatever you think it will take to help your child be successful. They can say no, but you can make alternative suggestions and chances are, they will say yes to something. I pretty much got most things set up the way I wanted even though they 'didn't like to do it.' It's OKAY to not be their favorite parent. I have gone from a floundering apologizing parent, to one they ask for materials about ADD. It's exciting to be your own child's expert. I hope my experience will be of help to you. You *can* develop an IEP for your child."

༄

Writing Objectives for the IEP. In her guidelines, *Honorable Intentions*, Dixie Jordan, coordinator of a project for children who have serious emotional problems, identifies some typical problems in developing relevant goals and objectives for an IEP:

"A common problem associated with developing appropriate goals and objectives for students who exhibit undesirable behaviors is the *lack of specificity* with which the behavior is often described. Words like off-task, disruptive, aggressive, non-compliant, lazy, or unmotivated do not lend themselves to the development of specific goals to correct the behavior. For example, does "off task" mean out of seat, non-responsive, not making eye contact, not responding to questions or directions? For my son, walking around the classroom during teacher lectures was *how he stayed on task*. Likewise, disruptive behavior is in the mind of the beholder. For some teachers, disruptive may mean that the student is tapping a pencil, leaning a chair on two legs, humming, which are all behaviors that other teachers may ignore. Obviously, such words should be accompanied by an explanation, including: *What* the behavior was; *where* it occurred; its *frequency, intensity, and duration* (compared to regular students); *when* the behavior occurred; a *hypothesis* or guess about why the behavior occurred; the *outcome* of the behavior (suspension, detention, peer approval).

"It is important that parents and school agree on the specific behaviors of concern so that goals can be directed toward *instructing* the student to learn more desirable behaviors, *not just punishing* the absence of such skills."

The issue of "developing a hypothesis" mentioned above is also addressed in Chapter 5 as the need to identify what triggers or may cause the problem (antecedent behavior).

Selecting Effective Interventions and Adaptations. One of the most difficult challenges is to identify specific interventions and adaptations for addressing problem behaviors. The interventions listed in many IEPs are too general and may not identify the specific classroom adaptations needed. To guard against this problem, *come to the IEP meeting prepared to suggest specific classroom adaptations* such as those that are discussed in this book (untimed tests, modified homework assignments).

A major issue in the sample IEP presented above was the failure to develop an adequate "individualized behavior management plan" to prevent reoccurrence of the problem behaviors resulting in suspension from school. For example, having a substitute teacher or guest speaker often triggered problems at school. School officials were aware of this problem, but no intervention strategies were developed to reduce the likelihood of it happening again.

Strategies that could be used to help this child include: 1) substitutes will be notified of potential problems and told how to best work with this child, 2) a classroom aide or other school official may sit in on the class(es) he has with a substitute, 3) the child is allowed to return to a former teacher's classroom for the periods a substitute is present, 4) the child is taught how to handle having a substitute teacher, and 5) the child is taught the procedure he should follow when a substitute is present and he feels he may blow up, such as going to the guidance counselor's office until the period is over.

As discussed in a later section on suspensions, *depriving a student of an education because of misbehavior related to his disability*, particularly if no attempt has been made to teach the student the proper behavior, *is discriminatory under civil rights law (Section 504).*

Monitor Development of the IEP. Parents should monitor the IEP process. You need to make certain the system is working in your child's best interests. All adaptations that your child is to receive—even those he will receive in the regular classroom—must be included in the IEP, in writing. When you get your copy of the IEP, check to see that all services are written down. Ask questions and don't be afraid to request services you think your teenager needs.

Signing the IEP. After the IEP is finalized, you will be asked to sign it. Technically, parents are *not* required by federal law to sign the IEP. If it is your child's first IEP, however, *the school* must *obtain your written permission before they can* place your teenager in a *special education class.* If the plan is an updated version of a previous plan, however, the school *can* implement the IEP without your written permission. In this case, if you disagree with the IEP that has been developed, you should state this in writing. Or sign the IEP but with a written note that you do not agree with it. Unless you object in writing, the school may, after 10 days, implement the IEP without your permission. Therefore, *it is critical that you state any objections to the IEP in* writing *and request a meeting to resolve points of disagreement.*

Implementation of the IEP. Under federal law, the IEP must be implemented immediately.

Annual Updating of the IEP. Each student who is receiving services under IDEA must have a valid IEP in effect at the beginning of each school year. If you or school personnel feel that your teenager's educational needs have changed or that he is not progressing satisfactorily, you may also request a meeting to review and revise the IEP at any time.

Under IDEA, students *must* be provided special education services until: 1) the student has met the goals and objectives stated in the IEP and parents and school agree the services are no longer needed, 2) the student graduates, or 3) the student turns 22.

5. An Education in the Least Restrictive Environment (LRE)

IDEA guarantees a free appropriate education in the least restrictive environment (LRE). The LRE is defined as the educational setting that allows the student with special needs to be educated, "to the maximum extent appropriate," with children who don't have disabilities. In other words, qualifying for special education under IDEA *does not* automatically mean placement in a special education classroom. *If a student can make good progress in the regular classroom with some modifications, adaptations, or supports, that is where he should be served.* Or if he only needs to leave the regular classroom for special instruction in one or two subjects, then he should still spend the majority of his time with classmates who don't have disabilities. A full continuum of options ranging from classroom adaptations to placement in a self-contained special education classroom must be available. Students should be provided services in the least restrictive environment in which they can succeed academically.

6. A Right to Remedy or Due Process

If you and the school system disagree about your child's educational plan, you can follow formal and informal avenues of complaint. On an informal basis, you may be able to iron things out with your teenager's teacher, principal, or director of special education simply by *notifying them that you disagree with your child's plan and are requesting a meeting* to talk things over.

Many school districts have a procedure called *"mediation"* that parents can use to informally resolve complaints fairly quickly and with a minimum of antagonism. In Georgia, mediation services are offered free at the local level for children eligible for services under IDEA. A mediator meets with you and school officials to: 1) discuss the points of disagreement, 2) listen to possible alternatives suggested by you and the school, 3) suggest other alternatives, and 4) help you and the school system agree upon a compromise. Frequently, mediation is preferable to filing for a due process hearing. You may be more likely to get services you want through mediation than a due proc-

ess hearing. For example, last year in Georgia, parents won only 2 of 23 due process hearings.

If local mediation fails, or you choose not to try it, you can request a *due process hearing* by notifying the superintendent of schools in writing. A hearing must then be scheduled within 20 calendar days from the date your request is received. You can request a due process hearing when you have a dispute about almost any aspect of your child's educational program, including identification, evaluation, placement, and provision of educational services.

A due process hearing has all the major elements of most legal court procedures. Parents and school officials each have an opportunity to argue their case before a hearing officer, often an attorney or administrative law judge who is not a state employee. This hearing officer must be impartial—he or she must not have a stake in one or the other side's winning. In some states, parents may select a hearing officer from a list supplied by the school system.

Parents may 1) access all school records, 2) present testimony and evidence, 3) bring witnesses to testify, 4) subpoena or compel witnesses to appear, 5) cross examine witnesses, and 6) present results of an independent evaluation. They can also hire an attorney at their *own* expense. Presentation of evidence that has not been disclosed at least five days prior to the hearing is prohibited. The hearing officer must present his findings within 25 calendar days after the hearing. This ruling is binding, unless appealed within 30 days. (The results of the hearing may be appealed in federal court). When the parents win, the school system *may* be required to reimburse their attorney's fees. Unless otherwise agreed, the *student will remain in his current education placement* until completion of the due process hearing.

※

"In our community, the most common reason parents have filed for due process hearings is because the school system refused to evaluate a child pursuant to IDEA or Section 504. School officials have said ADD is a medical problem that they cannot diagnose. Obviously, school personnel can diagnose ADD but the student must be referred to a physician for further evaluation and prescription of medications, if appropri-

ate. In some cases, student support teams have met and said the child wasn't eligible for services. We felt that they did not evaluate the student properly. Consequently, we requested an evaluation pursuant to 504. If they do not complete a more thorough evaluation, then we will file for a due process hearing."

— Jerry and Creasa Reed, Parent Advocates and parents of a child with ADD, Wichita, KS

Whenever possible, parents should try to resolve conflicts with the school quickly and with as little antagonism as possible. If parents have to use a "sledge hammer" to obtain services, the relationship between the family and school may be damaged forever. Unfortunately, if the school system is refusing to provide services that the student is eligible for, the family is probably dealing with a pretty damaged and entrenched system. Other students who come along after a due process hearing may benefit—although the student initiating a due process hearing may suffer. Systems change is often glacially slow.

Section 504 of the Rehabilitation Act of 1973

Section 504 of the Rehabilitation Act (P.L. 93–112) is a *civil rights law which prohibits discrimination* against people with disabilities. Section 504 is aimed at eliminating discrimination by any program or activity that receives funding from the federal government. Since most schools in the United States receive at least some federal funding, this law can be used to obtain many important educational rights and benefits for students with disabilities.

Section 504 states: "No otherwise qualified handicapped individual shall, solely by reason of his/her handicap, be excluded from the participation in, be denied the benefits of, or be subject to discrimination under any program or activity receiving federal financial assistance." Among other things, Section 504 provides an equal opportunity for a student with a disability to benefit from educational programs offered other students.

Under Section 504, a person with a disability is considered to be anyone with a physical or mental impairment that substantially limits one or more "life activities." Life activities include: walking, breathing, speaking and/or hearing, seeing, *learning*, performing manual tasks, and caring for oneself.

Many of the rights and safeguards mandated by Section 504 are the same as those in IDEA. For example, Subpart D - Preschool, Elementary, and Secondary Education - guarantees "a free appropriate public education to each qualified person with a disability . . . regardless of the nature or severity of the person's disability." Section 504 requires:

• Free appropriate public education (FAPE);
• Placement in the least restrictive environment (LRE);
• Nondiscrimination in assessment and evaluation;
• Periodic reevaluations of students receiving related special education services;
• Opportunities to take part in extracurricular and non-academic activities.

Even though development of a written "504 plan" is *not* required, you may ask the school to develop one anyway. Most likely, you will have a planning meeting to discuss your child's academic needs with his teacher(s) and other school personnel. So development of a written plan, based upon that meeting, would be a logical action. Ultimately, *an IEP or "504 plan" may be required as documentation for taking an untimed SAT or ACT.* If, for whatever reason, the school doesn't develop a written plan, you can *write the plan yourself* built upon the issues discussed at the school meeting. Summarize a list of classroom adaptations that are supposed to be implemented plus any other steps agreed to by members of the group. Send a copy to the teachers and school with a note. "Just thought I would summarize my son's learning problems and classroom adaptations we orally agreed upon at our meeting last week. Please let me know if there are any corrections. If I do not hear from you within ten days, I will assume that my letter is accurate."

Sometimes schools may be slow to provide services under Section 504, primarily because the educational ramifications of this civil rights law are still unfolding. Every education agency is required to have a *local 504 coordinator* on staff to respond to questions and concerns from families. Some local school systems are just now coming into compliance by hiring or identifying an existing staff person as their 504 coordinator. These coordinators are struggling to develop guidelines for their roles, plus guidelines for principals and teachers regarding provisions of services under 504. If you have questions about Section 504, talk with staff at your local school first. If they are unable to answer your questions satisfactorily, call your local 504 coordinator about rights and possible resolution of problems. If you are not satisfied with the coordinator's response, you can contact the regional Office for Civil Rights (a federal agency) for additional information.

Comparing IDEA and Section 504. Although these two federal laws are similar in many ways, there are also several important differences. First, *the eligibility criteria for Section 504 are broader* than those for IDEA. Often, teenagers with ADD who are unable to qualify for services under IDEA can qualify under Section 504. (But teenagers who qualify under IDEA are always eligible under Section 504.) Second, the effectiveness of services delivered under IDEA are held to a *higher standard* than under Section 504. Educational services offered under IDEA must be sufficient to allow the student to "benefit" from his schooling. Under Section 504, educational services must be "comparable" to those received by non-handicapped students, with no requirement that the student benefit from the services. Third, *IDEA only covers students through high school*, whereas Section 504 covers students in technical school, colleges, and universities, as well.

Violations of IDEA are often violations of Section 504 also; most due process appeals may be filed under one or both laws. One exception would be a dispute over the timeliness of a school's evaluations or reports, since Section 504 does not contain any required timelines. Another exception would be development of a written IEP, since this is required by IDEA but not Section 504.

Qualifying for Assistance under IDEA or 504

It may be crystal clear to you that your teenager should be eligible for assistance under either or both of the laws described above. But it may *not* be as clear to school personnel. Until recently, it could be especially difficult to convince a school that students whose sole diagnosis was ADD should be covered by IDEA. One reason was that IDEA lists 12 specific "handicapping conditions" that automatically qualify a student for special educational assistance. ADD is *not* one of these conditions. Consequently, the only way many students with ADD could get services was to be diagnosed with one of the listed conditions in addition to ADD. The most frequently used secondary diagnoses were specific learning disability (SLD) and emotional and behavioral disorder (EBD)—both of which are covered by IDEA.

Students with ADD may still pursue services on the basis of a diagnosis of SLD or EBD, if appropriate. But two new routes to eligibility are also now available, thanks to the work of national advocacy organizations such as CHADD and NADDA, as well as parents and other interested parties. Originally, these advocates sought to get ADD listed as one of the handicapping conditions under IDEA. Instead, on September 16, 1991, the U.S. Department of Education and Office for Civil Rights issued a joint policy memo. This memo indicated that ADD was already covered under IDEA (under the category of "other health impaired") and under Section 504 of the Rehabilitation Act of 1973. A copy of the US DOE memo is contained in Appendix B.

The **US DOE memo** is the *single most important document* ever issued regarding the education of children and adolescents with attention deficit disorder. It states that youngsters with ADD who experience **"limited alertness, which adversely affects their educational performance"** should be eligible for extra supports and adaptations under the IDEA category of **"other health impaired."** The memo further states that if a student is not eligible for services under IDEA, he may be eligible under **Section 504:** "'*Handicapped person*' is defined in the Section 504 regulation as any person who has a physical or mental impairment which substantially limits a major life activity (e.g., *learning*). 34 CFR s104.3(j). Thus depending on the severity of their condition, children with ADD *may* fit within that definition."

According to the US DOE memo, "The child's education must be provided in the regular education classroom unless it is demonstrated that education in the regular environment with the use of supplementary aides and services cannot be achieved satisfactorily." The memo goes on to list specific classroom adaptations that might be appropriate:

"providing a structured learning environment; repeating and simplifying instructions about in-class and homework assignments; supplementing verbal instructions with visual instructions; using behavioral management techniques; adjusting class schedules; and modifying test delivery; using tape recorders, computer-aided instruction, and other audio-visual equipment; selecting modified textbooks or workbooks; and tailoring homework assignments.

"Other provisions range from consultation to special resources and may include reducing class size; use of one-on-one tutorials; classroom aides and note takers; involvement of a 'services coordinator' to oversee implementation of special programs, and services, and possible modification of nonacademic times such as lunchroom, recess, and physical education."

A summary of these recommendations plus other possible classroom adaptations are included in Table 11–4 at the end of the chapter. The memo also clarifies parents' rights to request an evaluation of their child: "Under Section 504, if parents believe that their child is handicapped by ADD, the local education authority (LEA) must evaluate the child to determine whether he or she is handicapped as defined by Section 504." Parents may also request an evaluation under IDEA. A school system may, on rare occasions, however, refuse to do an evaluation if they are positive that the ADD is not affecting a child's school performance—he is making straight A's and is working above grade level.

As a result of this memo, many local school systems have been more responsive to teenagers with ADD. An additional incentive for local schools to respond to these teenagers' needs was created by a recent *U.S. Supreme Court ruling*. In November 1993, the Supreme Court ruled that a school system in South Carolina did not meet the special needs of a student with dyslexia and ADD and must reimburse the parents in full for the teenager's private schooling. The parents were dissatisfied with the educational plan developed by

special education officials because their daughter was not making educational progress, and placed her in a private school. The suit, filed in 1986, sought $36,000 for three years' tuition at the private school. The ruling was made even though the private school was not approved by state officials and did not meet all federal regulations. Of course, the problem with case law (the ruling in one specific case) is that it may not generalize to all other children with ADD.

Most school systems are knowledgeable about the US DOE policy memo and Supreme Court ruling and are providing improved services to teenagers with ADD. However, if your school system is not responsive, it may help to educate yourself about these statutes/rulings and use them for leverage to get services for your teenager.

Some local schools have already developed criteria for identifying ADD and others will complete this process during the coming months. It will be helpful if parents provide input to their school system on these criteria to ensure that DSM IV criteria for ADD are included instead of the outdated DSM III-R criteria. Although local school systems are not required to accept a medical diagnosis of ADD to consider a student eligible for services under Section 504, some schools have elected to do so. This has been done in situations where the doctor, teacher, or school psychologist indicated that ADD was adversely affecting a student's ability to learn.

🦋

"Some schools are still reluctant to serve children with ADD under IDEA or Section 504. Part of the problem is that ADD is not a visible disability. It is easy to see what accommodations are needed for a person who is physically disabled and in a wheelchair. The door must be wider or an elevator must be installed. That which we can see, we are more likely to accept. Conversely, if the disability is not visible, we are less likely to believe it exists. We have had to use IDEA and Section 504 regulations more than once to help parents get the educational services that their teenager needed."

— Jerry and Creasa Reed

The Right to Participate in Extracurricular Activities

Taking part in extracurricular and non-academic activities such as sports, band, debate team, cheerleading, or clubs, is very important to most adolescents. Unfortunately, some teenagers with ADD are denied the opportunity to participate in activities because of poor grades. A student who is eligible for services as a disabled student under either IDEA or Section 504, however, *may not be discriminated against in determining eligibility for sports or other activities*. That is, eligibility cannot be based upon the student's grades without regard to the disabling condition.

As of this writing, very little case law—rulings in lawsuits—has been issued regarding discrimination in extracurricular activities. Parents are breaking new ground in this area. You are encouraged to work with your school system, using 504 to allow your child to participate in extracurricular activities.

One scenario that might be considered as discriminatory against a child with ADD and thus provide potential grounds for a *civil rights complaint* is as follows: A teenager is on the swim team and fails two classes. He is declared ineligible to swim because of "no pass, no play" regulations. Two reasons parents might approach the school and ask for a reconsideration of their teenager's unique situation are: 1) if ADD has only recently been diagnosed during the grading period (academic problems have been present all along but no one recognized that ADD was the underlying problem), or 2) if ADD was previously diagnosed but related learning problems have only recently been identified.

The first step you could take is to approach school personnel and explain that this appears to be discriminatory (not allowing your child to swim) under Section 504, since adaptations have not been made at school. Obviously, this is not an issue of bad faith on either side, because you both have overlooked the diagnosis of ADD. Next, ask what suggestions they have for solving this problem. Finally, if they have none, you could suggest that they allow your child to take a grade of incomplete and make up any classwork or tests. If your child then completed the required schoolwork, his grade

could be revised, making him eligible to continue participating in the sport.

In many ways, you are on the *cutting edge of legal interpretations clarifying federal laws* regarding the educational rights of children with ADD. The truth is, the school system often doesn't know whether your issue will be ruled a civil rights violation or not. But it may be more costly for them to go to court to find out than to give you the modest adaptations you request. See how much you can get your local school system to agree to do to resolve problems of this nature. These situations are best resolved at the local level, since you have no idea how the regional Office for Civil Rights will rule. Filing a civil rights complaint should be done as a last resort, after all diplomacy and efforts to work with the school system have failed.

⚏

"A high school sophomore with ADD was not allowed to swim on the swim team because he failed two classes. He was the fastest swimmer on the team. Although the student made 87 on the final exam in geography, he 'forgot' to make up two tests he missed. He was allowed to make up the tests, but failed the class with a 69 average. This occurred prior to the 1991 US DOE memo, so he had not been declared eligible for services under Section 504. No special adaptations had been made in the regular classroom during the semester. Currently, under Section 504, parents could have requested that the teenager be allowed to make up classwork and tests."

⚏

"A high school junior with ADD did not wrestle in the state championship wrestling tournament. He failed chemistry because he 'forgot' to turn in a chemistry project that was due after Christmas. Subsequently, he started taking Ritalin his senior year and passed all his classes. He won the state tournament in his weight class his senior year. No special adaptations had been made in the regular classroom."

Suspensions and Expulsions of Students with ADD

Teenagers with ADD who are impulsive, argumentative, and easily frustrated are likely to have conflicts with school officials. The potential for conflict grows when school administrators do not understand ADD and incorrectly perceive the teenager's non-compliance, anger, and defiance as willful, malicious misbehavior. As discussed earlier, 46 percent of the students with ADD in a study of Dr. Russell Barkley had been *suspended* from school. Eleven percent had been *expelled* from school.

Some teenagers with ADD have been suspended or expelled inappropriately for long periods of time for non-dangerous misbehavior that is linked directly to their disability. Some of the examples given below fall in this category, but occurred prior to the US DOE memo. As clarified by a Supreme Court ruling, *children who are covered by IDEA or Section 504 cannot be suspended for more than ten days for an infraction related to their disability.* School systems must also abide by a variety of other safeguards in determining how to discipline a student with special needs.

❦

"A high school student was suspended for 15 days for fighting, his first ever disciplinary offense. No one was hurt, no blood was shed, and no weapon was involved. The student cursed at a teacher and did not stop fighting immediately. His medication had worn off and his guidance counselor was unavailable before the fight. In an effort to break up the fight, a school official grabbed the student from behind. The student was so caught up in the heat of the moment, he thought another student had grabbed him. He resisted momentarily. The administrator overreacted and called the police. The teenager and parents were hu-

miliated. School officials refused to utilize in-school suspension."

❦

"A middle school student was expelled the remainder of the school year for a collection of less serious, defiant behaviors. He refused to take a bandanna off his head as he was waiting for a bus after school."

❦

"A high school student was expelled for the remainder of the school year for a collection of non-compliant behaviors. The student was expelled because he got off the bus, left school property, and crossed the street to a convenience store. He was offered the option of attending an alternative night school. He was having tremendous academic problems but no adaptations had been made to the regular classroom."

❦

To cut down on behaviors that could result in suspensions, Dixie Jordan advocates addressing these behaviors in a student's IEP or Section 504 plan. She suggests that goals be written to specifically instruct the student in acquiring the necessary behavior or skills. She says that punishing a student with ADD for a lack of social behavior skills is "akin to punishing a child with a visual impairment for not being able to read."

As a result of the US DOE memo, many local school systems are struggling to develop an appropriate policy for disciplining adolescents with ADD. Obviously, these teenagers should not be allowed to misbehave, any more than other students should. But on the other hand, neither should they be made to feel they are bad or are criminals. *Reasonable consequences, which are instructive not just punitive, should be used.* For example, don't just suspend or send the teenager to detention because he misbehaved when a substitute was present. As discussed earlier, teach him how to handle this problem in the future or give him a safety release valve—going to the guidance counselor's office. Because many teenagers with ADD are struggling academically, suspending them does not improve their chances of succeeding in school.

Dealing with the issue of misbehavior of students with ADD is difficult right now because of the epidemic of school violence. School officials are justifiably afraid and may be more likely to over-react to misbehavior from students with ADD. Your job as an advocate is made harder when you try to explain that your teenager's ADD is the major cause of his misbehavior. Obviously, if the aggression is potentially life-threatening, school officials must act. Unfortunately, it is sometimes difficult to know if a crisis situation is life-threatening when you are in the middle of it.

A U.S. Supreme Court Ruling Regarding Suspensions and Expulsions. As the result of a 1988 Supreme Court decision (Honig vs. DOE), the Office for Civil Rights (OCR) issued a memo clarifying how suspensions and expulsions for special education students should be handled. A student with ADD who qualifies for services under Section 504 or IDEA has the following safeguards regarding suspensions and expulsions:

• Protected students may not be suspended or expelled, for more than 10 days, without a re-evaluation, and without affording the due process procedure required by 504. A suspension/expulsion for more than 10 days constitutes a "significant change in placement," which is prohibited by federal law.

• Students may be suspended for 10 days or less with no need to determine if misconduct is caused by their disability.

• Schools cannot impose a series of suspensions that are each of 10 days or fewer in duration.

• Reassessment must involve review of current information to determine if "misconduct is caused by the child's handicapping conditions."

• If misconduct is caused by a handicapping condition, the evaluation team must "determine whether the child's current educational placement is appropriate." A member of the evaluation team must be knowledgeable about the child's disability.

If parents disagree with the decision to expel, they may request a due process hearing.

Before a student is readmitted after a suspension or expulsion, a meeting should be held to address the behavior which resulted in the suspension. If necessary, objectives in the IEP or 504 plan should be rewritten to prevent misbehavior that may cause another suspension.

Provision of an Education During an Expulsion. Federal guidelines from the U.S. Department of Education, Office of Special Education and Rehabilitative Services (OSERS) require that *if there is a relationship between the disability and the misbehavior, the school* must *continue to provide educational services during the period of expulsion.* How educational services are provided during this period varies from state to state. As an example, however, here is what Texas administrative school rules provide for:

"The IEP committee must write an IEP to govern the instructional and related services that will be carried out during the expulsion, and that IEP must have goals and objectives which will assist the child's return to school at the end of the expulsion period and which will prevent significant regression during the expulsion."

Ordinarily, homebound instruction may be limited to only one or two hours of instruction per day for students without disabilities. Unless parents agree to an amended IEP, *schools* must *implement the existing IEP during the period of homebound instruction.* That means that your child could receive up to five or six hours instruction per day. The circumstances surrounding the home schooling of two teenagers are described below.

᪥

"A family filed for a due process hearing when their son was expelled from school. The school system refused to provide educational services to the student while he was expelled. He had been suspended a couple of times, been in fights, and had taken a 'weapon' (butter knife) to school. Although it has never been diagnosed, we think he has ADD. His parents requested home schooling plus an evaluation, but the school system refused. The parents put their request in writing and when the school refused again, they filed for a due process hearing and early complaint resolution (20 days) through the Office for Civil Rights pursuant to Section 504. The Office for Civil Rights advised us they had jurisdiction and would schedule a hearing. In the meantime, the school system contacted the parents and agreed to provide homebound schooling."

—*Jerry and Creasa Reed*

᪥

"A student with ADD (formerly in an EBD class) was expelled for four months for bringing a knife to school. He indicated he was carrying the knife for protection. He did not pull the knife or threaten anyone with it. A sympathetic county special education director arranged for county staff to provide home schooling for the teenager with plans to reenter the regular school in January at the beginning of the new semester. In the interim, he was reevaluated for special education eligibility. The homebound teacher visited the home three times a week for a couple of hours, gave homework assignments from his teachers, taught the lesson, and collected his completed homework. Since the student completed most of his school work, he was able to pass most of his subjects and continue earning credits toward graduation. Otherwise, he might have been pushed one step closer to dropping out of school."

🐾

Occasionally, the educational philosophy of a school system as a whole may not be carried out by individual schools. For some school officials, the answer to coping with non-compliant teenagers is still to suspend or expel them from school. These school administrators need to be educated about the impulsive characteristics and typical behaviors of teenagers with ADD, and about alternative ways of coping with them. If you run into this problem, your local CHADD chapter may be able to jointly develop, with your school psychologists or special educators, an in-service training for both teachers and administrators.

Working in Good Faith with School Officials

Now that all the legal issues are out on the table, let's talk about the *common struggles parents and school staff share* as they deal with ADD and the importance of parents and teachers *treating each other with mutual respect*. Together you must learn to manage ADD, to understand the emotional aspects of coping with ADD, and implement new federal mandates.

Because ADD can be a difficult and frustrating disability for both the parents and school, the potential exists for *hostile confrontations*. When nerves

are frayed, tempers may flare on either side, especially during crises such as school suspensions or expulsions. Clearly, the parents of most students with ADD have the legal backing of IDEA and Section 504 and are negotiating from a position of strength with their local school system. Most of the time, parents can get what they need from the school with a positive but firm approach. Parents may actually get more services, more rapidly by using this approach. Mutual respect and courtesy are appropriate in these negotiations, until or unless school officials refuse to cooperate. Assume good intentions of others until proven wrong. The comments from a county director of special education below convey a willingness to work with parents that is shared by many educators. You have to find a "voice of reason" within your school system.

🐾

"I really appreciate parents who come to me, without hostility, and are willing to work together toward a positive solution for the student. If parents feel the school is not responding properly, I encourage them to find a higher level official (director of special education, school superintendent, or school board member) and give school people the opportunity to do the right thing."

—*Dick Downey, Ph.D., Director of Special Education, Gwinnett County, GA*

🐾

Many caring and well-intentioned educators are eager to help students with ADD. You should first try to work in good faith with local school officials to develop an appropriate educational plan for your teenager. However, if your child's needs continue to be unmet, other options are open to your family. 1) Talk with school officials who are higher up the ladder—director of special education, 504 coordinator, or superintendent. 2) If you believe that a school or community program receiving federal funds is violating the civil rights of your teenager and is unwilling to work with you, contact the 504 coordinator for the school. 3) Next you may request local mediation. 4) If you are unable to resolve the problem with local officials, then you can file for a due process hearing under IDEA or Section 504. Contact your superintendent of schools, state director of special education, or regional Office for Civil Rights to find out procedures for filing a formal complaint.

An Educational Dilemma for Parents

If your teenager with ADD is struggling in school, you must make several important decisions. First, should you pursue special educational services for him? If the answer is yes, then secondly, should you pursue services under IDEA or Section 504? Third, should your child be placed in a special education classroom or receive services in the regular classroom? Last, if you are dissatisfied with public schools, should you seek private school placement?

Pros and Cons of IDEA and/or 504 Eligibility

If your child is struggling academically or behaviorally, you should consider requesting services under IDEA or Section 504, but not necessarily special education *placement*. Going through the process of having your teenager declared eligible for services under IDEA or Section 504 is especially important if you are concerned that he may fail classes or act out and be at risk of suspension or expulsion. As explained above, federal IDEA and 504 guidelines *require* school personnel to be flexible with academic and behavioral requirements and interventions for eligible students. This eligibility may give the school administrator the legal reason he needs to treat these students differently—for example, by changing classes or teachers, or providing a more appropriate consequence for misbehavior (in-school suspension instead of at-home suspension).

⚓

"If a teenager with ADD is struggling academically or behaviorally in school, it is a signal to me that he needs supports and adaptations pursuant to IDEA or Section 504. Frustration related to learning problems or school failure may escalate, resulting in increased misbehavior at home and school.

⚓

"I talked with one mother whose 13–year-old son with ADD was suspended for the last month of the school year. He had not committed any major offenses but rather a collection of defiant misbehaviors. I tried to explain that the school system was not providing this teenager services he had a right to receive. She was very 'beaten down' and was apologetic for her son's defiant behavior. She expressed a lot of guilt because she felt she had not been a better mother and had let him get away with too much. She accepted the school system's decision to suspend her son for the last month of school without question. She was attempting to provide 'home schooling' while working full-time.

"What she didn't seem to realize was that defiant, acting-out behavior may well be related to frustration due to an attention deficit or undiagnosed learning problems. This teenager is being denied his guaranteed right to a free appropriate education."

⚓

Advantages and Disadvantages of IDEA and Section 504 Eligibility. There are advantages and disadvantages to having your teenager with ADD declared eligible for services under IDEA or Section 504. Advantages include:

• Eligible students may participate in *regular classes* and still receive services under IDEA or Section 504. The adolescent does not have to be placed in a separate, "self-contained" classroom.

• IEPs must be developed which document all needed services and adaptations to the teenager's academic program. Even though it is not required, a plan should also be developed for services delivered under Section 504. If the planning team agrees, certain protections may be written in the IEP. For example, if suspension is necessary, it must be in-school suspension.

• Each school system has guidelines for disciplinary actions that can be taken against special education students. A student cannot be suspended long-term if his problem behaviors are caused by his disability, unless he presents a danger to himself or others. Students may be exempt from standard disciplinary actions and follow individualized expectations written into an IEP or 504 plan. For example, if the teenager talks back to a teacher, the special education teacher will determine appropriate discipline. It may be apologizing to the teacher, plus changing the time his medication is taken so his impulsive talking back to teachers is reduced."

• In some school systems, students protected by IDEA or 504 may transfer to another school more easily without requiring school board approval. Some teenagers have burned so many bridges within a school that transferring to a new school for a fresh start may be appropriate.

Three potential disadvantages of placement in special education classes are stigma, the risk that the special education class may be worse or no better than a regular class, and learning worse misbehavior from others in the class. Unfortunately, most adolescents feel a degree of stigma, whether real or imagined, if they are placed in part-time resource or self-contained special education classes. Students are usually more receptive to help from special classes in elementary school. When these students reach middle and high school, they don't want to be different from their friends and may be too embarrassed to participate.

"In second grade they found out I had a learning disability. I thought I was in 'dumb classes.' People started making fun of me. I'm in high school now and I don't want people to know I'm in a resource room except my close friends."

In addition, if students are forced into SLD or EBD classes, they may become more aggressive and resentful, causing even more problems at school. A student with ADD who is placed in one of these special education classes may feel he has nothing in common with the other students.

Sometimes after a student is declared eligible for EBD or SLD, other problems arise. Eligibility for special education is reevaluated at regular intervals. If the student's academic performance and behavior improves significantly, the school may say that he no longer meets eligibility criteria for special education services. In addition, eligibility for EBD and SLD may vary from state to state or even within a state. For example, a teenager in SLD

classes in one state may not be eligible if he moves to another state. Of course, this should not be a problem if the student is declared eligible for services under OHI or Section 504.

"In middle school the resource class really helped. The problem was she got better on test scores and didn't continue to qualify for SLD classes—that didn't make the ADD go away!"

Should You Pursue Eligibility Under IDEA or Section 504?

From a practical standpoint, you may find some advantages to seeking 504 eligibility first:

1) Because Section 504 eligibility criteria are very broad, it is *easier* for students with ADD to qualify for services under 504 than under IDEA.

2) Adaptations may be implemented in the regular classroom more *rapidly* under Section 504. Whereas the evaluation and eligibility procedure under IDEA may take two to three months, Section 504 requires no lengthy evaluation. Rapid provision of services under Section 504 should occur. If it does not, it may be because the school is unsure about how to proceed. Your child's planning team should be able to make the decision to implement needed services without requiring county level approval. Near the end of the planning meeting for your child, you might say, "As I understand this, Section 504 services may be offered immediately. When do you think you will be able to begin these services? Is this week a possibility?"

Pursuing Services under Section 504. Many school systems are uncertain how to respond when a parent says, "My child has ADD and I want services under Section 504." Whereas eligibility criteria for IDEA are very specific, many school systems have no guidelines or very limited ones for Section 504. After all, Section 504 is a civil rights law, not an education law. This confusion and lack of clarity can be to the parent's advantage. The Office for Civil Rights has not established any eligibility criteria other than the broad statement ". . .

mental impairment which substantially limits one or more life activities, e.g., learning." Essentially, the primary eligibility criteria is that the student has ADD and is having trouble succeeding in school. As one special educator explained, "Parents hold the trump cards with Section 504. Hopefully, they will use it with finesse rather than as a club. Parents should pursue a path of progressive assertiveness."

Below are some steps to follow in seeking Section 504 eligibility for your teenager:

1. Schedule a Teacher Conference: Schedule a conference with your adolescent's teacher to discuss his ADD and how it adversely affects his education and ability to learn. You could casually explain, "I am requesting help for my son through Section 504 of the Rehabilitation Act." Later, if necessary, you could say, "The joint memo from the U.S. Department of Education and Office for Civil Rights in September 1991 clarified that students with ADD whose ability to learn is adversely affected by ADD must be provided adaptations to their regular classroom setting."

2. Bring Documentation of ADD. Bring a *letter* from your psychiatrist, physician, or psychologist which documents that your teenager has ADD. Bring any *test results* completed by your doctor or counselor or previous evaluations done by other schools. If they have assessed academic issues, ask them to include a statement regarding any potential learning problems and possible adaptations, similar to those described in the OHI medical report (Table 11–2) or the revised IEP (Table 11–5) or OHI medical report.

3. Bring Documentation of Learning Problems. Begin to build a case that ADD has adversely affected your teenager's ability to learn. Identify areas where your teenager has learning problems and potential adaptations. Discuss your teenager's learning problems and underachievement based upon:

- *past academic performance* that shows a *discrepancy* between intelligence and grades. Your child is bright but making failing grades, has failed classes, frequently receives 0's for homework, makes erratic grades from A's to F's even though he has average or above average IQ;

- results of *standardized tests* such as the IOWA that may show *discrepancy* between intelligence and expected academic achievement. For example, math computation scores are well below other scores;

- *scores on subsections* of tests showing *variability* that may be indicative of learning problems. For example, variability in scale scores on subtests of the Weschler Intelligence Scale for Children (WISC), a commonly administered IQ test, may be present (a 7 on the Coding and a 19 on the Vocabulary subtests). Identify low subtests scores on the WISC and explain what learning problem may be present. (See Chapter 2 for more information on score variability.)

- a *list of learning problems* you have identified from observing your teenager do homework, grades and comments on old report cards, and past teacher conferences. For example, you may have observed that it takes him forever to do homework or that even with practice he can't memorize multiplication tables. Reading Chapter 10 should help you identify learning problems plus potential adaptations that may help. You can complete the blank forms in this book regarding learning problems and adaptations and take them to school to use as a springboard for discussion with a teacher. The completed form looks professional and sends a message to the teacher, "You are dealing with an informed parent who is very knowledgeable about the learning problems associated with ADD."

If the teacher will make modifications based on this meeting, then you may not need to go any further than this step. If the teacher seems reluctant or unclear about how to proceed, continue with the next step:

4. Request a Student Support Team Staffing for Your Teenager: Many schools have established a team of educational professionals—teachers, special education teachers, guidance counselor, vice principal, social worker, and/or school psychologist—who meet to discuss the special needs of students. You may request this type of staff meeting from the teacher, guidance counselor, or principal. Again, you should be prepared to *document* your teenager's ADD and learning problems. Keep in mind that under Section 504, a student may receive adaptations for learning problems without meeting school criteria for specific learning disabilities. Also take along a copy of the US DOE memo and relevant sections of this book, just in case you need it. Hopefully, adaptations will be agreed to at this meeting and you will not have to pursue the issue any further.

5. Request Help Through Higher Level Educators: If the teacher does not respond to your requests, you may pursue help through the school principal, the county director of special education, the superintendent of schools, school board members, and/or the county section 504 coordinator. When asking for their help, explain that your child has ADD plus learning problems and that you think he is eligible for services under 504. Later you will have the opportunity to explain which learning problems are significant and suggest adaptations.

Pursuing Services Under IDEA. If your teenager's learning and behavioral problems are more serious and may result in academic failure or suspensions, you should seek evaluation pursuant to IDEA. To get the process started, simply *tell the teacher* that you would like to have your teenager evaluated for special education services. If the teacher doesn't act promptly, *give her your request in writing.* Since the evaluation and eligibility processes may take several months or more, depending on your state's rules, seek an evaluation early before a crisis occurs. Procedures for the evaluation, follow-up, and appeals were discussed earlier in the chapter.

Generally speaking, it is best to work with the school system to arrange appropriate testing for special education eligibility. If a long delay in testing is anticipated, work with the school system to see 1) whether the evaluation procedure can be accelerated, or 2) whether Section 504 eligibility should trigger prompt provision of services. You

may want to *pursue services under Section 504 first,* so that your child receives services while participating in IDEA evaluation and awaiting the final decision about eligibility. Some schools will provide "pre-referral interventions" such as adaptations to the classroom even before the evaluation is started. Thus, some corrective actions are being taken while waiting for completion of the evaluation. Monitoring timelines may keep the process from dragging on indefinitely. If you child is eligible under IDEA, OHI is probably the most appropriate category.

Who Is Eligible Under "Other Health Impaired" (OHI)?

A more in-depth discussion of the Other Health Impaired (OHI) category is provided here because it is an important new avenue for children with ADD to access services. According to IDEA, Other Health Impaired *"means having limited strength, vitality, or* alertness *due to chronic or acute health problems that adversely affect a student's education performance."* Qualifying for special education eligibility under OHI should be easier than for SLD or EBD. The characteristics of ADD, such as inattention and impulsivity, can be important diagnostic criteria for OHI. These same characteristics are not particularly significant in determining eligibility under the SLD or EBD categories.

In Georgia, two key steps in determining OHI eligibility include completion of: 1) a medical report from your teenager's physician, and 2) the school eligibility report. Below are some suggestions for information that could be included in a medical report to help your child obtain services. Ask your local school or superintendent's office whether they have a specific medical report form for doctors to fill out when a child is believed to be OHI, or whether they have specific guidelines to follow.

Medical report. Your child's physician will need to fill out and sign a medical evaluation form. De-

---

Table 11–2

_____ **COUNTY SCHOOLS MEDICAL REPORT**

Name: Bert   **Date: 7/14/95**

1. Diagnosis and medical history: *ADD diagnosed at age 12, have treated child since 1986; learning problems as described below; sleep disturbance.*

  [A diagnosis of ADD should be listed, plus any learning problems. The doctor can give a diagnosis of any "Learning Disorders" he has detected from his evaluation such as "Mathematics Disorder" (DSM IV). See Chapter 8 for more details.]

2. Current medication/list side-effects: *Dexedrine SR 5 mg once daily (a.m.); Dexedrine 5 mg regular twice daily, morning and afternoon; Tofranil 50 mg near bedtime. If he forgets his medication, he may be inattentive and impulsive at school.*

  [Medications should be listed, and related problems mentioned: rebound, irritability in the afternoon as medication is wearing off; loss of appetite.]

3. Describe any condition which may interfere with regular attendance or functioning in school: *Even with medication, inattention and impulsivity may still present a problem at school. Medication may wear off during the day increasing the likelihood of problems with inattention and impulsivity. Bert has learning problems that interfere with his ability to do well at school; slow cognitive processing (reads and writes slowly, slow calculation of math problems, will produce less written work); poor memory (difficulty memorizing multiplication tables, spelling, and foreign languages); inattentive and forgetful; impulsivity and low frustration tolerance (says or does things without thinking, is more likely to blow up when upset); a sleep disturbance (sometimes can't fall asleep at night and has trouble waking up the next morning, may sleep in class or be irritable at school the next day, or may be late.) A copy of our psychological and academic assessment is attached.*

Bert may be inattentive or act or speak impulsively when his medication is wearing off. If he is having problems only during certain times of the day, you may want to double check to see if medication has worn off. If this is a problem I will work with you to correct the problem by changing the medication, dose, or time it is administered.

  [Some doctors can explain how your teenager's learning problems will adversely affect his performance at school. They may obtain information from an in-depth evaluation, including intellectual (IQ) or academic functioning as assessed by their staff. Or you may provide them information (old school psychological evaluations, IOWA scores, report cards) and point out areas of academic deficits, or share information from Table 10–2 about common learning problems and adaptations.]

4. Medical Prognosis: *Good, if the teenager continues to take medication and the school provides appropriate classroom adaptations.*

5. Recommendations and Comments: *Based upon our evaluation, this child will need some adaptations to succeed in school. The following adaptations should be extremely helpful: untimed tests, use of a calculator, written homework assignments, and procedures for him to follow when he feels he is about to lose control. I have prescribed medication which should help reduce problems with his emotional outbursts and sleep disturbances. It would be helpful if his most important academic classes are scheduled for times when his medication is at maximum effectiveness. Placing him with teachers who are positive but flexible and understand ADD is important. Try to schedule a reasonable lunch shift. If lunch is too late—after 1:00–and a noon dose is needed, he will be attempting significant amounts of schoolwork without the benefit of medication.*

_____ *(Signature of M.D.)*

---

pending on your relationship with your teenager's doctor, you might photocopy the medical report form and fill it out for him to use as a reference. You might say something like, "I know you're very busy and I have tried to save you some time by jotting down some ideas that may help you complete this medical form. Based upon my discussion with school personnel, I believe these are the type of is-

sues that need to be addressed. Feel free to use whatever information you want from my form."

School Eligibility Report. Next, the school will take your doctor's medical report, gather relevant school data, and complete an eligibility report. Georgia's eligibility report includes the following issues that are relevant to ADD:

Table 11–3

**SCHOOL ELIGIBILITY REPORT (GA)
OTHER HEALTH IMPAIRED**

I. Educational and Assessment Data

A. Medical evaluation (less than one year old. This section will be a summary of the information from your doctor's medical report.)
- Date of evaluation:
- Diagnosis/prognosis of health impairment:
- Information regarding limitations to alertness. Also information on medications.

B. Educational evaluation: Dates, instruments [tests], results
- Informal assessment of education performance; date & results

C. Psychological evaluation: Dates, instruments, results

D. Based upon the above information, education deficits are noted in the following areas:

_____ academic functioning_____ adaptive behavior
_____ gross/fine-motor development_____ communication skills
_____ social/emotional development_____ other areas; specify

II. Conclusion:
Summarize the documentation that educational deficits have resulted from the health impairment.

_____ The student *does (does not)* meet OHI eligibility criteria.

Consider having your child's eligibility changed to OHI. If your teenager is currently classified as EBD or SLD, you may want to ask that his classification be changed to OHI. He can continue with the same IEP and services, but the potential stigma associated with an EBD classification will be reduced. *The IEP should be driven by the child's needs, not the disability label.*

To Place or Not To Place . . . In a Special Education Classroom?

If your teenager has severe learning disabilities or serious behavioral problems, he may not be able to learn in a regular classroom. If so, you must weigh the pros and cons of placement in an IDEA special education program (SLD or EBD). Services offered in a special education class include individualized educational planning and teaching, identification of learning problems, and adaptations to the student's instructional program. The major advantage of a self-contained special education class is *reduced teacher-to-child ratio*, usually with ten or fewer students. In addition, teachers have received

special training for teaching students with special needs.

It is true that many experienced classroom teachers are applying the same teaching techniques used by special education teachers in regular classroom settings. And it is also true that *a good teacher who has this knowledge and skill can teach most adolescents with ADD in a regular classroom.* However, most special education teachers have had more training regarding the educational adaptations described in this book. In addition, they have learned to use behavior management, positive reinforcement, and other child management techniques, plus understand the dynamics of behaviors associated with various disabilities.

Teachers who pursue a career in special education tend to be more flexible, accommodating, aware of differences in individual learning style and abilities, and willing to work with students who are struggling. Many special education teachers may be more tolerant of, and experienced in, dealing with the emotionality (low frustration tolerance, arguing, talking back, defiance) associated with ADD than teachers in a regular classroom. The special education teacher may be the key to gradually returning a student with ADD to the regular classroom.

If you are considering placement in a special education class, first *find out about the class and teacher* to determine if it is in your teenager's best interest to participate. Ask friends or a trusted former teacher their opinion of the quality of the class. It is a good idea for you to *meet the special education teacher*. If you can't get an opinion from someone else you trust, *observe her teaching students*. When observing the class, ask yourself: 1) Does the special education teacher appear effective and seem to understand the special needs of students with disabilities? 2) Is she positive, firm but pleasant with her students? 3) Does she treat them with respect and seem to enjoy her students and work? 4) Do her students seem to like her? 5) Do you think she can meet your child's needs? 6) Are other students in the class reasonable classmates for your teenager? 7) Will he be safe? 8) Will a plan be developed to phase him back into regular classes as soon as possible? 9) Do the behavior and grades of students participating in this class improve?

For some adolescents, placement in a special education classroom may be an excellent choice. This may mean participation in a part-time resource room or placement in a self-contained classroom. However, participation in special education classes is no guarantee that your child's academic or emotional needs will be met. For example, an intellectually gifted adolescent who reads and writes very slowly and has organizational problems may not be helped by being placed in a self-contained SLD class. The decision to seek placement in a special education class is a difficult one and must be based upon each student's unique situation.

⚜

"Kansas's special education teacher has been a guardian angel. She has been the 'voice of reason' at school and has believed in him when no one else at school did. She helped him gradually transition back into as many regular classes as he could handle. He started with one regular class and then successfully kept adding more classes. Now he spends only one hour a day with her. She serves as an 'emotional anchor' for him. She understands and believes in him when no one else at school does."

⚜

Placement in SLD vs. EBD Classes. If you do choose for your child to be placed in a self-contained classroom or resource room, you may have a choice of an SLD or EBD class placement. Typically, no separate classes are available for OHI. Request placement in the class that can best meet your teen's educational needs.

Placement in an SLD class may be preferable for many children with ADD. As Chapter 8 discusses, many teens with ADD have learning problems linked to ADD. However, if behavior problems are present, school staff may lean toward EBD placement. Yet, these behavior problems may improve significantly when academic help is provided.

The term "serious emotional disturbance" (SED) is currently used in IDEA to describe emotional and behavioral problems. New federal legislation, however, has been proposed to change the name to emotional and behavior disorder (EBD). You might hear either term, depending on where you live.

Special educators have identified several problems with the present definitions of SED/EBD. The present criteria are vague and do not accurately describe the emotional and behavioral problems seen at school. SED is defined in IDEA as: "(1) an inability to learn which cannot be explained by intellectual, sensory, or health factors; (b) an inability to build or maintain satisfactory relationships with peers and teachers; (c) inappropriate types of behavior or feelings under normal circumstances; (d) a general pervasive mood of unhappiness or depression; or (e) a tendency to develop physical symptoms for fears associated with personal or school problems."

Placement in a good SED/EBD class can be an excellent choice if that is what your teenager needs and services in regular classroom have not been effective. One major advantage is that teachers in EBD classes usually have had the specialized training described earlier which enables them to effectively deal with students with special needs.

Despite possible advantages, many parents seek SED/EBD eligibility only as a last resort—for example, to prevent placement in a psychiatric hospital. One reason is that drop-out rates in SED classrooms are the highest of all special education categories—48 percent. This is not to say that EBD classes are bad, but rather that many schools must not be meeting the academic and emotional needs of students in these classes. Teenagers may also feel stigmatized if they are placed in these classes. This special education category is not used very often but when it is used, the students tend to have more serious problems. Although an estimated 5 percent of teenagers in this country have serious emotional problems, only 1 percent are served through classes for SED.

Some students with ADD and a diagnosis of conduct disorder may actually be excluded from SED/EBD services. Schools do not have to serve students who are socially maladjusted, "unless it is determined that they are seriously emotionally disturbed." Consequently, some schools use this as a loophole to avoid serving any student who is diagnosed as having a conduct disorder. As Chapter 2 discusses, the label of conduct disorder could hinder your child's access to educational services. If a professional has used this diagnosis with your teenager, you may need to explain the problems this may create at school. Remember, though: state regulations vary and a diagnosis of conduct disorder may not be a problem in all states.

Undiagnosed ADD in Special Education Students

If you are reading this book, chances are you already know or have good reason to believe that your teenager has ADD. If he is receiving special education for some other reason, however, you need to bear in mind something that has been stressed in previous chapters: ADD frequently slips through the cracks. Even though your child may be receiving special education services on the basis of a diagnosis of learning disabilities, for example, it is quite possible that he also has ADD. The experience of Lewis's family, below, underscores this possibility:

❧

"Lewis's learning disability was diagnosed when he was in the second grade and he has been in a learning disabilities class or resource room since then.

"In the first grade Lewis was considered a behavior problem. He also had severe astigmatism and had to wear an eye patch. He has always been very active. Lewis makes a great 'class clown.' He loves to en- tertain. The teacher called one day to tell me he was dancing on a car to entertain the other children. Sometimes he had to sit at a desk with high sides so he would not be distracted or distract others. He was placed in a self-contained special class until fourth grade and then mainstreamed for some regular classes.

"Nothing was ever mentioned by special education teachers or in psychological evaluations about the possibility of ADD. Lewis's high school teachers made comments like 'Lewis has trouble concentrating'; 'He doesn't finish his work'; or 'He gets distracted easily.' Apparently, it never occurred to them to have Lewis checked for ADD. Yet as part of authorization for participation in special education, school personnel indicated that Lewis showed 'weakness in attending, sequencing, and auditory short-term memory,' which are common problems for teenagers with ADD.

"His ADD was finally diagnosed at age 16 by a physician who specializes in treating teenagers with ADD. The Ritalin has helped Lewis very much. Since Lewis has been on Ritalin, he has made his first two A's ever. He is so proud of himself. It has opened a door for him. He does not seem to be going in 50 directions at once now. He can listen better, give feedback, and remember."

❧

It is difficult to understand how Lewis's high school teachers could have overlooked his ADD. Perhaps they believed the myths about outgrowing ADD in adolescence or that Ritalin no longer works for teenagers. Sometimes, middle and high school teachers incorrectly assume that if a student has ADD it would have been diagnosed in elementary school.

Placement in Private School— Another Dilemma

When public schools aren't providing needed supports and accommodations, some parents consider placing their teenager in a private school. You may want to think twice, however, before choosing this option. Private schools that specialize in educating teenagers with ADD are *rare*. And traditional private schools may *not* be a good choice, especially for teenagers with moderate to severe problems with ADD. Placing a student in a highly

---

Table 11–4

SUMMARY OF US DOE MEMO
CLASSROOM ADAPTATIONS FOR STUDENTS WITH ADD

Several examples of adaptations that may be used in regular classrooms are listed below. The adaptations listed in the left column were recommended in the landmark US DOE 1991 policy memo. Some of the classroom adaptations discussed earlier are listed in the column on the right. You may need to read Chapter 10 for a more detailed explanation for the adaptation. Obviously, adaptations are selected based upon each child's individual needs, learning problems and symptoms of ADD.

US DOE Suggestions:	Other Adaptations:
- structured learning environment	- seat near teacher
- repeat and simplify instructions	- seat positive role models nearby
- provide visual aids	- reduce distractions
- use behavior management	- pair students to check work
- adjust class schedules	- pair with student who checks to see if assignment is written down
- modify test delivery	
- use tape recorder	- give untimed tests
- computer aided instruction	- use calculator
- audio-visual equipment	- give guided lecture notes
- modified textbooks or workbooks	- provide chapter outline
- tailor homework assignments	- simplify directions
- consultation	- don't reduce grade for handwriting
- reduce class size	- consider multiple choice tests
- one-on-one tutors	- use Books on Tape
- special resources	- use extra set of books at home
- classroom aides	- use weekly progress reports
- notetaker	- consider oral tests
- services coordinator	- teach study skills
- modify nonacademic times: lunchroom, recess, PE	- put assignments in writing for month
	- use color to highlight info. to be memorized, or common errors
	- use flash cards

competitive private school, for example, may only exacerbate the problem. The teenager may not be able to keep up in highly competitive academic and sports situations and may experience even more failure. A more rigid, highly disciplined private religious school may not be the best choice, either. Such schools may lack flexibility. Too many demands may be placed on the student and the parents may be criticized for not "disciplining" him enough.

🦭

"We struggled for years trying to decide whether to place our son in a private school. Finally, in the middle of his junior year, we placed him in a private

school. Even the private school we selected wasn't the perfect choice. They didn't really understand ADD or know how to work with students who have it. They kept waiting for him to take the initiative to independently get organized and complete the required graduation requirements. They did not recognize these deficits were part of his disability and they would need to provide more structure and guidance. On the plus side, the private school *was* more flexible and staff were willing to accommodate our requests. Although, the school wasn't perfect, it was better than the public school."

🦭

Table 11–5

IEP Revisions Requested by Morris's Parents

Student: Morris	DOB:	
IEP Coordinator:	School:	Age: 13
Parent/Guardian:	Grade: 7	
Address:		
Phone:	Psychological evaluation:__/__/__	Screening:__/__/__

<u>Present Levels of Performance:</u> Summarize the student's current performance in academic/learning. Also describe behaviors directly related to learning such as study skills, task completion, etc.

- a bright student but has some problems academically
- inattention/poor concentration
- poor memory
- easily distracted
- slow processing, auditory and visual (reading, writing, listening)
- problems with listening comprehension
- weak language skills
- poor spelling skills
- poor fine motor coordination

as a result he

- forgets assignments
- is not always listening when directions are given
- doesn't always follow directions because of slow processing
- misunderstands directions
- reads and writes slowly
- has poor handwriting
- avoids writing
- produces less written work
- has difficulty taking notes
- doesn't always finish work

Summarize the student's current performance in other areas such as social skills, behavior, adaptive skills, motor abilities, medication condition, self-help skills, etc.

- impulsive
- low frustration tolerance
- sometimes forgets to take medication
- verbally aggressive
- poor self-esteem
- low frustration tolerance
- doesn't handle transitions or change very well
- sleep disturbance, can't fall asleep, difficulty waking up

as a result he

- loses his temper easily

- has difficulty waiting
- talks back, says no, while doing as teacher asks
- has trouble working well with others
- gets into fights
- brags, makes up accomplishments
- gets into trouble when substitute teachers or guest speakers are at school
- is sometimes tired and irritable at school
- may fall asleep in class

Strengths:

- very bright
- outgoing/talkative
- good sense of humor
- personable
- good with computers
- good in math
- looked up to as a leader
- likes to please adults
- likes to do things to help teachers
- enjoys being the center of attention

Weaknesses:

- lacks self-control (verbally and physically)
- loses temper, blows up
- walks out of class
- talks back to teachers
- these problems frequently occur with a substitute teacher
- problems relating to peers
- argues and fights

Recommended Program:

Special Education: Other Health Impaired (OHI), 30–60 minutes a week.
There are several different ways this time could be spent. He could start, and if needed, end each day going by his former special education teacher's classroom. Each morning, the teacher can assess his frame of mind and perhaps be able to tell if he took his medicine. Keep extra medicine at school, in case he forgets it. If a crisis is brewing, he may need to see the guidance counselor. At the end of the day, they can review assignments and make certain he has everything he needs to take home.

Regular Education: Make adaptations in regular classes. (Some schools may avoid including this level of detail in an IEP. Usually, if parents insist, the school will incorporate the information or add it as an addendum to the IEP.)

Substitute teacher present	• give substitute suggestions for dealing with this student
	• or send to his former special ed teacher for one period
	• or pay classroom aid to be in class when substitute is present
Slow processing (slow reading and writing) difficulty following directions	• keep instructions brief
	• give written instructions
	• be specific, 1,2,3

- use Post-it notes
- may need to remind him of homework

hates being rushed	• have another student remind him • reduce assignment • give more time to respond to questions • ask questions, let him think, come back to him
Poor concentration easily distracted	• check to see when it is a problem, meds may have worn off • check to see he has taken meds each day • give high interest work • use computer programs • use color to highlight important information • use books on tape • use touch on shoulder to pull back to task

Poor short-term memory
  forgets homework & books
  weak spelling skills
	• use flash cards and color to help
	learn spelling words
	• use spell checker
	• don't count off grade for spelling

Poor fine motor coordination poor handwriting	• accept poor handwriting • use computer • do not ask to write sentences as punishment
Doesn't complete homework	• modify homework assignment • find agency (CMHC) or relative who will pay for meds for evening homework • use weekly or daily report • keep extra set of books at home • have student check to see that homework assignments are written down • have phone numbers for students in class to confirm homework

Impulsive
  does things without anticipating
  consequences
	• make certain takes medicine
	• check to see that med dosage will provide all-day coverage
	• keep extra medicine at school

Verbal aggression says no but does as asked	• if possible ignore verbal comments • if he blows up, stay calm lower your voice • teach anger control techniques in Chapter 5 • ask if he can tell when he is about to blow up • find out what triggers blow ups • can you anticipate when problems will occur and send to guidance office • develop procedure for verbal blow ups, "If you blow up, I will ask you to go to the guidance office."

Most families are able to work successfully with the public schools. However, if your teenager's school experiences are extremely negative for a whole grading period or longer and you feel the school is unable or unwilling to meet your child's needs, it is time to take action: 1) Request a school meeting to discuss problems and *develop a new IEP* or revise the 504 plan. 2) If the school does not meet your teenager's needs as required by IDEA or Section 504, *contact* the director of special education, the local 504 coordinator, the superintendent, or school board member for advice. 3) Consider *mediation* to resolve your differences with the school system. 4) If you and the school cannot agree on your child's needs, or if you believe that the proposed program will not meet his needs, consider requesting a *due process hearing*. 5) If you want your child to remain in the public school but want to avoid a confrontation with the school, consider *other options*: hiring a tutor, hiring a psychologist to go to school and work with the teacher and/or your child in the classroom, or requesting a change in teachers. 6) *Seek placement* in an alternative public school or a private school, if possible, with the agreement of your local school system, so they will pay for your teenager's education.

CHAPTER TWELVE

AFTER HIGH SCHOOL . . . WHAT NEXT?

Many teenagers with ADD feel anxious about what they will do after high school graduation. Those who have had a terrible struggle in school may dread thinking about additional education, especially college or even classes at a technical school. Although most of them are aware that additional education will help them get a better paying job, they may doubt their ability to do the required school work.

❧

"At the end of Cassie's junior year in high school she started worrying, 'What will I do after high school? I'm too dumb to go to college. It's not possible. I don't know what I want to be or I don't know what I want to do.' We did a lot of talking about how everyone feels that way and it's okay to feel that way. As long as you have parents who are willing to support you in college, you might as well give that a try. You might as well figure out what you want to do and we'll help you get there.

"Cassie said that college wasn't a bad place to spend time while you were trying to figure out what you wanted to do with your life."

❧

"My son asked me if I ever worried about my grades when I was in high school. I replied that I did and asked if he worried about his grades. He does worry about his grades and getting into college although you would never know it by his actions."

❧

Obviously, one major advantage to additional schooling is the potential to earn a higher income. Just as important, your teenager may be able to select a more satisfying career than doing unskilled labor. Another advantage is that your teenager has more time to mature while in a somewhat protected school or college environment. At age 18, he may not be ready for the routine and monotony of a traditional 40–hour work week. By the time he reaches 21, however, he may be acting more like a typical 17– or 18–year-old. So between the ages of 18 and 21, he will become more mature and, perhaps, be ready to tackle technical school or college. Or he may make a more successful transition to the adult work world. But be patient. You may end up on a "six- or eight-year" college plan.

Educational Opportunities after High School

There are three general options for post high school training and education: *technical institutes*, two-year *community colleges*, and four-year *colleges and universities*. In some states, these three levels of higher education are closely interrelated. Students can earn an Associate of Applied Arts (AAS) degree jointly from a technical institute program and a two-year community college. Community colleges offer two types of two-year degrees: 1) degrees such as the AAS, which require no further training; and 2) degrees such as Associate of Arts (AA) or Associate of Science (AS) that can be used as a stepping stone toward a bachelor's degree at a four-year college or university.

Although college is not appropriate for every student with ADD, the majority of these teenagers would benefit from some specialized training after high school. You and your teenager should consider these three educational options and decide which one is most appropriate for your family.

Your teenager should not be afraid to consider college as an option if he has average intelligence or above; has adequate reading, writing, and math skills; adequate SAT/ACT scores; and is willing to attempt college-level work. Some students with ADD are extremely smart and have mastered academic skills in spite of not making good grades in high school. Some teenagers thrive in technical institutes or college and actually make better grades than they did in high school. They especially like the increased freedom college offers, flexibility in scheduling classes, fewer hours spent in class each day, plus being treated with greater respect by college faculty than by their high school teachers.

Many families are not aware that under Section 504, special supports and adaptations are available for students with ADD in all these programs. Some provisions of Section 504 are discussed in Chapters 10 and 11, as well as in this chapter.

Bear in mind that *timetables for starting and actually graduating from a technical institute or college may vary* among teenagers with ADD. Because they may be sick of 12 years of school, some students may prefer to take a year off and work first. Others may attend a technical institute or college for a year, work for awhile, and then return to school. Attending school on a co-op program—attending school while also getting credit for working in a related field—is also an option. Some start and go straight through to graduation, even though it may take six or eight years to graduate. However long it may take, remember that a couple extra years is not much time when compared with the rest of one's life.

What If Your Teenager Didn't Finish High School?

Teenagers may be surprised to learn that they can go to college or a technical institute even if they didn't graduate from high school. An impor-

tant first step will be to take a test that documents that he has an education that is the equivalent of a high school degree. Once he has passed a high school equivalency test he may be able to get a better job or apply to a technical institute or college.

Nationally, a high school equivalency test, the *GED (General Education Development)*, is available for students who didn't graduate from high school. The same GED test is administered in each state. Students must make a score of 225 to pass it. The GED test includes five sections: writing, social studies, science, literature and the arts, and mathematics. Students must obtain passing scores on each section, although the cut-off score may vary from state to state. In Georgia, students must score 35 on each section in order to pass, but in Florida a score of 40 is required. If a student passes some sections of the test, he is only required to retake the sections he failed. Accommodations, such as untimed tests or oral administration, may be made for students who have learning problems and are eligible for services under Section 504.

If your child is interested in getting a GED, there are a variety of ways to go. He can just sign up to take the test and see how he does. Or he can take a pre-test and then attend sessions at a community school, community technical institute, or community college to master areas of deficiency. As of 1995, a fee of $25 is charged for administering the whole test, or $5 per section. (If a student passes three of the five sections, he has to pay a total of $10 to retake the two sections he failed.) The GED may be administered daily, weekly, or less frequently. Check with your local vocational institute to determine the specific guidelines and fees in your state. Some states have incentive programs for completing a GED. When a student completes his GED in Georgia, for instance, he is given a voucher for $500 to use toward continuing his education.

Is Technical Training the Way to Go?

Because of the burgeoning employment opportunities in technical fields, the role of technical institutes is becoming increasingly important. Technical institutes provide training for a wide variety of careers in business and industry (See Table 12–1.) Students can obtain several levels of training, although the names of these levels may vary

Table 12-1

PROGRAMS OF STUDY AT GWINNETT TECHNICAL INSTITUTE

ASSOCIATE IN APPLIED TECHNOLOGY DEGREE (AAT)*

Accounting Technology
Automated Manufacturing Technology
Automotive Service Technology
Automotive Technology
Commercial Photography
Computer Programming Technology
Construction Management
Dental Laboratory Technology
Distribution and Materials Management
Interiors

Electronic Technology
Environmental Horticulture
Fashion Merchandising
Hotel, Restaurant, and Travel Management
Management and Supervisory Development
Marketing Management
Physical Therapist Assistant
Radiologic Technology
Secretarial Sciences
Telecommunications Technology

DIPLOMA AND ASSOCIATE IN APPLIED SCIENCE DEGREE (AAS)
JOINTLY AWARDED WITH COMMUNITY COLLEGE

Advanced Machine Tool Technology
Commercial Photography
Dental Assisting
Drafting
Electronics Technology
Environmental Horticulture
Fashion Merchandising
Hotel, Restaurant, and Travel Management
Information and Office technology
Interiors

Machine Tool Technology
Marketing Management
Medical Assisting
Microcomputer Specialist
Paramedic Technology
Physical Therapist Assistant
Radiologic Technology
Respiratory Therapy Technology
Surgical Technology
Telecommunications Technology

DIPLOMA PROGRAMS

Accounting
Air Conditioning Technology
Automated Manufacturing Technology
Automotive Technology
Carpentry
Cosmetology

Cosmetology Teacher Training
Dental Laboratory
Dental Laboratory Technology
Management & Supervision
Practical Nursing
Welding and Joining Technology

TECHNICAL CERTIFICATE PROGRAMS

Basic Emergency Medical Technology
General Office Assistant
Legal Office Assistant

Medical Transcription
Organizational Leadership
Warehouse Management

* Associate degree awarded by DeKalb College in conjunction with Gwinnett Tech.

from state to state. For example, *a certificate, a diploma, or associate degree* may be awarded. Associate degrees that may be awarded by a technical institute include an associate of applied technology (AAT), or an associate of applied sciences (AAS) degree. These training programs certify that graduates have specialized skills in any one of several areas: business sciences, health sciences, industrial technologies, and arts and sciences.

Most diploma programs may be completed in a year (four quarters) to a year and a half (six quarters). Completing classes for a degree may require six to eight quarters. The AAT or AAS degree requires basic academic classes such as English composition, math, algebra, and psychology, in addition to basic technical classes. Many four-year colleges and universities accept credits from the associate degree programs toward their own graduation requirements.

Admission requirements vary, but may include: a high school diploma or equivalent (GED), minimum age of 16 (some programs such as emergency medical technician may require 18), and scores from a state placement exam. For students seeking a degree rather than a diploma or certificate, SAT or ACT scores may also be required. Entry into some programs of study may be open at the beginning of each quarter. Other programs may have limited admission only during the Fall quarter.

Parents will probably need to help their teenager plan ahead, identify key deadlines, submit an application, and link them with staff at school who can help them make choices about classes and a program of study. If your teenager is interested, *you may have to take the initiative to get the ball rolling*. You can request a catalog which explains admission requirements and programs offered. You may even have to help him fill out the application and mail it in. Special supports provided under Section 504 are usually described under sections related to student services.

Many teenagers with ADD do well in technical institutes for several reasons. First, they are taking courses they really want to take. Second, most classes involve more action and hands-on learning and less reading and written paper work than high school classes. Third, the time required for completion of a certificate or diploma is shorter than for a four-year college degree. For example, certificate programs may only take two or three quarters; a di-

ploma, a year; and an associate degree, two years. Some students may have taken some vocational classes in high school, but this is not necessary for admission to a technical institute.

Two other services that are also available through most technical institutes and colleges are financial aid, such as low interest loans and scholarships, plus job placement services.

Are Low Grades an Obstacle to Admission?

Many teenagers with ADD do not have very high grades when they graduate from high school. Fortunately, most colleges consider both grade point averages and scores on the SAT (Scholastic Assessment Test) or ACT (American College Testing). Although making good scores on the SAT or ACT is important, a student who makes low scores on these tests should not be discouraged. They can still be accepted into certain colleges. Admissions criteria vary from school to school.

Admission Criteria. Students who make low scores on the SAT or ACT tests have other options that may help them get into college. First, students who have documented learning disabilities or ADD which adversely affects their ability to learn may be given *extra time on the SAT and ACT*. Second, students may be *admitted on the basis of high school grades alone*, assuming their grades are pretty good, but test scores are low. Finally, if both the SAT/ACT and grades are low, the student may be *admitted on conditional status*.

Untimed SAT or ACT. Students with ADD are encouraged to take the timed, regularly administered SAT or ACT first, perhaps in the Spring of their junior year or Fall of their senior year. Then if needed, untimed testing may be scheduled. If the teenager does well on the regularly administered SAT/ACT, he may not even need to take an untimed version. The difference between the two scores may give a better indication of the student's academic potential when adaptations are made for the learning problem. So it should be helpful for the college to compare scores for both the timed and untimed tests. When you request that scores for untimed SAT or ACT tests be sent to colleges your teenager is considering attending, the term

"Nonstandard administration" will appear on the SAT report and "Special" on the ACT.

❧

"According to SAT data, the average student who re-takes the test shows an increase of 15 to 20 points on each of the verbal and math sections. My son who has ADD/I/WO with slow cognitive processing took the SAT untimed and scored an increase of 270 total points over the timed testing session."

❧

The SAT. Two plans are available for administering the SAT to students with disabilities: *Plan A (Special Accommodations)* and *Plan B (Extended Time Only-90 extra minutes)*. Talk with the school guidance counselor to determine if your child should apply for Plan A or Plan B. Students with ADD that severely affects their academic performance, especially if they read or write slowly, should probably select untimed testing under Plan A. Under these Special Accommodations, the untimed SAT is administered at the teenager's home school by a local guidance counselor at a time convenient for both of them. The student may be tested alone or with several other students. A student may request a range of special accommodations such as an untimed test, a taped SAT, or, if needed, a reader.

Under Plan B *(Extended Time Only)*, the student applies directly to the College Board for extended time. Plan B is only scheduled by SAT twice annually, in November and May. The teenager will take the SAT at a designated test center and is given 90 minutes extra to complete the test. Students who receive extended time will be tested in a room separate from other students taking the regular SAT. They can spend the extra 90 minutes on any portion of the SAT they wish. Applications must be submitted at least six weeks prior to the test date

To sign up for extra time on the SAT, a student may request assistance from his high school guidance counselor or staff at a technical school or college. Parents may also submit an application directly. The College Board, which administers the SAT, requires documentation that a learning problem exists from *two specialists*, such as a physician, school psychologist, learning disabilities specialist, or child study team. The documentation must pro-

vide 1) a description of the disability (ADD), 2) the name and results of tests that were administered, and 3) the accommodations that the student is currently receiving in his regular classes. The evaluation cannot be more than three years old.

The documentation submitted to SAT should also *state the accommodation needed* (untimed testing). It is important to state that these adaptations are currently being provided for the student in regular or special education classes. According to SAT guidelines, the student *must currently be receiving the same accommodations* for tests in school that he is requesting for the SAT. All students are now allowed to use a calculator on the mathematics portion of the SAT, so that accommodation does not need to be requested.

If adaptations have never been provided at school, it will be more difficult to get SAT accommodations. Perhaps you can work with school officials to establish eligibility and provide needed adaptations at school as quickly as possible. Then you can send a statement to SAT that the teenager is receiving (even though recently determined) or will begin receiving, as of a certain date, extended time on tests.

The College Board is considering revisions to the SAT for 1995–96 that may change the required eligibility criteria, plus address the growing number of students requesting special accommodation.

The ACT. A student with ADD can apply for ACT Special Testing accommodations, which may include extended time and use of a calculator. Each student is responsible for finding someone at his school or a local college or technical school, perhaps a guidance counselor, who will agree to be his supervisor and administer the test. Then the supervisor must submit a request for special testing to ACT approximately four to six weeks before the test. The test can be given at a time that is mutually convenient for the student and supervisor. Call the ACT office and request an application to determine who qualifies to be a supervisor for testing.

Documentation for special testing is simpler for the ACT. The ACT application must include: 1) the proposed testing date, 2) the name of the disability, 3) a brief statement of when the disability was originally diagnosed, 4) name of tests and results, and 5) who gave them. A *copy of an IEP*, completed within the last three years, or *letter* from a school official showing the current use of accommodations, such as extended times or use of a calculator for tests, is acceptable documentation.

Be certain to look over the test booklets for both the ACT and SAT to see if you should make suggestions to your teenager. For example, it's okay to guess on the ACT since a student's score is not penalized for incorrect responses. However, wrong answers are penalized on the SAT. Computer programs and books are available for your teenager to work on as a practice exam for both the SAT and ACT.

Conditional Admissions. Some community colleges and smaller four-year colleges may accept students with SAT scores as low as 350 (out of a possible 800) on either the Math or Verbal sections and a combined score of 700 (out of 1600). Basically, this is a conditional acceptance. That is, the student is accepted into college but first must take remedial courses in those areas where he is deficient. If he is required to take only one remedial class such as algebra, then he may also take another regular college course. Some colleges and universities have lower SAT admission scores for students who have documented learning disabilities. Prior to their enrollment, students may have to take a placement exam covering basic math and English concepts. Students who score well on placement exams may not have to take remedial classes.

Remedial Classes. Students with low scores may be placed in remedial classes, or *developmental studies,* for no credit during the first quarter. Remedial classes are typically required for two or three basic academic areas—for example, English composition and algebra. In addition, students may be required to take a reading or basic study skills course.

Taking a developmental studies course can be advantageous for students with ADD because it gives them an opportunity to adjust to college life while taking non-credit courses. The student continues taking the class until skill mastery is achieved. At the end of the quarter, if mastery is not achieved, the grade report indicates "course in progress." If skills are mastered, a "satisfactory" (S) grade is given and the student moves into the next remedial class or regular college classes. Students may take the same remedial class for three or four quarters until they master the course content. If a student can't master the content in that time, the college may place him on probation and ask him to stay out of school for a year.

Making Up High School Deficiencies. Students who do not take all the necessary college preparation classes in high school can still go to college. The student may be given a conditional admission and allowed to make up any deficiencies during his first year in school. For example, if he did not take a foreign language, he might take one college-level course to make up for the deficiency. Developmental studies classes in math may help a student who did not take all the proper algebra courses. If your child is not required to make up difficult deficiencies during his first year at school, he may want to put it off as long as possible to give himself time to adjust to school and develop confidence that he can handle college-level work.

Making the Grade

Most colleges require students to maintain a certain cumulative grade point average (GPA) to stay in school, participate in extracurricular activities such as sports or fraternities, and also to graduate. If the GPA drops too low, the student is given an academic warning. If grades are low for two consecutive quarters or semesters—below a C average—he may be placed on probation and ultimately asked to leave school for a quarter or longer. Since no grades are given for developmental studies classes, the cumulative GPA is not brought down before the teenager has a chance to adjust and succeed in a college environment.

How the GPA is figured may vary from college to college. On a four-point system, the GPA is calculated by first multiplying the *credit hours* for each course by the *grade points* earned. Next divide the total *grade points* by the number of *credit hours,* which gives the GPA. The grade points for letter grades are usually: A - 4; B - 3; C - 2, D - 1; F - 0. For example, a student who was taking 11 hours of classes and received a B and a C in the 5 hour courses and a D in a one hour course would have a 2.36 GPA (5x3 + 5x2 + 1x1 = 26; 26÷11 = 2.36). To be "in good academic standing," students must usually maintain a 2.0 (C) average.

Seek Help from Student Services. Most colleges and universities have a student services department that offers *counseling* and other supportive services such as *tutoring, class and teacher advisement, and early registration.* Each college must have a Section 504 coordinator, who may also be located in the student services department. Typically there will be one person who is the major contact person and advisor for each student with a learning disability. This person can familiarize you and your teenager with various procedures at the college. Encourage your teenager to work closely with his advisor in the student services office.

Assuming you have your teenager's permission, you should feel free to call the advisor and ask questions occasionally as needed. Since most teenagers in college are 18 and legally adults, however, faculty members cannot disclose information about their academic performance without their permission. Grades are mailed to the student, not the parents.

Educational Expenses

Expenses will vary depending upon where the student attends school. Classes at a technical institute should be the cheapest. One technical institute estimated that the total cost of tuition, books, and tools for a four-quarter program would be approximately $1,500. Expenses are somewhat higher at a community college. Since the student generally lives at home, however, he does not incur any extra expenses for housing or food.

Expenses at public universities are significantly less than those at private universities. Tuition and fees at a moderately priced public college may be $500 or $600 per quarter. If you live on campus, dormitory rent, food, books, dates, and general living expenses may total another $1,000 to $1,500 for the quarter (more if the school is on a semester plan). So you may anticipate costs of $4,500 to $6,000 for a school year (three quarters) or $18,000 to $24,000 for four years. Out-of-state students generally have to pay extra, possibly $1,500 a year.

Seek Financial Aid. Your child may be eligible for low interest loans, grants, or scholarships. Grants and scholarships do not have to be repaid. If your child's grades are not good enough to get a scholarship his first year in college, he may consider applying the next year if his grades improve. Loans are available from a variety of sources and most must be repaid after graduation. Low interest loans are available to most students when starting college and may be continued as long as they are maintaining passing grades.

To find out what financial aid your child may qualify for, contact the director of financial aid at your child's college. The director should know if special scholarships or other sources of financial aid are available for students with disabilities. The high school guidance counselor may also know about sources of financial aid, particularly at state and local colleges. You can also consult a book such as *College Costs and Financial Aid Handbook*, published by the College Board (the company that developed the SAT). This book lists grants, scholarships, and loans available, includes a worksheet to determine financial need, and gives step-by-step directions on how to apply.

Community College vs. a Four-Year College

The key elements that help students with ADD achieve academic success after high school are: *classroom adaptations, staff guidance in course and faculty selection, and monitoring and support* during the first year in college. These elements can be found in many technical institutes, community colleges, and larger four-year universities. Some universities have highly specialized and intensive programs for students with documented learning problems. You and your teenager will need to do your homework and decide which program meets his needs.

Perhaps the biggest issue to consider in deciding between a community college and four-year college is whether your teenager is ready to live away from home. Students who attend a nearby community college often live at home, while those who attend four-year colleges often move away and live on campus. There are advantages to both options and your family must decide which option is best for your teenager.

Living at home may be a good choice for students: 1) who need and are willing to accept additional academic supports from their family, 2) who have limited financial resources, or 3) whose families are reluctant to pay for housing expenses when they are not certain that their teenager can cope successfully with the demands of college classes. Some parents may feel more comfortable with the teenager living at home for the first few quarters until he demonstrates he can handle college class work. Sometimes the curriculum at a community college may be geared to meet the needs of students with weaker academic backgrounds. In addition, faculty at community colleges may teach smaller classes and offer more individualized attention.

You may want to encourage your teenager to go away to college if you feel he can handle college classes, especially with Section 504 supports in place. There are some advantages to letting students with ADD begin taking on the responsibilities of living on their own in a somewhat sheltered college environment. In addition to learning academics, college students develop important life skills, such as getting their own meals, managing money, keeping their room clean (maybe, maybe not), and paying bills on time. Forgive me for saying this, but conflict in the family may also be reduced when the teenager is no longer living at home. Parents don't have to deal with the little things that drive them to distraction: leaving clothes all over the floor, coming in late, being late for meals, not completing chores, and arguing over school work. Typical problems these teenagers face living on campus plus suggestions for handling them are discussed later in the chapter.

Selecting a College

When selecting a college, students with ADD should consider many of the same factors that other students do: geographical location, cost, co-ed vs. single sex, and college majors offered. Other critical considerations for students with ADD include the college's responsiveness to students with special needs such as ADD, and the level of support it provides. Ideally, during the junior year of high school, you and your teenager will identify a few schools or colleges, visit their campuses, and talk with student services staff. Granted, it is sometimes difficult to do things in an ideal sequence with teenagers with ADD. So if you start later, during the senior year or after high school graduation, don't panic. It is never too late.

Because of the US DOE memo discussed in Chapter 11, colleges are trying harder to meet the needs of young people with learning problems and ADD. *Some colleges specialize in educating young people with learning disabilities.* These colleges offer special assistance and adaptations such as untimed tests, use of calculators, computer lab, tutoring, and individual student monitoring. The University of Georgia and West Virginia Wesleyan, for example, have full-fledged programs for students with learning disabilities. Annual projected cost for a freshman at WVW is approximately $20,000, with costs decreasing each year as less supervision is needed. Landmark College in Vermont is also well known because it exclusively serves students with dyslexia and learning disabilities ($26,500 annually). If the Landmark program interests you, you may want to follow up on their assertion that since they serve diagnosed dyslexic students, tuition and fees may be deductible as a medical expense for federal income tax purposes. Bear in mind that Landmark is a two-year college, so you would need to make sure that credits earned there would be accepted by the four-year college your child would attend afterwards.

Some colleges, even those that don't specialize in serving LD students, let students with learning disabilities take extra time for completing tests or let them take smaller class loads and still be considered full-time students. Special academic advisors may be available to advise them and consult with their professors. Other colleges provide limited supports as required by Section 504, but do not offer a full range of services. Several guides, including *Peterson's Guide to Colleges with Programs for Learning-Disabled Students,* list all universities/colleges, the services they provide for students with learning problems, expenses, housing, majors, graduation requirements, and a profile of their students. These guides are available at most local libraries.

Generally speaking, if your teenager does not select a college with a specialized program for students with learning disabilities, *a smaller college may be a wise choice,* at least for the first two years. Typically, classes are smaller and faculty may be more willing to provide support to students with ADD. Some smaller colleges, such as Reinhardt College in Georgia, have developed more intensive programs to closely monitor students with learning problems. Parents pay double the regular tuition to receive this intensive service. West Georgia College is an example of a small public college (7,000 students) that has provided excellent supports to students with learning disabilities even though they do not have a comprehensive program. One family found the College of Charleston (South Carolina) responsive to working with students with

ADD. Administrators were willing to make classroom adaptations, and were flexible in allowing waivers and course substitutions in students' areas of disability.

Once your teenager has an idea of what he wants to major in (or even if he doesn't), you can help him start searching for a suitable college program. Sometimes talking with people who currently work in his field of interest can help him identify colleges that offer a suitable program. Some teenagers may start college and have no idea what their major will be. Usually, this is not a problem.

✺

"Our son was interested in a major in printing management because he wanted to work in the paperboard packaging industry. We found out that Georgia Southern University and Clemson (SC) offer printing management degrees. Our son earned his degree from Georgia Southern and is working for Rock-Tenn Company."

✺

Visit the School. You may want to review Peterson's guide and decide which colleges look interesting in your own home state. Then contact a few and ask what services they offer for students with learning disabilities including ADD. If possible, visit the colleges and meet with the Section 504 coordinator or staff in the student services office. Ask what services and adaptations can be provided for your teenager.

Quarter vs. Semester System. At one time, schools that operated on a quarter system may have been a slightly better choice for students with ADD, since classes typically met more frequently (daily), for shorter periods of time (one hour), and ended sooner (ten weeks). Final exams were completed before Christmas and students could relax and enjoy the holidays without worrying about returning to finals. Under a semester system, classes met two or three times a week for one hour and the semester lasted fourteen weeks, ending in mid-January. However, some colleges are modifying their systems so that a quarter and semester system are more similar. One advantage the semester system offers is the novelty of not having to go to the same class, five days a week. Find out what

class schedules are available at the colleges of your choice.

✺

"Recently, my son's college shifted to a modified quarter system. I guess faculty prefer to have more than the allotted 50-minute class period for teaching. One of his major classes (Spanish) meets for one and a half hours three days a week and the other (Computer programming) meets two hours twice a week.

Of course, the first week after the change, he forgot to go to his computer class. He took awhile to get used to the schedule change and having to attend classes only three days a week."

✺

Cooperative Education (Co-op) Programs. Some colleges offer a combination of degree-related work experience interspersed with college classes. Co-op programs and internships offer several advantages for students with ADD. Students make business contacts with potential employers. Learning is more meaningful because it is done in a real world setting, not just an abstract educational setting. Some students with ADD need variety and tire of the monotony of classes, quarter after quarter. Your teenager can apply for a co-op program through his college, which will help him find an employer. Or you may know a business that would be a good match for his career interests and arrange the placement yourself.

The co-op program may be arranged several different ways: a student may work alternating quarters, six-month rotations, or work for a year and then return to school the following year. There are also parallel programs in which the student takes classes and works at the same time. This combination may be difficult for some students with ADD to juggle. Students may opt to get academic credit for their co-op work by signing up for individual study with faculty in their major field. In that case, they would have to pay tuition. Some students don't pursue a co-op program until their junior or senior years when they have taken more courses in their major field and have more skills to offer a potential co-op employer.

Scheduling Classes

Schedule a Lighter Class Load. When scheduling classes the first year, you may want to advise your teenager to *take a lighter load*. Usually, 12 credit hours is considered a full academic load. That may mean two five-hour courses and two hours of P.E. on a quarter system or four three-hour courses on a semester system. At some colleges, students with learning disabilities may be considered full-time students with fewer hours, perhaps eight.

For students who struggled in high school, taking a lighter academic load will reduce stress plus increase the likelihood of success and help build self-esteem. (Being considered a full-time student may be important if your teenager's car insurance rates are lower as a full-time student and if you want to continue to cover him under your health insurance policy.) Although your teenager may take longer to graduate, you are buying time for him to mature, develop better study habits, and take increasing responsibility for his school performance and career selection.

Balance Degree of Class Difficulty. Your child may need to balance his academic load with difficult and easier courses, especially during his first year in college. He should schedule at least one class he enjoys, plus consider taking a P.E. class. If possible, he should *avoid taking several demanding academic courses such as English 101 and college algebra during the same quarter.* Your child should be aware that some faculty may push him to follow a standard class schedule so as to keep him on track for graduation in four years. This might require him to take English 101 and algebra the same quarter. You and your child should hold firm in asking for a schedule that is best suited to his needs. It may help to explain that graduating is more important than the length of time required.

⧜

"My son took a computer class, developmental studies algebra, and a P.E. class his first quarter in college. I knew he loved computers so it only made sense to get him into those classes as soon as possible. My son lacked confidence in his ability to make it in college. He needed to have a successful first quarter under his belt to get hooked on believing he could actually pass college classes and eventually graduate."

⧜

Schedule Personal Growth or Career Planning Courses. You and your teenager may want to review a list of potential courses before he meets with his advisor to schedule classes. A brief description of the content of each class is offered in the college catalog. He may want to consider taking career studies or psychology courses designed to introduce career options, give students personal insight into their own behavior, or teach study skills. These courses are excellent because they have valuable practical application to everyday life. Plus, the class may be less demanding academically and may be paired with more demanding academic courses such as college algebra.

To Work or Not to Work. Something else to consider in helping your teenager schedule his time is whether or not he should also have a part-time job. Some students with ADD can manage jobs in addition to attending school. Often, teenagers who were formerly hyperactive have enough extra energy to also juggle a job. You may, however, want to encourage your child to wait until his second or third year in college until he is certain he can master the academics.

Supports under Section 504

Section 504 of the Rehabilitation Act requires that all technical institutes and colleges receiving any federal funds must provide special supports for students with learning problems. Schools that are recipients of federal funds usually have a statement in the front of their school catalog indicating that they are in compliance with Section 504 or other appropriate federal laws. If ADD adversely affects a student's ability to learn, these institutions must make *adaptations* in his environment similar to those listed in Chapter 10, Table 10–2.

Applying for Section 504 Supports

Ideally, your teenager should contact the college early, six months to a year prior to entry, to apply for admissions, and, once accepted, to request special supports and adaptations under Section 504. If your teenager hasn't planned ahead, this process can be completed at some colleges within

Table 12–2

**DOCTOR'S LETTER TO COLLEGE
DOCUMENTING AND REQUESTING ADAPTATIONS**

Richard Jones, Ph.D.
College/University
Director, Student Support Services
City, State

Dear Dr. Jones:

Tom Smith has been under my care since his ADD was diagnosed in 1987. Although ADD was not diagnosed until sixth grade, academic difficulties were reported as early as first grade. ADD has adversely affected his ability to learn throughout his academic career. Although he is extremely bright, he has consistently been an underachiever in school. In spite of low grades, however, he has several academic strengths, including reading skills above grade level.

He participated in classes for gifted children in public schools based upon his scores on the WISC in 1984 (full scale IQ of 141). When he was retested in May 1987, his full scale IQ score was 124. Results of the evaluation are included in the enclosed psychological evaluation report.

In addition to being intellectually gifted and having ADD, Tom has learning disabilities which prevent him from achieving academically at a level commensurate with his intellectual ability. The discrepancy between his intellectual ability, academic achievement, and test performance reflects the severity of his learning disabilities. Tom also has a sleep disturbance, which means that he frequently has trouble falling asleep and waking up, and may still be tired when he wakes up.

In addition to the typical problems with inattention, our psychologist identified two major deficits during the evaluation: 1) slow cognitive processing and 2) poor short-term memory. Practical implications of these deficits and services needed to ameliorate them are described below.

1) Slow Cognitive Processing: Tom reads and writes very slowly. He has difficulty organizing his thoughts when writing. Consequently, time required for homework, composition of themes, and test taking will be almost twice that required for the average student. Listening to lectures and simultaneously taking notes will also be difficult.

Services Required: Allow extended time for writing English compostions and taking tests. Multiple choice rather than essay tests are preferable, since they do not require as much writing. Tailoring homework assignments would be beneficial, especially if homework assignments become unduly burdensome because of the processing deficit. Allow him to record lecture classes, provide him with a note-taker.

2) Poor Short-Term Memory: Tom has a serious problem memorizing and retaining information. This problem is especially apparent in math calculation, classes requiring memorization of facts (history), and foreign languages. Although bright, he processes basic math facts very slowly.

Services Required: Tom will need to use a calculator in math and related classes. For foreign languages, special tutoring and testing procedures may be needed. Written rather than verbally presented tests may be required. If these adaptations are not effective, he may need to seek a waiver of foreign language requirements. He will also benefit from having a written course syllabus for every class, clearly listing assignments, tests dates, and due dates for special reports or projects.

As a result of his inattention, he may have difficulty paying attention in class and remembering assignments. Remembering to take his medication each day may also present problems.

It will be important for his instructors to be notified of these issues and make appropriate classroom adaptations. With these supports, Tom should have a successful college experience. Please advise us if you need additional information.

Sincerely,
Pamela Long, M.D.

TABLE 12–3

STUDENT DISABILITY REPORT
Report date: October 19, 1994
Joanna Jordan, Coordinator
_____ **College**

Student's Name: _____   **SS#:** _____

Major: _____   **Minor:** _____   **Advisor:** _____

Kind of Disability: Attention Deficit Disorder, Learning Disability

General Description of Student's Disability:

Tom is easily sidetracked. His processing of the written word, both in reading and writing, takes longer than usual.

How the Disability Affects Student in Class:

1. He takes a long time to read a test, write answers, and proof what he has written.
2. He has a hard time keeping his attention on the class content.
3. He has problems with organization and self-starting.
4. He takes a very long time to organize thoughts and get them on paper.
5. He is unable to calculate basic math quickly, despite high intelligence.
6. He has test anxiety as a major consequence of contending with ADD and LD during his school years.

Strengths and Additional Resources:

1. He will have his textbooks on tape.
2. Electronics and computer science are strengths.
3. He has a personal computer for word processing.
4. The untimed SAT was 270 points higher than the timed SAT.

Classroom Accommodations That Can Aid the Student in Reaching Standards and Requirements of His Courses:

1. Tom should have extended time on all tests.
2. He should have extended time for all in-class compositions.
3. He should have extra time on the Regents' Test.
4. He should have the use of a calculator on math tests.
5. Special test situations can be arranged with Mrs. Frances Martin, Office of Testing and Developmental Studies, ext. 555.

If you have questions or wish further information, please call Joanna Jordan, Student Development Center, ext. 554.

---

three to six months. You will need to provide documentation of the adverse effects of ADD on his ability to learn.

Requirements for documentation vary from state to state. Ask faculty in the student services office what information is required. You will probably need a _letter from a physician_ stating that your teenager has ADD that adversely affects his learning. The letter should also list specific learning problems and desired adaptations. The letter should be sent to your contact person in the student services office. Your teenager will likely also need a _psychological evaluation_, including 1) an intelligence test such as the WISC, and 2) an academic assessment such as the Woodcock Johnson. Some universities conduct their own evaluations and will not accept evaluations from other sources. A sample letter from a physician documenting ADD, learning problems, and needed adaptations is shown in Table 12–2.

Staff in student services will develop a letter stating your teenager's learning problems and needed adaptations. Your teenager will be responsible for taking this letter to his professors at the beginning of each quarter. (Sample letter–Table 12–3)

You and your teenager should not be embarrassed to ask for support under Section 504. Faculty can discreetly provide assistance so that no one realizes your child is receiving adaptations. He will participate in regular college classes with all other students. He will not be placed in self-contained special education classes.

Section 504: Aids and Adaptations

Institutions vary in the sophistication and intensity of services and adaptations offered. Any of the adaptations listed below are pretty basic, however, and should be available if your child qualifies for services under Section 504.

Request Extended Test Time/Use of Calculator. If your child needed these adaptations in high school, there's a good chance he may also need them in college. Talk with your teenager and ask him what supports he thinks he may need. If he doesn't want any adaptations, he doesn't have to give the letters from student services to any of his professors. But if he realizes three weeks into a class that he is in trouble, he can turn them in then.

※

"My son has short-term memory problems, can't memorize his multiplication tables, and reads and writes slowly. The college agreed to give extended time for tests, use of a calculator, and were flexible in requirements for English 101 regarding compositions that must be written in class. He had problems organizing his thoughts and getting them down on paper. The professor worked with him and provided him a written outline for preparing his themes. By the final exam, he was complying with the same requirements for all other students. The professor was flexible and

supportive. This enabled him to overcome his deficits in this area."

※

Use a Laptop Computer for Composition. Some colleges require that the majority of themes for English 101 be written in class. This ensures that the composition is actually written by the student and not someone else. If a student has ADD and slow cognitive processing, he will have a hard time finishing a composition in a one-hour class period. Having a laptop computer would be an excellent resource for students with this problem. The only worry for parents who actually invest in a laptop is that these students are sometimes forgetful and may lose it. If you do buy one, alert the professor that the computer may be accidently left behind.

※

"We tried to check out a laptop computer to use for English composition but there was only one available for students to check out in the whole college. Technically, the college should have provided a laptop. However, they have been so good to our son that we hated to 'rock the boat' and alienate those who have been so supportive."

※

Use Technology. Take advantage of the technology available today. Obviously, having a computer to use in his dorm room would be wonderful. Some software programs include access to encyclopedias. This could be a real asset to a student who occasionally forgets or puts off going to the library to research a report. If your teenager will accept help from you, he could send English themes to you for editing via modem or fax. Your child could fax difficult assignments to you at work, to be discussed later that night. Many school bookstores have fax machines that students can use at a nominal cost. The big question is how much extra academic help your child will accept. The advantage here is that high tech equipment is novel and exciting, so teenagers may be more likely to use it.

Seek Computer-Aided Instruction. As discussed in Chapter 10, students with ADD may do better in classes in which lessons and exercises can be completed on a computer.

▨

"Students in Spanish classes have access to computer instruction. Participation in foreign language computer lab is a mandatory part of the class."

▨

Ask for a Notetaker. Students may request a notetaker for them. Non carbon replica paper can be used so that the student immediately has access to a copy of the class notes each day (Chapter 10). Colleges will usually make arrangements for a notetaker for the student. Often, the notetaker won't even know your teenager's identity. Some professors may be willing to give the student a copy of their class notes.

Ask for Tutoring. Most colleges and universities offer free tutoring. Your teenager can ask his professor or the counselor for details about obtaining assistance. Encourage him to take as much responsibility for getting help as possible. Remember, however, that even if he is willing to accept this responsibility, he may continually forget to ask for help. Sometimes teenagers with ADD have trouble starting new things on their own. You may need to make the initial call to find out details about tutoring and then give your child the phone number to make a follow-up call to schedule an appointment. You may have to remind him to follow through.

Participate in Early Registration/Class and Professor Selection. Students who qualify for 504 supports are often eligible for early registration, which gives them first choice of class times and professors. If your child has a sleep disturbance or trouble getting organized in the morning, being able to choose classes with a later starting time can be a real boon. He can ask his advisor to help select professors who work well with and are supportive of students with learning disabilities. If faculty members are unknown, or if the college is too small to provide this service, either you or your teenager could call the chairman of a department and ask which faculty members work best with learning disabled students.

▨

"Our son has some sleep disturbance problems. He made certain none of his classes started before 11:00 his first quarter at school."

▨

Make Schedule Adjustments. If your teenager discovers a scheduling problem, his advisor may, with permission from the professor, "force" him into a class that is full and closed to other students. This may be helpful if your teenager forgets to go to early registration or has to drop and add a class at the beginning of a quarter and the class he wants is already "filled."

Drop and Add. Most colleges have a cut-off date after which a student may no longer "drop" a class without receiving an F. It is important to be aware of this date, especially if your child has enrolled in a difficult class. Most of the time, your child should know if he is in danger of failing a class. If he tells you he needs to drop a class, you should ask when the cut-off date is. If you have a college catalog, you can look the date up for yourself. And of course, remind him to complete the proper paperwork—a drop/add form signed by the instructor and taken to the registrar's office.

If the professor is willing, exceptions may be made for students who have learning problems. They may be permitted to withdraw after the cut-off date without having their grade point average penalized with an F. You shouldn't count on this option as a routine way of dropping a class, but it could be used occasionally in unusual circumstances. Your child should talk with his advisor in the student services office whenever he is considering this option.

It may be advantageous at times to allow your teenager to drop a course he is failing. Receiving an F significantly lowers a student's grade point average. As a result, a student with ADD may find that he is unable to graduate because his grade point average is too low. The student may need to take unnecessary courses with the added pressure of having to make an A or B to pull up his average.

Consider Requesting a Waiver. Some colleges will allow a teenager with serious learning problems to apply for a waiver and exempt a subject related to their learning deficit. For example, a waiver for foreign languages or math is allowed at some colleges. The decision is typically made on a case-by-case basis after considering a student's specific learning problems and his major. Obviously, it would be difficult to exempt math if you were planning to be an engineer. Obtaining a waiver for a student with ADD is still a relatively new procedure, so it may not be easy. But if that is what your teenager needs, go for it—be tenacious!

Potential Pitfalls

The symptoms of ADD continue to affect many teenagers with ADD in college and their chosen career. The same characteristics of ADD that made high school difficult may continue to pose problems in college: *difficulty concentrating, forgetting assignments, difficulty completing written schoolwork, difficulty being organized, poor self-control, mood swings, getting angry quickly, and poor frustration tolerance.* As a parent, you need to be knowledgeable and anticipate the challenges ADD will bring in these areas.

Many teenagers with ADD recognize their strengths and "challenge areas." For example, they probably know that they are forgetful and are distracted easily. It is important to show respect for this awareness and involve your child in the problem-solving process. As discussed in Chapter 10, you might say something like: "Sometimes you have difficulty remembering things. Would you like me to remind you when your psychology report is due, or what the deadline is for paying your parking ticket?"

If your teenager made passing grades in high school, you may let him tackle the first quarter or semester on his own before you rush in to help him. Talk with him to see how much help he needs and is willing to accept. Perhaps you may help him make arrangements for classroom adaptations and special supports. Don't be surprised if your teenager doesn't want any help. He may be hesitant or embarrassed to ask for assistance because he doesn't want to be different from other students. Sometimes this reluctance or refusal to ask for help is difficult for parents to accept. Understandably, you may become very frustrated or angry. You might try reasoning with your teenager and then wait for him to seek you out. Be aware that he may be more likely to ask if he knows he is in control and the final decision to request help is his. If he reaches a point where he is in danger of

failing a class, he will probably agree to accept assistance.

"When my son went away to college, I told him I would help him as much or as little as he wanted. He was an adult now and I would trust his judgment. We made arrangements for adaptations such as untimed testing, use of calculator, and teacher and class selection assistance. Then as the quarter progressed, I asked low-key questions and kept an eye on things. 'How did you do on your first test?' As long as he was passing, I didn't have much to say. When he started struggling in college algebra, I asked him if he thought he needed help from a tutor. At first he said no, but eventually he agreed. When he was ready, I made the first call to the tutor, found out the details, called my son, and gave him the number. He followed up and made the appointment. Sometimes, my son is shy about taking the first step. I didn't push him. The decision was his but I helped him follow up on the details."

Being Disorganized

Your teenager's ability to get organized and stay on top of his schoolwork may need monitoring on a limited basis, especially during his freshman year. Try to spot problems early so appropriate help can be provided. Although it will be more difficult for you to provide support or prompt your teenager about due dates on assignments, it can be done even if he is living away at school.

Teach Self-Monitoring. As always, allow your teenager to monitor his own progress, unless he requests your assistance. This is especially important if he is passing his courses. You may need to remind him of events occasionally. Some of the following suggestions may be helpful to him.

Keep 'A Month at a Glance' Calendar. You may suggest that your teenager write all his major assignments and test dates on his monthly calendar. This calendar will enable him to see assignments and tests plus due dates at a glance during the next 30 days. With a weekly calendar, he may fail to see a test that is scheduled on Monday of next week until too little time is left for studying. A small calendar that he can keep in his book bag or notebook may be easiest to manage. If needed, you may also make note of key dates and remind your teenager. As discussed later in this chapter, you could ask your teenager for a copy of the class syllabus—an outline of class assignments, tests, reports, and projects, and their due dates.

Use Time Management. The information in Chapter 5 regarding time management may be helpful to college students. You may help your child learn to fill out his month-at-a-glance calendar, especially in planning backwards from an assignment due date to allow enough time to complete a report or project.

Seek Help from the College. Universities with comprehensive programs for students with learning disabilities monitor each student's progress closely. Although colleges vary, some smaller institutions offer similar help. Students may schedule regular meetings with their advisor in student services to review their weekly calendar, to assess progress and identify problem areas, to monitor homework assignments, to help schedule time for studying, or developing timelines for completion of major class projects. Some colleges may arrange for a student volunteer to call or meet with a student with learning problems at least once a week to discuss their school progress.

Consider a Coach. If your teenager is struggling academically in college or feels he needs help, you might hire a coach to assist with either academics or activities of everyday living, as described in Chapters 4 and 8. Having a coach may be preferable to having a more traditional tutor. Although tutoring in specific subjects is often free, it is usually offered at set times and set locations. Sometimes, your teenager may have trouble getting organized to go to the location where tutoring is offered. He may be embarrassed and find ex-cuses not to go. So even though tutoring may be free, he may not take advantage of this service for a variety of reasons.

An academic coach can help your teenager organize assignments, monitor completion of homework, provide some tutoring or editing, and offer encouragement and moral support. If your child is willing to work with a coach, talk with someone in the student services department, the college tutoring service, or the psychology or social work departments to see if any graduate students may be interested in the job. You may pay $15 to $25 an hour for this service. Once you find a coach, you and your teenager will have to explain what you want him to do, plus brief him on ADD.

Inattention/Forgetfulness

Inattention can cause significant problems, especially during the freshman year. Students with ADD are forgetful, don't plan ahead, and seldom complete assignments ahead of due dates. They are more likely to remember routine assignments such as writing a theme every week. However, they may forget one-time special assignments.

Notify Professor of ADD. Your teenager may have to take the letter from student services regarding needed adaptations to his professor at the beginning of every quarter. Don't be surprised if he forgets the letter. You will probably need to remind him to give it to his professors.

Obtain a Copy of the Class Syllabus. Many faculty members provide each student with a class syllabus. This should make it easier for your teenager to know what assignments are due and when. If he agrees to accept some prompting about his school work, ask him to give you a copy of the syllabus. You can then remind him *before* major assignments are due. At the beginning of the quarter, you can also discuss all assignments for the class with your teenager, pointing out those that look like they will take extra time. As your teenager gets used to the college routine and takes on more responsibility, you can phase out this assistance.

Ask for a List of All Assignments. If the professor doesn't give a syllabus, your teenager should probably ask for a written list of all class assignments at the beginning of the quarter. This request could be included in his 504 letter to the faculty as an adaptation.

Record All Test and Project Due Dates.
Your child should record all test dates, special projects, and reports and their due dates in his month-at-a-glance book. You may want to review this with him by phone or on a weekend visit early in the quarter. With his permission, photocopy his schedule and help him monitor test and due dates. It is not unusual for a student with ADD to walk into class totally unaware that the test is "today" rather than tomorrow.

Monitor Key Events. With your teenager's consent, you or the coach may help monitor key activities. For example, "Have you taken your letter about classroom adaptations from the Student Services Office to each teacher? When is your meeting with your advisor for early registration? What classes do you want to take next quarter? When is your deposit due to guarantee your dormitory room?"

It is especially important to make sure your teenager fulfills all the requirements needed for graduation. Usually, a number of core courses, such as English, math, history, and science, must be completed prior to graduation. Your teenager and his advisor must check to see that he has taken all the core curriculum. If your child enters college with a deficiency in high school graduation requirements, he will have to take those make-up courses early in his college career.

In some states or universities, students must pass tests demonstrating that they have mastered basic skills, or they cannot graduate. In Georgia, for example, students must sign up for the Regents exam in writing after completion of English 102. They must write a standard five-paragraph theme in an hour. The theme is graded by faculty from other colleges in the state. If a student forgets to take the exam before he has earned a certain number of hours, he may not be allowed to take additional courses or may have to take unnecessary remedial courses.

Use Audio Tapes with Texts. If your teenager has a lot of required reading for class but has trouble concentrating when he reads, audio tapes may be helpful. Books on tape may help him read and comprehend material in college texts, particularly in subjects such as literature and history that require more reading and memorization. Recording

for the Blind & Dyslexic is the only national group that records college texts on tapes. (See Chapter 10.) They have a large collection of college books on tape and can mail them within 24 hours.

Books that aren't currently on tape may require three to four months advance notice. Under Section 504, students register early, usually a month or so before the next quarter. So, as soon as your child signs up for his next quarter classes, ask for the title of his textbooks. If he doesn't know the names of his books, call the school bookstore and they can give you the title. Call Recording for the Blind & Dyslexic and ask if the book is available. If it isn't, your child could drop the course and take it the following quarter. By then a copy can be made. If you plan too far ahead, books change and you may request a tape for a book that is no longer in use.

Although this is a wonderful service, some students may not want to use it. As long as they are passing the class, *they* should make the decision about whether or not to use the service.

Can't Get Started on Homework

Some college students with ADD report difficulty getting started on homework. They may not always complete their homework but continue their high school habits of trying to pass on the basis of what they learn in class. Although they may still be able to do this in some college classes, it will be increasingly difficult. They will encounter more challenging classes such as college algebra or physics which will require more studying and completion of homework.

Prompt Getting Started. If your teenager is struggling, an academic coach can prompt him to get started on homework. With your teenager's permission, the coach will call and remind him to start homework at the same time each day. Setting aside a couple of hours to study each day (2:00 to 4:00) should be helpful. If a coach isn't available, you may prompt your child, if needed, during the freshman year to ensure he gets off on the right foot.

❧

"Sometimes I remind my son to start his homework, get up, or take his medication by dialing his beeper number and entering a special code."

Forgetting to Take Medication

Remembering to take medication while living away at school may be a major problem for teenagers with ADD. Taking medication, however, may mean the difference between passing and failing classes. If your teenager continually forgets his medication, first ask *him* how he would suggest solving the problem.

⚜

"One teenager took his medication during the first two quarters of his freshman year. He passed his classes. The third quarter his prescription ran out and he kept forgetting to ask his dad to get it refilled. He failed a couple of classes."

⚜

Remind to Take Medication. Ideally, your teenager will remember on his own. If he doesn't, try some of the same tips provided in Chapter 4. Suggest that he put his medicine in a weekly pill box with compartments for each day. Then put the box in the same place each day. Put the meds where he is most likely to see them and remember to take them—by the bathroom sink, kitchen table, or bed. You may have to remind him to fill the containers each weekend. If he comes home every weekend, fill the weekly container for him then. Call or beep him each morning to remind him to take the medication, especially his freshman year, until he gets into a routine of taking his medicine regularly.

Perhaps he can find someone at school such as his coach, girlfriend, or roommate who will be willing to remind him to take his medicine.

Provide Medical Supervision. It may be best if your teenager continues with his present family doctor even if he goes away to school. His physician knows him and his needs best, since they have worked together for a number of years. You and your teenager can monitor the effectiveness of medication and talk with your doctor about any needed adjustments. Typically, by this age, your child doesn't visit his pediatrician very often, perhaps once a year for his annual physical and monitoring of his stimulant medication.

On the other hand, you may decide that your teenager should have a physician at school, particu-larly if he is going to school out of state and seldom comes home. Or if he is interested and wants counseling on a regular basis, you may ask the student services advisor for names of a good psychiatrist, counselor, or physician. You will need to find a doctor who specializes in ADD, make an appointment, and sign a release to have copies of your records sent from your family doctor. Otherwise, a doctor in another town will probably be reluctant to prescribe stimulant medications for a new patient without their medical records or a complete evaluation. If your teenager is pleased with the doctor at the college infirmary, he could serve as his doctor away from home.

Getting Prescriptions Filled. If your child is away at school for weeks at a time, you could have his prescription mailed to him at college and let him get it refilled there. Of course, he may have trouble remembering to get the prescription filled and then to put meds in his weekly container. If your teenager is going to school in another state, pharmacists won't fill out-of-state prescriptions. So you will need a local physician. Or in case of an emergency, you could get the prescription refilled and mail it overnight to him.

Monitor Medication Needs. Your child's medication needs may change over time. Some teens will continue the same medication throughout their high school and college careers. Others may not need any medication, especially as a junior or senior, if they are taking high-interest, active courses in their major field. As time goes on, your child may feel he can study and pay attention in class without medication. Or he may need to take meds less often, perhaps only on those days he has challenging subjects. Your child may be the best judge of his need for medicine. Obviously, if he stops taking his Ritalin or Dexedrine and begins failing his classes, you would discuss this with him. State the obvious: "Your grades started going downhill when you stopped taking your Dexedrine. What do you think is the problem? Do you think you need to start taking it again?"

Experiencing an Emotional Crisis

If your teenager fails a test or breaks up with his girlfriend, he may experience an emotional crisis while he is miles away from home. Hopefully, you have helped him understand that the characteristics of ADD—impulsivity, forgetfulness, difficulty getting started, and low frustration tolerance—may cause problems that eventually snowball into a major crisis. Your teachings may have also included helping him develop coping skills.

Call Home and Develop a Plan. Many times calling home and talking with you may help your child cope with his crisis. Remember that you can try several techniques discussed in Chapters 5 and 6: use active listening, then develop a plan to cope with the problem so he doesn't feel powerless and depressed. For example, a crisis may be triggered because he forgot he was having a test, didn't study, and failed an exam. Listen while he tells you his feelings about the pain, self-doubt, embarrassment, and fears about failure. This may take awhile—maybe even an hour. Next you begin the process of problem solving. Ask him what he can do to correct the problem or what would make him feel better? One thing he may do is take the "504 letter" about adaptations to the professor if he forgot to turn it in earlier in the quarter. He could start taking his medication again if he has not been taking it regularly. He can schedule a conference with his professor, explain what happened, and ask if he can do work for extra credit. He may schedule an appointment with his student services advisor. Or do something physical—swim, play tennis, or lift weights. Or spend time with a friend or girlfriend.

Handling a Crisis. If your teenager is experiencing a major crisis and you are concerned, encourage him to talk with his student services advisor. With his permission, you may call his advisor to get her opinion on how serious the problem is. Or you may decide to drive to school and see him yourself. Teenagers with ADD may be reluctant to open up and discuss painful problems with someone they don't know. As my colleague Karl Dennis says, "The last person you want to see during a crisis is some stranger." If he needs to see a doctor, the advisor may send him to a local doctor, emergency room, or to the college infirmary, if staff are properly trained.

Career Choices

Teenagers with ADD have a wide variety of intellectual abilities and interests, and may therefore pursue a wide variety of vocations. There are adults with ADD in traditional careers such as medicine or law, as well as those with jobs which tap their creative and physical abilities, such as art, modeling, electronics, music, computers, or working on cars. Finding a job that can hold their interest and commitment for a long time is critically important. Many prefer jobs that are active, include changes in routine, and involve a variety of different issues or people throughout the work week.

❦

"When Steven graduated from high school, he didn't know what he wanted to do. In some ways he was afraid to try college but he decided to go for one year. At the end of the first year of college, he dropped out. He knew he liked "detailing" cars, which includes thorough hand washing, waxing, and buffing. He went to work at a shop that specialized in detailing cars and worked there for three months. He pursued his dream, grew tired of it, and realized he did not want to do that for the rest of his life. Next, he got a job with a manufacturing company that made dies for printing companies.

"Subsequently, his ADD was diagnosed when he was 20. He went back to college on Ritalin and graduated with a degree in printing management. This job is ideal for him. It requires a lot of activity, both interpersonal and physical. He must interact with many people, plus he has the opportunity to move around a lot. It is not a traditional nine-to-five paper-pushing desk job."

❦

Selecting the right career is crucial and will require more planning for students who have ADD. The career your teenager selects should maximize his strengths and minimize deficits such as poor organizational skills or lack of attention to detail.

❦

"One day when Cassie came home and saw a stack of papers I had to read for work she said, 'If I had to read a six-inch stack of papers to make a living, I'd kill myself.'"

⚜

"At 16, Alex seems to feel trapped in his career choices. He told me that all my husband and I do is sit and work at a desk and how boring that was to him. Yet he feels the only way he can make money is to get a job that requires sitting behind a desk. We discussed other career options which don't just require people to sit behind desks."

⚜

"After high school graduation, my daughter who has ADHD took a job working for a company that provides temporary office help. It is a perfect job for her. She is enthusiastic about going to work each Monday and doesn't get tired of the job because she meets a new group of people and assignments every two weeks or so. They love the work she does. She is very bright and is a quick study in a new office."

⚜

Please keep in mind that some extremely bright teenagers with ADD excel academically in both high school and college. They may be skilled at many things and have trouble narrowing their job options. And then again, they may have trouble staying focused long enough to make a career decision.

⚜

"I thought it was interesting that the only two high school Merit Scholars I know both diagnosed themselves as having ADD. Both were struggling to select a career path. One had difficulty selecting a college and the other struggled with the decision about what he wanted to do after graduation."

Identify Skills and Interests

Identifying your teenager's skills and interests should be helpful in finding a good career match for him. You and your teenager can begin talking informally about these issues in high school. What does he enjoy doing? What special skills does he have? What vocations match his strengths and interests? What does he do with his spare time? Does he install stereo equipment for other friends?

Perhaps a job installing stereo equipment or working as a computer technician might be a good idea for him. Is he outgoing and does he enjoy talking a lot? Work in sales might be a perfect choice.

⚜

"My sister (ADHD) has a job that is perfect for her. She is a chiropractor. She is very outgoing, sees lots of different patients each day, is active and moving around all day long, and enjoys the diversity of her patients' problems. She is always upbeat and witty. Her patients love her entertaining personality. Now the down side is that she avoids paperwork like the plague. Ironically, our mother is her office manager and after 40 years she is still stuck with the job of trying to get my sister to do her 'homework.'"

⚜

Listed below are several steps you and your teenager can take to help find the most appropriate career.

Vocational Testing. Vocational interest testing can be conducted in either high school, technical institute, or college to help identify a student's strengths and career interests. In college or technical school, the student services section can help schedule the testing; in high school, the guidance counselor can. This testing is usually free.

The *Strong Interest Inventory* is one vocational test that some colleges use. Students answer questions about things they like or dislike. The scores give them a pattern of interests and show how their interests compare with those of successful people in different occupations. Scores are obtained for six general occupational themes: Realistic, Investigative, Artistic, Social, Enterprising, and Conventional. Approximately 115 possible occupations are listed within these themes.

⚜

"My son's best scores were found in the Realistic and Investigative Occupational Themes. He scored very high on the Basic Interest Scales for <u>Adventure</u> and average on <u>Nature, Agriculture, Military Activities, Mechanical Activities, Medical Science,</u> and Medical Service. Vocations in which he scored similarly to successful people currently working in the field included emergency medical technician, radiological technologist, veterinarian, electrician, computer programmer, farmer, police officer, enlisted military personnel, geologist, optometrist, bus driver, and photographer.

"He received a very low score on the Conventional Occupational theme of the <u>Office Practices</u> scale. Specific occupations in which he received lower scores and probably would not be well suited were accountant, business education teacher, public administrator, foreign languages teacher, minister, social worker, elected public official, and, not surprisingly, school administrator."

🕮

Computerized Career Programs. Some colleges have interactive computer programs available that explain details regarding various careers. For example, Educational Testing Services has developed SIGI PLUS, which describes detailed aspects of numerous occupations: work activities, settings, educational requirements, average income, top earning potential, average work week, and employment outlook.

Personality Testing. Another test that may be helpful is the *Myers-Briggs Personality Inventory*. The teenager answers approximately 100 questions about himself and the way he conducts his daily life. Based upon his scores, one of sixteen personality styles which describes him will be identified. This test provides labels for differences in personality that we observe in work colleagues and family on a day-to-day basis.

This is an interesting exercise that may help a teenager with ADD gain insight into his personality, how he thinks, makes decisions, and lives. The more he understands about himself and how he relates to others, the more he may learn to get along better with people and be more productive at work. One teenager with ADD who took the test was astounded that the test described him so well. Many young adults in the 18–22 age bracket are curious about who they are and what makes them tick. This test takes advantage of their natural curiosity.

Opposite extremes of four basic categories are identified on the Myers-Briggs: 1) Energy preferences: *Extrovert -Introvert;* 2) Perceptual preferences: *Sensing (realistic)-Intuitive;* 3) Decision-making preferences: *Thinking (Objective)- Feeling;* and 4) Lifestyle preference: *Judging (goal directed)-Perceiving (flexible/spontaneous).* Some teenagers with

ADHD may be described as an Extrovert, Intuitive, Feeling, and Perceiving (spontaneous). Certain personality types are better suited to particular careers. For example, as noted in the Strong Inventory, the teenager who had ADD would not make a good accountant because he would have to pay attention to details, be objective, deal with routine, and finish up quickly. This information may also explain why people with different personality types have problems in relationships. Obviously, conflicts may result between a teenager and his parents if they have the opposite characteristics of Introverted, Sensing (realistic), Thinking (objective), and Judging (goal directed).

🕮

"My son's personality type is Introvert, Intuitive, Thinking, and Perceiving. I am an Introvert, Sensing, Feeling, and Judging. Sometimes we drive each other crazy because I want to make a list, start work immediately, finish, and mark things off my list. Being organized is very important to me."

🕮

Special Courses. Teenagers can continue to explore job options in college through career study and personal development classes. Students don't have to declare a major upon entering college. During the first two years, most students take basic core academic requirements anyway, such as algebra, English, and history. Some college courses offer an opportunity to explore career options and to make decisions about a college major. The curriculum may include vocational testing, career discussions, filling out job applications, strategies for job interviews, and writing resumes and letters for job interviews.

Some colleges offer psychology courses related to interpersonal relationships and personal growth and development. A course of this nature should be helpful to a teenager with ADD. Typically, the classes are more interactive and require less written homework. Class participation is the key variable in the student's grade. If the student attends class every day and actively participates, he should receive a good grade. An A or B added to his grade point average would be a wonderful bonus.

Summer Jobs. Summer jobs offer an important opportunity to explore career options and mas-

ter basic work ethic skills. Seemingly simple job skills, such as getting up, being on time to work, and remembering and following directions, are important skills for *any* teenager to learn, especially if he has ADD. Administrative and organizational skills may also be learned on the job. In addition, working during the summers can help students obtain first-hand knowledge about various careers.

Exploring vocational interests is an extremely important benefit of a summer job. For example, some teenage boys may be drawn to jobs that don't require a postsecondary education. Once a teenager actually does the work eight hours a day, some of the appeal may wear off. He may realize that he doesn't want to spend the rest of his life doing that kind of work.

It is important for your teenager to select a job that he enjoys so that he will want to go to work. You may need to help teach him responsible work habits. Make certain he has his own alarm clock. Wake him up if he oversleeps. If sleeping late becomes a major problem, discuss it with him and develop a plan to solve the problem. See Chapter 6 for more information on handling sleep problems.

Dr. Barkley has found that teenagers with ADD do as well with summer jobs as teenagers who don't have ADD. Perhaps the short duration

of the job, the nature of the job (unskilled work with more activity involved than sitting in a classroom), having a job they like, and novelty make it easier for them to hold summer jobs successfully.

◪

"Steven worked as a lifeguard during the summers. Even with his ADHD, he did an excellent job. He had to open and close the pool on his own, watch all the children, monitor the chemicals, schedule the other lifeguards, and relate to the homeowner association president and members. He passed difficult lifeguarding classes, and first aid and CPR classes. His ego was boosted by this experience."

◪

Meeting Professionals in the Field. Another way to find out more about various careers is to talk with professionals currently working in the field. If your teenager expresses interest in such a meeting, you might line up informal interviews through your personal and professional contacts.

◪

"My son struggled finding a career after high school. After talking with a friend of mine who is a nurse, he thought that sounded really interesting. He recently started training as a nurse and loves it."

Life's Other Important Lessons

Teenagers with ADD experience tremendous changes when they go away to college. Just living on their own for the first time is a major adjustment. Getting up and going to class is a demanding endeavor for many. Writing checks, balancing checkbooks, washing clothes, and keeping up with homework assignments are a lot for these teenagers to juggle, especially with the organizational problems so many of them have.

◪

"Our daughter received numerous parking tickets that she never paid. One day the campus police impounded her car and towed it away. She called home all upset, asking if she could borrow $500 to pay parking fines and charges to get the car back."

Do Checkbooks Balance?

The answer to this question is an emphatic "No" if it is directed to a college freshman with ADD. Knowing how much money is in his bank account is a complete mystery. Even remembering to record basic information about checks, such as to whom they were written and the amount, may be difficult. Some students may use bank automatic teller machine (ATM) cards almost exclusively. If the teller machine indicates that money is in the account, they withdraw it. They may forget they wrote a check the day before that has not cleared yet. "Bounced" checks due to insufficient funds may cost an additional twenty dollars. A student may write a six-dollar check that ends up costing twenty dollars extra.

Obviously, this behavior can be very irritating to parents. Fortunately, the ability to manage money tends to improve with age. By the time your child is a senior, he should be able to manage his money much more effectively. In the interim, however, you must come up with a plan to teach him how to handle his finances.

Parents must decide how to deal with money matters. Some parents are so worried about their teenager succeeding academically, they cut the student some slack with his finances, especially during the first couple of years. If he has problems managing his money, ask him to help solve the problem. Just punishing him will not help him learn to manage his money better.

Teach Money Management. Spend some time with your teenager before he goes away to college and teach him how to handle his check book—filling out a check, listing the check and number in the checkbook, subtracting the check, and keeping a running balance. Explain how a checking account and ATM cards work. "It takes one to three days for a check to be subtracted from your account. So just because you use your bank card and it indicates that you have money in your account it may not be accurate. A check you have written recently may not have cleared."

Limit Access to Checking Account. You may decide to give your child a limited number of checks and to pay major bills such as tuition, dorm room, and a college meal plan yourself. He can pay for his books or other designated expenses. Then you can allow him to withdraw a set amount of money each week from the ATM for an allowance. You could try transferring the money in a week at a time. He can withdraw his weekly allowance on Saturday and pay his miscellaneous expenses in cash. Or you could send him his allowance in a weekly check. As long as he has a meal plan, he won't starve if he runs out of cash. Sometimes a girlfriend may be the lifesaver who helps him balance his checkbook and be aware of how much money he has in the bank. Another option is to deposit money in a savings account, rather than a checking account, so he has to go to the bank to withdraw funds. This way he can't write checks or use an ATM card.

Use a Check Card. One new service that banks are offering is a check card. It looks like a credit card but actually works like a check. The advantage of the check card is that it is declined or approved when you try to pay for a purchase. If you do not have enough money in your account, your check card will be declined. You will then avoid bounced-check charges from the bank, returned-check charges to the merchant, and the hassle of having to make the check good.

Deposit Extra Money. You or your child might deposit a little extra money in his account. One teenager told me he put $50 extra in his account as a safety cushion. If he makes a mistake on his account balance, he won't bounce any checks. This assumes that he is organized enough to keep a running account of his finances. Otherwise, he will just spend the $50 cushion.

Use Overdraft Protection. Another option is to obtain overdraft protection or a personal line of credit. With this protection, a check will not bounce. The only cost will be interest, usually only a few dollars or cents, for money the bank advanced to the account to cover the check. However, if your teenager knows about this service, he may take advantage of it and write checks for more money than he has available.

Managing Personal Earnings or Scholarship Funds. Your teenager may have a job or receive a check from a school loan or scholarship. Regardless of where the funds come from, he will need help managing his money. Sit down with him and explain how to develop a budget. Show him how to write down the exact amount of each monthly expense such as the phone, cable TV, rent, or quarterly expenses such as books and class registration fees. Then when he subtracts expenses from his income, he knows how much money he will typically have left to spend after bills are paid. If he is earning his own money, he will probably be more cautious about spending it. But he may still have problems managing it very well.

To Charge or Not To Charge?

College students often receive applications for credit cards. Some parents may *want* their teenager to have a card, perhaps for safety reasons and convenience. They may not want their teenager to drive home from college without a credit card in the event he needs gas or has car trouble. If you allow your child to have credit cards, you will need to closely monitor their use since most of these teenagers have trouble using a credit card wisely.

Set Guidelines for Credit Card Usage. Talk with your teenager about proper use of a credit card. You may teach the importance of keeping charges at a minimum and paying them off each month. You may also explain that some teenagers with ADD are prone to impulsive spending and may run up credit card bills. Express your hope that he will avoid that pitfall. Explain how much you pay for interest when you don't pay the card off each month.

Limit and Monitor Card Use. Let your teenager know what he should and shouldn't use his credit cards for. For example, you may want to designate their use only for emergencies or for expenditures you authorize in advance. You may also explain that you intend to monitor monthly statements and then review charge card expenditures with him. If bills are sent to a school address and you are paying the bill, you should review them with him each month. This may prevent his running up a huge credit card bill without your knowledge. If he is paying the bill but has a high balance, you could talk with him about ways to reduce his debt, such as paying more than the minimum required each month.

Will He Remember to Pay Fees and Bills?

No, he probably won't remember to pay his bills without being reminded. He may forget to pay his school fees, tuition, and other bills. And if he lives off campus in an apartment, he may also forget that rent, utilities, cable TV, and telephone bills must be paid. To keep your teenager from running up late payment fees or having services disconnected, you may have to step in and help, especially the first year or two.

Remind about Bill Payment. Since there is a good chance that your teenager may forget to pay his bills, you may need to remind him of due dates, such as rent due the first day of the month. You may need to ask for registration forms and bills for tuition and pay them yourself. Students don't always realize that bouncing too many checks and failing to pay bills may result in a bad credit rating for both themselves and their parents, if they have co-signed.

Bill Parents Directly. If your child often forgets to pay bills, you may want to have some bills sent directly to you and gradually phase in his full responsibility for payment by his senior year.

Can He Get Along with a Roommate?

Sometimes relationships between a teenager with ADD and his roommate can be strained. Teenagers with ADD are not known for their neatness. Clothes and possessions can pile up quickly when two people share a room measuring 10 by 12. Thoughtfulness or an awareness of how they affect others is not usually one of their strong suits. Loud music or talking while their roommate is trying to study is not going to go over real well. The teenage "night owl" may also create problems for his roommate. Sometimes both roommates may have ADD, which creates another set of problems. If you are lucky, your teenager's college will send out surveys before school begins in an effort to match roommates who have similar living and study habits. Still, there is no guarantee that your teenager and his roommate will hit it off.

Talk with Your Teenager. Before your child leaves home, you may want to talk to him about the need to respect the rights of his roommate and discuss potential areas of conflict.

Talk with the Resident Assistant (R.A.). Most colleges have resident assistants (R.A.'s) who live on each floor of a dorm. These upper-class students receive a free room in exchange for providing support, mediation, and supervision for students who live on their hall. If your child runs into problems with his roommate, suggest that he talk to his R.A. and ask for assistance in resolving their problems.

Change Roommates. If serious problems arise, your child may be able to change roommates immediately. He may feel, however, that he can wait for a new quarter or school year. He can begin looking for someone more compatible who shares common interests.

Request a Private Room. Sometimes when a teen with ADD finally gets around to studying, his roommate may be watching a movie or talking on the phone. It doesn't take much to get a teen with ADD distracted. The first thing you know, good intentions for studying are down the tube and your son is watching the movie with his roommate. If available and you can afford it, your child may be better off in a private room. One public college charges an extra $165 quarterly for a private room—$665 total compared to $500 with a roommate.

Get an Apartment or Live at a Fraternity House. Thankfully, most parents won't have to deal with this issue until their child's second year, since most colleges require freshmen to live in dormitories. However, many students may want to live off campus in an apartment or at a fraternity during their sophomore year. This final symbolic step of living out from under any adult supervision may be difficult for you to accept. You will have to make a judgment call as to whether or not your teenager is ready for this level of independent living.

The first question to ask yourself is, has he been responsible about studying during his freshman year and passed the majority of his classes? If so, chances are that he will manage living in an apartment successfully. You might tell him: "As long as you study and pass your classes, I'll support your living in an apartment." Second, are family finances sufficient to pay for an apartment or will he get a job to help pay? His share of a two-person dorm room may cost $500 for a quarter compared with $600 (or more) a quarter for an apartment with several roommates. Third, do you think your child can be responsible about paying bills? Remember: if needed, you can handle this by direct billing and paying the rent, phone, power, or cable TV bills yourself.

When students live in their first apartment, their sense of pride in living on their own may mean they keep their place fairly clean. Then again, your child's room may be a pig sty, but if he can live in it and get his studies done, so be it.

Should He Drive a Car to School?

As Chapter 7 discusses, driving can land many teenagers with ADD in difficulties ranging from minor parking violations to serious accidents. In deciding whether your teenager should have access to a car at college, think carefully about his ability to handle this privilege responsibly. In particular, ask yourself how likely he is to drive when his medication has worn off, and how likely he is to have an accident.

Allow Limited Driving. If you have serious reservations about your teenager driving a car to school, you might let him take a car his second quarter at school and see how well he handles it. After the quarter is over, does he have passing grades? Did he get any tickets or have any accidents? Has he received a ticket for DUI? A logical consequence for any problems in these areas may be reduced driving privileges.

Establish a Gas Allowance. Some students get jobs so that they can earn money to help pay for their gas. Other parents prefer to have their children focus all their energies on schoolwork and give them an allowance for gas each month. Any charges over that amount must be paid for by the student. If you want to encourage your child to come home more often, you could offer to pay for the gas required for the trip home.

Encourage Him to Ride with Others. If he has received an occasional ticket or had an accident, encourage him to ride with others at night (if these problems occur at night). He may be willing to ride with his girlfriend or roommate. Or encourage him to take his medication at 5:00 p.m. or so when he is driving after dark.

Talk about Drinking and Driving. As discussed in Chapter 7, tell him that drinking and driving is a non-negotiable area. Explain that you love him too much to allow him to risk his life while drinking and driving. If he is with someone who is drinking, get out of the car. Call a taxi or friend to come get him.

Should Your Teenager Join a Fraternity or Sorority?

Some teenagers will want to join a fraternity or sorority. One advantage to joining a fraternity is that students must maintain passing grades to be eligible to join and participate in fraternity activities. In addition, teenagers make a lot of new friends who can provide important social and business contacts in the future. They are also encouraged to participate in intra-fraternity sports.

Although parents may worry about drug and alcohol abuse, fraternities are under strong pressure from college officials to prohibit use of illicit substances. Sanctions are stiff for violations, especially use of drugs. Fraternities may be placed on probation or banned from campus for a year or more. On the minus side, a fraternity may demand so much time or put such an emphasis on partying that members may fail some of their classes. Your teenager is going to be drawn to people he enjoys and with whom he feels comfortable. You will probably not have much influence over the fraternity he selects. The good news is that a student can't remain active in the fraternity if he fails classes. Remember also, that most fraternities are okay or else they will have been disbanded.

〽

"At first I worried about my son joining a fraternity. When he decided he wanted to join, I agreed with some reservations. However, it has been a great experience for him. He actually worries about his grade point average so that he can be active in the fraternity. He tends to be introverted and it has helped him become more outgoing. The fraternity has given him certain responsibilities. He had to clean the fraternity house and participate in a pledge class project to improve the house. He has helped wire stereo systems and outside lights. He participates in inter-fraternity sports. He acts as photographer for the fraternity. He has been able to use so many of his talents. It has been a great confidence builder."

〽

Before your teen joins a fraternity, be sure he knows the costs involved. Costs vary from college to college. Some smaller colleges have a one-time initiation fee ranging from $150 to $225—plus monthly dues of from $25 to $40. At universities, some fraternities have new, elegant houses. They offer a wider range of optional services, that will, of course, cost more money—nicer rooms, a full-time house mother, cook, prepared group meals, etc. In some instances, living in a fraternity house may cost no more than living in an apartment or dorm. Being a member of a fraternity is important enough to some teenagers that they are willing to work a part-time job so they can belong to one.

Parental Involvement: When to Let Go?

Because some teenagers with ADD have struggled so much in high school, both parents and teenagers may face college with a great deal of anxiety. Some parents may think that their teenager should be independent, now that he is 18 and legally an adult. Yet, they also realize that he is not quite ready for total independence.

〽

"As a mental health professional, I have felt very guilty about my involvement in my son's academic life. All through high school, I kept trying to find someone else to be his 'academic coach' but never found anyone to replace me. Although my son was bright, high school was such a struggle for him. If I had totally stopped monitoring his performance, I'm not certain he would have graduated.

"A few months ago I talked to a mental health professional in another state who also has a son with ADD. We discovered we have both struggled with and felt a lot of guilt about this same dilemma. When do we let go? She told me how her son had called her from college, really upset about his first big test in history, a subject that was very difficult for him and required a lot of memorization. They talked by phone and she decided to go down to the college and help him study. After they made the decision, they both cried. She decided then that <u>you stop helping them when they no longer need help.</u> He is making every effort to make it academically on his own. There is no reason to feel guilty for helping him.

"From a practical financial perspective, parents are paying several thousand dollars a year for their child's education. What would be gained by letting him fail the class?"

❧

Faculty at West Virginia Wesleyan have found that students with learning disabilities usually need the most assistance their first year in college. As students learn how to study and gain confidence, they need fewer supports each subsequent year. As a result, special fees for extra supervision decline each year. *Getting over the hurdle of his first year in college may well be the most critical challenge your teenager faces.* After a successful quarter or two, he should build confidence in his ability to make it on his own.

❧

"Although I still feel guilty at times that I am so involved in my son's life, the good news is that each year he needs less help from me. He has assumed increasing responsibility for his schoolwork, payment of rent, and self-care. Now that he knows how to seek help from student services, he is helping his girlfriend, who is a freshman, do all her paperwork for special adaptations for her ADD."

❧

As a parent, you must identify your top priorities for your teenager and address those issues first. Do you want your child to do as well as possible with his academics? Or do you want him to learn to handle his own finances? Or keep his room clean? Sometimes mastering academics may come first and other things second.

❧

"Because our son's confidence in his ability to do college work was so tenuous, academics were our greatest concern. We made certain our son was on solid ground academically before we began pressing him for greater financial responsibility. When he was a junior, we gave him a set allowance and told him he had to live within that amount. Although he was somewhat resentful at that time, he later thanked us."

❧

You must be careful about how involved you get in your teenager's college career. If you are too controlling or demanding, your teenager may rebel. Power struggles may undermine and detract from his academic efforts. On the other hand, if you are paying for your child's education, you certainly have a right to expect a certain level of effort from him. But if he is doing his best and still fails a class because of learning problems, the best course is usually to be as supportive as possible and make sure that appropriate adaptations are provided.

CHAPTER THIRTEEN

PARENTS HAVE PERMISSION TO TAKE CHARGE

"Parents are probably the greatest single factor in determining whether or not a teenager with ADD receives needed services."

⚞

Some teenagers with ADD need little outside help to succeed at school and at home. Perhaps they need their parents to monitor their progress in a regular education program or to oversee their medication, but can otherwise manage on their own. Other teenagers, however, must struggle to cope with their ADD, even with a variety of interventions at home and at school.

If your teenager is struggling, give yourself permission to become more involved and to take charge of coordinating services if need be. You are probably the best person to take charge, anyway. *First,* you know your teenager best and have a tremendous emotional investment in his success! *Second,* because of the parent-child bond, you will stick with your child long after others have given up and are no longer involved. As a parent you have an intense emotional investment that enables you to be creative and tenacious, just as this book strongly advises. Remember, do whatever it takes to help your teenager succeed! After reading this book, you should feel comfortable developing a plan to help your teenager adjust successfully at home, school, and in the community. And you should understand and appreciate your own critical role in this process.

⚞

"I decided after five psychologists, four pediatricians, one neurologist, and many others that <u>I was my daughter's best case manager.</u> It was up to us to decide what to do. We know our daughter best. Professionals leave—parents stay!!!"

—*Beth Dague, Director, Stark County Ohio Family Council and mother of two daughters with ADD*

⚞

If your teenager is receiving specialized services from a variety of professionals, *someone must coordinate the services they provide.* Typically, each professional is a specialist in his own field and may not be knowledgeable or feel comfortable monitoring your teenager's progress in other areas. For example, the doctor may not know if your teenager has learning problems or whether classroom adaptations are needed. The teacher may not know that your teenager is on medication, whether it is effective, when medication changes are made, the time of day medication wears off, or whether your teenager has sleep disturbances that affect his schoolwork.

Ideally, the doctor and school personnel *should* communicate with each other periodically. For example, exchanging information about the effectiveness of medication at school is very important. With this information, adjustments can be made to the medicine, dosage amounts, and the time administered to maximize medication benefits. Unfortunately, this communication seldom occurs. Consequently, someone must look at the whole child, monitor his functioning in every setting, and provide feedback to all professionals involved. You, as a parent, are often the best person to take on this responsibility.

❧

"In Kansas, thanks to a federal grant, some parents are being trained to act as case managers for their children who have serious emotional problems. They have been extremely effective in coordinating services."

❧

If your teenager is struggling at home or school, you need to work *together* with the teacher, counselor, and physician to develop an individualized treatment plan. As discussed throughout the book, the family/school/physician partnership is the *cornerstone* of successful home and school experiences for teenagers with ADD. This partnership must truly include the parents and teenager as respected members of the treatment team. The critical role the family plays in treatment must not be underestimated.

❧

"Parents and teenagers have great inner strength and ability that frequently are overlooked in the traditional therapeutic process."

❧

School personnel may be extremely valuable allies who can ensure a successful academic experience for your teenager. Approaching them with a positive attitude, expecting them to cooperate fully, is very important. Chapters 8 through 10 offer guidance on working with school personnel to make sure that your teenager's learning problems are identified and that appropriate adaptations are provided in the classroom. The federal laws discussed in Chapter 11 should provide legal leverage, if needed, to obtain appropriate services at school.

Building a strong partnership with the physician is also crucial. As Chapter 4 explains, this partnership is the key to finding the right medication regimen. Your family must work with the doctor to determine which medications and dosages seem to work best. If maximum benefits are not obtained from medication, your family may need to talk with your physician about making adjustments. If

these changes are still not successful, you can request a consultation with a psychiatrist in hopes of finding a more effective medication regimen.

As a parent, you may want to get counseling for yourself to help you be a more effective parent and advocate. In fact, this tactic may result in greater long-term dividends than sending your teenager to someone to be "fixed." You will be better prepared to handle crises if you have developed effective communication and parenting skills.

Developing an Individualized Treatment Plan

This chapter will help you develop an individualized treatment plan for your teenager. By filling out the blank forms in this chapter, you can address each of five potential problem areas: 1) your teenager's self-esteem and coping skills; 2) family life; 3) medication; 4) school performance; and 5) community activities. It may help to refer to completed sample forms contained in earlier chapters. If need be, remember to ask for help from your teenager's physician, teacher, school counselor, social worker, or psychologist to complete the treatment plan. Other parents may also be able to help you develop a plan. You can meet parents through programs at CHADD, Federation of Families, ADDA, Mental Health Association, AMI-CAN, or other support meetings. Addresses for these organizations are listed in Appendix D.

As you develop your treatment plan, remember that you should seek services in the most normal manner possible. It is important that services not be stigmatizing, traumatizing, intrusive, or overly restrictive. Try first to obtain services for your teenager in his natural environment . . . through supportive services offered at home and in a regular classroom at school, rather than through residential treatment.

Do not feel as if you have to complete all the forms or try all the strategies recommended in this book. If your child's problems are simple, you may decide to fill out only a few forms. You may even be able to develop an informal plan in your head. Use this material in whatever way is helpful to you. Again, do not feel guilty if you cannot complete this process alone. Complete as much as you can and then ask someone else for help.

❦

"At first I thought there was no way I could develop an individualized treatment plan for my son. When I realized how useful it would be for my son, I felt compelled to get it done. I sat down and worked and worked with it. My advice to other parents is to go somewhere and find another parent who has been through all this. Have them hold your hand while you go through this process.

"The individualized treatment plan worked perfectly for my son. Of course, we had periods of adjustment and it took awhile to get the details worked out. When I showed the school people all these forms I'd completed for the individualized treatment plan, they were really impressed and treated me with more respect. Once we all agreed on a plan, things worked much better at school. They were more in tune with what was going on because we worked hard to put the plan into action. We had really begun to work as a team. When a crisis came up, we handled it together."

❦

You may find it helpful to complete the action steps listed below:

Identify Strengths/Build Self-Esteem

Develop a Unique Profile (Form 1). Each teenager with ADD is unique. Some have serious learning problems; others do not. The many factors listed on this form can all affect a teenager's self-esteem, performance in school, and outcome in life. Some problem behaviors, such as academic failure or friends who are a bad influence, can be changed; others cannot. Identify those things you can control and make an effort to change them. Completing this form will increase your awareness of your teenager's unique characteristics. (See sample Table 1–2, Chapter 1.)

Identify Strengths (Form 2). Teenagers with ADD can be extremely charming and creative. Take the time to identify *your* teenager's strengths by completing Form 2. It is also important to make your teenager more aware of his strengths. Many teenagers may only see their failures and shortcomings. Parents, too, may tend to focus on problem behaviors. Reading about the concept of reframing negative characteristics, as discussed in Chapter 3, should help you and your teenager redirect your thinking in a more positive way. (See Sample Table 3–1, Chapter 3.)

Follow the Guiding Principles for Interactions. Guiding principles for parent/teenager interactions are discussed in Chapter 5: give unconditional positive regard, treat as an equal partner, maintain good communication, provide structure and supervision, look for the good, be positive, help build self-esteem, avoid negatives, weather each crisis as it occurs, and nurture yourself. Obviously, it is important to encourage your teenager to move toward independence, accepting increased responsibility over time. In addition, treat him with respect by involving him in decisions affecting his life. (See summary Table 5–5, Chapter 5.)

Build Self-Esteem (Form 3). Develop a plan to build self-esteem, as discussed in Chapter 5. Encourage your teenager to pursue his interests. Give him an opportunity to participate in activities that make him feel special. Identify interests or talents such as sports, art, and music in which he can develop skills through special training. Let him select those activities he likes best. Completing this form will help guide your efforts. (See sample Table 5–4, Chapter 5)

Provide Appropriate Medication

Assess the Effectiveness of Medication (Form 4). Monitoring your teenager's response to medication is critical and is discussed in detail in Chapter 4. Finding the right medication(s) requires fine tuning; seldom will a family luck out and find the right medication and dosage on the first try. Informal reports from parents, teachers, and the teenager are needed to determine whether academics and behavior have improved. Completing this form can help you judge whether medication is working to improve behavior and school performance. Your physician may also monitor possible effects and effectiveness of medication through use of formal measures such as behavior rating scales. Most behavior rating scales, however, can pick up a reduction in inappropriate behavior, but may not capture increases in attention and improvement in school work. Both parents and teachers should complete this form. If improvement is not significant, go back to the drawing board and fine tune medications or make classroom adaptations. (See sample Table 4–4, Chapter 4.)

Chart Peak Medication Time (Form 5). Sometimes it helps to chart the period of time when medication is effective. Once stimulant medications are absorbed, they reach a peak time of effectiveness and then gradually decline until they no longer work. For example, the effects of regular Ritalin and Dexedrine can be felt within 30 minutes or so, reach optimum effectiveness for approximately 2 hours, and then rapidly decline during the next hour. If your teenager is having problems at school, check to see if his problems are related to times when his medication has worn off or he has totally forgotten to take his medicine. Note the time he takes medication, how long it takes to become effective, when it wears off, and time of each class. Then compare this with which classes he may be failing or where behavior problems occur. For example, you may discover that he is failing English, which is at 11:00, or is talking back to teachers in algebra at 2:00, when medication has worn off. You may need to reschedule classes or times for taking medication. (See sample Table 4–5, Chapter 4.)

Discuss Medication Change with Your Physician. If anger, irritability, frustration, or aggressive behaviors continue to cause problems at home and school, changes in medication may be needed. "Rebound" or academic frustration may be causing the problem, or the right medication or correct dosage may not yet have been found. Talk with your physician about the possibility of adjusting current medication. Don't be afraid to tactfully suggest changes: "A speaker at CHADD mentioned that Dexedrine SR lasts several hours, eliminating the need for a noon dose. Could we try it?"

᛬

"When a teenager says, 'Ritalin didn't work' or 'I don't like the way it makes me feel,' parents need to ask questions and get more details. This doesn't necessarily mean that the medication isn't working. The frequency, dosage, or medication strength may be wrong. Respond to the teenager's comments by asking him to work with you and the doctor. 'We should

be able to make adjustments in the medication to address your concerns.'"

᛬

As discussed in Chapter 4, the doctor may explore a variety of options: 1) increase the dosage; 2) give stimulants more frequently during the day (3 or 4 doses); 3) give smaller doses later in the day; 4) combine regular and sustained release (SR) stimulants; and 5) prescribe stimulants plus an antidepressant. Although other interventions such as a positive behavior modification program should be tried first, medication may be helpful if those efforts fail to bring about significant changes in behavior.

Consider a Psychiatric Consultation. If you and your family physician are unable to resolve the problems with anger, aggression, impulsivity, irritability, or sleep disturbances, you might consider a psychiatric consultation. As discussed in Chapter 4, psychiatrists are sometimes more knowledgeable about a broader range of medications that may be used to treat coexisting problems. When Ritalin or Dexedrine is not enough, medications such as Tofranil, Zoloft, Clonidine, or Lithium may help. Sometimes combinations of these medications may be prescribed.

Seek Additional Treatment Resources as Needed. If your teenager continues to struggle with some of the more serious problems discussed in Chapter 7 (suicide risk, drug abuse), you may need to consider other treatment options that are discussed in Chapter 4. Options include special education classes, a classroom companion, an academic coach, respite, intensive in-home services, a day treatment program, after school programs, summer programs, and as a last resort, residential treatment. Again, remember to ask first for services that will enable your teenager to remain in his home and local school.

Identify Challenging Behaviors

Identify Challenging Behaviors at Home and School (Form 6). You and your teenager should identify the behaviors that are most challenging at home. Teachers should help identify the behaviors that are most challenging at school. Completing this form should help you identify these behaviors and possible intervention strategies. If there are several problems, pick one or two behaviors of greatest concern to start working on and develop a plan for intervention. (See sample Table 6–2, Chapter 6.)

Select Appropriate Interventions. Chapter 5 discusses general principles helpful in raising a teenager with ADD. In addition, intervention strategies for dealing with common behaviors are included in Chapter 6 (Table 6–1) and more serious problem behaviors in Chapter 7 (Table 7–4). Remember, if you can't change your child, change the environment. Work with the school to anticipate problem situations and develop a plan to cope with them.

Eliminate Academic Agony

Make School More Positive (Form 7). As explained in Chapter 8, you can take several steps to help make school a more positive place for your teenager. Decide which action steps you should take on Form 7 and check them off when you have finished them.

Identify Learning Problems and Make Adaptations (Form 8). Although you *could* leave your teenager's education up to his teachers, he will be much more likely to succeed in school if you get involved. Along with teachers, you should identify your teenager's academic strengths, learning problems, and possible classroom adaptations. This form can help you to do so. To complete Form 8, you will need to review several documents: old report cards (teacher comments and grades); standardized test scores; IQ test scores, such as the WISC, subtest scale scores if available; academic achievement tests, such as the IOWA; and Table 10–2, "Common Learning Problems of Teenagers with ADD" in Chapter 10. (See sample Table 9–2, Chapter 9; Tables 10–1 & 10–2, Chapter 10.)

It may take several attempts, with input from trusted teachers, doctors, and other professionals, to fine tune the information. Once the form is completed, however, it will be invaluable during future school years. You can use it to discuss the best teaching strategies with new teachers at the beginning of each school year.

Make needed adaptations to the regular classroom as soon as possible. Then monitor your child's progress to determine if adaptations are effective. Does his academic performance improve? If not, go back to the drawing board. Adjustments to the original treatment plan may be needed. Remember to ask your teenager which interventions and adaptations he needs and is willing to accept.

Work on the Home Front to Avoid Academic Hassles. Chapter 9 suggests specific strategies for ensuring that your teenager completes his homework assignments and improves his performance at school. If needed, you can identify which strategies to use by checking off needed interventions on Table 9–2 in Chapter 9.

Use Federal Laws to Obtain Educational Services. Many teenagers with ADD have serious learning problems that interfere with their ability to learn. Remember that the federal laws discussed in Chapter 11 guarantee that students with disabilities, including ADD, have a right to a free appropriate public education. This includes providing adaptations in the regular classroom.

Treat Teachers as Respected Allies. How you approach school personnel about potential learning problems and adaptations is extremely important! Treating the teacher as an ally and partner is more likely to be successful. Most people do not respond favorably to a confrontive, adversarial approach. You may want to try an approach similar to the one described below:

"My son has some serious learning problems which are causing him problems at school. I have tried to identify his learning problems and some potential adaptations that may help him do better academically. The information contained in this chart [Form 8] reflects information you have provided me, plus input from several other sources: previous teacher conferences, standardized tests, past homework efforts, report cards, past academic and intellectual assessments, and my own observations. I need your help to fine tune this document and make it more accurate and helpful. You may have some ideas I haven't even thought of."

(Or, if form is completed near the end of the school year):

"Identifying learning problems and adaptations now should help him next year when we start off the new school year. We will have this information to help the next teacher."

Determine Who Will Monitor and Provide Support to Improve School Performance. Some parents avoid involvement in school-related work because it becomes such a hostile battlefield. Instead, they hire someone, such as a relative, friend, a private tutor, or staff at an after school program, to take on these responsibilities. Other parents are actively involved, even in high school and college. These parents are able to monitor and tutor their teenager without major battles.

Plan for the Future

When the time is right, begin planning for your teenager's future after high school. Information in Chapter 12 will help you schedule an untimed SAT or ACT if needed, explore career options, and learn about technical school or college. Don't forget that protections under Section 504, including classroom adaptations such as untimed tests, continue through technical school and college. Apply early and provide documentation to support your request for adaptations.

Nurture Yourself

Parents can burn out from the demands of raising a child with ADD. As discussed in Chapters 3 and 5, if you don't nurture yourself, you won't have any emotional energy to give to your child. This makes taking good care of yourself a crucial element of the treatment program for your child. Sometimes what you may need most is for someone to listen with a sympathetic ear while you vent your emotions. If you have emotional support, plus information learned from other parents, a teacher,

counselor, or your doctor, then you can be more patient and understanding, and can take crisis situations in stride more easily.

Participate in Parent Groups. You may benefit from participating in local parent education and support groups such as those offered by CHADD, Federation of Families, MHA, or AMI-CAN. These groups are a wonderful source of information and support for families. Other suggestions for nurturing yourself are offered in Chapter 5.

Learn New Parenting Skills. Becoming a more effective parent will give you greater confidence as you face the challenge of raising a teenager with ADD. Suggestions for improving your parenting skills are given throughout this book.

Some Final Thoughts for Parents

Sometimes it is difficult for parents to know when their teenager has reached his maximum potential. When have the best medications plus right dosages been prescribed? When have all learning problems been identified and proper adaptations made? When should parents stop pushing the system to help their teenager?

Keep pushing the system until your teenager succeeds!

🎗

"As a parent of a teenager with ADD, I didn't know how long to keep pushing for answers to my son's problems. I wondered, 'Maybe this is as good as we can make it for him.' Things had improved at home and medication helped him concentrate better at school. But his grades were still terrible and he was just barely getting by in school. I stopped pushing for answers because I thought he had reached his optimum level of functioning.

"In retrospect, I realize he had serious learning problems that were never identified or treated. His big academic breakthrough came in college when adaptations such as extended test time and use of a calculator were made pursuant to Section 504 of the Rehab Act. After barely graduating from high school, he has just finished a successful freshman year in college. My son was unable to articulate his learning problems and their negative impact until he was a col-

lege freshman. He is so much happier and self-confident now.

"My advice to parents is, 'If your teenager isn't doing well at home and school, something is still wrong. Keep searching for answers, such as adjustments in medication or classroom adaptations, until your teenager succeeds in both environments!!'"

In trying to help your teenager cope with ADD successfully, you may need to play the role of a detective who is trying to solve a mystery. You will have to continue to ask questions and seek answers as you unravel the mysteries of ADD and your teenager's unique problems and needs. For some parents, answers won't come easy. You may have to be tenacious in seeking solutions to your child's problems. The good news, however, is that parents of teenagers with ADD are no longer alone. Thanks to many parents who have traveled this lonely road and coped successfully, more information than ever is now available about teenagers with ADD. Hopefully, the information learned from other parents and professionals which is shared in this book will make your search less lonely and overwhelming.

Form 1

Understanding the Teenager with ADD

NAME: AGE: DATE:

By completing this form, parents should gain a better understanding of their teenager's unique characteristics, personality, strengths, difficulties, and how he is different from other teenagers with ADD. In addition to the symptoms of ADD, all the factors listed below also influence the teenager's behavior, self-esteem, and ability to cope successfully with ADD. The severity of behaviors will vary. Please circle words that best describe your teenager.

DIAGNOSIS: Symptoms of ADD may range from mild to severe.

ADD/Hyperactive (ADD/H)	mild	moderate	severe
ADD/Inattentive (ADD/I/WO)			
without Hyperactivity	mild	moderate	severe
ADD/Combined (ADHD)	mild	moderate	severe

COEXISTING DIAGNOSIS: ADD frequently coexists with other disorders.

Anxiety	mild	moderate	severe
Depression	mild	moderate	severe
Oppositional Defiant	mild	moderate	severe
Conduct Disorder	mild	moderate	severe
Learning Disability	mild	moderate	severe
Learning Problems	mild	moderate	severe
Sleep Disturbance	mild	moderate	severe

FACTORS INFLUENCING ADD: Other factors influence a teenager's personality and ability to cope successfully with ADD. These factors may also vary in intensity: mild/moderate/severe. Teenagers with ADHD and ADD/I/WO may be almost exact opposites in some behaviors. Circle the word that describes your teenager's behavior most of the time.

TEMPERAMENT	GENERAL ISSUES	FAMILY STRESS FACTORS
calm/fidgets	self esteem: good/fair	two parent family: yes/no
easy going/aggressive	intelligence: average/high	step-parents: yes/no
high energy/lethargic	gets along with friends: yes/no	family understands ADD
happy/depressed	inattentive: yes/no	(supportive): yes/no
pleasant/irritable	impulsive: yes/no	reasonable discipline: yes/no
charming/sullen	disorganized: yes/no	(not too harsh or lenient)
class clown/shy	loses things: yes/no	open communication: yes/no
relaxed/anxious	forgets things: yes/no	few hostile inteactions between
cautious/daring	complies with requests: yes/no	teenager and parents: yes/no
tenacious/gives up easily	will do chores: yes/no	relatives understand ADD
compliant/defiant	truthful: yes/no	(supportive): yes/no
copes well/easily frustrated	response to medication: good/fair	family stresses (money, illness,
angry outbursts/calm	difficulty falling asleep: yes/no	divorce, remarriage): yes/no
talks a lot/quiet & low key	difficulty waking up: yes/no	moved to new community: yes/no
	restless: yes/no	attending same school: yes/no
	self-centered: yes/no	
	accident prone: yes/no	
	interrupts/butts in: yes/no	

AREAS OF SUCCESS	POTENTIAL PROBLEM AREAS	MORE SERIOUS PROBLEMS

sports: yes/no
computers/Nintendo: yes/no
music/art: yes/no
religious activities: yes/no
hunting/fishing: yes/no
others:
	defies/disobeys adults: yes/no
	argues with adults: yes/no
	loses temper: yes/no
	blames others: yes/no
	intentionally annoys others: yes/no
	touchy or easily annoyed: yes/no
	angry & resentful: yes/no
	spiteful or vindictive: yes/no
	speeding tickets: yes/no
	substance abuse: yes/no
	sexually active: yes/no
	skips school: yes/no
	school suspension: yes/no
	school expulsion: yes/no
	drops out of school: yes/no
	access to weapons: yes/no
		bullies or threatens others: yes/no
		starts fights: yes/no
		uses weapon to harm others: yes/no
		physically cruel to others: yes/no
		physically cruel to animals: yes/no
		forces others to have sex: yes/no
		lies or "cons" others: yes/no
		steals without confronting: yes/no
		   (shoplifting, credit card fraud)
		robs someone: yes/no
		sets fires: yes/no
		breaks into houses, cars, etc.: yes/no
		destroys other's property: yes/no
		substance abuse: yes/no
		runs away from home: yes/no
		pregnancy: yes/no
		suicide risk: yes/no
		car accidents: yes/no
		
		before age 13:
		stays out all night w/o permission:
		   yes/no
		truant from school: yes/no

SCHOOL PERFORMANCE	LEARNING PROBLEMS	SPECIFIC LEARNING DISABILITY

poor handwriting: yes/no
reading skills: strong/weak
writing skills: strong/weak
can organize themes: yes/no
vocabulary: strong/weak
spelling skills: strong/weak
math skills: strong/weak
knows multiplication tables: yes/no
history/social studies: strong/weak
foreign language skills:
   strong/weak
passes all classes: yes/no
failed a grade: yes/no
test anxiety: yes/no
likes to go to school: yes/no
forgets homework assigned: yes/no
forgets make-up work: yes/no
forgets special projects: yes/no
remembers teacher instructions:
   yes/no
difficulty getting started: yes/no
	poor organizational skills: yes/no
	poor fine motor coordination:
	   yes/no
	poor memory: yes/no
	lacks attention to detail: yes/no
	poor concentration: yes/no
	slow reading: yes/no
	slow math calculation: yes/no
	slow writing: yes/no
	poor reading comprehension:
	   yes/no
	
	SCHOOL ENVIRONMENT
	
	school personnel:
	   positive/hostile
	   flexible/rigid
	   will make adaptions: yes/no
	   use reasonable discipline: yes/no
	special education eligible: yes/no
		Oral Expression: yes/no
		Listening Comprehension: yes/no
		Written Expression: yes/no
		Basic Reading Skills: yes/no
		Reading Comprehension: yes/no
		Mathematics Calculation: yes/no
		Mathematical Reasoning: yes/no

Form 2

DISCOVERING THE TEENAGER'S STRENGTHS
INDIVIDUALIZED TREATMENT PLANNING: "DO WHATEVER IT TAKES"

List your teenager's strengths that you observe at home, school, and in the community. Remember to reframe negative behaviors more positively as described in Chapter 5.

NAME: _____ **AGE:** _____ **GRADE:** _____ **DATE:** _____

STRENGTHS	
Home/Community	**School**
1.	1.
2.	2.
3.	3.
4.	4.
5.	5.
6.	6.
7.	7.
8.	8.
9.	9.
10.	10.

EXAMPLES OF REFRAMING NEGATIVE BEHAVIOR

Examples of reframing negative behaviors may help you develop a list of your teenager's strengths. Remember, the desirability of behaviors changes over time. Characteristics that are not valued in children in school may be valued in the adult business world. Discuss the teenager's strengths with him. Ask him to add to the list.

bossiness	"leadership" (albeit carried too far)
hyperactivity	"energetic," "high energy," "does ten projects at one time," "works long hours"
strong willed	"tenacious"
day dreamers	"creative," "innovative," "imaginative"
daring	"risk taker," "willing to try new things"
laziness	"laid-back," "Type B personalities live longer"
instigator	"initiator," "innovative"
manipulative	"delegates," "gets others to do the job"
aggressive	"assertive," "doesn't let people take advantage of him"
questions authority	"independent," "free thinker," "makes own decisions"
argumentative	"persuasive," "may be attorney material"
poor handwriting	"maybe they'll be a doctor one day"

Form 3
BUILDING SELF-ESTEEM
INDIVIDUALIZED TREATMENT PLANNING: "DO WHATEVER IT TAKES"

NAME: _____ AGE: _____ DATE: _____

IDENTIFY INTERESTS: Encourage your teenager to pursue his interests. Give him the opportunity to participate in activities that make him feel special. Build on strengths listed in Table 3-1. List interests or talents such as sports, art, music, in which skills could be developed further through special training.

* _____   * _____
* _____   * _____
* _____   * _____
* _____   * _____

PARTICIPATE IN ACTIVITIES TO BUILD SELF-ESTEEM: Parents may arrange for their teenager to participate in a variety of activities: a summer computer class, art classes, scuba diving class, modeling, boy or girl scouts, acting in school plays, hunting, fishing, motorcycle racing, water or snow skiing, canoeing, baseball/football/wrestling teams, tennis or golf lessons, summer sports camps, gymnastics, karate, cheerleading camp. Religious activities should also be considered if appropriate: summer camps, Bible school, singing in a choir, public speaking on programs, or activity retreats (snow skiing, camping). Let the teenager select those activities he likes best. If he has no special interests, parents may sign him up for variety of activities and see what skills emerge as strengths.

* _____   * _____
* _____   * _____
* _____   * _____
* _____   * _____
* _____   * _____

Form 4

ASSESS MEDICATION EFFECTIVENESS AT HOME AND SCHOOL—INDIVIDUALIZED TREATMENT PLANNING: "DO WHATEVER IT TAKES."

NAME: _____ AGE: _____ HEIGHT & WEIGHT: _____

<u>MEDICATION HISTORY:</u> List medication(s) currently being taken, dosage, frequency and describe how effective it is. Circle the number that describes the effectiveness of the medication.

Medication/Dosage/Frequency	Not Effective			Very Effective	
1._____	1	2	3	4	5
_____	1	2	3	4	5
2._____	1	2	3	4	5
_____	1	2	3	4	5
3._____	1	2	3	4	5
_____	1	2	3	4	5

<u>EFFECTIVENESS OF MEDICATION:</u> When medication is working properly and learning problems have been identified, most of the problem behaviors described below should decrease and academic performance should improve. Remember that it will take time to "fine-tune" the medication regimen. Even small adjustments such as changing the time of day or increasing the amount of medication may make a major difference in your teenager's behavior at home and school. Circle the correct number (5 if you strongly agree and 1 if you strongly disagree). Parents should ask teachers to complete this form to determine if behavior is improving at school.

When my teenager takes medication, s/he:

	Strongly Disagree	Disagree	Neutral	Agree	Strongly Agree	Comments (Optional)
1. Makes better grades	1	2	3	4	5	_____
2. Passes subjects	1	2	3	4	5	_____
3. Finishes homework	1	2	3	4	5	_____
4. Finishes classwork	1	2	3	4	5	_____
5. Pays attention in class	1	2	3	4	5	_____
6. Participates in class	1	2	3	4	5	_____
7. Obeys school rules	1	2	3	4	5	_____
8. Gets along with friends	1	2	3	4	5	_____
9. Stays awake in class	1	2	3	4	5	_____
10. Wakes up easily	1	2	3	4	5	_____
11. Listens when adults talk	1	2	3	4	5	_____
12. Obeys adults	1	2	3	4	5	_____
13. Is easily distracted	1	2	3	4	5	_____
14. Is forgetful	1	2	3	4	5	_____
15. Is irritable	1	2	3	4	5	_____
16. Is aggressive	1	2	3	4	5	_____
17. Is impulsive	1	2	3	4	5	_____
18. Talks back to adults	1	2	3	4	5	_____
19. Is easily frustrated	1	2	3	4	5	_____
20. Is hyperactive	1	2	3	4	5	_____

Comments:_____

If problems are continuing at school, one logical area to explore further is identification of learning problems and making appropriate classroom adaptations. Even if the teenager is doing okay academically, the current medication may need to be changed or adjusted if sleep disturbances, irritability, or aggression continue to be problems.

Form 5

PEAK MEDICATION TIME
INDIVIDUALIZED TREATMENT PLANNING: "DO WHATEVER IT TAKES"

Name: _____ Age: _____ Grade: _____ Date: _____

Medication name and dosage: _____

Chart the period of time each day when medication is effective. Compare this with when misbehavior or class failure is a problem. Medication wearing off may be a major contributing factor. Classes or times for taking medication may need to be changed. Please note time when: (1) Meds are taken; (2) Meds start to work; (3) Meds have worn off; and (4) Each class is scheduled. Give same information if a second dose is given at school.

Time	Meds (10 mg Ritalin)	Classes	Meds Status
7:00 AM			
7:30			
8:00			
8:30			
9:00			
9:30			
10:00			
10:30			
11:00			
11:30			
12:00 PM			
12:30			
1:00			
1:30			
2:00			
2:30			
3:00			
3:30			
4:00			
5:00			
6:00			
6:30			

Form 6

IDENTIFYING CHALLENGING BEHAVIORS
INDIVIDUALIZED TREATMENT PLANNING: "DO WHATEVER IT TAKES"

Identify challenging behaviors at both home and school and select intervention strategies. Information in Chapters 5–9 should be helpful in completion of this form.

Name: _____   Grade: _____   Date: _____

CHALLENGING BEHAVIORS

At Home/School	Intervention/comments
1.	
2.	
3.	
4.	

Form 7

MAKE SCHOOL MORE POSITIVE
INDIVIDUALIZED TREATMENT PLANNING: "DO WHATEVER IT TAKES"

Determine which of these action steps will increase academic successes and help make school a more positive place to be. Then check each step off as it is completed.

<u>Chapter 8</u>

_____Educate School Personnel about ADD

_____Educate Self about School Philosophy

_____Request Teacher Assignment

_____Schedule a Conference

_____Notify School Officials That Your Teenager Has ADD

_____Treat Teachers with Respect

_____Build Rapport with School Before a Crisis

_____Find the "Voice of Reason"

_____Work through Guidance Counselor

_____Phase Out Interventions Over Time

_____Be Knowledgeable: Sound Knowledgeable!!!

_____Express Appreciation

<u>Chapter 9</u>

_____Provide Assistance with Homework

<u>Chapter 10</u>

_____Identify Learning Problems

_____Identify Adaptations Needed at School

_____Request Services in Regular Classroom

_____Obtain Assistance with or without IDEA Eligibility

_____Request Teacher Change

_____Develop a Contingency Plan for Crisis

<u>Chapter 11</u>

_____Know Provisions of IDEA, Part B; Section 504, and the DOE/OCR Memo (Chapter 11 & Appendix B)

_____Request Evaluation for Services under IDEA or Section 504

_____Participate in Development of IEP

Form 8

IDENTIFYING LEARNING PROBLEMS AND SCHOOL ADAPTATIONS
INDIVIDUALIZED TREATMENT PLANNING: "DO WHATEVER IT TAKES"

Identify potential learning problems and possible classroom adaptions. Material in Chapter 10 should be helpful in completion of this form. After you have done the first draft, discuss it with a trusted former teacher, a counselor, guidance counselor, school psychologist, a child study team at school, or your teenager's physician to confirm, and, if needed, correct your assessment.

Name: Grade: Date:

Learning Problem/Behavior Observed	Adaptations
1.	
2.	
3.	
4.	
Other Comments:	

CHAPTER FOURTEEN

WORDS OF WISDOM FROM THE KIDS

Our sons, Alex and Steven, both have ADD. As teenagers, Steven and Alex shared many of the typical characteristics of ADD. However, their personalities were also different in many ways. One has ADHD and the other ADD/Inattentive (formerly ADD without hyperactivity). One has coexisting learning problems and the other does not. This chapter includes interviews with both of them which may help highlight the uniqueness of each teenager with ADD. The contrasts in their experiences may help parents understand the differences between the types of ADD, the complications that arise when ADD is accompanied by learning disabilities or other problems, and the frustrations of dealing with the disorder.

Actually, Alex and Steven "inherited" each other as brothers by virtue of my marriage in 1986. Alex's ADD/I/WO was diagnosed in 1986, when he was 12 years old. Steven was diagnosed as having ADHD in 1989, when he was 20 years old. You can imagine our surprise and disbelief when my husband and I realized we both had sons with ADD. Although the disorder appears to have skipped both of us, we each have relatives we believe have ADD.

Both our sons seem to be drawn to friends who also have ADD. Over a period of several years, we observed that several of our sons' friends appeared to have similar symptoms. At first we thought it was our imagination—projection possibly—but referral to a physician confirmed a diagnosis of ADD for six or seven of their friends. As discussed in Chapter 6, these young people may feel more comfortable with teenagers who think and act like them and tend to gravitate toward each other as friends.

My circle of friends and professional colleagues who have children with ADD has broadened considerably over the past eight years. Through this communication network, I have had the opportunity to interview several teenagers with ADD from across the country. Each teenager's story and experiences are similar yet different in some ways. Some of the young men and women have co-occurring learning disabilities, anxiety, depression, or oppositional defiant disorder, and others do not.

The young people who contributed to this chapter range in age from 14 to 25. The feelings they describe—their pain, confusion, anxiety, fears, and joys—as well as their academic difficulties despite good intentions, touch the heart. Their stories of living with ADD are sensitive and insightful, and reflect their courageous spirits. Having ADD isn't easy, but these teenagers have developed a better understanding of their disorder and have learned to cope with ADD successfully. You may want to share these inspiring stories with your teenager.

ALEX (Sixteen)............

Profile: Alex has ADD/I/WO (without hyperactivity) and has learning problems that include slow cognitive processing and poor short-term memory. He is 20 now and has successfully finished his first two years in college. He was diagnosed at age 12.

When you have a disability like ADD, you don't know what "normal" attention and concentration are. You just assume that everyone concentrates the same way you do. It's like having a vision problem. You don't know what the real world looks like or that you have a vision problem until you are tested and get glasses. In the same way, you don't know you have ADD and problems with attention and concentration until you take Ritalin and find out what is it like to be able to concentrate.

Second grade is where the trouble started. This is where I discovered writing, and that I didn't like it. One day when I was frustrated, I stopped writing. When the teacher asked me to do the work, I told her to do it herself.

Third grade I didn't get along with my teacher at all. She couldn't understand why I was so slow, so I spent a lot of time with the principal. This teacher was so bad that even my mom didn't like this woman.

I wasn't doing so well in school and they referred me to be tested. I scored pretty high and they said I was eligible for the gifted program.

Fourth grade I was moved to a new school. This school was much more fun and easier than my old school. I liked my teacher that year. She was nice to me.

Fifth grade I was lucky enough to get the same teacher again. This class helped me with my work habits. The thing I liked best about this class was its pets, especially the snakes. I liked taming wild snakes, and I was bitten almost every day.

I was not prepared for sixth grade. It was exactly like high school. I had six classes, six teachers, and six homework assignments every day. This was a very big change for me, but I hung in there.

Seventh grade I moved to Georgia from Tallahassee, Florida. The schools became a little bit less like high school since I had three teachers instead of six. I again got myself into trouble by cursing at a teacher. This incident helped me in a way, because I became good friends with the principal.

Eighth grade I was transferred to another school. Mr. Ford, the principal, also transferred to this new school. That year one of my teachers was not a friendly teacher, but I controlled my temper this time.

Ninth grade wasn't as bad as I had thought it would be. Some of the work was harder for me, which caused me to slack off a little bit. The Ritalin helped me a lot when trying to stay on task.

My sophomore year seemed to be a little bit easier, but I still slacked off some. I would usually have low grades that I would pull up near the end of the semester. My grades were pretty much borderline, but I had a few high grades.

So far my junior year has been the same with borderline grades.

Sometimes I was a troublemaker at school. I didn't like to do the work. Sometimes I made fun of the teacher. Teachers said I didn't assert myself very much. Mom said that teachers told her that I was never a discipline problem. I guess the things I did to make them mad were pretty subtle. I didn't do anything real bad.

I like for my teachers to treat me with respect. If a teacher is nice to me, then I usually do better in that class. If I don't like them and I think they're mean, sometimes I will fail the class.

When I'm not on Ritalin, I tend to be more impulsive and more aggressive. I go on instinct. When I am on my medicine, I actually think about my decisions more clearly and what will happen if I do something. I can do my work. I can really concentrate a lot better. I can sit for two or three hours and work on my homework.

I am not constantly on Ritalin so I can't constantly think about what will happen. I forget why I was grounded and feel like my parents are just being mean to me. It doesn't connect in my mind that I really did something wrong. Punishment doesn't work a lot of times because it doesn't connect in my mind.

I've been stopped for speeding lots of times. I hate to tell you but I was stopped for speeding seven times in the first seven months I was driving. I have slowed down a lot. Tickets and speeding are starting to connect in my mind a little more now. I have to go to court and pay money. They take my license away. But once you get your license back and are out driving, you forget. You don't realize that they can take it away again. I always say I won't do this again after I get a ticket. Getting a ticket really upsets me and I feel really stressed out. My Toyota 4-runner is the love of my life. I live to drive.

If you asked me to describe myself, I'd say I try to be generous to other people a lot. I get along well with a lot of people. I have a lot of friends. My friends say I'm a take-charge kind of guy. I am adventuresome. I like to come up with ideas. I try to make things fun.

LEWIS (Seventeen)...........

Profile: Lewis has ADHD and learning disabilities. His learning disabilities were diagnosed in second grade, but ADHD wasn't diagnosed until he was a junior in high school. He is 20, has graduated from high school, is working, and plans to attend a local technical school/community college.

My mom tells me I was born two months premature. I weighed 2 pounds 11 ounces. I had to stay at the hospital for six weeks before I could go home.

I was always getting into stuff. I was always curious about things and had to explore or check out everything. My mom must have thought I was a terror. Once I vacuumed all the water out of the toilet. One time I got a can of mace and accidentally sprayed it in my face.

I stuck rings in light sockets and knives in the toaster . . . I got shocked. I did it at least four more times even though I got shocked. Once I played in a big bed of fire ants. I was covered with bites. I ran in the house and jumped in the bathtub.

I used to talk a lot when I was little. Kids in school called me "motor mouth." If I thought of something, I just said it. I wouldn't think twice. It would just come out.

When I was growing up, people say I was in constant motion. I guess some people thought I was "hyper." Some people thought I was downright "crazy." I couldn't sit down for a long time. I had trouble sitting down even when I wanted to. I couldn't sit still for school, reading, or even watching TV.

I have always loved entertaining people and making them laugh. When I was in elementary school, I got on top of a car and started dancing just to make people laugh. Unfortunately, my mom and dad weren't laughing when the principal had them come to school to talk about my antics. I have always had a lot of friends.

Teachers have told me that they can see I'll be famous someday. I had long talks with my teachers while I was standing in the hall. Since I was in the hall almost every day, I had my own special spot in the hall. I would peek in the room and make faces. The other students would laugh a lot. I would wander off and peek in the bathroom. I'd run in, flush all the toilets, put soap in all the sinks and on the mirrors, and run back to my spot in the hall.

Usually, teachers seated me up front near their desk or back in the cubbyhole. Sometimes I had to sit in the corner. I'd get mad. It didn't work. I'd still turn around and get someone's attention. I had to sit in a cubicle with high sides in third through seventh grades. They put me there so I wouldn't disturb the other students.

In the second grade they found out I had a learning disability. I thought I was in "dumb classes." People started making fun of me. They thought I was abnormal. That's why I guess I kept being funny: to let them know I was just like them . . . maybe even better.

I am still in a resource room. In one way I am glad I am getting extra help. On the other hand, I don't like getting put down by other students asking why are you in that class? Are you dumb? Are you abnormal? I don't want people to know I'm in a resource room except my close friends. But I am coping better with being in the resource room.

Once I asked my teacher a question about a math problem. In front of the whole class, she asked my why I needed so much extra help. She said, "If you need extra help, then you need to go to the resource room." I was embarrassed and very angry with my teacher for being so insensitive.

I never made very good grades in school when I was little. Now that my ADD has been diagnosed, I have made better grades. I made my first A in a class . . . biology. Ritalin lets me concentrate better and focus on what I am doing. I don't shout out in class. I raise my hand. I think my temper is going down. I take time to do my work right rather than doing it half way. When I'm on time-release Ritalin, I can actually feel it kick in. In class one day I was making chicken noises. About three minutes later I felt it kick in and I started doing my work. Teachers ask me if I have taken my medicine. They know when I have and when I haven't. In fact, if I hadn't taken my medicine, I wouldn't be able to sit here long enough to write this story about my life.

When I started taking Ritalin, I took it only when I went to school. My mom had never been around me when I was on Ritalin. Then one day I started a new job and took my medicine before I went to work. So when I came home, the medicine was still working. My mom said that I could actually stand still long enough to have a conversation with her.

Although my family knew I had a learning disability when I was real young, no one ever even mentioned that I might have ADD. When I was 16, I met a friend in driver's ed class and spent the night the first night I met him. His mom, Ms. Dendy, got to know me and asked if I had ever been checked for ADD. I found out that Alex and a lot of my friends also had ADD. It made me feel more confident in myself when I knew that it wasn't me alone in the dark. Other friends were in the same boat with me.

STEVEN (twenty-three)............

Profile: Steven has ADHD, which was diagnosed in 1989 when he was 20 years old. He graduated from college with a degree in printing management in 1993.

I thought school was hard. I never really knew why school was so hard for me. I felt left behind when my friends were in advanced classes. I was stuck in regular class. Sometimes I thought I was doing really good in school. Then when report cards came home, I didn't understand why I didn't make good grades. I'd say I never had a lot of book smarts but I had a lot of common sense. For example, I never read a book on how to fix a bicycle, but I could take the whole thing apart and put it back together.

My dad thought I was pure lazy. My mother wanted to have me tested but my dad said that was ridiculous. I needed discipline. I did well in subjects that interested me, such as history. I did all right in math depending on what it was. I made stupid errors because I didn't listen well. I forgot to watch for changes in signs. In algebra, plus and minus signs change a lot.

I was a daydreamer in school. In middle school, I daydreamed about bicycles. In high school, I daydreamed about cars and girls. Through college, my daydreaming usually dealt with hunting.

I never wanted to miss school. I was afraid I would miss something. I missed only two days my freshman year and that was because my mom made me stay home. I missed a total of five days in four years in high school. I enjoyed school. I got along with my teachers even though I didn't make good grades. I was always well liked. I was always the class clown.

My handwriting is okay but I write a combination of printing and cursive. It's never consistent either way. I was also a doodler. I still doodle a lot.

I remember I didn't have any problems with school up until sixth grade. Until I got to sixth grade, I never had to study. I always got by with what I could remember. Sixth grade was also a "goody, goody" stage. If I did well on a test, other people who didn't do well kidded me. They wanted to bring me down to their level. So I didn't want to study. Later in seventh grade, I didn't want to study when I got home. If I went up to my room and studied for 15 minutes, I felt like I had spent a lifetime up there.

I earned the money and bought a BMX bicycle when I was in seventh grade. I loved to ride it every day. I worked on it all the time and was always wanting new stuff for it. When I got home from school, all I did was ride it. I read two or three bicycle magazines. If I didn't make my grade or I smarted off, my parents punished me by putting my bicycle in the attic for several weeks. I could go and visit my bicycle, but I couldn't work on it or ride it.

My senior year in high school, I had an easier year. I really liked social studies classes. I had two study halls. I wanted a B average bad enough my senior year, so I put in extra effort. I never really studied in high school. I got by on what I heard in class. If the class interested me, I would remember it. I never had a problem with wanting to drink a lot in high school. I never did any illegal drugs.

When I got my first speeding ticket, I was in my sister's car and some guy was racing me. I thought I had beat him, so I slowed down. A car was coming up fast on me, so I speeded up. It was a police officer. I got my second speeding ticket within 20 feet of my first ticket. I just really wasn't paying attention and was just cruising along. I used to drive faster, but now I roll down my window to stay awake.

I can't stand to be out of control in a situation, like in traffic. I'm a very vocal driver. I tend to yell a lot, blow my horn. I can't stand incompetence. I get irritated by things I think are stupid.

After high school, I went to Georgia Southern University. That was honestly the first time I ever had to really study. But even in college, I couldn't keep my attention focused long enough. Something was always going on. I always wanted to play golf or do something else. The first subject in college I ever studied for was probably a history class, my second quarter there. It was the first time I ever, ever, studied for a history class. It was the first time I hadn't made an A on anything related to social studies. I made a D. I barely passed.

After the low grades I made my first year in college, I thought books weren't for me. I could learn better from someone showing me. I felt totally out of it. No matter what I did or how hard I tried, I would get a bad grade. My grade point average was low enough that I had to sit out of college a quarter on probation. I chose not to go back to school.

I worked for a year and contemplated opening my own mechanic's shop. After having been out of school almost a year, I decided I would like to go back to school. My parents asked me before I went back to go get tested for ADD. I thought it was kind of dumb. I went to a pediatrician's office. Since I was 20 years old, 6'1" tall, weighed 205 lbs, and had a full beard, the nurse thought I was in the wrong place. When she asked why I was there, I said, "I'm here because my Dad told me to come." After the doctor tested me, he told me about Ritalin and we decided to give it a try.

I returned for my sophomore year at Georgia Southern at the end of August 1989. I started taking Ritalin then. I went back on probation because of my grade point average from my freshman year. I took psychology, government, plus repeated my history class. Straight out of the shoot, I made a B and two Cs. I brought myself off probation.

During my psychology class, we came to a section where they talked about ADD and Ritalin. The professor asked if anyone had ever taken Ritalin. Four or five of us raised our hands. She asked when was the last time we had taken it. I looked at my watch and said about an hour and a half ago. She was really shocked. Then she asked when I started taking Ritalin. When I told her I started taking it about four weeks ago, she was even more surprised.

The best way I can describe how Ritalin affects me is by telling this story. When I am sitting in class and my stomach starts growling, before I started taking Ritalin, I would sit there and think: "When I get home, I'll have me a ham sandwich, with mayonnaise and mustard, two slices of cheese, lettuce, some Fritos, and I'm gonna watch TV." I visually built the sandwich in my mind.

Then I would realize I had just missed 30 minutes worth of notes. Ritalin keeps me focused. Sometimes, it can make me focus so much, that any disturbance can grate on my nerves. If I am really concentrating on something, I tend to get angry and say, "What do you want?" Ritalin also makes me worry more, if anything is bothering me. Sometimes it makes me dwell on things and puts me in a depression.

I especially like Ritalin for two things: long trips in my car and long hours in my deer stand. If I take my Ritalin, I can sit for hours, as long as there's gas in the car. Ritalin puts me in a state of mind that I lose track of time. I can sit in my deer stand from dawn 'til past 10:00 a.m. without looking at my watch. I usually come out of my deer stand at 10:30.

I finished college with a Bachelor of Science in printing management. My junior and senior year I maintained a B average. I brought my grade point average from a 1.95 to a graduation level of 2.6. During my junior and senior years, I was able to work and go to school at the same time and still keep my grades up.

I feel that I am a technical person. With a technology degree, I actually get to do hands-on work. Dealing with a lot of theory like business classes doesn't seem practical. I really feel that people in the business field live in a glass house.

I'm married now and working as a management trainee at a folding carton plant. I love my work and put in between 50 to 60 hours a week. I work a lot on Saturdays too.

My wife says I've got a temper. All my friends tell me I'm obnoxious. That means I'm loud and boisterous. I have an "attitude." The ability to work with people is one of my strengths. I am a leader. I don't follow people.

TONYA (eighteen)...........

Profile: Tonya's ADD/I/WO was diagnosed in 1994 when she was a senior in high school. She is now a freshman in college.

My boyfriend kept telling me that I had ADD and needed to go to a doctor. At first I didn't think I had it, but he pointed out things I was doing. I had trouble concentrating, didn't listen, was forgetful and impatient, and daydreamed a lot. When I finally went to the doctor, he said I did have ADD.

My brother has ADD too but I think I must have a milder case.

I don't listen when people talk to me. When my mom calls me from work and tells me to do something, I sit on the phone and say, "Yeah, yeah, yeah." But I don't really hear her. I ignore her, I guess.

My friends think I listen but I don't hear everything they tell me. Half the time I'm not even thinking about what they are telling me. I'll be thinking about where I'm going and what I'm going to do. My friend will be telling me a long story and then will say, "What do you think I should do?" And I'll say, "About what?" Sometimes my boyfriend will be talking to me and I won't be listening. He'll say, "Tonya, where are you?" I daydream bad but nobody notices when I space out. I'm real quiet around most people so they don't notice.

Sometimes when I drive down the road, I'll be in the biggest daydream. I kind of know what is going on around me but I don't really. My driving makes me a little nervous. I don't like to drive because I don't think I pay attention enough. It scares me when I get in the car. I had my first wreck because I was daydreaming. I was pulling out of the parking lot at school. The guy in front of me looked like he was going to pull out. Then he slammed on his brakes. I was in another world. I mashed on the gas and hit him. Sometimes I like to drive if I'm depressed. I want to be alone. I'll get in the car, turn on the radio, and just drive.

I'm bad about forgetting things. My mother is my memory. Every time there is something important going on, I always tell Mom, because she will remind me. When someone tells me something, it goes in one ear and out the other. Even if I write something down, I usually lose the piece of paper I wrote it on. It's just easier to tell Mom. She has learned to have me repeat to her what she said. I have to do things right away or I'll forget.

In high school, I always forgot my homework assignments even though I wanted to do them. I always felt like my homework helped me. Plus, I didn't want to get to school and have to say I didn't have my homework. I would be embarrassed. At the end of the day, I'd stand at the locker trying to remember what we did in class. Some nights I wouldn't remember my homework assignments until nine o'clock. I would have my

Dad go get my books out of my locker. I was lucky, he had a key to my school.

One way I handled my homework was to ask my friends what our assignments were. We would all get to school early and stand by our lockers. Someone in my class would say, "Did you do your homework for Spanish?" I'd be in a panic. I would end up doing my homework during lunch or copy their homework. Sometimes I'd work on it in other classes.

I really didn't like school very much. I liked it pretty well my first two years in high school. After that I dreaded getting up and going to school. My junior year was my hardest year. I bought an assignment book and wrote everything down. I wrote down my assignments and what books I needed to bring home. I had to carry that book with me everywhere I went. It really helped a lot. I wish I had thought of it sooner.

If I can use a calculator, math is one of my strongest subjects. I have always liked math. I made A's and B's in first-year algebra and geometry. When I have to do my math in my head, I work slowly. I had trouble memorizing my multiplication tables. When I was in elementary school, we would have multiplication tests each week. I'd go home and memorize them but it wasn't really registering in my brain. It would take me the whole week to do it. I would memorize them just to get by on the test. The next week I would remember only one or two. I couldn't use a calculator on the SAT and I did so horrible.

My lack of concentration is a real problem. If I paid attention more in class, I would have made better grades. I drifted off or wrote a note to a friend while the teacher was talking.

I read real slowly. Reading slowly always made me get behind. In English class, we would have an essay to read. Everyone else would be done and I would still be reading. The teacher would give us a time limit and then would call out questions. Whoever raised their hand first would get extra credit. I never did earn extra credit because I would still be reading.

Writing stories was hard for me. I write slowly and my thoughts were going fast in my mind. By the time I was ready to write my ideas down, I had forgotten what I was going to write. Remembering subjects, verbs, and pronouns and distinguishing between them is hard for me.

I have trouble taking notes because I write so slowly. I write down half of what the teacher said and then I'll forget the other half. I can't write fast enough. That's why I wanted to have a tape recorder in Spanish. My teacher talked real fast. My mom and I had to go to the principal's office to get permission to use a tape recorder. The teacher didn't want me to use one in her classroom. In my chemistry class, the teacher went so much faster than the speed I learn at. He would lose me 15 minutes into class and then I wouldn't pay attention from then on. My handwriting is not real neat for a girl.

If something interests me, I can make good grades. I made bad grades in History and English because they bore me. I couldn't get into them and I wouldn't listen. I didn't care about things that happened years and years ago. I just barely passed three social studies classes with a 70 average. I always felt like my social studies teacher didn't like me. He always knew when I didn't know the answer and he would call on me. I'd have a blank look on my face and he would say "Come on, Tonya." Then he'd wait and wait forever. He made me feel real dumb.

I love danger and excitement. I try things that other girls don't try. I guess I like the rush I get. Once several of us went to the lake because one of the guys said there was a really cool bridge that people jumped off of. You have to jump quick or you could get caught and get a ticket. When you jump 60 feet off a bridge, you feel free. It's thrilling knowing it's something you could get into trouble for. Sometimes we hang onto a rope, swing out, and let go over the water.

I got caught when my aunt saw me and told my mother. When I got home Mom asked what I had been doing. I told her about jumping off the bridge. She told my Dad to get on to me. Dad said he couldn't get on to me because he jumped off the same bridge when he was a kid.

I also like to ride motorcycles. My boyfriend always told me his dirt bike was too big for me to ride and I might get hurt. I talked him into teaching me how to change gears with my foot. We went out riding and I rode the motorcycle. It was really easy. When you ride up a jump, you worry if you'll land right and not wreck. I rode it up a steep hill. The first time I tried it, I didn't go fast enough.

The motorcycle rolled back down the hill and I had to jump off.

My mom suggested that I try modeling since she felt I wasn't very confident in myself. She thought it would help build my confidence. Modeling is kind of exciting with all the lights around you. One photographer works with you. You get pictures back and they look so good. The pictures look so pretty it's like it's not really me. It helped my self-esteem a lot. I was real quiet and bashful.

During the modeling training, my instructor would take a video camera and we had to do a fake commercial in front of 30 people. We stood in front of the camera and had to say a paragraph. This helped me feel confident talking in front of people. I learned if I make a mistake not to worry. Everyone makes mistakes.

The first medication I took was Paxil. The doctor wanted to try it first because of my anxiety. When I have a test, I get real nervous. I forget everything even though I studied the night before. Paxil didn't help my attention or concentration. I asked my doctor if I could try Dexedrine. I started taking Dexedrine when I went away to college last fall. It works much better. I can concentrate.

TRAVIS (fourteen)............

Profile: Travis has ADD *combined with hyperactivity and inattention, which was diagnosed when he was nine years old.*

I want to be an Air Force pilot when I graduate from college. I have always wanted to fly airplanes, especially sophisticated aircraft. You have to be in the Air Force to do that. Civilian pilots can't fly sophisticated planes. I like the military because most of my family have been in the service. I love to build models of military armor and aircraft. Actually, I am making a diorama of Desert Storm right now. I am building an old city in Desert Storm with U.S. soldiers walking through town. There will also be M1-A1 Abrams tanks and behind them there will be M-1-113 troop carriers. I am setting it up on my modeling table downstairs. To build the diorama, I will fill a picture frame with Elmer's glue and then pour real fine powder over it for the sand. Everything is built to scale.

In my room, I have 32 model airplanes hanging from the ceiling. There are 16 other models on shelves, including tanks, ships, cars, and a model of the "Alien" from the movie. I can sit for hours and do models because I enjoy it so much. It may take hours and hours or even months to finish a model. Once when I was four years old and was bored, my Mom bought me a snap-type model. I loved it and have been building models ever since. I have sat up all night to work on a model.

When I build models, I don't follow the directions. The best thing to do is *never* follow directions. That will mess you up. I use pictures of the real tank to build from. For example, I have eight books with pictures of the M1-A1 Abrams tank. As I build the tank, I will set up pictures all around me to see what the actual tank looks like.

I love drawing too. I'm pretty good at drawing comic book characters, military aircraft, and tanks.

School is not my favorite thing to do. Some things I like about it, some things I don't. I liked it in fifth grade when I made all A's and B's. I notice I get in trouble at school more than other people do. When everyone else in class is working, I'm the one trying to get their attention. The teacher will say, "Sit down and be quiet." Five minutes later, I'm talking again. I really like to talk to people.

Most of my friends say I'm funny. I like to make them laugh a lot. Some people say I'm the class clown. Sometimes I make comments out of something the teacher said. For example, the bus driver said, "If we have a fire, you two in the back seat should be the first ones out of the bus." Everyone laughed when I said, "You're darn right I'll be first one out of this bus."

I have a hard time getting along with teachers because they don't understand ADD. I disturb class. Sometimes I get in trouble when I forget my medicine. I'll say, "Maybe if I take my medicine now it will help me calm down." The teacher will say, "That's no excuse and has nothing to do with it."

Teachers are always watching me. If something happens, they blame me. Today this boy was talking in class. The teacher told me to leave class without even asking who was talking. Other people told her it wasn't me. Finally, she let me come back in the room when she realized it wasn't me talking. I like it when my teachers understand ADD. They are more patient, tolerate me a lot more, and know how to help me with my problems. They notice when I get too wild and ask me if I have taken my medicine today. Then they say,

"It's time to go take your medicine. You need to calm down."

This year I want to make all B's and above because next year I want to go to a private military academy.

My strongest subject is language arts. Teachers say I have incredible writing skills. It seems like everything I write about is military, though. I wrote a 20-page theme on Viet Nam. I wrote it like I was on a tour of duty there.

I write real slow and my handwriting is not good. It's sloppy. I read slowly too, but I understand what I read. I have read some of Tom Clancy's books. I liked *Red Storm Rising,* which was about nuclear war, Navy Seals, and World War III. I like to read the book before I see the movie. I read *Jurassic Park,* and the book and movie were totally different.

My worst subject is math. I can't answer math problems real quick. I have never been good at memorizing my times tables or division tables. That really messes me up in math. I have been taken out of resource class and we are doing harder stuff. Last year in resource we were allowed to talk if we did our work. Now we have to do our work in total silence. I am allowed to use a calculator now and that really helps. But we had to do a test to find out how much we know about math. I know a lot but sometimes I still have to use my fingers when doing addition.

We have a routine every night about homework. Mom will say it's time to get started on my homework. Then she asks me what my homework is. "Let me see your assignment book." It takes forever to do my homework. We both get frustrated. We fight over homework all the time. Sometimes I may work close to four or five hours. I have to do all the problems in the assignment. For example, today the teacher assigned 4 pages of math with 30 problems on each page.

Sometimes it is hard to keep calmed down and work on my homework. I'll sit down and work for five minutes and then start looking around. My mind goes off somewhere else. I am thinking about my day, the things I did, and the people I saw.

I always do my homework because Mom will check it. I can't just give up and say I'm done, because Mom *always* checks.

Sometimes I forget my homework or books. We have assignment notebooks at school. Even when I fill it out, I often leave stuff out. The teacher will tell us our homework at the end of class. By then, I have all my stuff packed up and ready to go. Sometimes when she tells us our assignments, I don't write them down. When I get home, I don't have a clue what my assignments are. We have a real neat system now. We have a homework hotline. Each team of teachers has a different phone number and it says what our homework is. That works out for us a lot.

Right now the only medication I am taking is Zoloft. This year I am trying not to take any medicine. To get into the private military school, I have to cut back and not take anything. The military won't let anyone fly an airplane while taking medicine. Ritalin helps me a lot. It helps me concentrate and get my work done. It even helped me when I played sports. In basketball when I didn't take my medicine, I would get wild and just start shooting whenever I got the ball. In soccer, I couldn't concentrate on dribbling and just kicked the ball around. When I take my medicine, I think about moves I'm going to make. When people are coming at me, I concentrate on my shots. When I don't have my Ritalin, I can never hit my goal. When I take Ritalin, I can hit almost any goal. I may take Ritalin when I go hunting. I will be able to stay up in the deer stand longer and not get anxious and talk.

I just finished a hunting test and made a 100. I am an extremely good shot and can hit almost anything. I am not bragging or anything, but I can hit a bull's-eye on any target within range. At the military academy I attend during the summer, I am an expert marksman. When I was four years old, I shot my first turkey. Dad held the gun and I told him when the shot was lined up.

SHAWN (sixteen)............

Profile: Shawn has ADD/I/WO (without any apparent learning problems), which was diagnosed when he was 15. After graduating from high school, he attended college on an academic scholarship.

My ADD without hyperactivity was diagnosed when I was 15, and I started taking Ritalin then. Up until that time I had never done very well in school and it seemed like I was always in trouble with my parents.

I guess I thought I was lazy and stupid. I couldn't concentrate. Like, when I was reading, I would be thinking about something else. After I read something, I would realize I couldn't remember what it was about. My handwriting was never very good. My parents had me checked for learning disabilities when I was in the sixth grade but they couldn't find any.

I used to think, "I can get one zero in class and it won't hurt." One zero turned into more and more. Then it got to where I didn't really care. I would get too far behind and couldn't catch up.

During class I tended to be real tired and sleep a lot. I tended to sleep in classes like English that have a lot of book work. If teachers talked too much, it seemed like it just went right through my brain. If I missed a little, I couldn't catch back up.

When I came home from school each day, I was in a real bad mood. I would start yelling over the least little thing. My grades got worse in school as time went by. I got C's in elementary school, some D's and F's in middle school, and then mostly D's and F's my freshman year in high school, except in wood shop. I've always been good working with my hands so I made good grades in shop.

I always had trouble getting started on my homework. I would write down my assignments and bring them home. Then I would forget to bring my book home. Sometimes I remembered my homework at bedtime or in the morning just before I went to school. In elementary school, I had to go to after-school detention for not doing my homework at least once a week. My teachers said I was never a discipline problem, though.

I used to start a lot of projects but never seemed to get them finished. I would start out with lots of good ideas and good intentions. They I would slack off and do a crappy job. It was the same with sports. I'd go out for soccer, baseball, and football, do real well for a little while, then get bored with it and want to do something else.

I wanted to do better in school, but somehow I never could. I would start out okay the first two weeks. Then I slacked off. We moved around a lot and I thought that was why I had so many problems at school. I know I have developed bad work and study habits. I missed out on a lot of basic skills in math and English.

I forgot my chores a lot. If Dad asked me to bring my dirty clothes down within the next hour,

I forgot to do it. I forgot to bring in the newspaper. I forgot to clean my room. I never seemed to think about the consequences.

I felt like my parents didn't trust me. Sometimes I didn't always tell them the truth because I knew they didn't trust me anyway. Sometimes I'd tell them I was spending the night with one friend, but really stay with another. I knew they wouldn't let me stay with that friend. I got in so much trouble that at one point it felt like I had been grounded my whole life. I guess my parents just thought I was lazy. They were worried about what I would do in life when I grew up. At times they may have been ashamed of me. Thank goodness, things are a lot happier now. Since I've been taking Ritalin, I have not been grounded.

When I turned 15, my parents wouldn't let me get my learner's permit to drive. I had to wait until I was 16. They were worried about the way I drove. When I'm not on my medicine, I drive real bad. I forget to stop at red lights and sometimes I stop at green lights.

Besides making me a better driver, Ritalin has made a big difference in my grades. My grades went from D's and F's my freshman year to mostly A's and B's my sophomore year when I started taking Ritalin.

Now I go to school early. I always look at my books to make certain I haven't forgotten something. If I have forgotten something, I can do the work then before I go to class.

I really like my grades now. I have more free time. I can get most of my work done in class. My parents let me do more things. They trust me more and are real proud of me. They are very happy about my grades.

If I had to describe myself, I would say that I am quiet and easygoing. Most of the time I go with the flow. I don't argue a lot. I'm not hyperactive. People seem to like me a lot. I get along with most everyone. My friends say that they have never seen me angry. My friends can count on me. I like to try exciting things. If someone tries something new I want to try it too.

I have had a job for several months now and I love it. They really like my work and trust me and put me in charge sometimes if they are gone for a while. I don't like to have a lot of free time and just sit around home. I am saving up my money for a car.

ELIZABETH (nineteen)............

Profile: Elizabeth was diagnosed as having ADHD just before she started the third grade. She has graduated from high school and coordinates camp and meeting schedules for children with emotional problems and their counselors. She also volunteers with some of the children.

I'm not really sure I have ADD. But I've been told I do. In elementary school, I was a chatterbox but I wasn't disruptive or hyperactive. I was talkative, but everyone else was like that too. I didn't think I had ADD because I wasn't hyper.

I started having trouble in third grade. I transferred schools and had to take an entrance exam. I couldn't enter third grade at the new school without knowing my multiplication tables. They hadn't been introduced at the old school. I had to go to summer school to get caught up with the rest of my new class. Going to summer school was traumatic too. It was the first of many years in summer school.

I started taking Ritalin that summer before third grade. It helped me pay attention. But it didn't help me learn multiplication tables. Since Ritalin didn't help me learn my multiplication tables, I figured I didn't have ADD. I didn't like to take Ritalin. I don't even like to take aspirin. Ritalin took away my alertness and my fun. I focused only on school. I never saw anything but the teacher. I was bored and wanted to have more fun at school. Because Ritalin made me feel different, I felt like I lost several months of my life. I will never ever touch Ritalin again. I feel that I have no personality when I take it. I don't want to miss anything.

I noticed how much less observant I was in fourth grade. It was almost like I wasn't able to feel loose and fun and silly. I was such a loner when I took my medicine. I didn't want to take my Ritalin so I would give my medicine to my friends who asked to try it. Sometimes my friends would act like me because they took my pills.

In seventh grade, I finally had an adult who was a teacher who agreed with me. He agreed that I was much more lively and happy when I was not taking the Ritalin. I was glad that someone else saw what I felt.

In eighth grade, I made good grades. It just happened. I wasn't on Ritalin. I made my best grades and was on the honor roll.

I was on the high school speech and debate team for three years. My senior year I was captain and was co-captain my junior year. I started off with original oratory and had to give a speech that was 5-10 minutes long. I had to memorize it. I was under so much pressure I forgot my speech. I switched to prose and poetry and selected different poems. I did well on that. I did great on impromptu speaking. They give you part of a sentence or phrase and you have to speak for five minutes. I attended statewide speech and debate Congress and was elected Head of the House. I was popular with my friends. They respected my public speaking abilities.

The worst thing in high school was not knowing until graduation practice if I would graduate or not. I had a 69.5 average in English and my teacher wouldn't tell me if I was going to pass. She did pass me and I graduated with my class. English was so hard for me. Mother sent me to a learning center to help with my English. I had English teachers at the learning center review my papers, and my teacher still gave me failing grades. She didn't like females. I was afraid to go to college because of English. I had trouble with geometry too. I failed it twice.

I have always worked. I have a lot of energy and often have two jobs. One thing I am good at is working with people's hair and make-up. I have been in cosmetology school for several months and have a 98 average. My instructor made me angry one day. She told me I had messed something up but she didn't come back to help me. She made me wait. I was upset and left ten minutes before lunch.

I think I would be good at sales too. I have learned that I don't want to work for someone else. I want to work for myself.

I get tired of people saying, "You've got ADD," when I do something that any other teenager would do. For instance, I remember once my parents were out of town and my friends and I had a party at my house. The house was locked but we climbed up a ladder, got on the roof, and climbed in a window. We had a fight and were throwing grapes at each other. I didn't think Mother would ever find out, but she found the grapes smushed on her closet door and one on the couch in the den. My parents think I need friends who are calmer to keep me in line, to give me balance. My parents are conservative and I'm not. Sometimes I forget to call home and tell my parents where I am when I am coming home late. I don't realize how late it is. If I had a wreck, I would call them, or the cops would.

My mother kids me sometimes and calls me "Susie social worker." I really care about other people and want to help solve their problems. I am very loyal and protective of my friends. I would give people the shirt off my back. I have loaned friends money to help them out. I am a fun-loving person who enjoys life. I have a good personality.

ROBERT (Eighteen)............

Profile: Robert has ADHD, which was diagnosed when he was a junior in high school. He is currently attending college on a football scholarship.

When I was little, none of my toys lasted very long. I would take parts off one and put it on another. The toy I had the longest was an all-metal toy Tonka dump truck. A few days after I got the truck I had pulled off the rubber tail pipe and the rubber steering wheel. When I got older, my Dad would buy me model cars with up to 200 pieces. I would assemble them completely by the instructions. Then, I would start modifying them, adding pieces, taking pieces off, and putting bigger wheels on them. Anything to change them from the ordinary.

In school, I guess my biggest problems were being hyper and having teachers who didn't understand me. I would finish my work quicker than others. I never understood why my teachers wouldn't let me do something else when I finished my work. They always said that I was a nice kid, and I never caused any *intentional* trouble. But I was always curious and getting into things I wasn't supposed to get into. If I made a bad grade, teachers thought it was because of behavior.

When teachers used to put written comments on the back of report cards, they would say, "draws and daydreams, good student, can't sit still in a chair." When I got older, the hyperactivity faded away because of sports.

Teachers would say that I spent a lot of time drawing. Even on tests, on homework, anything I did, I'd get bored and draw pictures of what I was thinking about. I still do some art work. That's something that expresses me in every way. There are no limitations and my mind can skip from one thing to another without it really hurting my work.

Homework was always a problem, and still is a problem even in college. I was always getting in trouble about not doing my homework. It was easy work but I never got around to doing it. I couldn't understand the importance of something so easy. I could find better things that were more stimulating to do.

In the lower grades, school was too easy. Academically, school wasn't challenging. I didn't get any gratification out of the academics. I always had good intentions. I always felt I could do the work but I couldn't concentrate. I didn't feel I was motivated enough to do it.

I always wanted attention. I'd get attention from doing academics, but everyone got the same attention. I could get limitless attention if I misbehaved. I hated bad attention, but it was the only attention I could get. I misbehaved for attention mostly when I was in seventh grade and below. Then I got into sports in eighth and ninth grades, and could get attention that way. My athletics started out for attention and became more personal and more meaningful to me.

Because of my misbehavior, teachers would isolate me. They would turn my desk to the wall. They put me out in the hall and sent me to the principal's office numerous times. They gave me extra work to try to keep me occupied. That would only bore me more. I felt frustrated mostly. I always felt I was the same socially but different academically compared with other kids. I didn't think my behavior was out of the ordinary when I misbehaved. I just did it more frequently than the average kid. I think I depended on my behavior for acceptance by friends.

In high school, I didn't like to raise my hand in class and ask questions. I was afraid that my mind was drifting off and I might look dumb. I felt like I shouldn't ask questions about things the teacher already said. It would be redundant.

Social pressure can be devastating when you have ADD. It can destroy a kid having problems, everything from the way you dress to activities. Having ADD isolates you from the normal things the average kid does. It helps me to hang out with my other friends who have ADD. That's what makes me and my friends with ADD all different. We're all definitely different!!!

I have always done well in sports. I like sports that are mentally and physically stimulating and quick changing so you don't have to focus on anything for long. I never liked golf or tennis because you have to focus on only one thing. My senior year in high school I won the state wrestling championship in my weight class.

I think I was so tired from giving my heart out in sports, I would sleep in class. (I sleep in class even now.) Coaches would say my attention span was short. They would say, "If we can get you to focus on things, you'll be okay." It is hard for people who don't have short attention spans to understand how my attention can be so short.

My junior year, I had a better year in football than I did my senior year. There was so much frustration in the classroom and my parents and teachers were all on my back. They were trying to get me to do things right and I didn't understand how I could. I felt that there were so many things I couldn't do or couldn't remember to do in school. I got to where I didn't really care. After a stressful day I would get out on the football field. Football is not a love tap sport. It was a means for me to express my violence and frustration in a constructive way.

A lot of my frustration and confusion from the classroom would build up and football and wrestling would allow me to deal with that stress and frustration. Before the diagnosis I didn't know what the problem was. Everyone else seemed like they didn't care and they felt I needed to be isolated or something.

Well, then came the psychiatrist, psychologists, sports psychologist, and family counseling. All that was a hope at first. But then it was a failure because it didn't take care of the problems I was having. One doctor said I needed to take an antidepressant. I was strongly against that and I told my dad.

I was finally diagnosed with ADD the last semester of my junior year and started taking medication. The first half of the semester, I was having a lot of problems. The last half of the semester, teachers started saying that things were getting better and my attitude in class was getting better.

When I take Ritalin, physically it feels like taking caffeine to stay awake. It really perks me up and helps me stay awake. Mentally, I have a desire to concentrate on things. I don't have the desire to skip from one thought to another. I have a desire to stick on one thing and know what's going on.

During my senior year after my ADD was diagnosed, I was making A's and B's. Frustration and stress weren't there. I felt secure in the classroom and home life was secure. I didn't have fire, though, and didn't erupt on the football field. Some Fridays, game days, I wouldn't take Ritalin so maybe I would get pumped up for the game. But it didn't happen that way. My weeks were always going better. This made me understand why kids without ADD in hostile environments succeed so well in sports. They have some mental frustration built up. They have to let it out somehow.

Before I was diagnosed, I felt like I didn't know why things were happening the way they were. I couldn't express myself. After ADD was diagnosed, my parents were excited and relieved and had hope. They had been doubting my chances for a scholarship because of my grades. But they were excited about my grades my senior year.

I think I didn't have any long-term goals before I was diagnosed because of my short attention span. Everything was so stimulating and had to be dealt with at the same time. Afterwards, I could see more opportunity in the future and my goals broadened.

You forget things when you have ADD. So you forget to take your medication, which is supposed to help you remember things. *Dang, if I can just remember to take my medicine I would be fine.* When I was younger, people would always ask "Why? why? why?" And now I know why I had problems in school. But I still can't remember to take my medication.

In high school, there were people around me who reminded me of things, and I remembered stuff more frequently. Once I got home, it was a whole different life, and things were easily forgotten. I've always procrastinated and put things off until the day or night before. I remember when I was in sixth grade and had to make models of the universe. I was reminded the day before. It was the only time I remembered the project. My dad and I stayed up until one thirty or two o'clock in the morning to finish. I had such a great idea but it was so time consuming.

I don't know if this has anything to do with ADD, but I like to do things my own way. In sports, if I don't feel like a technique fit me personally, I modify it to how I think is the best way. I have always expressed the things I feel in my own words whether or not it was grammatically correct. That's how I can best express myself.

In college, I have to attend some classes on study skills. I guess it is because I didn't make such good grades last quarter in college. A counselor came in and spoke on learning disabilities. She mentioned that most students with ADD had learning disabilities or attention disabilities that they were unaware of. Even though I've been diagnosed, *I still need help school-wise.* I don't take medication 24 hours a day. At times I can't take it too late in the afternoon or I'll be up all night. I think the counselor can help me. Now if I can just remember to set up a meeting to go talk to her. . . .

Sometimes, I feel overwhelmed by my social life in college, which conflicts with taking medication. I'm afraid to take medication too late in the day or when we are going out partying.

I think I've always been someone who takes awhile to understand something or to get in the routine of things. Once I get in a routine, I have no conflicts. I haven't found my routine in college. If I can just get that medication in my body, however, I usually have no problems at all.

Sometimes ADD causes major problems in relationships. These problems are minor to me but major to the person who doesn't understand my ADD. For example, I have been going out with my girlfriend for two years and five months. She asked me on the phone today why I was talking to Ms. Dendy. I told her I was being interviewed for a book about ADD. She asked me if I had ADD. I told her a long time ago that I had ADD, but she didn't remember. She doesn't realize how much it affects me and our relationship. She gets so mad at me when I don't remember things that she tells me or the small things she asks me to do. She asked me to have a certain amount of money for a formal dance. She reminded me two weeks ago. When I didn't have the money, she thought I didn't want to go to the formal.

I forget things, important things. If we are trying to make plans for the weekend and my girlfriend asks me to check on reservations, I forget until the last minute. I forget until she asks me and reminds me again. Sometimes I don't remember what time I am supposed to be somewhere and I am late.

CHAD (Eighteen)...........

Profile: Chad has ADHD and was diagnosed when he was 17. He finished his freshman year in college and then decided to work awhile. He is working full-time and taking college courses at night.

When I was little, I was mischievous and always got in trouble. I got paddled all the time for being mean or calling someone a name. My Pawpaw would tell me not to go out of the yard or driveway and I would wander off somewhere. He would whip me.

Once I threatened to push the automatic trunk release while my grandmother was driving the car. She told me six or seven times not to do it. I didn't mind anybody except my dad.

They tested me in second grade but didn't find ADD. I just thought I didn't try hard enough in school and that I was lazy. Basically I always felt like I was lazy because people always told me that I was. I always made average grades in high school. I'd like to go back to high school on Ritalin and see what I could do. I feel I could do a whole lot better. I think I would have flunked out of college if I hadn't been on Ritalin.

In high school, my dad would put me on restrictions if I had low grades. He said I had a lot more potential than I was showing. I always said, "Come on, Dad, C is average." He told me that I wasn't average and I could do a lot better than that.

Sometimes when I spent the night with friends we would sneak out of the house. We would smoke cigarettes because we knew we weren't supposed to. One night, we sneaked out when it had snowed and threw snowballs at cars that passed.

My sister saw me smoking at the mall one night and told my dad. When we came home later, my dad asked me if I was smoking. I went on and on and told him I didn't smoke. I tried to lie my way out of it, but that didn't work. A friend was supposed to spend the night with me and Dad sent him home. He spanked me.

I always daydream a lot. I can't ever listen to the teacher more than fifteen minutes at a time. I find myself thinking about other things, things I'd rather be doing. When I don't take Ritalin, I can't stay focused in class. It seems like I'm not even there.

I am forgetful. Sometimes I forget big things. My memory is not totally bad, but sometimes I forget test dates and then haven't put aside enough time to study. I end up bombing the test. I almost forgot I was supposed to attend a meeting with my college advisor to preregister for next fall's classes.

I have trouble getting started on homework. I don't want to do it. It is real easy for me to find something more interesting to do. I put it off.

My doctor and my college advisor have gotten me thinking that I do have a learning disability and it's not really my fault. I still have a long way to go, but I am starting to accept the fact that I have a learning disability and I am trying to work with it.

In college, I took the SIGY test, which is supposed to help me find a suitable career. I thought it was extremely helpful. At first, I didn't even know what to major in. The test helped me narrow my field down to about three categories: sports medicine, physical therapy, and funeral director. When the instructor went over the test with me, the results predicted my personality right on the nose. I *am* introverted.

APPENDIX A
Sample Behavior Management Contract

CONTRACT

This contract between _____ (teenager) and
_____ (parents) is hereby entered into this _____
day of _____, 199___.

Whereas, _____ is a mature and responsible teenager;

Whereas, _____ is at least 16 years of age, has a driver's license, and wishes to drive a car;

Whereas, _____ likes to go to the mall, movie theater and participate in other activities with his
friends;

Whereas, _____ likes to spend time with friends, invite them on outings and to our home;

Whereas, _____ likes to watch TV in his room, talk on the telephone, play video games, and watch
movies on the VCR; and

Whereas, _____ likes to party, have a good time, buy cassette tapes, water ski, hunt, fish, swim, and
ride a dirt bike:

Therefore, be it agreed that _____ and parents have developed the following statements to help
ensure that s/he continues to enjoy the above listed activities and that the parents are able to enjoy being
parents. Both parties agree to do their best to comply with the following statements:

With regard to **school issues,** _____ **agrees to:**

1. complete school assignments and turn them in on time.

2. complete and turn in all homework.

3. start his homework after dinner. No TV or talking on the telephone until homework is completed except if s/he deems a break is necessary.

4. be responsible for finding out about and completing any make-up work or make-up tests.

5. make every effort to pass all subjects.

6. bring home a weekly report in any subject that s/he may be in danger of failing.

7. show parents completed homework assignments each evening.

In return, **the parents agree:**

1. not to nag him/her about school work.

2. to provide assistance if requested.

3. to ask to see completed homework daily (or once a week).

4. if necessary, to give one reminder after dinner that homework must be started.

5. if necessary, to check the weekly school report to see if all school work has been completed.

6. to allow him/her (on a school night) to use the telephone and watch TV in his room, drive with a parent, go to the mall, and spend time with friends, once all school assignments are completed.

If, in the unlikely event, _____ should fail a subject, allow him/her to drive and spend time with friends each week that he brings home a passing weekly progress report.

With regard to **driving privileges,** _____ **agrees to:**

1. wear a seat belt.

2. drive the speed limit or less.

3. take medication when driving.

4. be home by 10:30 on school nights or 12:30 on weekends.

5. pay for any gasoline used above gas allowance.

6. never drink and drive.

7. pay fines for any speeding tickets.

8. call parents for advice and/or transportation at any hour, from any place, if I am ever in a situation where I have been drinking or a friend or date who is driving me has been drinking.

In return, **parents agree to:**

1. provide a car to drive (or let you drive the family car or help teen pay).

2. pay for car insurance (or pay half the car insurance or teen pays all).

3. provide a gasoline allowance (one tank every two weeks or teen pays all).

4. come and get you at any hour, any place, no questions asked and no arguments at that time, or I will pay for a taxi to bring you home safely. I expect we would discuss this issue at a later time.

In the unlikely event _____ receives a speeding ticket, s/he will pay any fines, plus lose driving privileges for a week (a weekend, more or fewer days).

All parties signing this contract are doing so in good faith and with the belief that the terms of the agreement will be implemented in a fair manner. Exceptions to these rules shall be mutually agreed upon with the parents. If a dispute should arise, he/she can negotiate with parents to make changes to the contract. Let all men know by the signing of this document that these statements are agreed to by all parties.

_____   _____
(Teenager)   (parents)

_____   (Date)_____

Parents are encouraged to modify this contract to meet your family's needs. This contract can be helpful by stating guidelines for your teenager regarding school issues and driving privileges. Although the sample contract identifies important issues, you can design it specifically for your child. For example, curfews may be earlier or he may have more limits on his driving because he is only fifteen. Just having a contract will not magically make your teenager comply with these guidelines but will clearly state his privileges, limits, and responsibilities. You will need to remind him of responsibilities such as wearing a seat belt. The contract may also be modified if sections of it are not applicable or no longer effective. For example, in a large town, a tank of gas may only last a week. If your teenager has had numerous speeding tickets, you may need to talk to the doctor about giving him medication at night when he is driving, send him to another driver training course, or take driving privileges away for a longer period of time.

APPENDIX B
U.S. D.O.E. Memorandum on Educational Services for Students with ADD

I. Introduction

There is a growing awareness in the education community that attention deficit disorder (ADD) and attention deficit hyperactive disorder (ADHD) can result in significant learning problems for children with those conditions. While estimates of the prevalence of ADD vary widely, we believe that three to five percent of school-aged children may have significant educational problems related to this disorder. Because ADD has broad implications for education as a whole, the Department believes it should clarify State and local responsibility under Federal law for addressing the needs of children with ADD in the schools. Ensuring that these students are able to reach their fullest potential is an inherent part of the National education goals and AMERICA 2000. The National goals, and the strategy for achieving them, are based on the assumptions that: (1) all children can learn and benefit from their education; and (2) the educational community must work to improve the learning opportunities for all children.

This memorandum clarifies the circumstances under which children with ADD are eligible for special education services under Part B of the Individuals with Disabilities Education Act (Part B), as well as the Part B requirements for evaluation of such children's unique educational needs. This memorandum will also clarify the responsibility of State and local educational agencies (SEAs and LEAs) to provide special education and related services to eligible children with ADD under Part B. Finally, this memorandum clarifies the responsibilities of LEAs to provide regular or special education and related aids and services to those children with ADD who are not eligible under Part B, but who fall within the definition of "handicapped person" under Section 504 of the Rehabilitation Act of 1973. Because of the overall educational responsibility to provide services for these children, it is important that general and special education coordinate their efforts.

II. Eligibility for Special Education and Related Services under Part B

Last year during the reauthorization of the Education of the Handicapped Act (now the Individuals with Disabilities Education Act), Congress gave serious consideration to including ADD in the definition of "children with disabilities" in the statute. The Department took the position that ADD does not need to be added as a separate disability category in the statutory definition since children with ADD who require special education and related services can meet the eligibility criteria for services under Part B. This continues to be the Department's position.

No change with respect to ADD was made by Congress in the statutory definition of "children with disabilities"; however, language was included in Section 102(a) of the Education of the Handicapped Act Amendments of 1990 that required the Secretary to issue Notice of Inquiry (NOI) soliciting public comment on special education for children with ADD under Part B. In response to the NOI (published November 29, 1990 in the Federal Register), the Department received over 2000 written comments, which have been transmitted to the Congress. Our review of these written comments indicates that there is confusion in the field regarding the extent to which children with ADD may be served in special education programs conducted under Part B.

A. Description of Part B

Part B requires SEAs and LEAs to make a free appropriate public education (FAPE) available to all eligible children with disabilities and to ensure that the rights and protections of Part B are extended to those children and their parents 20 U.S.C. 1412(2); 34 CFR SS300.121 and 300.2. Under Part B, FAPE, among other elements, includes the provision of special education and related services, at no cost to parents, in conformity with an individualized education program (IEP). 34 CFR §300.4.

In order to be eligible under Part B, a child must be evaluated in accordance with 34 CFR §§300.530–300.534 as having one or more specified physical or mental impairments, and must be found to require special education and related services by reason of one or more of these impairments. 20 U.S.C. 1401 (a)(1); 34 CFR §300.5. SEAs and LEAs must ensure that children with ADD who are determined eligible for services under Part B receive special education and related services needs arising from the ADD. A full continuum of placement alternatives, including the regular classroom, must be available for providing special education and related services required in the IEP.

B. Eligibility for Part B services under the "Other Health Impaired" Category

The list of chronic or acute health problems included within the definition of "other health impaired" in the Part B regulations is not exhaustive. The term "other health impaired" includes chronic or acute impairments that result in limited alertness, which adversely affects educational performance. Thus, children with ADD should be classified as eligible for services under the "other health impaired" category in instances where the ADD is a chronic or acute health problem that results in limited alertness, which adversely affects educational performance. In other words, children with ADD, where the ADD is a chronic or acute health problem resulting in limited alertness, may be considered disabled under Part B solely on the basis of this disorder within the "other health impaired" category in situations where special education and related services are needed because of the ADD.

C. Eligibility for Part B services under Other Disability Categories

Children with ADD are also eligible for services under part B if the children satisfy the criteria applicable to other disability categories. For example, children with ADD are also eligible for services under the "specific learning disability" category of Part B if they meet the criteria stated in §§300.5(b) (9) and 300.541 or under the "seriously emotionally disturbed" category of Part B if they meet the criteria stated in §300.5(b) (8).

III. Evaluations under Part B

A. Requirements

SEAs and LEAs have an affirmative obligation to evaluate a child who is suspected of having a disability to determine the child's need for special education and related services. Under Part B, SEAs and LEAs are required to have procedures for locating, identifying and evaluating all children who have a disability or are suspected of having a disability and are in need of special education and related services. 34 CFR § §300.128 and 300.220. This responsibility, known as "child find," is applicable to all children from birth through 21, regardless of the severity of their disability.

Consistent with this responsibility and the obligation to make FAPE available to all eligible children with disabilities, SEAs and LEAs must ensure that evaluations of children who are suspected of needing special education and related services are conducted without undue delay. 20U.S.C.1412(2). Because of its responsibility resulting from the FAPE and child find requirements of Part B, an LEA may not refuse to evaluate the possible need for special education and related services of a child with a prior medical diagnosis of ADD solely by reason of that medical diagnosis. However, a medical diagnosis of ADD alone is not sufficient to render a child eligible for services under Part B.

Under Part B, before any action is taken with respect to the initial placement of a child with a disability in a program providing special education and related services, "a full and individual evaluation of the child's educational needs must be conducted in accordance with requirements of §300.532." 34 CFR §300.531. Section 300.532(a) requires that a child's evaluation must be conducted by a multidisciplinary team, including at least one teacher or other specialist with knowledge in the area of suspected disability.

B. Disagreements over Evaluations

Any proposal or refusal of an agency to initiate or change the identification, evaluation, or educational placement of the child, or the provision of FAPE to the child is subject to the written prior notice requirements of 34 CFR §§300.504–300.505. If a parent disagrees with the LEAs refusal to evaluate a child or the LEAs evaluation and determination that a child does not have a disability for which the child is eligible for services under Part B, the parent may request a due process hearing pursuant to 34 CFR §§300.506–300.513 of the Part B regulations.

IV. Obligations Under Section 504 of SEAs and LEAs to children with ADD Found Not To Require Special Education and Related Services under Part B.

Even if a child with ADD is found not to be eligible for services under Part B, the requirements of Section 504 of the Rehabilitation Act of 1973 (Section 504) and its implementing regulation at 34 CFR Part 104 may be applicable. Section 504 prohibits discrimination on the basis of handicap by recipients of Federal funds. Since Section 504 is a civil rights law, rather than a funding law, its requirements are framed in different terms than those of Part B. While the Section 504 regulation was written with an eye to consistency with Part B, it is more general, and there are some differences arising from the differing natures of the two laws. For instance, the protections of Section 504 extend to some children who do not fall within the disability categories specified in part B.

A. Definition

Section 504 requires every recipient that operates a public elementary or secondary education program to address the needs of children who are considered "handicapped persons" under Section 504 as adequately as the needs of nonhandicapped persons are met. "Handicapped person" is defined in the Section 504 regulation is any person who has a physical or mental impairment which substantially limits a major life activity (e.g., learning) 34 CFR §104.3(j). Thus, depending on the severity of their condition, children with ADD may fit within that definition.

B. Programs and Services Under Section 504

Under Section 504, an LEA must provide a free appropriate public education to each qualified handicapped child. A free appropriate public education, under Section 504, consists of regular or special education and related aids and services that are designed to meet the individual student's needs and based on adherence to the regulator requirements on educational setting, evaluation, placement, and procedural safeguards. 34 CFR §§104.33, 104.34, 104.35, and 104.36. A student may be handicapped within the meaning of Section 504, and therefore entitled to regular or special education and related aids and services under the Section 504 regulation, even though the student may not be eligible for special education and related services under Part B.

Under Section 504, if parents believe that their child is handicapped by ADD, the LEA must evaluate the child to determine whether he or she is handicapped as defined by Section 504. If an LEA determines that a child is not handicapped under Section 504, the parent has the right to contest that determination. If the child is determined to be handicapped under section 504, the LEA must make an individualized determination of the child's educational needs for regular or special education or related aids and services. 34 CFR §104.35. For children determined to be handicapped under Section 504, implementation of an individualized education program developed in accordance with Part B, although not required, is one means of meeting the free appropriate public education requirements of Section 504. The child's education must be provided in the regular education classroom unless it is demonstrated that education in the regular environment with the use of supplementary aids and services cannot be achieved satisfactorily. 34 CFR §104.34.

Should it be determined that the child with ADD is handicapped for purposes of Section 504 and needs only adjustments in the regular classroom, rather than special education, those adjustments are required by Section 504. A range of strategies is available to meet the educational needs of children with ADD. Regular classroom teachers are important in identifying the appropriate educational adaptions and interventions for many children with ADD.

SEAs and LEAs should take the necessary steps to promote coordination between special and regular education programs. Steps also should be taken to train regular education teachers and other personnel to develop their awareness about ADD and its manifestations and the adaptations that can be implemented in regular education programs to address the instructional needs of these children. Examples of adaptations in regular education programs could include the following:

> providing a structured learning environment; repeating and simplifying instructions about in-class and homework assignments; supplementing verbal instructions with visual instructions; using behavioral management techniques; adjusting class schedules; modifying test delivery; using tape recorders, computer-aided instruction, and other audiovisual equipment; selecting modified textbooks or workbooks; and tailoring homework assignments.

Other provisions range from consultation to special resources and may include reducing class size; use of one-on-one tutorials; classroom aides and note takers; involvement of a "services coordinator" to oversee implementation of special programs and services, and possible modification of nonacademic times such as lunchroom, recess, and physical education.

Through the use of appropriate adaptations and interventions in regular classes, many of which may be required by Section 504, the Department believes that LEAs will be able to effectively address the instructional needs of many children with ADD.

C. Procedural Safeguards Under Section 504

Procedural safeguards under the Section 504 regulation are stated more generally than in Part B. The Section 504 regulation requires the LEA to make available a system of procedural safeguards that permits parents to challenge actions regarding the identification, evaluation, or educational placement of their handicapped child whom they believe needs special education or related services. 34 CFR §104.36. The Section 504 regulation requires that the system of procedural safeguards include notice, an opportunity for the parents or guardian to examine relevant records, an impartial hearing with opportunity for participation by the parents or guardian and representation by counsel, and a review procedure. Compliance with procedural safeguards of Part B is one means of fulfilling the Section 504 requirements. However, if an impartial due process hearing raising issues under the Section 504 regulation, the impartial hearing officer must make a determination based upon that regulation.

V. Conclusion

Congress and the Department have recognized the need to provide information and assistance to teachers, administrators, parents and other interested persons regarding the identification, evaluation, and instructional needs of children with ADD. The Department has formed a work group to explore strategies across principal offices to address this issue. The work group also plans to identify some ways that the Department can work with the education associations to cooperatively consider the programs and services needed by children with ADD across special and regular education.

In fiscal year 1991, the Congress appropriated funds for the Department to synthesize and disseminate current knowledge related to ADD. Four centers will be established in Fall, 1991 to analyze and synthesize the current research literature on ADD relating to identification, assessment, and interventions. Research syntheses will be prepared in formats suitable for educators, parents and researchers. Existing clearinghouses and networks, as well as Federal, State and local organizations, will be utilized to disseminate these research syntheses to parents, educators and administrators, and other interested persons.

In addition, the Federal Resource Center will work with SEAs and the six regional resource centers authorized under the Individuals with Disabilities Education Act to identify effective identification and assessment procedures, as well as intervention strategies being implemented across the country for children with ADD. A document describing current practice will be developed and disseminated to parents, educators and administrators, and other interested persons through the regional resource centers, network, as well as by parent training centers, other parent and consumer organizations, and professional organization. Also, the Office for Civil Rights' ten regional offices stand ready to provide technical assistance to parents and educators.

It is our hope that the above information will be of assistance to your State as you plan for the needs of children with ADD who require special education and related services under Part B, as well as for the needs of the broader group of children with ADD who do not qualify for special education and related services under Part B, but for whom special education or adaptations in regular education programs are needed. If you have any questions, please contact Jean Peelen, Office for Civil Rights (Phone: 202/732–1635); Judy Schrag, Office of Special Education Programs (Phone: 202/732–1007); or Dan Bonner, Office of Elementary and Secondary Education (Phone: 202/401–0984).

APPENDIX C
Attention Deficit Disorder: Impact on School Performance

ADD is a neurobiological disorder which affects approximately 5 percent of all students. Researchers believe that neurotransmitters, the chemical messengers of the brain, do not work properly, causing symptoms of ADD. **Inattention and impulsivity,** the two major characteristics of ADD, can make succeeding in school more difficult for these students. Symptoms of ADD vary from mild to severe. These symptoms improve with age and approximately 50 percent of adults outgrow the disorder. Some students with ADD do extremely well in school and pursue demanding academic careers such as medicine or law. However, for many others, **underachievement in school is a hallmark characteristic of ADD.**

Three major types of ADD have been identified: **ADD/I/WO** (predominately inattentive); **ADD/H** (predominately hyperactive-impulsive); **plus ADHD** (a combination of both hyperactivity and inattention). Students who have ADD/H tend to be very energetic, talkative, and outgoing. In contrast, students with ADD/I/WO, previously called ADD without hyperactivity, tend to be lethargic, less likely to talk in class, and introverted. Although many students are diagnosed and treated in elementary school, some students, especially those with ADD/I/WO, may not be diagnosed until high school or college.

Although they may be bright intellectually, many students with ADD lag behind their peers developmentally (3–4 years). They are less likely to remember their assignments, complete their work independently, are more likely to say things or act impulsively before thinking, and the quality and amount of their work will fluctuate from day to day. Consequently, teachers may need to provide more positive feedback, supervise schoolwork more closely, give reminders of homework, and interact more frequently with parents to help the student cope with this disability.

Research has shown that **medication can help most students with ADD improve their performance at school.** Medications commonly used to treat ADD, such as Ritalin or Dexedrine, help the neurotransmitters norepinephrine, dopamine, and serotonin work properly. As a result, attention and concentration improve, more school work is completed, compliance with adult requests increases, hyperactivity and impulsivity decrease, and negative behaviors decrease.

Frequently, ADD may coexist with other problems—learning problems (25–50%), sleep disturbances (50%), anxiety, depression, or oppositional behavior (30–60%)—which further complicates their schoolwork and treatment.

Common learning problems and their practical implications for school performance are described below. However, keep in mind that each student with ADD is unique and may have some, but not all, of these problems.

1. *Inattention/poor concentration:* difficulty listening in class; may daydream; spaces out and misses lecture content or homework assignments; lack of attention to detail, makes careless mistakes in work, doesn't notice errors in grammar, punctuation, capitalization, spelling, or changes in signs (+,-) in math; difficulty staying on task and finishing schoolwork; distractible, moves from one uncompleted task to another; lack of awareness of time and grades, may not know if passing or failing class.

2. *Impulsivity:* rushes through work; doesn't double check work; doesn't read directions; takes short cuts in written work especially math (does it in his head); difficulty delaying gratification, hates waiting.

3. *Cognitive Processing Problems:* slow processing of information; reads, writes, and responds slowly; slow recall of facts; more likely to occur in students with ADD/I/WO.

Listening Comprehension: becomes confused with lengthy verbal directions; loses main point, difficulty taking notes; difficulty following directions; may not "hear" or pick out homework assignments from a teacher's lecture.

Spoken Language: talks a lot spontaneously (ADD/H); talks less in response to questions where must think and give organized, concise answer; avoids responding in class or gives rambling answers.

Written Language: slow reading and writing, takes longer to complete work, produces less written work; difficulty organizing themes; difficulty getting ideas out of head and on paper; written test answers or themes may be brief; poor reading comprehension, can't remember what is read.

4. *Poor Organizational Skills:* disorganized; difficulty getting started on tasks; difficulty knowing what steps should be taken first; difficulty organizing thoughts, sequencing ideas, writing themes, and planning ahead; loses homework; poor concept of time, doesn't manage time well, doesn't anticipate how long tasks will take.

5. *Poor Memory:* difficulty memorizing material such as multiplication tables, math facts or formulas, spelling words, foreign languages, and/or history dates; forgets homework assignments and to take right book home; forgets to turn in completed assignments to teacher; forgets special assignments or make-up work.

6. *Poor Fine Motor Coordination:* handwriting is poor, small, difficult to read; writes slowly; avoids writing and homework because it is difficult; prefers to print rather than write cursive; produces less written work; themes or discussion questions may be brief.

Difficulties in school may be caused by a combination of several learning problems: a student may not take good notes in class because he can't pay attention, can't pick out main points, and/or his motor coordination is poor. A student may not do well on a test because he reads, thinks, and writes slowly, has difficulty organizing his thoughts, and/or has difficulty memorizing and recalling the information. **Identification of learning problems plus implementation of appropriate adaptations in the regular classroom are critical. Under IDEA and/or Section 504, students with ADD whose ability to learn is adversely affected by the disorder are eligible for adaptations.**

Common classroom adaptations which are extremely helpful to students with ADD include: untimed tests; use of calculator or computer; modification of assignments (every 3rd math problem); elimination of unnecessary writing—write answers only not questions; written homework assignments given by teachers; utilization of notetakers or guided lecture notes. Adaptations should be individualized and made to accommodate each child's specific learning problems.

Other factors related to ADD may also influence the student's school work:

1. *Hyperactivity:* Can't sit still in seat long enough to complete work.

2. *Sleep Disturbances:* Students may come to school feeling tired; may sleep in class. Many students with ADD (50%) have difficulty falling asleep at night and waking up each morning. Approximately half of them wake up tired even after a full night's sleep. This suggests that there are problems with the neurotransmitter Serotonin.

3. *Medication Wears Off:* Since effects of medications such as Ritalin (regular tablets) wear off within three to four hours, students may begin having trouble paying attention around ten or eleven o'clock in the morning.

4. *Low Frustration Tolerance:* Students with ADD may become frustrated more easily and "blow-up" or impulsively say things they don't mean, especially as their medication is wearing off. They may blurt out answers in class or impulsively talk back to a teacher. Transitions or changes in routine, such as when substitute teachers are present, are also difficult for them.

Youngsters with ADD have many positive qualities and talents (high energy, outgoing charm, creativity, and figuring out new ways of doing things). Although these traits may be valued in the adult work world, they may cause difficulties for the student with ADD and his classroom teachers. Their high energy, if properly channelled, can be very productive. Although sometimes exasperating, they can also be extremely charming in their self-appointed role as class clown. Typically, students with ADD/I/WO tend to be quieter and present no discipline problems. When they graduate from school, these youngsters can do well in life.

Since most children with ADD are not as easily motivated by consequences (rewards and punishment) as other children, it is very difficult for them to have a natural love of learning. Although they would like very much to make good grades on a test or at the end of the semester, these rewards do not occur quickly enough nor are they strong enough to greatly influence their behavior. Frequently, they start out each new school year with the best intentions, but cannot sustain their efforts. Positive feedback or rewards are effective but must be given immediately, must be important to the child, and must occur more frequently than for other students. Consequently, sending home daily or weekly reports regarding school work should help improve grades.

Typically, their misbehavior is not malicious but rather the result of their inattention, impulsivity, and failure to anticipate the consequences of their actions. "Ready. Fire! And then Aim" may more accurately describe the behavior of students with ADD. Belatedly, and with remorse, they realize they should not have said or done certain things.

We, as parents, live with these children day-in and day-out and know how much attention and energy they require. We know that dealing with them can be very challenging at times. Consequently, we are extremely grateful to teachers who go above and beyond the call of duty to make school and learning a special and happy experience for our children!!!!

APPENDIX D
Resources

Organizations

The organizations listed below offer information and support to parents. You can call the national offices for a publications list, membership information, the answer to a specific question about ADD or LD, or to find out the location and phone number of the local chapter nearest you.

Children and Adults with Attention Deficit Disorder (CHADD)
8181 Professional Place, Suite 201
Landover, MD 20785
301-306-7070
www.Chadd.org

National Attention Deficit Disorders Association (ADDA)
1788 Second St., Suite 200
Highland Park, IL 60035
847-432-ADDA
www.add.org

Learning Disabilities Association of America
4156 Library Rd.
Pittsburgh, PA 15234
412-341-1515
www.ldanatl.org

If your child has more serious problems or is experiencing emotional problems, the following national organizations may be helpful. Again, call to see if there is a local branch near you.

Federation of Families for Children's Mental Health
1021 Prince St.
Alexandria, VA 22314–2971
703–519–9247

National Alliance for the Mentally Ill
NAMI-CAN
2101 Wilson Boulevard, Suite 302
Arlington, VA 22201
703–524–7600

National Mental Health Association
1021 Prince St.
Alexandria, VA 22314–2971
(703–684–7722)

Child and Adolescent Services System Program (CASSP)
Center for Mental Health Services (formerly part of National Institute of Mental Health)
5600 Fishers Lane
Room 11–C-09, Parklawn Building
Rockville, MD 20857
301–443–1333

For free information on special education, other kinds of special services for children and adolescents with disabilities, state resources for people with disabilities, or information on a specific disability, request a publication list or call for information from:

National Information Center for Children and Youth with Disabilities (NICHCY)
P.O. Box 1492
Washington, DC 20013–1492
(800–695–0285)

Publications

This is only a small sampling of the many books, journal articles, video tapes, and other materials available about ADD and related issues. To find out about other publications, visit your local bookstore or library, or contact the ADD WareHouse at the address below.

ADD in General

Barkley, Russell A. *Attention Deficit Hyperactivity Disorder: A Handbook for Diagnosis and Treatment*. New York: Guilford Press, 1990.

Brown, Tom. "Attention Deficit Disorders without Hyperactivity," *CHADDER Box*, Spring/Summer 1993, 7–10.

CHADD Facts: a series of 2–3 page fact sheets on different aspects of ADD. Available from CHADD, Plantation, FL.

Hallowell, Edward M. and John J. Ratey. *Driven to Distraction*. New York: Pantheon Books, 1994.

Phelan, Thomas W. "The Truth about Lying." *CHADDER Box*, February, 1991.

Weiss, Gabrielle and Lilly Hechtman. *Hyperactive Children Grown Up*. New York: Guilford Press, 1986.

Wender, Paul. *The Hyperactive Child, Adolescent and Adult*. New York: Oxford University Press, 1987.

Zametkin, Alan J. "Cerebral glucose metabolism in adults with hyperactivity of childhood onset." *The New England Journal of Medicine* 323 (November 1990): 1361–1367.

Children with ADD

Fowler, Mary. *Maybe You Know My Kid*. Secaucus, NJ: Carol Publishing Group, 1993.

Moss, Deborah. *Shelly the Hyperactive Turtle*. Bethesda, MD: Woodbine House, 1989.

Parker, Harvey C. *The ADD Hyperactivity Handbook for Schools*. Plantation, FL: Impact Publications, Inc. 1992.

Phelan, Thomas W. *1–2–3 Magic* (videorecording). Child Management, Inc., 1990.

Education and Special Services

Anderson, Winifred, Stephen Chitwood, and Deidre Hayden. *Negotiating the Special Education Maze: A Guide for Parents and Teachers*. Bethesda, MD: Woodbine House, 1990.

Jordan, Dixie. *Honorable Intentions*. Minneapolis: Pacer Center, 1995.

Karp, Naomi. "Inclusion: A Right, Not a Privilege." Farmington, CT: University of Connecticut, Child and Family Studies, 1993.

National Information Center for Children and Youth with Disabilities (NICHCY). "Individualized Education Programs." Washington, DC, 1990. (For a free copy, call 1–800–695–0285.)

Katz-Leavy, Judith, Ira S. Lourie, Beth A. Stroul, and Chris Zeigler Dendy. *Individualized Services in a System of Care*. Rockville, MD: 1991. Available from CASSP at address above.

General Parenting

Brooks, Robert. *The Self-esteem Teacher*. Circle Pines, MN: American Guidance Service, 1991.

Phelan, Thomas W. *Surviving Your Adolescents*. Glen Ellyn, IL: Child Management, Inc., 1991.

Newsletters and audiotapes

Many of the organizations listed above publish newsletters of interest to parents. Dr. Barkley also publishes a quarterly newsletter that summarizes the most current information and research regarding ADHD:

The ADHD Report
Guilford Press
72 Spring Street
New York, NY 10012
1–800–365–70061

Audio tapes of presentations made by national experts from each annual CHADD conference are available from CHADD. These are an excellent source of the most up-to-date information regarding ADD.

Catalog of ADD Materials

ADD WareHouse
300 N.W. 70th Ave., Suite 102
Plantation, FL 33317
305–792–8944
1–800–233–9273

INDEX